THE CIVIC CULTURE

THE
CIVIC CULTURE

POLITICAL ATTITUDES AND
DEMOCRACY IN FIVE NATIONS

BY GABRIEL A. *braham* ALMOND
AND SIDNEY VERBA

PRINCETON, NEW JERSEY
PRINCETON UNIVERSITY PRESS
1963

To Richard, Peter and Susan;
Margaret and Erica:
citizens and future citizens

".... *And this our form, as committed not to the few, but to the whole body of the people, is called a democracy*. ... *The offices of the State we go through without obstructions from one another; and live together in the mutual endearments of private life without suspicions; not angry with a neighbor for following the bent of his own humor, nor putting on that countenance of discontent, which pains though it cannot punish—so that in private life we converse without diffidence or damage, while we dare not on any account offend against the public, through the reverence we bear to the magistrates and the laws*. ... *There is visible in the same persons an attention to their own private concerns and those of the public; and in others engaged in the labor of life there is a competent skill in the affairs of government. For we are the only people who think him that does not meddle in state affairs—not indolent, but good for nothing."*

—PERICLES, *On the Causes of Athenian Greatness*

PREFACE

THIS STUDY of the political culture of democracy had its inspiration some thirty years ago in the Social Science Division of the University of Chicago. Much of what now goes under the name of the behavioral approach to the study of politics originated there in the period between the wars. It is a tribute to the vision of the men who created this leaven that it has taken three or four decades for their conception of political science to become a common possession. In particular, this study owes its inspiration to the work of Charles E. Merriam. His *Civic Training* series formulated many of the problems with which this study is concerned, and his *New Aspects of Politics* suggested the methods that have been used in its execution.

We are concerned in this book with a number of classic themes of political science: with what the Greeks called civic virtue and its consequences for the effectiveness and stability of the democratic polity; and with the kind of community life, social organization, and upbringing of children that fosters civic virtue. In using survey research to study these classic themes, we are also following the traditional practice of relying on the most precise methods available to us for the investigation of these problems. Perhaps Tocqueville and Bryce, were they living today, would have relied somewhat on the cross-section survey in their comparative studies of democratic attitudes.

Our study will suggest that there exists in Britain and the United States a pattern of political attitudes and an underlying set of social attitudes that is supportive of a stable democratic process. In the other three nations studied—Germany, Italy, and Mexico—this is less the case. But this conclusion ought not to lead the reader to despair about the prospects for democracy in the latter three nations. Our study is but a snapshot in a rapidly changing world, and though we can specify some serious problems these nations may have to overcome to achieve a more stable and democratic polity, we cannot and do not conclude that these problems are impossible of solution. Even more important, our conclusions ought not to lead the reader to complacency about democracy in the first two nations, Britain and the United States. As long as full participation in the political system and access to the channels of social betterment are denied to significant segments of their populations, their democratic promise remains unfulfilled.

Some five thousand people—Britons, Germans, Italians, Mexicans, and Americans—were interviewed to provide us with our data. We asked our respondents in the cities, towns, and villages of these five countries to cooperate with us in a scientific study, under university auspices, of problems of democracy and political participation. In a very real sense this is their book, and we as its authors hope we have kept faith with them.

Five years have transpired from the planning of this study to its completion, and our debts are many. We are pleased first to acknowledge the strong support given by the late Frederick S. Dunn, Director of the Center of International Studies at Princeton University when the study was begun, and by Klaus Knorr, Director of the Center during the later phases of the project. In the development of the research design and survey instrument, as well as in the administration of the project, we had the help of International Research Associates of New York; we acknowledge especially the collaboration of Elmo Wilson, Helen Dinerman, and Frank Bonilla. Morris Rosenberg of the National Institute of Mental Health made important contributions in the planning stage, in the construction of the research instrument, and in the analysis of the pretests. Herbert Hyman helped us greatly in the planning and pretesting stages of the study. Maurice and Ruth Farber and Robert E. Lane made original contributions to the construction of the survey instrument.

During the course of the study we benefited from the research assistance of a number of people. Louise K. Comfort took a major role in the planning and pretesting of the interview schedules and in the gathering of comparable material from other surveys. Anne Munholland provided general statistical assistance and performed the exacting task of rechecking our data for publication. Morris Davis contributed to our analysis of other survey material and prepared a memorandum on theories of citizenship. Annelisa Kelley helped with the gathering of other survey data and aided in the translation of the research instrument. Annette Ducey and William Flanagan supervised and carried out much of the statistical analysis of the data; Lotte Doverman and Peter Almond helped in the statistical analysis, and Mrs. Doverman prepared the first drafts of the illustrative case histories that appear in Chapter 14. We are grateful also for the aid of Robert Scott in the analysis of the Mexican life-history interviews.

For secretarial assistance we are grateful to Gail Ahlgren, Barbara Jacobs, and Sarah Bondy. The Center for Adanced Study in the Behavioral Sciences provided the facilities for the final preparation of the manuscript.

We are happy to acknowledge our collaboration with the interviewing agencies in each one of the nations studied. In the United States our survey was conducted by the National Opinion Research Center of the University of Chicago, and it was under the supervision of Selma Monsky and Jacob Feldman; in Great Britain, Research Services Ltd. of London conducted the survey under the supervision of Mark Abrams and A. E. S. Ehrenberg; in Germany the DIVO Institut, Frankfort, carried out the interviewing program under the direction of Gerhart Baumert and Peter Schmidt; in Italy the work was done by the Istituto Italiano Dell'Opinione Pubblica, Milan; under the direction of Ernesto Norbedo. The Mexican survey was carried out by International Research Associates of Mexico, Mexico City, under the supervision of George Gaither and Alfred Wilson.

An earlier draft of the manuscript benefited from the careful reading and valuable comments of Harry Eckstein, Herbert Hyman, Robert Scott, and Alex Inkeles.

This study was generously supported by the Carnegie Corporation of New York. We have many reasons to express our gratitude to its officers, in particular to John Gardner, William Marvel, and James Perkins. Needless to say, responsibility for the substance and the con·clusions of the study is ours.

G. A. A.
S. V.

August 1962

CONTENTS

CONTENTS

PART I

THE THEORY AND METHOD
OF THE STUDY

CHAPTER 1

AN APPROACH TO POLITICAL CULTURE

THIS IS a study of the political culture of democracy and of the social structures and processes that sustain it. The faith of the Enlightenment in the inevitable triumph of human reason and liberty has been twice shaken in recent decades. The development of Fascism and Communism after World War I raised serious doubts about the inevitability of democracy in the West; and we still cannot be certain that the continental European nations will discover a stable form of democratic process suitable to their particular cultures and social institutions; nor can we more than hope that together they will discover a European democracy.

Without having first resolved these doubts, the events since World War II have raised questions of the future of democracy on a world scale. The "national explosions" in Asia and Africa and the almost universal pressure by previously subjected and isolated peoples for admission into the modern world put this more special political question into the broader context of the future character of the world's culture. Culture change has acquired a new significance in world history. The groping toward enlightenment and control over nature that acquired momentum three or four centuries ago in the West has become a world-wide process, and its tempo has shifted from centuries to decades.

The central question of public policy in the next decades is what content this emerging world culture will have. We already have a partial answer to this question and could have predicted it from our knowledge of the processes of cultural diffusion.[1] Physical goods and their mode of production seem to present the least difficulties in diffusion. It is apparent that these aspects of Western culture are diffusing rapidly, along with the technology upon which they depend. Since economic modernization and national unification

[1] Ralph Linton, *The Study of Man: An Introduction*, New York, 1936, pp. 324-46.

3

require a large social overhead investment in transportation, communication, and education, and since this in turn calls for taxation, regulation, and administration, the model of a rational bureaucracy also diffuses relatively easily. The idea of an efficient bureaucracy has much in common with the idea of a rational technology. Lucian Pye refers to modern social organization as being based on an organizational technology.[2] What it has in common with engineering and technology is its mixture of rationality and authority. Engineering is the application of rationality and authority to material things; modern social organization is its application to human beings and social groups. While the non-Western world is far from having successfully developed an industrial technology and an efficient bureaucracy, there can be little question that it wants these institutions and has some understanding of them.

What is problematical about the content of the emerging world culture is its political character. While the movement toward technology and rationality of organization appears with great uniformity throughout the world, the direction of political change is less clear. But one aspect of this new world political culture is discernable: it will be a political culture of participation. If there is a political revolution going on throughout the world, it is what might be called the participation explosion. In all the new nations of the world the belief that the ordinary man is politically relevant—that he ought to be an involved participant in the political system—is widespread. Large groups of people who have been outside of politics are demanding entrance into the political system. And the political elites are rare who do not profess commitment to this goal.

Though this coming world political culture appears to be dominated by the participation explosion, what the mode of participation will be is uncertain. The emerging nations are presented with two different models of the modern participatory state, the democratic and the totalitarian. The democratic state offers the ordinary man the opportunity to take part in the political decision-making process as an influential citizen; the totalitarian offers him the role of the "participant subject."[3] Both modes have appeal to the new nations,

[2] Committee on Comparative Politics, Social Science Research Council, *Memorandum on the Concept of Modernization*, November 1961.

[3] See Frederick C. Barghoorn, "Soviet Political Culture," a paper prepared for the Summer Institute on Political Culture, sponsored by the Committee on Comparative Politics, Social Science Research Council, Summer 1962.

and which will win out—if indeed some amalgam of the two does not emerge—cannot be foretold.

If the democratic model of the participatory state is to develop in these new nations, it will require more than the formal institutions of democracy—universal suffrage, the political party, the elective legislature. These in fact are also part of the totalitarian participation pattern, in a formal if not functional sense. A democratic form of participatory political system requires as well a political culture consistent with it. But the transfer of the political culture of the Western democratic states to the emerging nations encounters serious difficulties. There are two principal reasons. The first of these concerns the nature of the democratic culture itself. The great ideas of democracy—the freedoms and dignities of the individual, the principle of government by consent of the governed —are elevating and inspiring concepts. They capture the imaginations of many of the leaders of the new states and of the modernizing older ones. But the working principles of the democratic polity and its civic culture—the ways in which political elites make decisions, their norms and attitudes, as well as the norms and attitudes of the ordinary citizen, his relation to government and to his fellow citizens—are subtler cultural components. They have the more diffuse properties of belief systems or of codes of personal relations, which the anthropologists tell us spread only with great difficulty, undergoing substantial change in the process.

Actually, Western social science has only begun to codify the operating characteristics of the democratic polity itself. The doctrine and practice of a rational bureaucracy as an instrument of the democratic political powers are less than a century old. Doubts about the possibility of a neutral bureaucracy were expressed in England as recently as the 1930's, and on the European continent such doubt is widespread today. The complex infrastructure of the democratic polity—political parties, interest groups, and the media of communications—and the understanding of their inner workings, operating norms, and social-psychological preconditions are only now being realized in the West. Thus the image of the democratic polity that is conveyed to the elites of the new nations is obscure and incomplete and heavily stresses ideology and legal norms. What must be learned about democracy is a matter of attitude and feeling, and this is harder to learn.

The second principal reason why the diffusion of democracy en-

THE THEORY AND METHOD OF THE STUDY

counters difficulties among the new nations concerns the objective problems confronting these nations. They are entering history with archaic technologies and social systems, drawn toward the gleam and power of the technological and scientific revolutions. It is not difficult to see why they should be drawn toward a technocratic image of the polity: a polity in which authoritarian bureaucracy predominates and political organization becomes a device for human and social engineering.

But in many cases, perhaps in all though in differing measure, the leaders of the modernizing nations appreciate the distortions and the risks in adopting an authoritarian form of polity. Though they cannot fully understand the subtle balances of the democratic polity and the nuances of the civic culture, they tend to acknowledge their legitimacy as the expression of an impulse toward the humane polity. In characterizing their situation, we have left out a significant element. For while it is true that they are fascinated by science and technology and are drawn to an impatient technocratic polity as a means of attaining the new things of this world, they are also the creatures of their own traditional cultures and would prefer to deal gently with these cultures if this choice were available.

The Civic Culture

It is as an answer to this ambivalence that the civic culture recommends itself. For the civic culture is not a modern culture, but a mixed modernizing-traditional one. C. P. Snow, with his gift for surgical prose, has confronted us with an exaggerated dichotomy between the humanistic and the scientific-technological cultures. Shils takes issue with Snow, arguing that he has missed a third culture— the civic culture—which, because it contains both the scientific and humanistic-traditional cultures, enables them to interact and interchange without destroying or polarizing each other.[4]

Herring, responding similarly to Snow's dichotomy, argues that

[4] C. P. Snow, *The Two Cultures and the Scientific Revolution*, New York, 1961, and Edward A. Shils, *Demagogues and Cadres In the Political Development of the New States*, a memorandum prepared for the Committee on Comparative Politics, Social Science Research Council, September 1961, pp. 20-21. The title of our book has been taken from this passage of the Shils paper, as well as from earlier uses of this concept of "civility" in other writings of his. For an excellent discussion of the relations between the scientific and humanistic cultures, see Shils, "The Calling of Sociology," in T. Parsons, E. Shils, K. Naegele, and J. Pitts, *Theories of Society*, New York, 1961, Vol. II, pp. 1,414 ff.

the culture of the West is pluralistic, and that Snow's representation of the sharp conflict between science and the more traditional humanism overlooks the cultural diversity of Western society, especially the quality that the cultures of science and democracy share in common: the experimental attitude. Herring suggests that science and democracy have a common origin in the humanistic culture of the West. But because they have different functions they diverge in important respects. Science is rational, straightforward, ". . . it abhors half-way measures." The democratic or civic culture emerged as a mode of "economic" and humane culture change. It takes the slow course and "seeks the common denominator."[5]

The development of the civic culture in Britain may be understood as the product of a series of encounters between modernization and traditionalism—encounters sharp enough to effect significant change but not so sharp or so concentrated in time as to create disintegration or polarization. Partly because of her insular security, Britain came into the era of national unification and of absolutism able to tolerate a greater measure of aristocratic, local, and corporate autonomy than could continental Europe. A first step toward secularization was the separation from the Church of Rome and the beginnings of toleration of religious diversity. A second step was the emergence of a thriving and self-confident merchant class, and the involvement of court and aristocracy in the risks and calculations of trade and commerce.

Independent aristocrats with secure local power in the countryside, courageous nonconformists, rich and self-confident merchants —these were the forces that transformed the tradition of the feudal estates into the parliamentary tradition and enabled Britain to pass through the era of absolutism without destroying her pluralism. Britain thus entered the industrial revolution with a political culture among its elites which made it possible to assimilate the gross and rapid changes in social structure in the eighteenth and nineteenth centuries without sharp discontinuities. The aristocratic Whigs found it possible to enter a coalition with nonconformist merchants and industrialists, to establish securely the principles of parliamentary supremacy and representation. The traditional aristocratic and monarchic forces assimilated enough of this civic culture to compete with the secularist tendencies for popular sup-

[5] E. P. Herring, "On Science and the Polity," *Items*, Social Science Research Council, Vol. xv, No. 1, Part 2, March 1961, p. 1.

port and, indeed, to mitigate their rationalism and impart to them a love and respect for the sacredness of the nation and its ancient institutions.

What emerged was a third culture, neither traditional nor modern but partaking of both; a pluralistic culture based on communication and persuasion, a culture of consensus and diversity, a culture that permitted change but moderated it. This was the civic culture. With this civic culture already consolidated, the working classes could enter into politics and, in a process of trial and error, find the language in which to couch their demands and the means to make them effective. It was in this culture of diversity and consensualism, rationalism and traditionalism, that the structure of British democracy could develop: parliamentarism and representation, the aggregative political party and the responsible and neutral bureaucracy, the associational and bargaining interest groups, and the autonomous and neutral media of communication. English parliamentarism included the traditional and modern forces; the party system aggregated and combined them; the bureaucracy became responsible to the new political forces; and the political parties, interest groups, and neutral media of communication meshed continuously with the diffuse interest groupings of the community and with its primary communications networks.

We have concentrated on British experience because the whole story of the emergence of the civic culture is told in British history, while developments in the United States and the countries of the "Old Commonwealth" began after some of the major battles had been won. Actually, in the course of the nineteenth century the development of the democratic culture and infrastructure was more rapid and more unequivocal in the United States than in Britain, since the United States was a new and rapidly expanding society and relatively unimpeded by traditional institutions. Though their basic patterns are similar, the civic cultures of Britain and the United States have somewhat different contents, reflecting these differences in national histories and social structures.

On the European continent the record is more mixed. Though their patterns differ in many respects from those of Britain and America, the Scandinavian countries, Low Countries, and Switzerland appear to have worked out their own version of a political culture and practice of accommodation and compromise. In France,

Germany, and Italy the encounters between modernizing tendencies and the traditional powers seem to have been too massive and too uncompromising to permit the emergence of a shared culture of political accommodation. The civic culture is present in the form of aspiration, and the democratic infrastructure is still far from being attained.

The civic culture and the open polity, then, represent the great and problematic gifts of the West. The technology and science of the West have now already passed out of her unique possession and everywhere are destroying and transforming traditional societies and cultures. Can the open polity and the civic culture—man's discovery of a humane and conservative way to handle social change and participation—spread as well?

As we consider the origin of the open polity and the civic culture —indeed, as we consider the areas in the West where their emergence is still in doubt—we may fall victim to one or both of two moods. The first is one of mystery or awe over a process whereby mankind on only a small part of the earth's surface muddled toward a humane and reasoned taming of violence and groped toward its transformation into a constructive instrument available to all interests. As mystery, it becomes a unique cultural heritage unavailable to foreigners. The second mood is one of pessimism, which seems to have replaced the mood of democratic optimism that existed before World War I. How can a set of arrangements and attitudes so fragile, so intricate, and so subtle be transplanted out of historical and cultural context? Or, how can these subtleties and these humane etiquettes survive even among ourselves in a world caught in the grip of a science and technology run wild, destructive of tradition and of community and possibly of life itself?

No one can provide definitive answers to these questions. But as social scientists we can put the questions in such a way as to get useful answers. While we may share the mood of wonder and awe at the intricacy of the democratic mechanisms and the unique historical experience out of which they emerged, we are confronted with a contemporary historical challenge for which mood by itself is an inadequate response. If we are to come closer to understanding the problems of the diffusion of democratic culture, we have to be able to specify the content of *what* has to be diffused, to develop appropriate measures for it, to discover its quantitative incidence and demographic distribution in countries with a wide range of experience with democracy. With such knowledge we can speculate intelligently about "how much of what" must be present in a country before democratic institutions take root in congruent attitudes and expectations.

Efforts to deal with this problem have usually been based on impressions and inferences from history, on inferences from democratic ideology, on certain kinds of sociological analysis, or on psychological insights. Thus in our efforts to estimate the prospects of democracy in countries such as Germany and Italy, or in the developing areas of the non-Western world, we frequently try to draw "lessons" from British and American history. It has been argued, for example, that the long continuity of British and American political experience and the gradual process of change have both contributed to effective democratization. Similarly, the growth of a vigorous and numerous middle class, the development of Protestantism, and in particular the nonconformist sects, have been considered vital to the development of stable democratic institutions in Britain, the Old Commonwealth, and the United States. There have been efforts to derive from these experiences some standards as to what attitudes and behavior must be present in other countries if they are to become democratic.

Even more common than drawing inferences from history has been our tendency to derive criteria of what has to be diffused from the institutional and ideological norms of democracy itself. It is argued that if a democratic system is based on the sharing of influence among the adult population as a whole, then, if the system is not to be subverted, the individual must use his power intelligently for the good of the polity. Theorists of democracy from Aristotle to Bryce have stressed that democracies are maintained by active citizen participation in civic affairs, by a high level of information about public affairs, and by a widespread sense of civic responsibility. These doctrines tell us what a democratic citizen ought to be like if he is to behave according to the requirements of the system.

Still a third type of investigation of the conditions favoring the development of stable democracy are studies of the economic and social conditions associated with democratic systems. This continues an old Aristotelian tradition. Lipset classified the nations of Europe (including the Old Commonwealth) and of Latin America into "stable democracies" and "unstable democracies and dictatorships."[6] Assignment to one or the other category was based on the historical

6 Seymour M. Lipset, *Political Man*, New York, 1960, pp. 45 ff.

record of these countries. He then drew together the available statistical information on economic and social conditions in these countries, the degree of industrialization and urbanization, literacy rates, and educational patterns. His findings show a relatively convincing correlation between these indices of "modernization" and stable democratization. James Coleman, in a similar analysis that included Southeast Asia, South Asia, the Middle East, Africa and Latin America, also found a strong correlation between indices of modernization and democratization.[7] The main problem presented by these studies is that the cultural and psychological consequences of "modern" technologies and processes are left to inference. We know that democracies, in comparison to other political systems, tend to have more literate and educated people, that their per capita income and wealth are higher, and that they enjoy in greater proportions the amenities of modern civilization. But this type of analysis not only omits the psychological basis of democratization, it cannot explain the significant deviant cases. Thus Germany and France, which rank high on the indices of modernization, are classified by Lipset as unstable democracies. Cuba and Venezuela, both of which rank high in economic development in Latin America, have long histories of dictatorship and instability. This kind of study is suggestive of hypotheses but does not tell us directly what kind of cluster of attitudes is associated with democracy.

Another type of approach to the culture and psychology of democracy is based on the insights of psychoanalysis. Harold Lasswell has gone furthest in specifying the personality characteristics of the "democrat."[8] In his list of democratic character qualities he includes (1) an "open ego," by which he means a warm and inclusive attitude toward other human beings; (2) a capacity for sharing values with others; (3) a multivalued rather than a single-valued orientation; (4) trust and confidence in the human environment, and (5) relative freedom from anxiety. While the relation between these characteristics and democratic behavior seems to be clear, Lasswell's democratic qualities are not specifically *political* attitudes and feelings, and they may actually be encountered in great frequency in societies that are not democratic in structure.

Our study grows out of this body of theory about the character-

[7] Gabriel A. Almond and James Coleman, *The Politics of the Developing Areas,* Princeton, N.J., 1960, pp. 538 ff.

[8] *The Political Writings of Harold D. Lasswell,* Glencoe, Ill., 1951, pp. 495 ff.; Lasswell, *Power and Personality,* New York, 1946, pp. 148 ff.

11

istics and preconditions of the culture of democracy. What we have done amounts to a series of experiments intended to test some of these hypotheses. Rather than inferring the properties of democratic culture from political institutions or social conditions, we have attempted to specify its content by examining attitudes in a number of operating democratic systems. And rather than deriving the social-psychological preconditions of democracy from psychological theory, we have sought to determine whether and to what extent these relations actually exist in functioning democratic systems. We do not argue that our study will shut off speculation and provide the precise and tested propositions of a complete theory of democracy, but, rather, that some of these propositions will survive the test of empirical-quantitative analysis and some will not. This stage of experiment should focus and direct inquiry by providing some answers to old questions and suggesting some new questions.

In still another respect we hope to contribute to the development of a scientific theory of democracy. By far the greatest amount of empirical research on democratic attitudes has been done in the United States. In our study we have included, in addition to our own country, Britain, Germany, Italy, and Mexico. Why we selected these particular countries is discussed below. Our five-country study offers us the opportunity to escape from this American parochialism and to discover whether relations found in the American data are also encountered in democratic countries whose historical experiences and political and social structures differ from one another.

Types of Political Culture

In our comparison of the political cultures of five contemporary democracies, we employ a number of concepts and classifications which it will be useful to specify and define. We speak of the "political culture" of a nation rather than the "national character" or "modal personality," and of "political socialization" rather than of child development or child rearing in general terms. This is not because we reject the psychological and anthropological theories that relate political attitudes to other components of personality, or because we reject those theories that stress the relationship between child development in general terms and the induction of the child into his adult political roles and attitudes. Indeed, this study could

12

not have been made without the prior work of those historians, social philosophers, anthropologists, sociologists, psychologists, and psychiatrists who have been concerned with the relations between the psychological and political characteristics of nations. In particular, this study has been greatly influenced by the "culture-personality" or "psychocultural approach" to the study of political phenomena. This approach has developed a substantial theoretical and monographic literature in the past twenty-five years.[9]

We employ the term political culture for two reasons. First, if we are to ascertain the relations between political and nonpolitical attitudes and developmental patterns, we have to separate the former from the latter even though the boundary between them is not as sharp as our terminology would suggest. The term political culture thus refers to the specifically political orientations—attitudes toward the political system and its various parts, and attitudes toward the role of the self in the system. We speak of a political culture just as we can speak of an economic culture or a religious culture. It is a set of orientations toward a special set of social objects and processes.

But we also choose political *culture*, rather than some other special concept, because it enables us to utilize the conceptual frameworks and approaches of anthropology, sociology, and psychology. Our thinking is enriched when we employ, for example, such categories of anthropology and psychology as socialization, culture conflict, and acculturation. Similarly, our capacity to understand the emergence and transformation of political systems grows

[9] General theoretical statements of this approach are to be found *inter alia* in Ruth Benedict, *Patterns of Culture*, New York 1934; Alex Inkeles and Daniel Levinson, "National Character: The Study of Modal Personality and Socio-Cultural Systems," in Gardner Lindzey (ed.), *Handbook of Social Psychology*, Cambridge, Mass., 1954, Vol. II; Bert Kaplan (ed.), *Studying Personality Cross-Culturally*, Evanston, Ill., 1961; Abram Kardiner, *The Psychological Frontiers of Society*, New York, 1939; Kardiner, *The Individual and His Society*, New York, 1945; Clyde Kluckhohn, Henry Murray, and David Schneider, *Personality in Nature, Society, and Culture*, New York, 1955; Harold D. Lasswell, *Psychopathology and Politics* in *Political Writings;* Nathan Leites, "Psychocultural Hypotheses About Political Acts," in *World Politics*, Vol. I, 1948; Ralph Linton, *The Cultural Background of Personality*, New York, 1945; Margaret Mead, "The Study of National Character," in Daniel Lerner and Harold D. Lasswell, *The Policy Sciences*, Stanford, 1951. Particularly relevant to our work is Alex Inkeles, "National Character and Modern Political Systems," in Francis L. K. Hsu (ed.), *Psychological Anthropology*, Homewood, Ill., 1961. And one of the most important recent contributions to the theory of national character and political culture is Lucian W. Pye's *Politics, Personality, and Nation Building*, New Haven, 1962, which both develops a general theory of personality and political attitudes and applies this to a study of Burmese patterns.

Studies of Germany include: R. Brickner, *Is Germany Incurable?*, Philadelphia, 1943;

when we draw upon the body of theory and speculation concerned with the general phenomena of social structure and process.

We appreciate the fact that anthropologists use the term culture in a variety of ways,. and that by bringing it into the conceptual vocabulary of political science we are in danger of importing its ambiguities as well as its advantages. Here we can only stress that we employ the concept of culture in only one of its many meanings: that of *psychological orientation toward social objects.* When we speak of the political culture of a society, we refer to the political system as internalized in the cognitions, feelings, and evaluations of its population. People are inducted into it just as they are socialized into nonpolitical roles and social systems. Conflicts of political cultures have much in common with other culture conflicts, and political acculturative processes are more understandable if we view them in terms of the resistances and the fusional and incorporative tendencies of cultural change in general.

Thus the concept of political culture helps us to escape from the diffuseness of such general anthropological terms as cultural ethos and from the assumption of homogeneity that the concept implies. It enables us to formulate hypotheses about relationships among the different components of culture and to test these hypotheses empirically. With the concept of political socialization we can go beyond the rather simple assumptions of the psychocultural school regarding relationships between general child development patterns and adult political attitudes. We can relate specific adult political attitudes and behavioral propensities to the manifest and latent political socialization experiences of childhood.

The political culture of a nation is the particular distribution of

---

H. V. Dicks, "Personality Traits and National Socialist Ideology," *Human Relations,* Vol. III, 1950; David Rodnick, *Postwar Germans,* New Haven, 1948, and Bertram Schaffner, *Fatherland. A Study of Authoritarianism in the German Family,* New York, 1948.

Studies of the United States include: Geoffrey Gorer, *The American People,* New York, 1948; Margaret Mead, *And Keep Your Powder Dry,* New York, 1942, and David Riesman, *The Lonely Crowd,* New Haven, 1950.

Studies of Russia include: H. V. Dicks, "Observations on Contemporary Russian Behavior," *Human Relations,* Vol. v, 1952; Geoffrey Gorer and John Rickman, *The People of Great Russia,* London, 1949; Nathan Leites, *A Study of Bolshevism,* Glencoe, Ill., 1953; Margaret Mead, *Soviet Attitudes Toward Authority,* New York, 1951, and Dinko Tomasic, *The Impact of Russian Culture on Soviet Communism,* Glencoe, 1953.

For England, see Geoffrey Gorer, *Exploring English Character,* New York, 1955. For France, see Nathan Leites, *On the Game of Politics in France,* Stanford, 1959; Rhoda Metraux and Margaret Mead, *Themes in French Culture,* Stanford, 1954, and Lawrence Wylie, *Village in The Vaucluse,* Cambridge, Mass., 1957. And for Japan, see Ruth F. Benedict, *The Chrysanthemum and The Sword,* Boston, 1946.

patterns of orientation toward political objects among the members of the nation. Before we can arrive at such distributions, we need to have some way of systematically tapping individual orientations toward political objects. In other words, we need to define and specify modes of political orientation and classes of political objects. Our definition and classification of types of political orientation follow Parsons and Shils, as has been suggested elsewhere.[10] Orientation refers to the internalized aspects of objects and relationships. It includes (1) "cognitive orientation," that is, knowledge of and belief about the political system, its roles and the incumbents of these roles, its inputs, and its outputs; (2) "affective orientation," or feelings about the political system, its roles, personnel, and performance, and (3) "evaluational orientation," the judgments and opinions about political objects that typically involve the combination of value standards and criteria with information and feelings.

In classifying objects of political orientation, we start with the "general" political system. We deal here with the system as a whole and include such feelings as patriotism or alienation, such cognitions and evaluations of the nation as "large" or "small," "strong" or "weak," and of the polity as "democratic," "constitutional," or "socialistic." At the other extreme we distinguish orientations toward the "self" as political actor; the content and quality of norms of personal political obligation, and the content and quality of the sense of personal competence vis-à-vis the political system. In treating the component parts of the political system we distinguish, first, three broad classes of objects: (1) specific *roles* or *structures,* such as legislative bodies, executives, or bureaucracies; (2) *incumbents* of roles, such as particular monarchs, legislators, and administrators, and (3) particular public *policies, decisions,* or *enforcements* of decisions. These structures, incumbents, and decisions may in turn be classified broadly by whether they are involved either in the political or "input" process or in the adminstrative or "output" process. By political or input process we refer to the flow of demands from the society into the polity and the conversion of these demands into authoritative policies. Some structures that are predominantly involved in the input process are

[10] Gabriel A. Almond, "Comparative Political Systems," *Journal of Politics, Vol.* xviii, 1956; Talcott Parsons and Edward A. Shils, *Toward a General Theory of Action,* Cambridge, Mass., 1951, pp. 53 ff.

political parties, interest groups, and the media of communication. By the administrative or output process we refer to that process by which authoritative policies are applied or enforced. Structures predominantly involved in this process would include bureaucracies and courts.

We realize that any such distinction does violence to the actual continuity of the political process and to the multifunctionality of political structures. Much broad policy is made in bureaucracies and by courts; and structures that we label as input, such as interest groups and political parties, are often concerned with the details of

FIGURE 1

Dimensions of Political Orientation

	1. System as General Object	2. Input Objects	3. Output Objects	4. Self as Object
Cognition				
Affect				
Evaluation				

administration and enforcement. What we are referring to is a difference in emphasis, and one that is of great importance in the classification of political cultures. The distinction we draw between participant and subject political cultures turns in part on the presence or absence of orientation toward specialized input structures. For our classification of political cultures it is not of great importance that these specialized input structures are also involved in the performance of enforcement functions and that the specialized administrative ones are involved in the performance of input functions. The important thing for our classification is what political objects individuals are oriented to, how they are oriented to them, and whether these objects are predominantly involved in the "upward" flow of policy making or in the "downward" flow of policy enforcement. We shall treat this problem in greater detail when we define the major classes of political culture.

We can consolidate what we have thus far said about individual orientations toward the polity in a simple 3 x 4 matrix. Figure I tells us that the political orientation of an individual can be tapped systematically if we explore the following:

1. What knowledge does he have of his nation and of his political

16

system in general terms, its history, size, location, power, "constitutional" characteristics, and the like? What are his feelings toward these systemic characteristics? What are his more or less considered opinions and judgments of them?

2. What knowledge does he have of the structures and roles, the various political elites, and the policy proposals that are involved in the upward flow of policy making? What are his feelings and opinions about these structures, leaders, and policy proposals?

3. What knowledge does he have of the downward flow of policy enforcement, the structures, individuals, and decisions involved in these processes? What are his feelings and opinions of them?

FIGURE 2
Types of Political Culture

	System as General Object	Input Objects	Output Objects	Self as Active Participant
Parochial	0	0	0	0
Subject	1	0	1	0
Participant	1	1	1	1

4. How does he perceive of himself as a member of his political system? What knowledge does he have of his rights, powers, obligations, and of strategies of access to influence? How does he feel about his capabilities? What norms of participation or of performance does he acknowledge and employ in formulating political judgments, or in arriving at opinions?

Characterizing the political culture of a nation means, in effect, filling in such a matrix for a valid sample of its population. The political culture becomes the frequency of different kinds of cognitive, affective, and evaluative orientations toward the political system in general, its input and output aspects, and the self as political actor.

Parochial Political Culture. When this frequency of orientations to specialized political objects of the four kinds specified in Figure 1 approaches zero, we can speak of the political culture as a parochial one. The political cultures of African tribal societies and autonomous local communities referred to by Coleman[11] would fall into this category. In these societies there are no specialized political roles: headmanship, chieftainship, "shamanship" are diffuse politi-

[11] Almond and Coleman, *Politics of the Developing Areas,* p. 254.

cal-economic-religious roles, and for members of these societies the political orientations to these roles are not separated from their religious and social orientations. A parochial orientation also implies the comparative absence of expectations of change initiated by the political system. The parochial expects nothing from the political system. Similarly, in the centralized African chiefdoms and kingdoms to which Coleman refers, the political cultures would be predominantly parochial, although the development of somewhat more specialized roles in these societies might mean the beginnings of more differentiated political orientations. Even larger-scale and more differentiated polities, however, may have predominantly parochial cultures. Rustow's characterization of the Ottoman Empire gives us an example:

"The authority of government, based almost entirely on taxation, the maintenance of an army, and an age-old tradition of dynastic rule, was felt most immediately in the towns, less directly in the villages, and hardly at all among the tribes. The provinces were ruled by military governors or landed feudatories with only occasional interference from the capital. The nomadic tribes lived in what an apt Arabic idiom calls the 'land of insolence,' respecting no outside authority. The city economies were largely regulated by the autonomous guilds of the craftsmen. In the country at large, each village was a self-contained unit economically as well as politically. The principal emissary of authority to the village, the tax gatherer, was less of a government official than a private contractor or subcontractor who recompensed himself as liberally as he could for the advances he had paid to his employers. Often the village was responsible for tax payments collectively—a circumstance which further reduced the control of authority over the *individual* peasant. Law itself was largely beyond the scope of the ruler, whose decrees in a few points supplanted or modified a universal structure of religious law and local custom."[12]

In this kind of polity the specialized agencies of central government might hardly touch the consciousness of townsmen, villagers, and tribesmen. Their orientations would tend to be unspecialized political-economic-religious ones, congruently related to the similarly unspecialized structures and operations of their tribal, religious, occupational, and local communities.

What we have been describing is extreme or pure parochialism

[12] *Ibid.*, pp. 378-79.

that occurs in simpler traditional systems where political speciali-
zation is minimal. Parochialism in more differentiated political
systems is likely to be affective and normative rather than cognitive.
That is to say, the remote tribesmen in Nigeria or Ghana may be
aware in a dim sort of way of the existence of a central political
regime. But his feelings toward it are uncertain or negative, and he
has not internalized any norms to regulate his relations to it.

The Subject Political Culture. The second major type of political
culture listed in Figure 2 is the subject culture. Here there is a
high frequency of orientations toward a differentiated political
system and toward the output aspects of the system, but orientations
toward specifically input objects, and toward the self as an active
participant, approach zero. The subject is aware of specialized
governmental authority; he is affectively oriented to it, perhaps
taking pride in it, perhaps disliking it; and he evaluates it either as
legitimate or as not. But the relationship is toward the system on
the general level, and toward the output, administrative, or "downward flow" side of the political system; it is essentially a passive relationship, although there is, as we shall show below, a limited
form of competence that is appropriate in a subject culture.

Again we are speaking of the pure subject orientation that is
likely to exist in a society where there is no differentiated input
structure. The subject orientation in political systems that have developed democratic institutions is likely to be affective and normative rather than cognitive. Thus a French royalist is aware of
democratic institutions; he simply does not accord legitimacy to
them.

The Participant Political Culture. The third major type of political culture, the participant culture, is one in which the members of
the society tend to be explicitly oriented to the system as a whole
and to both the political and administrative structures and processes: in other words, to both the input and output aspects of the
political system. Individual members of the participant polity may
be favorably or unfavorably oriented to the various classes of political objects. They tend to be oriented toward an "activist" role of
the self in the polity, though their feelings and evaluations of such
a role may vary from acceptance to rejection, as we shall show
below.

This threefold classification of political cultures does not assume
that one orientation replaces the others. The subject culture does

19

not eliminate diffuse orientations to the primary and intimate structures of community. To the diffuse orientations to lineage groups, religious community, and village it adds a specialized subject orientation to the governmental institutions. Similarly, the participant culture does not supplant the subject and parochial patterns of orientation. The participant culture is an additional stratum that may be added to and combined with the subject and parochial cultures. Thus the citizen of a participant polity is not only oriented toward active participation in politics, but is subject to law and authority and is a member of more diffuse primary groups.

To be sure, adding participant orientations to subject and parochial orientations does not leave these "earlier" orientations unchanged. The parochial orientations must adapt when new and more specialized orientations enter into the picture, just as both parochial and subject orientations change when participant orientations are acquired. Actually, some of the most significant differences in the political cultures of the five democracies included in our study turn on the extent and the way that parochial, subject, and participant orientations have combined, fused, or meshed together within the individuals of the polity.[13]

Another caution is necessary. Our classification does not imply homogeneity or uniformity of political cultures. Thus political systems with predominantly participant cultures will, even in the limiting case, include both subjects and parochials. The imperfections of the processes of political socialization, personal preferences, and limitations in intelligence or in opportunities to learn will continue to produce subjects and parochials, even in well-established and stable democracies. Similarly, parochials will continue to exist even in "high" subject cultures.

Thus there are two aspects of cultural heterogeneity or cultural "mix." The "citizen" is a particular mix of participant, subject, and parochial orientations, and the civic culture is a particular mix of citizens, subjects, and parochials. For the citizen we need concepts of proportions, thresholds, and congruence to handle the ways in which his constellation of participant, subject, and parochial attitudes is related to effective performance. For the civic culture, which we shall treat in detail below, we need the same concepts of proportions, thresholds, and congruence to handle the problem of what "mix" of citizens, subjects, and parochials is related to the ef-

13 See below, chaps. viii and x.

20

fective performance of democratic systems. When we compare the political cultures of our five countries we shall have the occasion to discuss these questions again.

Our threefold classification of participant, subject, and parochial is only the beginning of a classification of political cultures. Each one of these major classes has its subclasses, and our classification has left out entirely the dimension of political development and cultural change. Let us look into this latter question first, since it will enable us to handle the problem of subclassification with a better set of conceptual tools.

Political cultures may or may not be congruent with the structures of the political system. A congruent political structure would be one appropriate for the culture: in other words, where political cognition in the population would tend to be accurate and where affect and evaluation would tend to be favorable. In general, a parochial, subject, or participant culture would be most congruent with, respectively, a traditional political structure, a centralized authoritarian structure, and a democratic political structure. A parochial political culture that was congruent with its structure would have a high rate of cognitive orientations and high rates of positive affective and evaluative orientations to the diffuse structures of the tribal or village community. A subject political culture congruent with its system would have a high rate of cognition and high positive rates of the other two types of orientation to the specialized political system as a whole, and to its administrative or output aspects; while the congruent participant culture would be characterized by high and positive rates of orientation to all four classes of political objects.

Political systems change, and we are justified in assuming that culture and structure are often incongruent with each other. Particularly in these decades of rapid cultural change, the most numerous political systems may be those that have failed to attain congruence, or are moving from one form of polity to another.

To represent schematically these relations of congruence/incongruence between political structure and culture, we present Figure 3.

Any one of the three major types of political cultures may be located on the matrix in Figure 3. Thus we may speak of "allegiant"[14] parochial, subject, and participant cultures when cognitive, affective, and evaluative orientations to the appropriate

[14] We have borrowed the concept "Allegiant" from Robert E. Lane's book, *Political Ideology*, New York, 1962, pp. 170 ff.

21

objects of the polity approach unity, or perfect congruence between culture and structure. But congruence between culture and structure may be best represented in the form of a scale. The limits of congruence between culture and structure are established in columns 1 and 2 of the figure. The congruence is strong when the frequencies of positive orientations approach unity (+); the congruence is weak when the political structure is cognized but the frequency of positive feeling and evaluation approaches indifference or zero. Incongruence between political culture and structure begins when the indifference point is passed and negative affect and evaluation

FIGURE 3

Congruence/Incongruence Between Political Culture and Structure*

	Allegiance	Apathy	Alienation
Cognitive Orientation	+	+	+
Affective Orientation	+	0	–
Evaluative Orientation	+	0	–

* A (+) sign means a high frequency of awareness, or of positive feeling, or of evaluation toward political objects. A (–) sign means a high frequency of negative evaluations or feelings. A (0) means a high frequency of indifference.

grow in frequency (—). We may also think of this scale as one of stability/instability. As we move toward the first column in the figure, we are moving toward an allegiant situation: one in which attitudes and institutions match; as we move toward the third column, we are moving toward alienation: where attitudes tend to reject political institutions or structures.

But this scale is only a beginning, since the incongruence may take the form of a simple rejection of a particular set of role incumbents (e.g., a particular dynasty and its bureaucracy); or it may be an aspect of a systemic change, that is, a shift from a simpler pattern of political culture to a more complex one. We have already suggested that all political cultures (with the exception of the simple parochial ones) are mixed. Thus a participant culture contains individuals who are oriented as subjects and parochials; and a subject culture will contain some parochials. We use the term "systemically mixed" political cultures to refer to those in which there are significant proportions of both the simpler and more complex patterns of orientations. When we say these cultures are systemically mixed, we do not intend to suggest that there is an inevitable tendency for the development to complete itself. The

22

process of political culture change may stabilize at a point that falls short of congruence with a centralized authoritarian structure or a democratic one; or the development may take a course such as in Britain, where a slow, continuous pattern of cultural change was accompanied by correspondingly continuous changes in structure. Political cultures may remain systemically mixed for a very long time indeed, as witnessed by the experience of France, Germany, and Italy in the nineteenth and present centuries. When they do remain mixed, however, there are inevitable strains between culture and structure, and a characteristic tendency toward structural instability.

If the three types of political culture represented in Figure 2 are the pure forms of political culture, we may distinguish three types of systemically mixed political cultures: (1) the parochial-subject culture, (2) the subject-participant culture, and (3) the parochial-participant culture.

The Parochial-Subject Culture. This is a type of political culture in which a substantial portion of the population has rejected the exclusive claims of diffuse tribal, village, or feudal authority and has developed allegiance toward a more complex political system with specialized central governmental structures. This is the classic case of kingdom building out of relatively undifferentiated units. The chronicles and histories of most nations include this early stage of shift from local parochialism to centralized authority. But the shift may stabilize at a point that falls short of a fully developed subject culture. The loosely articulated African kingdoms, and even the Ottoman Empire, are examples of stable, mixed subject-parochial cultures where the latter predominates and central authority takes the form of a primarily extractive, dimly cognized set of political objects. The problem of cultural change from parochial to subject patterns is a difficult one, and unstable moves back and forth are common in the early history of nations.[15]

What we are suggesting is that the composition of this class may be viewed as subvarieties arranged on a continuum. At one ex-

[15] The classic case is that of the succession to King Solomon in the kingdom of Israel. When Solomon died, the parochial (tribal and lineage) leaders of Israel came to his son Rehoboam, saying, "Thy father made our yoke hard; but do thou now make lighter the hard service of thy father, and his heavy yoke which he put upon us and we will serve thee." Rehoboam's older counselors advised him to lighten the yoke and pay more respect to the autonomy of the persisting parochial tribal and lineage groups. His younger men—fanatical modernizers—offered him the celebrated advice to tell the traditional leaders of the people, "My little finger is thicker than my father's loins. . . . If

treme we might place the political culture under Prussian absolutism, which went rather far in suppressing parochial orientations; at the other, the political culture in the Ottoman Empire, which never went further than an extractive external relationship to its constituent, more or less parochial units. The contrast between Prussian and British absolutism is an interesting one from this point of view. We have already made the point that even "high" political cultures are mixes, and that the individual orientations comprising them are also mixes. In Prussia, in the typical individual case, we may assume that the intensity of the subject orientation was much stronger than that of the parochial, while in Britain we suggest there was greater balance, and, furthermore, the parochial and subject strata were more congruent. These *psychological* mixes may explain the contrast between the eighteenth century Prussian and British authority images: the first, of *Kadavergehorsam;* the second, of the self-confident, if deferential, country squire, merchant, and yeoman. Similarly, the *cultural* mix in Prussia probably involved more of a polarization between a persisting parochial subculture—exemplified in the extreme case by the peasantry on the East German estates—and a subject subculture among those groups most affected by the impact of Prussian absolutism: the bureaucracy down to the lowest levels and the increasingly large proportion of Prussian manpower undergoing the Prussian army experience.

Thus change from a parochial to a subject political culture may stabilize at a number of points on the continuum and produce different political, psychological, and cultural mixes. We also suggest that the kind of mix that results has great significance for the stability and performance of the political system.

The Subject-Participant Culture. The way in which the shift from a parochial to a subject culture is solved greatly affects the way in which the shift from a subject to a participant culture takes place. As Pye points out, the inculcation of a sense of national loyalty and identification, and of a propensity to obey the regulations of central authority, is the first priority problem in the

---

my father has burdened you with a heavy yoke, I will add to your yoke; if my father hath chastised you with whips, then will I chastise you with scorpion thorns" (I Kings 12:4-11). The consequences of Rehoboam's acceptance of the advice of the young modernizers, as told in the rest of *Kings,* suggest that too violent an attack on parochialism may cause both parochial and subject orientations to decline to apathy and alienation. The results are political fragmentation and national destruction.

24

emerging nations.[16] In the shift from a subject to a participant culture, the parochial and local autonomies, if they survive, may contribute to the development of a democratic infrastructure. Certainly this is what happened in the British case. Local authorities, municipal corporations, religious communities, and merchant groups in which the tradition of guild freedoms still persisted became the first interest groups in the developing British democracy. The lesson is a significant one. Precisely because the development of a subject culture in England stopped short of destroying local and parochial structures and cultures, these could become available at a later time and in modified form as an influence network that could relate Britons as competent citizens to their government. The more massive impact of the Prussian state authority drove parochial institutions into privacy, or assimilated them to state authority. Thus the era of democratization in Germany began with a great gap between the private and public spheres, and the infrastructure that emerged failed to arc across from individual, family, and community to the institutions of governmental authority.

In the mixed subject-participant culture a substantial part of the population has acquired specialized input orientations and an activist set of self-orientations, while most of the remainder of the population continue to be oriented toward an authoritarian governmental structure and have a relatively passive set of self-orientations. In the Western European examples of this type of political culture —France, Germany, and Italy in the nineteenth and present centuries—there was a characteristic pattern of structural instability with an alternation of authoritarian and democratic governments. But more than structural instability results from this kind of cultural mix. The cultural patterns themselves are influenced by the structural instability and the cultural stalemate. Because participant orientations have spread among only a part of the population, and because their legitimacy is challenged by the persisting subject subculture and suspended during authoritarian interludes, the participant-oriented stratum of the population cannot become a competent, self-confident, experienced body of citizens. They tend to remain democratic aspirants. That is, they accept the norms of a participant culture, but their sense of competence is not based on experience or on a confident sense of legitimacy. Furthermore, the structural instabilities that frequently accompany the mixed sub-

[16] Pye, *Politics, Personality, and Nation Building*, pp. 3 ff.

ject-participant culture, the frequent ineffectiveness of the democratic infrastructure and of the governmental system, tend to produce alienative tendencies among the democratically oriented elements of the population. Taken together, this kind of a political cultural stalemate may produce a syndrome with components of idealist-aspiration and alienation from the political system, including the infrastructure of parties, interest groups, and press.

The mixed subject-participant culture, if it persists over a long period of time, also changes the character of the subject subculture. During the democratic interludes the authoritarian-oriented groups must compete with the democratic ones within a formally democratic framework. In other words, they must develop a defensive political infrastructure of their own. While this does not transform the subject subculture into a democratic one, it certainly changes it, often to a significant degree. It is not accidental that authoritarian regimes that arise in political systems with mixed subject-participant cultures tend to have populistic overtones, and in the more recent period of totalitarianism these regimes have even adopted the democratic infrastructure in a grossly distorted form.

The Parochial-Participant Culture. In the parochial-participant culture we have the contemporary problem of cultural development in many of the emerging nations. In most of these countries the political culture is predominantly parochial. The structural norms that have been introduced are usually participant; for congruence, therefore, they require a participant culture. Thus the problem is to develop specialized output and input orientations simultaneously. It is not surprising that most of these political systems, always threatened by parochial fragmentation, teeter like acrobats on tightropes, leaning precariously at one time toward authoritarianism, at another toward democracy. There is no structure on either side to lean on, neither a bureaucracy resting upon loyal subjects, nor an infrastructure arising from responsible and competent citizens. The problem of development from parochial to participant culture seems, on first look, to be a hopeless one; but if we remember that most parochial autonomies and loyalties survive, we may at least say that the development of participant cultures in some of the emerging nations has not yet been precluded. The problems are to penetrate the parochial systems without destroying them on the output side, and to transform them into interest groups on the input side.

26

Political Subculture and Role Culture

We have already made the point that most political cultures are heterogeneous. Even the most fully developed participant cultures will contain surviving strata of subjects and parochials. And even within that part of the culture that is oriented toward participation there will be persistent and significant differences in political orientation. Adapting the terminology of Ralph Linton to our purposes, we use the term "subculture" to refer to these component parts of political cultures.[17] But we have to distinguish at least two types of subcultural cleavage. First, the term may be used to refer to population strata that are persistently oriented in one way toward policy inputs and outputs, but are "allegiantly" oriented toward the political structure. Thus in the United States the left wing of the Democratic party and the right wing of the Republican party accept as legitimate the structures of American politics and government, but differ persistently from each other on a whole range of domestic and foreign policy issues. We refer to these as policy subcultures.

But the kind of cleavage we are most interested in is that which occurs in systemically mixed systems. Thus in a mixed parochial-subject culture one part of the population would be oriented toward diffuse traditional authorities, and another toward the specialized structure of the central authoritarian system. A mixed parochial-subject culture may actually be characterized by a "vertical" as well as a horizontal cleavage. Thus if the polity includes two or more traditional components, then there will be, in addition to the emerging subject subculture, the persisting separate cultures of the formally merged traditional units.

The mixed subject-participant culture is a more familiar and even more contemporary problem in the West. A successful shift from a subject to a participant culture involves the diffusion of positive orientations toward a democratic infrastructure, the acceptance of norms of civic obligation, and the development of a sense of civic competence among a substantial proportion of the population. These orientations may combine with subject and parochial orientations, or they may conflict. England in the nineteenth and present centuries moved toward and attained a political culture that combined these orientations. It is true, of course,

---

[17] Ralph Linton, *The Cultural Background of Personality*.

27

that the Radicals in the first part of the nineteenth century and the Socialist and Labour left-wing groups at a later time were opposed to the monarchy and the House of Lords. But these tendencies resulted in the transformation, not the elimination, of these institutions. Political subcultures in England, consequently, are examples of our first type of cleavage, the one based on persistent policy differences rather than upon fundamentally different orientations toward political structure.

France is the classic case of the second type of political cultural heterogeneity. The French Revolution did not result in a homogeneous orientation toward a republican political structure; instead, it polarized the French population into two subcultures, one of participant aspiration and one dominated by subject and parochial orientations. The structure of the French political system has been at issue ever since that time, and what was at first a bipolarization of political culture was followed by further fragmentations, as the Socialists followed the Jacobins, and the Communists the Socialists, and as the right wing divided into a "rallied" and an "unrallied" part.

Vertical subcultural phenomena of this kind may be encountered in subject and participant cultures, or may compound the cultural fragmentation of mixed subject-participant cultures. We refer to the patterns of orientation in multinational polities, such as the Russian and the Austro-Hungarian empires. Here members of special ethnic-linguistic-national groups rejected the legitimacy of the polity that assimilated them, and persisted in their allegiance to their earlier political systems. Thus a vertical fragmentation combined with a subject-participant fragmentation to produce structural instabilities and disintegrative tendencies of a very high order.

On the other hand, policy subcultures may turn into structural ones, as, for example, in the case of the Confederacy during the American Civil War. Here the alternative appeared to be the formation of a separate polity. In many European countries the failure of the dominant elites to respond to the moderate demands for structural and policy changes put forward by the left in the first half of the nineteenth century led to the development of the structurally alienated, revolutionary socialist, syndicalist, and anarchist left of the second half of the nineteenth century.

In England, the Old Commonwealth, the United States, and the Scandinavian countries, the issues of political structure were resolved in the course of the nineteenth and early twentieth centuries: what emerged were homogeneous political cultures, in the sense of structural orientation. The subcultural phenomena in these countries turn on persistent policy differences. Left and right both tend to accept the existing political structure and differ only on the substance of policy and political personnel. What is most interesting is that in this group of countries in the last decades, the policy differences have tended to become less sharp, and there is a larger common body of agreement. In other words, subcultural cleavage has attenuated and cultural homogeneity has extended from structural orientation into policy orientation.

This brief discussion of political subculture serves only to introduce the concept. Some of its implications and consequences will be considered at later points in the book. But we would mislead the reader if we were to suggest that our study treats proportionally each aspect of political culture. Our study stresses orientation to political structure and process, not orientation to the substance of political demands and outputs. We need not apologize for this emphasis, but must point out how this choice may tend to obscure significant dimensions of political culture, and significant relationships between general psychocultural patterns and the substance of politics and public policy. A study that stresses orientation to public policy would require at least as much of a major effort as the present one. It would have to relate systematically types of public policy orientations to types of social structure and cultural values, as well as to the socialization processes with which they are related. A similarly rigorous separation of public policy orientation, general culture orientation, and socialization patterns would also be necessary, in order for us to discover the real character and direction of relationships among these phenomena.

We have to introduce still another complication, that of "role culture." The more complex political systems are characterized by specialized structures of roles—bureaucratic, military, political executive, party, interest group, media of communication. These centers of initiative and influence in the political system also produce cultural heterogeneity. The heterogeneity results from two sources. First, the elites who perform these roles may be recruited from particular political subcultures; and second, the process of induction and socialization into these roles produces different

29

values, skills, loyalties, and cognitive maps. Since these elites are crucial in the formulation and execution of policy, the kinds of cultural differences existing among them may seriously affect the performance of political systems.

For example, in both Germany and France the bureaucratic and military elites were traditionally recruited from the aristocratic and authoritarian subcultures. In addition, the role socialization of these elites reinforced the antidemocratic tendencies and were significant obstacles to the emergence of homogeneous participant cultures.

But role culture can be "progressive" as well as "regressive" from a developmental point of view. In many of the contemporary emerging nations the impulse toward political modernization is concentrated in the civil and military bureaucracy and among the political party elites. These elites may aspire toward the develop- ment of powerful authoritarian political systems, toward democratic ones, or some combination of the two, without fully appreciating the complexities involved in this pattern of cultural change.

In stable, legitimate political systems, role cultures vary in con- tent simply because the tasks performed by these role incumbents and the "corps spirit" to which they are exposed produce differences in cognition, affect, and evaluation. But again we may differentiate patterns of role cleavage according to whether they involve dif- ferences in structural orientation or simply in policy orientation. In a stable political system, differences in role culture tend to be limited to the substance of policy. The legitimacy of the structure of the system is accepted. In unstable ones policy differences com- bine with differences in structural orientation and may result in cultural fragmentation at the elite level. Thus the fragmentation of general political culture in France was compounded by fragmen- tation in role cultures, with the higher civil service and the officer corps oriented to an authoritarian structure, and a large part of the political party, interest groups, and communications elites oriented to a democratic structure. Indeed, fragmentation at the level of political elites may persist simultaneously with a trend toward homogeneity at the mass cultural level. The recent experience of the British Labour party is a case in point. Sharp differences with the Conservative party over domestic and foreign policy are concen- trated among the constituency militants. For the rank-and-file

Labour party voter these issues tend to have little salience. His ties with both class and party have tended to loosen as his economic and social opportunities have improved.

The Civic Culture: A Mixed Political Culture

At an earlier point we discussed the historical origins of the civic culture and the functions of that culture in the process of social change. Much of this book will offer an analysis and description of the culture and of the role it plays in the maintenance of a democratic political system. It will be useful therefore to spell out, if only briefly, some of its main characteristics.

The civic culture is not the political culture that one finds described in civics textbooks, which prescribe the way in which citizens ought to act in a democracy. The norms of citizen behavior found in these texts stress the participant aspects of political culture. The democratic citizen is expected to be active in politics and to be involved. Furthermore, he is supposed to be rational in his approach to politics, guided by reason, not by emotion. He is supposed to be well informed and to make decisions—for instance, his decision on how to vote—on the basis of careful calculation as to the interests and the principles he would like to see furthered. This culture, with its stress on rational participation within the input structures of politics, we can label the "rationality-activist" model of political culture. The civic culture shares much with this rationality-activist model; it is, in fact, such a culture *plus something else.* It does stress the participation of individuals in the political input process. In the civic cultures described in this volume we shall find high frequencies of political activity, of exposure to political communications, of political discussion, of concern with political affairs. But there is *something else.*

In the first place, the civic culture is an allegiant participant culture. Individuals are not only oriented to political input, they are oriented positively to the input structures and the input process. In other words, to use the terms introduced earlier, the civic culture is a participant political culture in which the political culture and political structure are congruent.

More important, in the civic culture participant political orientations combine with and do not replace subject and parochial political orientations. Individuals become participants in the politi-

31

cal process, but they do not give up their orientations as subjects nor as parochials. Furthermore, not only are these earlier orientations maintained, alongside the participant political orientations, but the subject and parochial orientations are congruent with the participant political orientations. The nonparticipant, more traditional political orientations tend to limit the individual's commitment to politics and to make that commitment milder. In a sense, the subject and parochial orientations "manage" or keep in place the participant political orientations. Thus attitudes favorable to participation within the political system play a major role in the civic culture, but so do such nonpolitical attitudes as trust in other people and social participation in general. The maintenance of these more traditional attitudes *and their fusion* with the participant orientations lead to a balanced political culture in which political activity, involvement, and rationality exist but are balanced by passivity, traditionality, and commitment to parochial values.

A more precise description of the civic culture and of its relevance for democracy forms the major substance of this volume.

Micro- and Macropolitics.
Political Culture as the Connecting Link

Developments in social science methods in recent decades have enabled us to penetrate more deeply into the motivational basis of the political attitudes and behavior of individuals and groups. A substantial literature has accumulated, which includes studies of electoral attitudes and behavior, analyses of the relations between ideological and public policy tendencies and deeper attitude or personality characteristics, psychopolitical biographies of political leaders, studies of political attitudes in particular social groupings, and the like. Rokkan and Campbell refer to this focus on the individual, his political attitudes and motivations, whether as individual or as a member of a sample of a larger population, as "micropolitics," distinguishing it as a research approach from "macropolitics," or the more traditional concern of the student of politics with the structure and function of political systems, institutions, and agencies, and their effects on public policy.[18]

While the relationship between individual political psychology and the behavior of political systems and subsystems is clear in

[18] Stein Rokkan and Angus Campbell, "Norway And the United States of America," in *International Social Science Journal*, Vol. xii, No. 1, 1960, pp. 69 ff.

principle, much of the micropolitical literature is content to assert this relationship in general terms. The implication is given that since political systems are made up of individuals, it may be taken for granted that particular psychological tendencies in individuals or among social groups are important for the functioning of political systems and their outputs. This may indeed be the case when the researcher is concerned with the psychological conditions affecting the behavior of a particular role incumbent or incumbents, such as a particular political decision-maker at one extreme, or an electorate at the other. On the other hand, much of this literature fails to make the connection between the psychological tendencies of individuals and groups, and political structure and process. In other words, the currency of political psychology, while it has undoubted value, is not made exchangeable in terms of political process and performance.[19]

We would like to suggest that this relationship between the attitudes and motivations of the discrete individuals who make up political systems and the character and performance of political systems may be discovered systematically through the concepts of political culture that we have sketched out above. In other words, the connecting link between micro- and macropolitics is political culture. At an earlier point we stressed that individual political orientations must be separated analytically from other kinds of psychological orientations, in order for us to test hypotheses about the relationship between political and other attitudes. We also defined the political culture as the particular incidence of patterns of political orientation in the population of a political system. Now, through the concepts of political subculture and role culture, we can locate special attitudes and propensities for political behavior among parts of the population, or in particular roles, structures, or subsystems of the political system. These concepts of political culture allow us to establish what propensities for political behavior exist in the political system as a whole, and in its various parts, among special orientation groupings (i.e., subcultures), or at key points of initiative or decision in the political structure (i.e., role cultures). In other words, we can relate political psychology to political system performance by locating attitudinal and behavioral propensities in the political structure of the system.

Thus any polity may be described and compared with other

[19] For a valuable analysis of the problem of "linkage" between public opinion and governmental action, see V. O. Key, *Public Opinion And American Democracy*, New York, 1961, chaps. xvi ff.

polities in terms of (1) its structural-functional characteristics, and (2) its cultural, subcultural, and role-cultural characteristics. Our analysis of types of political culture is a first effort at treating the phenomena of individual political orientation in such a way as to relate them systematically to the phenomena of political structure. It enables us to escape from the oversimplifications of the psycho-cultural literature in two significant ways. By separating political orientation from general psychological orientation, we can avoid the assumption of the homogeneity of orientation, and look at this instead as a researchable relationship. And by examining the relationship between political cultural tendencies and political structural patterns, we can avoid the assumption of congruence between political culture and political structure. The relationship between political culture and political structure becomes one of the most significant researchable aspects of the problem of political stability and change. Rather than assuming congruence, we must ascertain the extent and character of the congruence or incongruence, and the trends in political cultural and structural development that may affect the "fit" between culture and structure.

We suggest that this research strategy will enable us to realize the full creative potentialities of the great insights of the psychocultural approach to the study of political phenomena. It is our own hypothesis that such research will show that *the importance of specific learning of orientations to politics and of experience with the political system* has been seriously underemphasized. Such learning is not only cognitive in character, but involves political feelings, expectations, and evaluations that result largely from political experiences rather than from the simple projection into political orientation of basic needs and attitudes that are the product of childhood socialization.

In still another respect our theory of political culture may serve to make the psychocultural approach more directly relevant to the study of the political system. In our discussion of types of political culture and the problem of congruence between culture and structure, we have pointed out that congruence is a relationship of affective and evaluative allegiance between culture and structure. Each kind of polity—traditional, authoritarian, and democratic—has one form of culture that is congruent with its own structure. Starting from the orientation and psychological requirements of different types of political structure, we are in a better position to formulate hypotheses about the kinds of personality tendencies and socialization practices that are likely to produce congruent political cultures and stable polities. Thus in the case of the civic culture, we may say that a pattern of socialization which enables the individual to manage the inevitable dissonances among his diffuse primary, his obedient output, and activist input roles supports a democratic polity. We can then look at socialization patterns and personality tendencies and ask just which of these qualities are crucial, to what extent they must be present, and what kinds of experience are most likely to produce this capacity for dissonant political role management. Our findings will show that the civic orientation is widespread in Britain and the United States and relatively infrequent in the other three countries, but we would be most hesitant to attribute these gross differences in political culture to the relatively slight differences in childhood socialization brought to light in our findings. They seem more clearly to be related to characteristics of the social environment and patterns of social interaction, to specifically political memories, and to differences in experience with political structure and performance. The most productive research on political psychology in the future will treat childhood socialization, modal personality tendencies, political orientation, and political structure and process as separate variables in a complex, multidirectional system of causality.

In one class of political contexts, however, the relations between political structure and culture, on the one hand, and character and personality, on the other, are relatively clear and dramatic. This is in our category of mixed political cultures. Here, in the parochial-subject, the subject-participant, and the parochial-participant cultures, we are dealing with societies that are either undergoing rapid systemic cultural-structural change or else have stabilized in a condition of subcultural fragmentation and structural instability. Fragmentation of political culture is also associated with general cultural fragmentation (e.g., the sharp division between the modernizing urban society and the traditional countryside; between the industrial economy and the traditional agrarian economy). We may assume that in these rapidly changing and fragmented societies, cultural heterogeneity and the high incidence of discontinuity in socialization produce a high incidence of psychological confusion and instability. Nowhere would this be more marked than in the parochial-participant cultures of the emerging nations of Asia and

35

Africa. Lucian Pye has provided us with a dramatic study of this kind of discontinuity in culture and socialization, its consequences for personality development and for the characteristics and performance of the Burmese political system.[20]

The Political Systems Included in Our Study

The test of this theory of political culture is its usefulness in explaining the properties and performance of different kinds of political systems. Thus far we have been operating with a simple threefold scheme of political culture and with three varieties of cultural mixture. Actually, our scheme is capable of handling more refined discrimination. The introduction of the concepts of sub-culture and role culture has already complicated the scheme and taken us beyond our simple matrices. In addition, these matrices were made up of "sets" rather than "elements"; thus in order to make precise discriminations, we would need to subcategorize each of the categories of orientation to political objects. Cognition, then, would include not only the quantity of information, but its specificity and accuracy, as well as the ability to organize and process information. Affect would include different intensities as well as different qualities, such as anger, enjoyment, contempt, and the like. Evaluative orientation is the most complex of all, since it would involve the use of different value standards in formulation of opinions and judgments.

Similarly, the categories of political objects can be dismantled into component elements. Thus the political system in the general sense would at the minimum be classifiable into "nation" and "political system." Input objects would include the media of communication, interest groups, political parties, legislatures, and the executive in its political aspect. And output objects would be classifiable in a variety of ways. Obvious subcategories would include the military, police, and the many functional varieties of civil roles, such as tax authorities, welfare authorities, educational authorities, and the like.

In the body of our study we deal mainly with these subcategories of orientations and objects, and the classification we have developed in the present chapter provides us simply with a logic for summarizing the cultural aspects of political systems. How to categorize

[20] *Op. cit.*, pp. 52-53 and 287 ff.

a given empirical political system is a decision that must be built up from frequencies of specified kinds of orientation toward the various subclasses of political objects. The dismantled scheme that we use in the substantive chapters of the book enables us to discuss subclasses of political culture, and indeed to specify the more minute differences between individual political cultures of the same subclass.

Our comparative study of political culture includes five democracies—the United States, Great Britain, Germany, Italy, and Mexico—selected because they represent a wide range of political-historical experience. At one extreme we selected the United States and Britain, both representing relatively successful experiments in democratic government. An analysis of these two cases will tell us what kinds of attitudes are associated with stably functioning democratic systems, the quantitative incidence of these attitudes, and their distribution among different groups in the population.

At the same time, a comparison of Britain and the United States might be useful as a test of some of the speculation about the differences between these two often-compared countries. Two recent writers on British politics comment on the persistence of traditional attitudes toward authority in that country. Brogan points out that in the historical development of Britain the culture of democratic citizenship, with is emphasis on initiative and participation, was amalgamated with an older political culture that stressed the obligations and rights of the subject.[21] Eckstein points out that the British political culture combines deference toward authority with a lively sense of the rights of citizen initiative.[22]

In the United States, on the other hand, independent government began with republican institutions, in a mood that rejected the majesty and sacredness of traditional institutions, and without a privileged aristocratic class. The functions of government tended to be relatively limited, and bureaucratic authority was the object of distrust. The American populist ideology rejected the conception of a professional, authoritative governmental service and the corresponding role of the obedient subject. The spoils system and political corruption further undermined the prestige of governmental authority. In an even broader sense, and for reasons we cannot deal

[21] D. W. Brogan, *Citizenship Today*, (Chapel Hill, N.C., 1960, pp. 9 ff.
[22] Harry Eckstein, "The British Political System," in S. Beer and A. Ulam, *The Major Political Systems of Europe*, New York, 1958, pp. 59 ff.

with here, the general pattern of authority in American social systems, including the family, tended to stress political competence and participation rather than obedience to legitimate authority.

In our comparison of the British and American political cultures, then, can we establish that Englishmen are more likely than Americans to have incorporated allegiant subject orientations as well as participant ones? And are they better able than Americans to manage the dissonances between democratic activism and "subject obedience"?

Several considerations led us to select Germany in our comparative study. Prussia, like Britain, had a relatively long period of effective, legitimate government before the introduction of democratic institutions. During the German unification in the nineteenth century, the Prussian bureaucratic authoritarian pattern was imposed more or less successfully on the other German states included in the nation. It has been argued that while Germany developed both a *Rechtsstaat* and a subject political culture, the experiments with democratic participation in the late nineteenth century and in the Weimar period never developed a participant political culture necessary to sustain these democratic institutions and give them force and legitimacy. Much of the speculation about the stability of contemporary democratic institutions in Germany turns on the question of the extent to which a sense of the responsibilities and opportunities of citizenship and mutual trust among political groupings have actually taken root among the German people.

One might conclude from an examination of their histories that Britain and Germany have in common deferential attitudes toward authority, growing out of their long predemocratic experiences with authoritarian control. But examination of history brings out one most significant difference. British government control in its predemocratic period never became as complete or as exhaustive of initiative as did the German. Brogan points out that even in the centuries when Englishmen were "subjects" there was a broad area of autonomy, freedom to form societies and engage in limited self-government.[23] In other words, even in the long centuries of British authoritarian government there was a limited participant component in the British political culture. Thus the amalgamation of citizen attitudes with subject attitudes is a centuries-old process, long predating the parliamentary and suffrage reforms of the

[23] Brogan, *op. cit.*, pp. 14 ff.

seventeenth, eighteenth, and nineteenth centuries. These reforms did not founder on a hard and unyielding subject culture, but could root themselves on a long-existent culture of pluralism and initiative.

As Krieger points out in his penetrating analysis of the development of German political ideas and movements, the German conception of liberty—from the days of the struggle of the princes against the imperial authority to the attainment of nationhood in the nineteenth century—was identified with the freedom of the state from external limitations rather than with the initiative and participation of individuals.[24] However, democratic political culture tendencies have been, and are, present in German society. They were present in the nineteenth century, in the Weimar period, and are to be observed today. Our study will enable us to establish which elements of a participant culture are present in the German population and which are lacking.

We have included Italy and Mexico in our study, as examples of less well-developed societies with transitional political systems. Italy, at least in the South and the islands, has a premodern social and political structure. If we consider Italian political history for a moment, it is evident that Italy never really developed an allegiant national political culture in modern times. The Italian monarchy of the pre-World War I period was denied legitimacy by the Church. The rule of *non expedit* required that the faithful refuse to accord legitimacy to the new state, refuse to participate in its processes.[25] During the Fascist interlude an effective state apparatus developed, but it was more the external control of a society by a coercive authority than a relatively free according of legitimacy to an established political system. In this respect Italy is unlike Britain and Germany, both of which had integrated and legitimate authoritarian systems before the introduction of democratic institutions.

In his study of a village in the southern Italian province of Lucania, Banfield characterizes the political culture of this area as "amoral familism," according legitimacy neither to the bureaucratic authoritarian organs of the state, nor to the civic-political organs of party, interest group, or local community.[26] It would be incorrect to view all of Italy in these terms, but our own data will tend to sup-

[24] Leonard Krieger, *The German Idea of Freedom*, Boston, 1957, *passim* and pp. 458 ff.
[25] D. A. Binchy, *Church and State in Fascist Italy*, London, 1941.
[26] Edward C. Banfield, *The Moral Basis of a Backward Society*, Glencoe, Ill., 1958, pp. 7 ff.

port Banfield's claim that the Italian political culture contains unusually strong parochial, alienative subject, and alienative participant components. Democratic aspirational tendencies are also present, primarily concentrated on the left, but these are relatively weak in comparison with the widespread mood of rejection that affects the attitudes of the great majority of Italians toward their political system in all its aspects.

We selected Mexico as our fifth country in order to have at least one "non-Atlantic community" democracy. Mexico can hardly be viewed as representing the emerging nations of Asia and Africa, yet no single country could possibly represent the variety of socio-political structures and historical experiences of the emerging nations. It has in common with many of these nations a high rate of industrialization, urbanization, and increased literacy and education. Before the revolution, Mexican government and politics were essentially alien, extractive, and exploitative structures resting uneasily on a society made up essentially of kinsmen, villagers, and ethnic and status groups. In the last thirty or forty years, however, the Mexican Revolution has deeply affected the social and political structure and has stimulated modern and democratic aspirations and expectations.[27]

In contrast to Italy, where a large portion of the population tends to view the political system as an alien, exploitative force, many Mexicans tend to view their revolution as an instrument of ultimate democratization and economic and social modernization. At the same time, the Mexican democratic infrastructure is relatively new. Freedom of political organization is more formal than real, and corruption is widespread throughout the whole political system. These conditions may explain the interesting ambivalence in Mexican political culture: many Mexicans lack political experience and skill, yet their hope and confidence are high; combined with these widespread participant aspirational tendencies, however, are cynicism about and alienation from the political infrastructure and bureaucracy. In addition, Mexico is the least "modern" of our five countries; that is, there is still a relatively large tradition-oriented village population and a high illiteracy rate. Perhaps the Mexican case will provide useful leads about the characteristics of political culture in non-Western countries undergoing similar experiences in modernization and democratization.

[27] Robert E. Scott, *Mexican Government in Transition*, Urbana, Ill., 1959, pp. 56 ff.

In this brief comparison of the political-historical experience of our five countries, we have been formulating hypotheses about the differences in political culture we might expect to find among them. However, inferences about political culture drawn from history leave unanswered the question of how much of a country's historical experience lives on in the memories, feelings, and expectations of its population, in what form it can be said to live on, which elements of the population are the bearers of which historical memories, and with what intensity. Here newer scientific methods can combine with the more traditional approaches, in our search for living history in the political cultures of peoples. Our survey will translate the rather simple and massive expectations inferred from history into quantities, demographic distributions, and regularities or relations. There is no necessary conflict between the methods of history and those of the behavioral sciences; they are actually supplemental and mutually supportive.

The results of our survey are reported in five parts. Part I is introductory, presenting the general theory of the study as well as an analysis of the methodological problems that arose in the planning and execution of a comparative study of this scale.

Part II presents the main body of descriptive data on the differences and similarities in the political cultures of our five countries. It begins with the dimension of knowledge of the political system in its governmental and political aspects, proceeds with an analysis of feelings toward and evaluations of the political system as a whole and of its various parts, and concludes with an analysis of attitudes toward the self as a political actor. A final chapter shows how these attitudes are related to one another in all five countries, and in particular how subjective political competence is related to political awareness, involvement, and morale.

In Part III we deal with the factors that affect political culture. In particular we examine the relationships between patterns of social interaction and of political culture, the relation between organizational affiliation and activity and political competence and participation, and the effects of patterns of participation in family, school, and work group on political attitudes.

In Part IV we discuss some of the group differences in our five countries and present summary profiles of the political cultures of our five countries as well as illustrative case histories.

Part V is a concluding chapter, which analyzes the relationship between the civic culture and the effective functioning of a democratic political system. It also evaluates the prospects for such a culture in the unstable democracies of Western Europe and among the new nations.

CHAPTER 2

CROSS-NATIONAL RESEARCH AND
POLITICAL BEHAVIOR: SOME
CONSIDERATIONS OF METHOD

ONE of the most significant recent developments in the social sciences is the revolution in data gathering and data evaluation.[1] This revolution depends on developments in the techniques by which data can be collected and analyzed: developments in the theory and method of sampling and in methods of statistical analysis, as well as in the mechanical equipment needed to handle large amounts of data. But the change depends upon more than the availability of research tools; it depends upon a new attitude toward the use of data. The social scientist no longer assumes that the facts of social or political life are known, or that they are easily accessible through casual observation, introspection, or systematic reading. One questions not merely the interpretation of facts, but in the first instance the facts themselves. Most important, perhaps, the criteria by which one accepts or rejects statements about social life are of a special nature. The ultimate criterion is the method by which they are gathered. The method should be relatively systematic and relatively reliable. And it ought to be amenable to replication, so that some other researcher looking at the same body of material would come up with roughly the same facts. Of course all this implies that the method be public and explicit.

An important aspect of the new concern with systematically gathered data is the relationship between the facts presented about social life and the universe of facts from which these are drawn. One

[1] On the "revolution" in social science, particularly in political science, see, among many others: David Truman, "The Impact on Political Science of the Revolution in the Behavioral Sciences," in the Brookings Institution, *Research Frontiers in Government and Politics*, Washington, D.C., 1955, pp. 202-31; Vernon Van Dyke, *Political Science: A Philosophical Analysis*, Stanford, 1960, and Roland Young (ed.), *Approaches to the Study of Politics*, Evanston, Ill., 1958.

does not ask merely if the facts presented are correct—if such-and-such people said so-and-so; or if certain events happened on certain days—but if the selection of facts is made in such a way as to allow generalizations about all the people one is interested in or all the events one is trying to describe. Has the researcher spoken to all relevant people or looked at all relevant events? Or if this is not possible, as it usually is not, are the people or events representative of the population in which he is interested? As Glazer points out, this approach to the selection of the facts of social life (or of political life) is quite new in social thought. "Whether one considers Aristotle or Montesquieu, one will find history or existing social life considered as simply a storehouse of examples to illustrate presumed truths."[2] And of course such a rich storehouse of material as history or social life can produce examples to satisfy anyone's preconceived notions. A systematic collection of data, on the other hand, refers to a set of explicit rules for fact gathering that limit the freedom of the researcher. He cannot select from the storehouse of events only those that support his preconceived notions. He must look at everything that is relevant or, if there is too much to look at, at a representative sample.

A further difference associated with the data-gathering revolution in the social sciences involves the origination of data by the researcher. He does not rely necessarily on that which is written or that which is known by savants. He may go out and "create" data that did not previously exist. The usual way this is done is to ask people questions as the survey researcher does (and as we did to prepare this book); questioning them, not as one might question a book or a man particularly learned in a specific field in order to get expert opinion on the subject, but in order to find out at firsthand what their own attitudes are on the particular subject.[3] By the "creation" of data about social attitudes or behaviors, we (hopefully) do not mean the creation of the attitudes and behaviors themselves. That this may also occur—that an attitude which did not previously exist may be created in an interview situation—is a danger in any research of this sort.

In the study of political science, the data-gathering revolution has had its major impact in the field of voting behavior. One reason for

[2] Nathan Glazer, "The Rise of Social Research in Europe," in Daniel Lerner (ed.), *The Human Meaning of the Social Sciences,* New York, 1959, p. 46.
[3] Glazer, *ibid.*

this is clear. Elections are easily amenable to statistical analysis: one deals with a large number of formally similar events (voting decisions), a situation that is perfect for statistical analysis. The first studies of voting behavior utilized available data (essentially voting statistics and ecological data), but since World War II there has been a growing body of studies that create data through survey analysis of the voting decision.[4] And these voting studies have expanded in scope; they attempt to explain more than voting behavior. Studies of voting behavior and other political surveys deal with political participation in general, political information, the satisfactions that individuals derive from politics, their motives in participating, and so forth.[5] They represent a major contribution to the systematic analysis of politics.

The present work attempts to apply some of the methods developed in the field of systematic survey research to the study of comparative politics. Ours is not specifically a voting study; we do not concentrate on any particular election, nor are we mainly interested in explaining the voting decision. Yet, in terms of the attitudes we are interested in and the techniques used, our work has been greatly influenced by these voting studies. Unlike other studies of political attitudes, however, ours is cross-national. Most survey studies of voting behavior or of other political attitudes have taken place within a single nation, the bulk of them in the United States.[6] Our study is multicontextual—a study of five nations. Throughout this book we shall concentrate on those nations—on their similarities and their differences. Because of our comparative approach, we must regretfully bypass interesting problems within the individual countries.

[4] The classic work using election statistics is Herbert Tingsten, *Political Behavior: Studies in Election Statistics*, London, 1937, while the pioneering work in election surveys has been done by Lazarsfeld and his associates and by Angus Campbell and his associates. See especially Bernard Berelson, Paul Lazarsfeld, and William McPhee, *Voting*, Chicago, 1954; Angus Campbell *et al.*, *The American Voter*, New York, 1960, and Paul Lazarsfeld, Bernard Berelson, and Hazel Gaudet, *The People's Choice*, New York, 1944. For a general discussion and citation of much of the relevant literature, see S. M. Lipset *et al.*, "The Psychology of Voting," in Gardner Lindzey (ed.), *The Handbook of Social Psychology*, Cambridge, Mass., 1954, Vol. II.

[5] See Robert Lane, *Political Life*, Glencoe, Ill., 1959, for a discussion of the various types of studies that have been undertaken.

[6] Some exceptions are: William Buchanan and Hadley Cantril, *How Nations See Each Other*, Urbana, Ill., 1953; The International Teacher's Study, reported in Eugene Jacobson and Stanley Schachter (eds.), "Cross-National Research: A Case Study," *Journal of Social Issues*, x (1954). See also Stein Rokkan, "Comparative Cross National Research: II Bibliography," *International Social Science Bulletin*, VII (1955), pp. 622-41.

In applying to the study of comparative politics a method that has been used with eminent success in studies of particular nations, we are following an old trend. The comparative study of politics has often developed by the adoption, after some time lag, of methods developed in the study of individual nations. The comparative approach to political parties and to pressure groups developed out of similar approaches within single nations—and incidentally enriched the study of comparative politics as well as of parties and pressure groups.[7] Hopefully, the present work will also enrich both fields of study.

A Description of the Citizenship Study

The present book is based upon about one thousand interviews carried on in each of five nations (about five thousand interviews in all). The nations were the United States, Great Britain, Germany, Italy, and Mexico. In each case an attempt was made to obtain a national cross-section sample.[8] The interviews ranged in length from about forty minutes to somewhat over an hour, though in some cases they lasted much longer. The interviews were largely structured, with about ten per cent of the questions open-ended in form. In each nation a small proportion of the respondents interviewed as part of the national cross-section were reinterviewed with a longer and less structured interview, which attempted to elicit more material of the sort dealt with in the cross-section interview, as well as to obtain a description of what we call an individual's "political life history."[9] The respondents for the follow-up interviews were selected on the basis of their answers in the cross-section interview. We tried to obtain a sample of various "citizen-types" (see above, Chapter 1) for reinterview. And within the categories of the various citizen-types we tried to achieve some demographic balance—some with high and low education, some men and women, and so forth.

[7] For a discussion of the trends in the study of comparative government, see Harry Eckstein and David E. Apter (eds.), *Reader in Comparative Politics*, New York, 1963, Introduction.

[8] For technical details about the sampling procedures, the interview form, and so forth, see the Appendices below. In Mexico the sample is of cities of 10,000 or more population.

[9] The original plan was to obtain 125 such interviews in each country. For a variety of reasons it was impossible to reinterview that many. The number of reinterviews actually completed were: United States, 49; United Kingdom, 114; Germany, 135; Italy, 121, and Mexico, 120. See Appendix A for a discussion of the selection of these respondents.

Since the selection of respondents for follow-up interviewing is based on their answers in the first wave of interviews, these second interviews cannot be considered a representative sample of our original sample.

The cross-section interviews were carried on in June and July of 1959 in all of the nations except the United States; the interviews in the United States were carried on in March 1960. In most cases the follow-up interviews took place about six months to a year after the first interviews. Interviewing was done by professional polling agencies in each of the countries (see above, pp. vii-viii); of these agencies, all but the National Opinion Research Center, University of Chicago, are affiliates of International Research Associates of New York, which participated in the supervision of the study in its planning and field stages.

The interviews were coded in each of the countries on the basis of a uniform set of coding instructions. IBM punch cards from the individual nations were sent to the United States, and the bulk of the analysis of the data was carried on at Princeton and Yale universities.

Such, in very brief outline, is a description of a research endeavor that began long before the interviewing itself was carried on, and, as is often the case, continued longer than the authors expected. The study began with a concern with the quality of data on political attitudes as well as with the explanations of democratic government based on such attitudes. Distinctions between political attitudes in modern democracies are often made on the basis of inadequate information or unsystematic impressions. Furthermore, the explanations of the effect of such attitudes on political structures often has an unfortunate circularity. In the absence of direct data on political attitudes, one often infers political attitudes from political structures. The stability of the British political system, for example, might be explained in terms of a basic consensus among the British people. But what is the evidence for the consensus? If one looks carefully, it is often the existence of a stable political system. To avoid such circularity, we decided to look directly, if we could, at political attitudes; to describe them, and to relate them to the functioning of political systems. And the original desire to be both descriptive and analytical is reflected in the organization of the book—the first half being largely descriptive of attitude patterns, the second somewhat more analytical.

The interview schedule that was sent into the field in 1959 and 1960 was the seventh version, the first version having been drawn up over a year before in Princeton. Each successive version was tested out in trial interviews; at first a few interviews were held in the Princeton area, and later, with the fifth and sixth versions, full-scale field pretests in the five nations were carried on. During these successive waves of interviewing, the interview schedule underwent substantial changes. The most obvious change was in length. In the first version the study directors followed up all their theoretical interests wherever they might lead. We also experimented with the possibility of obtaining in brief form a political biography of the individual—what political events he remembered, what political experiences he had. The result was anything but brief. The first interviews lasted more than a day. But each successive interview became shorter and more structured as we adjusted what we originally wanted to what we could reasonably obtain.

The third version of the interview, completed in the fall of 1958, was the first that was translated and tested outside of the United States: in Germany, Italy, Britain, and Sweden. (Shortly thereafter the decision was made to substitute Mexico for Sweden.) At this point we began the difficult process of adjusting the research instrument for simultaneous use in a number of societies. In a later section of this chapter we shall analyze some of the serious difficulties this entails. Suffice to mention here that the process of adjusting what we wanted in terms of what we could reasonably obtain was accelerated by the need for a research instrument applicable in several different contexts.

In the winter and early spring of 1958-1959 two successive waves of pretest interviews were carried on by the research agencies cooperating in the study. These brought to light many problems in translation as well as in cross-national applicability. Furthermore, the interviews revealed certain significant differences in the interviewing practices in the various nations—differences that necessitated more complete central control over the interviewing than was originally planned. It was necessary, for instance, to specify precisely the number of times an interviewer could probe for further information in an open-ended question, as well as the content of that probing. In this way, the extent to which a sophisticated interviewer could obtain a full response in a particular area through extensive follow-up questions was circumscribed, but the comparability of the results was increased.

The attempt to achieve comparability led, as we have suggested, to a constant adjustment of research goals. In the process of tightening the interview, some interests had to be pushed aside and some hypotheses had to be left untested. And the theoretical framework with which we started went through numerous modifications as we were faced with the task of designing a research instrument to test the theory. Such modifications are perhaps inevitable in social research; yet they are not all to the bad. In designing an actual research instrument, one is forced to consider the meaning and precision of one's concepts and of the relations among them. A concept that appears intuitively clear and precise may suddenly turn out to be quite ambiguous when one considers how to develop research operations to define it. There is a loss involved here. Theories in the social sciences that can be tested, even in a rough way, tend to be less general and more "middle-range" than those that are never subjected to any attempts at confirmation. But the loss is balanced by the fact that one attempts to combine theory with empirical research—a combination that is the goal of a science of politics. And one can hope to build more general theories out of more limited ones; the two do not necessarily conflict.

As we have mentioned, the interviewing was done by natives of each country. All interviewers had had previous experience, most in interviewing of a political nature. They all received special instructions and training in the particular problems associated with this survey, as did the coders in each country. The overall goal was to obtain results as comparable as possible.

This brief description cannot convey the excitement of the planning and administration of a large cross-national survey. Interviewers' reports are full of vignettes of attempts to trace respondents who are difficult to find; of the receptions interviewers received— usually friendly, sometimes hostile; of interviewers in Southern Italy traveling with sleeping bags because of the uncertainty of accommodations, and of interviewers jailed in Mexico and Louisiana because of suspicion about their purposes. Nor will we attempt to describe the excitement involved in attempting to analyze the results of five thousand interviews in five nations. Hopefully, this excitement will be conveyed by the analysis reported below.

The Uses of Comparative Survey Research

A cross-national survey of the type described in this book involves great labor and expense. It requires elaborate advanced planning, careful coordination, and substantial risk of a serious misstep at a number of points. And the difficulties of administering such a survey are fully matched by the difficulties of analysis once the data are gathered. Before cataloging some of the problems involved in a research operation of this sort—a catalog that might lead the reader to give up in despair—it might be well to suggest why such an endeavor was thought useful despite the difficulties it entails.

A cross-national study of political attitudes was felt to serve a variety of purposes and to be of use both to the student of comparative politics as well as to the student of political attitudes. One purpose of such a study is descriptive.

There exists very little systematic evidence about political attitudes for most nations, and even less (if any at all) that is comparable across nations. Yet much is written about political attitudes and the impact of these attitudes on political systems. In most cases the evidence for the existence of a particular type of political orientation among the citizens of a nation is indirect. Studies are made of the attitudes expressed in the writings of intellectuals; in the novels or poetry or even political science of a nation. One may also look at patterns of political behavior or political structure. The evidence of an alienative political orientation among a populace, for instance, might be the existence of frequent strikes or political violence. Or a high degree of political consensus among the citizens of a society might be inferred from the existence of a stable two-party system. It may be reasonable to infer political attitudes from such evidence, as the anthropologist infers attitudes from a society's folklore or institutionalized patterns of behavior. But these inferences need careful qualifications. And if one's goal is to explain a particular pattern of behavior in terms of a set of attitudes (as much political science implicitly attempts to do), one cannot use as evidence for those attitudes the very behavior patterns one is trying to explain. Thus a direct look at political attitudes, such as we attempt in this study, is useful in order to validate the inferences we have made about them from other material, and to develop independent measures that can be used to explain other phenomena.

Our interest was in political orientations, and it was to evidence about political orientations that we turned.

This brings up another advantage of such a study. Others have studied citizens' political attitudes in these five countries, not by inferring them from institutions, but by talking to Englishmen or to Mexicans. But in most cases this evidence, though direct, is un-systematic—based on casual conversation or inadequate samples. It is rather hard to stay what the "typical" Englishman encountered in a pub is typical of. We hoped to gather data about political attitudes that was at once both direct and more precise. By "pre-cise" we mean that (hopefully) our statements about the political orientations held by a population of a particular nation are likely to be closer to the "real" attitudes of that population than are state-ments based on unsystematic observation. We also mean that the reader can see and evaluate the evidence we have for a proposition. If we say, for instance, that cynicism is a characteristic of Italian attitudes toward politics, the reader should be aware that by "cynicism" we refer to the fact that people responded to a certain question a certain way; and by "characteristic" we mean a particular percentage of our sample answered the question a particular way. In this way the basis for our inferences will be laid bare for the reader's evaluation.

The fact that we can give some quantitative meaning to such words as "characteristic" or "usual" found in studies of political attitudes is important. In many cases we will describe differences in general political attitudes among the nations; in many of these cases the differences are quite striking. But with almost no excep-tions these statements refer to the frequency of a particular po-litical attitude in a nation. If we say that Britons and Mexicans differ in a particular attitude, this does not mean that all Britons think one thing and all Mexicans something else; there is usually a substantial overlap between the nations, as well as great variation within each one. What differs is the frequency with which a particular attitude is expressed. This allows us to talk of attitudes that are "characteristic" of a nation and to say *how* characteristic they are—without having to posit any uniformity of political at-titudes within that nation. Thus in the previous chapter we dis-cussed several types of political orientation. Each type is found in varying degrees in each of the several nations. But no single nation is composed of all one type, and in all there are some of each type.

That we have cross-national data on the same attitudes becomes important when we attempt to characterize nations by the patterns of attitudes found therein. In many single-nation studies of attitudes, the frequency with which citizens of one nation hold an attitude is given significance through implicit comparisons with the citizens of another country. Geoffrey Gorer, for instance, in his study of the "English character" (based on questionnaires distributed in Britain), assumes implicitly (and at times explicitly) that people in other nations would respond quite differently to the same question; for this reason he believes that his findings about English attitudes are significant.[10] With cross-national data we can test such assumptions.

To what extent is there uniformity of psychological type in a nation? This problem, raised in studies of national character, might be approached through the use of explicitly parallel cross-national data. (The parallel question for us is the extent of uniformity in political attitudes in a nation.) Much of the literature on national character assumes that there is a modal character type in each society; others argue that the distribution of character types has greater variability, that it is probably multimodal. Inkeles and Levinson, in their analysis of this literature, suggest that the data collected so far are inadequate to reveal which point of view is correct.[11] One reason for this is that the degree of variability of psychological types or of political attitudes depends heavily upon the nature of the measures used. Consider, for instance, the use of a systematic survey to discover whether political attitudes in a particular nation are uni- or multimodal. There are two reasons why it would be difficult to learn about the uniformity of attitudes in that way. In the first place, what is the index of deviance that would determine if there is uniformity on an attitude? Must 100 per cent of the people agree? 80 per cent? or perhaps 51 per cent? Clearly the percentage of deviants that will represent substantial nonuniformity will depend upon the centrality of the attitude to the attitude structure of the nation. Second, the type of question one asks determines to a large extent the number of modal attitudes one finds. Ask a question that allows the respondent to answer only yes or no, and you are likely to get a majority on one side or

---

[10] Geoffrey Gorer, *Exploring English Character*, New York, 1955.
[11] See Inkeles and Levinson, "National Character," in Lindzey, *Handbook of Social Psychology*, p. 982.

the other. But give respondents ten choices and the number of groups will increase, while the number of respondents in the largest group will decrease. If, however, one can carry on a cross-national survey and can make comparative statements—for example: in relation to a particular attitude tapped by a particular type of question, there is greater uniformity in one nation than in another —then one can make meaningful statements about the *relative* uniformity in attitude within nations.[12]

Thus through the use of a cross-national survey we hope to improve our ability to describe the state of attitudes in various nations —both because the attitudes are discovered through a systematic questioning of a representative sample of the nation, which makes the statements about attitudes more accurate; and because the data are from several nations at once, which gives us a bench mark for interpreting the meaning of different distributions of attitudes.

But our interest is only partly to describe attitudes in the nations we study. Our goal is to analyze attitudes as well as to explain why attitudes are the way they are. For comparative analysis of political behavior the use of a cross-national survey seems quite apt. In the first place, the statistical methods by which one analyzes the results of survey research are essentially comparative. In the analysis of survey research one cannot say that two attributes are associated because they exist frequently together. They must exist more frequently together than one would expect by chance. If, for instance, a large number of the alienated vote for a radical party, one does not assume that there is an association between political alienation measured on an attitude scale and voting for radical parties. It is only when a significantly *larger* number of the alienated vote for such a party than vote for radical parties among the non-alienated, that one can say these attitudes are associated—essentially a comparative statement.[13]

The above suggests that there is nothing particularly new in using survey research for comparative analysis. Almost all such re-

[12] However, even this apparently simple operation of comparing results on the same question asked in a number of countries is not as easy as it sounds, as will be pointed out below.

[13] As Yule and Kendall put it: ". . . in statistics the word 'association' has a technical meaning different from the one current in ordinary speech. In common language one speaks of 'A' and 'B' as being associated if they appear together in a number of cases. But in statistics 'A' and 'B' are associated only if they appear together in a greater number of cases than is to be expected if they are independent. Thus, if we consider

search is analyzed comparatively: men are compared with women, Republicans with Democrats, Catholics with Protestants. A cross-national survey differs from surveys within one nation, not by being comparative, but by using the same logic as is used in a single-nation survey to focus attention on *cross-national* comparisons.[14] This focus has a significant advantage if one wants to analyze political attitudes and behavior. In a survey within a single nation the explanatory factors that are introduced to explain an individual's political attitudes or behavior tend to be characteristics of the individual himself, not of the political system. An individual's vote or his interest in politics is explained in terms of his personality, his social class, his place of residence, the voting preferences of those within his primary group, his perceptions of candidates, parties, or issues. It is not explained in terms of the characteristics of the political system—the governmental structure, the electoral system, the structure of partisan conflict, and so forth. The reason why such "macrocharacteristics" of the political system are not introduced to explain individual attitudes ought to be clear. When one is dealing with a single system, the characteristics of that system are, in effect, held constant. As the comparative nature of statistical analysis indicates, one can estimate the relationship of one variable to another only if there is a comparable situation in which one of the variables is missing. On the individual level one can estimate the relationship between higher education and political participation only if there exists within the country a group with lower education. On the systemic level one can estimate

---

means of land transportation as dichotomized into road and rail travel, we may say, in the customary use of the term, that road transport is associated with speed. But it does not follow that the two are statistically associated, because rail transport may be equally associated with speed and, in fact, the attribute may be independent of the means of travel in these two manners." C. Udny Yule and M. G. Kendall, *An Introduction to the Theory of Statistics*, London, 1937, p. 37.

[14] For those unfamiliar with the logic of the statistical analysis of the sort of survey research carried on in this book, good sources are Herbert Hyman, *Survey Design and Analysis*, Glencoe, Ill., 1955, Part III, and Paul Lazarsfeld, "Interpretation of Statistical Relations as a Research Operation," in Lazarsfeld and Morris Rosenberg (eds.), *The Language of Social Research*, Glencoe, Ill., 1955, pp. 115-24.

In a sense we are using the word comparative in two different ways: to refer to the study of politics across national borders, and also to refer to comparative analysis (comparison of any relevant categories) of survey research. The word is probably more appropriate to the latter field, and for the former we should perhaps speak of "cross-national" research as the particular branch of political science in which we are working. All political science that aspires to be scientific must be comparative. In an attempt to develop general propositions it may compare nations, regions, political parties, different types of organizations, stable with unstable societies, men with women—it may

the effect of a two-party system on voting behavior only if there is in another country another type of party system with which to compare it.

If there are several political systems available for analysis, the characteristics of one system can be used directly to explain individual behavior, and can also help make more precise the relationships discovered among characteristics of the individual. We can begin to estimate the systemic conditions under which characteristics of individuals are related. The proposition, derived from numerous studies of voting behavior in the United States, that higher-status individuals participate most in politics might, for instance, not hold in political systems with other party structures. Or the relationship between interest in politics and partisan affiliation (the finding that "independents" are less politically interested) might not apply to societies whose political histories differ from that of the United States. Without comparative data one cannot know. By focusing attention on the characteristics of political systems, cross-national surveys can add a significantly new dimension to the analysis of individual political behavior; and they can do much to bring more closely together the analysis of individual political behavior with that of political systems.[15]

Cross-national survey work has another advantage. In order to compare political behavior cross-nationally, one must be able to specify dimensions of political behavior that apply to all the systems studied. One must therefore undertake a very important task for comparative analysis: the development of a means of conceptualizing politics in ways that have wide applicability.

---

make any comparison that appears important. But the logic of survey research—that one can find association among attributes (i.e., that one can find useful general propositions) only in a comparative context—is but one specific form of the logic of all social research. On the use of the term "cross-national" rather than "comparative" to describe the type of research we are discussing, see H. C. J. Duijker and Stein Rokkan, "Organizational Aspects of Cross-National Social Research," *Journal of Social Issues*, x (1954), pp. 8-24.

[15] On this general topic, and especially on the problem of how micro- and macro-explanations of political behavior differ, see Stein Rokkan, "The Comparative Study of Political Participation: Notes Toward a Perspective on Current Research," in Austin Ranney (ed.), *Recent Developments in the Behavioral Study of Politics*, Urbana, Ill., 1962. Rokkan's is the best discussion of the problems of analyzing cross-national research in political behavior.

Estimating the impact of structural constraints on political attitudes does not have to be done cross-nationally. One can compare political attitudes under differing structural conditions within a single nation. One can, for instance, compare cities with differing social structures, or electoral districts with differing party structures, or states

Some Problems in Cross-National Survey Research

The cross-national survey faces all the problems of the national survey—problems of conceptualization, sampling, interview design, interviewer training, and so forth. There is, however, one major difference. In the cross-national survey all these problems, with the possible exception of devising the questionnaire, are multiplied by the number of nations studied: in this case five samples were drawn, the no-response problem had to be faced five times, five interviewing staffs had to be trained, and so on. In effect, then, we are presenting the results of five simultaneous surveys.

But this in itself would introduce no new problems over ordinary single-nation survey research if the five surveys were treated and analyzed independently. The new and intriguing problems begin when one attempts to treat the five surveys as comparable, and to concentrate, not on individual nations, but on comparisons across nations. In most cases, however, even these problems are not different in *kind* from those encountered in systematic research in a single nation: they are the same difficulties, only much more so. For example, one problem in cross-national research is the possible lack of standardization in the interview situation. Attitudes toward interviewing may vary from one nation to another: in some nations it may be better known than in others, or the relationship between the interviewer and the respondent may not be uniform in all nations. And these differences may act to lower the comparability of the interviews. This is a serious problem, but is no different in kind from the problem of standardization within individual nations. Just as the "Italian" interview situation may differ from the "British," so may interviews with upper-class respondents differ from those with respondents of lower status within the same nation; likewise, interviews may differ between regions of the same nation. Even the most striking problem in cross-national research, that of the use of

---

with differing election laws. Studies of this kind include: Angus Campbell *et al., The American Voter,* chap. xi, and Daniel Katz and Samuel Eldersveld, "The Impact of Local Party Activity on the Electorate," *Public Opinion Quarterly,* xxv (1961), pp. 1-24. The Campbell work compares states with differing election laws; Katz and Eldersveld compare precincts with differentially active local party organizations.

Thus the kind of comparative research we are conducting does not have to be cross-national. However, the focus on the nation-state as the primary structural unit for analysis is of obvious use and needs little justification; an example of one study with such a focus is Angus Campbell and Stein Rokkan, "Norway and the United States," *International Social Science Journal,* pp. 69-99.

more than one language, resembles in kind the problem of regional dialect or of differences in the uses of words among the strata of one society.

But though the problems differ more often in degree than in kind, the difference in degree is so great as to make it worthwhile to look more closely at some of these problems. In fact, one possible methodological advantage of the cross-national survey is that many of the problems that can be ignored when one is dealing with a single nation must now be faced explicitly. If the meaning of questions varies among the geographical regions or the social strata of a nation, this may receive little consideration; but if one must write an equivalent interview schedule in English, Italian, German, and Spanish, such problems must be carefully considered.

The Problem of Equivalence

The two broad problems in comparative research are the standardization of the interview situation and the interpretation of the data gathered through the interviews.

The interview carried on with each of the five thousand respondents is essentially a stimulus that produces responses. The responses are the data we analyze. But for these responses to be comparable, the stimulus situation itself must be comparable. The differences that are found in response patterns from nation to nation or group to group within nations have little meaning if they are artifacts of the interview situation: that is, if the situation changes from nation to nation or group to group. The first task, then, in cross-national survey research is to develop a research instrument that will represent an equivalent stimulus in each nation.

In achieving such equivalence, the most obvious problem faced by the practitioner of cross-national research is that of language. Can one translate an interview from one language to another so that it represents an equivalent instrument in both languages? The answer is probably "no." Obviously one wants not a literal translation but an equivalent translation. What exactly is equivalence? In the first place, the words used must refer to equivalent objects in the several languages. But this is not enough. Even if words with equivalent meaning can be found, they may not be equivalent stimuli in the interview situation. They may, for instance, differ in the frequency with which they are used in the respective languages, and hence in the extent to which they are familiar to respondents. Or, though the words refer to equivalent objects, they may in one language have a wider range of meanings than in another; and the other meanings of the word may affect responses. Furthermore, the desire to obtain words of equal familiarity may conflict with the desire to obtain words that are both equally precise in referring to an object and "uncontaminated" by other meanings. For example: one set of questions in our survey has to do with attitudes toward the local government under which the respondent lives. Interviewers were instructed in the selection of the governmental unit about which questions were to be asked. In most cases the names of the local units were well known and caused little problem. But in the common parlance of Mexico City the local government (essentially the government of the Federal District) is identified with the name of the extremely popular governor of the district, Ernesto Uruchurtu. Our pretest suggested that if we asked about the government of the Federal District we would find many residents in Mexico City who had never heard of it or confused it with the federal government itself. Everyone, however, knew of *"el gobierno de Uruchurtu,"* and it was in this form that the question was asked. But though in the familiarity of the terms we achieved rough equivalence with other nations (and other locales in Mexico), we obviously introduced new problems of nonequivalence through the use of the name of a specific man.

Other examples of this sort could be mustered from our experience with translation—and there are probably many others of which we do not know, since information on the relative familiarity of words is not readily available. In fact, the most serious problem in attempting to attain equivalence is that there is no way of recognizing it when one has attained it. When one uses linguistic stimuli such as questions, there are no rules that specify when one has equivalent stimuli.[16]

The problem of language illustrates the difficulty of achieving equivalent stimuli from nation to nation. Yet the researcher has control (though not complete control) over a number of other factors that make equivalence possible. These include the level of

[16] For other problems involved in obtaining equivalent meanings, see Susan Ervin and Robert T. Bower, "Translation Problems in International Surveys," *Public Opinion Quarterly*, xvi (1952-1953), pp. 595-604, and Eugene Jacobson, Hideya Kumata, and Jeanne E. Gullahorn, "Cross-Cultural Contributions to Attitude Research," *ibid.*, xxiv (1960), pp. 205-23.

skills of the interviewers, the training they receive, the "tightness" of control over their actions, and so forth. One attempt to achieve equivalence—by controlling the interviewer's behavior somewhat more tightly than would be necessary in a single-nation survey—was described above in the discussion of the modification of our research instrument in response to the results of our pretest. When it became apparent that interviewers in different countries used different practices in following up the answer to an open-ended question, it was possible for the research directors to specify more precisely the exact nature of the follow-up questions to be used. Other differences in the interview situation are not under as close control of the researcher. One such factor is the familiarity of populations in various nations with political surveys. It is not so much that populations differ in the frequency of the experience itself; it is unlikely that more than a handful of respondents in any of the nations studied had ever been interviewed before in a social survey. But the nations do differ in the extent to which social surveys are well known; in our case, in the United States, Britain, and perhaps Germany, pre-election surveys are quite familiar. In the other two nations they are not. Differences in reactions to the interview situation, or perhaps general differences in willingness to talk to strangers, can affect the results of a cross-national survey and are hard to eliminate.[17]

One other possible source of nonequivalence is the time at which the survey is carried on. This too is difficult to standardize from nation to nation. Even if all five surveys are carried on simultaneously, there may be events taking place in one nation that temporarily affect political attitudes in ways that are relevant to the concerns of the researcher. The height of an election campaign and the aftermath of a major crisis are clearly noncomparable situations in which to survey the extent of interest in politics. And again, it is impossible for the researcher to standardize the situation in the several nations.[18]

[17] See below, chap. iv, for a discussion of national differences in the willingness to express one's partisan preferences in an interview.
[18] As was pointed out above, in four of the nations our interviews were carried out simultaneously in June-July, 1959; in the United States they were carried out in April 1960. In Mexico the interviewing took place during a crisis over fishing rights with Guatemala (and the Mexican press carried rumors of a possible war). Obviously an event of this sort, if it had any effect at all, would affect political interest—and only in Mexico and Guatamala. Similarly, the interviewing in Britain and the United States took place several months before a general election, though in both cases well before

What then can one do? Equivalent questionnaires—that one is *sure* are equivalent—appear impossible to obtain. Two possible approaches suggest themselves. First, one can let the availability of methods dictate one's approach; one can aim at developing stimuli that are as cross-national as possible. This can be accomplished, perhaps, by dropping the use of ordinary questions or by using non-verbal techniques. It may be that one significant future task of political science is to develop such techniques. But the techniques of this sort that are currently available are not applicable to many substantive problems. To use them would increase cross-national comparability, but would limit the range of one's substantive interests.[19]

The second possible approach—and the one we have used in our study—is to follow one's substantive interests wherever they lead, in full realization that even the best available techniques are far from perfect. And though one cannot achieve perfect comparability, there are a number of ways in which one can hope to come somewhat closer to it. By careful translation, for instance, one can attempt to minimize linguistic problems.[20] Furthermore, there is some evidence that the difficulty of achieving equivalent meanings diminishes as one moves from abstract words to concrete ones. If the questions can be kept simple and relatively straightforward, it is easier to attain some degree of equivalence.[21] The desire to avoid ambiguity in the results often means that subtle distinctions in the data must be ignored. Intensity questions—where respondents are asked if they agree with a statement "strongly," "somewhat," and so forth—can be dichotomized into positive and negative answers. This may

---

the beginning of the campaign; while in Mexico the interviewing occurred in the year following a general election. Though it is impossible to dismiss the possible contaminating effects of these events, there is little evidence that these events had any effect on the interviews.

[19] Some possible nonverbal techniques that have been used cross-culturally include the thematic apperception test and the Rorschach test. See J. Henry and M. E. Spiro, "Psychological Techniques: Projective Tests in Field Work," in A. L. Krocher (ed.), *Anthropology Today*, Chicago, 1953, pp. 417-29. As yet they are of limited usefulness in the analysis of political attitudes. In fact, there is some evidence that even these nonverbal techniques do not have equivalent meaning cross-nationally.

A very promising approach to cross-national equivalence is the semantic differential. Osgood and his associates, using pairs of opposite adjectives that appear to be cross-cultural, have found common judgment dimensions. See Charles E. Osgood, "The Cross-Cultural Generality of Visual-Verbal Synethestic Tendencies," *Behavioral Science*, v (1960), pp. 146-61, and Howard Maclay and Edward E. Ware, "Cross-Cultural Use of the Semantic Differential," *Behavioral Science*, vi (1961), pp. 185-90.

[20] The interviews used in this study were translated from English into the foreign

eliminate any differences among nations in their propensity to use extreme language (as in slang, where even the "mildly good" becomes the "greatest"). The use of open-ended questions, where the respondent has the opportunity to respond freely, may also improve comparability. The questions may still be nonequivalent, but the free responses allow one to catch at least gross deviation from equivalence. And lastly, there are ways of analyzing the resulting data that reduce the extent to which one is dependent on complete equivalence; this we shall discuss in the following section.

So much for the mechanical difficulties in designing an equivalent stimulus situation when one is using an interview cross-nationally. The reader should consider himself forewarned as to the limitations of our data. We shall present many tables with cold and solid figures as to the numbers who said such-and-such in a nation. The figures may not be as solid as they appear. On the other hand, this warning ought not to lead the reader to despair. Though the material presented in here is far from perfect, it does have the advantage that its weaknesses can be at least made explicit. In fact, one can certainly argue that *no* cross-national study can avoid the problems listed above—problems of translation from one language to another, temporary differences in the situation at the time the material is gathered, and so forth. No matter what sort of study is contemplated, one must contend with these difficulties.

The Interpretation of Results

The search for equivalent questions and an equivalent interview situation is but the first step toward meaningful comparisons of the political behavior of citizens in various nations. One must still select equivalent dimensions of political behavior, as well as indicators

---

language by bilinguals. They were then "blindly" translated back to English by other bilinguals who were not familiar with the original English version. This process was repeated several times. Furthermore, the several pretest waves of interviews were also translated, and the responses to these interviews highlighted some translation problems.

[21] Buchanan and Cantril found that words such as "peace" and "democracy" were likely to cause the most trouble in attempts to find equivalent meanings (see Buchanan and Cantril, *How Nations See Each Other*, pp. 106-7). Yet in one of the first international surveys it was discovered that as concrete a word as "washing machine" meant different things in different countries. In some it was an expensive electrical appliance; in others it referred to any hand-turned device, however simple. See D. Wallace *et al.*, "Experience in the *Time* International Survey," *Public Opinion Quarterly*, XII (1947), pp. 8-21.

for those dimensions. Assume, for example, that a question on some aspect of political behavior (say, on the frequency of political discussion) is translated accurately; that the German respondent who says he discussed politics means by this what the Mexican respondent does (perhaps any informal discussion in which politics or public affairs is mentioned); assume that there are no differences in ease of interviewing, in the respondent's honesty, and so forth. Nevertheless, the problem of inference from the response is still difficult, because the dimensions and indicators of political behavior are being applied to differing political systems.

The more general a dimension, the more likely it is to have cross-national validity. One can, for instance, place American voters on a dimension that ranges from "strong Republican" to "strong Democrat," with various levels of partisan affiliation in between. Such a scale is useful in the United States, but obviously makes no sense elsewhere; either other nations will have no two parties with those names, or, even if there are parties with similar names (as in Turkey), these parties may be of so different a nature from those in America that it would make no sense to compare the dimensions. Or one might array voters on a left-right continuum, but even this more general dimension might not apply to all nations. On a more general level one might use, as we have done, the dimensions of activity-passivity, awareness-unawareness, or alienation-nonalienation. It is likely that individuals in all political systems can be arrayed along these.

But if the use of general dimensions solves some of the problems of cross-national comparability, these problems re-emerge when one attempts to find precise indicators for the dimension. Consider the dimension of "political activity." As in all social research one does not observe "political activity" directly, but tries to develop *indicators* of political activity. Does a man report he discusses politics? This might indicate that he is active politically. Does he vote? This might be another indicator. Yet the problem always arises as to the relationship of a particular indicator to the underlying dimension. Is the respondent who discusses politics more "active" than the man who does not? That we are dealing with five different political systems complicates this relationship even further.

Though one can easily think of indicators of political activity, it is a subtler problem to find indicators of equivalent meaning cross-nationally. Assume that a particular type of behavior—let us call it "be-

CROSS-NATIONAL RESEARCH AND POLITICAL BEHAVIOR

havior A"—is of political significance. We want to compare the rates of performance of "behavior A" in a variety of countries. The important point is that, if the comparison is to be meaningful, the behavior must be the same in each country. We obviously will learn little if we compare the rate of "behavior A" in one country with that of "behavior B" in another—it makes little sense to compare the rate of voting turnout in Germany with the rate of party membership in Italy. This is clear and obvious, but we stress the point here because, not only may voting be different from party membership, but voting in one country may differ from voting in another country, just as party membership in one country may differ from party membership in another. In other words, what we label "behavior A" in one country may appear the same as, yet differ sharply from, that to which we commonly give the same label in another.[22]

It may differ in two ways: in its meaning for the individual who is acting, or in its meaning for the political system in which the act is performed. Consider voting as an example. As far as the individual is concerned, the vote may represent a conscious attempt to bring into power a party or candidate who stands for policies the individual desires; or it may involve ritualistic conformity to traditional party affiliations. Similarly, the vote may involve a great effort for some individuals or a minimum effort for others. Surely the Southern Negro in America who registers and votes at great personal risk is participating in a much more intense way than is the voter who lives in a situation where voting is relatively easy and expected. These variations in the meaning of the vote or of other political acts occur within nations, but they also occur, often more sharply, between nations. It would make little sense to compare the rate of voting in Australia, where voting is compulsory by law, with the rate of voting in a nation that has no such legal provision—especially if one wants to use the frequency of voting participation as an indicator of political interest and activity.[23]

In its impact upon the political system in which it takes place,

[22] On this general subject, see Campbell and Rokkan, "Norway and the United States," *International Social Science Journal*.

[23] This problem is an old one for those anthropologists who have wanted to make cross-national comparisons. As Whiting points out, physiologically a belch is a belch in any society, but in one society it may be a compliment and in another an insult. But this, he goes on to say, does not eliminate the possibility of cross-national comparisons. A belch may not always be a belch, but an insult is always an insult. One can compare insults, if one can find some adequate index. See John W. M. Whiting, "The Cross-Cultural Method," in Lindzey (ed.), *Handbook of Social Psychology*, I, p. 528.

voting has another kind of differential meaning. Under an authoritarian government the vote is essentially a symbol of solidarity; in a multiparty democracy, however, it has an effect on who runs the country. Certainly the vote cannot be considered the same act in those two circumstances. (It must be noted that the countries dealt with in this book, though they might be considered democracies, all differ in this respect. There are, for instance, large one-party areas in the United States. And Mexico is essentially a one-party system.)

What has been said about voting applies with more or less validity to other forms of political behavior: party membership, organizational membership, even media exposure and knowledge of politics. Party membership, for instance, represents one act for the individual who is in a mass party with structures of indirect membership, and another act for someone who is in a party with no structure of mass membership. From the point of view of the political system, these two kinds of membership mean something else. Lastly, it should be pointed out that the individual and systemic meanings of an act, though usually related, may vary independently. Thus the vote may mean different things to two different individuals but have identical effects on the political system: to one individual it may be a highly affect-laden protest against the current government, to another it may be traditional conformity to family voting patterns. But both may vote for the same party. Or the vote may mean the same to two individuals and different things to the system: two civic-minded citizens may vote on the basis of careful calculation, but one may live in a community where, unknown to him, his vote is not counted.[24]

That an act may mean one thing in regard to the political system and another in regard to the individual suggests that differences in the frequencies of particular behavior from nation to nation may reflect differences in the political systems as much as in the perspectives and attitudes of individuals. For example, we asked about watching

[24] A related problem, which does not raise such serious methodological difficulties, is that the relationship between a particular behavior and a set of attitudes (or among attitudes) may differ from nation to nation. Rates of voting and attitudes toward voting, for instance, may vary independently. A high frequency of voting may not be matched by a high frequency of interest in the vote or of belief in the efficacy of the vote. It may well be that in some nations or among some groups, frequent voting is associated with lack of interest in the vote (one votes for other reasons).

However, this problem can be handled by comparing attitudes and behavior within nations, to see what attitudes are associated with what behavior, or with what other attitudes. A further discussion of the advantages of this approach will appear below; and numerous examples of such analyses will be found in the text.

news broadcasts on television and learned that a much higher proportion of Americans than Mexicans watch such programs. There is little doubt that our data are correct on this point (there are no particular translation problems, for example,) ; but how does one interpret such a result? One could not conclude from this that Americans are more interested in politics and involved in governmental affairs. The bulk of the difference in watching broadcasts is probably due to the greater ease of access to television sets in the United States. This does not mean that one can infer nothing from the difference. If one is interested in the amount of time spent exposed to communications about politics, the difference will be important. On the other hand, one cannot very well use these data to infer differences in the level of motivation to obtain information about politics in these two countries.

The same problem applies to the interpretation of differences in frequency of political attitudes. Here the major difficulty is that the *object of orientation* for the attitude differs from nation to nation— that is, Italians were asked about Italian government and Britons were asked about British government. Again if we solve the mechanical problems of creating a similar stimulus situation, we are still faced with the problems of interpretation. If the citizens in one country report more frequently than those in another that their government operates in their interest or that it can be trusted, this is a real difference in attitude with real consequences. But because the object of orientation differs (we are not, for instance, comparing, as one does in a single-nation survey, the attitudes of men and women toward the same government) , it is more difficult to explain these differences in attitude toward government. To some extent the explanation may lie among the factors usually adduced in surveys to explain attitudes—social group, personality, other attitudes, and so forth. On the other hand, it may simply be that one government is in fact more beneficial in its operation or more to be trusted than another. Or it may be both—the two types of explanation do not necessarily contradict each other. Again the differences are real, but what they mean is harder to say.[25]

Finally, there is the difficulty in attaining comparable social cate-

[25] Here, the problems in cross-national survey research seem to differ in kind from those in single-nation research. Yet single-nation surveys have this in common with cross-national surveys: in the first place, from the subjective points of view of the respondents, the objects of orientation may differ. One Mexican, when asked about his government, might have one view of it; another might have a different view. Further-

gories for matching respondents across national lines. In all survey research analysis one attempts to compare matched subgroups of a sample in order to isolate nonspurious relationships among variables. If one wants to estimate the impact of income on political participation, one compares various income groups within matched educational groups to eliminate the possibility that what appears to be a relationship between income and political participation is, instead, largely due to the fact that those with higher income are likely also to have more education. In cross-national research in political behavior the isolation of such matching groups is useful. If one can compare matching groups cross-nationally—Americans with Italians of similar educational attainment; British working-class men with German working-class men—one can begin to estimate the extent to which differences between the average responses in a cross-section sample can be explained by the uneven distribution of some important social attribute in the cross-section samples. For instance, a much larger proportion of respondents in the United States than in Italy reported exposure to political communications. One reason for this might be that a much higher proportion of Italians than of Americans reported no formal education or only primary education (both samples seem fairly accurately to reflect the distribution of educational attainment in the two nations). If one can show that a larger proportion of American respondents are exposed to political communications, whereas among American and Italian respondents of equivalent educational attainment there is little or no difference in rate of exposure, then one has gone a long way toward explaining why the two nations differ in this aspect of political behavior. The difference in exposure would appear to be due to differences in educational levels from one nation to another rather than to some aspect of Italian politics or Italian "national character." In fact, if, when one controls for a demographic characteristic or some other attribute, one can remove the differences among the response patterns in the various nations, one has a powerful tool for explaining the differences among various nations. (The difference in, say, exposure to political communications remains, however, a "real" difference between the nations; as real as the difference in the educational systems.)

Though achieving matched subgroups cross-nationally would be

more, one often asks about objects that differ from respondent to respondent. This is true when one asks the respondent about himself or his family. And as will be discussed below, this raises similar problems in single-nation and cross-national surveys.

desirable, it is very difficult. This is not because the measures are inaccurate, but because again the interpretation is difficult. One cannot, of course, "translate literally" demographic measures from nation to nation. Such a translation would involve, for instance, matching income groups by their equivalence in each other's currency at the going rate of exchange. This would lead to such obvious distortion as matching respondents whose positions in the income hierarchy within each nation were quite different. A better way would be to match respondents by their position on the income ladder in each country—compare those in the top twenty per cent of earners in each nation, and so forth. But even this does not produce equivalent groups. Real incomes will differ, as will perhaps such important characteristics as the difference in income from that of people lower on the scale.

This problem can best be illustrated by considering how to obtain matched educational groups cross-nationally.[26] One approach would be to match groups in terms of number of school years completed. Yet obviously the quality and content of education differ from nation to nation. (Again this is a problem found within nations as well.) More important, perhaps, the social implications of equivalent levels of education, in terms of number of years, may differ as well. In a nation where secondary education is almost universal and college education widespread, higher educational attainment is not as clear an indicator of higher social status as it would be in nations where there is a generally lower level of education.[27] The problem of matching groups cross-nationally, like the problem of equivalent indicators, is probably insoluble *if one is looking for complete equivalence.* (As we shall suggest below, one can get by with much less.)

The above discussion should make it clear that cross-national systematic comparisons are difficult indeed. The problem in finding equivalent indicators from nation to nation is, however, not spe-

[26] This is a useful example, for educational attainment seems to be the most significant demographic variable in our study, and the one most able to explain differences among nations. It is also the demographic control we use most frequently.

[27] We are dealing here with "composition" effects: that is, the impact on an individual, not of his own position on a variable (e.g., his level of educational attainment), but of the distribution of that variable in the group to which he belongs (e.g., the proportion of university educated within the group). Composition effects have obvious relevance to cross-national research. See Peter M. Blau, "Structural Effects," *American Sociological Review,* xxv (1960), pp. 178-93, and James A. Davies, *Great Books and Small Groups,* New York, 1961, chap. i.

cific to this type of research (although, as suggested earlier, it may be most explicit in this sort of research endeavor). In all comparative research we have to isolate comparable variables: one cannot simply compare "totalities." Yet in the social sciences this isolation of variables is difficult. As yet we cannot adequately separate those aspects of politics that we want to compare from other aspects; we cannot hold constant or ignore the large number of aspects of a phenomenon that the natural scientists can leave out of his calculations. Most of the variables we attempt to isolate are completely meaningful only when considered in their contexts, but to compare complete contexts is not really possible. Is there any way out of this dilemma—the general social science dilemma or the specific one of cross-national research in political behavior? The answer is "no" if we are looking for a perfect solution, but "yes" if we are looking for a reasonable solution: a solution through which we pursue problems of substantive interest with as much rigor as possible, but do not let the concern for rigor dominate our willingness to tackle problems of significance.

Maximizing Comparability

There are a number of ways to maximize comparability in survey research. One way, as was suggested above, is to take general dimensions of political behavior. As will be seen, many of the variables we use—such as the activity-passivity dimension—are of this sort. Second, if we want data on individual political orientations and not on the political structures of the system (the latter might better be studied by some means other than a systematic survey), it is well to concentrate on the behavior or attitudes that are least determined by the structure of the situation. Of course, all the attitudes we deal with are in part situationally determined. If one is interested in political orientation and not in basic dimensions of personality, one must expect to study attitudes and behavior that are affected by structural characteristics. Nevertheless, one can search for that type of attitude or behavior that is relatively independent of structural constraints.

That frequency of exposure to news broadcasts on television was found inappropriate as a measure of political interest suggests what sort of behavior one ought to concentrate on. If television sets are more widely distributed in one nation than another, there is clear structural constraint on the relative ability of individuals to watch television. Assume that individuals in the United States and Mexico have the same desire to watch news broadcasts on television (if that could be measured independently of actual watching); it would take much more effort by the average Mexican than by the average American to overcome structural resistance to his desire to watch. Similarly, given the same level of intensity of desire to vote, the force required to vote is greater for a Southern Negro than for a Northern Negro. Thus one cannot infer differences in intensity of political affiliation from lower voting rates among Southern Negroes. If, then, one wants to compare the rates of political acts cross-nationally in order to infer the nature of political orientation in various countries, one ought to compare acts to which the social structural obstacles to performance are minimal or roughly the same from nation to nation. Rather than concentrating on voting behavior or party membership or exposure to formal media of communications, one might concentrate on more informal political acts. Political discussion might be this kind of act. Or one might concentrate on expressed political attitudes, such as political interest. Behavior and attitudes of this sort are not independent of various social pressures and structural constraints: they do not spring solely from some internal individual mechanism. It is more difficult to discuss politics even if one so desires if there are few others interested in such discussion. Yet the constraints on such informal activities and attitudes are not as clear and insuperable as are structural obstacles in other fields.[28]

Differences in political structure can also be minimized, at least in part, by concentrating on the individual as object of orientation.

[28] However, comparison of the rates of formal activity, such as voting behavior, party membership, or exposure to formal media of communications, is still important if one recognizes the uses to which it can be put. That these data cannot be used to infer national differences in political attitudes or perspectives does not mean that the formal differences, in exposure to a particular type of communications, for example, do not have real effects on the nature of political communication and on the way a political system operates. Furthermore, the fact that more Americans than Mexicans watch the news on television, or that more British workers than American workers are members of a political party, or that more Northern than Southern Negroes vote (all of these differences could be traced mostly to structural inhibitions that operate regardless of individual propensities) does have significant implications for the political behavior of individuals. For even if a particular behavior varies from group to group because of structural differences, the chain of causality does not end there. The behavior, no matter why it is performed, affects the individual who performs it. Thus the Northern Negro who votes may not have started out any more involved in politics than his Southern counterpart. But the act of voting makes him a different political person. If greater involvement did not lead him to vote, voting may lead to greater involvement. Whatever their origin, differences in rates of behavior have different effects upon the political system and upon the individuals within that system.

One asks questions, not about the government nor even about the individual's perception of the government, but about the individual's perception of *himself* in relation to the government. Does the individual believe the government benefits *him?* Does he think *he* can influence it? With questions of this sort one focuses attention on the individual's subjective view of the political system and compares these subjective views cross-nationally. While this does not eliminate the fact that one is dealing with differing political systems, it does make the measures used somewhat more comparable.

Though the judicious choice of indicators helps eliminate some of the problems of nonequivalence in cross-national research, perhaps the most important way in which such problems must be handled is in the analysis of the data. The fact that a particular indicator has to be interpreted to some extent in terms of its context has led those interested in cross-national comparisons to stress, not direct comparisons of variables cross-nationally, but cross-national comparisons of the *pattern* of relations among variables.[29] For instance, one does not compare the rate of performance of a particular act or of expression of a particular attitude from nation to nation; instead, one compares cross-nationally the differences among groups within each nation. The question is not whether Germans more frequently vote or more frequently report interest in politics than do Italians, or even if German and Italian males differ in these respects. Rather, one asks if males vote more frequently than females in both countries, or if those with high income are more interested in politics in both countries. By phrasing the comparison *between* nations in terms of the similarities and differences in the *patterns* of relations *among* variables *within* each country, one controls somewhat for the difference in meaning that these variables may have from one nation to another.

Even if an activity (say, voting) has a somewhat different meaning from nation to nation, this does not invalidate cross-national comparisons of the internal distribution of voting behavior in a nation. The differences in voting rates that one compares are differences among various groups within each nation, and one can assume the meaning of the variable has greater stability within than across nations. Furthermore, the variables presented to explain the polit-

[29] See Rokkan, "Comparative Study of Political Participation," in Ranney, *Behavioral Study of Politics,* and Campbell and Rokkan, "Norway and the United States," *International Social Science Journal.*

ical activity or attitude (the independent variables) can be made more comparable when patterns of relationships are compared. The difficulty of obtaining matched groups on such characteristics as education or income is eased. Even though one does not know what constitutes an equivalent level of income or education cross-nationally, one can without much difficulty locate individuals within each nation on an income or educational hierarchy. Though university education is not the same in the United States as in Italy, it is in both countries a higher level of education than primary or secondary education. And this is the only assumption one needs to make for this type of comparison. The same applies to the use of variables of political behavior or attitude as independent variables to explain other political behavior or attitudes. Just as it is easier to rank individuals in a single society in terms of educational attainment or income than to compare income or educational levels across societies, so it is easier to rank individuals on dimensions of political behavior than to compare levels of political behavior cross-nationally. It is more difficult to say what are equivalent levels of political interest, or political information, or exposure to political communications from nation to nation than it is to rank individuals within each nation in terms of their interest, or information, or exposure. Ranking individuals within each nation, one can then raise such questions as: "How do those who are more highly exposed to political communications differ in their political attitudes from those less exposed?" And one can compare cross-nationally the differences in political attitudes between those well exposed to political communications and those not so well exposed. This approach partially eases the problem that the meaning of each variable depends somewhat upon the political system in which it is embedded. By comparing patterns of relationships, one has to some extent placed the relevant variables into their context before drawing comparisons.

Many of the comparisons made in this book will be of the pattern of relationship among variables. We shall compare demographic distribution of attitudes and behavior, as well as the ways in which several attitudes and behaviors are related. In this way we hope to increase the cross-national validity of our comparisons.[30]

---

[30] Though cross-national comparison of the pattern of relations among variables eases some of the problems mentioned above, it does not completely eliminate them. For instance, if such patterned comparison allows one to consider particular variables within their own context, it does not eliminate the fact that the variables must be comparable to begin with. If the meaning of an indicator is not related to some underlying dimen-

Having argued for the greater validity of cross-national comparisons of patterns, we must warn the reader that we shall also present a large number of direct comparisons of rates of adherence to a particular attitude or performance of a particular act—direct comparisons either among entire samples or among particular subgroups. These comparisons can answer a number of descriptive questions about differences among nations that could not be answered through the patterned comparisons described above. The direct comparisons must, however, be viewed with caution. In particular, it is important to look, not merely for differences among nations on a particular measure, but for a consistent set of differences among nations on a number of measures. If a particular measure of political activity tends to inflate the level of participation in one nation over another—due perhaps to some translation problem, or some characteristic of the political system—there is no reason to expect a distortion in the same direction on another measure of activity. Therefore, if we can locate consistent differences in political orientation among nations on a variety of measures, we can have somewhat more confidence that our observation is a real difference among the nations and not merely an artifact of the interview situation.[31] Throughout this volume, then, we shall look for patterns of consistent differences in order to characterize the sets of political attitudes we study.

---

sion—if the vote, for instance, cannot even be considered a measure of activity in *one* of the nations—then any cross-national comparison will be meaningless.

Second, there is the danger that national differences in a political act or attitude will mean differences, not only in the absolute *frequency* of performance of the act or of adherence to the attitude, but also in the *distribution* of that act or attitude. For instance, we argued earlier that comparative rates of party membership in Britain and the United States could not be used as an index of political activity, since membership in Britain meant something quite different from membership in the United States. This difference in meaning (the particular example given was the existence in Britain of a large amount of nonindividual affiliation through trade unions) describes the national differences in absolute level of membership. But it also describes national differences in the class distribution of membership. The inflation of British membership figures through the existence of nonindividual membership has a differential effect on members of the various classes. Cross-national comparisons of class patterns of activity on this measure would therefore be distorted.

[31] For a discussion of a particularly useful technique for locating measures that represent "real" differences among nations by comparing the demographic distributions of different variables, see chap. vii.

Political Culture and Political Systems

The present work is partly a study in what has been called "micro-politics." It deals with the political orientations and behavior of a cross-section sample. The one thousand or so respondents in each country are viewed in the first instance as individuals. They have no relationship to one another; one respondent has no knowledge of the other respondents and no interaction with them—certainly none that is explored in our study. Yet we are interested in the respondents, not as individuals, but as members of complex social systems. We wish to make statements, based on those separate interviews, about the general state of attitudes in these nations. And we wish to make statements about the relationship between these attitudes and the way in which the political systems operate. In particular, we are interested in understanding democratic political systems; and these systems consist of much more than the individual or collective attitudes of their members. They consist as well of formal structures of government, political parties, structures of power and influence, shared norms, patterns of policy, communication, interaction, and so forth. The major problem of analysis is, therefore, how to use responses from one thousand individuals who have never met to answer questions about the characteristics of a political system. It is as if that system were a large map on the wall of a darkened room, and all we know of it is what is revealed by one thousand separate pinpoints of light. These points of light (our interviews) illuminate the spots on the map that they touch. But they light up only a small part of the map and leave the areas between the dots completely dark. We want to say something, not merely about the points that are illuminated, but about the entire map itself.

There are a number of ways in which one may use the individual pinpoints of light to illuminate the territory between them. In the first place, one assumes that the results of interviews with one thousand individuals can be generalized to the entire population—with, of course, the usual allowances made for errors. Second, though we only talk to individuals and do not observe them interacting with others or engaged in political activity, we do ask them about their attitudes toward others, their relations with others, their social activities, their organizational memberships, and their political activities. If we can generalize about the respondents' answers, we can make statements about the number of people in each nation who hold to certain attitudes and engage in certain behavior; we can also describe the network of relations among people: the frequencies of such behavior as organizational membership, informal social contact, and political activity, and the frequencies of such attitudes as interpersonal trust and cooperativeness that refer, not merely to single individuals, but to the relations among individuals.

The third and crucial point is that one must assume that the attitudes we report have some significant relationship to the way the political system operates—to its stability, effectiveness, and so forth. The distribution in a society of such attitudes as the belief that the political system is legitimate, that it operates effectively, that it is amenable to the ordinary man's influence; or the frequency of such activities as organizational membership or political participation—clearly all these have important effects on the way the political system operates. It is somewhat more difficult to pin down the precise relationship between these attitudes and behaviors of ordinary citizens and the ways in which political democracies operate. The major problem is that, though we have about five thousand individual respondents, we have only five nations. Thus if we want to test statistically the relationship between two attributes of the individuals in our sample—say, the relationship between social class and political participation—we have a large number of cases with which to do this. But if we want to test the relationship between a pattern of attitudes in a nation and some characteristic of a political system—say, the relationship between frequency of political alienation and the stability of the political system—we have few cases in which to test this. This is no new problem in political analysis, and we are in fact five times as well off as most studies of this sort. What we can do is to consider our five nations as examples of types of political democracy—more or less stable democracies, more or less effective, more or less participatory. Which of these nations is highest on any dimension can be assessed either on the basis of data outside of our study (a brief glance at history will tell which of these are more stable, or an analysis of the party structures will allow a classification by type of party system), or on data within our study (one might use the frequency of various types of political activity to rank the nations by the extent to which they are characterized by high or low rates of participation). If one can then show, for instance, that in the more stable democracies there does exist a particular set of political attitudes that could theoretically further the chances of stable democracy; or that in those nations where participation is most frequent there does in fact exist a particular set of interpersonal attitudes that could theoretically further political participation, then one has come a long way toward demonstrating the probability of some connection between attitudinal patterns and systemic qualities. Furthermore, these connections between sets of attitudes and the characteristics of the political system can be made more convincing by internal analysis of the attitudes within the nations. Suppose one finds that a particular attitude toward interpersonal relations exists most frequently in a system where political participation of a particular sort is most frequent; if one also finds that it is precisely those individuals who hold that attitude who are more likely to be the political participants, one can then support the hypothesis that the particular attitude is connected with a particular kind of participatory system. By moving constantly from characteristics of the political system to frequencies of particular attitudes within the system to the pattern of attitudes within the individual members of the system, one can hope to develop plausible, testable (and perhaps, in a preliminary way, tested) hypotheses about the relationship between what we have called political culture and the workings of political systems.

We hope to have shown in the above discussion that the sort of data reported here makes sense only if interpreted in terms of other types of material about the systems we study. Thus the information we have about the five political systems is not limited to areas directly under the little pinpoints of light. One must integrate into a study of this sort findings about the general shape of the system, the institutions, the history of their development, and so forth. One advantage of a cross-national study, we have suggested, is that it forces one to look at systemic characteristics. Our findings are intended, not to replace, but to supplement other materials used for the analysis of political systems. It is only if material of the sort we have can be combined with other materials that we will have made progress.

The above discussion should suggest to the reader that there are many difficulties in cross-national research in political behavior and that he ought to proceed into the substance of this book with care. Such a warning is, we hope, not a sign of the weakness of the study to follow, but an indication of its strength. The problems raised above are not specific to cross-national surveys of the sort carried on here. They exist, we would argue, for all types of comparative political research. The problems of equivalent indicators, of the variation in context, of sampling, of translation, exist even in unsystematic comparative studies; they just appear to be less salient since they can more easily be ignored. To be able to explicate the ways in which our knowledge is limited and the reasons for that limitation is to have raised the level of our knowledge.

That the data reported here have limitations is not a reason for us to apologize. Nor do we apologize for another limitation of the study. In dealing with the relations between political and social attitudes on the one hand, and political systems on the other, we shall probably raise more questions in the readers mind than we shall answer. The explanation for many of the findings in this book will leave many problems unsolved. Does this mean that our explanations are inadequate? Yes, it does. They are inadequate not because one can raise further questions about them—as we know from little children, one can always ask "Why?" even when what appears to be a full explanation is given. Our explanations are inadequate because one is left unsatisfied—the authors were and the reader probably will be. One will want to raise further questions, to probe deeper into the results. With Hume, we believe that an explanation is adequate when the mind comes to rest. And few minds will be put to rest by the present study.

PART II

PATTERNS OF POLITICAL CULTURE

CHAPTER 3

PATTERNS OF POLITICAL COGNITION

IN OUR classification of types of political culture, we have referred to the dimension of cognition. A participant is assumed to be aware of and informed about the political system in both its governmental and political aspects. A subject tends to be cognitively oriented primarily to the output side of government: the executive, bureaucracy, and judiciary. The parochial tends to be unaware, or only dimly aware, of the political system in all its aspects. In the five countries in our study, pure parochials and subjects are rare. Even the Mexican Indian villager has had some exposure to specialized governmental authority; and the Italian rural housewife may have some knowledge of political parties. In the five democracies we study, the parochial and subject orientations tend to rest primarily upon affective and evaluative tendencies. The Mexican villager may feel no loyalty or involvement with the Mexican nation and government. He may view it as an alien force to be avoided. His loyalty and sense of obligation go to his village, and to its norms and structures. Nevertheless, these affective and evaluative parochial and subject patterns have cognitive consequences. When affect and norms are lacking, the motivation to acquire information is weak, and thus cognition, while it may be present, tends to be vague.

In the present analysis of cognitive patterns, we do not claim to present an exhaustive description of the political "cognitive maps" of Americans, Britons, Germans, Italians, and Mexicans. What we have to offer, rather, is a limited number of measures of cognitive content and processes, which is nevertheless sufficient to bring out some of the significant differences among our countries. Four of such measures are presented in this chapter.

The first of these is an attempt to discover how much importance is attributed to national and local government in each of our five countries. The second is a measure of awareness of and exposure to politics and public affairs. The third is a political information test intended to get at differences among countries in the amount of political information their adult populations possess. And the fourth is a measure of the readiness of these populations to make choices or entertain opinions about political issues and problems. Needless to say, this represents only the shallowest probing of the dimension of political cognition. But it does bring out some rather striking differences among our countries in the objects of political cognition, in the intensity and quantity of cognition, and in the sense of cognitive competence.

TABLE 1

Estimated Degree of Impact of National Government on Daily Life, by Nation[a]
(in per cent)

Per Cent of Respondents who say National Government has	U.S.	U.K.	Germany	Italy	Mexico
Great effect	41	33	38	23	7
Some effect	44	40	32	31	23
No effect	11	23	17	19	66
Other	0	–	–	3	–
Don't know	4	4	12	24	3
Total per cent[b]	100	100	99	100	99
Total number of cases	970	963	955	995	1,007

[a] Actual text of the question: "Thinking now about the national government [in Washington, London, Bonn, Rome, Mexico City], about how much effect do you think its activities, the laws passed and so on, have on your day-to-day life? Do they have a great effect, some effect, or none?"

[b] In this and subsequent tables, variations in total percentages from one hundred per cent are due to rounding.

The Impact of Government

The first aspect of the cognitive dimension we shall examine is that of knowledge of governmental output. To what extent do the people in these countries perceive government as having an effect on them as individuals? To what extent do they see their lives as related to the activities of government? One of the questions asked of all respondents was designed to discover how much effect they thought the activities of their national governments had on their daily lives. The results are reported in Table 1.

Large majorities of Americans, Britons, and Germans see their national government as having some impact on their lives. The Mexicans are at the opposite extreme, with 66 per cent attributing no effect to their national government. The Italians are in-between, with just a little more than half attributing some or great importance to national government, and a little less than half attributing no importance to the national government or stating that they did not know what importance the national government had for them. Table 2 reports the responses to a similar question regarding the effect of local government. The pattern is almost the same as that for the national government, except that a slightly higher proportion of American, Italian, and German respondents attribute importance to their local governments.

TABLE 2
Estimated Degree of Impact of Local Government on Daily Life, by Nation*
(in per cent)

Per Cent who say Local Government has	U.S.	U.K.	Germany	Italy	Mexico
Great effect	35	23	33	19	6
Some effect	53	51	41	39	23
No effect	10	23	18	22	67
Other	–	–	–	2	–
Don't know	2	3	8	18	3
Total per cent	100	100	100	99	100
Total number	970	963	955	995	1,007

* Actual text of the question: "Now take the local government. About how much effect do you think its activities have on your day-to-day life? Do they have a great effect, some effect, or none?"

What these figures suggest is that the large majority of Americans, Britons, and Germans are cognitively oriented to governmental action. That is, they perceive government as influencing their lives. Italians and Mexicans, and particularly the latter, are either less frequently aware of the impact of government or are aware of it but reject it as having no significance for them.

We are also in a position to determine whether or not the impact of government in these countries is considered favorable. A follow-up question was asked: "On the whole, do the activities of the national government tend to improve conditions in this country, or would we be better off without them?" Table 3 shows that large majorities in the United States, Britain, Germany, and Italy who said the national government effected their daily lives also viewed this effect as beneficial. The Mexicans showed the lowest frequency of favorable responses; they, more than the others, said that they would be better off without the activities of the national government. The same pattern came out in the follow-up question on the impact of the local government.

If we combine the results of these two questions on the impact of national and local government and the character of impact, the following points are suggested. The American and British respondents in the great majority perceive an impact of their national and local governments and view that impact as favorable. The German re-

TABLE 3

Character of Impact of National Government, by Nation*
(in per cent)

Per Cent who say	U.S.	U.K.	Germany	Italy	Mexico
National govt. improves conditions	76	77	61	66	58
Sometimes improves conditions, sometimes does not	19	15	30	20	18
Better off without national govt.	3	3	3	5	19
National govt. makes no difference	1	1	1	1	2
Other	0	1	0	2	1
Don't know	1	2	4	5	2
Total per cent	100	99	99	99	100
Total number	821	707	676	534	301

* As described by those respondents who attribute some impact to national government.

spondents resemble them, except that a larger percentage takes the skeptical position that the national and local governments sometimes improve conditions and sometimes do not. Those Italians who do attribute significance to their national and local governments (a little more than half) also attribute a favorable impact to them. On the other hand, only a minority of the Mexicans (less than one-third) attributes significance to the government, and even among this third a substantial proportion either takes a skeptical position on the benefits of government or rejects it as largely harmful in its effects.

The broad picture presented thus far suggests that in the United States, Britain, and Germany, the bulk of the population are "allegiants" in the output sense; that is, they are aware of and evaluate favorably the governmental output. In Italy and particularly Mexico, there is a high incidence of alienated subjects and parochials. Our regular interview enabled us merely to say that around two-thirds of the Mexicans and a little less than half of the Italians either attributed no significance to government or said they didn't know if it had any significance. Our life-history interviews will help us fill in the meaning of our quantitative data.

In each of the countries we reinterviewed some ten per cent of our respondents, repeating some of the same questions but probing more deeply and recording their responses verbatim. What we discovered in this freer, open-ended material is that those respondents in Mexico and Italy who said that government had no impact on them or that they did not know how much impact it had included both "parochials" and "alienates." Some parochial statements follow.

Asked whether government is necessary, a Mexican house servant who lives with her family in her mistress's house in Mexico City replied, "I won't answer this as I don't know what to say." She attributed no significance to government for her and her family. Asked what taxes are used for, she replied, "What are they? I don't know." She can neither read nor write and has never voted. A Mexican housewife in San Luis Potosi replied to the question on the effect of government by saying, "Its activities have no effect on me as I have nothing to do with government." She reported that she has too many children to be able to think about anything else. She has few friends and no trust in people outside her family. The only occasion when she would consider approaching a governmental official would be if there were some possibility of getting a job for a member of her family. Insofar as the parochial is aware of government, he tends to see it in relation to family interests. Thus a poor Mexican tailor living in Oaxaca said about the government: "It has no effect. I have no family or job connections with the government."

An elderly Italian widow living in Milan not only displayed parochialism herself, but appeared to argue that the poor should be content with their parochial lot. Answering the question on the effect of the national government on people like her, she remarked, "It has no effect. Madame Gronchi the President's wife has become a lady, and I am poor, but perhaps I am better off than she is. She has satisfactions in her life. She has been presented to queens. But I don't envy her. She wasn't born a lady, and when she makes a 'gaffe,' everybody laughs."

Much more frequent among the Mexican and Italian cases were explicitly alienated respondents. Most of them were "output" alienates: government should do things for themselves and for people like them, they believed, but it was indifferent to the interests of poor people, or it was corrupt and responsive only to bribes or family connections.

Here are a few examples of the theme of governmental corruption among our Mexican respondents.

A Mexican Housewife, on the effect of local government on her life:
"It has an effect for them. They take all the money."

A Mexican Secretary, on what taxes are used for:
"Public officials say they are for improvements for the town, which seems incredible since each new governor increases taxes and does nothing for the town, only for his pockets."

A Mexican Shoemaker, on the chances for government reform:
"If they wanted to, they could improve things. They could do it by keeping the money from the hands of unscrupulous people who take the funds that belong to the people."

Another theme of alienation is neglect.

A Mexican Bricklayer, on the effect of local government on him:
"There is no water in the house and my wife has to go somewhere else to get it."

A Mexican Schoolteacher in a small village, on the effect of local government on him:
"It doesn't effect me in any form; it sometimes seems there is no local authority."

A Mexican Female White-collar Worker, on the effect of local government:
"They have neglected the food shops and the markets where the merchandise is not of good quality and expensive. Vegetables are sometimes rotten but are sold just the same and this causes sickness among the people."

The same themes of corruption and neglect appear among the Italian alienated respondents. Thus an Italian cab-driver in Bari replied impatiently to the question on the effect of the national government on people like himself: "Of course, it has an influence, but we don't have any influence. The government officials have influence to fill up their own pockets. What effect can they have? There is nothing that one can do. My family keeps its place and is not interested." Questioned further about the local government, he replied: "All local activities are for interested parties. They make a lot of propaganda; they promise many things, but nobody does anything for the people. How can I approach the mayor, or join a party, if nobody thinks about us?"

A tailor living in Platania in the province of Calabria replied: ". . . the activities of the government should be important, but they aren't. Many new regulations have been made in the last ten years, but the poor people are not affected by them. Millions have been spent uselessly, ending up in the pockets of the rich. The rich had money and land, and obtained financial aid from the government to build houses for the farmers. But if you noticed on your way here to Platania, there are many lovely new houses, but they are closed since the owners only come here fifteen or twenty days a year. The rest of the time the houses are closed while the farmers live six to ten in a room, and these rooms are like holes in the ground. When funds are raised, they are lost on the way, and the poor never profit by it. . . . The government is taking measures against this. There is too much corruption among officials. For example, there is a law that says that workmen have to receive a minimum per month, but nobody pays any attention to it. If a workman refuses to work for 20,000 lire a month, they send him away and immediately find someone who will work for 15,000 lire. There is too much misery, too many people without work, and too few people to defend us."

Parochialism and alienation are not peculiar to Italy and Mexico, however. We encountered both phenomena in Germany, Britain, and the United States. Tables 1 and 2 suggested that these attitudes occur far less frequently in the latter three countries. But a few examples may help to make the point that the differences are relative and not absolute.

An English Female Garment Worker, on the effect of the national government on her:
"I don't know. I don't bother. They don't affect us at all. If we don't work, they don't give us anything."
An English Cook, on the effect of the national government:
"I should say, quite a lot . . . well, I don't know that they affect me in particular. The only thing I'm up against is that those who have been thrifty all their lives, they let them get on with it—but those who haven't, they help. That's what I don't like."
A German Laborer, on the influence of the national government:
"There is little influence. The main influence is that everyone has to pay taxes. It hardly touches my life."
A German Refugee Housewife, on the effect of government on her family life:

85

"When my husband brings home his pay envelope and we see the deductions—then we are in touch with the government."

Thus far we have been analyzing questions about governmental output. Those respondents who attribute significance to national and local government and who can provide examples of this significant impact are at least subjects. If they are aware of the impact of government but are dissatisfied, we can call them alienated subjects. If they are not aware at all or only dimly aware, we can call them parochials. It is of interest that many respondents, particularly among the British, answered these output questions with gratuitous input content. In other words, their "democratic" orientation spilled over into a subject context. Thus a Scottish steel worker attributed great significance to the local government, and when pressed for an example he remarked, "Well, the people are interested in things that want doing and they are not long in waiting to bring it up to the local Council or in wanting to publish it in the local paper." To the question on whether or not government was necessary a British laborer from Gloucester replied: "We have got to have governments or there would be chaos. One party should be in power and another in opposition to keep the balance, otherwise the Communists would step in." A B.B.C. employee in London added to her comments on the need for government, "It's a good way of running a country, by enabling people of opposing views to discuss things; people of higher education, especially." And a lower-level British civil servant, replying to the same question, said, "You must have a government . . . the same as at work. You must have management or directors. The government we have is the best. It's elected by the people. The people put them in and the people can put them out."

Awareness of the significance of government impact varies sharply with the level of education (see Table 4). Thus in the United States 89 per cent of those who had had some secondary school education were aware of the significance of the national government, as compared with 73 per cent of those who had had only primary school education. In England the percentages were 76 for the university educated to 70 for the primary school educated, and in Germany the figures were 83 per cent to 66 per cent.

While the differences are large among these three countries, the important point is that even among the minimally-educated Americans, Britons, and Germans, the perception that government is significant for one's daily life is extremely widespread. The point might also be made that in all three of these countries the overwhelming majority of the population has had some schooling; thus almost no respondents turned up in our samples in these three coun-

TABLE 4

Educational Differences in Estimation of Impact of National Government
in the United States, Great Britain, and Germany
(in per cent)

Per Cent who say National Government has	U.S.			U.K.			Germany		
	Prim. or Less	Some Sec.	Some Univ.	Prim. or Less	Some Sec.	Some Univ.	Prim. or Less	Some Sec.	Some Univ.
Some effect	73	89	96	70	76	92	69	83	92
No effect	17	10	4	25	21	8	18	14	8
Other	0	0	0	0	1	0	0	0	0
Don't know	10	1	0	4	2	0	14	2	0
Total per cent	100	100	100	99	100	100	101	99	100
Total number*	339	443	188	593	322	24	792	123	26

* On this and other tables broken down into separate educational groups, the numbers add to a few less than the total sample since the educational level of some respondents was not ascertained.

TABLE 5

Educational Differences in Estimation of Impact of National Government
in Italy and Mexico
(in per cent)

Per Cent who say National Government has	Italy				Mexico			
	None	Prim. or Less	Some Sec.	Some Univ.	None	Prim. or Less	Some Sec.	Some Univ.
Some effect	24	48	72	85	25	30	35	57
No effect	17	20	19	13	65	68	62	41
Other	6	3	2	2	–	–	2	–
Don't know	53	29	7	–	10	2	1	3
Total per cent	100	100	100	100	100	100	100	101
Total number	88	604	245	54	221	656	103	24

tries who had not had some formal schooling. In Italy and Mexico a substantial percentage of the respondents had had no schooling (9 per cent in Italy, 20 per cent in Mexico). Among those formally-uneducated Italians and Mexicans, the incidence of awareness of the significance of national and local government was extremely low: 24 per cent for Italy and 25 per cent for Mexico (see Table 5).

Italians with secondary school education had an incidence of awareness of 72 per cent, and those with university education 85 per cent. What is striking about the results for Mexico is that even the secondary- and university-educated showed a relatively low incidence of awareness of the significance of government: 35 per cent for the secondary-educated Mexicans and 57 per cent for the university-educated Mexicans.

Awareness of Politics

Our first series of questions was intended to ascertain patterns of "output cognition." We were concerned with whether people perceived government as having an effect on them, their families, and their communities. In another series of questions we sought to determine whether or not they followed or paid attention to political and governmental affairs (including political campaigns). These questions come closer to testing the frequency of participant orientations in the five countries, for they get at the dimension of attentiveness to political input. We may assume that if people follow political and governmental affairs, they are in some sense involved in the process by which decisions are made. To be sure, it is a minimal degree of involvement. The civic culture, as we use the term, includes a sense of obligation to participate in political input activities, as well as a sense of competence to participate. Following governmental and political affairs and paying attention to politics are limited civic commitments indeed, and yet there would be no civic culture without them. They represent the cognitive component of the civic orientation.

Table 6 tells us something about the incidence of civic cognition in the five countries. In general, the picture in Table 6 coincides with the one reported in the discussion of subject or output cognition. The United States, Britain, and Germany are high in following political and governmental affairs, and Italy and Mexico are low. But there are two interesting qualifications to this general pattern. First, the Germans more frequently follow political affairs than do the English. And second, the Italians follow political affairs far less frequently than do the Mexicans.

A similar general pattern is seen in Table 7, which reports data on the frequency with which respondents pay attention to election campaigns. In Italy and Mexico election campaigns are more likely to be ignored than in the other three nations, with the Italians reporting somewhat more frequently that they pay no attention to such campaigns. The proportion of respondents who pay no atten-

TABLE 6

Following Accounts of Political and Governmental Affairs, by Nation*
(in per cent)

Per Cent who report they Follow Accounts	U.S.	U.K.	Germany	Italy	Mexico
Regularly	27	23	34	11	15
From time to time	53	45	38	26	40
Never	19	32	25	62	44
Other and don't know	1	1	3	1	1
Total per cent	100	100	100	100	100
Total number	970	963	955	995	1,007

* Actual text of the question: "Do you follow the accounts of political and governmental affairs? Would you say you follow them regularly, from time to time, or never?"

TABLE 7

Paying Attention to Political Campaigns, by Nation*
(in per cent)

Per Cent who say they	U.S.	U.K.	Germany	Italy	Mexico
Pay much attention	43	25	34	17	15
Pay little attention	44	47	34	25	38
Pay no attention	12	29	27	54	45
Other and don't know	1	0	5	4	2
Total per cent	100	101	100	100	100
Total number	970	963	955	995	1,007

* Actual text of the question: "What about the campaigning that goes on at the time of a national election—do you pay much attention to what goes on, just a little, or none at all?"

tion to election campaigns is smaller in America than in any of the other nations, while the percentages in Britain and Germany are quite similar to each other.

The relatively high frequency with which German respondents report that they are cognitively oriented to the governmental input process—a frequency as great as or greater than that in Britain—suggests that at least in the cognitive dimension there may well be civic tendencies in Germany. If democracy does not seem to have struck deep roots in German society, it is not because of lack of exposure to politics or lack of political information.

The Italian and Mexican data present an interesting contrast. On the questions about output cognition and input cognition these two nations scored lower than the other three. But in terms of their cognition of government output, the Italians much more frequently than the Mexicans expressed awareness of such activities. However, in terms of their cognition of government input—their exposure to political affairs and to political campaigns—the Italians much less frequently than the Mexicans indicated such exposure. Thus more than half of the Italian respondents said that the government had an impact on their lives; but almost two-thirds said that they never follow politics or governmental affairs, and more than half said they do not pay attention to election campaigns. In Mexico, on the other hand, a much larger proportion pays attention to campaigns and follows politics than attributes significance to the government.[1]

This Mexican characteristic appears with greater clarity in Table 8. In the other four nations there is a substantial probability that if a respondent is cognitively oriented toward political input, he will also be cognitively oriented toward governmental output. Thus in the United States 89 per cent of those who both follow political and governmental affairs and pay attention to political campaigns also attribute significance to both their national and local governments, while only 3 per cent of those who are high in political exposure are low in attributing significance to their national and local governments. Britain, Germany, and Italy show similar ratios. In Mexico, on the other hand, of those scoring high in exposure to politics 56 per cent attribute significance to neither their national nor local government. The striking character of the Mexican finding is suggested by the fact that in the other four countries the proportion of those who score high in political exposure and low on governmental significance is in every case below 10 per cent. We suggest again, although our evidence has only been partly presented, that Mexico

[1] In chapter 2 we pointed out that the Mexican sample did not include that part of the Mexican population living in towns whose population was under 10,000. Since this might have affected the Mexican results, particularly in the dimension of exposure to political communication, and thus rendered invalid our Mexican-Italian comparison, we compared the Mexican sample with that part of the Italian sample living in towns of 10,000 and over. The results differed only by a small number of percentage points and confirmed the conclusion discussed here.

TABLE 8

Awareness of Government Impact, by Nation and Exposure to Politics*
(in per cent)

Per Cent of who report They are Affected by	U.S. Exposure			U.K. Exposure			Germany Exposure			Italy Exposure			Mexico Exposure		
	Low	Med.	High	Low	Med.	High	Low	Med.	High	Low	Med.	High	Low	Med.	High
Both national and local govt.	57	82	89	54	65	75	45	62	75	33	62	69	14	29	27
Either national or local govt.	21	13	7	21	20	17	24	23	18	23	28	19	18	19	17
Neither national nor local govt.	16	4	3	23	13	6	16	12	6	19	6	8	64	49	56
Other and don't know	7	1	–	3	2	2	15	3	–	23	3	3	3	3	–
Total per cent	101	100	99	101	100	100	100	100	99	98	99	99	99	100	100
Total number	194	315	461	385	290	288	324	231	400	672	173	150	584	257	167

* As revealed by respondents whose exposure to politics varies in three ways: *low* exposure to politics means negative responses to both the question on following political and governmental affairs and on paying attention to campaigns; *medium* exposure means a positive response to one question and a negative to the other; *high* exposure means two positive responses.

has an individual pattern of political culture: one marked by high output alienation and/or parochialism, along with a high, though diffuse, political involvement in the input structure.

A few comments from our life-history interviews may illustrate the difference between the Mexican and Italian patterns. A Mexican truck driver, when asked whether he was interested in political and governmental affairs, replied, "Very much, because the government can help the general conditions of life of all the Mexicans. At least this is what I wish." Asked when he first became interested in politics, he said, "About ten years ago, when I began to realize that our governors tend to benefit themselves economically without considering the needs of the other citizens." A Mexican shoemaker replied to the same question, "Yes, I like politics. I am very interested in it, because I want to see improvements and also because I want to see that everything goes well, because many political leaders, rather than help the worker, hurt him." And a Mexican stenographer commented, "I have an interest in my town that is neglected by its governor. I have compared it with other cities that were at the same level as Pueblo and now they have gone way ahead in culture and beauty." She first became interested in politics when she visited Guadalajara" . . . and saw how it had improved. I remember that last year Pueblo had the second place in the republic for its beauty and now she has lost it because her governors have neglected her."

While there were Italian respondents who described themselves as interested in politics, the more typical reply stressed the danger and futility of interesting oneself in politics:

An Italian Retired Worker, on his interest in politics:
"Reading the paper is the most that I do, and when I read it, I read it very slowly. It takes me a whole day to read it. I don't like to take part in discussions. As I told you before, they are very lively and at times even dangerous."

An Italian Mechanic, on who is interested in politics:
"The fanatics who believe in what they are doing and in their aspirations, or the ignorant people who are behind and pushed by the first."

An Italian Housewife who waits on customers in the family grocery store:
"None! I have an aversion for it, because I feel nothing is just."

An Italian Bookkeeper:
"No! I don't want to get mixed up in it. Who is interested? Educated people. Who is not interested? Peaceful people."

The British responses, though characterized by understatement, reflected relatively high standards of political interest:

A British Housewife:
"I'm not an avid follower of government. I do read newspapers. I do take quite a big interest. As my own party is in, I'm quite happy to let them get on with it. But if Labour were in, I would take much more interest, I suppose."

A British Civil Servant, on who is interested in politics:
"I don't know. The average Tom, Dick and Harry, the ordinary fellow. In the pub, the average bloke used to talk politics. It's fifty-fifty I say. At election nearly everyone, ninety per cent, use their vote. Whether they vote because their father did or what, I don't know. Ninety per cent vote, and fifty per cent are interested in politics."

A British Bartender:
"An average interest. Because you like to know how the country is being run . . . whether for their own good or for the people. . . . Through working in a bar you hear so many points of view from customers. You get discussions all over the bar. You hear more politics in a bar than anywhere . . . just people talking to you."

A British Housewife working as a Secretary:
"Well, not too much. Sufficient interest. You don't want to waste too much time on it. There are many other things of more interest. . . . You've got to have a certain amount of interest. . . . I think everybody should be interested without being rabid. Everybody must be, because it affects your life."

In the German life-history interviews the participant respondents, in discussing their political obligations, stressed the historical experience of their country:

A German White-collar Worker:
"I am greatly interested in political matters. A good democratic citizen must concern himself with political matters. In a democratic state everyone shares the responsibility for what happens."

A German Baker:
"I have great interest because the kind of government we have concerns me too. Actually, everyone should pay more attention to it."

A German Housewife:
"I am very much interested in politics today. Through the developments since 1914 one sees things quite differently. They should put greater emphasis on the various connections in the schools. You have to have your eye on politics nowadays."

When we use other measures of political cognition, the same national patterns are repeated. Thus when we compare exposure to political communication in the various mass media (Table 9), the

Germans come out ahead of the British, and the Mexicans better than the Italians.

We have already seen that output cognition is closely related to level of educational attainment and socio-economic position. It also appears that education is strongly correlated with civic cognition

TABLE 9

Following Reports of Public Affairs in the Various Media, by Nation*
(in per cent)

Per Cent who Follow Accounts	U.S.	U.K.	Germany	Italy	Mexico
In newspapers at least weekly	49	43	53	16	31
On radio or television at least weekly	58	36	52	20	28
In magazine (ever)	57	21	45	26	25
Total number	970	963	955	995	1,007

* Actual text of the questions: "What about newspapers (radio or television, magazines)? Do you follow (listen to, read about) public affairs in newspapers (radio or television, magazines) nearly every day, about once a week, from time to time, or never?" Only the per cents for those who report exposure are reported here.

TABLE 10

Following Politics Regularly or from Time to Time, by Nation and Education

Nation	Total (%)	(No.)*	Prim. or Less (%)	(No.)	Some Sec. (%)	(No.)	Some Univ. (%)	(No.)
United States	80	(970)	67	(339)	84	(442)	96	(188)
Great Britain	68	(963)	60	(593)	77	(322)	92	(24)
Germany	72	(955)	69	(790)	89	(124)	100	(26)
Italy	36	(995)	24	(692)	58	(245)	87	(54)
Mexico	55	(1,007)	51	(877)	76	(103)	92	(24)

* Numbers in parentheses refer to the bases upon which percentages are calculated.

(see Table 10). On the university level almost all respondents in each country follow politics. On the secondary level the countries are, with the exception of Italy, uniformly high in the proportions who follow politics; and even in relation to Italy the difference between secondary-school Italians and secondary-school respondents in other countries is much less than the difference between primary-school Italians and primary-school respondents in other countries. Thus on the higher levels of education one finds in all nations a uniformly high proportion who follow politics. Among those with lower educational attainment the national differences are greater. In the United States, Britain, and Germany, and to a lesser extent in Mexico, those with little education still follow politics; but in Italy few respondents on the lower level are exposed to political communication.

Having Information and Opinions

Our measures of knowledge or cognition of the political system thus far have been subjective estimates of the significance of government and subjective estimates of exposure to political and governmental affairs. We have not yet tried to ascertain the amount of information about government and politics that the respondents actually have. Democratic competence is closely related to having valid information about political issues and processes, and to the ability to use information in the analysis of issues and the devising of influence strategies. Our survey contained two measures of information: one was based on ability to identify the national leaders of the principal parties in each country, and the second was based on ability to identify cabinet offices or departments at the national level of government.

These are simple measures of quantity of a certain kind of information. They tap only a limited aspect of the dimension of knowledge, and they tell us nothing about the capacity to use knowledge intelligently. Furthermore, since the governmental and party structures of the five countries differ, we cannot assume that these quantitative measures of political information are strictly comparable. The ability to identify leaders of the smaller parties in Italy and Mexico may represent a higher order of cognition than the ability to identify a larger number of leaders in the American two-party system. However, when we compare the proportions at the extremes—those having either no correct information or a great deal of information—these structural differences are of less significance and our comparisons are more reliable.

The results in Table 11 show that Germans, English, and Americans have the largest proportion of well-informed respondents by this measure of political information. The high frequency of uninformed Italian respondents is consistent with the high percentage of Italians who describe themselves as not following politics and political campaigns. On the other hand, the Mexican figures are again of great interest. Though reporting with relatively great frequency that they follow politics and political campaigns, the Mexicans show themselves to be the most poorly informed of all our national groups. Approximately half the Mexican respondents—including many who say they follow politics—could not name correctly any political leader or any government department.

If we can demonstrate this Mexican pattern, we shall have added another significant item to our characterization of the Mexican political culture. We have hypothesized that Mexican political culture

TABLE 11

Ability to Name Party Leaders and Governmental Ministries, by Nation[a]
(in per cent)

| Nation | Percentage of total sample who could[b] | | | |
	Name Four or More Party Leaders	Name No Party Leader	Name Four or More Ministries	Name No Ministry
United States	65	16	34	28
Great Britain	42	20	34	23
Germany	69	12	40	20
Italy	36	40	23	53
Mexico	5	53	21	47

[a] Those with medium levels of information (i.e., who could name one to three in each category) have been left off the table.

[b] Percentages in each case are of the total sample.

combines high cognitive self-appraisal with poor cognitive performance. One way of testing this would be to determine the extent to which poorly informed respondents in our five countries are ready to express political opinions. We shall use as a measure of readiness to express political opinions a "range of political opinion" index. This index is based upon the frequency with which respondents, rather than saying they did not know, expressed opinions on a series of six general political attitude questions. These questions dealt with such matters as the content of civic obligations, judgments of interest groups and political parties, and the need for political campaigning.[2] That this combination of high cognitive

[2] The six questions used to compute the "range of political opinion" index were as follows:

"1. One sometimes hears that some people or groups have so much influence on the way the government is run that the interests of the majority are ignored. Do you agree or disagree that there are such groups?

self-appraisal with low information is especially characteristic of Mexico is suggested by Table 12, which reports how frequently respondents answered these opinion questions.

It appears that the Mexicans are almost as frequently willing to express opinions on all six questions as are the Germans, even though the Germans have the largest proportion of persons with high information scores and the Mexicans have the smallest. But to provide further confirmation that Mexico contains a larger

TABLE 12
Range of Political Opinions, by Nation
(in per cent)

Per Cent who	U.S.	U.K.	Germany	Italy	Mexico
Answered all six political questions	63	56	47	26	46
Said "Don't know" to one or two questions	29	37	46	37	35
Said "Don't know" to three or more questions	7	7	7	36	19
Total per cent	99	100	100	99	100
Total number	970	963	955	995	1,007

proportion of "low information-high opinion" respondents than do any of the other countries, we must ascertain what percentage of respondents in each country *combines* these qualities of low information and high willingness to express opinions. This analysis, expressed in Table 13, brings out a number of points. First, it appears that in all the countries except Italy, persons who score low in information score high in the expression of opinions. Thus two out of three poorly informed Mexicans and almost all of the

---

"2. We know that the ordinary person has many problems that take his time. In view of this, what part do you think the ordinary person ought to play in the community affairs of his town or district?

"3. People speak of the obligations that they owe to their country. In your opinion, what are the obligations that every man owes his country?

"4. Some people say that campaigning is needed so the public can judge candidates and issues. Others say that it causes so much bitterness and is so unreliable that we'd be better off without it. What do you think—is it needed or would we be better off without it?

"5. The _____ party now controls the government. Do you think that its policies and activities would ever seriously endanger the country's welfare? Do you think that this *probably* would happen, that it *might* happen, or that it *probably wouldn't* happen?

"6. Same as question 5, but with reference to chief opposition party."

poorly informed Americans, British, and Germans gave some answer to four or more of the six opinion questions. On the other hand, only one out of three poorly informed Italians expressed opinions in four or more of the questions. This would seem to suggest that in all the countries but Italy, the willingness to express political opinions is widespread, affecting even the uninformed. The striking thing is that the poorly informed Mexicans are in this respect like the Americans, British, and Germans and unlike the Italians. There

TABLE 13

Willingness to express Political Opinions among Respondents
with Little Political Information, by Nation
(in per cent)[a]

Nation	Percentage of Total Sample Low on Political Info.[b]	Percentage of Total Sample Low on Info. But Answered Four or More Opinion Question
United States	13	11
Great Britain	13	10
Germany	8	8
Italy	33	11
Mexico	36	23

[a] Percentages in each case are of the total sample.
[b] Low on political information means that the respondent could name neither any party leaders nor any government ministerial post.

were almost as many poorly informed respondents in Italy as in Mexico, but most of the former refrained from offering opinions on political questions. Two inferences are suggested: first, Mexico is like the more "developed democracies," for even the cognitively incompetent feel free to express opinions, and, second, there are many more such "aspiring citizens" in Mexico than in any of our other countries. These Mexicans (about one-fourth of the sample) are in almost all cases persons of primary or no education; persons possessing little information about the larger world of public affairs, yet quite willing to take a position on general political questions.[3] Such persons appear in all of our countries, but they appear twice as frequently in Mexico as in any of the other nations. Their

[3] It is important to note that we are dealing with the extent to which respondents felt *free* to express opinions, not with the extent to which they actually had opinions. Thus one reason for the infrequency of opinions among Italian respondents may be their greater unease in an interview situation. This point is discussed further in Chapter 4.

existence in such large proportion in Mexico supports our interpretation that the political culture of that country contains a large aspirational component—a tendency to be willing to express opinions—along with poverty of information.

In general our findings on political cognition show the British, Americans, and Germans to be predominantly oriented toward their

TABLE 14

Summary of Patterns of Political Cognition, by Nation
(in per cent)[a]

Nation	Percentage Alienated or Parochial in terms of Govt. Output[b]	Percentage Alienated or Parochial in terms of Govt. Input[c]	Percentage Alienated or Parochial in terms of Both Input and Output[d]
United States	12	20	7
Great Britain	26	33	14
Germany	26	28	13
Italy	42	63	38
Mexico	71	45	35

[a] Percentages in each case are of the total national sample.
[b] Negative or don't know answers on local government impact
[c] Negative or don't know answers on following politics
[d] Negative or don't know answers on both local government impact and following politics

political systems in both the political and governmental sense. Or to use our jargon, they are cognitively oriented toward the political system in its output and input aspects. The Mexicans and Italians, on the other hand, include large numbers who are alienated or parochial. Table 14 provides a convenient summary of much of the argument that has been presented in this chapter. It shows that more than a third of the Italians and Mexicans are fully alienated or parochial, as compared with far smaller proportions for the other three countries. It also brings out quite clearly the imbalances in the Italian and Mexican patterns of orientation, and it summarizes evidence we have thus far presented on the predominance of aspirational tendencies among the Mexicans and of alienated tendencies among the Italians. If to the evidence summarized in Table 14 we add our demonstration of the low political information level in Mexico, combined with an unusually frequent willingness to express political opinions, our theory of Mexican civic aspiration begins to assume a structurally elaborated form.

However, there is more to political culture than knowledge or cognition. How people *feel* about their political systems is an important component of political culture. The state of feeling or political emotion in a country is perhaps the most important test of the legitimacy of its political system. It is also the most important measure of political alienation and aspiration. This is the aspect of political culture to which we now turn.

CHAPTER 4

FEELINGS TOWARD GOVERNMENT
AND POLITICS

ALTHOUGH we stressed the dimension of knowledge or cognition in the preceding chapter, we included data and drew inferences about the state of feeling about government and politics in our five countries. Thus when we spoke of Italy and Mexico as having large proportions of alienates, we were implying that the citizens of these countries are cognitively oriented toward their political systems, yet they reject them either completely or in some of their aspects. In this and the following chapters we shall consider the affective dimension more directly.

In the present chapter we shall deal with generalized attitudes toward the system as a whole: toward the "nation," its virtues, accomplishments, and the like. We call this "system affect." We shall also deal with "output affect," or the kinds of expectations people have of treatment at the hands of government officials. Here we shall be describing the attitudes people have toward the executive or administrative agencies that enforce laws and toward regulations affecting them: that is, that part of the political system in relation to which they have a predominantly passive role. Finally, we shall treat "input affect," or the feelings people have both about those agencies and processes that are involved in the election of public officials, and about the enactment of general public policies. In the present chapter we shall introduce the dimension of input affect with an analysis of attitudes toward communicating about politics. In the chapter that follows we shall deal in detail with partisan attitudes and feelings in election campaigns.

We shall first treat the general dimension of "system affect," using as our measure the objects of national pride in our five countries.

101

System Affect: National Pride

Quite early in our interview we asked our respondents, "Speaking generally, what are the things about this country that you are most proud of?" In replying to this question, the respondents were not directed in any way to select political characteristics. When they gave political responses, we may assume that the expression of political pride was spontaneous. Table 1 summarizes the results. Eighty-five per cent of the American respondents cited some feature

TABLE 1

Aspects of Nation in which Respondents report Pride, by Nation
(in per cent)

Per Cent who say they are proud of	U.S.	U.K.	Germany	Italy	Mexico
Governmental, political institutions	85	46	7	3	30
Social legislation	13	18	6	1	2
Position in international affairs	5	11	5	2	3
Economic system	23	10	33	3	24
Characteristics of people	7	18	36	11	15
Spiritual virtues and religion	3	1	3	6	8
Contributions to the arts	1	6	11	16	9
Contributions to science	3	7	12	3	1
Physical attributes of country	5	10	17	25	22
Nothing or don't know	4	10	15	27	16
Other	9	11	3	21	14
Total % of responses*	158	148	148	118	144
Total % of respondents	100	100	100	100	100
Total number of cases	970	963	955	995	1,007

* Percentages exceed one hundred because of multiple responses.

of the American government or political tradition—the Constitution, political freedom, democracy, and the like—as compared with 46 per cent for the British, 7 per cent for the Germans, 3 per cent for the Italians, and 30 per cent for the Mexicans. In addition, the Americans and the British referred more frequently to public policy accomplishments than did the respondents in the other countries. At the other extreme, the Italian respondents, who included the smallest number of persons taking pride in their political system, had the largest number of respondents who reported that they took pride in nothing (8 per cent) or "didn't know" what they took pride in (19 per cent). The Italians had the highest proportion of "other" responses (21 per cent) and almost all of these were general statements of pride in the fact of having been born Italians.

Table 1 also reports the nations' nonpolitical attributes in which the five peoples take pride. The German respondents, who infrequently took pride in their political system, included the largest proportion who took pride in their national economic accomplishments. They also included the largest proportion who expressed pride in the characteristics of Germans as people (frugality, cleanliness, hard work, and efficiency). Italians cited their country's contributions to the arts, the physical beauty of the country, and its cultural treasures most frequently. Mexican pride was more or less equally distributed among the political system, the economic system, the virtues of the people, and the physical beauties of the country.

On the whole, these findings in Table 1 support the characterizations of the political culture of our five countries presented in the preceding chapter. Thus the Americans and the British with greatest frequency take pride in their political systems, social legislation, and international prestige. Italians in the overwhelming majority take no pride in their political system, nor even in their economy or society. To the extent that they have national pride at all, it is in their history, the physical beauty of their country, or in the fact of being Italian. Thus the picture of Italian alienation is deepened.

It is of great interest that Germany parts company with American and British democracy in the dimension of national pride. Germans see the significance of governmental output and they expose themselves to information about political input, but they express little pride in their political system as a whole and focus their national pride on the German economy, on the personal virtues of Germans, and on their scientific and artistic accomplishments.

The Mexican results provide a striking confirmation of the pattern presented in the preceding chapter. While overwhelmingly alienated or parochial in relation to governmental output, the Mexicans show a relatively high frequency of interest in politics. Table 1 also shows that, as compared with the Italians and Germans, the Mexicans have a relatively high frequency of political pride. This pattern of high system affect coupled with rejection of the actual performance of the government is, we have argued, what one might expect in a nation characterized by a continuing attachment to a set of revolutionary ideals. Such a pattern of attitudes is what one might expect from people suddenly drawn into politics by a revolutionary upheaval. It is, of course, impossible to trace this set

103

of attitudes solely to the Mexican Revolution, for it probably has many roots. But there is some evidence that the continuing impact of the Revolution as an ongoing process explains in part the type of attachment to their political system that Mexican respondents manifest. These respondents were asked if they could name some of the ideals and goals of the Mexican Revolution.[1] Thirty-five per cent could name none of the goals, while the remaining 65 per cent listed democracy, political liberty and equality, economic welfare, agrarian reform, social equality, and national freedom. What is of interest here is that, when asked what they were proud of as Mexicans, 34 per cent of those who could name some of the Revolution's goals or ideals—in contrast with only 19 per cent of those who could not name any—were proud of some political aspect of their nation.

But even more interesting are the results of a follow-up question to the one on the goals of the Mexican Revolution. Those respondents who mentioned some goal of the Revolution were then asked if these goals had been realized, or forgotten, or if people were still working to achieve them. Of the respondents who could name a goal of the Revolution (n: 614), 25 per cent thought the goals had been realized, 61 per cent thought that people were still working to attain them, and 14 per cent thought they had been forgotten. As one would expect, those respondents who thought that the goals of the Revolution had been forgotten were the least likely of the three groups to express pride in their political system. Thirty-one per cent (n: 84) of this group said they were proud of the Mexican political system. But in connection with our hypothesis about the effects of the Mexican Revolution as an ongoing process, it is interesting that, though the difference is slight, those respondents who believe that people are still working to accomplish the goals of the Revolution, rather than those who believe the goals have already been accomplished, express pride most frequently in the political system: 39 per cent of the former (n: 379) express such political pride, in comparison with 34 per cent of those who do not see the Revolution as a continuing process (n: 151). Mexican pride in nation, thus, does seem to depend to some extent on the continuing symbolic identification with the Mexican Revolution.

[1] The text of the question was: "Our Mexican Revolution is a very important event which is always much discussed. Could you tell me, in your opinion, what the principal ideals and goals of the Mexican Revolution are?"

In the United States and Britain, where a large proportion of the respondents express pride in the political characteristics of their nation, this proportion was higher among the better-educated respondents. In the United States 92 per cent of those with some university education responded with political objects of pride, as compared with 81 per cent for those who did not get beyond primary school. In Britain 75 per cent of the university educated took pride in political characteristics, as compared with 41 per cent of those with only primary education. Similarly, in Mexico, 22 per cent of those with no education expressed political pride, as compared with 38 per cent of the university educated. In Germany and Italy, on the other hand, level of education seems to have little relationship to the frequency with which political pride was expressed.

Similarly, persons in the more skilled and better-rewarded occupations in Britain, the United States, and Mexico were more frequently proud of their political systems, while occupation made relatively little difference in this respect in Germany and Italy. The main difference in objects of pride in each of the latter two countries was that the better-educated and the skilled, managerial, and professional respondents more often expressed pride in their country's achievements in the arts and sciences than did those with relatively little education or those employed in manual occupations.

The fact that education and occupational level have so little effect on national pride in Germany and Italy suggests alienation from the political system rather than parochialism or lack of awareness of the system. Higher education opens the minds of individuals to the secondary structures of their society, to the dimension of historical depth, and to the wider perspectives of the world scene. If higher-educated Germans and Italians fail to be significantly more political in their choice of objects of pride than their lower-educated compatriots, we have to conclude that the political system of each country is given a low order of preference, or is negatively appraised among those social groupings who are aware of it and follow its activities. Furthermore, we are now in a position to point out that political alienation in Germany differs from that in Italy. Alienation in Italy involves the withdrawal of attention as well as the absence of political pride. In Germany we have the interesting combination of high exposure and attentiveness to the political system, along with an absence of pride in it.

Output Affect: Expectations of Treatment
  by Government and Police

The feelings that people have toward governmental authorities may be inferred from their expectations of how they will be treated by them. In constructing our interview we assumed that most people preferred to be treated fairly and considerately when in contact with officials. If they expected fair and considerate treatment, we could safely assume that at least in these respects they were favorably disposed toward governmental authority. And in the opposite case, we could assume that they were unfavorably disposed. Thus our questions were intended to discover what qualities our respondents imputed to the executive side of government.

We confronted our respondents with two hypothetical situations. In the first they were asked to imagine themselves in a government office with a problem that called for official action. How did they think they would be treated? Would they be treated equally, like everyone else? We then asked them to imagine that they were explaining their point of view to the official or officials. Did they expect that they would be listened to attentively and considerately? In the second situation they were asked to imagine themselves as having some minor trouble with the police. Did they expect to be treated equally and considerately by the police? The results of the questions on equality of treatment are summarized in Table 2.

The pattern that emerges is of great interest. The Americans and the British, who in large majorities perceived the significance of national and local government for their daily lives, who said they followed politics and political campaigns, and who most often spontaneously expressed pride in their political systems, also in large majorities expect equality of treatment at the hands of government. In theoretical terms we can say that the British and Americans are high in output and input cognition, high in system affect, and high in output affect. The Germans again conform to the British and American pattern, although the proportions expecting equal treatment are somewhat lower. Though they are low in system affect, they are high in output affect, just as they were high in output and input cognition.

The responses in Italy and Mexico confirm the high incidence of output alienation in these countries. These people are alienated in their expectations of treatment at the hands of governmental

106

authority and police. Again, on the output side, the Mexicans show more frequent alienation than the Italians—a repetition of the pattern in the dimension of output cognition.

Table 3 reports the frequency of expectations of considerate treatment at the hands of governmental officials and the police. Here we were concerned with whether or not our respondents imputed responsiveness to government officials, whether they felt they would be treated with dignity, on a "give and take" basis. Although there are structural differences in the bureaucratic and police organizations among our five countries, our questions were directed at those bureaucratic and police authorities with whom the respondents might come in contact in the hypothetical situations set up by the questions. (A more discriminating series of questions, which would get at differences in expectations of treatment by different levels of bureaucratic authority and different types of bureaucratic or police agencies, would no doubt have produced a more complex pattern and more reliable body of information.) Given the problem of interview length, we sought to attain comparability by specifying the type of problem (e.g., taxation, housing) or the type of offense (traffic violation, misdemeanor) that occasioned the bureaucratic or police encounter.

In all of our countries, with the exception of Mexico, the police were often viewed with as much favor as—if not more favor than —the general governmental authority. Mexican cynicism is particularly marked vis-à-vis the police, while in Britain the reported general confidence in the considerateness and responsiveness of the police is strikingly documented. It is of great interest that the Germans come out somewhat better than the Americans on expectations of considerate treatment at the hands of government and the police. Why Americans should, on the one hand, expect equality of treatment in such overwhelming proportions and then drop to only around 50 per cent for expectations of considerate treatment is an intriguing question. We would like to suggest, though it will be treated in detail below, that Americans have not as fully assimilated the role of subject in relation to administrative authorities as have the Germans and the British. Certainly these data seem to support popular impressions of the American as uneasy in bureaucratic situations, fuming over inefficiency and red tape.

A comparison of Tables 2 and 3 brings out an important point. In all countries the proportion expecting considerateness and re-

TABLE 2

Expectation of Treatment by Governmental Bureaucracy and Police, by Nation*
(in per cent)

Per Cent who say	U.S. Bureauc.	U.S. Pol.	U.K. Bureauc.	U.K. Pol.	Germany Bureauc.	Germany Pol.	Italy Bureauc.	Italy Pol.	Mexico Bureauc.	Mexico Pol.
They expect equal treatment	83	85	83	89	65	72	53	56	42	32
They don't expect equal treatment	9	8	7	6	9	5	13	10	50	57
Depends	4	5	6	4	19	15	17	15	5	5
Other	–	–	–	–	–	–	6	6	–	–
Don't know	4	2	2	0	7	8	11	13	3	5
Total per cent	100	100	98	99	100	100	100	100	100	99
Total number	970	970	963	963	955	955	995	995	1,007	1,007

* Actual texts of the questions: "Suppose there were some question that you had to take to a government office—for example, a tax question or housing regulation. Do you think you would be given equal treatment—I mean, would you be treated as well as anyone else?" "If you had some trouble with the police—a traffic violation maybe, or being accused of a minor offense—do you think you would be given equal treatment? That is, would you be treated as well as anyone else?"

TABLE 3

Amount of Consideration expected for Point of View from Bureaucracy and Police, by Nation*
(in per cent)

Per Cent *who expect*	U.S. Bureauc.	Pol.	U.K. Bureauc.	Pol.	Germany Bureauc.	Pol.	Italy Bureauc.	Pol.	Mexico Bureauc.	Pol.
Serious consideration for point of view	48	56	59	74	53	59	35	35	14	12
A little attention	31	22	22	13	18	11	15	13	48	46
To be ignored	6	11	5	5	5	4	11	12	27	29
Depends	11	9	10	6	15	13	21	20	6	7
Other	0	–	–	–	1	2	6	6	–	1
Don't know	4	2	2	1	8	11	12	14	3	4
Total per cent	100	100	98	99	100	100	100	100	98	99
Total number	970	970	963	963	955	955	995	995	1,007	1,007

* Actual texts of the questions: "If you explained your point of view to the officials, what effect do you think it would have? Would they give your point of view serious consideration, would they pay only a little attention, or would they ignore what you had to say?" "If you explained your point of view to the police, what effect do you think it would have? Would they . . . [same choices as before]?"

sponsiveness from governmental and police authority is substantially lower than the proportion expecting equality of treatment. The average for all five countries for equality of treatment is 66 per cent; for responsiveness and considerateness it is 45 per cent. This suggests that, while equality of treatment seems to be a general expectation of bureaucracy, responsiveness and considerateness are far less frequently expected of bureaucratic authority. At the same time, there are sharp differences between countries. The distinction

TABLE 4

Expectation of Treatment by Governmental Authorities and Police, by Education in the United States, United Kingdom, and Germany (in per cent)

Per Cent who expect	U.S.			U.K.			Germany		
	Prim. or Less	Some Sec.	Some Univ.	Prim. or Less	Some Sec.	Some Univ.	Prim. or Less	Some Sec.	Some Univ.
Equal treatment in govt. office	80	84	88	81	87	88	64	73	77
Equal treatment by police	81	87	89	88	90	96	70	81	88
Consideration in govt. office	44	46	58	60	58	75	51	62	81
Consideration by police	50	59	60	75	72	71	58	65	81
Total number	338	443	188	593	321	24	788	123	26

between the United States, Britain, and Germany, on the one hand, and Italy and Mexico, on the other, still holds. Only 35 per cent of the Italians and 12 to 14 per cent of the Mexicans expect serious consideration from governmental and police authority, should they try to explain their point of view, in contrast with 48 per cent or more for the respondents in the other three countries.

Expectation of treatment by government and police also varies among educational levels. Table 4 shows these differences for the United States, Britain, and Germany. In the United States the proportion of university-educated respondents expecting equal and considerate treatment by the government and police ranges from 8 to 12 percentage points higher than for those respondents having primary school education or less. In England the difference is similarly small, and in the case of expectations of considerateness by the police the poorly educated come out better than the well educated. This suggests that in these two countries, not only is there

110

a general widespread expectation of equal and considerate treatment, but the less educated have these expectations almost as frequently as the more educated. Table 4 also shows that Germany, which was high on the overall national percentage for expectations of treatment, has a sharper difference in expectation among educational levels. Furthermore, this difference is more marked in the dimension of considerate treatment than in equality of treatment. While there is a difference of 13 to 18 percentage points in expectations of equality of treatment between Germans with primary school and those with university education, still around two-thirds of the less well-educated Germans expect to be treated equally by the government and the police. But only 51 per cent of the less well-educated Germans expect to be considerately treated by governmental authorities, as compared with 81 per cent of the university educated. The difference between these two groups with respect to considerate treatment by the police is also large—23 per cent. The British figures present a striking contrast. While almost three-fourths of all the British respondents expect to be considerately treated by the police, it would appear that this expectation is somewhat more widely distributed among poorly-educated Britons than among the university educated.

These findings show that in the United States and Britain both the educated and the less well educated, in large and approximately equal proportions, tend to expect "good" treatment from government. In Germany the less well educated expect to be treated equally by governmental authorities, but the expectation of considerate treatment is more frequently concentrated among the educated elements of the population.

As Table 5 indicates, in Italy and Mexico the overall percentage of those expecting fair and considerate treatment is low, but the differences between the advantaged and disadvantaged groups is relatively large. Thus in Italy 30 per cent of those with no formal education expect to be treated equally by the police, as compared with 74 per cent for those with some university education—a difference of 44 percentage points. In Mexico only 19 per cent of those with no education expect equal treatment by government, as compared with 68 per cent for the university educated—a percentage spread of 49 points. The difference among educational groups in expectations of equal treatment by the police is similarly high in both countries. Even on the upper levels of education, the expectations of considerate treatment are low in both countries, but particularly in Mexico, where only 20 per cent of the university educated expect considerate treatment at the hands of the government and the police.

From our analysis thus far we see that the American and British respondents tend, on the whole, to have relatively favorable expectations of government; and educational differences have a relatively small effect on such expectations. In Germany overall expectations

TABLE 5

Expectation of Treatment by Governmental Authorities and
Police, by Education in Italy and Mexico
(in per cent)

	Italy				Mexico			
Per Cent who expect	None	Some Prim.	Some Sec.	Some Univ.	None	Some Prim.	Some Sec.	Some Univ.
Equal treatment in govt. office	30	51	65	59	19	45	58	68
Equal treatment by police	27	53	68	74	14	33	54	51
Consideration in govt. office	20	34	38	44	5	16	18	22
Consideration by police	17	34	43	48	8	13	17	22
Total number	88	604	245	54	221	656	103	24

proved to be relatively high, but class differences in expectations of considerateness of treatment are also relatively large. In Mexico and Italy, and particularly in the former, overall expectations of favorable treatment are relatively low, and educational differences in expectations tend to be relatively extreme.

In our life-history interviews we pursued a similar line of questioning, but in these cases we asked our respondents whether they had ever had any direct contact with government officials. We then pressed them to describe their experiences and indicate whether they were satisfied with the treatment they received. The life-history material, consequently, can provide us with reports of personal experience at the hands of governmental authority.

The pattern in Britain is illustrated in the experience of a British house painter who approached an official of the Inland Revenue. He asked him ". . . about starting our business. He was very fair. I asked him about scales for house purchase and rates of loan." When asked whether he was satisfied or felt fairly treated, he replied, "Very satisfied. It seemed too good to be true, this about housing loans." A garage mechanic referred to an experience with the police involving a "no parking" violation. When asked whether he was satisfied with his treatment, he replied, "Well, honestly, satisfied. I didn't like it at the time." When asked if he had been treated efficiently, he replied, "Yes, too much so." There were cases of dissatisfaction among the British respondents. Perhaps the strongest case of dissatisfaction was that of a small businessman. He referred to a contact with income tax officials: "The only way was to browbeat them. Politeness didn't work at all. In the long run, I was quite satisfied, but only through my own endeavors. I find the more minor the official you deal with, the less satisfaction you get." When asked whether he had been fairly treated, he replied, "Yes, I don't think there's any distinction made between various people. Only in the case of personal friendships, which is not only done in government offices."

The American respondents similarly reported favorable contacts on the whole, but with qualifications. Thus a salesman referring to his experiences with traffic tickets said his experiences had varied. "In some ways it was ideal, in others it was disgraceful the way I was treated. One guy was looking to give a ticket and he gave it. But the police force is adequate as could be expected. Some can be very arrogant." A manufacturer's representative referred to contacts with both an alderman and the sewer department. He reported: "The alderman fixed me up fine. As to the other—yes and no. Yes, insofar as the explanation I got. No, in that I was told the City Hall had to take care of the problem—this entailed much travelling." Pressed to state whether he was fairly treated, he replied, "Yes. That's the way everyone's treated." Southern Negroes' experiences of governmental treatment are illustrated in the case of a Negro woman who reported her effort to register as a voter. "The men were so harsh and gruff, I don't know. I mean, they used that tone of voice to me I guess trying to frighten me, but I just smiled to myself and acted like I did not notice it." When asked whether she was satisfied, she replied, "No, they could have been more pleasant."

The Italian and Mexican cases bring out a general pattern of experience with corruption, discrimination, and unresponsiveness:

An Italian Housewife:
"I have spoken very often to governmental officials, but they take no interest in this town. My husband tried to get a pension for his father, but spent so much money that he had to stop. They don't take us into consideration. Here we advance only by recommendation."

An Italian Tree Surgeon:
". . . my wife was sent back from the tax office. In the employment office things are not done right. . . . It is a month that I am without work, and am not on the employment list, as there is favoritism. The friends of the officials will be signed up first, and they will get the first jobs available. We are put on the list with a month and one-half delay."

An Italian Gymnastic Instructor (Communist):
"For Heaven's sake! The last time I was at a government office there was a poor man with a paper to fill out. He was asking the official how to fill it out. The official wouldn't pay attention but told him, 'Fill this paper out and that paper out and come back to-morrow.' The poor man did not know what to do. So I told the official he was there because I was paying him; everyone was paying him to be there and give explanations. He didn't open his mouth, and filled out the paper for the man."

The themes are similar among the Mexicans.

A Mexican Small Businessman:
"Normally the officials are not very competent. One doesn't see individuals with much education in the municipality. They are not very efficient in the way they do their business. But in the local government they will do their duty for money. . . ."

A Mexican Blacksmith:
". . . the people that work in those places are not attentive. They don't do it willingly. They are despots and get angry."

A Mexican Schoolteacher:
". . . the judges operate through money. As far as the state employees are concerned, they are generally just although they take into account your personal appearance."

A Mexican housewife said she would go to the government authorities only if a member of her family was arrested. ". . . I would go to a judge or to a lawyer. If he [member of family] was guilty, they would let him free if I paid a big sum. If he was innocent, they would help me."

114

Patterns of Political Communication

We turn now to the dimension of feelings about politics, or input affect. Here and in the following chapter we present a variety of measures, including attitudes toward political communication, intensity of partisanship, feelings about voting and election campaigns. In the present chapter we deal with communication patterns in our five countries. Our treatment of political communication covers more than the dimension of input affect; we are concerned with discovering the differences in the direct (face-to-face) political communications processes among the five countries. Our questions seek to get at communications behavior as well as feelings about political communication.

If ordinary men and women are to participate in a democratic political process, they must have the feeling that it is safe to do so, that they do not assume great risks when they express political opinions, and that they can be relatively free about whom they talk to. To the extent that these expectations are not present, impulses to communicate politically are suppressed, and what political communication there is tends to be restricted, covert, confined to family, or "ideologically trustworthy" groups; people are not on "speaking terms" politically. Whether or not people are on "political speaking terms," whether or not there is an overt and relatively unrestricted communications process, will in turn be related to the degree of development of the media of communication and their freedom and autonomy, the relative independence of interest groups from governmental and party control, the characteristics of the party system, and the relationship between parties.

The first measure we shall use of freedom of political communication is the extent to which people in our five countries report that they discuss politics. We have already examined exposure to political communication in the press, radio, and television. The same pattern that we found there emerges in our examination of informal, face-to-face communication (see Table 6). The chief exception is that Germany, which reported the highest frequency of following reports of public affairs in the mass media, comes out with a lower frequency of talking politics than that of either the United States or England. This is a finding of some interest. Talking politics with other people differs from exposure to political communication in the mass media in two respects. First, talking politics

115

is an active form of political participation; mass media exposure is relatively passive. Thus German political participation, which is extraordinarily high in the dimension of passive exposure, seems to drop substantially when it comes to active political communication. Second, talking politics with other people implies some sense of safety in political communication. No one can tell what thoughts pass through the minds of newspaper readers or television viewers. Talking politics means taking a chance; in totalitarian countries, a big chance. In democratic countries the risks may not be so high,

TABLE 6

Frequency of Talking Politics with Other People, by Nation*
(in per cent)

Per Cent who report they	U.S.	U.K.	Germany	Italy	Mexico
Never talk politics	24	29	39	66	61
Sometimes talk politics	76	70	60	32	38
Other and don't know	0	–	1	2	–
Total per cent	100	99	100	100	99
Total number	970	963	955	995	1,007

* Actual text of the question: "What about talking about public affairs to other people? Do you do that nearly every day, once a week, from time to time, or never?"

but there still are some risks. The higher frequency of talking politics in the United States and Britain than in Germany suggests that there is a a greater sense of safety in political communication in these countries, a greater tendency to involve family, friends, neighbors, and work-groups in the political communications process. But we shall return to this theme later.

The Mexican and Italian patterns of direct, face-to-face communication about politics and exposure to political communication in the mass media coincide. Roughly two-thirds of the respondents in each country report that they do not talk politics, and two-thirds say they do not follow political affairs through the mass media. Mexican respondents report somewhat higher percentages of inactivity.

But we are concerned here, not only with the frequency of talking politics, but with how people feel about discussing political and governmental affairs. We have a number of measures of this dimension of political feeling. One of them is the way in which people responded to our interviewers. In all of our countries we were interested in the party affiliations of our respondents. Not all of them were willing to reveal the party or parties for which they voted in recent elections. The same questions were asked in all of our countries, and the interviewers were in all cases natives of the countries in which they did their interviewing. In the United States, Britain, and Mexico, practically all the respondents reported

TABLE 7

Refusal to Report Voting Decision to Interviewer, by Nation
(in per cent)*

Nation	National Election		Local Election	
	Refuse to report Last National Vote	"Don't know"	Refuse to report Usual Local Vote	"Don't know"
United States	2	2	1	1
Great Britain	2	1	1	1
Germany	16	5	14	6
Italy	32	6	31	6
Mexico	1	3	1	6

* Percentages in each case are of the total sample.

the party they had voted for in the last national election and the party they usually vote for in local elections. In Italy 32 per cent refused to identify their national party choice, and another 6 per cent said they didn't know what party they had voted for. Similar percentages were recorded for local party choices. In Germany about 20 per cent either refused to talk about their national and local party choices or said they didn't know. The low percentage in Mexico is due no doubt to the fact that the overwhelming majority of Mexicans vote for the Revolutionary party, which is the dominant party in the country. In other words, Mexicans, unlike Italians of the extreme left, have nothing to conceal.

Those Italians and Germans who refused to identify the party of their choice in the last national election were relatively equally distributed among all the social strata and were not especially concentrated among the relatively poorer elements. Table 8 shows that the frequency of refusals among Italian skilled workers, white-collar workers, and professional and managerial personnel was almost as high as the frequency among unskilled workers. In Germany skilled workers, professional and managerial personnel, and small business-

117

men had the highest frequency of refusals. What this suggests is that political suspicion is generally distributed in both Italian and German society.

The findings in Tables 7 and 8 suggest that in Germany and Italy substantial numbers of people feel that identifying their political party is unsafe or inadvisable, even when they have been assured that the information is to be kept confidential and used only for scientific purposes. A direct question on feelings of freedom

TABLE 8

Refusal to Identify Party Last Voted For in National Elections
in Italy and Germany, by Breadwinner's Occupation[a]

| | Refuse to report vote | | | |
| | Italy | | Germany | |
Occupation	(%)	(No.)[b]	(%)	(No.)
Unskilled	37	(224)	13	(141)
Skilled	35	(77)	22	(203)
Artisans	44	(81)	21	(72)
White collar	33	(142)	13	(143)
Professional and managerial	36	(57)	22	(45)
Small business	25	(78)	24	(83)

[a] On this and succeeding tables where a "breadwinner's occupation" breakdown is used, data are reported for selected occupations only.

[b] Numbers in parentheses refer to the bases upon which percentages are calculated.

or restriction in communicating about politics supports the pattern suggested in these tables.

In all five countries our respondents were asked, "If you wanted to discuss political and governmental affairs, would there be some people you definitely wouldn't turn to—that is, people with whom you feel it would be better not to discuss such topics? About how many people would you say there are with whom you would avoid discussing politics?" The response was recorded by the interviewers and then coded under the categories listed in Table 9, which differentiates respondents according to the number of persons with whom they thought it better not to discuss political and governmental affairs.

Table 9 shows that, while almost two out of every three respondents in the United States and Britain feel relatively or completely free to discuss political and governmental affairs, only about one out of three of Germans and Italians indicated this degree of freedom about political communication. The Mexican distribution falls between, with almost equal numbers reporting feelings of freedom and limitation in political communication. The fact that both Germany and Italy show equally high proportions of respondents who feel greatly limited in political communication suggests that this kind of attitude can be associated with very different kinds of political structures. In Italy there is a fragmented party system with revolutionary parties on both right and left. In this situation of sharp interparty antagonism it is understandable that many people would conceal their party preferences and would be fearful of discussing politics with most other people. In Germany the trend has been toward the formation of a moderate two-party system and the development of autonomous interest groups and media of communication. But this and other evidence show that these institutions have not taken root in the Germans' feelings toward politics and partisanship; earlier attitude patterns seem to persist among the people. Thus the German pattern is one of incongruity between political structures and political culture, while the Italian pattern of party fragmentation and interpenetration of parties, interest groups, and the media of communication is matched by a cultural pattern of intensity of partisan antagonism, withdrawal from political communication, and withholding of feeling. It is also of importance that both Germans and Italians in recent decades have lived under totalitarian systems in which political communication was rigidly controlled and heavy sanctions were imposed on even moderate criticism of the regime. It is to be expected that the habits and feelings of these earlier Nazi and Fascist periods would persist into the present, despite the formal freedoms of the contemporary German and Italian political systems.

The question reported in Table 9 confronted respondents with the hypothetical situation: "If you wanted to discuss politics, how free or unrestricted would you feel?" We have already seen (Table 6) that about two-thirds of the Italians and Mexicans reported that they never talked politics. In other words, in response to the question of Table 9 a large proportion of the Italians and Mexicans who never talk politics were estimating how free they would feel to discuss political problems "if they wanted to." In order to control for this response, we next selected only those respondents who actually do talk politics with other people; their feelings of freedom in communication are reported in Table 10.

This table shows that about half of the American and British respondents both talk politics and feel relatively free to do so with most people. Less than one-third of the Germans showed this combination of communicating about politics and feeling free about it.

TABLE 9
Feeling of Restriction in Discussing Political and
Governmental Affairs, by Nation
(in per cent)

Per Cent who report they	U.S.	U.K.	Germany	Italy	Mexico
Don't feel free to discuss politics with anyone	18	12	32	34	21
Don't feel free to discuss it with many people	19	20	23	17	22
Feel free to discuss it with a few	34	35	14	15	22
Feel free to discuss it with anyone	29	29	23	22	19
Other	0	0	–	1	3
Don't know	0	4	8	11	13
Total per cent	100	100	100	100	100
Total number	970	963	955	995	1,007

TABLE 10
Political Discussion and Feelings of Freedom or Restriction
in Such Discussion, by Nation
(in per cent)

Per Cent who	U.S.	U.K.	Germany	Italy	Mexico
Discuss politics and feel they can talk to anyone or most people	54	50	32	21	18
Discuss politics and feel they must avoid it with many or almost all people	22	20	28	11	20
Never discuss politics	24	29	39	66	61
Total per cent	100	99	99	98	99
Total number	970	963	955	995	1,007

Only about one-fifth of the Italians and Mexicans had this combination.

These figures are of great interest, for they suggest the degree of openness of the political communications processes in these five countries. Thus in the United States and Britain around three-quarters of the respondents claimed they take part in the political communications process, and only a fifth in each country both take part and feel seriously restricted in discussing politics. In Germany, while 60 per cent claim they take part in political communication, almost half of these communications "activists" feel seriously restricted and avoid communicating about politics with many or most people. In Italy less than a third of the respondents are active in political communication, and two out of three of these activists feel free to discuss politics with most people. The Mexican pattern is

TABLE 11
Regular or Occasional Discussion of Politics, by Nation and Education

Nation	Total (%)	(No.)*	Prim. or Less (%)	(No.)	Some Sec. (%)	(No.)	Some Univ. (%)	(No.)
United States	76	(970)	63	(338)	83	(443)	93	(188)
Great Britain	70	(963)	64	(593)	81	(322)	83	(24)
Germany	60	(955)	56	(790)	80	(124)	96	(26)
Italy	32	(995)	22	(692)	42	(245)	76	(54)
Mexico	38	(1007)	34	(877)	67	(103)	65	(24)

* Numbers in parentheses refer to the bases upon which percentages are calculated.

similar to the Italian: only 38 per cent talk politics, and these are equally divided into those who feel relatively free and those who feel restricted. Mexico also has an historical background of violence and revolution; freedom of political organization and communications has only begun to develop in recent decades. Thus the Mexican pattern of communications freedom is similar to the Italian and German.

Both talking politics and feeling relatively unrestricted about whom one can safely discuss politics with are closely related to educational attainment. Interest in and awareness of national and international events rise as the educational level rises; this, along with the greater leisure and social contacts associated with higher education, create greater political motivation and opportunity. Those with higher education are also more likely to discuss these topics. Table 11 shows that the frequency of talking politics rises sharply from the primary to the secondary to the university levels in all five countries. But what also comes out quite clearly in Table 11 is the fact that the differences between the educational levels are least sharp in the United States and Britain and most sharp in the other three countries. It is also evident that participation in political discussion is more frequent at the secondary education level in Mexico than in Italy. Thus political discussion rises from one-third among Mexican primary-educated respondents to two-thirds of the secondary-educated Mexicans. Among the Italians the increase at this level is smaller. Only four out of ten Italians with some secondary education report they talk politics, as compared with the great majorities of secondary-educated respondents in the other four countries.

TABLE 12

Feeling of Relative Freedom to Discuss Politics, by Nation and Education

Nation	Total (%)	(No.)*	Prim. or Less (%)	(No.)	Some Sec. (%)	(No.)	Some Univ. (%)	(No.)
United States	63	(970)	49	(338)	70	(443)	71	(188)
Great Britain	64	(963)	59	(593)	70	(322)	83	(24)
Germany	37	(955)	35	(790)	52	(124)	60	(26)
Italy	37	(995)	30	(692)	53	(245)	59	(54)
Mexico	41	(1007)	39	(877)	54	(103)	54	(24)

* Numbers in parentheses refer to the bases upon which percentages are calculated.

We find a similar pattern of higher frequency of the sense of freedom to communicate about politics among the better-educated levels in all five countries (see Table 12). Here again we can see that, while there are educational differences in the United States and Britain, about one-half of the primary-educated Americans and British report feeling relatively unrestricted in their political communication, while in the other three countries only around one-third report this feeling of freedom. But there is a sense in which the Mexican pattern is somewhat more like the British and American than like the German and Italian. The percentage spread between levels of education is smaller in Mexico than in Germany and Italy. This higher incidence of communications freedom among the poorly educated in Mexico is another indication of the strength of the revolutionary aspirational tendency in Mexican political culture.

122

CHAPTER 5

PATTERNS OF PARTISANSHIP

POLITICAL theorists often discuss the kind of partisanship that is consistent with an effectively functioning, stable democracy. Common to most of these discussions is the view that the major parties accept, by and large, the rules of political competition laid down in constitution, laws, and custom; and that their goals and methods are such that either one or any of the major parties finds being in the minority or opposition an acceptable risk. This formal conception of the character of majority and opposition in effective democracies implies a particular state of popular feeling: it assumes the existence of partisan feeling. It implies taking sides, having convictions and feelings about the proper course of political action, supporting some groups and opposing others. But it also assumes a limited partisanship. A too-hostile partisanship might jeopardize the willingness to accept opposition, and could cause electoral decisions to be rejected or dispensed with altogether.

Democratic partisanship implies political feeling, and not indifference. It also implies a particular quality of feelings. They must be expressible openly. And the political atmosphere must be able to accept the expression of partisan feelings. Where either the tone of political life is so menacing that it requires, out of a concern for safety, the suppression of partisan feeling; or where partisan impulses are so negative and hostile as to require suppression (or expression only in limited and intimate circles), then the effective conditions necessary for an open and moderate partisanship are not present.

Open and moderate partisanship, then, are essential to a stable democracy. They are the "feeling correlates" of responsible majority and loyal opposition. We have already seen that there are marked differences among countries (and among groups within countries) in the respondents' feelings of freedom to communicate with others on political questions. We saw that in Britain and the United States the proportion of respondents who felt relatively unrestricted in communicating about politics was relatively high, while in Germany, Italy, and Mexico it was substantially lower.

Now we turn to the dimension of partisan feeling as such; to attitudes toward one's own party and other parties. We offer two measures of partisan feeling in the five democracies. The first is a comparison of "self" and "other" images: views of one's own party and of opposing parties. The second is a measure of the depth and severity of partisan cleavage, reflected in attitudes toward marriage across party lines.

Images of Party Supporters

All of our respondents were told, "We're interested in what sorts of people support and vote for the different parties." Then they were presented with a list of statements and asked to select those statements most appropriate to describing the supporters of the competing parties in their countries. In the tables that follow, our respondents have been divided according to their partisan affiliations. Hence we are in a position to compare people's views of their own and of opposed parties, and to measure the overlapping or polarization in these views. The list itself was a product of experimentation. In order to present the respondents with choices meaningful to them, the question was posed in open-ended form in the pretest and the list constructed from those judgments and appraisals. The list of judgments includes favorable, unfavorable, and neutral judgments.[1]

In its actual content this question is a cognitive one. The respondents were asked to pick statements that *described* the supporters of the main political parties in their countries. At the same time, most of these statements clearly reflected the respondents' emotional disposition toward these parties. When we interpret the responses as positive, negative, and neutral, we are, of course, drawing inferences about the feelings of the respondents.

Table 1 provides an analysis of the American responses to this question. It is of interest that the large percentages are all to be

[1] The actual interviewing instructions permitted the respondents to pick as many statements as they desired. Only the first two choices were coded and recorded for each party.

found in the positive or favorable cells. While Republican voters attribute patriotism, intelligence, and humanitarianism to Republicans more frequently, in large proportion they attribute these same qualities to Democrats. The same pattern is true of the Democratic

TABLE 1

Qualities Attributed to Republican and Democratic Supporters by
Republican and Democratic Voters in the United States[a]
(in per cent)

Per Cent describing Party Supporters as	Repub. Views of Repub.	Repub. Views of Dem.	Dem. Views of Repub.	Dem. Views of Dem.
POSITIVE QUALITIES				
Interested in defense and independence	63	49	44	52
Intelligent people	35	25	27	31
Interested in humanity	46	41	27	49
NEGATIVE QUALITIES				
Selfish people	3	14	23	4
Betrayers of freedom and welfare	1	4	4	2
Ignorant and misguided	0	8	6	1
Fascists, imperialists, etc.	0	1	2	0
Atheists	0	1	0	0
NEUTRAL QUALITIES				
Religious people	11	6	8	13
All sorts	13	15	15	13
Other	0	0	4	2
Total per cent[b]	172	164	160	167
Total number of cases	309	309	464	464

[a] For England, Germany, Italy, and Mexico, party affiliation was determined by the respondent's statement of the party voted for in the last national election. Party affiliation in the U.S. was based on responses to a question asking respondents whether they were "members" or "supporters of" or "leaned toward" the Republican or Democratic party. This applies to all tables in this chapter.

[b] Percentages in most cases exceed one hundred because of multiple responses. "Don't know" respondents omitted.

appraisal of themselves and of the Republicans. The strongest negative description made by supporters of either party about the supporters of the other party was "selfish people." Twenty-three per cent of the Democrats picked this statement to describe Republicans; 14 per cent of the Republicans picked it to describe the Democrats.

In the United Kingdom the polarization between the two major parties is somewhat sharper than that reported for the United States (see Table 2). Thus the percentages of respondents who view their political opponents in favorable terms are a good deal smaller than those in the United States. Similarly, the negative appraisals are somewhat more frequent in Britain than in the United States. Thus 28 per cent of the British Conservative respondents say that selfish people support the Labour party, and 29 per cent of the

TABLE 2

Qualities Attributed to Conservative and Labour Supporters
by Conservative and Labour Voters in Great Britain
(in per cent)

Per Cent describing Party Supporters as	Conserv. Views of Conserv.	Conserv. Views of Laborites	Labour Views of Conserv.	Labour Views of Laborites
POSITIVE QUALITIES				
Interested in defense and independence	47	8	22	27
Intelligent people	33	6	12	18
Interested in humanity	25	17	9	49
NEGATIVE QUALITIES				
Selfish people	2	28	29	3
Betrayers of freedom and welfare	1	3	3	1
Ignorant and misguided	0	23	6	1
Fascists, imperialists, etc.	1	0	10	0
Atheists	0	1	1	0
NEUTRAL QUALITIES				
Religious people	2	1	4	3
All sorts	6	13	9	8
Other	1	3	2	1
Total per cent*	118	103	107	111
Total number	358	358	376	376

* Percentages in most cases exceed one hundred because of multiple responses. "Don't know" respondents omitted.

Laborites return the compliment to the Conservatives. Almost one-fourth of the Conservative respondents view the Laborites as "ignorant and misguided," while the Laborites spread their negative characterizations, picking "militarists and imperialists" in 10 per cent of the cases and "ignorant and misguided" in 6 per cent of the cases.[2]

[2] Cf. Mark Abrams and Richard Rose, *Must Labour Lose?*, London, 1960, p. 19. In this survey a similar list question with different statements was used and showed a somewhat larger overlap between the supporters of the two major British parties. Mark Abrams comments, "The survey yielded striking evidence of the tolerance of the British electorate toward their political opponents and of agreement that links the supporters of both major parties. For example, between 40 per cent and 50 per cent of Labour supporters thought that the Conservatives could do as well as their own party in stand-

The German pattern (Table 3) shows just about the same degree of polarization as the British. Only one positive characteristic is attributed to the supporters of the opposition party by more than one-fifth of the voters for either party: 23 per cent of the Christian Democrats attribute humanitarianism to the SPD supporters. The negative attributions are about as frequent as in Britain and some-

TABLE 3

Qualities Attributed to Christian Democratic Union and Social Democratic Supporters by CDU and SPD Voters in Germany
(in per cent)

Per Cent describing Party Supporters as	CDU Views of CDU	CDU Views of SPD	SPD Views of CDU	SPD Views of SPD
POSITIVE QUALITIES				
Interested in defense and independence	35	16	15	40
Intelligent people	20	8	10	29
Interested in humanity	33	23	9	57
NEGATIVE QUALITIES				
Selfish people	1	19	25	2
Betrayers of freedom and welfare	0	3	1	0
Ignorant and misguided	0	10	10	0
Fascists, imperialists, etc.	0	0	4	0
Atheists	0	8	0	2
NEUTRAL QUALITIES				
Religious people	57	1	55	3
All sorts	12	20	13	14
Other	0	3	0	1
Total per cent*	158	111	142	148
Total number	333	333	235	235

* Percentages in most cases exceed one hundred because of multiple responses. "Don't know" respondents omitted.

what more frequent than in the United States. The striking difference between the German pattern, on the one hand, and the British and American, on the other, is the large percentage of Germans—almost identical for Christian Democrats and Socialists —who describe the supporters of the Christian Democratic party as "religious people." This clearly indicates that supporters of both major parties agree that the CDU receives support on religious

ing for the nation as a whole, in giving fair treatment to all races, in respecting British traditions, and in working for peace and against nuclear war. Of those who opposed Labour, at least 40 per cent were prepared to describe Labour as equally qualified with the Conservatives in giving fair treatment to all races, working for peace, and opposing nuclear war."

grounds, though the evaluation of that support may differ from party to party.

As we might expect, the Italian respondents show a far sharper polarization between right and left than do the Americans, British, and Germans (see Table 4). If we examine Table 4 from right to

TABLE 4

Qualities Attributed Christian Democratic, Nenni-Socialist, and
Communist Supporters by DC, PSI, and PCI Voters in Italy
(in per cent)

Per Cent describing Party Supporters as	Christian Democratic Views of			Nenni-Socialist Views of			Communist Views of		
	DC	PCI	PSI	DC	PCI	PSI	DC	PCI	PSI
POSITIVE QUALITIES									
Interested in defense and independence	16	2	4	4	13	5	0	14	16
Intelligent people	30	2	5	0	9	31	0	32	23
Interested in humanity	20	1	4	2	20	29	0	27	32
NEGATIVE QUALITIES									
Selfish people	0	21	17	18	4	2	25	0	0
Betrayers of freedom and welfare	0	18	11	6	2	2	9	0	0
Ignorant and misguided	1	24	20	9	7	0	18	0	0
Fascists, imperialists, etc.	1	2	1	2	0	2	2	0	0
Atheists	0	24	18	0	9	0	0	5	2
NEUTRAL QUALITIES									
Religious people	52	0	1	35	4	4	25	0	0
All sorts	11	9	18	27	26	29	7	14	20
Other	3	5	5	11	15	13	11	11	14
Total per cent*	134	108	104	114	109	117	97	103	107
Total number	353	353	353	55	55	55	44	44	44

* Percentages in most cases exceed one hundred because of multiple responses. "Don't know" respondents omitted.

left, we note that large percentages in the favorable cells and small percentages in the unfavorable cells appear in those columns that record the statements picked by the Christian Democratic (DC), Nenni-Socialist (PSI), and Communist (PCI) voters to describe themselves, as well as the statements picked by the Nenni-Socialists to describe their Communist allies and vice-versa. The two left parties' appraisals of the Christian Democrats and the Christian Democrats' appraisals of the two left parties (the second, third, fourth, and seventh columns) are extremely low in the favorable cells and high in the unfavorable ones. Again, as in Germany, all parties agree in associating religious characteristics with the Christian Democrats, though again the evaluative connotation may differ from party to party.

The Nenni-Socialists are intermediate in this pattern of polarization. Thus the Christian Democratic appraisal of the Communists is more negative and less neutral than is their appraisal of the PSI. The Nenni-Socialist appraisal of the *Democristiani* is less negative and more neutral than is the Communists'. Finally, the appraisal by the two left parties is of some interest.. If we compare the fifth column with the ninth, we find that the Nenni-Socialist respondents more often pick negative and neutral statements to describe the Communists than do the Communists to describe the Socialists. Also, the two left parties differ from each other in the frequency of unfavorable responses vis-à-vis the Christian Democrats (columns 4 and 7). Thus the Communist responses are more heavily weighted on the negative side, while the Nenni-Socialist statements are far more heavily concentrated in the neutral categories. Further, the Nenni-Socialists more frequently say that all sorts of people can be found supporting the various parties. Over one-fourth of the supporters of this party say that one cannot generalize about the supporters of either their own party or of the other two parties. This ambiguity of position is what one would expect from a party of the middle (not that the Nenni-Socialists are a middle-of-the-road party, but they are at least in-between the two other parties cited in the table).

These findings suggest that at the mass voting level there are significant differences between the left-Socialists and the Communists; that the PSI tends to be more open to right and left, and that the really sharp polarization is between the *Democristiani* and the Communists.

The Mexican pattern is of particular interest. It is more balanced between positive and negative than is the Italian, and if we exclude the ambiguous "religious people" category, it is less neutral (see Table 5). Positive views of the right are expressed more often by the Mexican left than by the Italian left; this may be due in part to the fact that the PRI (Mexican Revolutionary party) is in power in Mexico and consequently can afford to be more generous in appraising the right than can the Communists and left-Socialists in Italy. But it is probably largely due to the fact that the Mexican Revolutionary party is not very revolutionary. It includes the overwhelming majority of the voters and is consequently more heterogeneous in its social and ideological composition. Similarly, the fact that the Mexican right is more antagonistic to the left than the left is to the right may be because the PAN[3] has relatively small support, and this support is heavily upper class and clerical in character.

TABLE 5

Qualities Attributed to Supporters of the Mexican Revolutionary Party and
the Party of National Action by PRI and PAN Voters in Mexico
(in per cent)

Per Cent describing Party Supporters as	PRI Views of PRI	PRI Views of PAN	PAN Views of PRI	PAN Views of PAN
POSITIVE QUALITIES				
Interested in defense and independence	44	14	24	23
Intelligent people	38	14	16	26
Interested in humanity	31	19	15	50
NEGATIVE QUALITIES				
Selfish people	17	20	52	3
Betrayers of freedom and welfare	4	9	17	2
Ignorant and misguided	7	17	24	12
Fascists, imperialists, etc.	4	3	7	4
Atheists	1	5	8	1
NEUTRAL QUALITIES				
Religious people	17	36	7	52
All sorts	8	8	2	3
Other	2	2	5	0
Total per cent*	173	147	177	176
Total number	514	514	75	75

* Percentages in most cases exceed one hundred because of multiple responses. "Don't know" respondents omitted.

Table 6 summarizes the differences in party images among all five countries. Here we have included only the reciprocal appraisals and have aggregated the responses into positive, negative, and neutral categories (removing the religious category because of its ambiguity). The percentages are of responses, not of respondents. The American responses show the least antagonism or polarization between major parties. The Republicans appear to be somewhat more favorably disposed toward the Democrats than vice-versa. The antagonism between the British parties is greater than between the German. In view of other findings about the German pattern (see

[3] This is the *Partido de Accion Nacional,* the second largest party in Mexico.

TABLE 6

Distribution of Positive, Negative, and Neutral Statements about Opposition Parties, by Nation

(in per cent)

Percentage of Statements that were	United States		United Kingdom		Germany		Italy		Mexico	
	Repub. v. Dem.	Dem. v. Repub.	Conserv. v. Labour	Labour v. Conserv.	CDU v. SPD	SPD v. CDU	DC v. PCI & PSI	PCI & PSI v. DC	PRI v. PAN	PAN v. PRI
Positive	70	63	32	41	43	24	8	4	32	32
Negative	17	23	54	47	26	28	80	45	37	63
Neutral	9	9	13	9	18	9	12	19	6	1
Religious people*	4	5	1	4	1	39	0	32	25	4
Don't know	6	1	11	9	26	16	30	26	19	4
Total per cent	100	100	100	101	98	100	100	100	100	100
Total number of respondents	309	464	358	376	333	235	353	99	514	75
Total number of statements	507	726	349	395	366	335	780	95	737	129

* "Religious people" appears to have different evaluative connotations for different respondents.

Chap. 9), this may not mean that the German political system is more consensual than the British, but, rather, that there is a general withholding of affect from the political system in Germany: a withholding that influences partisan attitudes as well as more general attitudes toward the political system and the nation. It is also noteworthy that in Britain the right is more antagonistic to left than left is to right, which reverses the American pattern.

Italy clearly presents the most polarized pattern. In view of the extremely small proportions of positive statements, the Italian figures would suggest something approximating a "psychological clean break" between right and left. Mexico's pattern shows somewhat less antagonism than the Italian, but more than the American, British, and German. It is also of interest that the left in Mexico is less antagonistic to the right than the other way around. This appears to result from the fact that the PAN combines a conservative social policy with a proclerical position, while the PRI voters are a more mixed group, including some middle-class people as well as workers and farmers, and believing Catholics as well as anticlericals.

In all five countries interparty antagonism appears to be significantly reduced by education. Thus in the United States around 14 per cent more of the secondary educated than of the primary educated picked favorable statements to describe the opposing party. In Britain the increase was smaller (6 per cent), but the direction was the same for both parties. In Germany the average increase from primary to secondary educated was 7 per cent, and in Mexico the average increase was 13 per cent. The same pattern was manifested in Italy, except that here the increase was relatively small in the positive category. There was a decline in the proportion of negative statements and an increase in the neutral and "religious people" categories.

Psychological Distance Between Parties:
Marriage Within and Across Party Lines

Citizens of the great national societies are affiliated with many groups and associations. In addition to their national citizenship, they may have party affiliations, interest group memberships, religious affiliations, regional identifications, occupational and professional memberships, recreational and convivial associations, as well as family ties. It has been argued by Schattschneider that the fragmenting impact of interest groups in the political system is mitigated by the fact that individuals are members of many groups; these memberships are not politically cumulative but are often conflicting, thus individuals tend to moderate and combine interests in their own minds in order to reduce conflict.[4] Lane, summarizing the literature on "multiple group membership" and "cross-pressures," concludes that it is conflict on salient issues among primary and more intimate group memberships, rather than among categoric memberships (such as class, ethnic origins, and the like), that tends to make people withdraw from political choices. He also points out that political withdrawal is only one of the means available to persons confronted by this situation. Other solutions that he lists include identification with one of the conflicting groups, moderating one's viewpoint by synthesizing or diffusing, minimizing the issue, and the like.[5] Truman, drawing insights from Bentley,[6] Herring,[7] and a number of American sociologists and anthropologists, points out that multiple memberships and conflicts affect the political choices, not only of individuals, but of groups; that is, groups tend to moderate sharp choices based upon interest, avoid or postpone them when there is an expectation that memberships might be confronted with conflicts.[8] Truman's analysis is important, for he combines political-structural with psychological considerations, while purely psychological treatments tend to assume a static structure producing a "cross-pressured" individual psychology. In actual fact, where there are overlapping and competing structures, the structures themselves are responsive to the multiple-membership phenomenon and tend to avoid pressing for extreme positions and exclusive loyalties.

The theory of group membership and cross-pressures is largely based upon American experience. Truman is an exception in that he sought to include non-American experience, but he found little data to work with. In actual fact, membership patterns differ from one country to the next. In the European Catholic countries, for example, the pattern tends to be ideologically cumulative. Family, church, interest group, and party membership tend to coincide in their ideological and policy characteristics and to reinforce one

---

[4] E. E. Schattschneider, *Party Government*, New York, 1942, pp. 33 ff.
[5] Robert E. Lane, *Political Life*, Glencoe, Ill., 1959, pp. 197 ff.
[6] A. F. Bentley, *The Process of Government*, Chicago, 1908.
[7] Pendleton Herring, *Group Representation Before Congress*, Baltimore, 1929.
[8] David B. Truman, *The Governmental Process*, New York, 1951, chap. vi.

another in their effects on opinion. In the United States and Britain, however, the overlapping pattern appears to be more common. As Schattschneider points out, where memberships tend to be politically cumulative, the impact of group membership tends to be fragmenting; where it is overlapping, there tends to be less political polarization.

In Chapter 12 we shall treat in detail the patterns of voluntary association membership. Here we are concerned with the capacity of the family to tolerate partisan differences. One of our questions confronted the respondents with the hypothetical situation of the marriage of a son or daughter. The respondent was then asked: "How would you feel if he or she married a supporter of the —————————party? [The question was repeated for each of the larger parties.] Would you be pleased, would you be displeased, or would it make no difference?"

Because of its hypothetical character, the question does not measure behavior, that is, the actual extent to which interparty marriage has occurred among our respondents or their children. Rather, it measures the respondents' estimates of the effects on family ties of marriage across political party lines. Since we can safely assume that parents prefer to maintain close relations with their children, their response to our question will be an estimate of the degree to which family ties would be either impaired by marriage outside the party or safeguarded by marriage within the party. This, in turn, reflects the intensity of partisan antagonism. It also reflects the characteristics of the family as a part of the political system. If the family can bear political heterogeneity, we may entertain the hypothesis that the family tends intermittently to be drawn into the interest articulation and aggregation processes of the polity; that is, becomes part of the interest group and party systems. (In Chapter 12 we shall show that the American and British families tend to be drawn into the political communications process.)

Another way of saying this is to point out that where political feelings are relatively cool, the large, impersonal structures of the polity can mesh with the personal and intimate ones without damaging them. If this is the case, then the family can provide a relatively smooth and continuous political socialization of children into a political system characterized by competitive political parties. It can inculcate, not only pride in nation, but also a form of partisanship that is tolerant of opposition, ambiguity, and contingency.

134

Where the edge of partisanship is too sharp, however, the family either remains out of the political system or simply increases the impact of this form of partisanship. Furthermore, given a moderate atmosphere of partisanship, we may assume that it becomes possible to bring the family and the other intimate relationships of friendship and community into the political system as informal groups in situations of special need or stress. This point is dealt with in detail in Chapter 7. Here we need only point out that the ability to

TABLE 7

How Supporters of Major Parties Would View Marriage of Son or Daughter
Within or Across Party Lines in the United States
(in per cent)

Per Cent who would feel	Repub. toward Repub. Marriage	Repub. toward Dem. Marriage	Dem. toward Dem. Marriage	Dem. toward Repub. Marriage
Pleased	16	3	11	3
Displeased	0	4	0	4
Indifferent	84	93	89	92
Other and don't know	0	0	0	1
Total per cent	100	100	100	100
Total number	309	309	464	464

cooperate politically with one's fellow citizens is associated with a kind of partisanship that does not threaten intimate ties.

Table 7 shows us how Republican and Democratic party supporters in the United States view the possible marriage of their children across party lines. Overwhelming majorities of the respondents of both parties expressed indifference regarding the partisan affiliations of the future mates of their children. Small percentages of the respondents of both parties expressed pleasure at the thought that a son or daughter would marry within the party they support, and very few respondents expressed displeasure over marriage outside the party.

The percentage among the British respondents who said that the party affiliations of marriage partners for their children made some difference was higher than among the Americans (see Table 8). But it was more a Conservative than a Labour party concern. Twenty-three percent of the Conservative respondents stated they would be pleased by a marriage with a Conservative. The Labour respondents overwhelmingly expressed indifference.

The German respondents expressed more concern than the British and far more concern than the Americans about marriage across party lines (see Table 9). Thus 42 per cent of the CDU respondents expressed pleasure at the thought of a Christian Demo-

TABLE 8

How Supporters of Major Parties Would View Marriage of Son or Daughter
Within or Across Party Lines in Great Britain
(in per cent)

Per Cent who would feel	Conserv. toward Conserv. Marr.	Conserv. toward Labour Marr.	Labour toward Labour Marr.	Labour toward Conserv. Marr.
Pleased	23	0	7	0
Displeased	0	12	0	3
Indifferent	77	87	92	97
Other and don't know	0	1	1	0
Total per cent	100	100	100	100
Total number	358	358	376	376

TABLE 9

How Supporters of Major Parties Would View Marriage of Son or Daughter
Within or Across Party Lines in Germany
(in per cent)

Per Cent who would feel	CDU toward CDU Marriage	CDU toward SPD Marriage	SPD toward SPD Marriage	SPD toward CDU Marriage
Pleased	42	1	25	3
Displeased	0	19	0	8
Indifferent	48	61	62	74
Other and don't know	10	19	13	15
Total per cent	100	100	100	100
Total number	333	333	235	235

cratic marriage, and 19 per cent expressed displeasure regarding a Social Democratic marriage. Similarly, the percentage of Socialist respondents favoring a Socialist marriage was relatively high as compared with the British and American left-wing attitudes. What we are encountering here is the cumulative impact of group affiliations. The relation between religion and party affiliation is closer in Germany than in either Britain or the United States. Hence marriage out of the CDU and into the SPD may be viewed as a double strain—that of religion and party—on family ties. Still, in Germany this reaction is more frequently expressed positively as pleasure over marriage *within* the party rather than displeasure over marriage *out of* the party.

Table 10 shows that among Italian Christian Democratic voters the reaction is both strongly positive toward in-party marriage and strongly negative toward marriage with Communists; it is not quite as strongly negative toward marriage with left-Socialists. What account for this pattern in Italy are the revolutionary and anticlerical

TABLE 10

How Supporters of Major Parties Would View Marriage of Son or Daughter Within or Across Party Lines in Italy
(in per cent)

Per Cent who would feel	DC toward DC Marr.	DC toward PCI Marr.	DC toward PSI Marr.	PCI toward PCI Marr.	PCI toward DC Marr.	PCI toward PSI Marr.	PSI toward PSI Marr.	PSI toward DC Marr.	PSI toward PCI Marr.
Pleased	59	1	1	27	2	23	16	6	4
Displeased	1	58	46	0	14	2	0	6	7
Indifferent	29	28	39	59	73	64	67	71	71
Other and don't know	11	13	14	14	11	12	16	17	18
Total per cent	100	100	100	100	100	100	100	100	100
Total number	353	353	353	44	44	44	55	55	55

character of the left and the closeness of the Christian Democratic party to the Catholic Church. Since the Vatican and the Italian heirarchy have declared voting for the Communist and left-Socialist parties a mortal sin and have threatened to deny the sacraments to persons voting for these parties, it is not surprising that family ties would be threatened by the marriage of a member of a Christian Democratic family with a Communist. Not all Christian Democrats are hostile, however: almost one-third of the DC respondents expressed indifference regarding such a marriage. But again, these are the less devoted Catholic Christian Democrats, as measured by frequency of church attendance (see Table 12). Communist respondents, on the other hand, express greater indifference toward intermarriage with *Democristiani* (see Table 10).

In Mexico about one-fifth to one-fourth of the supporters of the major parties express hostility toward interparty marriage—a figure larger than in the United States, Britain, or Germany, but not as large as the proportion of Italian Christian Democrats who oppose cross-party marriage. Nevertheless, indifference is the most frequent response, which may reflect the recent moderation of church-state tension. Something approximating a modus vivendi has been reached between the regime and the church hierarchy.[9] This seems to be reflected in the high rate of indifference regarding interparty marriage among both PRI and PAN voters.

In general, this series of tables tends to support the points made above. Partisanship in the United States and Britain appears to be

TABLE 11

How Supporters of Major Parties Would View Marriage of Son or Daughter
Within or Across Party Lines in Mexico
(in per cent)

Per Cent who would feel	PAN toward PAN Marriage	PAN toward PRI Marriage	PRI toward PRI Marriage	PRI toward PAN Marriage
Pleased	23	2	22	8
Displeased	7	22	11	24
Indifferent	65	70	61	63
Other and don't know	5	6	6	5
Total per cent	100	100	100	100
Total number	75	75	514	514

sufficiently moderate to be combined with intimate family ties without seriously threatening them. This is less true in Germany, Mexico, and Italy. A more detailed analysis suggests that in all the countries, save the United States, these attitudes are affected by the interplay of three types of membership: political, religious, and family. Thus if we control for frequency of church attendance (Table 12), it is evident that conservative voters who attend church every week or more frequently in Britain, Germany, Italy, and Mexico are more opposed to interparty marriage than are those who attend church less frequently or not at all. It is of interest that this relationship between frequency of church attendance and opposition to interparty marriage is almost as strong in Britain as in Germany. However, the data also show that conservative voters in Germany, Italy, and Mexico include a far larger proportion of frequent church attenders than in Britain, so the incidence of marital parochialism is far higher in these countries than in Britain.

[9] Robert E. Scott, *Mexican Government in Transition*, p. 174.

It is also of interest that in all five countries the left appears to be more open to marriage with the right than the other way around. This is true even in the United States, although the difference between the parties in this respect is small. This imbalance in party attitudes toward intermarriage increases in Britain, is even larger in Germany and Mexico, and becomes quite extreme in Italy. This general pattern of greater left openness to marriage with the right

TABLE 12

Frequency of Church Attendance[a] and Displeasure toward Political Party
Intermarriage (Right v. Left), by Nation

Nation	Per Cent of Right Displeased at Marriage into Left Party			
	Attend Church Weekly or More Often		Attend Church Less Than Weekly or Never	
	(%)	(No.)[b]	(%)	(No.)
United States (Republicans displeased at Democratic marriage)	3	(143)	4	(156)
Great Britain (Conservatives displeased at Labour marriage)	23	(74)	10	(246)
Germany (CDU displeased at SPD marriage)	25	(166)	13	(162)
Italy (DC displeased at PCI-PSI marriage)	60	(296)	44	(55)
Mexico (PAN displeased at PRI marriage)	24	(48)	[18	(13)]

[a] Data only for respondents who reported some religious affiliation
[b] Numbers in parentheses refer to bases upon which percentages were calculated

may perhaps be explained in ideological and social mobility terms. Generally speaking, conservative movements are more traditionally oriented than are left-wing movements. Traditionality implies religious or status exclusiveness. Hence we might expect supporters of conservative parties, more frequently than supporters of left parties, to have an in-group feeling about marriage across party lines. But this attitude on the part of conservative supporters may also be due to status differences. Since the supporters of the left parties tend more frequently to be lower class, in social and economic terms, they view marriage of a son or daughter with a son or daughter of the conservative party as upward social mobility. The contrary attitude on the part of the right may also be a status reaction; that is, they may view such an interparty marriage as a social step down.

National differences in feelings about parties may be illustrated by our life-history material. Our respondents were asked, not about party intermarriage, but about how they would feel if a son or daughter joined their own party or one of the other principal political parties. The British and American responses about the opposition party reflected tolerance of freedom of party choice for their children:

An American Housewife (Democrat):
"Well, I'd feel that was up to her. She has to make her own choice. Just because I'm a Democrat doesn't mean she has to be one too."

An American Employee in a Trucking Firm (Democrat):
[If his children should become Republicans] "It may have its merits which I don't know about. I would like to discuss it with them to see what part they are taking in it. That would probably be my incentive to get interested in politics."

A Southern Negro Housewife (Democrat):
[If her child became Republican] "Just fine. I think everyone should be active in his government. I think the Republican party is a wonderful political party. Just because I made this statement about the last eight years I did not mean I did not like the Republican party. Sometimes both parties have leaders who do not seem to do as much as we think they ought to do, but sometimes they are doing the best they can do under the circumstances." [If he became a Democrat] "Fine, too, if that was the party of his choice. Just so he is interested in one of the parties."

An English Housewife (Conservative):
[If her children joined the Labour party] "If they're responsible, that's their choice. If they were irresponsible, I would have to give them a guiding hand."

An English Draughtsman (Conservative):
"I would be pleased to think they were taking an interest in politics —no matter which party."

An English Small Businessman (Liberal):
"If they were old enough to join the [opposed] party, they would be old enough to know their own mind."

More of the English respondents than the American expressed concern, but it was a moderate concern:

An English House Painter (Conservative):
[If his son became a Conservative] "Very pleased about it. Because he is on the right road." [If his son joined the Labour party] "Not too badly. He has to make his own choice. There are good chaps in the Labour party."

140

An English Truck Driver (Conservative):
[If his children became Conservative] "I'd advise them for this, but apart from this I'd not worry." [If his children became Labourites] "They would have their choice at this age. I wouldn't mind one way or other."

An English Skilled Worker (Labour):
[If his son became a Conservative] "I should say I had done a darn good job of bringing him up, if he could mix with them, but I would be disappointed."

A common German response reflected opposition to joining any party, or recommended the purest kind of expediential behavior.

A German Postal Employee:
"I should warn them of any party ties, but the CDU would still be the most bearable."

A German Housewife:
"It's better for him to stay away. Under Hitler we went through that mess. I hardly think that it would be any better today."

A German Clothing Store Owner:
"My son is opposed to all parties. He leaves them strictly alone. As a businessman, you can't get involved with that sort of thing."

A German Businessman:
"According to my experience I should say: If you are wise, join where-ever they have the most power—but not out of idealism. I don't believe that anymore."

A number of CDU parents expressed strong opposition to a child's joining the SPD. Thus a Christian Democratic housewife commented about the possibility of her son's joining the SPD, "That should not happen, and that would hardly be the case in our family. We are Christians—for us, there is only the CDU."

The most common German response reflected a qualified neu-trality. Thus a German policeman who votes SPD said, in response to the question regarding his child's joining the CDU, "I should be very surprised, but I shouldn't object." If his child were to join the SPD, he would ". . . approve strongly." If he were to join the FDP or DRP, he said, "I'd never be able to understand that." A headwaiter whose party preference was CDU remarked, "if I had the impression that my child was taking this step out of full conviction, and that he was wholly conscious of his action and had given the matter ample thought—I should have nothing against it."

141

More extreme comments were encountered among the Italian respondents, especially regarding the Communist party:

An Italian Petty Government Official (Christian Democrat):
"If I knew about it, I would tell them to choose a party of the right, never of the left. If they became Communists, I would beat them like dogs and hate them."
An Italian Baker (Christian Democrat):
[If his children joined the DC] "I would try to bring them up the right way. If he signed up with the DC, I would be pleased." [If they became Communists] "If they wanted to sign up, I would disown them."
An Italian Carpenter (Christian Democrat):
[If his son became a Communist] "Well, I would try to prevent him, as they say so many things, and one can see that they never go to Mass."

Italian left-wing respondents were less extreme in their statements:

An Italian Housewife with left sympathies:
[If her son joined the DC] "I would say: Poor son! I don't sympathize very much with the DC. I consider them hypocrites."
An Italian Farmer (Communist):
[If his children joined the DC] "As long as things are done in the right way, it doesn't matter whether they are Communists, Socialists, or Christian Democrats."

The Mexican respondents, like the Germans, included a substantial proportion who opposed party affiliations in principle.

A Mexican Worker:
[On any kind of party affiliation] "Not good. I think that to have tranquillity, it is necessary to keep away from this, since in politics one has to be very skillful and lucky enough to fall on one's feet."
A Mexican Housewife:
"I wouldn't like it if they entered politics because it always brings problems. If one is honest, the rest don't agree with you; if one is a rascal, the people realize it and don't like you."
A Mexican Blacksmith:
"I wouldn't like my children to get into politics. I would like one of my children to study law. If they were in politics, they should be very honest about it, and take no personal advantage."

142

A number of Mexicans expressed approval of their children's joining their own party and disapproval if they joined the opposing party, but the disapproval was less extreme than that expressed by the Italians. There were also a substantial number of Mexicans who expressed neutrality about the party affiliations of their children. The comment of a Mexican social worker may illustrate this. "They are free to choose. One party or another is the same for me. They are free in politics as well as in religion."

The Flow of Feeling From Community to Polity

What we have demonstrated so far is that people in the United States and Britain more frequently feel free to express their political opinions openly, and that the edge of partisanship in these countries is less sharp than it is in Germany, Italy, and Mexico. At the same time, our data show that these national differences are differences in degree, with the United States and Britain at one extreme, the Italians at the other, and Germany and Mexico in the middle.

What we are in the process of uncovering is the "capillary" structure of democracy and the affective culture that is associated with it. The analogy is a useful one if we do not press it too far. The great secondary components of the democratic infrastructure—political parties, interest groups, and the media of communication—are analogous to the veins and arteries of a circulatory system. Unless they are connected effectively with the primary structure of community—family, friendship, neighborhood, religious groups, work groups, and the like—there can be no effective flow of individual impulses, needs, demands, and preferences from the individual and his primary groups into the political system. The overwhelming majority of the members of all political systems live out their lives, discover, develop, and express their feelings and aspirations in the intimate groups of the community. It is the rare individual who is fully recruited into the political system and becomes a political man. In those societies in which the secondary political structures effectively mesh with the intimate primary structures, there is a gradation from "public" to "private"; from the full-time professional politician to the intermittently active citizen. Where the primary structures remain outside the polity or are passive objects of the polity rather than active participants within it, then the individual has only three choices: to fully involve himself in politics, withdraw from it, or become a passive object of it.

In other words, an effectively functioning democracy implies that a substantial proportion of its members are involved in the political system through the meshing of the more diffuse structures of the community with the more differentiated ones of the polity. Only through this engagement of family and community by the polity can the impulses, needs, complaints, and aspirations of the average man flow into the polity and affect the form and content of political controversy and policy making. The flow of demands and claims is sustained in a flow of feeling—pleasure in attaining one's ends or in the excitement of a political contest, anger over political defeat, frustration at the chicanery of politicians, contempt over demagogy, dishonesty, or corruption. The tissue of a democracy in which the primary structures are well articulated with the secondary ones has the flush of health, the "tone" of a good circulation.

Where for one reason or another the political system fails to integrate with the intimate community structures, then the demands and feelings do not flow readily into the political system and the polity may lose touch with the intimate moods and needs of its members. People may withdraw emotionally from the political system or relate themselves to it by passively accepting the displacements, projections, and other irrationalities of extremist movements. The success of Communist movements in such countries may be attributed to the Communist technique of creating its own infrastructure, particularly its own primary infrastructure (the cell), which taps into these negative feelings and channels them *against* the legitimate structures of the polity rather than *into* them.

Lest there be any ambiguity on this score, it should be recognized that a political system such as the Italian which contains large extremist movements of the left and the right can hardly be described as lacking in political feelings. The critical point made here has to do with the *flow* of affect from the individual and the community into the legitimate political institutions. Undoubtedly, the activists and some of the supporters of the Communist, Left Socialist, and MSI parties have, and express, strong negative feelings about governmental and social institutions, and positive ones about alternative forms of political and social organization. The press, parliamentary debates, party meetings, and demonstrations document the high incidence of negative affect and evaluation at the level of elite communications. Our data will suggest that this elite pattern of partisan antagonism is associated with a withdrawn and perhaps mutinous mood among large numbers of ordinary people, a tendency to withhold loyalty from the political system (which we have already discussed), and to avoid emotional involvement in electoral contests.

Several questions in our survey sought to get at the flow of affect into and out of the polity. The great act of mass participation in a democracy is the election. Consequently, our questions dealt with feelings in election campaigns. The first of the series of four questions sought to get at feelings about voting. The respondents were asked: "Which one of these statements comes closest to describing your feelings when you go to the polls to cast your ballot?" Then they were presented with a list of statements, which included the following: "I get a feeling of satisfaction out of it; I do it only because it is my duty; I feel annoyed, it is a waste of time; I don't feel anything in particular."

The respondents were later asked the following three questions about the kind of feelings they had during election campaigns: "Do you ever get angry at some of the things that go on in election campaigns? Do you ever find election campaigns pleasant and enjoyable? Do you ever find election campaigns silly or ridiculous?" On each question the respondent could indicate whether he experienced the particular feelings often, sometimes, or never. Table 13 shows the percentages in each of the five countries of those reporting they felt satisfaction while voting, and occasionally or frequently felt anger, pleasure, or contempt.

A number of important country differences appear in the table. The United States is high in the expression of all feelings. Almost three-quarters of the American respondents reported feelings of satisfaction when going to the polls. Two-thirds of the Americans reported enjoying election campaigns, and more than half reported sometimes feeling angry or feeling that what went on was silly or ridiculous. Only 12 per cent of the American respondents reported having none of these feelings during election campaigns. England was second highest in expressing satisfaction about voting and about election campaigns. Germany was third highest, but there was an interesting reversal. Whereas in the United States and United Kingdom a higher percentage enjoyed election campaigns than felt anger and contempt, in Germany the percentages reporting negative

145

affect were greater than those reporting pleasure. Italy was low in all these emotions, and 54 per cent of the respondents reported never having any of these feelings about election campaigns. Mexico was also low in reported feelings about voting and elections, but not quite as low as Italy.

The Italian pattern of low affect in election campaigns is of

TABLE 13

Attitudes and Feelings About Voting and Election Campaigns
in Five Nations
(in per cent)

Per Cent who report they	U.S.	U.K.	Germany	Italy	Mexico
Feel satisfaction when going to polls*	71	43	35	30	34
Sometimes find election campaigns pleasant and enjoyable	66	52	28	18	34
Sometimes get angry during campaigns	57	41	46	20	26
Sometimes find campaigns silly or ridiculous	58	37	46	15	32
Never enjoy, never get angry, and never feel contempt during campaigns	12	26	35	54	41
Total number of respondents for each question	970	963	955	995	1,007

* This question was asked only of those who had voted in one or more of the last three national elections or in recent local elections. Number of cases for this question: U.S., 693; U.K., 959; Germany, 869; Italy, 923, and Mexico, 652.

interest when we compare it with our earlier measures of partisanship. In the extent of cleavage between the right and left parties—as measured by the reciprocal party images and the incidence of negative attitudes toward marriage across party lines—the Italians came out very high. How can we reconcile the low frequency of expressions of emotional involvement in election campaigns with the high frequency of antagonistic partisanship? The explanation would appear to lie in the fact that Italians, by and large, are not oriented toward election campaigns as contests. They do not view election campaigns as necessary; and the proportion of those who report paying no attention to election campaigns is far larger than that of any other country (see Table 14).

In other words, the Italians tend to be withdrawn from the electoral process, just as they tend to be withdrawn from govern-

146

ment and nation. One might even view the intensity of their commitment to their own party as a rejection of the *system* of parties, a rejection of the other parties as members of a system of interaction; also, they regard their own party, not as an electoral contestant, but as a church or a "way of life." Partisanship is a full and

TABLE 14

Need for Election Campaigning and Attentiveness to Elections, by Nation
(in per cent)[a]

Nation	Percentage Who Say Election Campaigning Necessary[b]	Percentage Who Pay No Attention to Election Campaigning[c]
United States	74	12
Great Britain	63	29
Germany	42	27
Italy	29	54
Mexico	61	45

[a] Percentages in each case are of the total sample.

[b] Actual text of the question: "Some people feel that campaigning is needed so the public can judge candidates and issues. Others say it causes so much bitterness and is so unreliable that we'd be better off without it. What do you think? Is it needed, or would we be better off without it?"

[c] Actual text of the question: "What about the campaigning that goes on at the time of a national election? Do you pay much attention to what goes on, just a little, or none at all?"

intense commitment—intensively negative because the opposing movements are in another, and threatening, moral dimension; intensively positive because one's own party is really the church, or its secular equivalent on the left.

In our life-history interviews we asked our respondents when they had last voted and what thoughts had gone through their minds while they were casting their ballots. The Italian respondents rarely reported positive reactions. More common were expressions of anxiety or of indifference:

An Italian Housewife (Christian Democrat):
"I thought I had to vote, but I thought that perhaps I didn't want to vote, as often for one vote we might ruin a family. A government might get into power that will have war and the husband will be called in the army."

An Italian Accountant (Christian Democrat):
"I thought, what if I didn't vote for the DC? I was not sure how to vote. I was afraid I wasn't doing the right thing."

An Italian Housewife (Christian Democrat):
"I am afraid. I always worry about voting and that I might do the wrong thing."
An Italian School Official (nonparty):
"The last time I went to the polls with a feeling almost of disgrace, of indifference."
An Italian Workman (Communist):
"I felt I was doing my duty even if it was useless."

Here and there one encountered ideological comments, particularly among the few survivors of Italian liberalism and idealistic socialism who turned up in the sample:

An Italian Physician (Liberal):
"I felt I was contributing to the assertion of certain principles."
An Old Italian Socialist:
"I thought I was making a contribution to the achievement of a more humane society."

Among the Germans one frequently encountered feelings of distrust, futility, or of voting simply to conform:

A German Police Officer (SPD):
"I wondered whether and how much people could cheat."
A German Housewife (nonparty):
"It has never been quite clear to me what all that is supposed to be good for. Those who have been elected will do what they want to, anyway, once they are in."
A German Retired Miner (CDU):
"You can't stay away or you become conspicuous."

And in a more personal vein—

A German Widow (SPD):
"I felt somehow obligated, especially since the Mayor had helped me so much. I have to thank him for my little pension, and so I felt like a citizen who has to vote."

But there were also Germans who expressed satisfaction at being able to participate.

A Young German Salesman (CDU):
"It was an elevating feeling now to be able to participate and have one's own views count."

148

A German White-Collar Worker (nonparty):
"It was wonderful for me to know that we can vote here in freedom and that we have no dictatorship."

A German Locksmith; a Refugee from the Eastern Zone (SPD):
"Here I went to the polls free and unburdened, differently from over there where you trembled when you went to the polls because you had to be afraid to be arrested for the least remark. Over there, they stood nearby and observed everyone individually—what kind of a face he made and whether he said anything. There were no voting booths there and a secret ballot not at all."

A German Painter (SPD):
"I thought quietly that my vote counted, too."

Among the Mexican respondents one frequently encountered the feeling that the electoral process was corrupt.

A Mexican Blacksmith (PRI):
"I felt bad. I don't think that the law of voting is respected."

A Mexican Schoolteacher (PAN):
"I was very excited about the election even though all our ballots were torn up."

Mexican female respondents often reported anxiety at the strangeness of the voting experience, having been enfranchised only in 1956.

A Mexican Nurse:
"I felt nervous as it was the first time I voted. I was afraid since I was not used to voting. I thought I would make a mistake."

A Mexican Housewife:
". . . they gave me many papers. The one I liked best was the PRI. I felt very nervous. I thought that everyone was looking at me as if I was doing something wrong."

There were also Mexicans who expressed satisfaction at the opportunity to vote.

A Mexican Shoemaker:
"I felt satisfaction because registration now gives one the feeling of being a patriot, of being able to elect a president. I thought with satisfaction about the fact that the majority were in favor of the President [of the state government], Jesus Torres."

A Mexican Housewife:
"I voted two years ago for Ruiz Cortinez and he came here. I was pleased because we voted for what belonged to us, for what we liked."

149

The American and British comments were predominantly expressions of pleasure and satisfaction.

A British Civil Servant (Conservative):
"It's funny you ask that. You think what a wonderful fellow you are. You really think you've done something. I expect everybody is the same."

A British Housewife (Conservative):
"I kept thinking, was it worth my while voting, will it make any difference? You see, it's a strong Labour seat here, Mr. Gaitskell has it. And then I thought, it's my vote. I'll use it—it might be of some use."

A British Housewife (Labour):
"I never miss. I felt very happy, and very disappointed when things went wrong. I watched it on TV all the time, and I was hoping the man I voted for would get in. . . . I feel happy with everybody when I go to the polls. When I come home again, my mind is going all the time, 'Please God, Please God.' "

An American Housewife (Democrat):
"I felt important. That's all, just important. I don't know, I just felt important to be able to cast the vote."

An American Assembly-Line Worker (Republican):
"I felt good. I think you feel a little more important that day than you ordinarily do."

An American Postal Clerk (Republican):
"I felt more encouraged. That the Republicans had a better chance. Not good enough, maybe, but better."

But there were many Americans and Englishmen who expressed indifference or brought up personal considerations.

An English Cinema Projectionist (Labour):
"I felt the same as always; it's your duty. I was worrying about my bike outside."

An English Housewife (Liberal):
"I voted for the person, not the party. He was a doctor (a chest specialist). And since my son has been cured of a chest complaint, I voted for him. He also seemed a nice, unassuming man."

An American Nurse (Republican):
"I stood there and prayed and asked God's guidance and He gave it to me. And He didn't direct me to vote for Terry Sanford."

In the United States and Britain the proportion of respondents reporting that they have feelings about voting and election increases with education (see Table 15). It is of some interest that the expression of political anger is most sharply affected by education, not only in the United States and Britain, but in Germany, Italy, and Mexico as well (see Table 16). The important point to be noted in Table 16, however, is that in the United States and Britain all of the "affects" rise substantially with increased educa-

TABLE 15

Attitudes and Feelings About Voting and Election Campaigns in the United States, Great Britain, and Germany, by Education
(in per cent)

Per Cent who report they	U.S.			U.K.			Germany		
	Some Prim.	Some Sec.	Some Univ.	Some Prim.	Some Sec.	Some Univ.	Some Prim.	Some Sec.	Some Univ.
Feel satisfaction when going to polls*	58	75	82	41	47	57	35	37	26
Sometimes find campaigns pleasant and enjoyable	60	67	77	52	54	62	37	47	27
Sometimes get angry during campaigns	43	62	71	37	47	62	43	63	73
Sometimes find campaigns silly or ridiculous	53	56	73	37	37	54	44	51	42
Total number of respondents	338	443	188	593	322	24	790	124	26

* Shown in order of columns above, the number of cases for this question (asked only of voters): *U.S.*, 226, 309, and 151; *Great Britain*, 552, 264, and 23, and *Germany*, 729, 102, and 23.

tion. In Germany it is of great significance that only anger increases substantially with high education: from 43 per cent for those with some primary education to 73 per cent for those with some university education. The frequency of respondents expressing satisfaction over casting the ballot, finding elections enjoyable, or sometimes silly or ridiculous, rises somewhat with secondary education and drops with university education. It would appear, therefore, that the German pattern of high negative affect is most marked among the better-educated, "upper-class" Germans. That political anger is a characteristic of class as well as of education is indicated when we control for occupation. Thus the frequency of anger doubles from 34 per cent among German unskilled laborers to 68 per cent among professional and managerial personnel. The increases in the frequency of the other affects among German professional groups are of a far smaller order.

We can now add another feature to the German political-cultural profile. We have already seen that German national pride is in economic and character attributes rather than political ones. At the

TABLE 16

Attitudes and Feelings About Voting and Election Campaigns
in Italy and Mexico, by Education
(in per cent)

	Italy					Mexico			
Per Cent who report they	No Educ.	Some Prim.	Low Sec.	High Sec.	Some Univ.	No Educ.	Some Prim.	Some Sec.	Some Univ.
Feel satisfaction when going to polls*	10	28	29	26	25	12	24	28	49
Sometimes find campaigns pleasant and enjoyable	9	16	24	31	35	26	36	37	46
Sometimes get angry during campaigns	12	19	23	26	39	18	25	40	65
Sometimes find campaigns silly or ridiculous	9	17	29	23	39	24	31	50	55
Total number of respondents	88	604	148	97	54	221	656	103	24

* Shown in order of columns above, the number of cases for this question (asked only of voters): Italy, 85, 583, 129, 93, and 50; Mexico, 103, 456, 75, and 18.

same time, we have seen that Germans appreciate the impact of government on their lives and expect equal and responsive treatment from their bureaucracy and police. Now we discover that German feelings about the specifically political aspects of their governmental system tend to be negative, and that this negativism tends to be most marked among the educated middle and upper middle classes. In other words, it is precisely among these elements which in most democratic countries tend to support democratic processes that contemporary German democracy appears to have least support.

The political cultural characteristics of educated Germans reflect ambivalence. On the one hand, political cognition rises with education. Thus educated Germans have higher political information scores, more frequently follow discussions of public affairs in the media of communication, and more frequently talk politics with other people. They also accept democratic values more frequently than the less well educated; but wherever political feelings are concerned, the educated Germans show greater alienation and negativism than the less well educated. Thus pride in the political aspects of nation and feelings of satisfaction while voting decrease with education. And now we discover that only the emotion of anger in election campaigns increases sharply with education.

Two possible explanations may be made of this German phenomenon. First, the educated middle class in Germany never developed a fully democratic culture. What we may be observing in our data is the persistence of this authoritarian subject culture, which involves imparting legitimacy to authority and bureaucracy, but not to political parties and competitive elections.

But there is another explanation of these tendencies. The German educated middle classes were deeply compromised by National Socialism and in many cases penalized (if only briefly) during the early phases of the Occupation. Their withholding of feeling toward the German nation and toward the political process may be an expression of anxiety about being involved once again in a risky business. Perhaps both factors are present: a sense of discomfort over the disorderliness and lack of dignity of democratic politics, and anxiety about any kind of political involvement, based on the Nazi trauma.

Table 16, showing the relation between education and electoral feeling in Italy and Mexico, reveals the same trends that were manifested in the United States and Britain, though the magnitudes of the percentages are substantially smaller. Thus the frequencies of all the affects in Italy at the university level are below 40 per cent, as compared with the "no education" group, where they are below 15 per cent. Mexico shows the same trend, with the range in general being substantially higher than in Italy, but lower than in the other countries. At the university level the Mexican respondents range from 46 per cent for enjoying elections to 65 per cent who report sometimes getting angry at events during election campaigns.

Our analysis of national differences in feelings about politics and partisanship has brought out the following patterns. In the United States and Britain there is a widespread sense of freedom and safety in political communication; partisan feelings are relatively cool, and feelings of all kinds flow relatively freely into the political system. In Germany people seem to feel more restricted in these communications, partisanship appears to be more intense, and anger and contempt seem to be the emotions most frequently expressed in election compaigns. In Italy the proportion of the population that feels free to communicate about politics and admits to having feelings about elections is extremely small. At the same time, the intensity of partisanship is extremely high. In Mexico political communication is restricted, but not to the same extent as in Italy. The expression of feelings about elections is also low, but not as low as in Italy, and the level of partisanship is high, but again not so high as in Italy.

Types of Partisans

At the beginning of this chapter we suggested that an effectively functioning democracy required a form of partisanship that avoided intense antagonism at one extreme and political indifference at the other. In the preceding pages we have described the incidence of extreme partisan cleavage in our five countries, as measured by attitudes toward interparty marriage and the kinds of feelings that partisans have toward electoral contests.

We are now in a position to present a typology of partisanship based on a score that combines these two measures of attitudes. If we dichotomize the responses to both sets of questions, we have a fourfold typology, as follows:

1. The Open Partisan. This is the respondent who expresses indifference toward interparty marriage yet describes himself as emotionally involved in election compaigns. This "open partisan" is emotionally involved in electoral contests but not so intensely partisan as to cut himself off from relations with members of the opposing party. Table 17 shows that 82 per cent of the Americans, 61 per cent of the British, 44 per cent of the Germans, and 42 per cent of the Mexicans manifest this kind of partisanship, while only 14 per cent of the Italians fall into this category.

2. The Apathetic Partisan. It may seem a contradiction in terms to speak of an "apathetic partisan," but this is the respondent who voted for one of the major parties, who expressed indifference about interparty marriage, and who denied having any of the three feelings about elections covered in our interview (anger, pleasure, contempt). He is the indifferent voter, found in any polity, who casts his ballot but feels little involvement in the electoral contest. We see that Italy has the highest proportion of apathetic partisans and the United States the lowest, with the other countries in-between.

3. The Intense Partisan. This is the respondent who is concerned about marriage across party lines and who also is emotionally involved in elections. He is both sharply divided from his party

TABLE 17

Types of Partisanship, by Nation

(in per cent)

Per Cent who are	U.S.	U.K.	Germany	Italy	Mexico
Open partisans	82	61	44	14	42
Apathetic partisans	8	22	18	30	24
Intense partisans	10	14	25	20	25
Parochial partisans	0	3	13	36	9
Total per cent	100	100	100	100	100
Total number (all admitted major party adherents or voters, omitting those who had no opinion on interparty marriage or on the emotions they felt at campaign time)	736	719	485	300	489

opponents and emotionally involved in electoral contests. We see in Table 17 that this type is most frequently encountered in Germany and Mexico, with Italy, Britain, and the United States following in that order.

4. The Parochial Partisan. This is the respondent who, though concerned about interparty marriage, is indifferent about election campaigns. This class of partisans is relatively uninvolved in politics; we speak of them as "parochial partisans." As will be shown below, they are predominantly religious women. Their partisanship is not a political phenomenon, but a cultural-religious one. We encounter this type in large numbers only in Italy, where 36 per cent fall into this category.

What strikes the eye in Table 17 is the sharp difference between Italy and all the other countries. This extreme deviation in the Italian pattern may be due in part to the very high incidence of refusals among Italian left-wing party voters to disclose their party preference. This is brought out in Table 22, where we have broken down the four types in Italy by party preference. We know from election results that approximately four out of ten Italian voters support the Christian Democratic party, while approximately one-third support the left parties (the Communists and Nenni-Socialists). In our sample 35 per cent of the respondents identified them-

TABLE 18

Demographic Characteristics of Types of American Partisans
(in per cent)

Demographic Characteristics	Open Partisans	Apathetic Partisans	Intense Partisans	Parochial Partisans	Total Per Cent	Total Number[a]
(Per Cent of Total Sample)	82	7	10	1	100	736
SEX						
Male	85	6	9	0	100	345
Female	79	9	10	1	99	391
CHURCH ATTENDANCE[b]						
At least weekly	83	7	9	0	99	341
Occasionally	81	7	10	1	99	320
Never	78	10	10	2	100	51
PARTY SUPPORT						
Republican	79	7	13	1	100	339
Democrat	83	8	7	1	99	194
EDUCATION						
Primary or less	78	9	10	1	98	389
Secondary or above	85	6	9	0	100	351

[a] For major party supporters only, omitting those who have no opinion of interparty marriage or on emotions they feel at election campaigns.

[b] Only for those who report religious affiliation.

selves as Christian Democratic voters and 10 per cent as left party voters. Hence the Italian pattern presented in Table 17 is heavily biased in the Christian Democratic direction. Table 22 shows that almost half of the Christian Democratic respondents are parochial partisans, while 27 per cent are apathetic partisans, and 21 per cent are intense partisans. In contrast, the Nenni-Socialist respondents are almost entirely open or apathetic partisans, and the Communists tend to fall in the open, apathetic, and intense categories.

Table 17 illustrates the gross distribution of these types of partisanship in the five countries. It would also be useful to determine which social elements these types are composed of. In the United States there is relatively little difference between men and women in their patterns of partisanship (see Table 18). There is also relatively little difference based on frequency of church attendance, party preference, or educational level. In Britain, on the other hand, proportionately fewer women than men are open partisans (56 per cent to 68 per cent). And British women are found more frequently in the apathetic partisan category. Conservatives are more likely to be intense partisans or parochial partisans than

TABLE 19
Demographic Characteristics of Types of British Partisans
(in per cent)

Demographic Characteristics	Open Partisans	Apathetic Partisans	Intense Partisans	Parochial Partisans	Total Per Cent	Total Number[a]
(Per Cent of Total Sample)	61	22	14	3	100	719
SEX						
Male	68	17	13	1	99	341
Female	56	26	14	4	100	378
CHURCH ATTENDANCE[b]						
At least weekly	54	22	21	3	100	160
Occasionally	63	19	14	3	99	387
Never	60	28	8	3	99	89
PARTY VOTE						
Conservative	56	18	21	5	100	340
Labour	68	24	7	1	100	361
EDUCATION						
Primary or less	59	24	14	3	100	466
Secondary or above	67	17	14	3	101	234

[a] For major party supporters only, omitting those who have no opinion of interparty marriage or on emotions they feel at election campaigns.
[b] Only for those who report religious affiliation.

are Laborites. These data suggest a higher incidence of traditionalism in Britain than in the United States, although the pattern is not strongly pronounced (see Table 19).

In Germany the contrasts become sharper. Only 37 per cent of German women are open partisans, as compared with 51 per cent of the men. Furthermore, 20 per cent of the German women are parochial partisans. Frequency of church attendance affects partisanship strongly. Thus 26 per cent of those who attend church weekly or more often are parochial partisans. Similarly, party vote has a strong relationship to types of partisanship. Thus only 38 per cent of the CDU respondents are open partisans, as compared with 53 per cent of the SPD respondents. The higher incidence of parochial partisanship among women, frequent churchgoers, and CDU voters suggests the persistence of a fairly strong clerico-traditional tendency in the right wing of German politics (see Table 20).

The Mexican pattern is in some respects much like the German, with the exception that German males are more likely to be intense partisans than are Mexican males, and German females are more likely to be parochial partisans than are Mexican females. Clerical-

TABLE 20

Demographic Characteristics of Types of German Partisans
(in per cent)

Demographic Characteristics	Open Partisans	Apathetic Partisans	Intense Partisans	Parochial Partisans	Total Per Cent	Total Number[a]
(Per Cent of Total Sample)	44	18	25	13	100	485
SEX						
Male	51	13	29	6	99	224
Female	37	22	21	20	100	261
CHURCH ATTENDANCE[b]						
At least weekly	33	15	25	26	99	163
Occasionally	50	18	24	8	100	259
Never	46	30	19	5	100	43
PARTY VOTE						
CDU	38	17	27	18	100	288
SPD	53	19	21	7	100	197
EDUCATION						
Primary or less	41	20	24	14	99	415
Secondary or above	57	6	30	7	100	67

[a] For major party supporters only, omitting those who have no opinion of interparty marriage or on emotions they feel at election campaigns.
[b] Only for those who report religious affiliation.

ism appears to be stronger in Germany than in Mexico, which suggests that the anticlericalism of the Mexican Revolution has produced a rather thoroughgoing political secularization. This is also reflected in the fact that the two Mexican political parties are unusually alike in their distribution of types of partisanship, unlike the German situation, where the CDU has a lower incidence of open partisanship and a higher incidence of intense and parochial partisanship than the SPD (see Table 21).

But the Italian pattern shows the most extreme contrasts and the highest incidence of clerico-traditional conservatism (see Table 22). Forty-eight per cent of the Italian women are parochial partisans and only 7 per cent are open partisans. While only small proportions of Italian respondents report themselves as rarely or never attending church, church attendance is strikingly correlated with partisanship: half of those who never attend church are open partisans, and almost half of those who attend church weekly are parochial partisans. We have already seen the striking difference in party pattern, with the Christian Democrats most frequently manifesting parochial partisanship, the Communists and left-Socialists

TABLE 21

Demographic Characteristics of Types of Mexican Partisans
(in per cent)

Demographic Characteristics	Open Partisans	Apathetic Partisans	Intense Partisans	Parochial Partisans	Total Per Cent	Total Number[a]
(Per Cent of Total Sample)	42	24	25	9	100	489
SEX						
Male	52	22	19	6	99	246
Female	31	27	31	11	100	243
CHURCH ATTENDANCE[b]						
At least weekly	36	28	28	9	101	351
Occasionally	49	18	25	9	101	113
Never	(too few cases)					
PARTY VOTE						
PRI	40	25	26	9	100	320
PAN	45	23	25	7	100	62
EDUCATION						
Primary or less	40	26	24	10	100	414
Secondary or above	52	16	29	3	100	75

[a] For major party supporters only, omitting those who have no opinion of interparty marriage or on emotions they feel at election campaigns.
[b] Only for those who report religious affiliation.

open partisanship. We can provide a summary answer to the question we first raised when we discovered the unusually high incidence of parochial partisanship in Italy. This substantial component of the Italian electorate consists predominantly of women, frequent churchgoers, and Christian Democratic voters.

Through this analysis of the distribution of types of partisans and their demographic characteristics, we are enabled to locate our five countries on a continuum of moderate pragmatic partisanship. The United States is at one extreme, with a relatively homogeneous pattern of open partisanship, involvement of low intensity, and interparty social mobility. This is a kind of partisanship that is consistent with an aggregative, bargaining party system. Britain is much like the United States, though there is some evidence that a clerical-traditional tendency persists in the right wing of British politics. That is to say, there is a tendency among some British conservatives—women and frequent churchgoers—to be conservative for religious rather than political reasons. Mexico would seem to follow Britain in the incidence of clerical-traditional tendencies. Germany shows a relatively strong tendency toward clerical-traditionalism, particularly among churchgoing Catholic women.

TABLE 22

Demographic Characteristics of Types of Italian Partisans
(in per cent)

Demographic Characteristics	Open Partisans	Apathetic Partisans	Intense Partisans	Parochial Partisans	Total Per Cent	Total Number[a]
(Per Cent of Total Sample)	14	30	20	36	100	300
SEX						
Male	23	33	23	21	100	126
Female	7	27	18	48	100	174
CHURCH ATTENDANCE[b]						
At least weekly	6	26	20	47	99	201
Occasionally	24	42	18	16	100	76
Never	50	25	25	0	100	16
PARTY VOTE						
DC	5	27	21	46	99	229
PCI	39	26	26	10	101	31
PSI	46	44	10	0	100	39
EDUCATION						
Primary or less	12	31	19	37	99	225
Secondary or above	19	26	22	33	100	73

[a] For major party supporters only, omitting those who have no opinion of interparty marriage or on emotions they feel at election campaigns.
[b] Only for those who report religious affiliation.

Italy presents us with the curious anomaly of a political system in which the formal democratic constitution is supported in large part by traditional-clerical elements who are not democratic at all, and not even political in a specialized sense of the term. Opposed to the constitution is a left wing, which, at least in part and at the rank-and-file voter level rather than among the party elite, manifests a form of open partisanship that is consistent with a democratic system.

CHAPTER 6

THE OBLIGATION TO PARTICIPATE

THE CITIZEN, unlike the subject, is an active participant in the political input process—the process by which political decisions are made. But the citizen role, as we have suggested, does not replace the subject role or the parochial role: it is added to them. Only the rare individual considers his role as citizen more important and salient than his role as subject or parochial; for whom politics is a matter of first priority. This has been corroborated in many surveys of political opinion. When asked general questions about what worries them, or what they consider important, people usually mention family problems, job problems, economic problems, but rarely political problems.[1] Furthermore, if the ordinary man is interested in political matters, he is more likely to be interested in the output than in the input process. He is concerned about who wins the election, not about how it is carried on; he cares about who is benefited by legislation, not about how legislation is passed. Even in relation to his vote—an act that is designed to make him an active participant in the decision-making processes of his nation—he may behave routinely, voting for a party because of traditional allegiance or for other reasons not connected with a desire to guide the course of policy.

That most men orient themselves more as subjects than as citizens is a familiar theme. Much has been written describing this fact, sometimes deploring it. Interest in and criticism of the role of the ordinary man in his political system is especially characteristic of those writers and thinkers concerned with the problems of democracy —from the ancient Greeks to current writers on American civic af-

[1] In our survey, when respondents were asked what they spent their free time on, no more than three per cent in any of the five nations mentioned something to do with politics; and in most cases the percentage was smaller. Other survey results show almost universally that politics is not uppermost in the minds of people.

161

fairs; for it is in a democracy that the role of the ordinary man as a participant in the political affairs of his country is significant. The man whose relation to his government is that of a subject—a passive beneficiary or victim of routine governmental actions—would not be found wanting in a traditional, nondemocratic society. Moreover, this relationship would exhaust what is expected of him. What the government does affects him, but why or how the government decides to do what it does is outside his sphere of competence. He has obligations, but the obligations are passive—he should be loyal and respectful of authority. "All that is necessary for salvation is contained in two virtues, *faith* in Christ and *obedience* to laws."[2] As a subject he may be more or less competent, but his competence will be "subject competence." He will not attempt to influence the decisions of his government, but will try to see that he is treated properly once the decision is made. It is not in his sphere of competence to say what taxes should be levied, but once these are decided the competent subject will see that he is treated fairly within the boundaries of that decision. The law is something he obeys, not something he helps shape. If he is competent, he knows the law, knows what he must do, and what is due him.

In democratic societies, on the other hand, his role as subject does not exhaust what is expected of him. He is expected to have the virtues of the subject—to obey the law, to be loyal—but he is also expected to take some part in the formation of decisions. The common thread running through the many definitions of democracy is that a democracy is a society in which ". . . ordinary citizens exert a relatively high degree of control over leaders."[3] Democracy is thus characterized by the fact that power over significant authoritative decisions in a society is distributed among the population. The ordinary man is expected to take an active part in governmental affairs, to be aware of how decisions are made, and to make his views known.

The fact that the ordinary man does not live up to the ideal set by the normative theory of democracy has led to much criticism of his passivity and indifference. Our goal is to describe and analyze, however, and not to assign praise or blame. In any case, normative questions about the role of the individual in his political system are by no means unrelated to more descriptive and analytic questions. Certainly the political moralist in describing what an in-

[2] Thomas Hobbes, *Leviathan*, London, 1945, Book III, p. 385.
[3] Robert A. Dahl, *A Preface to Democratic Theory*, Chicago, 1956, p. 3.

dividual *should* do will probably not be unaffected by what individuals actually *do,* and certainly he will consider what he believes they *can* do. The three types of questions are not identical, but they affect one another. This is especially the case if we switch our perspective to that of the ordinary man himself. So far we have talked about the gap between what scholars, philosophers, and teachers have said the ordinary man ought to do in a democracy and what in fact he does. But what about the ordinary man himself? What does *he* think he *should* do? And how does this compare with what he thinks he *can* do and with what he does?

This chapter will deal with the first question: What does the ordinary man think he should do? Philosophers and democratic ideologists have written at length about the obligations of the citizen, but what is the ordinary man's conception of his role in politics? If the model democratic citizen is active, participating, and influential, is this what the ordinary man aspires to be? And, what may be more important, does he think of himself as capable of influencing and participating in the decisions of his government? In this chapter we shall look at the ordinary man's conception of the role he ought to play, and in the next at the conception of the role he thinks he can play.

What Is The Good Citizen?

The good citizen does not equal the good man. No zealous advocate of good citizenship would argue that political participation ought to be pursued at the neglect of all other obligations. The active influential citizen described in normative political theory is not excused from the obligations of the subject. If he participates in the making of the law, he is also expected to obey the law. It has, in fact, been argued that he has greater obligation to obey because of his participation. Nor would one want his civic activity to be at the expense of his private obligations. Surely the lady described by Riesman who left her screaming children locked in their room while she attended a meeting of a neighborhood improvement association does not represent the ideal toward which the advocates of good citizenship are striving.[4] There will, of course, always be conflicts between the demands of different roles, but the obligations of one role do not replace those of another.

This point is stressed here because it introduces a complexity

[4] David Riesman, *Faces in the Crowd,* New Haven, 1952, pp. 82-83.

163

into our attempt to measure the extent to which the ideal of the participating citizen exists in the minds of men; for the man who believes that he should be upright in his personal life—work for the good of his family or, to quote one of our respondents, "If he is a carpenter, he should be a good carpenter"—may also believe that he should be a participating and active citizen. Similarly, the man who believes that he should pay taxes and obey the laws is a "good subject." The same man may also be a "good citizen." It is only when the individual thinks of his family's advantage as the only goal to pursue, or conceives of his role in the political system in familistic terms, that he is a parochial and not also a citizen. And it is only when an individual thinks of his relationship to his state as being exhausted by his role as subject that he is subject and not also citizen.

Attempting to see how much the role of participant has been added to those of parochial and subject in our five countries, we examined our respondents' relations with their local community. We were interested in the extent to which respondents considered themselves to have some sort of responsibility to be active in their community—either in a formal or informal way; either in relation to local government or in relation to fellow citizens. The local community seemed to be a good place to begin, since political and governmental problems tend to be more understandable, the organs of government less distant, the chances of effective participation for the individual citizen greater on the local level than on the level of national government. It has, in fact, often been argued that effective democracy rests on the ability of the individual to participate locally, for it is only here that he can develop some sense of mastery over political affairs. As Bryce put it (and as defenders of local autonomy have constantly argued), "An essential ingredient of a satisfactory democracy is that a considerable proportion should have experience of active participation in the work of small self-governing groups, whether in connection with local government, trade unions, cooperatives or other forms of activity."[5]

National Differences in the Characteristics of Local Government

In this chapter and in a good part of the next, we shall deal with attitudes toward the local government. In interpreting the responses

[5] James Bryce, *Modern Democracies*, New York, 1921, I, p. 132. (See below, chap. 7.)

to questions about the local government, we are faced with the problem that the structures of local government differ from nation to nation and within the nations as well. And these differences in structure partially explain differences in attitudes found among the nations. (As we pointed out in Chapter 2, this is a general problem in the interpretation of cross-national data.) It is important that these differences be kept in mind. While it would be impossible to describe fully the patterns of local government within the five nations—there are numerous levels of local government in all five nations and substantial variation among regions—one can specify certain similarities and differences among them.

In the first place, all five nations have some form of local government. (It is important to note here that we are dealing with the most local governmental units: units below the level of state, or *Land*, or province.) And the local unit, whether it be a commune, *municipio, Gemeinde*, township, or noncounty borough, almost invariably has some sort of locally elected council or set of officials. Thus in each country there is a set of locally elected units on which we can focus.

But despite this similarity, local government differs sharply among the five nations. From the point of view of respondents' attitudes toward participation within the local community, there are two types of structural differences that are particularly significant: the degree of local autonomy and the degree to which local structures foster citizen participation. It is difficult to measure precisely the extent of autonomy of local governmental units within nations; there are variations within nations, the criteria of autonomy are not clear, and the data are often lacking. Nevertheless, the five nations do differ so substantially in this respect—and the variations among the nations are generally larger than the variations within each nation—that one can rank the nations with some confidence in terms of local autonomy. It is clear that at one extreme the pattern of local government in the United States represents the greatest amount of local autonomy. The range of subject matter over which the local communities have control—the police and schools are two important examples (and the communities not only handle administration of the schools, but in many cases they actually formulate educational policy)—as well as the extent of the local governments' freedom from external control appear to be much greater in the United States than elsewhere.

165

It would appear that Great Britain ranks next to the United States in degree of local autonomy. The range of issues over which the local government has control is smaller—educational policy, for instance, is controlled by central government agencies to a much larger degree—and within the unitary British system of government, local autonomy is not provided for formally by home rule provisions, as it is in the constitutions of a number of American states. Nevertheless, the British have a long tradition of local self-government. And local councils are active in administrative work as well as in some limited areas of legislation where permission is given by the central government.[6]

It is difficult to rank the other three nations precisely. In terms of the formal structure of local government, however, it is relatively easy to specify which ranks lowest. The existence of the prefect system in Italy limits substantially any opportunity for local self-government. The communes in Italy have locally elected councils, but they have little freedom of action. All acts must be submitted to the centrally appointed prefect of the province, who passes on their legality; and certain significant matters, such as the municipal budget and the levying of taxes, must be approved by the provincial administrative committee (*Giunta Provinciale Amministrativa*), which passes on both the legality and the merit of the act. It is quite unlikely that a local government structure of this sort, in which there is a centrally appointed official with powers to oversee the activities of the locality, would foster a high level of autonomous local activity. Though there is some evidence of more local autonomy than one would expect, given the formal structure, the degree of autonomy is probably least of all the five nations.[7]

As in most cases when one is trying to array a series of units along a scale, it is the units near the middle of the scale that present the more difficult problems in categorization. In terms of the degree of local

[6] See, for instance, W. Eric Jackson, *Local Government in England and Wales*, London, 1960. This is not to argue that in the United States and Britain there is no external control over local government. There is obviously a large amount of external control and this control is steadily growing—a point whose implications will be discussed below. But relatively speaking, local government in these two nations has a vigor missing in the other three.

[7] See Samuel Humes and Eileen M. Martin, *The Structure of Local Governments Throughout the World*, The Hague, 1961, pp. 319-24; Harold Zink et al., *Rural Local Government in Sweden, Italy and India*, London, 1957, and Edward Banfield, *The Moral Basis of a Backward Society*, Glencoe, Ill., 1958. See, also, Robert C. Fried, *The Italian Prefects*, unpublished Ph.D. dissertation, Yale University, 1961.

governmental autonomy, it is probably accurate to place Germany and Mexico between the United States and Britain on the one hand and Italy on the other. But one must approach the characterization of these two nations with somewhat more caution. One reason is the wide range of variation possible within a federal system, a situation heightened in Germany by differing regional traditions and by the somewhat different heritages from the three occupying powers. There is in many areas of Germany a strong tradition of local autonomy, as well as a tendency for local communities to engage in a wide range of activities. This is especially true among many of the older northern German cities, which have long histories of local self-government.[8] It is, however, difficult to estimate in any precise way the extent to which local self-government is firmly entrenched in other areas in Germany.

Mexico, unlike Italy but like the other three nations, has legal provision for relatively autonomous local governments on the level of the *municipio*. In actual practice, however, these local governments have been relatively uninfluential and relatively nonautonomous. This has been largely due to central control over local finances and the pervasive influence of the PRI, the single important Mexican political party. Local government in Mexico has rarely been of great significance.[9]

The nations also differ in the extent to which the local decision-making apparatus is accessible to participation by local residents. In some communities—and again this varies within nations, but perhaps more sharply among nations—there will be greater opportunity for the individual to participate in decisions. It is somewhat more difficult to compare the nations in this respect than it was to compare them in respect to local autonomy. There are fewer studies of the degree to which individuals actually participate in local affairs, for such participation depends largely upon informal as well as formal channels of participation. Some data from our own study, to be presented in the next chapter, will be useful for such categor-

[8] See, for instance, Lorenz Fischer and Peter Van Hauten, "Cologne," in William A. Robson (ed.), *Great Cities of the World*, London, 1957, pp. 645-82.

[9] For a consideration of the influence of the PRI in the politics of one Mexican city, see Scott, *Mexican Government in Transition*, pp. 44-55; and William H. Form and William V. d'Antonio, "Integration and Cleavage Among Community Influentials in Two Border Cities," *American Sociological Review*, xxiv (1959), pp. 804-14. If our knowledge of and ability to measure this dimension were more precise it is possible that we might rank Mexico close to, or even below, Italy. However, more precise descriptions will depend on more precise research.

ization. In general, one would expect that the extent to which the local government is open to citizen participation in decisions would be closely related to the extent of local autonomy; and impressions of community life in these five nations, as well as the data to be presented in the next chapter, support this proposition.[10]

Consequently, in interpreting the data in this and the next chapter, we shall have to keep in mind that one reason why individuals differ in the frequency with which they adhere to participatory norms is that the structure of government and community organization changes from one nation to another. This does not make the attitudinal data any less significant. As we have suggested earlier, even if the attitudes we describe are in part determined by the structure of government and social system in each nation, this does not remove the fact that these attitudes in turn affect these same structures. The norms to which an individual adheres are largely determined by the role that the system allows him to play (though the fit between norms and structure will rarely be perfect); but these norms in turn have a feedback effect on the structure, reinforcing the structure if the fit between norms and structure is a good one; introducing strain into the system if norms and structure fit less well. And lastly, as we shall attempt to demonstrate below, attitudes toward the local government cannot be explained solely by the relation between the individual and the local governmental structure (and the same point can and will be made about the national government as well). We shall attempt to show, for instance, that the extent to which individuals believe they can influence the government, and in particular the ways in which they would attempt to exert that influence, depend, not only on the governmental system, but upon certain social and attitudinal characteristics of the individuals.

National Differences in Sense of Civic Obligation

Our question to the respondents dealt with participation in local

[10] But the degree of local self-government and the degree to which individuals can participate within that government may be independent of each other. It would be possible, for instance, to draw the conclusion from John Gimbel's study of *A German Community Under American Occupation: Marburg, 1945-1952*, Stanford, 1961, that the American Occupation's attempt to introduce local democracy failed for the simple reason that, though they gave power to local elites, these elites were not committed to furthering citizen participation.

affairs. We were interested, not only in political participation, but in any sort of outgoing activity the individual might mention. We wanted to know the extent to which individuals believe they have any sort of obligation to the community—to care about more than the personal problems of the family life and job.[11]

Table 1 summarizes the responses we received as to the role individuals should play within their local community.

TABLE 1
How Active Should the Ordinary Man be in his Local Community, by Nation
(in per cent)

Per Cent who say the Ordinary Man Should	U.S.	U.K.	Germany	Italy	Mexico
Be active in his community	51	39	22	10	26
Only participate passively*	27	31	38	22	33
Only participate in church affairs*	5	2	1	*	–
Total who mention some outgoing activity	83	72	61	32	59
Only be upright in personal life*	1	1	11	15	2
Do nothing in local community	3	6	7	11	2
Don't know	11	17	21	35	30
Other	2	5	1	7	7
Total per cent	100	100	100	100	100
Total number of cases	970	963	955	995	1,007

* Multiple answers were possible, but we have eliminated them from this table by listing respondents' *most active* response only (i.e., the response that would fall highest on the table). Thus an individual who mentioned active as well as passive participation would be listed under active participation only; one who mentioned church activities as well as an upright private life would be listed under the former and not the latter.

We have classified our respondents into those who believe that the ordinary man should take some active part in his community (this includes those who say the ordinary man should attend meetings, join organizations involved in community affairs, and the like); those who believe that one ought to participate more passively in community activities (for example: one ought to be interested in

[11] The question read: "We know that the ordinary person has many problems that take his time. In view of this, what part do you think the ordinary person ought to play in the local affairs of his town or district?" The interviewer attempted to find out as closely as possible what the respondent specifically felt one ought to do in his community.

local affairs, try to understand them and keep informed, vote); those who feel that the ordinary man ought to participate only in church and religious activities; and those who do not think the ordinary man has any responsibility that involves him in the affairs of his community (here we include the respondents who feel that the ordinary man ought to maintain an upright personal life; who say that he ought to take no part in the affairs of his community; and who do not know what role the individual ought to play in his community).

Clearly from this table, the image of the citizen-as-participant is more widespread in some countries than in others. In the United States and Britain a large number of respondents believe that the individual should be an active participant in the affairs of his community. Half of the Americans interviewed and 39 per cent of the British mention some active role that the individual ought to play. In Italy, at the other extreme, there are few who conceive of the citizen as active participant. Only one in ten Italians believes that the ordinary man has an obligation to take an active role in his community. The proportions of German and Mexican respondents who have some image of the active citizen lie in-between the American and British proportions on the one hand and the Italian on the other. One out of five of our German respondents and one out of four of our Mexicans conceive of the ordinary man as having some obligation to participate.[12]

"One ought at least to take an interest in what goes on in the community"; or, "One ought to be active in church and religious affairs": if we consider these statements an indicator (albeit a weaker one) of the existence of some norm of participation, then the contrasts among the nations are still striking. In the United States 83 per cent of the respondents talk of the ordinary man as having some commitment to his community that takes him out of involvement in purely personal affairs—even if the responsibility is minimal. The proportion in Britain is somewhat smaller at 72 per cent; in Mexico and Germany about 60 percent talk of some outgoing role for the individual, while in Italy only 32 per cent do.

What sorts of community activities do our respondents have in

[12] The Mexican pattern is interesting here, and we shall return to it later. Mexican respondents mention an obligation to participate more frequently than do German respondents and much more frequently than do Italian respondents. This relatively high sense of obligation, coupled, as we shall discuss, with lower activity and information, is an aspect of the civic aspirational tendency among the Mexicans.

mind when they say the ordinary man ought to play some part in his local community? As Table 2 shows, only a small number of respondents in each country mention partisan activity as the responsibility of the individual to his community. In the United States and Britain

TABLE 2

What Role Should the Ordinary Man Play in his Local Community, by Nation
(in per cent)

Per Cent who choose	U.S.	U.K.	Germany	Italy	Mexico
ACTIVE PARTICIPATION IN LOCAL COMMUNITY[a]					
Take part in activities of local government	21	22	13	5	11
Take part in activities of political parties	6	4	4	1	5
Take part in nongovernmental activity and in organizations interested in local affairs	32	17	9	5	10
MORE PASSIVE COMMUNITY ACTIVITIES[a]					
Try to understand and keep informed	21	11	24	6	29
Vote	40	18	15	2	1
Take an interest in what is going on	3	13	6	15	4
PARTICIPATION IN CHURCH AND RELIGIOUS ACTIVITIES[a]	12	2	2	–	–
Total percentage of respondents who mention some outgoing activity[b]	83	72	61	32	59
Total number of respondents	970	963	955	995	1,007

[a] The percentages in these categories are somewhat larger than in Table 1, since this table contains all the responses of individuals, rather than their most active responses.

[b] Total percentages are less than the total of the individual cells, since the latter involve multiple responses.

respondents frequently mention taking part in local government bodies, attending meetings, and the like. In Germany and Mexico this is less frequently mentioned, but is mentioned more frequently than in Italy. Active community participation in a nongovernmental sense—participation in civic groups and organizations, or informal activity to help the community—is quite frequently mentioned in the United States. Such nongovernmental activity is again least mentioned in Italy, with Germany and Mexico trailing Britain. In

171

terms of active participation, then, the five countries can be roughly grouped: the United States and Britain are the countries in which the image of the active participating citizen is most often the normative ideal; in Germany and Mexico the ideal receives mention, but less often; and in Italy this ideal is least widespread.

Some illustrations may be useful in making explicit the specific areas of activity respondents had in mind:

A British Housewife:
"He should take some part in public life and have a say in town-planning, education, and religion."

An American Housewife:
"Everyone should take part in church and community affairs. . . . We should take an active part in making our schools better."

A Mexican Housewife:
"People should have diversion, but have enough free time to occupy themselves with political and social things."

A German Worker:
"Organizations should be formed that would enable [people] to discuss their problems together—for instance, parents' advisory councils [*Elternbeiräte*] at schools."

An Italian Teacher:
"Each individual should be interested in an active way and should criticize justly and severely when it is necessary."

An American Postmaster:
"A citizen should play an active part. . . . He might hold a local office. Other civic work such as drives, such as Red Cross. Here we have a volunteer fire company; he could help out with that."

The last quotation, from an American postmaster, suggests how the existence of structures in which one can participate affects the norms of participation that individuals hold. One would certainly not expect an individual to feel an obligation to participate in such activities as "drives," the Red Cross, and volunteer fire companies in communities where such activities were nonexistent.

One theme running through many of the answers that stress active participation in the local community—a theme found largely among activists in the United States and Britain—is that the individual ought to be active as a participant in decisions; that he ought, in a rather independent way, to take part in the running of the community:

An English Female Worker:
"Everyone should take a part. . . . They should get together and give opinions as to why and how this and that should be worked."
An American Housewife:
"I think a person should vote. If there are any town meetings he should attend them. . . . If everyone does things in his own small way, it would add up to something big. Many people sit back and let others do things for them, then complain."
A German Farmer:
"He should discuss politics, but shouldn't just accept everything, but [should] speak up too."

On the other hand, local activity means for some respondents more informal social participation, perhaps to help out one's neighbors:

A German Chauffeur:
"He should not just talk, but should act too. For instance, during hay harvesting time, one should not just stick his hands in his pockets and watch the farmers exerting themselves, but should pitch in. After all, it's a matter of community welfare."
An English Businessman:
"He should help in local organizations—children's clubs, boy scouts. He should help his neighbors and be a good living person."

A number of respondents, as shown in Table 2, thought of the individual as having a more passive sort of obligation to participate in his community; this usually involved some obligation to be informed of what is going on or to be interested in it:

A Mexican Housewife:
"[He should] be interested in how the government is formed, and be active by studying books and newspapers."
An English Housewife:
"He ought to know what is going on. Go to the occasional meeting to find out."
An Italian Worker:
"Simply be interested."

Though the degree of autonomy of local government differs from nation to nation, in all five nations there are elections for some sort of local or communal council. For many respondents, as Table 2 indicates, voting in these elections was considered a responsibility

173

of the individual to his community. But insofar as the individual considered his local responsibility to be exhausted by the act of voting, we have listed this as a relatively passive form of participation in community life—though a form of participation it certainly is. In some cases, particularly among those German respondents who mention voting as an obligation, this interpretation is made explicit. The responsibility to vote is explicitly stated as exhausting the individual's responsibility and, in fact, is invoked as an act that absolves one of all other community responsibilities:

An American Disabled Worker:
"I think they should do their part. Outside of voting there isn't too much the average fellow can do. . . . You ought to vote and then support any worthwhile thing your community is trying to do."

An Italian Veterinarian:
"What should an individual do? Elect his representatives. That's all."

A German Retired Worker:
"Choose a mayor at election time. That's all one need to do. The mayor takes care of everything."

A German House Painter:
"He should vote—that's the most important thing. But he should not be politically active himself."

A German Housewife:
"I don't understand that. We have to work. The people in the council are cleverer after all. They'll do a good job. You just have to vote for the right ones."

As was pointed out earlier, not all respondents think of the individual as having any outgoing responsibility within his local community. As Table 1 indicated, there were a substantial number of respondents in Germany and Mexico, and particularly in Italy, who admitted to no sense of local civic obligation. In this sense, the norms that they accept in relation to their community are certainly not those of the participating citizen. They are quite probably oriented to their communities as subjects or parochials. These can be found in all five nations, but they are most frequent in Italy (where 15 per cent of the respondents invoke these parochial values—a larger group than those who think the individual ought to be an active participant) and in Germany (where 11 per cent of the respondents talk of such parochial values). The following are some examples of the ways in which one's responsibility to the community is interpreted as an essentially parochial or subject responsibility to one's personal life:

An English Housewife:
"It's as much as my husband can do to go to work, never mind taking part in local affairs. We appoint councillors and leave everything to them."

A German Mechanic:
"Take care of one's family by working. Make one's children into decent people."

A German Farmer:
"I pay my taxes, go to my church, and do my work as a farmer."

A German Mechanic:
"Work and support one's family decently. If everyone did that, the state would have less trouble and expense."

A German Housewife:
"Everyone should do his work."

An Italian Worker:
"[He] should attend to his work . . . be a good citizen, and take care of [his] family."

An Italian Artisan:
"[He should be] honest and concerned about his work."

One important point about the relationship among civic, subject, and parochial norms is suggested by the data in Table 2. If the values of active participation are widespread in a country, this does not mean that the valuation of more passive participation is missing, or that subject and parochial values are missing. In the United States, for instance, where active participation is most frequently mentioned, the more passive political participation of voting is also frequently mentioned, as is participation in church and religious activities. And many respondents who mention active participation also mention the more parochial norms. This accords with our notion that the citizen role is built on but does not replace the roles of subject and parochial.

Our data clearly suggest sharp differences among the nations in the roles that respondents think individuals ought to play in their local communities. However, our data do not suggest that all those who think the individual ought to take an active part do in fact take such active roles. The gap between civic norms and civic behavior is, as we all know, large. As one American businessman who stressed the obligation to participate actively put it, "I'm saying what he ought to do, not what I do." We are not saying that one out of every two Americans is an active participant in the affairs of his local community or that four out of ten Britons are. Rather, we suggest that in these countries the norm of active citizenship is widespread. And this is congruent with the structure of government.

TABLE 3

Per Cent who say the Ordinary Man Should be Active in his Local Community, by Nation and Education

Nation	Total (%) (No.)*		Prim. or less (%) (No.)		Some Sec. (%) (No.)		Some Univ. (%) (No.)	
United States	51	(970)	35	(339)	56	(443)	66	(188)
Great Britain	39	(963)	37	(593)	42	(322)	42	(24)
Germany	22	(955)	21	(792)	32	(123)	38	(26)
Italy	10	(995)	7	(692)	17	(245)	22	(54)
Mexico	26	(1,007)	24	(877)	37	(103)	38	(24)

* Numbers in parentheses refer to the bases upon which percentages are calculated.

TABLE 4

Per Cent who say the Ordinary Man Should be Active in his Local Community, by Nation and Occupation of Family Breadwinner

Nation	Total (%) (No.)*		Unskilled (%) (No.)		Skilled (%) (No.)		White Collar (%) (No.)		Professional & Managerial (%) (No.)	
United States	51	(970)	34	(208)	52	(177)	59	(194)	73	(101)
Great Britain	39	(963)	31	(224)	43	(289)	50	(123)	42	(106)
Germany	12	(955)	18	(141)	20	(203)	31	(143)	33	(45)
Italy	10	(995)	8	(223)	6	(77)	24	(142)	14	(57)
Mexico	26	(1,007)	26	(120)	25	(294)	25	(148)	42	(59)

* Numbers in parentheses refer to the bases upon which percentages are calculated.

The actual opportunities to participate and the norms that one ought to participate mutually reinforce each other to foster a high level of citizen participation. In Italy, on the other hand, the relative lack of opportunity to participate in an autonomous local community is accompanied the absence of a set of norms favoring such participation.

Demographic Patterns

Who within each country hold to the ideal of the citizen as participant? The middle class? or those with higher education? As Table 3 indicates, in each of the five nations it is those with some higher education who are most likely to express adherence to the norms of participation; and the least likely to report that the individual has some responsibility to participate actively in his local community are those with primary school education or less.

TABLE 5

Per Cent who say the Ordinary Man Should be Active in his Local Community, by Nation and Sex

Nation	Total (%) (No.)*		Male (%) (No.)		Female (%) (No.)	
United States	51	(970)	52	(455)	50	(515)
Great Britain	39	(963)	43	(460)	36	(503)
Germany	22	(955)	31	(449)	16	(506)
Italy	10	(995)	14	(471)	6	(524)
Mexico	26	(1,007)	31	(355)	24	(652)

* Numbers in parentheses refer to the bases upon which percentages are calculated.

Nevertheless, despite the fact that the distribution of adherence to participatory norms is similar in the five nations, the differences in absolute levels of such expressed adherence are still great even within similar education groups. And within each educational group the relationship among the nations is roughly the same— American respondents tend most frequently to express adherence to such norms, followed by British, Mexican, German, and Italian respondents in that order. Furthermore, unlike some other variables, where the differences among nations tend to disappear when the all-important characteristic of education is controlled, differences still remain in the frequency of adherence to the norms of participation. In fact, a university-educated person in Germany or Mexico is no more likely to express adherence to these norms than is a primary-educated person in the United States or Britain; and the Italian university-educated respondent is less likely.

In regard to occupational groups (see Table 4), there is a tendency in the United States for the acceptance of the norm to be more general among those with higher-status occupations. In the other countries the relationship between occupation and belief in the

177

norm is relatively weak, but it does tend to be in the same direction. Thus in all countries, save Mexico, white-collar workers are more likely than unskilled or skilled workers to believe that the ordinary man should be an active participant in his local community.

Lastly, if one compares the sexes (see Table 5) in terms of the degree to which they hold participatory norms, it becomes clear that in all countries except the United States these norms are more frequently held by men than by women. Thus the extent to which the norms are widespread differs from nation to nation, but the patterns of who accepts the norms are the same in all the nations.

If a democratic political system is one in which the ordinary citizen participates in political decisions, a democratic political culture should consist of a set of beliefs, attitudes, norms, perceptions, and the like, that support participation. Of course, the frequency of adherence to this norm will be affected by the structures of the local community. But if the norm of participation is not widespread, institutional change in the direction of fostering participation will not in itself create a participatory democracy.

It is impossible to say what is the requisite level of participatory norms and of participation in political affairs for an effective democracy. Americans more often accept norms of participation than do individuals in the other four countries, yet they have often been accused of not being civic enough. But while our findings cannot tell us whether the level of participation in the United States or Britain is "good enough," they do tell us that it is certainly higher than in Germany, Mexico, and Italy. And as this and other data on participation will suggest, where norms of participation, perceived ability to participate, and actual participation are high, effective democracy is more likely to flourish.

That an individual believes he ought to participate in the political life of his community or nation does not mean that he will in fact do so. Before the norm that one ought to participate can be translated into the act itself, the individual will probably have to perceive that he is able to act. And though the two are related, they are by no means identical. One can believe he ought to participate, but perceive himself as unable to do so. Or one can perceive himself as able to participate but not feel any obligation to do so. Certainly a great source of political discontent is the acceptance of the norms of participation coupled with the belief that one cannot in fact participate. This, it has been suggested, is the danger of overselling the norms of political democracy in the schools. When the myth of democracy comes into serious conflict with the realities of politics, the results are cynicism. The society in which individuals do in fact participate in decisions—that is, the democratic society—is likely to be the society in which individuals believe they ought to participate. It is also likely to be the society in which they think they can participate and know how to go about it. It is to these questions of subjective civic competence that we now turn.

CHAPTER 7

THE SENSE OF CIVIC COMPETENCE

DEMOCRACY is a political system in which ordinary citizens exercise control over elites; and such control is legitimate, that is, supported by norms that are accepted by elites and nonelites. In all societies, of course, the making of specific decisions is concentrated in the hands of very few people. Neither the ordinary citizen nor "public opinion" can make policy. If this is the case, the problem of assessing the degree of democracy in a nation becomes one of measuring the degree to which ordinary citizens control those who make the significant decisions for a society—in most cases, governmental elites.

Recent work on the theory of influence suggests that there are numerous means by which interpersonal influence can be exerted, and that it makes a difference which means are used. In this chapter we shall be concerned with a particular type of influence that non-elites may exert on elites: a type that we label *political* influence. We shall roughly define the political influence of a group or individual over a governmental decision as equal to the degree to which governmental officials act to benefit that group or individual because the officials believe that they will risk some deprivation (they will risk their jobs, be criticized, lose votes) if they do not so act. Thus we define political influence in terms of both the outcome of the decision and the motives of the decision makers. The outcome will benefit the influential groups or individuals more than it would if the influence were not exercised. And the decision makers act to benefit the groups or individuals because they believe they will suffer some deprivation or, what amounts to the same thing, fail to gain a reward. The latter criterion is important. Officials may act to benefit a particular group for a variety of reasons: out of a feeling of paternalism, for instance. But it is only when officials act because they fear the consequences of not acting that a group

180

may be considered to be politically influential and a participant in the decision.[1] If the individual can exert such influence, we shall consider him to be *politically competent;* or if he *believes* he can exert such influence, he will be *subjectively competent.*

So far we have defined political influence in terms of the way in which governmental elites make decisions. Our study, however, concentrates upon the perceptions and behaviors, not of governmental elites, but of the ordinary citizen. We are concerned with the ordinary man's perception of his own influence. Thinking that one can influence the government or even attempting to influence government is not the same as actually influencing it. A citizen may think he has influence over decisions, or he may attempt to exert influence over decisions, and the government official may be unmoved. Conversely, a citizen may believe that all government decisions are made without any consideration of his needs and desires or of the needs and desires of his fellow citizens, when, in fact, government officials constantly try to calculate the way groups will react to their acts.

If the degree to which citizens believe they can influence the course of governmental decisions is not necessarily related to their actual level of influence, why study their subjective views of their competence? In the first place, we are interested in the state of attitudes in a country. If democracy involves high levels of actual participation in decisions, then the attitudes of a democratic citizenry should include the perception that they in fact can participate. A democratic citizen speaks the language of demands. Government officials accede to his demands because they fear some loss otherwise—the loss of his vote perhaps—or because they consider it legitimate that he make such demands. The subject, too, may want and expect beneficial outputs from the government. But he does not expect these to be accorded him because he demands them. The government official who acts to benefit him responds, not to the subject's demands, but to some other force. In a tra-

[1] This model represents, of course, a great oversimplification. If one were studying the "real" influence situation, rather than the ordinary man's perception of that situation, one would have to complicate things quite a bit. Government officials respond to many different groups for many different reasons. Furthermore, even where democratic political influence by the populace exists, the government official will have reciprocal influence, and this leads to a complex bargaining situation. Since we are not studying the "real" influence situation, however, such complications are not necessary; nor are we forced to ask which citizens exert influence over which officials in relation to which issues.

ditional society with a highly developed set of norms as to what is due each member, the government official may be responding to these traditional rules when he acts in favor of an individual. Or in an authoritarian-legalistic political system in which the behavior of government officials is circumscribed by explicit rules, he may act as he does because the individual falls within a particular category, which, according to the rules, is to receive a certain type of treatment. In these situations the official is not acting capriciously. His decision to aid the individual is determined by a set of social or legal rules. And these rules may, of course, be enforced by an administrative hierarchy to which the subject may appeal. This kind of subject influence, or administrative competence, is more circumscribed, more passive than that of the citizen. It may set in motion an action that will affect the way in which a rule is interpreted or enforced against an individual. It is not a creative act of influence that can affect the content of the decisions themselves, except in an indirect way.

Second, the perception of the ability to exert political influence is significant even if individuals rarely try to use that influence, or are frequently unsuccessful when they do try. Much of the influence that our respondents believe they have over government probably represents a somewhat unrealistic belief in their opportunities to participate. It is likely that many who say they could influence the government would never attempt to exert such influence; and it is likely as well that if they tried they would not succeed. Yet such a belief in the ordinary man's ability to participate may have significant consequences for a political system. Though individuals' perceptions of their own political ability may not mirror the objective situation, it cannot be unrelated to that situation. If an individual believes he has influence, he is more likely to attempt to use it.[2] A subjectively competent citizen, therefore, is more likely to be an active citizen. And if government officials do not necessarily respond to active influence attempts, they are more likely to respond to them than to a passive citizenry that makes no demands. If the ordinary citizen, on the other hand, perceives that government policy is far outside his sphere of influence, he is unlikely to attempt to influence that policy, and government officials are unlikely to worry about the potential

[2] Evidence that those who believe they can influence are more likely to have actual experience in attempting to do so will be presented below, in Table 3.

182

pressure that can be brought to bear on them. Thus the extent to which citizens in a nation perceive themselves as competent to influence the government affects their political behavior.

Furthermore, the existence of a belief in the influence potential of citizens may affect the political system even if it does not affect the political activity of the ordinary man. If decision makers believe that the ordinary man *could* participate—and they certainly are not entirely cut off from the dominant social beliefs—they are likely to behave quite differently than if such a belief did not exist. Even if individuals do not act according to this belief, decision makers may act on the assumption that they can, and in this way be more responsive to the citizenry than they would be if the myth of participation did not exist. But whether myth or reality (and the statements we shall be talking about are probably a combination of both), the extent to which individuals think they can influence the government and the ways in which they believe they can do so are as we shall discuss further in Chapter 15, important elements of the civic culture.

In this chapter we are concerned with the perceptions that individuals have about the amount of influence they can exercise over governmental decisions. Several questions may be asked about their attempts to influence the government:

1. Under what circumstances will an individual make some conscious effort to influence the government? Direct political influence attempts are rare. For the ordinary citizen the activities of government—even local government—may seem quite distant. At the time that a decision is being made, the citizen is not aware that it is being made or of what its consequences for him are likely to be. It is probable, then, that only in situations of some stress, where a government activity is perceived to have a direct and serious impact upon the individual, will a direct influence attempt be stimulated.

2. What method will be used in the influence attempt? Some major dimensions in this respect include: the kinds of channels of influence that are used; whether the attempt is violent or nonviolent; and whether the individual attempts to influence the government alone or attempts to enlist the support of others.

3. What is the effect of the influence attempt? The extent to which the government official changes his behavior in response to some influence attempt by a citizen is a problem beyond the scope

of our study. However, since we are concentrating on the perspective of the citizen, we shall consider his view of the likelihood that an attempt made by him to influence the government will have any effect.

The Distribution of Subjective Competence

In developing our survey instrument, we took into account the fact that direct attempts to influence the government are more likely to arise in some stress situation, where an individual perceives that an activity of the government is threatening injury to him. Our questions attempted to place the individual in such a hypothetical stress situation, so that we could ascertain how he thought he would react. We asked him to suppose that his local government or his national legislature was considering a law that he thought was very unjust and harmful. What did he think he could do about it? If the respondent thought he could do something, we probed to find out what it was. We then asked him how much effect he thought any action he took would have, and how likely it was that he actually would do something. A similar set of questions was asked about an unjust and harmful regulation being considered by the most local governmental unit.[3] These questions were about the political branches of the government, the elected governments on the national and local levels. Through these questions we hoped to get some notion of the respondent's views on the extent of his political competence and, more important, on the strategy of influence open to him.

The results for these questions on local and national subjective competence are reported in Table 1. Two points call for comment. First, in all five countries the sense of subjective competence occurs

[3] The exact wording of these questions was:
On the national government—
Suppose a law were being considered by [appropriate national legislature specified for each nation] that you considered to be unjust or harmful. What do you think you could do?
If you made an effort to change this law, how likely is it that you would succeed?
If such a case arose, how likely is it you *would actually* try to do something about it?
On the local government—
Suppose a regulation were being considered by [most local governmental unit: town? village? etc. specified] that you considered very unjust or harmful. What do you think you could do?
If you made an effort to change this regulation, how likely is it that you would succeed?
If such a case arose, how likely is it that you *would actually* do something about it?

more frequently vis-à-vis the local government than the national government. This confirms widely-held views of the closer relatedness of citizens to their local governments because of their greater immediacy, accessibility, and familiarity. American and British respondents most frequently say that there is something they can do about an unjust local regulation. More than three-quarters of those we interviewed in each of the two countries expressed the opinion that they have some recourse if they believe the local government is considering a law they think unjust; only 17 per cent say that there is nothing they can do. In the other three countries over 30 per

TABLE 1

Per Cent who say they Can Do Something about an Unjust Local or
National Regulation, by Nation
(in per cent)*

Nation	Can Do Something about Local Regulation	Can Do Something about National Regulation
United States	77	75
Great Britain	78	62
Germany	62	38
Italy	51	28
Mexico	52	38

* Percentages in each case are of total sample.

cent of those interviewed report that there is nothing they can do in such a situation.[4]

The second point brought out in Table 1 is that, although in all five countries the proportion that says it can influence the local government is higher than the proportion expressing national competence, this difference is relatively small in the American, British, and Mexican samples, and relatively large in Germany and Italy. Put briefly, three-fourths of the American respondents express local and national competence; more than three-fourths and a little less than two-thirds of the British respondents express local and

[4] Many respondents make it quite clear that they believe there is nothing they can do, either because they consider themselves too powerless or because they consider government activities outside their sphere of competence. The following are some examples of these responses:

A German Housewife: "Nothing at all. The local council makes its decision, and there is nothing one can do about it."

A German Housewife: "I'd say nothing because I don't understand it, and I wouldn't do it right, anyway."

An American Semiretired: "Nothing. That's all because we put our trust in our

national competence, respectively. In Germany almost two-thirds of the respondents express local competence, while only a little more than one-third express national competence. In Italy the proportion drops from one-half to less than one-third. And in Mexico the proportion declines from a little more than one-half to a little more than one-third. The generalization about the greater sense of competence vis-à-vis the local government holds up in our findings, but it is most apparent in Italy and Germany.

The sense of ability to influence the government on both levels is

TABLE 2
Levels of Subjective Civic Competence, by Nation
(in per cent)

Per Cent who report	U.S.	U.K.	Germany	Italy	Mexico
National and local competence	67	57	33	25	33
National competence only	8	5	4	2	5
Local competence only	10	21	29	26	19
Neither national nor local competence	15	19	34	47	43
Total per cent	100	100	100	100	100
Total number of cases	970	963	955	955	1,007

summarized in Table 2. In that table we have divided the respondents in each country into four groups: (1) those who say they can influence both local and national governments; (2) those who express national competence only; (3) those who express local competence only, and (4) those who express neither form of competence. In the United States more than two-thirds of the respondents say they can influence both levels of government, and only 15 per cent say they can influence neither level. In Britain more than half say they can influence national and local government, but the percentage saying they can influence local government only or neither governmental level is higher than in the United States. In Germany only one-third of the respondents con-

elected people and we must feel they know more about these things than we do even though we don't always agree."
    An American Housewife: "Not anything. No 'mam' not nothing . . . Nothing at all."
    A British Retired Office Worker: "I wouldn't have much chance to do anything, being just one insignificant person."
    An Italian Housewife: "What do you want me to do? I don't count for anything."
    A Mexican Housewife: "Nothing. I have no one with whom to talk. I wouldn't know what to do in such a case."

sider themselves generally competent, and another third fall into the incompetent category. In Italy the percentage that considers itself incompetent at the local and national levels is twice as large (47 per cent) as the percentage showing both types of competence (25 per cent). Mexico falls midway between the German and Italian distributions, with 33 per cent competent at both levels and 43 per cent competent at neither.

That an individual is subjectively competent does not mean that he will in fact try to change what he considers an unfair law. Ours was a hypothetical situation, and we do not really know what our respondents would do if they ever were actually faced with such a challenging situation. But we did ask them for their opinions on whether or not they thought they would act. In all countries many who say they can do something about an unjust regulation report that in fact they probably would do nothing. But the number who report that there is at least some likelihood that they would make an effort reflects the same national pattern reported above. If we consider the responses about the local government (the responses about the national government form the same pattern), we find that 58 per cent of the American respondents and 50 per cent of those in Britain say there is some likelihood that they would actually make an effort to influence an unjust regulation. In Germany 44 per cent and in Italy 41 per cent make some such affirmation. (The question was, unfortunately, not asked in a comparable form in Mexico.)

Lastly, there is some evidence that the subjective estimate of one's propensity to act in this challenging political situation is closely related to actual attempts to influence the government. In all five nations a substantially larger proportion of those respondents who say there is something they can do about an unjust local regulation (let us, for convenience, call them "local competents") report some experience in attempting to influence the local government. (We find the same pattern in the national data.) These data are reported in Table 3. In all nations those who say they could influence the local government, in comparison with those who say they could not, are at least three times as likely to have attempted such influence.

Thus the sense of local and national civic competence is widely distributed among the American and British populations. In

Germany and Italy local competence is widely distributed, while this is much less the case with national competence. In Mexico, while the general level of civic competence is lower than in the United States and Britain, the discrepancy between the local and national level (as reported in Table 1) is less great than in Germany and Italy. It also appears that there is a relation between subjective competence and political action.

Local competence and national competence are, as one would expect, fairly closely related. The man who believes he can in-

TABLE 3

Per Cent who say they Have Attempted to Influence the Local Government, by Local Competents and Local Noncompetents

Nation	Local Competents		Local Noncompetents	
	(%)	(No.)*	(%)	(No.)
United States	33	(745)	10	(225)
Great Britain	18	(748)	3	(215)
Germany	21	(590)	2	(365)
Italy	13	(508)	4	(487)
Mexico	9	(531)	2	(476)

* Numbers in parentheses refer to the bases upon which percentages are calculated.

fluence the national government is more likely to think he can influence the local government than is the man who does not feel competent on the national level. Conversely, the man who feels competent locally is also more likely to believe he can influence the national government than is the man who does not have a sense of local competence. Earlier it was pointed out that local competence is more widespread than national competence. Furthermore, local competence is most widely distributed in those nations where local government autonomy and the accessibility of local government officials to ordinary citizens is most firmly institutionalized (see Chapter 6). Adding these three facts together—local and national competence are related, local competence is more widespread than national, and local competence is related to the institutional availability of opportunities to participate on the local level—one has an argument in favor of the classic position that political participation on the local level plays a major role in the development of a competent citizenry. As many writers have argued, local government may act as a training ground for political competence. Where local government allows participation, it may foster a sense of competence that then spreads to the national level—a sense of competence that would have had a harder time developing had the individual's only involvement with government been with the more distant and inaccessible structures of the national government. To argue this point is to speculate beyond our data on national and local competence. But in a later chapter we shall present data to the effect that the individual's belief in his ability to affect the government derives, at least in part, from opportunities to be influential within smaller authority structures such as the family, the school, and the place of work.[5]

The Strategy of Influence

Another aspect of political competence is the strategy an individual would use in attempting to influence the government. The *way* in which those who report that they could influence the government report they could exert this influence is, of course, important. It makes a difference whether someone has only the vaguest notion of what he can do, or a clear view of the channels open to him for expressing his point of view. It also makes a difference what resources he believes he has available to use. Furthermore, the strategy that an individual would use will naturally affect the extent to which his subjective view of his ability to influence represents real influence potential—that is, represents the sort of activity that has some chance of changing the behavior of the government officials. We shall deal primarily with those who think they have influence, the "competents," and ask how they would exert that influence.

The strategies of influence that individuals report they would use in connection with the local government are summarized in Table 4. (Comparable data on the national government will be presented below.) Let us look first at the question of what social resources the individual feels he has available to him. This is highly significant for understanding the nature of his perceived relationship to his government. Government organizations are large and powerful, especially when compared to the individual. This is especially true of the national government, but even local government represents an institution whose resources are much greater than those of the ordinary man. Looking at the individual and his

[5] See below, chap. 12.

government, one is tempted to see him as lonely, powerless, and somewhat frightened by the immensity of the powers he faces. This is in fact one of the most frequent descriptions of the average man in modern political societies. In the theory of the "mass society" the individual is described as related directly as individual to the state. He has no other social resources to support him in this relationship and naturally feels ineffective and anxious.[6] However valid this theory may be in terms of the actual amount of power the average man has and the social resources available to him, our data suggest that a large number of our respondents do not view themselves as the model of mass society describes them. In their relationship to their government they think of themselves as neither powerless nor, what is more important, alone.

This fact is reflected in the data reported in Table 4. A number of our respondents believe that they can enlist the support of others in their attempts to influence the government. What is most striking is the variation from country to country in the numbers who feel they can call on others to aid them. In the United States 59 per cent of our respondents indicated that they could attempt to enlist the support of others if they wished to change a regulation they considered unjust. At the other extreme, only 9 per cent of the Italians mentioned the use of this social resource. In the other countries the proportions reporting that they would try to enlist the support of others varied from 36 per cent in Britain, to 28 per cent in Mexico, to 21 per cent in Germany.[7]

Whom would citizens enlist to support them? Individuals as we know are members of a large number of social groups. They are not merely citizens of their nations; they are members of families, communities, churches, voluntary associations, trade unions, and a great variety of other groups and organizations. Basically these associations can be divided into two classes: formal organizations and informal face-to-face groups.

Much has been written about the important role of formal organizations in the political process—especially the role of politi-

[6] On this general topic see William Kornhauser, *The Politics of Mass Society*, Glencoe, Ill., 1959.

[7] Since question wording can seriously affect the response received, it is important to note here that the notion that one could enlist the support of others was in no way suggested by the question or by the interviewer's probing of the question. Interviewers were carefully instructed not to ask such questions as: "Is there anyone you could get to help you?" or "Would you attempt to do this alone or with other people?"

cal parties and associational interest groups. Both play major intervening roles between the individual and his government. They aggregate the demands of citizens and communicate these to government officials. Recently there has been growing interest in the informal face-to-face network of social groups to which an individual belongs—family, friends, work group, and neighbors. Here

TABLE 4

What Citizens Would Do to try to Influence their Local Government, by Nation
(in per cent)

What Citizens Would Do	U.S.	U.K.	Germany	Italy	Mexico
TRY TO ENLIST AID OF OTHERS					
Organize an informal group; arouse friends and neighbors, get them to write letters of protest or to sign a petition	56	34	13	7	26
Work through a political party	1	1	3	1	–
Work through a formal group (union, church, professional) to which they belong	4	3	5	1	2
Total per cent who would enlist others' aid[a]	59	36	21	9	28
ACT ALONE					
Directly contact political leaders (elected officials) or the press; write a letter to or visit a local political leader	20	45	15	12	15
Directly contact administrative (nonelected) officials	1	3	31	12	18
Consult a lawyer; appeal through courts	2	1	3	2	2
Vote against offending officials at next election	14	4	1	1	–
Take some violent action	1	1	1	1	1
Just protest	–	–	–	12	–
Other	1	2	–	3	5
Total per cent who would act alone[b]	18	41	41	43	24
Total per cent who would act with others or alone	77	78	62	51	53
Total number of respondents	970	963	955	995	1,007

[a] Total percentages are less than the total of the individual cells, since some respondents gave more than one answer.

[b] This row includes only the respondents who replied that they could do something but did not mention working with others. Hence the total is less than the sum of the individual cells, which contain respondents who may have mentioned both group and individual activity.

the main emphasis has been upon the impact of these groups on the political attitudes of their members, and on the process of communication downward: that is, to the individuals from such formal institutions as government, political parties, and the mass media.[8] Little has been said about the role of such informal associations in what we might call the "influence-upward" process: the process by which citizens in a democracy influence the attitudes and behavior of government officials. But our findings show most strikingly that, when it comes to the support that individuals believe they could enlist in a challenging political situation, they think much more often of enlisting support from the informal face-to-face groups of which they are members than from the formal organizations to which they belong or with which they are affiliated. In all countries except Germany, less than one per cent of the respondents indicate that they would work through their political party if they were attempting to counteract some unjust regulation being considered by the local government; the German figure is about three per cent. Clearly, no matter how important the role of political parties may be in democratic societies, relatively few citizens think of them first as the place where support may be enlisted for attempts to influence the government.[9]

In all countries more individuals report that they would attempt to work through other formal organized groups than through political parties. But when one considers the entire range of formal organizations to which people may belong, the number who report they would enlist their support is small: no more than five per cent of the respondents in any country. Of course, not all respondents have some formal organization at their disposal; such organizations are more frequent in some nations than in others. And the percentage who report membership differs substantially from country to country. Furthermore, not all formal organizations are equally politically relevant.

But even among those respondents who belong to a formal organization that they report is involved in politics, the number

[8] On the subject of the political functions of informal groups, see Sidney Verba, *Small Groups and Political Behavior*, Princeton, N. J., 1961, chap. 2.

[9] To some extent the infrequent mention of a political party in this context probably understates the role of parties in this influence process. Many more respondents mentioned contacting government officials. If they explicitly mentioned that the partisan affiliation of the official was relevant in their attaining access to him, they would be coded as working through a party. But many may have considered this affiliation relevant even if they did not mention it.

192

who would invoke such membership in a stress situation is much smaller than the number who are members. In the United States, where such memberships are most frequent, 228 respondents report membership in this kind of organization, but only 35 of these Americans report that they would work through that organization if they were trying to influence a local regulation. In Italy, where such memberships are least frequent, we find the same pattern. Fifty-six Italians belong to some organization they believe is involved in political affairs, but only thirteen of those members would work through it if they were trying to influence a local regulation. The aid of a formal organization would be called upon most frequently in Germany, but only half as frequently as the occurrence of membership in a politically relevant organization.

That formal organizations would be rarely invoked by individuals who were trying to influence the government does not mean, however, that these organizations are politically unimportant. They still may effect an individual's political influence, for he may have more influence over government officials merely by being a member of such a group, even if he makes no overt attempt to influence the government. And this sort of influence is of great significance—probably of greater overall significance than the overt influence attempts that ordinary citizens make from time to time. Furthermore, though an individual would not use his formal organization as the means to influence the government directly, his membership in itself enhances the prospects that he will believe himself capable of influencing the government and will actually make some such attempt. Thus he may, for a variety of reasons to be discussed below, develop greater self-confidence in his own political competence.[10]

Cooperative Political Behavior. As Table 4 indicates, in all nations respondents less frequently mention enlisting the support of formal groups than informal groups—arousing their neighbors, getting friends and acquaintances to support their position, circulating a petition. This in itself is striking, though it ought not, for reasons given above, to be taken to imply that these informal groups play a more significant role in the political process than do formal organizations. What is most striking is not the frequency with which informal groups are mentioned in all countries, but the sharp differences in frequency among the nations.

[10] See below, Chap. 11, for a discussion of the impact of voluntary associations.

Thus Table 5 shows that 56 per cent of the American respondents, 34 per cent of the British, and 26 per cent of the Mexicans reported that they would use this informal group strategy, as compared with 13 per cent of the Germans and 7 per cent of the Italians. If we consider the proportion of local competents who say they would cooperate with their fellow citizens in attempting to influence the government,[11] we find that 74 per cent of American local competents would use informal groups, whereas only 13 per cent of Italian local competents and 22 per cent of the Germans would do so. In Mexico,

TABLE 5

Those who would Enlist the Aid of an Informal Group
to Influence an Unjust Local Regulation

Nation	Percentage of Total Sample (%) (No.)*		Percentage of Local Competents (%) (No.)	
United States	56	(970)	74	(745)
Great Britain	34	(963)	43	(748)
Germany	13	(955)	22	(590)
Italy	7	(995)	13	(508)
Mexico	26	(1,007)	50	(531)

* Numbers in parentheses refer to the bases upon which percentages are calculated.

though the proportion of local competents is relatively low, the proportion of those local competents who would work through informal groups is quite high—50 per cent. And in Britain the proportion of local competents who say they would seek the cooperation of others is about as great—43 per cent.

The notions that one can cooperate with one's fellow citizens in attempting to influence the government and that such cooperation is an effective means of increasing one's own influence dominate the bulk of the responses of the local competents in the United States and play an important role in responses in Britain and Mexico. In all five countries, however, there are individuals who would work

[11] The percentage of respondents mentioning a particular strategy of influence can be computed either as a percentage of the entire population or as a percentage of the local competents only. Both figures are important. The first figure reflects the propensity for certain types of political behavior in a nation. But if we are interested in how nations differ in the strategies their citizens will use, we must use the second figure; for if we did not, the national differences in the percentage choosing a particular strategy might reflect merely that there are more in one country than in another who report that there is nothing they could do. In the following tables the percentages will be reported in both forms.

with others in attempting to influence the government. A few illustrations may help to convey that attitude:

An American Office Manager:
"You can't do anything individually. You'd have to get a group and all get together and go to the proper authorities to complain."

An American Salesman:
"Get up a petition. Get together with people who have the same objection. Taking it up with the responsible person like the mayor or police commissioner."

An American Housemaid:
"I could discuss it with others and see how many others felt the same about it as I did. We could then write a letter each to some government person in charge and let him know how we felt, or we could write one letter and get a lot of people to sign it."

An American Nurse:
"My main interest is my church . . . just about the only thing I do outside my work . . . and I wouldn't personally have much influence in politics. But I believe that if I thought anything was really harmful, a good many other people in my church would too, and I believe we could work together to do what we thought was right."

An English Coal Merchant:
"[You could do] little or nothing. Things are too much cut and dried beforehand. You have no chance, especially if you're on your own. I'd join up with other people."

An English Dispatch Clerk:
"Contact neighbors and friends and make a protest to the councillors. . . ."

An English Foreman Gardener:
"First thing—get a petition going. Take it up to the Council offices and make yourself spokesman of a group. You could try the local M.P."

An English House Painter:
"You could more or less get a petition up and show the feeling. You could discuss it with your workmates and your wife."

A Mexican Shoemaker:
"Protest, join a group of citizens, and personally go to the office where it was issued and talk about it to the authorities."

A Mexican Workman:
"I would form a group or would join a union to fight politically against the municipal government."

A Mexican Housewife:
"I would get together all the people and send a petition to the president or the governor of the state signed by all."

A Mexican Bricklayer:
"Protest with other people. . . ."

A German Teacher:
"I could petition, protest, collect signatures."

An English Retired Painter:
"Organize a petition to call a meeting."

A German Policeman:
"As an individual, one can't do anything at all. One could only get together with others who are of the same mind and consult about what to do. Then one could write a letter of complaint to the city administration."

A Retired Italian:
"Promote an action of protest together with citizens who, like me, were harmed by the decision of the administration."

A Retired Italian:
"I would protest through the administration, or, if necessary, by demonstrating with a group of people."

In a democratic political system, the belief that cooperation with one's fellow citizens is both a possible and an effective political action represents, we suggest, a highly significant orientation. The diffusion of influence over political decisions, by which we define democracy, implies some cooperative ability among the citizenry. This cooperation seems to be necessary, in terms of both the amount of influence the ordinary man can expect to have and the results of his influence on governmental decisions. By definition, the "average" man's influence over the government must be small. Compared with the forces of government—and this would apply to local as well as national government—he is a frail creature indeed. If the ordinary man is to have any political influence, it must be in concert with his fellows. Second, from the point of view of the output of a democratic government, noncooperative and completely individualistic influence attempts could lead only to dysfunctional results. Every individual demand cannot be met, or the result will be chaos. If the government is to be responsive to the demands of the ordinary man, these demands must be aggregated, and the aggregation of interests implies cooperation among men. The aggregation of interests involved in the cooperation of groups of like-minded individuals is aggregation on a rather low level, but it does suggest a propensity to work together with one's fellows, which is relevant for larger political structures as well. In any case, we may suggest that

196

the citizen who believes he can work cooperatively with others in his environment if he wants to engage in political activity has quite a different perspective on politics from the individual who thinks of himself as a lone political actor.

Furthermore, the notion that one can affect a government decision by bringing one's peers into the dispute is a highly political notion. It represents a fairly clear attempt to use political influence in one's relations with government officials. The threat that *many* make—whether it be the threatened loss of votes or of support, or the threat of public criticism—is, other things being equal, greater than the threat that *one* can make. Thus the individual who mentions getting others to join him in his dispute with the government is more likely to see himself as a citizen able to influence his government than as a subject who lacks such influence. And the variations among the five nations in the frequency with which such groups are mentioned reflect variations in such citizen competence.

It is particularly important to note what sorts of groups are involved here. The informal groups our respondents talk of forming do not exist, at least in a politically relevant sense, before the political stress situation arises. The individual perceives himself as able to create structures for the purposes of influencing the government. Those structures represent a form of influence that had not been committed to politics before the politically challenging situation arose. In this sense, the ability of the individual to create structures to aid him in his disputes with the government represents a reserve of influence on his part. He has not committed his complete support to some larger social system, as has the individual in the so-called mass society; nor is he cut off from contact with the government, as is the parochial.

That a large proportion of people in a country perceive that the informal face-to-face groups of which they are members can be rallied to their support in time of political stress represents a significant aspect of the political culture of that nation. It means that some of the most basic building blocks of the social structure have been incorporated into the political system. An individual's role as citizen, particularly as a democratic, influential citizen, fuses with his other social roles. The type of political activity sparking this fusion of informal group membership and political citizenship is also highly significant. The fusion takes place because of political demands being made by citizens upon their government. They invoke their friends and neighbors in an attempt to influence their government. Thus the fusion occurs at the heart of the democratic process—the process by which the ordinary citizen exercises some control over his government. This is profoundly different from the fusion between face-to-face groups and government that has been attempted within totalitarian states. Here the government has attempted to influence the individual: family and friendship groups are penetrated by the state to support its attempts to propagandize and control. The state attempts to control these informal groups. In the countries we studied the invocation of informal groups has a contrary meaning. It is an attempt to penetrate and control government. It represents a meshing together of polity and community, rather than an assimilation of community into the polity.

Lastly, we have stressed the importance of this propensity toward cooperation with one's fellow citizens, not merely because we believe that it has significant consequences for the political system, but because we feel it is a type of behavior that can best be understood and explained by the type of study contained in this book. In the first place, the frequency with which individuals talk of cooperating with their fellow citizens to influence the government is not as dependent upon the structure of government as is the frequency with which they say they can influence the government. Whether or not someone feels he can affect the course of government action obviously depends to a large extent upon the structure of government —the extent to which it provides citizen access. But the difference between the individual who responds that he would write a letter to the local council and the one who responds that he would write a letter to the local council *and try to induce his friends to do likewise* cannot be explained by national differences in the structure and powers of their respective local councils.[12] As we shall see

[12] This is not completely true. Governmental structure may be more amenable to group influence in some countries than in others. But this is more likely to occur because of the government's past experience with such groups than because of the government's formal structure. On the other hand, there is no doubt that certain structures of government foster such "banding together" protests more than do others. Structures where power is diffused among a large number of autonomous or semi-autonomous boards and councils and the like (especially elected boards and councils) are more likely to foster such protest than are structures dominated by a centrally appointed official whose domain includes a larger area (as with the Italian prefect system). But this is an example of the general proposition that interaction will occur between political orientation and political structure. In this case, however, to explain the origins of this group-forming attitude in terms of formal political structure alone would be unconvincing. One has to look beyond the structure of the local government. There is, however, another way in which governmental structure may foster or

shortly, these differing levels of social and economic development, while they can explain many of the political differences among the nations, cannot explain the propensity to cooperate politically. The origin of this propensity must be sought elsewhere. In a later chapter we shall try to trace it to social values and attitudes and to the degree of partisan fragmentation in society.[13]

Though the use of primary groups as a resource for influence is most common in the United States, Britain, and Mexico, there are several interesting differences between the United States and Britain on the one hand and Mexico on the other. The notion that one can mobilize an informal group as an aid in attempting to influence the government appears to be of greater significance for the actual exercise of influence in the former two countries. Earlier it was pointed out that those who report they can do something about an unjust local law (the local competents), compared with those who report the opposite, are much more likely to report some experience in attempting to influence the government. If we look only at the local competents and ask how those who would work through groups and those who would act alone differ in the extent of their experience in attempted local influence, we find that in the United States and Britain those who would work through groups are more likely to have had experience in these endeavors. In the United States 36 per cent of those who report they would work through informal groups (n: 547) also report that they have at some time actually attempted to influence the government, whereas only 25 per cent of those local competents who would use some other strategy (n: 198) report such experience. In Britain the parallel figures are 23 per cent for those who mention informal groups (n: 315) and 15 per cent for other local competents (n: 414). In Mexico, on the other hand, those who mention informal groups are a bit less likely to

---

inhibit the group forming propensities of a population. The legal systems of nations differ in the extent to which they ban, regulate, or in other ways make difficult the formation of non-governmental associations. Legal systems on the European continent have been more hostile to such groups than has the Anglo-American legal system. And though these regulations refer largely to formal organizations (to be discussed in Chapter 11, below), they might have an effect on informal groups as well. See on this point, Arnold Rose, "On Individualism and Social Responsibility," *Archives Européennes de Sociologie*, II (1961), pp. 163-69.

[13] The relationship between social and economic development and the propensity to form groups will be discussed at the end of the chapter. The explanation of this group-forming propensity in terms of social values and partisan fragmentation will be attempted in chapter 10.

be the experienced respondents: 7 per cent of those who mention informal groups (n: 264) report experience, as against 10 per cent of the other local competents (n: 267).[14]

Furthermore, in the former two countries the use of informal groups as a means of influencing the government is seen, not only as a means to protest, but as the key to effective protest. In order to test the extent to which individuals felt they could influence their local government, we asked another question after asking what respondents thought they could do about an unjust local law: "If you made an effort to change this regulation, how likely is it that you would succeed?" Of interest to us here is that a large number of American and British local competents volunteered the statement that their protest would have some likelihood of success only if others joined with them. (The percentages were 30 per cent in the United States and 20 per cent in Britain.) In Mexico, though a good percentage felt there was some likelihood that they would succeed if they attempted to influence their local government, fewer than one per cent of the respondents suggested that this would be the case only if they had the support of others. Though the use of informal groups is perceived as a means of influence in Mexico, it is not yet perceived as the key to effective influence.[15]

One further difference deserves mention. In the United States and Britain the use of informal groups as a means of influencing a governmental decision is considered much more appropriate on the local level than on the national level. In the United States 73 per cent of the local competents report that they would work through informal groups in attempting to influence the local government, whereas only 38 per cent of the national competents (i.e., those who believe they could do something if the national government were considering a law they thought unjust) would work through such groups. In Britain, similarly, 43 per cent of the local competents would work through informal groups, while only 28 per cent of the national competents would do so. In Mexico, on the other hand, the proportion of local and national competents who

[14] In Germany those local competents who mention informal groups are somewhat less likely to have had actual influence experience. Seventeen per cent of those who mention informal groups (n. 126) report past experience, as against 23 per cent of local competents who do not mention them (n. 460). In Italy those local competents who mention groups are somewhat more likely to be experienced: 16 per cent (n. 67), as against 13 per cent (n. 438) of those who do not mention groups.
[15] In Germany the percentage of local competents who mentioned that they would succeed only if others joined them was 12; in Italy it was 5.

would use informal groups is about the same—50 per cent of local competents would use this means to influence the local government, and 46 per cent of national competents say this is how they would try to influence the national government. The fact that in Britain and the United States, more than in Mexico, the use of such groups is closely related both to experience and to expectations of success, coupled with the fact that such strategy is considered more appropriate in connection with the local government in the former two countries, suggests that informal group strategy is based on a more realistic appraisal of the potentialities of such a strategy—a realistic appraisal deriving from actual experience with such groups on the local level. In Mexico this influence strategy is less well grounded in actual local experience. It appears to be another instance of the aspirational character of the Mexican political culture.

Individual Action. The respondents who spoke of themselves as acting alone in their attempt to influence the government show some variation, as Table 5 indicates, in the strategies they mention. In the United States and Britain respondents are more likely to say they would approach an elected government official rather than an appointed official of the bureaucracy. In Mexico and Italy respondents are as likely to say they would direct their protest toward one type of official as toward the other. In Germany, however, more respondents mention appointed officials than elected officials as the target of their protest. It is tempting to consider these results to be a reflection of a more highly developed political competence in the United States and Britain. A protest to an elected official seems to be inherently more of a political protest, in the sense of involving an implied threat of deprivation to the official if he does not comply —for the loss of the vote is the most usual deprivation with which the individual can threaten an offending official. This may partly explain the differences among the nations in the chosen targets of influence attempts; but it is more likely that these differences merely reflect national differences in the relative position and importance of elected and appointed officials within the structures of local government.

Lastly, not all of those who say they could do something about an unjust local regulation had any clear strategy in mind. As Table 4 indicates, 12 per cent of the Italian respondents said that they could protest if faced with a regulation they considered unjust, but when asked how or to whom they could protest, gave no more specific reply. The 12 per cent who would protest represent about one-fourth of all Italian local competents. While this answer shows a higher level of subjective competence than the answer that one could do nothing, it reflects little awareness of the political channels through which one might effectively approach the government.

National Competence

We saw in Table 1 that in all nations fewer respondents say they could influence the national legislature than the local government and more say there is nothing they could do. In Table 6 we report the strategies respondents say they would use vis-à-vis the national government. In all nations formal organizations are somewhat more often mentioned as a resource for influencing the national government than the local government. (And if one calculated the percentage as a proportion of "national competents" rather than as a proportion of the entire sample, the difference would be sharper.) Conversely, in all nations fewer respondents mention using informal groups in connection with the national government than mentioned them in connection with the local government, though the pattern is the same; these groups are mentioned most frequently in the United States, followed by Britain and Mexico, then Germany and Italy. Generally, national influence strategies tend to rely more on the organized structures of politics, such as interest groups, political parties, and the press, or on individual approaches to elected political leaders. As we have already pointed out, this probably reflects realistic calculations. It takes a larger group and greater political skill to bring influence to bear on the national than on the local government. However, our evidence suggests that informal group competence persists significantly at the national level in the United States and Britain, even if it does not bulk as large as it does at the local level.

Social Groups and Subjective Competence

Clearly the five nations differ in the extent to which their citizens believe themselves capable of doing something should government threaten their interests; they differ, too, in the strategies the citizens would use. Why are there such differences? The causes are many and we do not claim to deal with them all in this study. We shall concern ourselves with the more limited question of whether the differences observed are general differences among the political cul-

202

tures of our five countries, or are differences that vary sharply and
in the same way among subgroups themselves, whatever the country.
If the former is true, one would expect most Italians to respond in
the same way, no matter what their social position, and to differ
from Americans of all social groups. If the latter is true, one would

TABLE 6

What Citizens Would Do to try to Influence their
National Government, by Nation
(in per cent)

What Citizens Would Do	U.S.	U.K.	Germany	Italy	Mexico
TRY TO ENLIST AID OF OTHERS					
Organize an informal group; arouse friends and neighbors, get them to write letters of protest or to sign a petition	29	18	7	6	18
Work through a political party	1	2	6	2	–
Work through a formal group (union, church, professional) to which they belong	4	3	7	2	3
Total per cent who would enlist others' aid[a]	32	22	19	10	20
ACT ALONE					
Directly contact political leaders (elected officials) or the press; write a letter to or visit a local political leader	57	44	12	7	8
Directly contact administrative (nonelected) officials	–	1	4	4	6
Consult a lawyer; appeal through courts	–	–	1	1	4
Vote against offending officials at next election	7	3	4	1	–
Take some violent action	–	–	2	1	4
Just protest	–	–	–	3	–
Other	–	2	–	2	3
Total per cent who would act alone[b]	42	40	18	18	18
Nothing	21	32	56	50	50
Don't know	4	6	7	22	12
Total per cent[c]	123	111	106	101	108
Total number of respondents	970	963	955	995	1,007

[a] Total percentages are less than the total of the individual cells, since some respondents gave more than one answer.

[b] This row includes only the respondents who said they could do something but did
not mention working with others. Hence the total is less than sum of the individual
cells, which contain respondents who may have mentioned both group and individual
activity.

[c] Percentage more than 100% due to multiple responses.

expect upper-status Italians to differ significantly from Italians of lower status, and to resemble Americans of similar status. There are many difficulties in making such comparisons—not the least of which is the difficulty of getting equivalent status measures across societies; but by using roughly equivalent subgroups for comparisons, we shall attempt to make them. Furthermore, by using different measures to compare these results, one can begin to distinguish those patterns that seem to depend more upon the distribution of other social characteristics within a society. If the differences among the nations disappear when one considers only social groups that are roughly matched, one has an aspect of political culture that is less specific to the particular culture. On the other hand, if the nationals in a particular social grouping of one country still differ significantly from those of a similar social group in other countries, while resembling closely their fellow nationals of diverse social backgrounds, one is probably dealing with an aspect of political culture whose roots are in the unique experiences of that country, and not in the experiences common to all our countries.

Let us look first at the relationship between citizen competence and education. We choose education as the first variable to consider, because of its close relationship with the factors that would tend to make a man feel subjectively competent (we shall discuss this relationship more fully in Chapter 13). As Figure 1 clearly points out, in all countries the more education an individual has, the more likely he is to consider himself capable of influencing the local government: that is, to be what we have called a local competent. (The percentage of individuals who say they could affect a local law is measured on the vertical axis; the level of education on the horizontal.) In the United States 60 per cent of those who did not get beyond primary school and 95 per cent of those with some college education are local competents. And the pattern repeats itself in each country. This then is a clear uniformity across national lines. No matter what the frequency of local competence within a nation, the incidence of this competence is greater among those with higher education.

What about the differences among and within nations? The question is a bit harder to answer, for differences exist both among educational groups within the same country (as the slopes of the lines indicate) and within similar educational groups among nations (as the different heights of the lines indicate). Some differences among nations diminish significantly within similar educational groups. For instance, though the American and German national totals for local competents are quite different, the differences between the two countries almost disappear when similar educational groups are compared. The greatest similarity in national totals occurs between the United States and Britain, on the one hand, and Mexico and Italy, on the other; yet in each pair the members differ somewhat more from each other between similar educational groups than they do on the national level. When the primary educated of America and Britain are compared, those in Britain show a higher rate of citizen competence; and when the lower educational groups of Italy and Mexico are compared, those in Mexico show a somewhat higher competence on the lower two levels.

Thus education has a mixed effect on the differences among nations. But the following general statements can be made on the basis of Figure 1. On all levels of education Mexican and Italian respondents are less frequently local competents than are respondents on similar levels in the other three countries (though on the university level the difference becomes quite slight). Second, the higher the educational level, the less difference there is among nations. This fact comes out clearly if one looks at the range among the nations on each level of education. On the elementary school level the range between the nation with the greatest frequency of local competents (Britain) and the nation with the least frequency (Italy) is 29 percentage points; on the secondary school level there are 21 percentage points between the nations that have the greatest frequency (Britain and Germany) and the one with the least (Italy); and on the university level 19 percentage points separate the United States, on the one hand, from Italy and Mexico, on the other.

Which are greater, national or educational differences? The measure of these is rough, but if one compares the ranges between the highest and lowest nation within each educational group (as reported in the previous paragraph) with the ranges between the highest and lowest educational group within each nation, the results suggest that there is certainly as much—if not, on the average, more —variation among educational groups within a single nation than among individuals with similar educational attainment in different nations. In the frequency with which respondents believe themselves competent to influence the government, there is within each nation about as much, if not more, difference among the educational levels as there is cross-nationally on each educational level. The ranges between the educational group that most frequently reports itself

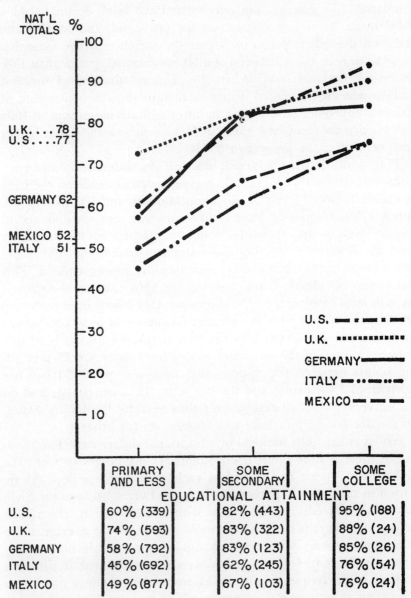

PERCENTAGE OF RESPONDENTS WHO SAY THAT THEY CAN DO SOMETHING ABOUT A LOCAL REGULATION THAT THEY CONSIDER UNJUST OR UNFAIR BY NATION AND EDUCATION

	PRIMARY AND LESS	SOME SECONDARY	SOME COLLEGE
U.S.	60% (339)	82% (443)	95% (188)
U.K.	74% (593)	83% (322)	88% (24)
GERMANY	58% (792)	83% (123)	85% (26)
ITALY	45% (692)	62% (245)	76% (54)
MEXICO	49% (877)	67% (103)	76% (24)

(NUMBERS IN PARENTHESES REFER TO THE BASE UPON WHICH PERCENTAGE IS CALCULATED).

FIG. I

PERCENTAGE OF LOCAL COMPETENTS WHO WOULD ENLIST THE
SUPPORT OF AN INFORMAL GROUP IN ORDER TO INFLUENCE A
LOCAL REGULATION THEY THOUGHT WAS UNJUST BY NATION
AND EDUCATION

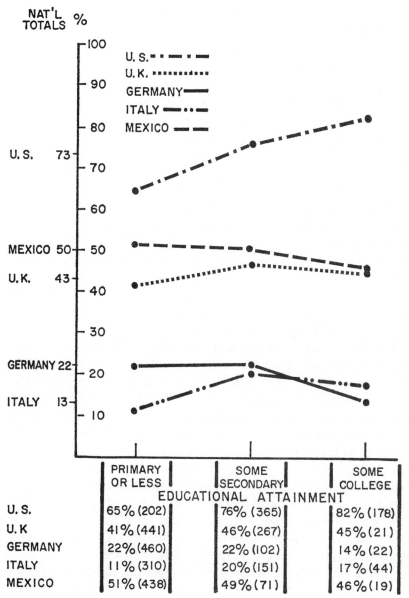

	PRIMARY OR LESS	SOME SECONDARY	SOME COLLEGE
U.S.	65% (202)	76% (365)	82% (178)
U.K	41% (441)	46% (267)	45% (21)
GERMANY	22% (460)	22% (102)	14% (22)
ITALY	11% (310)	20% (151)	17% (44)
MEXICO	51% (438)	49% (71)	46% (19)

(NUMBERS IN PARENTHESIS REFER TO THE BASE UPON WHICH PERCENTAGE
IS CALCULATED).

FIG. 2

competent to influence the government (those with some university education in each nation) and the group that least frequently reports such competence (those with only primary education or no education in each country) are: United States, 35 percentage points; Britain, 14 percentage points; Germany, 27 percentage points; Italy, 31 percentage points, and Mexico, 27 percentage points. These figures are rough, since they compare the extreme cases in terms of education and [in terms of] nation. But they do suggest that in terms of overall local competence, similar educational groups compared cross-nationally resemble one another at least as much as, and perhaps more than, do different educational groups within the same nation.

So far we have considered the extent to which individuals believe they can influence an unjust local regulation. But the strategy an individual would use may be more important than the simple distinction of whether or not he thinks he can do anything. In particular, the belief that one can cooperate with one's fellow citizen as a means of influencing the government appears to be important. Does this political strategy depend to as large an extent upon educational attainment as does the existence of local competence? The data in Figure 2 suggest that this is not the case.

The percentage of local competents who would work through informal groups varies sharply from country to country even within each educational group, but varies very little among educational groups within the individual countries.[16] Only in the United States does the frequency with which such activity is mentioned vary directly with educational attainment, and even here the relationship is not as strong as that between educational levels and local competence in general. Consider again the contrast between the United States and Germany. Within similar educational groups, German and American respondents hardly differ in the frequency with which they say that there is something they can do about an unjust local regulation. But if we compare the percentage of these local competents who would cooperate with their fellow citizens, we see that on each educational level German respondents are much less likely to mention such activity. Furthermore, well-educated German respond-

[16] The percentage is calculated as a percentage of local competents, not of the total population. This is to isolate the political strategy that competents would use from the fact that the frequency of competents differs from country to country.

ents are no more likely to talk of such activity than are less-educated ones. Unlike the situation in relation to overall local competence, where the range of difference among nations was no greater and perhaps a little less than the range of variation among one nation's educational groups, the variation among nations in the frequency with which political cooperation is mentioned is generally much greater on all educational levels than among educational groups within a nation. Here, then, may be a pattern of political culture the existence of which is independent of the educational attainment of an individual or the educational level in a nation. Education, our data suggest, may lead individuals to believe that they can influence their government, *no matter what country they live in* (providing, of course, that there is at least some institutional structure to support this attitude). Our data also suggests that as the overall educational level of nations rises, they will become more similar in this respect. But education does not necessarily increase the potentiality that individuals will create groups to support them. The ability to create political structures through cooperation with one's fellow citizens in time of stress seems to be typical of some nations and not of others. It is an element of political style, not a result of educational attainment.

Our discussion suggests that local competence varies with social grouping, while the use of informal groups as the strategy of influence is much more dependent upon national political style. This can be seen if we compare nations using another indicator of social group—the occupation of the family breadwinner. These data are presented in Figures 3 and 4. As Figure 3 shows, local competence in all countries is more frequent among those with higher-status occupations. And the range among occupations within a single country is approximately as large as the range among nations when occupation is held constant. On the other hand, Figure 4 shows that the selection of informal groups by local competents varies relatively little among occupational groups within a nation, but varies greatly among nations. In the United States and, to a slight extent, in Britain, the frequency with which competents talk of cooperation of this sort increases as one moves up the occupational ladder, but the relationship is not very strong. And in Germany the relationship is slightly in the opposite direction.

Finally, let us consider whether it makes any difference in political competence if one is male or female. It is clear from Table 7 that

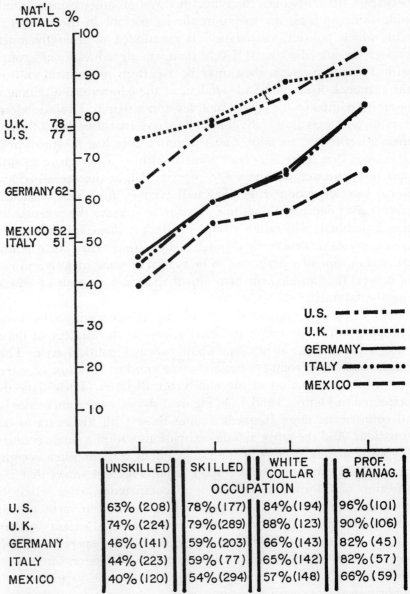

PERCENTAGE OF RESPONDENTS WHO SAY THAT THEY CAN DO SOMETHING ABOUT AN UNJUST LAW BY OCCUPATION OF FAMILY BREADWINNER

NAT'L TOTALS %

U.K. 78
U.S. 77

GERMANY 62

MEXICO 52
ITALY 51

U.S. — · — · —
U.K. ·················
GERMANY ————
ITALY — ·· — ··
MEXICO — — —

	UNSKILLED	SKILLED	WHITE COLLAR	PROF. & MANAG.
U.S.	63% (208)	78% (177)	84% (194)	96% (101)
U.K.	74% (224)	79% (289)	88% (123)	90% (106)
GERMANY	46% (141)	59% (203)	66% (143)	82% (45)
ITALY	44% (223)	59% (77)	65% (142)	82% (57)
MEXICO	40% (120)	54% (294)	57% (148)	66% (59)

OCCUPATION

(NUMBERS IN PARENTHESES REFER TO THE BASE UPON WHICH PERCENTAGE IS CALCULATED).

FIG. 3

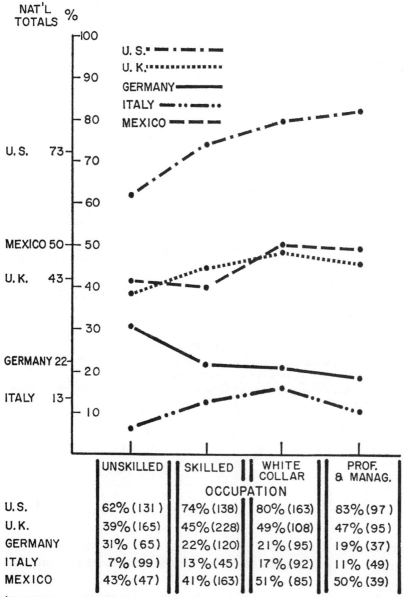

PERCENTAGE OF LOCAL COMPETENTS WHO SAY THEY WOULD ENLIST THE SUPPORT OF INFORMAL GROUPS BY OCCUPATION OF FAMILY BREADWINNER

	UNSKILLED	SKILLED	WHITE COLLAR	PROF. & MANAG.
U.S.	62% (131)	74% (138)	80% (163)	83% (97)
U.K.	39% (165)	45% (228)	49% (108)	47% (95)
GERMANY	31% (65)	22% (120)	21% (95)	19% (37)
ITALY	7% (99)	13% (45)	17% (92)	11% (49)
MEXICO	43% (47)	41% (163)	51% (85)	50% (39)

(NUMBERS IN PARENTHESES REFER TO THE BASE UPON WHICH PERCENTAGE IS CALCULATED).

FIG. 4

males in all countries are more likely to say they can influence the local government. But this difference occurs with least frequency in the two participatory democracies, the United States and Britain. However, if one compares this result with the proportion of male and female local competents who would work through informal

TABLE 7

Per Cent who say they Can Do Something about an Unjust Local Law, by Sex

Nation	Total (%)	(No.)*	Male (%)	(No.)	Female (%)	(No.)
United States	77	(970)	80	(455)	74	(515)
Great Britain	78	(963)	83	(460)	73	(503)
Germany	62	(955)	72	(449)	53	(506)
Italy	51	(995)	62	(471)	47	(524)
Mexico	53	(1,007)	63	(355)	46	(652)

* Numbers in parentheses refer to bases upon which percentages are calculated.

groups, one finds a pattern similar to that which obtains in relation to education and occupation. The use of informal groups is more homogeneous among groups within a nation than is overall local competence. As Table 8 shows, in those countries where informal groups are most frequently mentioned, the United States, Britain,

TABLE 8

Local Competents who would work through Informal Groups to try to Influence an Unjust Local Law, by Sex

Nation	Total (%)	(No.)*	Male (%)	(No.)	Female (%)	(No.)
United States	73	(745)	75	(366)	72	(379)
Great Britain	43	(748)	43	(383)	42	(365)
Germany	22	(590)	25	(322)	19	(268)
Italy	13	(508)	15	(291)	11	(217)
Mexico	50	(531)	52	(225)	49	(296)

* Numbers in parentheses refer to bases upon which percentages are calculated.

and Mexico, there is little or no difference between the sexes in terms of the proportions of males and females who would use such groups. And though in Germany and Italy men are more likely to use them than women, the differences are not great.

The data on educational, occupational, and sex differences in subjective competence suggest that whether or not one believes himself capable of influencing a local or national regulation depends a lot on who he is within his own country.[17] If he has more education, higher status, or is male, he is clearly more likely to consider himself competent. One's self-perceptions of his role as a citizen vary greatly with one's social position within a nation. But whether or not the local competent believes that his friends and neighbors are available to help him in a stress situation depends relatively little on his social position within a nation; more important is the nation he happens to live in. Political competence thus grows with higher education or occupational status, but cooperative competence seems to be rooted in specific national political cultures.

[17] The questions on "national competence" produce a similar pattern of response.

CHAPTER 8

CITIZEN COMPETENCE AND
SUBJECT COMPETENCE

THE ROLE of citizen represents in some sense the highest form of democratic participation. It is through such participation that the ordinary man gains influence over the course of governmental affairs. But men do not take part in political life only in their roles as citizens. As was suggested in the introductory chapter, they also remain in a subject relationship to government even after they have adopted the role of citizen. Though they may take part in the making of laws, they remain the subjects of laws. In many societies the opportunity for the individual to take on the role of the citizen may be very limited, but in all societies with any form of specialized political system, individuals are subjects.

Just as the citizen role may be performed more or less competently, so may the subject be more or less competent. But the competence of the subject is different from that of the citizen. The competent citizen has a role in the formation of general policy. Furthermore, he plays an *influential* role in this decision-making process: he participates through the use of explicit or implicit threats of some form of deprivation if the official does not comply with his demand. The subject does not participate in the making of rules, nor does his participation involve the use of political influence. His participation comes at the point at which general policy has been made and is being applied. The competence of the subject is more a matter of being aware of his rights under the rules than of participating in the making of the rule.[1] And though the subject may attempt to make the government official responsive, he appeals rather than demands. His appeal may be to the set of administrative

---

[1] Of course, there is no hard and fast line between the making of general rules and the application of them. General rules are usually made within the legislature, but administrative agencies often have discretion to formulate fairly general policy as well.

rules that are supposed to guide the action of the government official, or he may appeal to his considerateness. If the government official responds, it is because he is following these rules or because he is being considerate—not because influence has been applied to him. (Of course, administrative officials can be "influenced," as we define influence, but then one no longer has a subject relationship. We shall return to this point below.)

The civic culture, we have argued, is a political culture in which large numbers of individuals are competent as citizens: we call this competence *political* competence. But in the civic culture individuals would be competent as subjects as well (*administrative* competence). Whether or not individuals consider themselves competent in the administrative sense depends upon many factors, not the least of which are the responsiveness of the governmental bureaucracy to the individual and the existence of channels of appeal open to the ordinary man. Though we cannot measure the extent to which the governmental structure fosters a sense of administrative competence in a population, we can measure the extent of that sense of competence.

The Sense of Administrative Competence

Just as individuals may or may not perceive that the decision-making organs of government are amenable to political influence, so they may or may not perceive that those government officials with whom they stand in a subject relationship are responsive to their appeals. To test the extent of the sense of administrative competence, we attempted to find out what expectations respondents had of the responsiveness of government bureaucrats. The situation presented to them was an administrative one in which attempts at political influence would be inappropriate (though in the real world it may be and often is employed). What sort of treatment, we wanted to know, did individuals expect to receive from government administrative officials? In particular, we were interested in the extent to which individuals felt they could have some voice in the proceedings if they were involved in some question in a government office. We posed two hypothetical situations. In one we asked respondents: "Suppose there were some question you had to take to a government office—for example, a tax question or a housing regulation. . . ." In the other we asked them to suppose "you had some trouble with the police—a traffic violation, maybe, or being accused of a minor offense. . . ." In both cases we asked what sort of reaction they would expect if they explained their point of view to the government officials.[2]

The relevant data were reported in Chapter 4, Table 3. As the table showed, the type of response individuals expect varies from nation to nation. It is clear that Mexican respondents rarely expect to achieve much by expressing their point of view. Only 14 per cent expect that they will receive serious consideration, and almost twice as many expect that they will be ignored; most of the rest expect to receive little attention. Italian respondents follow the Mexicans in the frequency with which they expect to be ignored and in the infrequency with which they expect to receive serious consideration. The response patterns for the other three countries are similar, with the British most frequently expecting serious consideration, followed by Germans and then Americans.

As the table also revealed, the pattern is the same in relation to the police. Again the Mexicans expect very little: only 12 per cent believe they will receive serious consideration, and 29 per cent believe they will be ignored. Italian respondents again fall above the Mexicans in terms of their expectations, but below the respondents of the other three countries. American and German respondents report about as frequently that they would receive serious consideration, but Americans more frequently report that they would be ignored (11 per cent of American respondents believe they would be ignored, in comparison with only 4 per cent of the Germans). The expectations of serious consideration among British respondents is, however, well above that in any other country, with 74 per cent of British respondents expecting such treatment.

The divergences among the nations on this set of figures can hardly be overemphasized. Certainly the British live in an entirely different governmental world from that of the Mexicans or Italians. How different this is can be seen if we compare Britain and Mexico. Whereas three out of four Britons expect the police to give their point of view serious consideration and only a handful expect it to be ignored, little more than one in ten Mexicans expect such consideration and almost one in three expect their point of view to be ignored.

[2] These questions are discussed more fully in chapter 4, above.

Citizen and Subject Competence

Individuals, then, may believe themselves competent as citizens or as subjects. As competent citizens, they perceive themselves as able to affect governmental decisions through political influence: by forming groups, by threatening with the withdrawal of their vote or other reprisals. As competent subjects, they perceive themselves as able to appeal to a set of regular and orderly rules in their dealings with administrative officials. They will receive fair treatment from the administration, and their point of view will be considered, not because they attempt political influence, but because the administrative official is controlled by a set of rules that curbs his arbitrary power. The British, for instance, perceive themselves as able to count upon such treatment; the Mexicans clearly do not.

Citizen competence and subject competence differ but are not completely independent of each other. Nor is it likely that the existence of one type of competence will leave the other unaffected. One would expect a certain amount of spillover of political competence into administrative competence. The more politically competent a population is, the more inhibited is the bureaucracy in its ability to act arbitrarily and without consideration of the individual. But the spill-over from political into administrative competence can be of two types. On the one hand, a highly politically competent citizenry may exert pressure upon bureaucrats to follow the administrative rules. Their adherence to the rules of administrative procedure will be enforced, not merely by their own internalization of these rules or by the controls exercised upon them by administrative higher-ups, but by the threat of political reprisal: protest by citizens through political agencies if the officials do not follow these rules. In this way a high degree of citizen competence raises the level of subject competence, but it does not change the relationship of the individual to the administration—he still comes as a subject, albeit a competent one, whose appeal is to the rules of bureaucracy.

The second type of spill-over of political competence into the relations between individuals and administration is one in which political influence (and here our technical use of the term coincides with the everyday, pejorative use of the word) is brought to bear upon administrative officials, not to compel them to follow the bureaucratic rules, but to compel them to make a particular

217

decision in favor of a particular individual or group. Political influence acts directly to enforce individual demands, not indirectly to
enforce bureaucratic rules. In this way political competence does
not support and increase administrative competence; rather, it tends
to convert it into political competence as well. The role of citizen
overwhelms the role of subject.

The relationship between the two types of competence, we suggest, represents a significant aspect of the pattern of political orientation in a nation. Let us look first at the number of respondents in
each nation who consider themselves competent in the political
and administrative sense. As an indicator of those who consider
themselves politically competent, we shall take the responses to the
questions on whether the individual believes he can do something
about an unjust act contemplated by the local or national government. Political competents are those who believe there is something
they can do in relation to both levels of government. Administrative
competents, on the other hand, expect serious consideration both
from the police and in a governmental office.

Figure 1 reports the numbers of citizen and administrative competents in each nation. Some interesting differences emerge when
one compares the nations in terms of the number of individuals
who manifest these two types of subjective competence. In the
United States the number of politically competent respondents is
quite a bit greater than the number of administratively competent
ones. Sixty-six per cent of the Americans believe they can exert
some political influence over national and local government, while
only thirty-seven per cent expect serious consideration in the two
administrative situations. In Britain, on the other hand, there is
relatively little difference between the proportions of political and
administrative competents; though there are somewhat fewer administrative competents, both types are frequent. In Germany the
relationship between the numbers of political and administrative
competents is the reverse of that in the United States and Britain:
administrative competents are more frequent than political competents. In Italy there are about as many political as administrative
competents, but both types are relatively rare. And in Mexico, as
in the United States, there are more political than administrative
competents. However, both types of competents are less frequent
in Mexico than in the United States, and the ratio of political to
administrative competents is much greater: more than four times

CITIZEN COMPETENCE AND SUBJECT COMPETENCE
by Nation, Education, and Sex

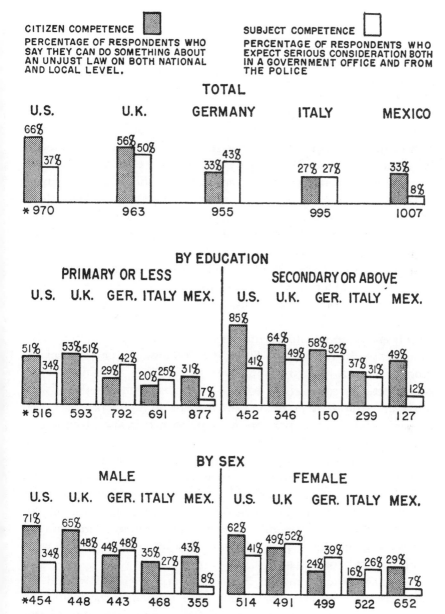

FIG. I

as many political competents as there are administrative competents.

This pattern of distribution of the two types of competence is generally apparent if we consider subgroups in the various nations —males and females and those with high and low education. In general, within all subgroups in the United States and Mexico the proportion of respondents who are politically competent is greater than the proportion who are administratively competent; the levels of both types of competence remain lower in Mexico. In Britain and Italy there are roughly equivalent proportions of political and administrative competents, but the frequency of both types is much lower in Italy. And in Germany the frequency of administrative competents is greater than the frequency of political competents.

Another interesting point emerges from Figure 1. Among those respondents whom one would expect generally to be more competent there appears to be a heavier stress on political competence. Compare those who have secondary education or better with those respondents who have less education. As one would expect, those who have a higher level of education are more frequently competent in both the administrative and the political sense. But the increase in competence from the lower to the higher educational level is much more manifest in terms of political than administrative competence. In the United States, for instance, 35 per cent of respondents with primary education or less are administratively competent, in comparison with 41 per cent among those with secondary education or better—an increase in frequency of 7 percentage points. But 51 per cent of those with primary education or less are politically competent, in contrast with 85 per cent among those with higher educational attainment—an increase of 34 percentage points. The parallel increases between educational levels in Italy are 6 percentage points for administrative competence and 17 percentage points for political competence. And though in Germany there are generally more administrative than political competents, on the higher educational level there are somewhat more political competents.

A similar pattern emerges if one compares men and women. In every nation men are more likely than women to be politically competent, and in most cases the differences in frequency of this form of competence are quite striking. But the differences between the sexes in terms of administrative competence are much smaller. In Mexico and Italy the differences in frequency of administrative competence are negligible, while in the United States and Britain women are somewhat more likely than men to consider themselves administratively competent.

The fact that female respondents and those respondents with lower education resemble male respondents and those with higher education much more in their administrative competence than in their political competence suggests that political competence in some way develops after administrative competence. As was suggested in Chapter 1, the role of citizen develops on top of the role of subject. Those groups whose induction into full political participation has generally lagged—women and those with lower education—are more fully inducted into the role of competent subject than into that of competent citizen. Thus the distribution of the two types of competence probably reflects the historical process by which various groups have come to take part in politics. Within each of the five nations the subject role has been more generally assimilated than the citizen role. Citizen participation is a more selective and more slowly developing type of participation. It spreads from the more easily politicized to those more difficult to bring into political life.

These subgroup differences within the nations in the distribution of the two types of competence suggest an historical pattern of the spread of citizen and subject competence. A similar historical pattern is suggested if we compare the nations in these terms. Consider the United States and Britain first. Both nations stand high on our measures of political competence. British and American respondents most frequently say that they can do something about an unjust local regulation and about an unjust national law. Furthermore, as pointed out in Chapter 7, they most frequently suggest that they would form groups as a means of increasing their influence. There is one important difference between the two countries in their patterns of political strategy: informal groups are more frequently invoked as a means of influence in the United States; for though the British rank second in the frequency with which respondents mention such groups (34 per cent of them do), they mention them much less frequently than do American respondents (56 per cent of whom do). On the other hand, the British much more frequently manifest what we have called administrative competence. In the frequencies with which they expect serious consideration from government and police officials they rank first of all the five nations. The American respondents, on the other hand, are less likely to expect serious consideration from government and police officials than are British or German respondents, and more likely than either group to expect that their point of view will be ignored.

In Britain, then, a high level of political competence coexists with a high level of administrative competence. In the United States the former type of competence is more widespread than the latter. This difference between the two countries reflects the way in which the development of political institutions in each country has interacted with individuals' attitudes toward these institutions to produce a current state of competence. The development of political competence in Britain (a development that can be roughly equated with the spread of the franchise and the formation of interest groups and of political parties with roots in a mass electorate) came gradually and on top of a previously existing idea of an independent government and sovereign whose powers over individuals were limited by the rules of law. Englishmen had what we would call subject competence long before they were politically competent. They had an elaborate set of rights dating at least from the seventeenth century (their legally enforceable common law went back to the twelfth century). These legal rights were enforced, not by political means, but through the independent courts of law. For our purposes the important historical development is that the political rights acquired by Britons in the nineteenth century did not come into conflict with the idea of an independent governmental authority limited by some higher law. The notion of the independent authority of government under law has continued to exist side by side with the notion of the political power of the people. The old authoritarian institutions and symbols were not replaced by democratization, but continued to coexist with the new institution. From the point of view of the individual, the political competence Britons received in the nineteenth century did not replace their competence as subjects under the rules of law. If anything, the growth of citizen competence raised the level of subject competence by adding a new force for the enforcement of the rules of law.[3]

[3] For a discussion of this development see Harry H. Eckstein, "The British Political System," in Samuel H. Beer and Adam B. Ulam (eds.), Patterns of Government, New York, 1958, pp. 57-74, and T. H. Marshall, Citizenship and Social Class, Cambridge, England, 1950, pp. 10-27.

In the United States, on the other hand, the development of political competence through the spread of the franchise, the growth of political parties, and the consequent induction of new groups into the political process has tended to conflict with Americans' subject competence. The idea of an independent governmental authority controlled by rules of law was affected by the spread of democratic participation. As popular political control over government increased, it clashed with the notion of independent government agencies that were controlled, not by popular political influence, but by a set of legal or administrative rules and norms. In the Jackson era, for instance, the franchise spread and new groups entered the political process. This increase in political democracy, however, was accompanied by a tendency for the administrative branches of the government to be subordinated to political considerations. Through the growth of the spoils system and the popular election of essentially administrative and judicial officers, popular influence over the governmental process came to mean political influence over the courts and administrative agencies. And throughout most of American political history, the spread of popular influence over the government has involved a diminution of the areas in which individuals stood in a subject relationship to the government. As new groups have been given political influence, this has meant control, not so much over legislative decisions through the right to elect representatives, as over the courts and bureaucracy through election, political pressure, and "pull." The traditional urban machine did not offer favorable social legislation to the new groups: it gave them influence over administrative decisions. The political machine offered favors in employment, "protection" by the police, aid before the courts or aid in becoming a citizen, and favors in the receipt of business. The sign that one had a voice in the affairs of government was not that the legislature was responding to one's needs through social legislation, but that one could have some trouble with the police "fixed." Thus as the American gained political competence, his role as subject declined; for political competence meant influence over just those institutions in relation to which one might expect the individual to stand as a subject.

Perhaps the major distinction between Britain and the United States in this aspect of their political histories turns on the existence of a revolutionary tradition in the United States. Whereas British political development has never involved the challenge of the existence of an independent governmental authority, the very founding of the American republic involved such a challenge. As Oscar and Mary Handlin have pointed out, the American colonists brought with them the European conception that government authority descended from the crown, but this view changed during the eighteenth century. "The marks of change were a growing habit of defiance or evasion of royal wishes, a steady loss of respect for the royal person and for the symbols of his majesty, and the disappearance of the charisma in which the throne had been enveloped. At the eve of the Revolution, the colonists could refer casually, without sense of *lèse-majesté,* to George III as a crowned ruffian. . . .

"By then Americans thought of authority, not as descending downward from the throne, but as derived from below from the choices of the people. The consent of the governed referred not to an abstract compact between ruler and governed, as in the long tradition of European political theory, but to a process by which the people delegated power to their governors."[4]

The contrast between British and American attitudes toward the police is especially relevant here. As the Handlins go on to state, Americans ". . . never acquired the respect for the cops that the English did for the Bobbies. The revolutionary experience persuaded the free citizens of the United States that a police force . . . was a threat to republican institutions."[5] Thus in the United States the revolutionary experience led to the view that there was no office that did not derive from the citizenry, hence no limit to the exercise of citizen competence. While in Britain the competent citizen and the competent subject coexist, in the United States the competent citizen has tended to replace the competent subject.

If this is true, one would expect to find a closer relationship between political and administrative competence in the United States than in Britain. Britons' expectations of their ability to affect administrative decisions ought not to depend on the extent to which they consider themselves politically competent. In the United States, on the other hand, one would expect the individual who believes himself politically competent to generalize his political competence into administrative competence as well. That such a difference in the relationship between the two forms of competence

4 Oscar and Mary Handlin, *The Dimensions of Liberty,* Cambridge, Mass., 1961, p. 32.
5 *Ibid.,* p. 39.

does indeed exist is shown on Table 1. This table relates political to administrative competence. On all levels of political competence Britons are more administratively competent. In the United States the respondents with high subjective political competence (those who believe that both the national and local governments would be amenable to their influence) are more likely to expect serious consideration from the police and government than are respondents with intermediate political competence (those who believe that one level of government—usually the local—is amenable to their influence) and are much more likely to expect such consideration than are those low in political competence (those who believe neither level of government would be responsive). Forty-four per cent of those high in political competence express high administrative competence, in contrast with 31 per cent of the intermediates and 19 per cent of the lows. In Britain, on the other hand, the relationship between the two forms of competence is not as close. Fifty-three per cent of those high in political competence expect serious consideration in both administrative situations, in contrast with 50 per cent of those intermediate and 38 per cent of those low in political competence.

The sharpest contrast between the two nations in the relationship between the two types of competence is found among those on the higher educational level. In Britain the relative independence between the two forms of competence is most clearly seen among this group: 50 per cent of those with high political competence are high on administrative competence, in comparison with 42 per cent among those low in political competence. In the United States the close relationship between these two forms of competence is most apparent among those with higher education: 44 per cent of those with high political competence also manifest administrative competence, in contrast with 16 per cent of those low in political competence. These data suggest that there is indeed greater independence between the roles of citizen and subject in Britain than in the United States.

The pattern of political and administrative competence in Germany contrasts sharply with that of the United States. Germany seems to be a nation in which the subject orientation is relatively frequent, as against the citizen orientation. Consider the treatment Germans expect in government offices or from the police. In both cases, they (after the British) most frequently expect serious con-

TABLE 1

Political and Administrative Competence,[a] by Nation and Education

Nation	Total			Primary or Less			Secondary or Above		
	Can Influence Local and National (%) (No.)[b]	Can Influence Local or National (%) (No.)	Can Influence Neither (%) (No.)	Both (%) (No.)	Either (%) (No.)	Neither (%) (No.)	Both (%) (No.)	Either (%) (No.)	Neither (%) (No.)
United States	44 (644)	31 (179)	19 (145)	43 (262)	32 (128)	19 (126)	44 (382)	22 (51)	16 (19)
Great Britain	53 (534)	50 (245)	38 (160)	55 (312)	52 (168)	37 (108)	50 (222)	47 (77)	42 (47)
Germany	55 (314)	42 (314)	33 (314)	53 (227)	41 (270)	33 (295)	59 (87)	45 (44)	37 (19)
Italy	29 (250)	28 (277)	25 (463)	30 (138)	25 (185)	23 (368)	28 (112)	33 (92)	35 (95)
Mexico	8 (337)	9 (239)	6 (431)	7 (273)	9 (211)	5 (395)	10 (64)	12 (28)	16 (36)

[a] I.e., the proportion of respondents who expect consideration for their point of view in a government office and by the police, measured among three groups of respondents: those who believe they can influence both the national and local government; those who believe they can influence either the national or local government, and those who believe they can influence neither.

[b] Numbers in parentheses refer to the bases upon which percentages are calculated.

sideration for their point of view. In contrast to this is their response to unjust legislative activity. In connection with an unjust local regulation, they rank third in the frequency with which individuals feel they can do something to redress such an act; in connection with an unjust national law, they rank fourth—slightly below the Mexicans. As Figure 1 indicated, it is only in Germany that more respondents could be described as administrative competents rather than political competents. However, that pattern appears to apply especially to those Germans of lower educational attainment. Just as important as the number who say they can influence an unjust law are the strategies they report. Relatively few would attempt to form groups for these purposes, and German respondents frequently talk of contacting administrative officials.

This pattern of competence seems to reflect the political history of Germany. Subject competence grew, as in Britain, before citizen competence. But whereas the development of political democracy in Britain has had a long history and has added a significant degree of citizen competence to subject competence, political democracy has had a far less orderly and successful development in Germany. While in the nineteenth century the British middle class, followed by the working class, was demanding and receiving political influence over the government, the German middle class accepted the law and the order of the German *Rechtsstaat*, under which it might prosper but have no political influence. Power over governmental decisions was left in the hands of competent governmental officials; it was not distributed among the populace. But though the German was not a competent citizen, he remained a competent subject. His rights under the law were clearly defined and carefully protected by a system of courts and administration free from political influences. In contrast with Britain, then, the belief in one's political competence has not taken a firm root among the population. If in the United States the competent citizen tends to replace the competent subject, and if in Britain the two tend to coexist in harmony, in Germany the competent subject remains the dominant form of competence.[6]

[6] But if in Germany the subject role is dominant and the role of citizen has not yet been completely assimilated, there does tend to be a relationship between these two roles—a relationship somewhat stronger than that in Britain but not as strong as that in the United States. Fifty-five per cent of those Germans high on political competence are also high on our measure of administrative competence, in contrast with 42 per cent of those who are intermediate on political competence and 33 per cent who are low on this measure.

If our above description is correct, then our data would seem to indicate the Italian citizens experience neither *Rechtsstaat* nor effective democracy. In terms of subject competence the Italians rank fourth, well below the United Kingdom, the United States, and Germany. Only about one in three expects serious consideration from the government or the police. On our measures of political competence the Italians rank last in the frequency with which respondents say that they can influence an unjust local or national regulation. And among the Italian local competents the strategies suggested reveal little political competence. Very few mention the possibility of forming groups. And one out of four of those who say they can do something about a local law they feel is unjust say that they can "protest" and that is all. Citizenship competence and subject competence seem equally retarded.

This pattern, too, is what one might expect in a nation with the political history of Italy. Before unification, Italy had experienced centuries of external tyranny by a variety of powers under whom Italians had neither political nor effective legal rights—they were competent neither as citizens nor as subjects. From such a history one would expect the development of neither citizen nor subject competence. One would expect, rather, as H. R. Spencer argues, that Italians would look upon government, not as a social institution amenable to their influence, but as a natural force—often catastrophic, like an earthquake—to be endured. "This tendency to acquiescence and submissiveness, this feeling of the individual's insignificance, this feeling that the affairs of men are governed by forces that may be endured but not swerved from their movement or organized for man's use, only taken advantage of, furtively and sporadically—is a natural conclusion for men of intelligence who are not men of political tradition."[7] The current political culture of Italy may be inappropriate for a healthy, functioning democracy. It is quite appropriate for a nation with Italy's political history.

Lastly, let us consider the pattern of subject and citizen competence in Mexico. In the frequency with which they would expect serious consideration from government officials or the police the Mexicans rank clearly the lowest. The figures, when compared with those of any of the other countries, are quite striking. On political competence, however, the data are not so bleak. In terms of the percentage who think they can do something about an unjust

[7] H. R. Spencer, *Government and Politics of Italy*, Yonkers, New York, 1932, p. 17.

regulation on the local level, the Mexicans rank slightly above the Italians; and more frequently than either the Italians or the Germans they report they can do something about an unjust national law. More important is the fact that their strategy of influence manifests some incipient political competence. The use of informal groups, for instance, is frequently mentioned.

The Mexican pattern is significant. Political competence, we have been arguing, is harder to acquire than subject competence; historically it has tended to develop later and to spread from the more politically "advantaged" groups in a society to the less advantaged. But in Mexico we seem to have the reverse situation. The explanation probably lies, once again, in the revolutionary political culture of Mexico. The Mexican pattern of more widespread political than administrative competence is paralleled only in the United States, the other nation whose political formation has represented, as has the Mexican Revolution, a rejection of traditional authority. The Mexican Revolution meant a sudden induction of individuals into the political system. Attention was turned to the national government as the vehicle of change and to the national heroes who guided the destiny of the country. Individuals did develop a subjective sense of political competence, but it was not a competence based on experience. As we have shown, the cooperative competence found in Mexico is not based on much actual group experience, and only 9 per cent of the Mexicans who believe they can influence the local government report some experience along these lines (in contrast with 33 per cent in the United States and 18 per cent in Britain). The Mexican Revolution created political competence, but it was an aspirational or mythic sense of competence. Furthermore, the Revolution took place in a society where the institution of an independent, rational bureaucracy had not taken root; local bureaucracy was the tool of the traditional political powers. Nor did the Revolution change this fundamentally. Bureaucracy remained subordinate to political forces and today is still an arena of political struggle. Thus subject competence never developed in Mexico. In contrast to Germans, Mexicans have started to become competent citizens before they are competent subjects.

CHAPTER 9

COMPETENCE, PARTICIPATION, AND
POLITICAL ALLEGIANCE

In earlier chapters we have shown that the frequency of various types of political attitudes and behavior differs from nation to nation. In Part III we shall consider the social and psychological conditions with which such attitudes and behavior are associated. In this concluding chapter of Part II we consider what is probably the most significant and certainly the most difficult question raised by the data thus far presented: how do political competence and participation affect a political system?

Though citizen competence and participation are at the heart of the definition of democracy, the problems faced by democratic governments would be much simpler than they are if their only concern was to maximize that competence and participation. In fact, however, the political system that attempted to maximize that goal at the expense of all others would not long survive. Political systems, if they are to survive, must also be relatively effective and relatively legitimate; that is, what the government accomplishes must be at least satisfying enough to the citizens so that they do not turn against the government; and the system, if it is to have a long-run potential of survival, must be generally accepted by citizens as the proper form of government per se.

These statements about political stability are so general as to be truistic. But they focus our attention on those aspects of a political system that are most crucially affected by political competence and participation. Political competence and participation will influence a system's effectiveness as well as its legitimacy, and it is this influence that we shall attempt to explore.

Our data enable us to explore this relationship only partially. The question we ask is not what happens to the political system in which there is participation in decisions, but what happens to the individual who believes himself competent to participate in decisions. As we pointed out earlier, our respondents differ in the extent to which they believe they can participate in political decisions: in what we have called their subjective competence as citizens. What, we may ask, goes along with this subjective political competence? Aside from his sense of ability to participate, in what way does the subjectively competent individual differ from someone who does not feel that the affairs of politics and government are amenable to his influence? This is clearly not the same as asking how a participatory political system will differ from one that involves less participation, but it is closely related to it. We want to know what set of political orientations is likely to be found among a citizenry that considers itself capable of participating in governmental decisions. And those orientations—whether they involve belief in either the effectiveness or ineffectiveness of the system, whether they involve allegiance to or rejection of the system—will have implications for the stability of that system.

To facilitate this analysis of the way in which subjective political competence affects other attitudes, a scale was devised to rate respondents on the extent to which they believe themselves competent in their relations with the government. The scale is based on their responses to five questions dealing with local government. We asked whether the respondent believed he could understand local politics; whether he felt he could and would act to influence the local government; whether he had any expectations of success in influencing the local government, and whether he had ever attempted such influence. The five questions formed an acceptable Guttman scale.[1]

The scale allows us to group our respondents into one of six

---

[1] The five questions used were the following:

"*1.* How about the local issues in this town or part of the country? How well do you understand them? [This question was asked as a follow-up question to the following two questions: "Some people say that politics and government are so complicated that the average man cannot really understand what is going on. In general, do you agree or disagree with that?" and "How well do you think you understand the important national and international issues facing this country?"]

"*2.* Suppose a regulation were being considered by [most local governmental unit specified by interviewer] that you considered very unjust or harmful. What do you think you could do?

"*3.* If such a case arose, how likely is it that you *would actually* do something about it?

"*4.* If you made an effort to change this regulation, how likely is it that you would succeed?

"*5.* Have you ever done anything to try to influence a local regulation?"

The responses were dichotomized into positive and negative responses. If a person

categories, ranging from a high score of five, for those with the highest degree of subjective competence, to a low score of zero, for those who expressed the least subjective competence. Figure 1 shows the distribution of these types within the five countries. Though our purpose is not to describe differences among nations in frequency of expressed competence, but, rather, to compare the competents with the noncompetents, it is interesting to note that the total distribution of scores on the scale for the five nations is what one would have expected from our earlier discussion of the distribution of political attitudes. The United States and Britain have the highest proportions of high scorers, Italy and Mexico the lowest, while the German respondents fall somewhat in-between the two pairs of nations.

On this scale we have used attitudes toward local rather than national government, because there is a substantially higher level of subjective competence in relation to the local government in all countries. This allows one to locate, in each nation, a group of respondents who express relatively high levels of subjective competence. If a scale based on the national government had been used, too many respondents would have fallen into the lower categories of subjective competence, and the scale would not have been useful to discriminate among various types of citizens. In any case, the score on the subjective competence scale for the local government is closely correlated with the extent of national competence, which suggests that we are measuring similar dimensions.

said he could understand local issues, no matter how well, his answer was considered positive. If he said he could not understand them, his answer was considered negative. The same dichotomy was used with answers on the likelihood of success and likelihood of action. When asked what one could do to affect an unjust local law, anyone who said he could do something was considered to have answered positively, no matter what he said he could do. (These people are the "local competents" discussed in chapter 7.)

Using the technique suggested by Ford, we combined the five items into a Guttman-type scale. (Robert N. Ford, "A Rapid Scoring Procedure for Scaling Attitude Questions," *Public Opinion Quarterly*, xiv, [Fall 1950], pp. 507-32.) Those patterns that were not perfect scale types were assigned to scale positions according to the "minimum error" criterion; where this criterion is ambiguous, patterns are assigned according to the "distribution of perfect types" criterion. See Andrew F. Henry, "A Method for Classifying Non-Scale Response Patterns in a Guttman Scale," *ibid.*, xvi (Spring 1952), pp. 94-106.

Scales were constructed for the data from the United States, Great Britain, Germany, and Italy. These scales met the criteria for acceptable Guttman scales. The coefficients of reproducibility were all above the .9 level suggested by Guttman for an acceptable scale (*U.S.*, .94; *U.K.*, .925; *Germany*, .97; and *Italy*, .96). To correct for the possibility of artificially high coefficients of reproducibility due to the extremeness of some of the

SUBJECTIVE COMPETENCE SCORE BY NATION

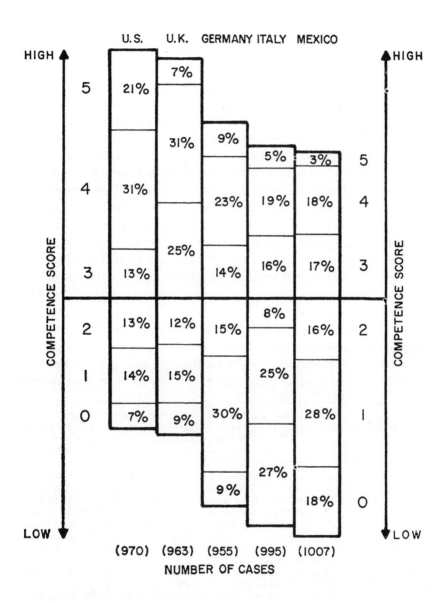

FIG. I

The use of a scale about local government, however, introduces some complexity into our analysis. Within each nation, individuals are asked their attitudes toward different governments—i.e., the local government under which they live—and these governments may differ even within nations in the extent to which they foster participation. Smaller governmental units might, for instance, lead to higher degrees of subjective political competence. The scale results would then be affected by the proportions of respondents living in towns and cities of various sizes. As Figure 2 indicates, however, the distribution of scores on the subjective competence scale is not affected by the size of the towns in which respondents live. Small-town dwellers and big-city dwellers, in each of the countries, appear to share similar levels of subjective competence toward their local government. There is some difference within nations in the regional distribution of scores on the subjective competence scale, but these differences parallel other differences between regions in levels of national competence, political activity, and the like. Thus it is probable that regional differences in attitudes toward local government are a function, not so much of differences in attitudes toward the local governments, but of differences in general attitudes toward government and politics.

The level of subjective competence does vary, as do so many of our political variables, with a number of significant demographic characteristics. There are sex, educational, and class differences in the level of subjective competence, and the same tendencies exist

---

items, a coefficient of scalability was also calculated. See Herbert Menzel, "A New Coefficient for Scalogram Analysis," *ibid.*, XVII (Summer 1953), pp. 268-80. This measure of scalability is essentially the same as the "plus percentage ration" suggested by J. M. Jackson; see Richard G. Pearson, "Plus Percentage Ratio and the Coefficient of Scalability," *ibid.*, XXI (Fall 1957), pp. 379-80. The coefficient of scalability is not based upon the ratio of errors to total responses, as is the coefficient of reproducibility, but upon the ratio of errors to the "maximum possible error." The latter is equal to the number of responses less the sum of the modal responses for each item. Menzel suggests that the minimum criterion for scalability should be about .60-.65. Jackson suggests a minimum of .70 for the "plus percentage ratio." The scales were all acceptable according to these criteria. The coefficients of scalability were: *U.S.*, .80; *U.K.*, .71; *Germany*, .90; and *Italy*, .87. An analysis of the individual items indicated that no item was contributing unduly to the error.

The result was a six-point scale, running from a high score of five to a low of zero. Due to linguistic difficulties, one of the five questions that made up the Guttman scale was not asked of all respondents in Mexico; question 3 above was not asked of those who on question 2 had responded that they could "do nothing." Because of this, the Mexican respondents were not assigned scale scores according to the Guttman technique, rather, they were assigned scores based on the simple arithmetic sum of their responses, with one point given for a positive answer and zero given for a negative

SUBJECTIVE COMPETENCE SCORE BY SIZE OF TOWN
PROPORTION OF RESPONDENTS SCORING HIGH ON SUBJECTIVE COMPETENCE SCALE BY SIZE OF TOWN

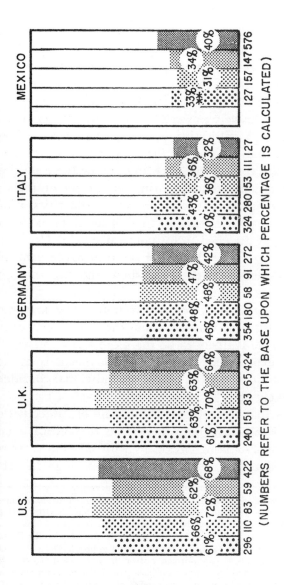

(NUMBERS REFER TO THE BASE UPON WHICH PERCENTAGE IS CALCULATED)

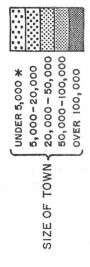

SIZE OF TOWN
- UNDER 5,000 *
- 5,000 – 20,000
- 20,000 – 50,000
- 50,000 – 100,000
- OVER 100,000

FIG. 2

* NOT IN MEXICAN SAMPLE
** CITIES OF 10,000 – 20,000

in each nation. Male respondents, respondents with higher levels of education, and respondents from families with a higher-status breadwinner are more likely to rank high on our competence scale. In particular, the differences among various educational groups are sharp, as Figure 3 shows. This suggests that in relating the sense of political competence to other political attitudes, it will be important to attempt to hold the level of education constant.

How does the self-confident citizen differ from the individual who considers himself relatively powerless? Respondents can be grouped into those with *high* subjective political competence (those who receive a score of four or five on the subjective competence scale), those with *medium* competence (scoring two or three on the scale) and those with *low* competence (scoring zero or one on the scale). Is the subjectively competent citizen more active in politics; is he more likely to think that politics benefits him; is he more likely to be in some way affectively attached to his political system? How, in short, does the man who considers himself a political participant differ in his political attitudes from the individual who does not consider himself competent?

Sense of Competence and Political Activity. The first and most obvious question that one may ask about the subjectively competent citizen is whether he is likely to be the more active citizen. This is what one would expect, and the data suggest that it is strongly the case. The more subjectively competent an individual considers himself, the more likely he is to be politically active.

Table 1 shows that those high on the scale of subjective competence are more likely to expose themselves to political communications. For instance, among Mexicans with no education or only primary school education, 34 per cent of those high in subjective

answer. Those who were not asked question 3 were assumed to have answered it negatively and assigned a score of zero for the question (which is what our Guttman scale in the other four countries would have predicted them to do based on their negative answer to question 2). To test whether the more arbitrary method of assigning individuals to scale positions in Mexico gives us a scale approximately like that in the other countries, a Guttman scale was formed out of the four questions that had been asked of all Mexican respondents. They were found to form an acceptable scale: the coefficient of reproducibility was .93 and the coefficient of scalability was .83. This suggests that our scale, based on the arbitrary assignment of one point for a positive answer and zero for a negative answer, yields a distribution of individuals similar to that which would have been obtained if the Guttman technique could have been applied to the Mexican responses as well. (Clearly, if the response patterns formed a perfect Guttman scale, the arbitrary point assignment technique and the Guttman technique would yield identical distributions of respondents.)

SUBJECTIVE COMPETENCE SCORE BY EDUCATION
PROPORTION OF RESPONDENTS SCORING HIGH ON SUBJECTIVE COMPETENCE SCORE BY EDUCATION

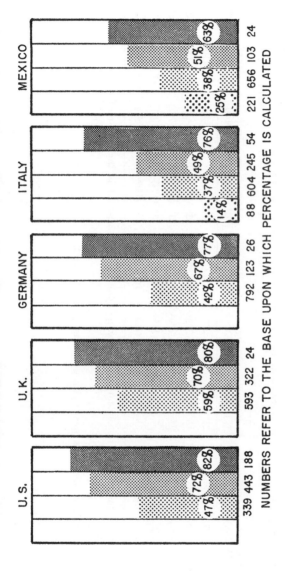

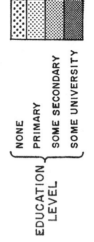

EDUCATION LEVEL
- NONE
- PRIMARY
- SOME SECONDARY
- SOME UNIVERSITY

NUMBERS REFER TO THE BASE UPON WHICH PERCENTAGE IS CALCULATED

FIG. 3

TABLE 1

Per Cent who report High Exposure to Political Communications[a] among Three Groups of Subjective Competents, by Nation and Education

Nation	Total			Primary or Less			Secondary or More		
	High[b] (%) (No.)[c]	Med. (%) (No.)	Low (%) (No.)	High (%) (No.)	Med. (%) (No.)	Low (%) (No.)	High (%) (No.)	Med. (%) (No.)	Low (%) (No.)
United States	59 (506)	46 (251)	21 (212)	51 (205)	40 (146)	15 (165)	65 (301)	54 (105)	40 (47)
Great Britain	36 (366)	33 (364)	16 (230)	29 (209)	29 (219)	13 (164)	44 (147)	40 (138)	22 (59)
Germany	57 (305)	51 (279)	23 (368)	51 (230)	49 (227)	21 (334)	77 (73)	56 (50)	50 (24)
Italy	26 (243)	25 (234)	5 (514)	13 (149)	14 (188)	3 (402)	46 (93)	41 (94)	12 (111)
Mexico	39 (201)	19 (332)	9 (474)	34 (153)	16 (287)	8 (436)	54 (47)	34 (45)	15 (35)

[a] "High" exposure to politics means that a respondent reports that he follows politics regularly in the mass media and that he pays attention to election campaigns.

[b] Level of Subjective Competence.

[c] Numbers in parentheses refer to the bases upon which percentages are calculated.

competence report that they follow politics and electoral campaigns regularly, in contrast with 8 per cent of those low on subjective competence. Or, to select an educational group that follows politics quite frequently: among the Germans with secondary education or better, 77 per cent of those of high subjective competence report that they follow politics regularly; in contrast, of those on the same educational level whose sense of subjective competence is lower, 50 per cent report following politics regularly. This pattern is noticeable in each nation.

The self-confident citizen is not only more likely to be the recipient of political communications: he is also more likely to take some part in the political communications process himself. As Table 2 shows, those respondents high on the subjective competence scale are more likely than those lower on the scale to engage in political discussion. This relationship applies to groups where such discussion is relatively rare. Italians with primary education or less are an example: 14 per cent of those low in subjective competence discuss politics, in contrast with 36 per cent high on this measure. It applies as well to groups where discussion is carried on more frequently. An example would be American respondents in the higher educational categories, among whom 64 per cent of those low in subjective competence discuss politics, as compared with 92 per cent of the highly subjectively competent citizens. Thus the self-confident citizen is more likely to be aware of what is going on in politics and to make his voice heard in political discussion.

Somewhat similar results are apparent in regard to partisan affiliation. Compared with those low in subjective competence, respondents higher on the scale are more likely to be party activists (either members of some political party or active campaign workers) and somewhat less likely to report no partisan affiliation. The relationship between partisan activity and sense of competence, however, is not as close as that between the measures of nonpartisan activity and sense of competence. Thus subjective competence has a definite effect upon the level and the kind of political activity within a society.

That the subjectively competent citizen is also likely to be the active citizen is not an unexpected finding. It is but the beginning of our inquiry into the implications of subjective competence. Of greater significance in understanding political participation is the

TABLE 2

Per Cent who report Political Discussion among Three Groups of Subjective Competents, by Nation and Education

	Total			Primary or Less			Secondary or More		
Nation	High[a] (%) (No.)[b]	Med. (%) (No.)	Low (%) (No.)	High (%) (No.)	Med. (%) (No.)	Low (%) (No.)	High (%) (No.)	Med. (%) (No.)	Low (%) (No.)
United States	87 (506)	80 (251)	44 (212)	79 (205)	73 (146)	39 (165)	92 (301)	90 (105)	64 (47)
Great Britain	81 (366)	74 (364)	46 (230)	74 (209)	69 (219)	45 (164)	88 (147)	81 (138)	49 (59)
Germany	76 (305)	68 (279)	41 (368)	72 (230)	65 (227)	40 (334)	92 (73)	84 (50)	54 (24)
Italy	46 (243)	47 (234)	18 (514)	36 (149)	33 (138)	14 (402)	62 (93)	66 (94)	33 (111)
Mexico	60 (201)	42 (332)	26 (474)	54 (153)	36 (287)	24 (436)	79 (47)	73 (45)	45 (35)

[a] Level of Subjective Competence.
[b] Numbers in parentheses refer to the bases upon which percentages are calculated.

relationship between sense of ability to participate and the individual's allegiance to the system, as reflected in his evaluation of the legitimacy and effectiveness of the system. One of the advantages a democratic political system is supposed to have over other systems is that those who are able to participate in decisions will thereby be more satisfied with the decisions, and will be more attached to the system than are those who cannot participate. According to this hypothesis, a mutually beneficial exchange occurs between the individual and the political system. In response to his influential inputs, the system produces outputs that are in some way more beneficial for the individual than they would be without those inputs. The beneficial outputs, in turn, lead the individual, through his satisfaction with the system, to a higher level of attachment to that system. In this way, if all else is equal, democratic political systems will be, from the point of view of the participants, both more effective (participants will be more satisfied with the output of the system) and more legitimate (participants will generally consider the political system to be the proper one per se).

With our data we can test the psychological form of this hypothesis. We cannot test the hypothesis that the more individuals participate in decisions, the more likely they are to receive beneficial outputs from the system in which they participate. As has been pointed out, measuring this kind of participation involves a much more complicated analysis of citizen-elite interaction than is possible in our study; and the techniques available for measuring the performance of systems are quite crude. We can, however, test the hypothesis that the perception that one can participate is related to greater satisfaction with the performance of the system and to a higher level of attachment to that system. And this psychological form of the participation hypothesis is significant for the democratic political system. It seems likely that the combination of high participation and high system performance will increase the chances of stable democracy only if both the high participation and the high system performance are perceived as such by the citizenry. If a citizenry does not consider the outputs of the system as beneficial, it is hard to see how participation can have any effect on system stability. Thus in testing the psychological form of the participation hypothesis—i.e., the relationship between participation and satisfaction with the political system, as viewed by our respondents—we are testing a crucial form of the hypothesis.

241

Satisfaction with the political system can take several forms. We have been dealing with three types of orientation to the political system: orientation to the structure of political influence (the input structure), orientation to the structure of governmental output (the output structure), and a more general, diffuse orientation to the political system as a whole. If one wants to relate satisfaction to the sense of competence to participate, it is useful to look at these three orientations. In the first place, the perceived ability to participate in decisions ought to be associated with greater satisfaction with an individual's role within the political input structure; that is, the more he thinks he has influence over the government, the more he ought to be satisfied with his role as participant. Second, one would expect that the individual who considers himself capable of affecting decisions, compared with the one who believes he has no voice, would be more likely to consider the output of those decisions favorable to him. Thus the subjective competent ought to be more positively oriented to his input role as well as to the output of the political system. But the effect of subjective competence upon his more general orientation to the system as a whole may be the most crucial issue in the relationship between participation and the potential for stability of a system. Satisfaction with governmental output may lead an individual to support his political system, and high levels of such satisfaction are therefore likely to foster political stability. For long-run stability, on the other hand, a more diffuse sense of attachment—one that is less closely tied to performance—may be more significant. Satisfaction with political output usually varies with system performance. The more diffuse sense of attachment to the system (or what we have called system affect), though in the long run not unrelated to specific output, can be expected to be a more stable kind of satisfaction. It is the kind of "rain or shine" attachment that will enable a system to weather a crisis in its performance.

Table 3 presents data on the relationship between the sense of ability to participate in politics and the satisfaction with the role of participant. To measure their satisfaction with participation in the political process, we asked respondents how they felt when they went to the polls to vote: did they have a feeling of satisfaction? a feeling that they were voting merely as a duty? did they feel annoyed at the effort it took to vote? or did they feel nothing in particular?

TABLE 3

Per Cent who report Satisfaction with their Voting Participation, among Three Groups of Subjective Competents, by Nation and Education

Nation	Total			Primary or Less			Secondary or More		
	High[a] (%) (No.)[b]	Med. (%) (No.)	Low (%) (No.)	High (%) (No.)	Med. (%) (No.)	Low (%) (No.)	High (%) (No.)	Med. (%) (No.)	Low (%) (No.)
United States	78 (400)	72 (183)	44 (109)	68 (164)	67 (111)	42 (85)	84 (237)	79 (72)	50 (24)
Great Britain	51 (330)	43 (330)	30 (198)	49 (195)	43 (205)	30 (149)	54 (126)	45 (119)	30 (44)
Germany	42 (284)	38 (251)	26 (332)	42 (219)	41 (208)	25 (303)	43 (63)	24 (41)	37 (19)
Italy	40 (225)	35 (218)	21 (476)	38 (145)	33 (135)	21 (385)	45 (80)	40 (81)	21 (90)
Mexico	50 (161)	32 (233)	26 (258)	50 (123)	30 (197)	25 (236)	51 (38)	38 (36)	34 (22)

[a] Level of Subjective Competence.
[b] Numbers in parentheses refer to the bases upon which percentages are calculated.

As Table 3 indicates, those voters higher in subjective competence are more likely to report a feeling of satisfaction with their vote. For instance, 26 per cent of the Mexican voters who are low in their sense of competence report satisfaction with their vote, whereas 50 per cent of those high in subjective competence report satisfaction. And this general pattern is found in all groups. Furthermore, fewer voters on the higher levels of subjective competence report that they feel nothing in particular or that they do not know what they feel at the polls. The self-confident citizen, this table suggests, is also the citizen who is most likely to derive satisfaction from his participation. In all nations subjective competents are more likely than others to find their role in the input structure a satisfying one.

Satisfaction with one's political role, however, is not the only satisfaction that might be related to the sense of ability to participate. One would also expect that the individual who believes himself capable of participating in decisions would be more likely to be satisfied with the outcome of those decisions. Table 4 indicates that this is generally the case. As an indicator of satisfaction with governmental output, we have taken a question on whether the activities of the local government tend to improve conditions in the area.[2] Thus we are comparing the individual's sense of competence *vis-à-vis* the local government with his evaluation of the output of the local government. In general, as Table 4 indicates, the more subjectively competent an individual feels, the more likely he is to report that the output of the local government tends to improve conditions in his area. Among Italian respondents with low levels of subjective competence, 63 per cent believe that the local government tends to improve things in the area, in contrast with 75 per cent of those high in subjective competence. The proportions of British respondents who attribute this beneficial impact to the local government are 63 per cent among those low on local competence and 74 per cent among those high on such competence. And the same pattern is found in the United States and Germany— those low on the subjective competence scale are less likely to say that the local government improves local conditions than are those high on the scale. When the level of subjective competence is held constant, the similarity among these four nations in the frequency

[2] For the purposes of this analysis, we consider only those respondents who on a previous question indicated that the activities of the local government had an impact on their lives. Further discussion of this question can be found in chapter 3.

TABLE 4

Per Cent who report Belief in the Beneficial Effect of Local Government Activities, among Three Groups of Subjective Competents,[a] by Nation and Education

Nation	Total			Primary or Less			Secondary or More		
	High[b] (%) (No.)[c]	Med. (%) (No.)	Low (%) (No.)	High (%) (No.)	Med. (%) (No.)	Low (%) (No.)	High (%) (No.)	Med. (%) (No.)	Low (%) (No.)
United States	76 (471)	72 (223)	57 (155)	73 (177)	67 (124)	58 (119)	78 (294)	78 (99)	53 (36)
Great Britain	74 (296)	68 (282)	63 (130)	74 (166)	67 (165)	64 (95)	75 (120)	68 (110)	61 (31)
Germany	75 (244)	61 (225)	62 (233)	72 (181)	62 (181)	61 (211)	84 (62)	57 (42)	76 (17)
Italy	75 (175)	69 (155)	63 (240)	72 (99)	67 (90)	62 (173)	79 (75)	72 (64)	66 (67)
Mexico	46 (79)	52 (109)	44 (122)	38 (61)	45 (91)	41 (112)	71 (17)	79 (18)	[71] (10)

[a] But only among those respondents who on a previous question indicated that the local government had an impact on their lives.
[b] Level of Subjective Competence.
[c] Numbers in parentheses refer to the bases upon which percentages are calculated.

with which local government activities are positively evaluated is quite striking.

The results for Mexico, however, form a sharp contrast to those in the other four nations. Here the sense of ability to participate is apparently unrelated to an individual's evaluation of the output of the government. Moving up the scale of subjective competence, one does not find an increasing proportion of respondents who express the belief that the activities of the local government tend to improve conditions in the area. Whereas in all the other nations the individual who believes himself to be capable of participating in decisions is more likely to evaluate the governmental output positively, the Mexican who considers himself competent to participate does not differ from others in his evaluation of the government's output. In regard to the degree of activity of citizens and their satisfaction with their participatory roles, the subjective competence scale produced a close relationship in all five nations. In regard to the evaluation of governmental output, we now find a break in the uniform pattern. In Mexico the competent citizen is not more likely to evaluate actual government performance positively. Before discussing this deviation from the pattern, let us look at the relationship between subjective competence and system affect.

The attitude most relevant to long-term political stability may not be the individual's level of satisfaction with governmental output or with his role as participant. Rather, long-run political stability may be more dependent on a more diffuse sense of attachment or loyalty to the political system—a loyalty not based specifically on system performance. The question that can be raised is: does the ability to participate within the political system lead to this kind of attachment? In contrast with, say, the individual's evaluation of system output, the more diffuse sense of attachment to the political system is somewhat hard to measure. To measure system affect we shall use our question on what the individual is proud of about his country; in particular, we shall use the frequency with which individuals report pride in some aspect of their political or governmental system. The advantage of using this question is that references to the political system are spontaneous. (For a fuller discussion of the response to this question, see Chapter 4.)

The relationship between subjective competence and pride in

246

one's political system is reported in Table 5. The most interesting point about this relationship is the difference between the United States, Britain, and Mexico, on the one hand, and Germany and Italy, on the other. In the United States, Britain, and Mexico those who consider themselves competent to participate in governmental decisions are more likely than those who do not feel this way to express pride in the political aspects of their nation. In Britain, for example, 50 per cent of those high in subjective competence indicate pride in their political system, as compared to 36 per cent of those low in subjective competence. And this generally applies to both levels of education. Furthermore, those on the high level of subjective competence are less likely than those below to say either that they are proud of nothing about their nation (a rather overt statement of alienation) or that they do not know if they are proud of anything or of what they are proud.

In Germany and Italy the pattern is quite different. There is apparently little relationship between one's sense of political competence and the likelihood that one will express pride in the political system. High scorers on the subjective competence scale are not more likely to say that they are proud of a political aspect of their nation than are low scorers on the scale. Furthermore, although the "high" competents are less likely than the "low" competents to say that they do not know what they are proud of as Italians or Germans, they are each as likely to give the rather extreme alienative response that they are proud of "nothing." In both countries the sense of political competence is related strongly to satisfaction with one's role as participant and to satisfaction with the specific output of the government. Unlike the situation in Britain, Mexico, and the United States, however, it does not appear to be related to more general system affect. Yet there is one difference between Italy and Germany in this respect. In Italy the lack of relationship between sense of competence and system affect is found on both educational levels. In Germany, on the other hand, this lack of relationship appears confined to those with no more than primary school education.

The data in Tables 3, 4, and 5 suggest that there is much validity to the hypothesis that the degree of participation in decisions affects the degree of satisfaction with the system in which one participates. In general, satisfaction increases with participation. In the United States and Britain the relationship between satis-

TABLE 5

Pride in Nation among Three Groups of Subjective Competents, by Nation and Education
(in per cent)

TOTAL

What Respondents are Proud of about their Country	United States			Great Britain			Germany			Italy			Mexico		
	High[a]	Med.	Low	High	Med.	Low	High	Med.	Low	High	Med.	Low	High	Med.	Low
Governmental and political system	92	87	67	50	49	36	9	5	6	3	8	2	38	31	26
Other aspects[b]	7	12	20	46	44	43	81	85	70	80	76	61	60	60	48
Nothing	0	0	4	2	4	8	5	3	9	8	4	11	0	2	5
Don't know	0	0	9	3	4	13	5	6	15	9	12	26	2	7	21
Total per cent	99	99	100	101	101	100	100	99	100	100	100	100	100	100	100
Total number of respondents	506	251	212	366	364	230	305	279	368	243	284	514	201	382	474

PRIMARY OR LESS

What Respondents are Proud of about their Country	United States			Great Britain			Germany			Italy			Mexico		
	High[a]	Med.	Low	High	Med.	Low	High	Med.	Low	High	Med.	Low	High	Med.	Low
Governmental and political system	87	86	64	47	44	34	8	5	7	3	4	2	35	30	25
Other aspects[b]	11	12	21	47	47	44	82	85	69	77	72	56	63	60	48
Nothing	1	0	5	1	5	9	6	4	10	10	5	11	0	3	4
Don't know	1	1	10	4	5	13	5	7	15	10	19	31	2	8	23
Total per cent	100	99	100	99	101	100	101	101	101	100	100	100	100	101	100
Total number of respondents	205	146	165	209	219	164	230	227	334	149	138	402	153	287	436

TABLE 5 (continued)

Per Cent who report Pride in Nation among Three Groups of Subjective Competents, by Nation and Education

(in per cent)

SECONDARY OR MORE

What Respondents are Proud of about their Country	United States High[a]	Med.	Low	Great Britain High	Med.	Low	Germany High	Med.	Low	Italy High	Med.	Low	Mexico High	Med.	Low
Governmental and political system	95	90	74	52	56	42	12	8	0	3	12	2	49	38	37
Other aspects[b]	4	10	15	44	40	41	79	88	96	85	83	80	51	59	50
Nothing	0	0	4	2	2	5	3	0	0	4	2	8	0	1	5
Don't know	0	0	6	2	2	12	5	4	4	8	3	10	0	1	8
Total per cent	99	100	99	100	100	100	99	100	100	99	100	100	100	99	100
Total number of respondents	301	105	47	147	138	59	73	50	24	93	94	111	47	45	35

[a] Level of Subjective Competence.
[b] "Other aspects" refers to those respondents who were proud of some other aspects rather than the political system. Respondents who report pride in the political system as well as something else are in the top row.

faction and a sense of participation is found on all three measures of satisfaction; in the other three nations the relationship is found on two of the three measures. In this respect, the democratic government that fosters a sense of ability to participate in decisions does appear to reap the benefit of this participation.

But the data do not unambiguously confirm the participation hypothesis. Rather, they suggest that the impact of an individual's sense of competence on his sense of satisfaction with and attachment to the political system may differ somewhat from nation to nation. In all five nations the citizen with a strong sense of ability to participate is more satisfied with his role as participant than is the citizen whose sense of ability is weaker. On the other hand, a positive relationship between sense of participation and satisfaction with the performance of the government is found in only four out of five nations. In Mexico the sense of competence is not related to output satisfaction. And the relationship between system affect and the sense of ability to participate is apparent in only three out of five of the nations. In Germany and Italy participation does not appear to lead to more frequent positive evaluation of the system as a whole.

These differences in the types of satisfaction associated with participation have important implications. As was reported and discussed in Chapter 4, German and Italian respondents report least frequently that they are proud of the political aspects of their nations. Expressions of pride are directed at other national objects, but not at the political system. This is readily understandable in light of the recent political histories of these two nations. The present systems of government are rather new and have been, to some extent, externally imposed. In contrast with the United States and Britain—and even in contrast with Mexico, whose government has undergone a rather gradual evolution for the past forty years or so since the Mexican Revolution—politics in Germany and Italy have shown sharp discontinuities.

But the absolute *level* of expression of national pride is not in question here. Granting the differences in absolute level, we are searching for the *relationship* between sense of participation and the expression of national pride. And here the important point emerges that, whereas in the other three nations the sense of ability to participate in political decisions seems to be translated to some degree into general pride in the political system, little of this process is apparent in Germany and Italy. In these two nations even the individual who considers himself highly capable of influencing the government is no more likely to express pride in the political aspects of his nation than is the individual who feels no such sense of competence; and the self-confident citizen is as likely as the other citizen to express alienation from his nation. In the United States, Britain, and Mexico the sense of ability to participate appears to yield a general attachment to the political system. In Germany and Italy, though there is some opportunity to participate and though there are respondents who consider themselves competent to do so, this participation has not led to a greater sense of identification with the political system. Thus the positive relationship between subjective competence and system affect found among Germans with secondary education or better becomes important. It suggests that the ability to participate is beginning to be translated into attachment to the political system among those who have attained some higher educational level. In Italy, on the other hand, the gap between participation and system affect is wider.

As the data for Germany and Italy suggest, any positive attachment to the political system that derives from participation in that system tends to be rather pragmatic. The citizen who believes himself capable of participation, compared with the one who holds no such belief, does tend to be more satisfied with his political system, but it is satisfaction with the specific performance of the system. If our hypothesis about the significance of system affect for the long-run success of a political system is correct, it would appear that the sense of ability to participate within governmental decision making —an attitude that has developed in Germany and Italy since the formation of democratic governments—will foster the stability of those democratic systems as long as the performance of the system is kept at a high level. If the performance of the system lags, the fact that some Italians and Germans consider themselves capable of participating within it might add little to the chances of survival of democracy in these two nations.

The relationship between satisfaction and sense of participation in Mexico differs significantly from that found in Germany and Italy. In Mexico, as in all the other nations, subjective competence is positively related to satisfaction with one's role as participant. Furthermore, in Mexico, as in the United States and Britain (but

251

unlike the pattern in Germany and Italy), the sense of political competence is related to general system affect. In Mexico, however, unlike the other four nations, there is no apparent relationship between sense of competence and satisfaction with the specific performance of the political system.

We cannot be sure why the pattern of Mexican responses should deviate from the participation hypothesis in this way, but the parallel between this finding and some earlier data suggests an explanation. In Mexico the sense of competence is related to general system affect, but not to a more favorable view of the actual performance of the system. This may be the pattern one would expect to find associated with a revolutionary or aspirational orientation to politics. Interest and involvement in politics, we have suggested, did not develop gradually among the Mexican people. Instead, the ordinary citizen's awareness of politics and, indeed, of his membership in a nation probably derived from the dramatic upheavals of the Mexican Revolution. Participation in politics did not spread gradually through the nation, nor was the first experience with political participation related to some specific issue.[3] Rather, the first sense of participation was in a heavily affective-laden nationalistic uprising. And the symbolic importance of the Revolution in Mexican politics has persisted to the present day. Participation, then, is not closely related to the day-to-day operations of the Mexican government; indeed, a highly active sense of participation and patriotism coexists with a low evaluation of actual government performance. Participation exists on an aspirational level. The Mexican with a strong sense of participation is positively oriented to his nation as symbol and to his political system on the more general level. He does not expect any better performance from the actual government.

The most thoroughgoing relationship between sense of ability to participate and satisfaction with the political system exists in the United States and Britain. The subjective competents are more likely to express satisfaction with their roles as participants and with the specific performance of the system; and they are also more likely to express general pride in the political system. In Britain and the United States one finds neither the gap between sense of participa-

[3] For an example of the way in which mobilization into politics may develop gradually, through the spread of the franchise and (what may not be the same) of voting from "central" to more "peripheral" segments of society, see Stein Rokkan, "Trends in Political Mobilization" (a paper prepared for a UNESCO Conference on Comparative Political Behavior, Bergen, Norway, June 1961, mimeographed).

tion and general attachment to the system apparent in Italy and Germany, nor the gap between sense of participation and satisfaction with the system performance apparent in Mexico. Participation is neither on the unreal aspirational level, as in Mexico, nor on the pragmatic level, as in Italy and Germany. Rather, it involves a more positive orientation to the state on the most general level, as well as more positive specific expectations of system performance.

Here then is striking evidence for the existence of a "balanced" democratic political orientation in the United States and Britain. Participation in politics in these two nations is linked with both affective orientation to the political system and specific pragmatic expectations of the system. One has neither political participation that is related only to specific system performance nor political participation related to the political system on the symbolic level but not to actual politics.

Competence and Democratic Values

If our data in the previous section are correct, democratic systems do have some of the advantages imputed to them. At least from the point of view of the individual participant, the opportunity to participate in political decisions is associated with greater satisfaction with that system and with greater general loyalty to the system. (This conclusion, though, requires all the qualifications introduced in the previous section.) Everything being equal, the sense of ability to participate in politics appears to increase the legitimacy of a system and to lead to political stability.[4]

If, in addition to being satisfied with their political system, subjective competents believe that a participatory system is the proper system to have, then the potential stability of a democratic system has been increased even more. If those who consider themselves more competent to participate also value the participation of their fellow citizens more highly—believe in electoral democracy, believe that the ordinary man ought to be a participant—then participation within politics will increase the democratic potential of a nation by increasing the citizens' commitment to democratic values.

The data in Table 6 indicate that those who consider themselves competent to participate are also more likely to believe that a dem-

---

[4] This point needs some qualification. High levels of participation may have unstabilizing effects on a system. But the *sense* of competence, especially when coupled with a somewhat lower actual fulfillment of this competence, does play an important role in political stability. See chapter 15 below for a further discussion of this point.

TABLE 6

Per Cent who report Belief that Elections are Necessary, among Three Groups of Subjective Competents, by Nation and Education

Nation	Total						Primary or Less						Secondary or More					
	High[a] (%)	(No.)[b]	Med. (%)	(No.)	Low (%)	(No.)	High (%)	(No.)	Med. (%)	(No.)	Low (%)	(No.)	High (%)	(No.)	Med. (%)	(No.)	Low (%)	(No.)
United States	81	(506)	74	(251)	58	(212)	77	(205)	71	(146)	57	(165)	84	(301)	78	(105)	64	(47)
Great Britain	70	(366)	64	(364)	52	(230)	63	(209)	63	(219)	51	(164)	80	(147)	64	(138)	58	(59)
Germany	53	(305)	46	(279)	29	(368)	52	(230)	45	(227)	30	(334)	59	(73)	48	(50)	29	(24)
Italy	53	(243)	49	(234)	28	(514)	46	(149)	46	(138)	24	(402)	62	(93)	55	(94)	40	(111)
Mexico	71	(201)	66	(332)	52	(474)	72	(153)	64	(287)	52	(436)	68	(47)	79	(45)	57	(35)

[a] Level of Subjective Competence.
[b] Numbers in parentheses refer to the bases upon which percentages are calculated.

ocratic participatory system is the proper system to have. In each nation those respondents higher on the subjective competence scale are more likely than those below to report that election campaigning is a good thing.[5] In Mexico, for instance, 71 per cent of the respondents high on the scale report that election campaigns are needed, whereas 52 per cent of those low on the scale hold this view.

That subjective competence seems to be related to adherence to formal democratic rules is shown perhaps more clearly in Table 7. This relates sense of political competence to the frequency with which respondents report that the average man has an obligation to be an active participant in his local community. As was reported in Chapter 6, there are national differences in the frequency with which respondents report that the citizen ought to participate in the affairs of his community. Table 7 indicates that despite these differences in evaluation, in all nations those who consider themselves most competent to participate are also most likely to believe that the ordinary man has an obligation to be a participating citizen. The relationship is quite close between the belief in one's own participatory capabilities and the norm that people ought to participate, and it is found both where adherence to the norm is widespread (e.g., America) and where it is less frequent (e.g., Italy). Among American respondents who most frequently report that the individual has an obligation to be a participant in his community, 61 per cent of those high on subjective competence report that the ordinary man has such an obligation, in contrast with 23 per cent of those low on the subjective competence scale. Of those Italians who are high in subjective competence, 19 per cent report that the individual has an obligation to be active in his local community, in contrast with 4 per cent of those low in subjective competence. In general, then, the individual who feels competent to participate is also more likely to place a high value on participation by the ordinary man.

The Self-Confident Citizen: Conclusion

The citizen, as he has been defined in this study, is the man able to take some part in the running of his political system. He has influ-

[5] The question was phrased so as to make it easy for those who were opposed to electoral campaigns to express their opposition. It read: "Some people feel that campaigning is needed so that the public can judge candidates and issues. Others say it causes so much bitterness and is so unreliable that we would be better off without it. What do you think—is it needed or would we be better off without it?"

TABLE 7

Per Cent who report Belief that the Ordinary Man Should be Active in his Community, among Three Groups of Subjective Competents, by Nation and Education

	Total			Primary or Less			Secondary or More		
Nation	High[a] (%) (No.)[b]	Med. (%) (No.)	Low (%) (No.)	High (%) (No.)	Med. (%) (No.)	Low (%) (No.)	High (%) (No.)	Med. (%) (No.)	Low (%) (No.)
United States	61 (506)	54 (251)	23 (212)	53 (205)	46 (146)	18 (165)	67 (301)	66 (105)	38 (47)
Great Britain	48 (366)	42 (364)	21 (230)	45 (209)	41 (219)	22 (164)	50 (147)	43 (138)	20 (59)
Germany	33 (305)	27 (279)	12 (368)	32 (230)	25 (227)	12 (334)	38 (73)	34 (50)	17 (24)
Italy	19 (243)	14 (234)	4 (514)	13 (149)	11 (138)	3 (402)	30 (93)	19 (94)	8 (111)
Mexico	35 (201)	32 (332)	19 (474)	34 (153)	30 (287)	17 (436)	40 (47)	39 (45)	33 (35)

[a] Level of Subjective Competence.
[b] Numbers in parentheses refer to the bases upon which percentages are calculated.

ence over the decisions that are made in it. Throughout this study we have stressed the importance of the extent to which individuals consider themselves to be citizens in this sense. The frequency with which they rate themselves competent to participate in their political system may be taken as an index of the extent to which they consider their nations democratic. Since these individuals may be wrong about their influence potential, it would be mistaken to take the frequency of positive self-evaluations as an objective index of democracy. Nevertheless, because we are studying the political orientation associated with democracy, data on citizens' subjective competence are crucial.

Besides being an index of the extent to which citizens consider their political systems democratic, subjective competence seems to be closely related to many other attitudes vital for understanding the nature of democratic political orientations.

Compared with the citizen whose subjective competence is low, the self-confident citizen is likely to be the active citizen: to follow politics, to discuss politics, to be a more active partisan. He is also more likely to be satisfied with his role as a participant and, subject to certain exceptions discussed above, likely to be more favorably disposed toward the performance of his political system and to have a generally more positive orientation toward it.

Finally, the self-confident citizen is more likely to express adherence to the values associated with a democratic system. He is more likely to believe that election campaigns are needed and to believe that the ordinary man has an obligation to participate in the affairs of his community.

In many ways, then, the belief in one's competence is a key political attitude. The self-confident citizen appears to be the democratic citizen. Not only does he think he can participate, he thinks that others ought to participate as well. Furthermore, he does not merely think he can take a part in politics: he is likely to *be* more active. And, perhaps most significant of all, the self-confident citizen is also likely to be the more satisfied and loyal citizen.

PART III

SOCIAL RELATIONS AND
POLITICAL CULTURE

CHAPTER 10

SOCIAL RELATIONS AND CIVIC COOPERATION

In Part II we discussed specifically political qualities and attitudes, their distribution in the five countries, and their interdependence as a democratic syndrome. To separate out political qualities and attitudes from general cultural characteristics is analytically justifiable. Only in that way can we treat political culture as a separate variable, examine its component parts and their interrelationships, and establish the ways in which national political cultures differ from one another. To do so, however, is not to imply that political attitudes are autonomous and unrelated to other social attitudes. They are in fact closely related to other social attitudes, but it is only by separating them out that we can then relate them to their more general social context.

In Part III we turn to this theme of the social and psychological conditions with which democratic culture is associated. Needless to say, the relation between forms of society and the polity has engrossed the efforts of political theorists from Aristotle down to Marx and Weber. More recently Lasswell, Lane, Rosenberg, and Lipset have dealt with aspects of this relationship. Lipset is concerned primarily with the relationship between economic modernization and democratic stability. Lasswell, Rosenberg, and Lane concern themselves with the social-psychological requisites of democracy. Lasswell argues the thesis that the "democratic community" is associated with a "democratic character," and that the central property of the democratic character is an "open ego," or a capacity to relate to others and share values with them, a sense of confidence in the benevolence of the human environment, and relative freedom from anxiety. Morris Rosenberg has shown that faith in people, as measured by an ingeniously constructed scale, is strongly correlated with belief in the democratic process. And Lane, writing in more general terms about the social psychological bases of democratic attitudes, stresses that "ego strength," or a general sense of personal effectiveness, and faith in people are essential to democratic participation. He provides evidence based on research in the United States to support these hypotheses.[1]

In order to analyze the relationship between such social and psychological variables and political attitudes, we shall first describe some findings on the differences in general social and interpersonal attitudes among the five nations. We concentrate on the individual's nonpolitical relations with his fellow man: the extent to which he is engaged in social relations with him, his attitudes toward him. These attitudes toward his social and interpersonal environment, we believe, might help explain the individual's view of the specifically political aspects of his environment. After describing these social and interpersonal attitudes and how they are distributed among the five nations, we shall turn to their relationship with political attitudes.

Leisure Time and Sociability

How can one measure the extent to which social interaction is valued in a society? Certain kinds of social relations are in a sense involuntary, and the actors' interest in them is not indicative of the value they place on social interaction. Interacting with members of one's family, for example, is unavoidable. Family members living in a household must interact with one another, though undoubtedly there are cultural differences in the extent to which family interaction or "togetherness" is valued, or in the extent to which the culture encourages individuation among the family members. Similarly, social interaction is unavoidable in many, perhaps most, work situations. Consequently, in our question designed to get at "sociability" or social interaction, we deliberately directed the respondent away from these more or less compulsory situations, and toward the leisure-time of his daily life; and we sought to discover whether he preferred the leisure activities of a group or of an individual sort. The question was asked at the very beginning of the interview and was open ended. Hence we may view the responses as

[1] Harold D. Lasswell, *Power and Personality*, pp. 148 ff., and *Political Writings*, pp. 465 ff.; Robert E. Lane, *Political Life*, pp. 163 ff.; Seymour M. Lipset, *Political Man*, pp. 45 ff., and Morris Rosenberg, "Misanthropy and Political Ideology," *American Sociological Review*, XXI (1956), p. 691.

spontaneous statements of preference and behavior. The actual text of the question with interviewer instructions was as follows:

"We'd like to start out by talking about some of your more general interests. Now aside from your work and your family, what are the activities that interest you most, that you spend your free time on? [Probe] Is there anything else?" [For those who say they have no free

TABLE 1

Preferred Leisure Activities, by Nation
(in per cent)

Per Cent interested in	U.S.	U.K.	Germany	Italy	Mexico
Civic-political activities	2	2	3	1	0
Economic interest groups	0	0	1	0	0
Other interest groups	3	0	0	0	0
Charitable and welfare activities	8	5	2	2	1
Religious activities	20	7	4	2	4
"Social" activities	18	18	8	3	6
Total per cent choosing outgoing activity**	40	30	16	7	11
Hobbies, sports, etc.	70	73	61	42	51
Cultural activities (reading, tv, radio, etc.)	33	44	52	33	58
Travel	0	3	7	8	13
Other only	0	5	15	17	4
Nothing	3	6	6	10	2
Don't know	0	0	1	3	1
Total number of respondents	970	963	955	995	1,007
Total per cent respondents	100	100	100	100	100
Total per cent responses*	157	163	160	121	140

* Percentages exceed one hundred because of multiple responses.

** Percentages in this row are less than the sum of those above since some respondents chose more than one outgoing activity.

time:] "If you had more free time and opportunity, which activities would you like to engage in?"

The responses were coded under the categories listed in Table 1. It is of interest that in all five countries the percentages of respondents expressing interest in specifically political activities during their leisure time are extremely small. The first three rows of the table recording the frequency of civic-political, economic interest group, and other interest group activity contain only very small percentages. This confirms the proposition that the proportion of individuals for whom civic activity is highly salient tends to be small in all countries. This is not the case, however, for social activity. In the United States and Britain the percentages of respondents reporting interest and participation in charitable and welfare activities, religious group activities (other than church attendance proper), and social activities are markedly higher than in Germany, Italy, and Mexico. If one considers all respondents who mention some activity that brings them into social interaction with other people, the proportions vary from 40 per cent in the United States to 7 per cent in Italy. The remainder of the activity categories are largely individual pursuits, such as hobbies of one kind or another, reading, viewing television, listening to the radio, or travelling.

TABLE 2

Per Cent Choosing Outgoing Activities, by Nation and Education

Nation	Total (%)	(No.)*	Prim. or Less (%)	(No.)	Some Sec. (%)	(No.)	Some Univ. (%)	(No.)
United States	40	(970)	32	(339)	45	(442)	41	(188)
Great Britain	30	(963)	29	(593)	31	(322)	33	(24)
Germany	16	(955)	15	(792)	22	(123)	12	(26)
Italy	7	(995)	8	(692)	5	(245)	11	(54)
Mexico	11	(1,007)	11	(877)	10	(127)	16	(24)

* Numbers in parentheses refer to the bases upon which percentages are calculated.

These data suggest that in the stable democracies there is a higher incidence of social interaction outside of the more or less compulsory relationships of family and work group. This voluntary social interaction expresses "moral" purposes (social, welfare, and religious) as well as more recreational and social purposes. One may infer that the pattern of voluntary social interaction is relatively well established in the stable democracies, and that this in turn reflects feelings of confidence and safety in the social environment. Thus in those countries where there is a higher incidence of cooperative civic competence, there also appears to be a higher incidence of social interaction in other than political contexts. Furthermore, as Table 2 points out, the frequency of mention of outgoing activities is relatively independent of educational attainment. There is some tendency for those with higher education to report such activities more frequently, but compared with other educational patterns the differences are slight.

Valuing Outgoing Character Qualities

Some writers have suggested that the populations of stable democracies place a high value on "open" or "outgoing" character qualities. The logic of this hypothesis is as follows. If an effectively functioning democracy requires a high incidence of civic competence, and if this in turn is based on a capacity to join with others in seeking civic and political goals, then we would expect to see a high value placed on character qualities that are related to cooperating and working with others.

TABLE 3

Per Cent Who Choose Generosity as Most Admired Quality,
by Nation and Education

Nation	Total (%)	(No.)*	Prim. or Less (%)	(No.)	Some Sec. (%)	(No.)	Some Univ. (%)	(No.)
United States	59	(970)	39	(339)	66	(442)	80	(188)
Great Britain	65	(963)	60	(593)	73	(322)	83	(24)
Germany	42	(955)	37	(792)	64	(123)	85	(26)
Italy	25	(995)	21	(692)	31	(245)	39	(54)
Mexico	36	(1,007)	35	(877)	44	(127)	34	(24)

* Numbers in parentheses refer to the bases upon which percentages are calculated.

In one of our questions we confronted our respondents with a list of statements describing different character qualities. Respondents were asked to choose the two characteristics they admired most.[2] The most decided difference among the nations lies in the greater frequency with which American and British respondents report that they admire generosity and considerateness. When asked to name the characteristic they admire most in people, 59 per cent of the American respondents and 65 per cent of the British mention these outgoing, interpersonal virtues; these characteristics are mentioned by 42 per cent in Germany, 25 per cent in Italy, and 36 per cent in Mexico. Furthermore, the selection of generosity and considerateness as admirable qualities rises sharply with educational and occupational status in the United States, Britain, Germany, and Italy (see Table 3).

In Mexico, on the other hand, higher education seems to have less

[2] Actual text of the question was: "All of us have ideas about what people should be like. Here is a list of characteristics you might find in people [see Appendix B, *List 1*, p. 527]. Could you select the quality you admire the most?"

effect on the frequency with which generosity and considerateness are selected. A similar national pattern emerges when we control for occupation. In the United States, Britain, and Germany we find a sharp rising curve as we move from unskilled workers to professional and managerial personnel, while in Italy and Mexico the differences are quite small. These findings would seem to suggest that in the United States, Britain, Germany, and, to a lesser extent, Italy, these "protocivic" or "precivic" qualities of valuing "outgoingness" exist most frequently among those whose educational and occupational advantages are greatest. But the sharpest variation in the frequency with which the "outgoing" virtues of generosity and considerateness are valued is not within, but among, the nations. In the United States and Britain these are more frequently mentioned even within matched educational and occupational groups.

Feelings of Safety and Responsiveness

The frequency with which people interact with one another and the kinds of character qualities they admire are in turn related to the qualities they impute to their social environments. We would expect that people who frequently engage in group activities and who place a high value on outgoing character qualities would also tend to view the human environment as safe and responsive. In order to get at these feelings and expectations about social relations in our five countries, we used a group of questions developed by Morris Rosenberg. In a series of articles Rosenberg has shown that "faith in people," as measured by responses to these questions, is related to democratic and internationalist values and attitudes. Rosenberg's populations consisted of American university students. In our study they were used for the first time on cross-section samples.[3]

[3] Rosenberg, "Misanthropy and Political Ideology," *American Sociological Review*, XXI pp. 690-95; and "Misanthropy and Attitudes Toward International Affairs," *Journal of Conflict Resolution*, I (1957), pp. 340-45.

The five items in the scale were:

"1. Some people say that most people can be trusted. Others say you can't be too careful in your dealings with people. How do you feel about it?

"2. Would you say that most people are more inclined to help others, or more inclined to look out for themselves?

"3. If you don't watch yourself, people will take advantage of you.

"4. No one is going to care much what happens to you, when you get right down to it.

"5. Human nature is fundamentally cooperative."

To form a "faith in people" scale, respondents were given one point for responding that "most people can be trusted," that "people are more inclined to help others"; for

The questions required the respondents to make sweeping judgments of human nature and behavior, in the form of simple yes or no, agree-disagree, statements. Nevertheless, we can infer mood and emotional "tone" from the response patterns. In addition, we shall have occasion to report more detailed responses to similar questions asked of a subsample in each country in our political life-history interviews.

In Table 4 we have grouped the questions into two classes. The

TABLE 4
Social Trust and Distrust, by Nation
(in per cent)

Per Cent who agree that	U.S.	U.K.	Germany	Italy	Mexico
STATEMENTS OF DISTRUST					
"No one is going to care much what happens to you, when you get right down to it."	38	45	72	61	78
"If you don't watch yourself, people will take advantage of you."	68	75	81	73	94
STATEMENTS OF TRUST					
"Most people can be trusted."	55	49	19	7	30
"Most people are more inclined to help others than to think of themselves first."	31	28	15	5	15
"Human nature is fundamentally cooperative."	80	84	58	55	82
Total numbers of respondents	970	963	955	995	1,007

first two are statements reflecting distrust of others; the first of this pair reflects alienation or distrust, and the second reflects the desirability of caution in dealing with others. The first statement of alienation brings out sharp differences between the American and British respondents, on the one hand, and the Germans, Italians, and Mexicans, on the other. The second statement of distrust, which gets at the desirability of being cautious in relation to others, seems to be almost universally supported in all five countries.

The more moderate of the two positive statements about social responsiveness and trust (i.e., the statement that most people can be

disagreeing with items *3* and *4*, and for agreeing with item *5*. Those who gave the opposite answers to those listed above were given a score of −1 for each of these answers. Equivocal answers, such as "it depends" or "some people can be trusted and others not," were given a score of zero. The respondents were then classified into three groups, depending on their level of "faith in people." In the high group are those whose scores ranged from +2 to +5; in the middle are those whose scores ranged from −2 to +1, and in the low group are those who scores ranged from −3 to −5. This scoring differs from that which Rosenberg used for his scale.

trusted) brings out sharp differences among the countries: the American and British respondents show the highest frequencies of trustfulness, the Italians and Germans the lowest, and the Mexicans are in-between. The stronger statement on interpersonal trust (most people are more inclined to help others) produces less frequent agreement, but again the percentages are higher for the American and British respondents. The fifth question, on whether or not human nature is fundamentally cooperative, offered in effect a "free ride" toward optimism and faith. It did not direct respondents' attention toward the immediate situation and realistic expectations. The percentages in all five countries are high, but again the German and Italian percentages are substantially lower than the American, British, and Mexican.

If we look down the columns we discover three national patterns. First, the American and British responses are on the whole at the low end of the continuum on the measures of social distrust and at the high end on the measures of trust. Second, the German and Italian responses show relatively high distrust and low trust. The Mexican pattern is mixed. More Mexicans than Italians and Germans agree with the alienative statements. And, with one exception, more Mexicans than Italians and Germans agree with the last three positive statements. In other words, the Americans and British tend to be consistently most positive about the safety and responsiveness of the human environment, the Germans and Italians more negative, and the Mexicans inconsistent.[4]

In all five countries confidence in the human environment tends to increase among the better educated and economically more privileged elements of the populations. This is indicated in Table 5, in which we have taken the statement that reflects the most extreme feeling of distrust and alienation: "No one cares what happens to you." The percentage of those who agree with this statement drops sharply in the United States and England as we move from the less

[4] In this chapter we shall relate political attitudes to these more general interpersonal attitudes of trust and confidence in other people. But it is useful to remember that these nonpolitical social attitudes may in turn be affected by the political experiences of a nation. The way in which an attitude such as trust in other people can be affected by political events is suggested by the results to a question on trust in other people asked in Germany in 1948, a decade before our study. Though in 1959 as many as 59 per cent of the Germans responded that people could *not* be trusted, in 1948 this negative response occured among 93 per cent of the respondents. This suggests that German distrust was at least partly engendered by the particularly harsh nature of the postwar environment in that country. (See *NORC Opinion News*, August 1948.)

to the better educated. In Germany, Italy, and Mexico there is a drop, but around two-thirds of the secondary-school respondents and around one-half of the university-educated respondents agree to this extreme statement of alienation and distrust. These data suggest that in Germany, Italy, and Mexico, even among the educated middle and upper classes, a feeling of suspicion about human relations tends to prevail. Interaction with others, outside the narrow circles of family and friends, is viewed as risky and dangerous.

In our life-history interviews we repeated two of the "faith in people" questions in open-ended form. We asked the smaller number

TABLE 5
Per Cent Saying "No One Cares," by Nation and Education

Nation	Prim. or Less (%)	(No.)*	Some Sec. (%)	(No.)	Some Univ. (%)	(No.)
United States	56	(338)	32	(443)	19	(188)
Great Britain	51	(593)	34	(322)	29	(24)
Germany	75	(790)	62	(124)	58	(26)
Italy	62	(692)	60	(245)	48	(54)
Mexico	81	(877)	65	(127)	59	(24)

* Numbers in parentheses refer to the bases upon which percentages are calculated.

of respondents whether they felt they could trust most people in their neighborhood or community, and whether their neighbors were more inclined to help others or to look out for themselves. In each case respondents were asked to give examples. While trustful and distrustful respondents turned up in all countries, they turned up most frequently among the Italians, Mexicans, and Germans. Furthermore, the statements of distrust coming from these three countries, compared with American and British distrust, appeared to reflect greater anxiety. Some responses may illustrate these points.

An Italian Local Government Messenger:
"To trust completely, no! Have friends but do not get intimate with anyone. We have seen friends deceive for greediness. So be friends, but at a distance."
An Italian Laborer:
"I am accustomed to mind my own business and not to mix with other people. I work, I eat, I sleep."
An Italian Shopowner:
"It is better to be reserved, on account of the political question, but

269

also one has to know how to live among people. We have all taken parts in fights. I fought too. I threw myself against my enemies. (I am thinking about political fights.) But today I have no rancor, while others do."

An Italian Retired Workman:
"On the whole we should be careful. Politics has something to do with it. Certainly, when politics enters in, one should be careful with whom one talks. Many things have happened, but it is useless to talk about it here."

An Italian Salesman:
"Never trust people of your own town. They taught us this way and so they tell us. It is better not to get in further trouble. We don't help each other. Sometimes yes, but then it is among us, a group of friends, almost a small society."

An Italian Housewife:
"One should always keep quiet, because people envy each other. The only thing is to keep quiet at home. The less they know, the better it is."

The Mexican cases frequently showed fear of actual violence.

A Mexican Peasant:
"To tell you the truth, I don't trust anyone. . . . I am afraid someone will try to kill me because I am not a Catholic."

A Mexican Housewife:
"As things are today it is better not to trust anyone. . . . People do many things, like stealing. I have seen them enter houses to steal and do atrocities to the women and children."

A Mexican Workman:
"One cannot trust the majority of the people. People here steal and kill. At night one cannot trust anybody. For example, one night at the corner I was attacked and they hit me and my friend."

The German respondents complained primarily of envy, indifference, and general malevolence in their communities.

A German Housewife:
"You can trust very few people. They are usually full of jealousy and ill feeling. Each one wants to have more than the other. Each one pretends to be more than he is. It's the same everywhere."

A German Metal Worker:
"It is best to rely on one's self, and to keep to one's self. You never know whom you can trust. You can't see inside people. . . . You never really know the other person."

A German Housewife:

"I wouldn't trust my best friend. They gossip about everything. If there's a quarrel they talk about everything. We have no time to talk with people anyway. . . . When some neighbors had gone away after the war, the others told such stories about them that I said, 'Let's have nothing more to do with these people.' "

A German Architect:

"The people around here are mostly civil servants. Everyone wants to have more but has a definite place in his salary group. They see that I work independently and can afford this and that. . . . These civil servants are incredibly jealous, mean, and without conscience. . . . We Germans envy others easily. . . . We always want to have more than others, and ambition, vanity, and overbearing attitude contribute their share."

There were, of course, Italian, Mexican, and German respondents who expressed trust of their neighbors and gave examples of helpfulness and reliability in their communities; just as there were American and British respondents who complained about the ill will and untrustworthiness of their neighbors.

A British Housewife:

"Oh, I wouldn't trust anybody, love. People are so made they'll take anything from you in front of your eyes. If I put a bit of carpet on the front step, it wouldn't last two minutes. Somebody would take it. Oh no! You can't trust them at all. I had a bit of coal at the back here. One day the woman next door said, 'I saw a lady and two kids out at the back stealing your coal!' I said, 'Why didn't you stop it?' They're like that around here, they'd steal the eyes out of your head and come back for the lashes."

An English Small Contractor:

"I think you should be careful. We have one man on the job who, though a friend in name, I feel sure was the person who robbed me of my pay packet, and I was so upset I felt I could not trust anyone wholly again."

An American Stenographer:

"From the little bit I've seen of the people around here they talk very nicely and as soon as you walk away they stick a knife in your back."

An American Negro Maid:

"They will give to the Red Cross and the United Appeal and things like that, but they see people right in their community who need help and they don't do a thing. . . . They rather say the father is no good and let the children suffer."

271

More typical of the American and British respondents were statements of confidence in the reliability and trustworthiness of neighbors.

A British Stenographer:
"We are friendly on each side of us. We've been to parties, and so
on, and they come in here, and also people on the other side of the
road. For instance, people ask Clem to go into their houses to see
to things that need repairing. And when I was ill after an operation
the women from around here came in and asked me into their
houses. When I was in the hospital I had lots of flowers."

A British Higher Civil Servant:
"In my relations with the trade union side I often tell them more
than I need to explain something, and they don't betray the confidence."

A British Bus Depot Superintendent:
"When I say they can be trusted, it's rather a sweeping statement.
You have to use a certain amount of intelligence and pick the individual out before you can trust them. You wouldn't ask a stranger
to hold fifty pounds for you. But you could trust him to give a mes-
sage or do a service for you. People are a bit on the reserved side."

A British Dressmaker:
"They neighbor more here than in better class districts. Everyone
knows each other's business. When they are having babies, the neighbors come to the rescue, as they cannot afford to have anyone to
look after them."

An American Housewife:
"I lived here four years and my husband's been sick two years. We
moved over to this part of the building only two years ago, and we
were here only six weeks when he had his first stroke. There wasn't
a person here who did not stop and want to know how he was. They
brought me lunch when I was not feeling well and they have helped
by staying with him when I wanted to get out."

An American Housewife:
"When the Williamson's house burned down we got up enough food,
furniture, and money to start them off again. I told you when you
were here before how we all helped each other out during the snow.
Why I could talk all day on this and not get through. You know how
people help out at death."

In all five countries statements about trustfulness and helpfulness
were frequently accompanied by qualifications. Thus some said
that people in small towns or villages could trust one another while
city people could not; or that working-class people and farmers

could trust one another but middle-class people could not; or that they could trust people in their own streets but didn't know about other areas. British and American respondents reported most frequently that they trust others in general. Statements of trust among the German, Italian, and Mexican respondents were most frequently accompanied by qualifications. There was irony, either intended or unintended, in the comment of an Italian tax official: "I have the impression that we can be trustful. In my work in the tax office I have never seen attempts to avoid payment that were either obvious or too frequent."

Social Attitudes and Political Cooperation

The data presented in the previous section suggest that the five nations differ in general social attitudes. Our next task is to see how these social attitudes relate to political attitudes. The particular political attitude whose roots we shall seek in social attitudes is what we have labeled "civic cooperation"—the propensity to work with others in attempting to influence the government. Why do some individuals believe that they can cooperate with their fellow citizens in political activity while others do not? Why is it, for instance, that the American who wants to get something accomplished politically thinks immediately of talking to his friends and neighbors about his problem and getting them to help him, while this possibility would rarely occur to an Italian?

In the following chapters we shall attempt to find some of the social sources of political activity and of the feeling of political competence. In this chapter we shall not deal with the roots of the belief in one's ability to affect the government, but, rather, with the question of why some people who think they can influence the government would attempt to do so alone, while others would cooperate with their fellow citizens. Thus we shall be looking, not only for the social roots of certain orientations toward the government, but for the roots of certain orientations toward one's fellow political actors.

Why concentrate on the sources of the propensity to work along with others in political affairs? There are several reasons. In the first place, one would expect political cooperation to be influenced by one's view of the social environment. And, furthermore, this type of political behavior has significant implications both for the

273

political perspectives of the individual who engages in it and for the political system in which such activity is common. The reasons why such cooperative political behavior is important were discussed at some length in Chapter 7, and they only need mention here. Briefly, these include: (1) cooperation with one's fellow citizens is a means of raising the individual's influence potential vis-à-vis the government; (2) the ability to form political groups in time of political stress represents a "reserve of influence" on the individual's part; (3) the belief that one's primary group affiliations are available to aid one politically represents an integration of some of the most basic social units with the political system—an integration that greatly affects the democratic potential of a nation, because it occurs in relation to the "input structure" of politics, the process whereby individuals attempt to influence their government; and (4) the belief that one's fellow political actors will cooperate with one represents at least an incipient tendency to aggregate one's demands on the government with the demands of one's fellows—a process that is necessary for democratic decision making.

The extent of political cooperation differs strikingly among the five nations—another reason for concentrating on this topic. As the data in Chapter 7 indicated, the propensity to form political groups is almost absent in some nations and exceedingly common in others. In fact, one has the impression that this propensity, in whatever degree it exists, is one of the most important aspects of political culture. This, of course, is a finding that other observers of politics have made. Tocqueville, for one, comments at length on the number of political groups observed in America:

"No sooner do you set foot upon American ground than you are stunned by a kind of tumult; a confused clamor is heard on every side, and a thousand simultaneous voices demand the satisfaction of their social wants. Everything is in motion around you; here the people of one quarter of a town are met to decide upon the building of a church; there the election of a representative is going on; a little farther, the delegates of a district are hastening to the town in order to consult upon some local improvements; in another place, the laborers of a village quit their plows to deliberate upon the project of a road or a public school. Meetings are called for the sole purpose of declaring their disapprobation of the conduct of the government; while in other assemblies citizens salute the authorities of the day as the fathers of their country. Societies are formed which regard drunkenness as the principal cause of the evils of the state, and solemnly bind themselves to give an example of temperance. . . ."[5]

And the vast difference in the tone of politics between a political system where such activity is rife and a system where it is rare can be illustrated by quoting at some length from the first few pages of a book on an Italian village by an acute student of American local politics:

"Americans are used to a buzz of activity having as its purpose, at least in part, the advancement of community welfare. For example, a single issue of the weekly newspaper published in St. George, Utah (population 4,562), reports a variety of public spirited undertakings. The Red Cross is conducting a membership drive. The Business and Professional Women's Club is raising funds to build an additional auditorium for the local junior college, by putting on a circus in which the members will be both clowns and 'animals.' The Future Farmers of America (whose purpose is to 'develop agricultural leadership, cooperation, and citizenship through individual and group leadership') are holding a father-son banquet. . . . The Chamber of Commerce is discussing the feasibility of building an all weather road between two nearby towns. 'Skywatch' volunteers are being signed up. . . . Meetings of the Parent Teachers Associations are being held in the schools. . . .

"Montegrano [the small Italian community] . . . presents a striking contrast. . . . Twenty-five upper class men constitute a 'circle' and maintain a clubroom where members play cards and chat. Theirs is the only association. None of the members has ever suggested that it concern itself with community affairs or that it undertake a 'project.' . . . There are no organized voluntary charities in Montegrano. . . .

"To the peasants, many of whom are desperately anxious for their children to get ahead, the lack of educational opportunity is one of the bitterest facts of life. Upper class people are affected too; some of them would like to live in Montegrano but cannot do so because it would cost too much to send their children away to a boarding school. One might think, then, that the improvement of the local school might be an important issue—one on which people would

[5] Alexis de Tocqueville, *Democracy in America*, ed. Phillips Bradley, New York, 1948, I, pp. 249-50.

unite in political parties or otherwise. . . . However, such possibilities have not been considered. . . ."[6]

The national differences in the propensity for civic cooperation take on heightened importance from the fact that cooperative political behavior appears to be of greatest significance in the two most successful democracies, the United States and Britain, and of relatively little significance in Germany and Italy. And it also appears to a significant degree in Mexico (the nation we have termed an "aspirational democracy"), though here it seems to be based on less actual experience with such groups than is the case in Britain and the United States.

Finally, the search for the sources of political cooperation is especially intriguing because the propensity to form political groups does not seem to depend on the differing levels of social and economic modernization within a country. Most other significant political attitudes and behavior—interest in politics, political discussion, voting, knowledge of politics, and general sense of competence to influence the government—were found to vary strongly with an individual's educational attainment or his socio-economic status. The relationship was often so close that one could expect that as education became more widespread, the degree of political participation and competence would increase substantially. But unlike the political attitudes and behavior that seem heavily dependent on social position within a nation, the strategy of using informal groups as a means of influencing the government seems to be relatively independent of social position. If an individual thinks he can influence his government, the probability that he will try to form a group for this purpose appears to depend on the nation in which he lives, and not on other social characteristics. If we are seeking the reason for differences in political "style" among societies, the search for the roots of this political style—a style that cannot be explained by level of economic development—should prove rewarding.

How can we explain why the "confused clamor" of group activity exists in some countries and not in others?[7] Though no final answer

[6] Edward C. Banfield, *The Moral Basis of a Backward Society*, Glencoe, Ill., 1958, pp. 15-17, 30-31.

[7] That this sort of question *can* be raised and that one can attempt to answer it illustrate, incidentally, the advantage of "discovering" the propensity to form groups in a study of this sort rather than through the keen but unsystematic observations of a Tocqueville. Not only can we now know about this propensity in some new way (those of us who work on studies of this sort like to believe the knowledge is now more reliable, if sometimes less colorful), but our knowledge is also more precise. We can

can be given to a question of this sort, our data do suggest some of the sources of the belief that one can cooperate with one's fellow citizens. We shall not, in this chapter, look for the sources of the belief that one can influence the government. Rather, we shall concentrate mostly on those who believe they have such potential influence, and seek some explanation of why they would attempt to exert it through the formation of groups.

As we suggested in Chapter 7, the informal groups that our respondents talk about forming are a social resource that they use in attempting to influence the government. If an individual attempts to use (or reports that he would attempt to use) a particular resource in relation to the government, one would expect: (1) that he believes that this resource offers a valuable base for influence over the government officials; (2) that the resource is available to him, and (3) that there is no special reason inhibiting the *political* use of this resource. Similarly, the individual who mentions that he would seek the cooperation of his peers in an attempt to influence the government must (if he is responding reasonably) believe: (1) that government officials are responsive to a group appeal (or, at least, more responsive to such appeals than to individual appeals); (2) that he has available to him such informal groups (i.e., that he has a family, friends, neighbors, whom he trusts and from whom he expects help), and (3) that these friends, neighbors, and other associates can be used for *political* activity. The last criterion is important. The man who is well integrated into a number of primary groups—values his membership in these groups, trusts the members of the group, believes he can depend on them for help— may still not think of those groups in time of political stress. He may consider politics a special realm, where the ordinary day-to-day relationships of trust and confidence are irrelevant. He may have a rich social life, yet may not translate this into political competence. Thus in searching for the roots of political cooperation, one has to look, not only at the extent of cooperative social activities in a nation, but at the extent to which these are translated into political resources. The propensity to cooperate with one's fellow citizens,

tell who it is that is likely to engage in such behavior—men or women, college graduates or those with less education. More important, we can go further in trying to find out how those who say they would work through groups differ from others who do not say this; that is, we can learn why such groups can be formed. Not only is the knowledge (hopefully) more reliable, it is also more useful, for it can lead to further knowledge.

we suggest, is based, not only on an individual's attitudes toward politics and his position in the political system, but on his attitudes toward his fellow citizens and his position in the social system as well.

The first requirement for the maintenance of a group-forming political style is that individuals believe such an influence strategy will work. This attitude is present in the United States and Britain to an extent not found in the other nations. As was pointed out in Chapter 7, when asked if there was any chance that an attempt to influence the government would succeed, a substantially larger proportion of American and British respondents than of any other respondents volunteered the statement that success was likely only if others joined them in making the attempt.[8] Other responses in our survey support the position that the formation of groups is considered highly effective in these two countries. In another question in the interview, subsequent to the open-response question on influence strategy, respondents were given a list of five possible strategies for influencing the government, and were asked to select the most effective. The five choices were: working through personal and family connections; writing to government officials; getting people interested and forming a group; working through a political party; and organizing a protest demonstration. In the United States, 37 per cent of the respondents selected "getting people interested and forming a group" as the most effective strategy. In Britain, 35 per cent selected this response. In Germany the proportion was 12 per cent, in Italy 13 per cent, and in Mexico 15 per cent. Clearly, one reason why individuals in the United States and Britain are more likely to think of using groups as a means of influencing the government is that they believe this method will work.[9]

Civic Cooperation and Freedom to Communicate

But even if one believes that with the help of others one can influence the government, one may still not believe that the help of

[8] See chapter 7 above.

[9] Again, we must point out that these beliefs do not exist in a vacuum. The respondents are probably right: government officials are probably more responsive to such group activity in Britain and the United States than in the other countries. And this is one source of the beliefs. But the effect of government action on political beliefs is probably reciprocal. Probably one reason why government officials are more likely to respond to group activity is that people believe that they will respond and therefore attempt such group pressure.

others is available to use in time of political stress. The perceived availability of others would appear to depend on a number of social characteristics. In the first place, of course, other people must be present. But more than physical presence is needed. There must also exist no severe impediments to communication among individuals. Whereas these informal political groups we have been considering may be created on the spot for political activity, group formation can probably only take place if there are pre-existing channels of communication among the potential members of the group; if there has been some previous contact among them. Table 6 suggests that this pre-existing communications network helps explain the existence of group competence. Among those who think they can influence the government (the local competents) in each country, those who report that they discuss political affairs are more likely to choose a group strategy as the means they would use. In Britain, for instance, 45 per cent of the local competents who discuss politics choose the group strategy, whereas 38 per cent of those who do not discuss politics choose such a strategy. And in each of the other countries those local competents who discuss politics are more likely to say they would work through some informal group than are those local competents who do not discuss politics. Though the differences are not great, the uniformity from nation to nation is convincing.[10]

The relationship is not as strong among those with secondary education or better. In terms of their propensity to form groups, there is no difference between the American local competents who discuss politics and those who do not; in Italy and Mexico there is a slight opposite tendency: those who do *not* talk politics invoke informal groups a bit more often. However, for each nation as a whole, and especially on the lower educational levels, the relationship holds. The existence of a political communications network (as roughly measured by our question on political discussion) does make it more likely than not that an individual will think of using his primary group relations in an attempt to influence the government. At best, however, the relationship is a mild one.

Table 6 divides respondents into those who discuss politics and those who do not. Thus it deals with the relationship between a

[10] It must be remembered that Table 6 analyzes local competents only. One would expect those who discuss politics to be the more competent citizens. Table 6 makes a more interesting point: those local competents who discuss politics are more likely than those who do not to say they would work with others in trying to exert political influence.

279

TABLE 6

Two Types of Local Competents and their Propensity to Form Groups, by Nation and Education

Nation	Total				Primary or Less				Secondary or More			
	Local Competents Who Discuss Politics		Local Competents Who Don't Discuss Politics		Discuss Politics		Don't Discuss Politics		Discuss Politics		Don't Discuss Politics	
	(%)	(No.)[a]	(%)	(No.)	(%)	(No.)	(%)	(No.)	(%)	(No.)	(%)	(No.)
United States	75[b]	(621)	68	(123)	68	(252)	62	(84)	79	(369)	79	(39)
Great Britain	45	(571)	38	(177)	45	(312)	36	(126)	45	(243)	38	(45)
Germany	24	(421)	17	(169)	24	(309)	18	(150)	22	(111)	[7	(14]
Italy	15	(221)	11	(275)	15	(102)	8	(202)	15	(119)	21	(73)
Mexico	50	(236)	48	(295)	53	(178)	48	(260)	47	(56)	51	(34)

[a] Numbers in parentheses refer to the bases upon which percentages are calculated.
[b] I.e., 75 per cent of local competents who discuss politics mentioned a group-forming strategy.

specifically political activity and civic cooperation, and not with more general social activities and attitudes. Yet we are interested in the sort of informal groups that are essentially nonpolitical but are mobilized for political activity in response to a particular challenge; thus one might expect to find that the availability of these groups derives, at least in part, from more general social and interpersonal attitudes. An individual may have a wide range of informal associations, but may believe that the individuals with whom he associates cannot be relied upon for cooperative political behavior, that they cannot be trusted, or that they are unlikely to be helpful.

Civic Cooperation and Social Values

Just as the United States and Britain differ from the other three nations in the frequency of cooperative political behavior, as evidenced by the propensity to form groups, so do they differ in the frequency of expression of cooperative interpersonal values and perceptions. We have already seen that British and American respondents value generous and considerate behavior more than do the respondents in other nations, and they are also more likely to perceive their fellow citizens as cooperative and trustworthy. This set of social attitudes, one might expect, would open the way for the individual to turn to his fellow citizens for political help. And it is perhaps this set of interpersonal perceptions and values that explains the propensity to engage in cooperative political behavior. Whether an individual attempts to form a group to influence the government would depend on his perception of the probable response of the government to such an appeal and on his ability to communicate with his fellow citizens. But it would also depend on his perception of the characteristics of his fellow actors in the political system.

Our questions about interpersonal values and perceptions were asked in a nonpolitical context; they were asked about people in general. We now ask how much these general and diffuse social and interpersonal attitudes are related to political attitudes. Since these interpersonal attitudes are nonpolitical in content, one must consider not only their frequency but the extent to which they have an effect upon or are translated into political attitudes. It is possible that general interpersonal trust is unrelated to the existence of a trusting attitude in political affairs. One might trust people in general, but not in relation to politics. Thus in order to see if the belief that one's fellow citizens can be called on for political aid is rooted in social and interpersonal attitudes, one would have to find (1) that social and interpersonal attitudes fostering cooperation and trust are widespread among those who believe in the political availability of their informal groups, and (2) that the existence of the cooperative interpersonal attitudes does indeed affect the belief in one's group-forming powers.

We have seen that the nations differ markedly in the frequency with which respondents report that they admire generosity and considerateness in people. In the two nations where the propensity toward cooperative political behavior is most widespread (America and Britain), admiration of general cooperativeness among people is, as we pointed out at the beginning of this chapter, also most widespread. To what extent are those related? Table 7 relates admiration of generosity and consideration to the frequency with which informal groups are mentioned as a means of influencing the government. In the United States and Britain there is some relationship between the admiration of such outgoing characteristics and the frequency with which local competents choose a strategy that involves the formation of groups. In the United States, for instance, 76 per cent of the local competents who say they admire generosity and considerateness would work through informal groups in trying to influence the government, in contrast to 68 per cent among those who admire less outgoing virtues. The relationship, though not a very strong one, exists on all educational levels. Thus in the United States and Britain, not only are supportive interpersonal activities admired by individuals more frequently than in the other three nations, but this admiration of generosity and consideration is related to the willingness of individuals to form political groups. Interpersonal consideration is highly valued and appears to be translated into a positive evaluation of the efficacy of cooperative activities in relation to the government.

In contrast to the pattern in the United States and Britain, the degree to which individuals of the other three nations value outgoing interpersonal activities is not related to their belief in the efficacy of cooperative political activity. In Italy those who value generosity and considerateness are no more likely than those who do not to suggest using a group strategy; and in Germany and Mexico the relationship is actually reversed: those who value cooperative,

TABLE 7

Two Types of Local Competents and their Propensity to Form Groups, by Nation and Education

Nation	Total		Primary or Less		Secondary or More	
	Local Competents Who Value Generosity (%) (No.)[a]	Local Competents Who Don't Value Generosity (%) (No.)	Value Generosity (%) (No.)	Don't Value Generosity (%) (No.)	Value Generosity (%) (No.)	Don't Value Generosity (%) (No.)
United States	76[b] (483)	68 (263)	68 (165)	65 (172)	81 (318)	75 (91)
Great Britain	46 (495)	39 (253)	46 (276)	38 (165)	45 (206)	43 (82)
Germany	18 (275)	25 (315)	18 (185)	25 (276)	16 (88)	30 (37)
Italy	14 (135)	13 (370)	10 (71)	11 (239)	19 (64)	17 (131)
Mexico	45 (190)	53 (341)	43 (151)	53 (287)	51 (38)	47 (52)

[a] Numbers in parentheses refer to the bases upon which percentages are calculated.
[b] I.e., 76 per cent of local competents who value generosity in others mentioned a group-forming strategy.

interpersonal behavior are less likely to invoke informal groups as a means of influencing the government. In the three countries where group formation is a relatively smaller part of the dominant political style, not only are interpersonal cooperative virtues less frequently admired, but admiration for them is not translated into political behavior.

Civic Cooperation and Trust in People

The tendency to engage in cooperative activity within the political influence process appears, therefore, to be rooted at least partially in a set of social values that stress cooperative behavior among individuals. In the two countries where this fusion is most complete the dominant social values stress cooperative behavior; and the degree to which cooperative interpersonal behavior is valued is directly related to the propensity to create political structures.

High valuation of cooperative behavior can be expected to affect actual interpersonal behavior if those who value such behavior also believe that people will in fact behave cooperatively in their relations with each other. In this respect as well, Britain and the United States differ from the other three nations as was shown above in Table 4. The responses to several questions dealing with their expectations of the behavior of others indicate that British and American respondents are more likely to expect other people to be trustworthy, helpful, and cooperative.

The relationship between the propensity to form political groups and the belief that one's fellow men are cooperative, trustworthy, and unselfish may be demonstrated by relating an individual's general "faith in people" to his expressed belief in his ability to form political groups. In order to tap the extent of our respondents' faith in people, we employed Rosenberg's "faith in people" scale, which consists of five items (reported above in Table 4). Each item dealt with the respondents' general attitudes toward their fellow citizens; none referred in any way to political activity. The respondents were then scored along a "faith in people" scale, according to how frequently they chose the question-response that indicated strong faith in people.[11]

How does one's generalized belief in the cooperativeness and unselfishness of human nature affect one's strategy of influence vis-à-vis

[11] See note 3 for a discussion of this scale.

the government? Table 8 indicates that in the United States and Britain the more one has such faith in people, the more likely he is to believe that he can work with his fellow citizen in attempting to influence the government. In the United States among those with strong faith in people, 80 per cent report that they would attempt to form a group to influence the local government, while this is reported by only 58 per cent of those low on faith in people. Those local competents whose faith in people is moderate are also moderate in the frequency with which they report they would attempt to form political groups. And in Britain the same pattern is apparent: 50 per cent of those local competents high in faith in people would form such groups, in contrast with 33 per cent of those low in faith in people. And the relationship persists on both higher and lower educational levels.

In contrast with the pattern in the United States and Britain, faith in people does not increase one's propensity to form political groups in the other three nations. In Germany and Mexico there is some tendency for those with stronger faith in people to be *less* prone to think of group strategies to influence the government, and in Italy there is little regular relationship between general trust in people and the ability to form groups.

In the United States and Britain the belief that people are generally cooperative, trustworthy, and helpful is frequent, and it has political consequences. Belief in the benignity of one's fellow citizen is directly related to one's propensity to join with others in political activity. General social trust is translated into politically relevant trust.[12] In the other three nations the absence of a cooperative, group-forming political style appears to be related, not only to the lower frequency of expression of general social trust, but to the fact that even that trust which is expressed does not increase the probability that an individual will think of working with others in trying to influence the government. A gap remains between general social attitudes and political attitudes. Politics appears to be

[12] Rosenberg reports a similar relationship between general social trust and political trust in an American sample. He finds that those who score high in "faith in people" are less likely than the low scorers to be cynical about politics and politicians; see his "Misanthropy and Political Ideology," *American Sociological Review, op. cit.*

A study carried on in a small city in the western United States yields similar results. A positive correlation was found between trust in people (as measured by a low score on a "personal cynicism" scale) and trust in politics. See Robert E. Agger, Marshall N. Goldstein, and Stanley A. Pearl, "Political Cynicism: Measurement and Meaning," *Journal of Politics*, XIII (1961), pp. 477-506.

TABLE 8

Three Types of Local Competents and their Propensity to Form Groups, by Nation and Education

Nation	Total						Primary or Less						Secondary or More					
	Faith in People						Faith in People						Faith in People					
	High		Med.		Low		High		Med.		Low		High		Med.		Low	
	%	No.[a]	%	No.	%	No.	%	No.	%	No.	%	No.	%	No.	%	No.	%	No.
United States	80[b]	(286)	73	(338)	58	(122)	74	(94)	70	(160)	51	(83)	83	(192)	76	(178)	74	(39)
Great Britain	50	(210)	44	(379)	33	(159)	50	(100)	44	(229)	34	(112)	49	(103)	45	(143)	29	(42)
Germany	22	(96)	20	(374)	27	(120)	22	(60)	20	(299)	27	(102)	22	(36)	18	(71)	22	(18)
Italy	19	(31)	12	(193)	14	(281)	[27	(11]	10	(116)	10	(183)	15	(20)	14	(77)	20	(98)
Mexico	41	(24)	47	(217)	54	(290)	[48	(14]	46	(170)	53	(254)	c		48	(46)	53	(36)

[a] Numbers in parentheses refer to the bases upon which percentages are calculated.
[b] I.e., 80 per cent of those "high" in "faith in people" mentioned a group-forming strategy.
c Too few cases.

a separate, independent sphere of activity for which one has a set of political attitudes not particularly grounded in general social attitudes. In the United States and Britain one's view of the realm of politics appears closely related to one's view of social life. In the other three nations there is less fusion between social and political attitudes.

The above data go a long way in explaining why there is a "buzz" of group activity in Britain and especially in the United States, and why this activity is not as apparent elsewhere. The explanation of the difference is intriguing: it is not only that general social values and attitudes that would foster cooperation with one's fellow citizens are more widespread in Britain and the United States; beyond that, these general social attitudes are more closely related to political attitudes in these two nations than in the other three nations. And this explanation adds weight to an interpretation we advanced earlier, of the meaning of the propensity to invoke one's primary group in time of political stress. This tendency to use one's primary associations in political influence attempts, we suggested, represented a close fusion of the basic primary group structures of society with the secondary structures of politics; a fusion that led to a more integrated political system. That the use of such primary groups does represent a fusion of this sort on the structural level is strongly supported by the discovery of a parallel fusion on the level of attitudes in the same nations where the integration of primary and political structures was most complete. The close overlap of society and polity that we have been suggesting for the United States and Britain is thus evidenced on the levels of both structure and attitude. Though the structures of government in both nations are modern, functionally specific, and formally differentiated from other social structures, they are linked to the primary units of the social structure by the use of these primary structures as a resource for political influence. And the political structures are linked with the rest of the social structure, as well, by a diffuse set of attitudes that apply both to general social relations and to political activities.[13]

[13] The next question that suggests itself is how this combination of trust in people and willingness to cooperate with them in political activities is learned. One possible answer is that from childhood on, individuals in the United States and Britain are given opportunities to take part in group activities with others. McClelland reports a study of secondary-school students in Germany and the United States, in which respondents were asked to list their leisure activities. American students mention on the

This suggested explanation of the sources of cooperative political behavior is particularly interesting because of the further questions it raises. Why, for instance, do British and American respondents express relatively higher degrees of interpersonal trust? And why is there no gap between these social attitudes and political attitudes, as there is in the other three nations? We leave the first question to others who are able to probe more deeply than we have into cross-national differences in social structure and personality. We shall attempt some answer to the second question.

The answer to such a complicated question can only be partial and tentative. In searching for the reason why general social attitudes are more closely related to political attitudes in some nations than in others, and why primary group affiliations are considered available for political activity in some nations but not in others, one might begin by looking at the political characteristics of Britain and the United States, to see if there is something about the way politics is carried on there that might explain the absence of a gap between primary social structures and attitudes and the political system.

Intensity of Partisanship and the Integration of Polity and Society

The state of partisanship in a nation may help us explain the way in which social relationships mesh with the political system. An individual's attitudes toward political parties and, more important, toward the supporters of political parties—his own and the opposition—are, in a sense, the political equivalent of his general attitudes toward people. If there is a disparity between general attitudes toward interpersonal relations and more specific attitudes toward relations with people when they are given a political label (identified in the mind of the individual as either politically sympathetic or hostile), this indicates a lack of integration of social structure with political system.

We have already seen that the structure of partisanship in the United States and Britain differs from that in Germany, Italy, and Mexico. The two former nations have had long and relatively

average five group activities (clubs, school publications, social gatherings and the like), while German students mention on the average one such activity; see David McClelland, *The Achieving Society*, Princeton, N. J., 1961, pp. 199-201. This early experience with groups—and one would assume it begins even earlier than secondary school —may be a major source of civic cooperation. See chapter 12 for a further consideration of political socialization in family and school.

stable political developments. Both systems have been able to manage problems of change and the entry of new groups into politics without resort to violence. And though there have been and still are partisan conflicts, these have rarely led to a fragmentation of society into deeply ideological, closed, and antagonistic political groups. The absence of partisan fragmentation in recent decades is reflected in our data. As was pointed out in Chapter 5, respondents in the United States and Britain are less likely than those in the other three nations to report that they consider supporters of an opposition political party ineligible for membership in the primary group. In response to a question on their reaction to the marriage of a son or daughter to a supporter of an opposition party, American and British respondents rarely said they would be opposed to such a marriage and almost invariably said that such partisan considerations do not matter in this situation. In Italy, on the contrary, a much higher level of partisan antagonism was observed; and the level of partisan antagonism in Germany and Mexico lay somewhere in-between the two extremes.

Can this lack of partisan fragmentation help explain both the propensity to cooperate politically with one's fellow citizens and the use of informal groups in the political influence process? At first glance, the data on the use of informal groups in Britain and the United States and the data on interparty marriage in these countries appear somewhat inconsistent with each other. We have argued that the propensity to form political groups represents a close meshing of primary structures and the political process. Yet the responses in Britain and the United States to the question on interparty marriage suggest that political affiliation is not considered a relevant criterion for membership in the primary group. This is, after all, what respondents are saying when they reply that it would not matter if their child married a supporter of the party they opposed. And other data in our study also suggest that this combination—a belief that one's primary group is available for aid in time of political stress and a desire to keep politics from disturbing primary group relationships—exists in these two nations. For instance, in response to a question on whether there are any people with whom they would avoid political discussion, the most frequent reason given by American and British respondents who say there are such people is that the discussion can cause disharmony within the primary group: it can create unnecessary arguments with friends or relatives. (In the other nations the most frequent reasons given for avoiding political discussion are that it is useless, that other people are too biased, ignorant, or fanatic, or that the discussion can get one into trouble.)

The data in our study indicate that there is no contradiction between the perceived availability of one's primary group in time of political stress and the beliefs that membership in the group ought not to depend on political affiliation and that the group ought not to

TABLE 9

Three Types of Local Competents and their Propensity to
Form Groups, by Nation
(Supporters of Major Parties Only)[a]

Nation	Oppose Marriage to an Opposition-Party Supporter (%) (No.)[b]		Favor Marriage within Own Party, but would Not Oppose Marriage Out (%) (No.)		Think Partisan Criteria Irrelevant for Primary Group Admission (%) (No.)	
United States	59[c]	(22)	73	(37)	74	(547)
Great Britain	26	(42)	44	(55)	44	(476)
Germany	16	(55)	24	(58)	24	(220)
Italy	8	(118)	[21	(14)]	14	(85)
Mexico	55	(84)	47	(16)	53	(206)

[a] There are too few cases to allow the usual educational control, but education has little relationship to either of the variables—social distance among political parties and the propensity to form informal groups—on this table.

[b] Numbers in parentheses refer to the bases upon which percentages are calculated.

[c] I.e., 59 per cent of local competents who oppose inter-party marriage mentioned a group-forming strategy.

be disrupted by political conflict; rather, it is these two beliefs that make the primary group available in time of political stress. If the criteria for entry into the primary group were partisan in nature, the ability to form groups easily in time of stress would be inhibited. Moreover, the usefulness of the group would be limited: it would be useful only if the government officials one wanted to contact were members of the same political party; whereas if the primary group is essentially nonpartisan, its usefulness is more general. In a sense, the intervention of the primary group in politics is made possible by the fact that it has no partisan commitment.

Table 9 shows the connection between the partisan fragmentation of social relationships (as measured by the extent to which respondents feel distant from opposition-party supporters) and respondents' propensity to form political groups. Respondents are divided into three types, according to the degree to which they accept partisan political affiliation as a criterion for admission to the primary group—that is, the degree to which they consider partisan affiliation a relevant criterion for the selection of a marriage partner by a son or daughter.[14] The three types of respondents are: (1) those who express opposition to marriage of a son or daughter with an adherent of the opposition party; (2) those who are not opposed to such marriage, but would be pleased if a son or daughter married a supporter of their own party; and (3) those who consider the partisan affiliation of a prospective family member to be irrelevant. The respondents in the first group prefer a social world that is relatively closed to cross-party affiliations; they express a negative reaction to those of other partisan affiliation. Those in the second group do not express hostility to people outside their own party, but they do express some positive affect toward their own party affiliation; they would be pleased if a child married someone of like political belief but not displeased if he or she married someone of opposing views. In the last group we have those who express indifference to the partisan affiliation of a potential family member.[15]

As Table 9 indicates, there is a relationship between the extent to which partisan criteria are considered relevant for primary group membership and the propensity to form political groups. Compare the column on the left of the table (those who oppose marriage into the family of a supporter of the opposition party) with the column on the far right (those who say that partisan criteria are irrelevant). In general, those whose primary groups are "closed," in the partisan sense, are less likely to think of cooperating with their fellow citizens in time of political stress than are those whose primary groups are "open." And in this case the relationship between attitudes toward one's fellow citizens and the propensity to cooperate with them politically is found, not only in the United States and Britain, but in Germany and Italy as well. In Britain, for instance, 26 per cent of those in closed primary groups report that they would try to enlist the cooperation of others in trying to influence the gov-

[14] See chapter 5 for a discussion of these questions.

[15] Table 9 reports attitudes toward party intermarriage among the supporters of the two largest parties in each nation: in America, Republicans' attitudes toward marriage of a child with a Democrat; in Britain, Conservatives toward Labour; in Germany, CDU toward SPD; in Mexico, PRI toward PAN; and vice versa in each case. In Italy three parties are involved. Table 15 reports the attitudes of DC supporters toward marriage with a Communist supporter, and the attitudes of PCI and PSI supporters toward marriage with a Christian Democrat.

SOCIAL RELATIONS AND POLITICAL CULTURE

ernment, in contrast to 44 per cent of those whose primary groups are open. And in Germany the respective proportions of respondents who would work with others in trying to influence the government are 16 per cent among those in closed primary groups and 24 per cent among those whose groups are not closed. In some cases the numbers upon which percentages are based are quite small, but the cross-national uniformity is convincing.

In terms of our hypothesis that a close relationship between social and political attitudes exists in Britain and the United States but not in the other nations, it is interesting to note that, whereas there was no relationship between general attitudes toward people and political cooperation in Italy and Germany, there is in these two countries a relationship between attitudes to people as political actors (i.e., people who are given a partisan label) and political cooperation. Unlike general interpersonal attitudes, political interpersonal attitudes are related to the propensity to cooperate in political action.

The deviant case in Table 9 is Mexico. Here those who have closed primary groups are as likely to speak of cooperation with their fellows as are those whose primary groups are open. One cannot, of course, be sure why this is so. But the most likely reason is that Mexico is essentially a one-party nation. Where there is only one party of significance, hostility to those outside the party cannot have as great an effect on one's ability to work with others as it would if there were more than one party. If, for instance, 85 per cent of the Mexicans who express support for some party express support for the major party, the PRI (as our data indicate they do), or if 90 per cent of the votes go to that party (as voting data on the 1958 election indicate),[16] then hostility to those outside the party cuts one off from few potential collaborators. And where all government, local and national, is controlled by this one party and appears likely to remain so indefinitely, partisan informal groups do not appear to be limited in the generality of their use. Thus the impact of partisanship in a one-party nation will obviously differ from that in a nation where there are competing parties with relatively large support, where there are at last some governments on the local level controlled

16 Though ours is a sample of little more than one thousand Mexicans, our data on party support may be somewhat more accurate than the voting statistics. Ballots in Mexico are counted by the incumbent party in what may not be a completely non-partisan manner.

by the opposition, and where the opposition is a possible successor to office on the national level.

One other aspect of the data in Table 9 is interesting. Consider the frequency with which those respondents in the middle column— i.e., those who say they would be pleased if a child married a supporter of their party, but who also say they would not be opposed to marriage with a supporter of the opposition party—report that they would cooperate with their fellow citizens. In the United States, Britain, Germany, and Italy the frequency with which this group mentions using primary group affiliation as a source of political influence is much closer to (and in Britain and Germany, exactly the same as) the frequency with which such groups are mentioned by those who consider partisan affiliation irrelevant (column 3) than to the frequency with which such groups are mentioned by those whose primary groups are "closed" to political opponents (column 1). This distinction is important, for it takes us one step further in our analysis of the relationship between partisanship and political cooperation. It helps specify what *type* of partisanship inhibits informal political cooperation. Those who say they would be pleased if a child married a supporter of their own party are expressing an affective orientation toward their own political party: they are saying that partisan affiliation is not completely irrelevant to primary group membership. But as long as this positive attachment to their party is not coupled with a negative reaction to those of an opposition party, their ability to form political groups does not appear to be impaired. The Conservative party supporter who would be pleased if his child married a Conservative but not displeased if the child married a Labourite appears as free to form political groups as is the Conservative party supporter who would be neither pleased by marriage to a Conservative nor displeased by a marriage to a Labourite.

It is not the existence of an affective tie to one's own political party or a preference for those of like mind that blocks the free formation of groups; it is only when these ties involve the *rejection* of those of opposing views that group formation is inhibited. This appears significant in understanding the relationship between affective orientation to politics and the maintenance of a participatory political system that is not rent by harsh political disputes. An intense affective orientation to politics, insofar as it involves rejection on personal grounds of those of opposite affiliation, is a barrier to the type of cooperative influence activity discussed in this chapter.

293

But if the affective orientation is a "managed" affective orientation—that is, if it involves essentially positive loyalty and attachment to one's own political views, but does not involve rejection of those with opposing views—then this orientation is not a hindrance to the free formation of political groups at times of political stress.

The hypothesis that it is not partisanship per se but negative or hostile partisanship that impedes political cooperation receives additional confirmation in Table 10. In Table 10 respondents are divided by another measure of partisanship: not their attitude toward others of opposing views, but their affiliation with their own party. Respondents are divided into "party activists," "party supporters," and "nonpartisans." Party activists are those who take an active role in their political party; party supporters express support for a party but are not active; and nonpartisans express support for no political party.[17] Table 10 indicates the frequency with which respondents in each group say they would cooperate with their fellow citizens in political activity. Apparently, the extent to which an individual is positively associated with a political party has little effect on his group-forming propensity. Party activists are generally as likely to speak of using informal groups as a means of influencing the government as are party supporters or nonpartisans. The fact that one is a partisan—that one is active in a political party or supports a political party—does not impede his ability to cooperate with one's fellow citizens. It is only when partisanship becomes so intense as to involve rejection, on personal grounds, of those of opposing political views that the state of partisanship in a nation may be said to limit the ability of its citizens to cooperate with each other in political affairs.

Conclusion

The data presented in this chapter offer some explanation for the phenomenon of group formation noticed by Tocqueville and by many others since then. In searching for the reasons why political cooperation with one's fellow citizens appears easier and more

[17] Party activists in Britain, Germany, Italy, and Mexico are those who report membership in a political party. Party activists in the United States are those who report having taken an active part in a political campaign for a party. Party supporters in all countries are those who say they support or lean toward a particular party but who report no activity. Nonpartisans are those who say they neither support nor lean toward a party. Respondents who refuse to answer on party affiliation are omitted from the table.

TABLE 10

Three Types of Local Competents and their Propensity to Form Groups, by Nation and Education

	Total						Primary or Less						Secondary or More					
	Party Activists[a]		Party Supporters		No Party		Party Activists		Party Supporters		No Party		Party Activists		Party Supporters		No Party	
Nation	%	No.[b]	%	No.	%	No.	%	No.	%	No.	%	No.	%	No.	%	No.	%	No.
United States	79[c]	(150)	71	(480)	79	(99)	69	(48)	64	(239)	80	(41)	83	(102)	77	(241)	78	(58)
Great Britain	47	(126)	43	(540)	45	(62)	42	(81)	42	(320)	42	(38)	46	(48)	43	(210)	50	(24)
Germany	31	(26)	21	(404)	24	(110)	33	(21)	19	(321)	28	(78)	[d]		25	(80)	10	(29)
Italy	13	(88)	15	(136)	14	(226)	11	(54)	12	(76)	10	(147)	11	(35)	18	(60)	22	(78)
Mexico	44	(46)	55	(164)	46	(201)	45	(41)	57	(181)	46	(178)	[d]		55	(25)	43	(20)

[a] Party activists are those who report membership in a political party in Britain, Germany, Italy, and Mexico. In the United States party activists are those who report having taken an active part in a political campaign for a party. Party supporters in all countries are those respondents who say they support or lean toward a particular party but who report no activity. Nonpartisans are those who say they neither support nor lean toward a party. Respondents who refuse to answer on party affiliation are omitted from the table.

[b] Numbers in parentheses refer to the bases upon which percentages are calculated.

[c] I.e., 79 per cent of local competents who are party activists mentioned a group-forming strategy.

[d] Too few cases.

frequent in some countries than in others, we have considered a number of important characteristics of basic social and political attitudes in five nations. We have paid special attention to certain general attitudes and values connected with interpersonal relations, and to attitudes connected with the state of partisanship in these nations. And in doing so we have had to consider some basic differences among the nations.

In Italy, Germany, and Mexico our data suggest that there is a gap between political attitudes and the more general attitudes toward interpersonal relations. Not only are the levels of interpersonal trust relatively low, but what interpersonal trust there is is not related to the willingness or ability to cooperate politically with one's fellow citizens. Nor are those who value such outgoing characteristics as considerateness and cooperation any more likely than those who do not value them to think of engaging in cooperative political activity as a means of influencing the government. Politics appears to be a special realm where the norms and attitudes of more general interpersonal relations do not prevail.

In Italy and Germany this lack of integration between general social attitudes and political attitudes appears explicable, at least in part, by the existence of a high degree of partisan fragmentation. Those who carry political antagonisms into their personal lives (and the proportions who do this are greater in Germany, and greater still in Italy, than they are in the United States and Britain), are less likely than others to think of cooperating with their fellow citizens in political activity.

These characteristics of the other three political systems highlight the pattern of attitudes in the United States and Britain that seem to explain the propensity for citizens to cooperate with one another in politics. In these two nations the ability freely to form groups for political activity appears to be related to the general nature of the citizens' commitment to politics: it is "balanced" or "managed." Americans and Britons are involved in politics, but the involvement is held within limits. They are neither parochials, cut off from politics, nor intensely partisan in ways that might lead to political fragmentation. And this balance, as we have said, is needed for a successful democracy: there must be involvement in politics if there is to be the sort of participation necessary for democratic decision making; yet the involvement must not be so intense as to endanger stability.

The balance between commitment to politics and autonomy from

296

politics is illustrated in our data on the relationship between primary groups and politics in America and Great Britain. On the one hand, these groups are a resource that is available to the individual in time of political stress. They are a means of increasing his influence vis-à-vis the state and of making him less dependent on "mass" political institutions. Furthermore, this balanced commitment to politics seems to be related to the existence of more basic social values—widespread social trust and a high evaluation of considerateness and generosity in people—*and* to the fact that these values permeate the political system. The latter point is the significant one. It is not just that there are many Americans and Britons who trust their fellow citizens: more important, this social trust affects political trust and the willingness to cooperate with others. The political system this suggests is penetrated by overarching social values.

These overarching social norms are reflected as well in the data on interparty marriage. One can infer that the 90 per cent or so of the respondents in the United States and Britain who say that it would make no difference if their child married a supporter of the opposition party are saying, in effect, that personal relationships ought to be governed by values other than political ones. The family ought not to be allowed to be divided by partisan considerations. It is not that partisan differences are unimportant, it is just that they are not absolute values. In certain social situations there are other, more general interpersonal attitudes that are considered binding.

In Germany and especially in Italy primary groups are also insulated from inharmonious political relationships that might strain the group. In fact, one would expect the primary groups of any society to be protected by some social mechanism—for the integration of the primary groups is of key social importance. But in Italy and Germany these groups are insulated by norms that bar from entry those of opposing political views.[18] Political conflict is probably so intense that the primary group can be protected from such conflict only by exclusion. In Britain and the United States partisanship has a more moderate character, and the challenge to primary group integration by divisive partisan attitudes can be met by less drastic means. Those of opposing views can be allowed into the primary group, but the potential fragmentation is managed by the set of norms that places integrative, primary group values above the partisan, divisive ones.

[18] Data on voting in the continental European countries, on the other hand, might suggest that there is quite a split within the family on partisan affiliation. Women in

SOCIAL RELATIONS AND POLITICAL CULTURE

This is not to say that politics is unimportant in Britain and America. Respondents report that it plays a significant role in their lives, it is of interest to the populace, it is a topic of conversation. It is all these things frequently—more frequently, in fact, than in the other three nations. Yet politics is "kept in its place." The values associated with it are subordinate in significant respects to more general social values, and these more general social values act to temper political controversy within the two nations. In this way, again, we have a "managed" or "balanced" involvement in politics: an involvement that is kept from challenging the integration and stability of the political system.

In this close relationship between primary groups and the polity, each modifies the other. On the one hand, partisanship tends to be less intense in these two countries, and therefore constitutes less of an objective threat to the stability of primary relationships. On the other hand, it would appear that the American and British families tend to be somewhat more "modern," more participating, more secularized in their communications patterns and decision-making mechanisms.[19] Consequently, they are better able to handle partisanship without being damaged. Perhaps what we are describing in these two countries is an overall pattern of greater secularization, which implies a great capacity for affective neutrality in all relationships, more of a multiple-value orientation, more tolerance of ambiguity. Furthermore, it may be that the greater secularization of the political market in England and the United States and the presence of primary-group protective mechanisms have a feedback effect, tending to mitigate conflict at the level of party elites. It is not accidental that the ritual of shaking hands by winner and loser and the sending of the congratulatory telegram by the loser to the winner are common occurrences in the United States and Britain, while they are rare on

general vote more heavily for the Christian parties, men more heavily for the left parties. In the German Bundestag election of 1953, for instance, the CDU received 2,200,000 more votes from women than from men. However, this difference in the voting behavior of men and women does not necessarily imply that this particular split occurs in many families. It has been pointed out that in Germany the bulk of this female surplus for the Christian parties comes from women who are unmarried, widowed, or divorced. (See Gabriele Bremme, *Die Politische Rolle der Frau in Deutschland* Göttingen, 1956, p. 98.) And Duverger makes a similar point for women and the MRP in France; see Maurice Duverger, *The Political Role of Women*, Paris, 1955, pp. 49 ff. It is likely that a similar pattern exists in Italy.

In any case, as we shall discuss in chapter 15, the norms relating to marriage of a child to an opposition party supporter may be more important than the actual behavior.

[19] See chapter 12 for a further discussion of family patterns in the five nations.

298

the European continent. It is almost as though a bargain had been struck between the community and the polity. If the primary group is to be open to the partisanship of the polity, then the polity must assimilate some of the cohesive properties of the primary group. In Britain this is effectively symbolized in the widespread acceptance of the quasi-sacredness of the Royal Family, a sacredness that makes "Her Majesty's government" and "Her Majesty's loyal opposition" members of the same national family. In the United States this quality of quasi-sacred community is symbolized in a number of roles and institutions—the national representative role of the presidency, the supralegal symbolic qualities of the Constitution, the special status of the Supreme Court, and the like.

It is this very mixture of the values of community and polity in Britain and the United States, this set of mechanisms that mitigate partisan cleavage, that create the psychological conditions necessary for the propensity to form informal groups. The nature of partisan and interest-group commitment is such that the individual can mobilize his own personal and community network in situations of political stress or threat. In a sense it is the old "right of revolution" now institutionalized in a widespread capability to act outside the organized infrastructure of democracy; the reserve power of the democratic citizen that gives him a right of independent access to political influence.

Thus the "buzz" of group activity in the United States and Britain, this characteristic tone of their politics, appears to be rooted in some fundamental characteristics of the social system. That people can so easily cooperate with each other in political activities is based on the fact that, despite political differences, they are tied to their fellow citizens by a set of interpersonal values, and these values overarch the political and nonpolitical aspects of the system. Though the two political systems are highly "modern"—highly differentiated, with functionally specific interest groups, political parties, and governmental agencies—they are in a sense embedded in a "national community." The "modern" political system has within it the seeds of great fragmentation—among political structures, along partisan lines, between polity and society. But in Britain and the United States this fragmentation is impeded by the force of shared social values and attitudes, which permeate all aspects of society.

299

CHAPTER 11

ORGANIZATIONAL MEMBERSHIP AND
CIVIC COMPETENCE

A CIVIC culture, we have argued, rests upon a set of nonpolitical attitudes and nonpolitical affiliations. Many of these attitudes that we have discussed—general attitudes toward other people, sense of social trust—have little explicit political content, and many of the affiliations we have dealt with—primary group affiliations in particular—are quite distant from the political system. Our concentration on this level of social structure has not meant to imply that larger, secondary, nonpolitical groups—voluntary associations are the main example—play an insignificant role in the democratic polity. Quite the contrary: though primary associations play an important role in the development of a citizen's sense of political competence and reflect an incipient capability to aggregate one's demands with others, they would, by themselves, represent a weak link between the individual and the polity. As Kornhauser has pointed out, primary groups are still small and powerless compared with the mass institutions of politics. Larger institutions, close enough to the individual to allow him some participation and yet close enough to the state to provide access to power, are also a necessary part of the democratic infrastructure.[1]

Voluntary associations are the prime means by which the function of mediating between the individual and the state is performed. Through them the individual is able to relate himself effectively and meaningfully to the political system. These associations help him avoid the dilemma of being either a parochial, cut off from political influence, or an isolated and powerless individual, manipulated and mobilized by the mass institutions of politics and government. The availability of his primary groups as a political resource in times of threat gives him an intermittent political resource. Membership in

[1] William Kornhauser, *The Politics of Mass Society*, Glencoe, Ill., 1959.

voluntary associations gives him a more structured set of political resources, growing out of his varied interests.

If the citizen is a member of some voluntary organization, he is involved in the broader social world but is less dependent upon and less controlled by his political system. This is so for several reasons. The association of which he is a member can represent his needs and demands before the government. It can make the government more chary of engaging in activities that would harm the individual. Furthermore, communications from central governmental authorities are mediated by the associational memberships of the individual. This is because individuals tend to interpret communications in terms of their memberships in social groupings—i.e., they are likely to reject communications that are unfavorable to the association to which they belong—and also because they may also receive communications from their associations and are thereby provided with alternate channels of political communication. Above all, from the point of view of the individual member, affiliation with some voluntary organization appears to have significant effects on his political attitudes. We shall try to specify these effects in this chapter.

In dealing with the data on associational membership, we must consider one further point. Associational membership may involve a low level of individual participation and competence: associations may be quite large; opportunities for participation limited. Thus the existence of a high frequency of membership may tell us more about the political institutions of a society than it does about the state of citizenship in that society. For the latter we shall have to know somewhat more about the nature of the membership—how active individuals are in their organizations and what effects their memberships have upon them.

The Distribution of Voluntary Association Membership

Voluntary association membership is more widespread in some countries than in others. This is apparent from Table 1. In the United States over half the respondents are members of some such organization.[2] In Britain and Germany somewhat less than half the

[2] These data are based on responses to this question: "Are you a member of any organizations now—trade or labor unions, business organizations, social groups, professional or farm organizations, cooperatives, fraternal or veterans' groups, athletic clubs, political, charitable, civic or religious organizations, or any other organized group?

respondents are members of some organization, while in Italy and Mexico the proportions are 29 per cent and 25 per cent, respectively.

To what sorts of organizations do individuals in the five countries belong? The range of specific organizations is wide. But Table 2 suggests some of the main types. In all countries organizations repre-

TABLE 1

Membership in Voluntary Associations, by Nation

Nation	(%)	(No.)*
United States	57	(970)
Great Britain	47	(963)
Germany	44	(955)
Italy	29	(995)
Mexico	25	(1,007)

* Numbers in parentheses refer to the bases upon which percentages are calculated.

TABLE 2

Membership in Various Types of Organizations, by Nation
(in per cent)

Organization	U.S.	U.K.	Germany	Italy	Mexico
Trade unions	14	22	15	6	11
Business	4	4	2	5	2
Professional	4	3	6	3	5
Farm	3	0	4	2	0
Social	13	14	10	3	4
Charitable	3	3	2	9	6
Religious[a]	19	4	3	6	5
Civic-political	11	3	3	8	3
Cooperative	6	3	2	2	0
Veterans'	6	5	1	4	0
Fraternal[b]	13				
Other	6	3	9	6	0
Total per cent members	57	47	44	30	24
Total number of respondents	970	963	955	995	1,007

[a] This refers to church-related organizations, not to church affiliation itself.
[b] U.S. only

Which ones?" The amount of voluntary association membership depends heavily upon the wording of the question and on the definition given the respondent of a voluntary association. The inclusion of trade unions, for instance, results in a somewhat higher figure than has been found in other studies. However, what is relevant here is not the absolute level of membership in any one nation, but the relative position of each of the five nations. What is significant, then, is that the same question was asked in all five nations.

senting economic interests—unions, business organizations, farm organizations, and, perhaps, professional organizations—are frequently reported. Social organizations are mentioned by 10 per cent or more of our sample in the United States, Britain, and Germany; and in the United States religious, civic-political, and fraternal organizations are also mentioned by 10 per cent or more of the respondents. One point to note is that the extent of "politicization" of these organizations, that is, the extent to which they are overtly engaged in politics, probably varies greatly. Some of the economic organizations are obviously deeply politicized; some of the social ones

TABLE 3

Percentage of Respondents who Belong to Some Organization, by Nation and Sex

Nation	Total		Male		Female	
	(%)	(No.)*	(%)	(No.)	(%)	(No.)
United States	57	(970)	68	(455)	47	(515)
Great Britain	47	(963)	66	(460)	30	(503)
Germany	44	(955)	66	(449)	24	(506)
Italy	30	(995)	41	(471)	19	(524)
Mexico	24	(1,007)	43	(355)	15	(652)

* Numbers in parentheses refer to the bases upon which percentages are calculated.

may be completely nonpolitical. We shall return below to the implications of this for political attitudes.

The distribution of organizational membership is also interesting. If we look at the proportion of men and women who are members of some organizations, we see some striking results (see Table 3). The national differences in the number of individuals participating in associations can be largely explained by differences in the proportion of women who report such membership. Thus the high level of associational membership in the United States depends to a large extent on the high level of female participation. If only males are considered, associational participation in the United States is no more frequent than it is in Britain or Germany. It is, in fact, striking how similar the frequency of membership is among the three nations: about two-thirds of male respondents in each of the three nations report such membership. Among females, on the other hand, participation in the United States is substantially more frequent than in Britain and about twice as frequent as in Germany. In Mexico and

Italy the level of participation by both males and females is lower than in the other three countries. However, a similar relationship between frequency of male participation and frequency of female participation is found in all nations except the United States; that is, men participate in voluntary organizations about two to three times as frequently as do women. In terms of the participatory role of women, then, the United States differs substantially from the other four countries, for American women, though they participate less frequently than American men in voluntary associations, do not

TABLE 4

Percentage of Respondents who Belong to Some
Organization, by Nation and Education

Nation	Total		Prim. or Less		Some Sec.		Some Univ.	
	(%)	(No.)*	(%)	(No.)	(%)	(No.)	(%)	(No.)
United States	57	(970)	46	(339)	55	(443)	80	(188)
Great Britain	47	(963)	41	(593)	55	(322)	92	(24)
Germany	44	(955)	41	(792)	63	(124)	62	(26)
Italy	30	(995)	25	(692)	37	(245)	46	(54)
Mexico	24	(1,007)	21	(877)	39	(103)	68	(24)

* Numbers in parentheses refer to the bases upon which percentages are calculated.

differ from men in this respect as much as do women in other countries.

Just as men participate more frequently in voluntary associations, so do individuals with higher education. This is seen in Table 4. In all countries there is a sharp increase in organizational membership as one moves up the educational ladder. Among those with primary school education, memberships are much less frequent than among those with higher education. This suggests one of the reasons for the close relationship between education and political competence. Education has compound effects upon political competence. Not only does the more highly educated individual learn politically relevant skills within the school, but he also is more likely to enter into other nonpolitical relationships that have the effect of further heightening his political competence. Associational membership is one form of such nonpolitical participation. The individual with less education, and therefore less political competence, is also less likely to enter into the sorts of relationships that would tend to develop political competence in later years. The data, then, do suggest that the various functions performed by voluntary associations are performed more frequently for those with higher education.[3]

We are interested in the way in which voluntary association membership affects political attitudes. But the types of associations we are dealing with are many and varied, and one would expect different effects from membership in different types of organization. One way in which the organizations vary is in the extent to which they are concerned with public affairs. Some of the associations are purely social, others are directly and overtly politically oriented. One can argue—and, indeed, this is one of the major hypotheses about voluntary association membership—that membership in even a nonpolitical organization will affect political attitudes. The experience with social interaction within the organization; the opportunity to participate in the decisions of the organization (if there is such participation); and the general broadening of perspectives that occurs in any sort of social activity—all would be expected to increase an individual's potential for political involvement and activity. Nevertheless, one would also expect to find that those organizations more directly involved in politics would have greater effects on the political perspectives of their members.[4]

Unfortunately, our data do not allow us objectively to divide the voluntary organizations into different types, based on the degree to which they take an active political role. We do, however, know whether or not the individual member perceives of his organization as taking some part in politics. Respondents were asked if any organization they belonged to was "in any way concerned with governmental, political, or public affairs; for instance, do they take stands on or discuss public issues or try to influence governmental decisions?" It must be remembered that this question probes the perceptions of the respondents: it asks for their own definition of political affairs. Furthermore, many members may not be aware of the activities of their organizations. A member of a veterans' group

[3] Similar data could be presented for the distribution of organizational membership among the occupational strata. Higher occupational status generally involves more frequent voluntary association membership, though the relationship is not as close as that between education and affiliation.

[4] Similarly, such organizations would probably also have greater effects on the operation of the political system. Even those that take no active role in politics—do not press for legislation, are politically unconcerned—may have a significant role in political decisions. Their very existence as *potential* political organizations may affect the decisions of government officials in ways that would not happen if these particular groups were not organized. Yet all else being equal, one would expect an overtly political group to have more of an impact on political decisions.

that is actively lobbying for veterans' benefits or for certain foreign policies may perceive his group in essentially social terms. Thus these data do not necessarily reflect the actual state of political activity by voluntary associations. But we are interested in the impact of membership in political and nonpolitical organizations on political attitudes, and so these data on the individual's perception of the political role of his organization may be sufficient.

Table 5 reports the frequency with which respondents in our five countries perceive that their organizations take some part in politics.

TABLE 5

Respondents who Believe an Organization of Theirs Is Involved
in Political Affairs, by Nation

Nation	% of Total Population (%) (No.)*		% of Organizational Members (%) (No.)	
United States	24	(970)	41	(551)
Great Britain	19	(963)	40	(453)
Germany	18	(955)	40	(419)
Italy	6	(995)	20	(291)
Mexico	11	(1,007)	46	(242)

* Numbers in parentheses refer to the bases upon which percentages are calculated.

In the United States about one in four respondents belongs to an organization that he perceives to be involved in politics.[5] This proportion falls off to six per cent in Italy. Though the nations differ in the percentage of the *total population* who perceive that an organization of theirs is involved in political affairs (column 1), the proportion of *organizational members* who hold this perception is strikingly uniform among the nations (column 2). With the exception of Italy, approximately the same proportion of organizational members in each country—40 to 45 per cent—perceives itself to be part of a politically active organization. For about one-fifth of the Italian members and about two-fifths of the members in

[5] That the frequency with which an individual reports affiliation with a political organization varies with his definition of politics is suggested by a finding made by Woodward and Roper: 31 per cent of their sample responded positively to the question, "Do you happen to belong to any organizations that sometimes take a stand on housing, better government, school problems, or other public issues?" In contrast, 24 per cent in our sample answered our question positively. The difference may be due to the fact that many of our respondents would not consider "school problems" a political question. See Julian L. Woodward and Elmo Roper, "Political Activity of American Citizens," *American Political Science Review*, XLIV (1950), pp. 872-85.

each of the other nations, being part of an organization does involve (in terms of the individual's awareness) recruitment into the political system.

Organizational Membership and Political Competence

Political and Nonpolitical Organizations. What effect, if any, does organizational membership have on political attitudes? Do those individuals who are members of some organization differ in their political perspectives from those who are not members? And does membership in any sort of organization, political as well as nonpolitical, affect one's political views? Or is it only membership in a politically relevant organization that influences one's perspectives on politics? The political attitudes we are interested in are those associated with democratic citizenship, as we have defined it. If organizational membership fosters the development of a democratic citizenry, one would expect the members, in comparison with those who are not members, to feel more confident of their ability to influence the government, to be more active in politics, more "open" in their political opinions, and, in general, more committed to democratic values.

Let us look first at the relationship between organizational membership and the individual's sense of ability to influence the government. This sense of competence, we have suggested earlier, is a major attitudinal variable in understanding the political perspectives of the individual, and it has significant implications for a wide range of other important political attitudes. Table 6 reports the proportion of respondents receiving high scores on the subjective competence scale among (1) those respondents who are members of organizations they consider to be involved in politics, (2) those who are members of nonpolitical organizations, and (3) those who are members of no organization. The results are striking, and quite uniform from nation to nation. In all nations those respondents who are members of no organization are generally lower in the scale than are organizational members. And among organizational members, those respondents who consider their organization to be involved in politics are most likely to receive high scores on the scale. In Great Britain, for instance, 80 per cent of the members of a politically oriented organization are to be found in the highest three scores of the subjective competence scale; 69 per cent of the

TABLE 6

Percentage of Respondents who Scored Highest in Subjective Competence[a] among Members of Political and Nonpolitical Organizations, by Nation and Education

Nation	Total Member Political Organiz. %	Total Member Political Organiz. No.[b]	Total Member Nonpolitical Organiz. %	Total Member Nonpolitical Organiz. No.	Total Non-member %	Total Non-member No.	Primary or Less Member Political Organiz. %	Primary or Less Member Political Organiz. No.	Primary or Less Member Nonpolitical Organiz. %	Primary or Less Member Nonpolitical Organiz. No.	Primary or Less Non-member %	Primary or Less Non-member No.	Secondary or More Member Political Organiz. %	Secondary or More Member Political Organiz. No.	Secondary or More Member Nonpolitical Organiz. %	Secondary or More Member Nonpolitical Organiz. No.	Secondary or More Non-member %	Secondary or More Non-member No.
United States	79	(228)	70	(322)	54	(418)	65	(91)	60	(163)	46	(263)	87	(137)	81	(160)	68	(156)
Great Britain	80	(193)	69	(157)	56	(510)	83	(97)	61	(144)	52	(352)	74	(86)	77	(112)	62	(148)
Germany	60	(172)	52	(246)	37	(534)	59	(137)	48	(184)	34	(471)	94	(32)	65	(63)	57	(55)
Italy	77	(56)	49	(234)	34	(701)	68	(25)	45	(148)	29	(519)	85	(31)	55	(85)	48	(183)
Mexico	57	(103)	45	(139)	33	(765)	54	(79)	40	(101)	33	(697)	64	(24)	58	(36)	46	(67)

[a] I.e., those who received three highest scores on the subjective competence scale
[b] Numbers in parentheses refer to the bases upon which percentages are calculated.

members of a nonpolitical organization are in these top three categories; while only 56 per cent of those who belong to no organization can be found in the highest categories of the scale. In Italy 77 per cent of the members of politically oriented organizations score high on the scale, in contrast with 49 per cent of those who belong to nonpolitical organizations, and 34 per cent of those who belong to no organization.

Both subjective competence and the frequency of organizational membership are related to educational attainment, thus it is important to note that this relationship between membership and sense of ability to influence the government persists when educational level is held constant. Only among British respondents with higher education is there a reversal of the trend: those respondents who are members of a nonpolitical organization score slightly better on the subjective competence scale than do the respondents who are members of a political organization. But the expected pattern is quite strong among British respondents in the lower educational group, and on both educational levels elsewhere.

Table 6 presents striking confirmation of the hypothesis about the impact of organizational membership on political attitudes. Such membership is indeed related to a citizen's self-confidence. The individual who belongs to an organization, compared with one who does not, is more likely to feel competent to influence the government. The table shows that the kind of organization one belongs to also makes a difference. Those who are members of a politically related organization are more likely to feel competent in their relations with the government than are those who belong to a nonpolitical organization. But the most striking finding is the contrast between those who are members of organizations that they do not perceive as being political and those who are members of no organization. In all nations, on both levels of education, those who are members of a nonpolitical organization are more likely to feel subjectively competent than are those who belong to no organization. This, then, appears to confirm the fact that latent political functions are performed by voluntary associations, whether these organizations are explicitly political or not. Those who are members of some organization, even if they report that it has no political role, have more political competence than those who have no such membership.

A similar pattern is reported in Table 7. Members of politically oriented organizations report more often than the other respondents that they discuss politics. This is to be expected, and it appears in all five nations and on both levels of education (with the exception of the Mexican respondents with higher education, where there is a slight reversal). And, as with the data on subjective competence, the individual who is a member of a nonpolitical organization is more likely to report he discusses politics than is the individual who belongs to no organization. Thus in Germany: 88 per cent of those who belong to a political organization discuss politics, in contrast with 70 per cent of the members of a nonpolitical organization. And both these percentages contrast with the figure that represents the frequency of such discussion among nonmembers: 47 per cent. Organizational membership, apparently, even if explicitly nonpolitical, makes it more likely that an individual will have a sense of ability to participate in politics and that he will actually participate in political discussion.

Organizational membership also seems to expand an individual's range of political opinion. In Table 8 we compare members of politically oriented organizations, members of nonpolitical organizations, and nonmembers, according to their willingness to express opinions on a variety of political questions. Members of political organizations were most likely to respond to all six questions; members of nonpolitical organizations and nonmembers followed in order. In Italy, for example, 68 per cent of the members of some politically oriented organization answered all six questions in this series, in contrast with 36 per cent of those who were members of a nonpolitical organization, and 20 per cent of those who belonged to no organization at all.[6]

Membership in an organization, political or not, appears therefore to be related to an increase in the political competence and activity of the individual.[7] The member, in contrast with the nonmember, appears to approximate more closely what we have called the democratic citizen. He is competent, active, and open with his opinions.

Active and Passive Membership. One reason why organizational membership might be expected to effect political competence and activity is that the members of such organizations receive training for participation within the organization, and this training is then

[6] See chapter 3 for a description of the questions that are involved.

[7] This relationship between group membership and political efficacy and activity is reported in some of the studies carried on by the Survey Research Center, and in other community studies. See Robert E. Lane, *Political Life,* p. 188.

TABLE 7
Percentage of Respondents who Discuss Politics among Members of Political and Nonpolitical Organizations, by Nation and Education

	Total			Primary or Less			Secondary or More		
Nation	Member Political Organiz. % No.*	Member Nonpolitical Organiz. % No.	Non-member % No.	Member Political Organiz. % No.	Member Nonpolitical Organiz. % No.	Non-member % No.	Member Political Organiz. % No.	Member Nonpolitical Organiz. % No.	Non-member % No.
United States	89 (228)	79 (322)	66 (418)	86 (91)	66 (163)	56 (263)	92 (137)	92 (160)	82 (156)
Great Britain	81 (193)	76 (257)	62 (510)	77 (97)	69 (144)	59 (352)	86 (86)	84 (112)	71 (148)
Germany	88 (172)	70 (246)	47 (534)	86 (137)	66 (184)	44 (471)	94 (32)	83 (63)	76 (55)
Italy	79 (56)	39 (254)	25 (701)	64 (25)	30 (148)	18 (519)	90 (31)	54 (85)	45 (183)
Mexico	64 (103)	61 (139)	31 (765)	61 (79)	54 (101)	27 (697)	74 (24)	79 (36)	59 (67)

* Numbers in parentheses refer to the bases upon which percentages are calculated.

TABLE 8

Percentage of Respondents Willing to Express Opinions on All Six Political Attitude Questions[a] among Members of Political and Nonpolitical Organizations, by Nation and Education

Nation	Total						Primary or Less						Secondary or More					
	Member Political Organiz.		Member Nonpolitical Organiz.		Non-member		Member Political Organiz.		Member Nonpolitical Organiz.		Non-member		Member Political Organiz.		Member Nonpolitical Organiz.		Non-member	
	%	No.[b]	%	No.	%	No.	%	No.	%	No.	%	No.	%	No.	%	No.	%	No.
United States	78	(228)	66	(322)	53	(418)	62	(91)	54	(163)	44	(263)	89	(137)	79	(160)	69	(156)
Great Britain	70	(193)	61	(257)	46	(510)	68	(97)	58	(144)	45	(352)	73	(86)	65	(112)	51	(148)
Germany	68	(172)	52	(246)	38	(534)	65	(137)	48	(184)	35	(471)	81	(32)	64	(63)	63	(55)
Italy	68	(56)	36	(234)	20	(701)	56	(25)	26	(148)	13	(519)	77	(31)	52	(85)	39	(183)
Mexico	75	(103)	60	(139)	40	(765)	71	(79)	60	(101)	37	(697)	87	(24)	62	(36)	63	(67)

[a] See above, p. 96, n.2.
[b] Numbers in parentheses refer to the base upon which percentages are calculated.

transferable to the political sphere. According to this argument, a member of an organization will have greater opportunity to participate actively within the organization than he would have within the larger political system. Organizations are, in a sense, small political systems, and both the skill in participation and the expectation that one can participate increase the individual's competence vis-à-vis the political system. Furthermore—and this is one of the most important effects imputed to organizational membership—training within these organizations means that there are alternate channels of recruitment into politics. If opportunities to participate in organizations did not exist, all such training for participation would have to take place within the political system itself, and would be dominated by the more general norms of that system. The existence of alternate channels means that the recruitment into political activity will not be as closely controlled by incumbent elites. In this way organizational participation leads to greater pluralism.

But we cannot assume that membership in a voluntary association necessarily involves active participation by the member. Many of these organizations are large and complex; to the individual member, perhaps they are as large and complex, with as distant centers of power, as his nation. Many of these organizations are centrally controlled, and allow little room for individual participation. Membership, then, offers very little training for political participation. A member of a large, centrally organized trade union, for example, may feel as passive a participant in his organization as does a subject in a large, authoritarian nation; and he may in fact have as little voice.

To trace the impact of organizational membership on political attitudes, therefore, it is important to consider the extent to which individuals take active roles in their organizations. The gross membership figures tell us nothing about this participation. In order to have some estimate of the extent to which membership involves active participation, those respondents who reported membership were asked if they took any active role within their organization: in particular, whether they had ever held any form of official position, high or low, in a local branch or in some central office.

The data bring out more striking differences among countries than did the figures on gross membership (see Table 9). In the United States 26 per cent of the respondents report that they have held some such position in an organization. In Britain the proportion, though lower (13 per cent), is substantially above that in the other countries (7 to 8 per cent). This suggests that the effect of voluntary associations upon the nature of citizenship may differ significantly from one country to another. In some countries there is a relatively large stratum of individuals who more or less actively participate in the decision making of voluntary associations; elsewhere, organizational membership may be relatively formal and lacking in participatory opportunities. Organizations in which there is some opportunity for the individual to take an active part may be as

TABLE 9

Respondents who Report they have ever been an Officer in one of their Organizations, by Nation

Nation	% of Total Population		% of Organizational Members	
	(%)	(No.)*	(%)	(No.)
United States	26	(970)	46	(551)
Great Britain	13	(963)	29	(453)
Germany	7	(955)	16	(419)
Italy	7	(995)	23	(291)
Mexico	8	(1,007)	34	(242)

* Numbers in parentheses refer to the bases upon which percentages are calculated.

significant for the development of democratic citizenship as are voluntary organizations in general.

These considerations add another link to our discussion of the nature of participation in the five countries. In particular, they point to a sharp distinction between the nature of participation in Germany, on the one hand, and Great Britain and the United States, on the other. All three countries are relatively high on organizational membership, especially among males. Yet the differences in the proportions of members who are active participating members (as measured by whether or not they have ever held an official position) are sharp. If we look at the second column of Table 9 (the proportion of members who have held some official position), we see that 46 per cent of American members and 29 per cent of British members have held some official position in one of the organizations to which they belong, while only 16 per cent of the German members have had experience in active participation. (In fact, the percentage of active group members is lower in Germany than in Mexico or Italy—although in the latter two countries we are dealing with a much smaller population of group members.) Here again is a reflection of the tendency for participation in Germany to be widespread but not intense. It tends to be formal in nature and involves little direct individual commitment and activity. Formal organizations in Germany, like those in Britain and the United States, are widespread and important in policy determination. But they differ in the degree to which they afford opportunities for their

TABLE 10

Organizational Members who were ever Officers, by Nation and Sex

Nation	Total		Male		Female	
	(%)	(No.)*	(%)	(No.)	(%)	(No.)
United States	46	(551)	41	(309)	52	(242)
Great Britain	29	(453)	32	(304)	22	(149)
Germany	16	(419)	18	(298)	9	(121)
Italy	23	(291)	24	(193)	19	(98)
Mexico	34	(242)	43	(146)	18	(96)

* Numbers in parentheses refer to the bases upon which percentages are calculated.

TABLE 11

Organizational Members who were ever Officers, by Nation and Education

Nation	Total		Prim. or Less		Some Sec.		Some Univ.	
	(%)	(No.)*	(%)	(No.)	(%)	(No.)	(%)	(No.)
United States	46	(551)	31	(156)	44	(245)	64	(150)
Great Britain	29	(453)	23	(241)	31	(176)	64	(22)
Germany	16	(419)	12	(321)	24	(79)	38	(16)
Italy	23	(291)	13	(173)	36	(91)	38	(26)
Mexico	33	(242)	30	(181)	39	(44)	52	(17)

* Numbers in parentheses refer to the bases upon which percentages are calculated.

members to participate in decisions. Once again we find that in Germany the structures of a democratic system are well developed, but they do not yet play significant roles in the perspectives and behavior of citizens. They are elements of a democratic political structure; they are not yet assimilated into a democratic political culture.

The differences in the frequency of participation within organizations are highlighted if we consider which members are likely to be active. In general, as the data in Tables 10 and 11 indicate, males and those with higher education are more likely to be active in their organizations than are female members and members with less education. An exception occurs in the United States, where female organizational members are more likely to be active participants than are men.[8]

It is of particular interest that the German pattern of frequent organizational membership, coupled with infrequent participation within the organization, is relatively uniform among all the German subgroups. While German males are members of organizations as frequently as are British or American males, and while Germans in particular educational groups are members as frequently as are their British or American counterparts, in no subgroup on Tables 10 or 11 do we find German respondents as frequently active within their organization as are American and British respondents. Compare, for example, male respondents in the three countries. German males are as likely as British or American males to be members of voluntary associations: the proportions who report membership are 68 per cent in the United States and 66 per cent in Britain and Germany. On the other hand, 41 per cent of American male members and 32 per cent of the British male members report that they have been active in their organizations, while only 18 per cent of the German male members report such participation. Similar contrasts can be found on Table 11 among the various educational groups, and can be observed as well within the various occupational groups.

The extent to which organizational membership involves some sort of active participation within that organization appears to vary significantly from nation to nation, and within nations among sex and educational groupings as well. Not all members take an active role in their organization. Furthermore, the extent to which an individual is active in the organization seems to be related to his political perspectives. This is suggested clearly in Table 12. Again we use the subjective competence score to measure this relationship (though measures of political activity would give similar results). Those organizational members who have held active positions in their organizations are more likely than rank-and-file members to receive high scores on this scale. In Italy, for instance, 76 per cent of these respondents who report some active participation within their organization score in the top three categories of our scale of sub-

[8] A similar relationship was found in a study by John C. Scott ("Membership and Participation in Voluntary Associations," *American Sociological Review*, XXII [1957], pp. 315-26). He found that male respondents in a New England town were more likely than female respondents to belong to an organization. But among the organizational members, women were more likely to be officers than men. One reason for this may be the smaller size of the organizations to which women belong.

TABLE 12

Percentage of Respondents who scored Highest in Subjective Competence[a] by the Extent of their Activity in Organizations, by Nation and Education

Nation	Total						Primary or Less						Secondary or More					
	Active Member		Passive Member		Non-member		Active Member		Passive Member		Non-Member		Active Member		Passive Member		Non-member	
	%	No.[b]	%	No.	%	No.	%	No.	%	No.	%	No.	%	No.	%	No.	%	No.
United States	82	(253)	66	(298)	54	(418)	68	(98)	55	(166)	46	(263)	85	(165)	80	(132)	69	(156)
Great Britain	84	(130)	69	(320)	55	(510)	86	(56)	66	(184)	52	(352)	84	(69)	73	(127)	62	(148)
Germany	72	(65)	55	(353)	37	(534)	69	(39)	50	(282)	35	(471)	80	(25)	74	(69)	55	(55)
Italy	76	(66)	48	(224)	34	(701)	53	(32)	44	(150)	29	(519)	74	(43)	56	(73)	49	(183)
Mexico	68	(83)	42	(159)	33	(765)	63	(56)	39	(124)	32	(697)	76	(27)	49	(33)	46	(67)

[a] I.e., those who received three highest scores on the subjective competence scale

[b] Numbers in parentheses refer to the bases upon which percentages are calculated.

jective competence, in contrast with 48 per cent of the more passive organizational members. However, even passive membership, when compared with nonmembership, appears to be associated with an increased sense of political competence. Whereas 48 per cent of the passive members score in the top three categories of the subjective competence scale, only 34 per cent of the nonmembers are in the higher levels. And the pattern for Italy is apparent in all nations, for individuals on both educational levels and for men and women. Apparently both the type of organization one belongs to and the intensity of one's activity within it are related to one's political attitudes. Yet organizational membership per se appears to have a residual effect on political competence and activity. The passive member as well as the member of a nonpolitical organization still differ from the individual who reports no such membership.[9]

These findings strongly support the proposition associated with the theory of mass society, that the existence of voluntary associations increases the democratic potential of a society. Democracy depends upon citizen participation, and it is clear that organizational membership is directly related to such participation. The organizational member is likely to be a self-confident citizen as well as an active one. We can also specify somewhat more precisely the impact on political competence of various types of organizational membership. Membership in a *politically oriented* organization appears to lead to greater political competence than does membership in a nonpolitical organization, and *active* membership in an organization has a greater impact on political competence than does passive membership. This fact is important because it helps explain the differential effect of organizational membership among the nations. Lipset, using data from a variety of surveys, points out that the frequency of voluntary association membership is about as great in such stable democracies

[9] In 1948 the American military government in Germany conducted a survey among German youth to evaluate how effective the newly formed youth organizations were in the inculcation of democratic attitudes. They found that there was relatively little difference between youth club members and non members in their adherence to democratic attitudes. For instance, 58 per cent of the youth club members and 55 per cent of the nonmembers believed it was better for a club to have a leader elected by majority rule rather than appointed. In contrast, 72 per cent of the club members whose own club leaders were elected favored election of leaders, in comparison with 48 per cent of the club members whose own leaders were appointed. Apparently the nature of the authority structure in the youth club had a greater effect on youth attitudes than did the fact of membership per se. See Office of Military Government for Germany (US), Opinion Survey Report No. 99, March 5, 1948, "A Report on German Youth." The survey of youth is based on 2,337 interviews with respondents between the ages of 10 and 25 years.

as the United States, Britain, and Sweden as it is in the relatively less stable democracies of Germany and France—a finding that seems to challenge the idea of a connection between stable democracy and organizational membership.[10] Our data for the United States, Britain, and Germany confirm that the rates of membership are similar for the three nations. But our findings also indicate that organizational membership may have quite different implications among the three nations. In Britain and the United States organizational membership much more frequently involves active participation within the organization than it does in Germany, where relatively few members appear to take an active part. And, as our data further show, the degree of activity within an organization has an effect upon political attitudes. The active member is more likely to be the competent democratic citizen.[11]

Multiple Membership. One other aspect of organizational participation must be considered to round out our picture of the differing patterns of participation and the impact of that participation on political attitudes among the nations. This is the number of organizations to which individuals belong. If one considers merely the frequency of membership and nonmembership among the nations, one finds some striking differences, yet this does not indicate the full extent of the differences in the amount of organizational participation. Nations differ, not only in the frequency with which respondents report membership, but also—and perhaps even more strikingly—in the frequency with which individuals report membership in more than one organization. This fact is illustrated in Table 13. In the United States about one-third of our total sample are members of more than one organization and, indeed, 9 per cent of the sample are members of four or more organizations. In Britain 16 per cent of the total sample are members of more than one organization. The figure falls off to 12 per cent of the total in Germany, 6 per cent in Italy, and 2 per cent in Mexico. Though on many measures of participation Great Britain and the United States were quite similar, on the question of organizational membership the

[10] See Lipset, *Political Man*, p. 67.

[11] We have no data that are comparable for Sweden or France, the other two nations cited by Lipset; but descriptions of French voluntary associations strongly suggest that, like the German and unlike the American and British, they tend to be highly centralized and to allow little opportunity for active participation. See in particular Arnold Rose, *Theory and Method in the Social Sciences*, Minneapolis, 1954, p. 74, and M. Crozier, "La France, Terre du Commandement," *Esprit*, xxv (1957), 779-98.

impressions of many observers prove correct. Organizational partici-pation in the United States, both in the total number who are members and the number who are members of several organizations, is much higher than that of any other country. This is reflected in the proportion of the total sample who are multiple members, as well as in the proportion of organization members who are members of more than one organization. In the United States 55 per cent of organizational members belong to more than one organization. The

TABLE 13

Respondents who Belong to One or More Organizations, by Nation
(in per cent)

Per Cent who	U.S.		U.K.		Germany		Italy		Mexico	
Belong to one organization	25		31		32		24		23	
Belong to two organizations	14		10		9		5		2	
Belong to three organizations	9		4		2		1		0	
Belong to four or more organizations	9		2		1		*		*	
Total per cent multiple members	32		16		12		6		2	
Total per cent members	57	(970) ª	47	(963)	44	(955)	30	(995)	25	(1007)

ª Numbers in parentheses refer to the bases upon which percentages are calculated.

other figures are: Britain, 34 per cent; Germany, 27 per cent; Italy, 20 per cent, and Mexico, 8 per cent.

The number of organizations to which an individual belongs also affects his political competence. Organizational membership appears to have a cumulative effect: that is, membership in one organization increases an individual's sense of political competence, and member-ship in more than one organization leads to even greater competence. This relationship is apparent in Table 14. Those who belong to an organization show higher political competence than those who are members of no organization, but the members of more than one organization show even higher competence than those whose af-filiation is limited to one. And in their political competence multiple members differ from members of a single organization about as much as, if not more than, single members differ from nonmembers.

What we have shown so far is that voluntary associations do play a major role in a democratic political culture. The organizational member, compared with the nonmember, is likely to consider him-self more competent as a citizen, to be a more active participant in

320

TABLE 14

Percentage of Respondents who scored Highest in Subjective Competence[a] among Members of One or More Organizations, by Nation and Education

Nation	Total						Primary or Less						Secondary or More					
	Multiple Member		Single Member		Non-member		Multiple Member		Single Member		Non-member		Multiple Member		Single Member		Non-member	
	%	No.[b]	%	No.	%	No.	%	No.	%	No.	%	No.	%	No.	%	No.	%	No.
United States	81	(314)	64	(242)	55	(418)	72	(106)	55	(150)	46	(263)	85	(208)	78	(92)	68	(156)
Great Britain	80	(160)	70	(294)	56	(510)	82	(77)	65	(165)	52	(352)	80	(79)	74	(119)	62	(148)
Germany	71	(111)	52	(308)	37	(534)	66	(82)	48	(239)	35	(471)	90	(27)	69	(68)	73	(55)
Italy	74	(55)	49	(240)	34	(701)	58	(26)	46	(150)	29	(519)	89	(28)	54	(90)	49	(183)
Mexico	61	(22)	50	(220)	34	(765)	[82	(11)]	45	(169)	32	(697)	[42	(10)]	64	(50)	48	(67)

a I.e., those who received three highest scores on the subjective competence scale.
b Numbers in parentheses refer to the bases upon which percentages are calculated.

politics, and to know and care more about politics. He is, therefore, more likely to be close to the model of the democratic citizen. We have also shown that it makes a difference which type of organization an individual belongs to; political organizations yield a larger political "dividend" than do nonpolitical organizations. And it makes a difference how active an individual is within his own organization: the active member displays a greater sense of political competence than does the passive member. But perhaps the most striking finding is that any membership—passive membership or membership in a nonpolitical organization—has an impact on political competence. Membership in some association, even if the individual does not consider the membership politically relevant and even if it does not involve his active participation, does lead to a more competent citizenry. Pluralism, even if not explicitly political pluralism, may indeed be one of the most important foundations of political democracy.

CHAPTER 12

POLITICAL SOCIALIZATION AND
CIVIC COMPETENCE

The Theory of Political Socialization

Recent discussions of the process involved in the formation of adult political attitudes suggest a complex set of relationships.[1] The earlier psychocultural approach to the subject regarded political socialization as a rather simple process. Three assumptions were usually made: (1) the significant socialization experiences that will affect later political behavior take place quite early in life; (2) these experiences are not manifestly political experiences, but they have latent political consequences—that is, they are neither intended to have political effects nor are these effects recognized, and (3) the direction of socialization is a unidirectional one: the more "basic" family experiences have a significant impact upon the secondary structures of politics but are not in turn affected by them. Thus the source of German attitudes toward authority was said to lie in the structure of authority in the German family and the expectations that derived from experiences with that authority structure; American and Russian political behavior could be traced to such early, non-political experiences as patterns of weaning or toilet training.[2]

This approach to an explanation of political attitudes was too simple. One could not make unambiguous connections between

[1] See, for example, the various criticisms of the "authoritarian personality" studies, especially: Richard Christie and Marie Jahoda (eds.), *Studies in the Scope and Method of the Authoritarian Personality*, Glencoe, Ill., 1954. The chapters by Edward A. Shils, Herbert H. Hyman and Paul B. Sheatsley, and Harold D. Lasswell are particularly relevant. See also Herbert Hyman, *Political Socialization*, Glencoe, Ill., 1959; Sidney Verba, *Small Groups and Political Behavior*, Princeton, N.J., 1961, pp. 29 ff.; Gabriel A. Almond and James S. Coleman, *The Politics of the Developing Areas*, Princeton, N.J., 1960, pp. 26-33.

[2] For examples of this approach, see the works by Schaffner, Mead, and Gorer cited above in chapter 1, note 9.

early socialization experiences and politics; the gap between the two was so great that it could be closed only by the use of somewhat imprecise analogies and a rather selective approach to evidence. But though it was wrong in its specific statements about political behavior (at least its more incautious adherents were wrong), this approach was a fruitful beginning. A number of the assumptions were correct and did suggest new insights into the sources of political attitudes. Attention was focused on pre-adult experiences as a source of political attitudes. It was also suggested that authority patterns in pre-adult social situations played a crucial role in the formation of political predispositions. In general, nonpolitical human relations became a source for understanding political relations.

Where this approach to political attitude formation went wrong was in narrowing the focus of these assumptions. Nonpolitical experiences in childhood may play an important part in later political attitudes and behavior, but the impact of these experiences on politics continues throughout the adolescent and adult years. In fact there is some evidence that later experiences have a more direct political implication. Early socialization experiences significantly affect an individual's basic personality predispositions and may therefore affect his political behavior, but numerous other factors intervene between these earliest experiences and later political behavior that greatly inhibit the impact of the former on the latter. Such basic dimensions of political behavior as the degree of activity or involvement in politics or the individual's partisan affiliation seem to be best explained in terms of later experiences.[3]

Another valuable insight of the psychocultural approach was that the nonpolitical authority patterns to which an individual is exposed have an important effect on his attitudes toward political authority. The authority patterns in the family are his first exposure to authority. And it is likely that his first view of the political system represents a generalization from these experiences.[4] But to think of the political system as the family writ large—as was essentially the view of those who saw the roots of the German authoritarian tradition within the German family—is too simple. In the first place, as

[3] For a discussion of the factors that can intervene between early socialization experiences and political behavior, see Nathan Leites, "Psycho-cultural Hypotheses About Political Acts," *World Politics*, I (1948), pp. 102 ff.

[4] Hess and Easton point out that the child's first image of the President represents a transfer from family experience, but he begins to differentiate between political and family roles as he grows older. See Robert D. Hess and David Easton, "The Child's Image of the President," *Public Opinion Quarterly*, XXIV (1960), pp. 632-44.

will be pointed out below, certain characteristics of family authority patterns make generalization to the political realm somewhat difficult. Furthermore, there are a host of other nongovernmental authority patterns to which the individual is exposed: in school, on the job, in the various organizations to which he belongs. And these other patterns, particularly those closer in time and in kind to the political system, may have greater importance for political behavior than have the patterns in the family.[5]

Like the emphasis on family authority patterns, the importance attached to nonpolitical experiences carrying latent political consequences represented a significant, but too narrow, insight. The latent political socialization that is involved in, say, experiences with family authority patterns may create certain predispositions toward political attitudes within the individual; his receptivity to particular types of political relationships may be increased. But this is obviously an inadequate explanation of his political attitudes, for there are other forms of political socialization. There is, for instance, manifest political socialization—the intentional teaching of political attitudes in the family and in school. Perhaps of greater importance is the unintentional exposure of a child to material that is explicitly political— the views he hears expressed about politics or political leaders, explicitly political views that are communicated to him without the express intent of forming his political attitudes. It is likely, for instance, that a good deal of the transfer of partisan allegiance from generation to generation does not depend upon the intentional teaching of political views, but upon the fact that children hear their parents discussing politics and adopt the views they hear. Or more general attitudes, such as respect or lack of respect for government, might be formed in this way. Wylie, for instance, reports that children in the French village he studied ". . . constantly hear adults referring to government as the source of evil and to the men who run it as instruments of evil. There is nothing personal in this belief. It does not concern one particular government composed of one particular group of men. It concerns government everywhere and at all times—French governments, American governments, Russian governments, all governments. Some are less bad than others, but all are essentially bad."[6]

<hr>

[5] See Harry Eckstein, *A Theory of Stable Democracy*, Princeton, N.J., 1961. Data to be presented later in this chapter will support Eckstein's point that the authority patterns closer to the political realm have a greater significance for political attitudes.

[6] Lawrence Wylie, *Village in the Vaucluse*, p. 208. It is interesting to note that this political lesson is effective despite the fact that it directly contrasts with the teachings

Such unintentional exposure to political attitudes may be a major way in which *incivism* is passed on from generation to generation.

Attitudes toward politics may therefore be formed by exposure to the political attitudes of others, whether the attitude formation is intentional or unintentional. And this formation on the basis of political experience must be added to the attitude formation that occurs through the transfer of attitudes from the nonpolitical to the political realm.

There is one last respect in which the theory of political socialization needs expansion. The flow of influence is not necessarily unidirectional. Not only may the authority patterns of family or school or occupation influence the political system, but it is also possible for the standards applied to the political system to influence authority patterns in these other areas. In the United States, for instance, the norms of *political* democracy are often used as arguments in favor of further democratization of school and employment relationships. Though much of this may have little effect on actual practice, it probably has more than a simple rhetorical significance.[7]

In expanding our view of political attitude formation from one that concentrated on early, latent political socialization, we gain in completeness of explanation, but clearly lose in neatness and simplicity. The sources of political attitudes appear to be many. They include early socialization experiences and late socialization experiences during adolescence, as well as postsocialization experiences as an adult. They include both political and nonpolitical experiences, experiences that are intended by others to have an effect on political attitudes as well as those that are unintended. Clearly many types of experience can affect basic political attitudes, and these experiences can come at a variety of times. Having thus complicated our model of political socialization, we face the problem of simplifying it again. If political attitudes are not derived from simply one source, we can at least attempt to find what sources appear most significant and for what sorts of people, and what combinations of experiences are most closely associated with particular types of political attitudes. It is this

in the civics textbooks (see pp. 106-7). It suggests that the explicitly political material that the child hears informally and that represents the real political attitudes of adults is more significant than the formal education he receives.

[7] The large body of literature concerned with the democratization of the German schools gives one the distinct impression that these authors think the schools ought to be democratic because this is what is appropriate for a democratic political system. See W. Stahl, *Education for Democracy in West Germany*, New York, 1961.

problem of specifying the impact of various types of nonpolitical experiences on political attitudes that we shall deal with in this chapter.

Of course, phrased as it is, the problem is complex and probably insoluble. We shall deal with it by concentrating on only a few types of nonpolitical authority patterns that might be expected to influence political attitudes: those patterns in the family, school, and work place. First, we shall briefly describe some differences among the five nations in the frequency with which respondents report that they were able to participate in family and school decisions as a child, and, in later life, at their place of work. We shall also examine the differences among educational and generational groups within each nation—differences that suggest important changes in participation opportunities over time. Second, we shall try to determine whether and to what extent those forms of social participation are related to political participation.

The essential question is whether there is a close relationship between the roles that a person plays in nonpolitical situations and his role in politics. Is there some strain toward homogeneity in these roles? This question suggests why the authority patterns within nonpolitical social groups may be the crucial variables to consider. These authority patterns represent, as it were, the political structures of these nonpolitical groups: if they are not identical to the authority and participatory patterns of government, they resemble them in form. They can, for instance, be more or less democratic: that is, they may allow the individual more or less opportunity to participate in decisions. Thus in concentrating on authority patterns in family, school, and job, we are concentrating on a set of relationships analogous to some basic political relationships.

There are a number of reasons why one might expect the authority patterns to which the individual is exposed outside of the political realm to have some influence on his attitudes toward politics. In the first place, the role that an individual plays within the family, the school, or the job may be considered training for the performance of political roles. He is likely to generalize from the former roles to the latter. If in most social situations the individual finds himself subservient to some authority figure, it is likely that he will expect such an authority relationship in the political sphere. On the other hand, if outside the political sphere he has opportunities to participate in a wide range of social decisions, he will probably expect to be

able to participate in political decisions as well. Furthermore, participation in nonpolitical decision making may give one the skills
needed to engage in political participation: the skills of self-expres-
sion and a sense of effective political tactics.

Because of the tendency to generalize from one social sphere to the
other, we may reasonably expect some strain toward homogeneity
among the authority relations to which an individual is exposed.
But we do not expect complete homogeneity. There is a wide gap
between family, school, and occupational participation and political
participation. In the first place, an individual who has had ample
opportunities to participate in a wide range of nonpolitical situations
may live within a political system that affords few opportunities to
participate. He may have the propensities for civic participation but
little opportunity to perform a civic role. Conversely, his prepolitical
experiences may give little encouragement for participation, but
other social characteristics or political characteristics may lead him
into participation. Furthermore, participation in the more intimate
situations of the family, the school and the job (particularly in the
family and perhaps the school) may differ markedly from participation in politics. The authority patterns within the smaller units may
take a different form from those in politics and thereby inhibit the
degree to which he will generalize from one social situation to the
other. The authority patterns of smaller, more intimate units tend
to be informal. Decisions may "emerge" from the group without ever
having been "decided" in any formal sense. The channels of influence are less clearly articulated. Because of this, the political socialization that occurs within more intimate social units may be inadequate training for the performance of civic activities within the
larger, secondary political system. Therefore, those institutions closer
to the political realm and in which authority patterns become more
similar in kind to authority patterns in the political system may be
more crucial for the formation of political attitudes.[8]

The above discussion suggests that the major difference between
nongovernmental and governmental authority patterns may be a
structural one: political decision making is a more formal process,
yet the opportunities for political participation may not differ from

[8] For a discussion of the differences between decision-making patterns in small primary groups and larger secondary groups, see Sidney Verba, *Small Groups and Political
Behavior*, chapter ii. For a further discussion of this point, see below.

those afforded by the nonpolitical social systems. But if, instead of looking at the *actual* amount of homogeneity, we look at the individual's subjective attitudes toward authority—that is, the extent to which he *thinks* there is such homology—we may expect to find a greater similarity between political and nonpolitical authority patterns. Though the individual may not have that much control over whether or not the structure of politics affords him many actual opportunities to participate, his expectations of whether or not he is able to participate (what we have called his "subjective competence") ought to be more amenable to influences from outside of the realm of politics.

Before describing some of the data relevant to this question, a few caveats are in order. As with much of our data on political participation, we shall be dealing in this chapter with respondents' reports on how much they were able to participate in decisions in the family, the school, and the job. And the relationship we are interested in is that between perceived ability to participate in these areas and perceived ability to participate in politics. We do not ask whether a man who participated in family decisions is more likely to participate in politics; we ask the more modest question of whether the man who *remembers* that he was able to participate in the family currently *believes* he is able to participate in politics. However, since the expectation that one can participate appears to be a major factor in leading to actual participation, our findings will be relevant, though not conclusive, in answering the question of the impact of nonpolitical authority experiences on political behavior. Another warning is in order regarding the problem of participation within the family and the school. In these cases we are asking respondents to remember the pattern of authority relations as they existed in what is often the rather distant past. Many of these reports must, therefore, be considered at best the approximations of past relationships. This problem of memory does not arise in regard to current job participation.

As was pointed out earlier, the patterns of interpersonal relations within the family, the school and, to a lesser extent, the job are likely to take different forms from those within the political system. They are likely to be less formal. Decision making in such situations does not involve membership in formal parties or participation in a formal election system; it is more likely to consist of an expectation that one will be consulted, if only tacitly, before decisions are made;

or that one is free to express one's point of view when decisions are being considered. Democracy in the more intimate primary group is expressed in the tone of relations and in implicit norms. If this form of participation affects political attitudes, it does so in the form of latent political socialization: that is, its explicit purpose is not to inculcate standards of political participation. However, political socialization may be explicit as well as implicit. Parents or teachers may explicitly attempt to teach norms of political behavior. The impact of this explicit civic training will be considered as well.

Early Participation in Decisions

Participation in Family Decisions. The two most significant institutions for the socialization of the child are the family and the school. In both, authority patterns are important and salient. Within the family and the school the child is first exposed to authority relationships. And though the authority patterns of both are necessarily hierarchical, involving relations between adults and children, the institutions may vary substantially in the extent to which they allow some freedom for children to participate. This participation may begin implicitly at a very early age. But since we felt that patterns of activity closer in time to political participation would be of greater significance and more reliably remembered, we decided to ask about participation within the family during adolescence. Respondents were asked if they could remember how much influence they had had in family decisions that concerned them when they were about sixteen. The results are reported in Table 1. In all countries but Italy, more than half of the respondents remember having some influence in family decisions, and in Italy the proportion is close to one-half. Respondents in the United States and Britain most frequently report (73 per cent and 69 per cent, respectively) that they had some influence over family decisions; German, Italian, and Mexican respondents in roughly equal frequency report that they had no influence. Respondents were also asked if they had had opportunities to complain about decisions. Had they felt free to complain if decisions were made that they did not like? And could they remember actually complaining? Within the informal structure of the family this freedom to dissent may be considered a form of participation.

The responses to these questions are reported in Tables 2 and 3.

In general, British and American respondents report the greatest ability to participate in family decisions in this way. British respondents report more frequently than others that they remember feeling free to complain, while the American respondents report somewhat more frequently than others that they remember actually complain-

TABLE 1

Remembered Influence in Family Decisions, by Nation
(in per cent)

Per Cent who Remember they had	U.S.	U.K.	Germany	Italy	Mexico
Some influence	73	69	54	48	57
No influence	22	26	37	37	40
Don't know, don't remember, and other	5	5	9	15	3
Total per cent	100	100	100	100	100
Total number of cases*	970	957	955	995	923

* On tables reporting data about remembered family experiences, those respondents who were not raised within a family (in an institution, for instance) are omitted.

TABLE 2

Remembered Freedom to Protest Family Decisions, by Nation
(in per cent)

Per Cent who Remember they felt	U.S.	U.K.	Germany	Italy	Mexico
Free to protest	52	63	42	41	30
Uneasy about protesting	13	10	19	16	14
It was better not to protest	29	24	27	29	50
Don't know, don't remember, and other	6	3	12	14	6
Total per cent	100	100	100	100	100
Total number	970	957	955	995	923

TABLE 3

Actual Protests about Family Decisions, by Nation
(in per cent)

Per Cent who Remember they	U.S.	U.K.	Germany	Italy	Mexico
Occasionally protested	66	61	45	53	41
Never protested	26	31	38	34	49
Don't know, don't remember, and other	8	7	17	13	10
Total per cent	100	99	100	100	100
Total number	970	957	955	995	923

ing. At the other extreme, about one-half of the Mexican respondents report that it was better not to complain and that they in fact did not complain. The frequencies with which German and Italian respondents report family participation lie between those of the United States and Britain, on the one hand, and Mexico, on the other; however, in the negative reply reported in Table 2 (row 3) all nations except Mexico report relatively similar proportions.

Participation in School. The data on participation within the family roughly parallel much of the data previously reported on

TABLE 4

Freedom to Discuss Unfair Treatment in School or to
Disagree with Teacher, by Nation
(in per cent)

Per Cent who Remember they felt	U.S.	U.K.	Germany	Italy	Mexico
Free	45	35	34	29	40
Uneasy	22	18	24	19	16
Better not to talk to teacher	25	41	30	36	39
Don't know, don't remember, and other	8	6	12	16	5
Total per cent	100	100	100	100	100
Total number	969	963	953	907	783

participation within politics: a relatively greater frequency of participation in Britain and the United States, intermediate participation in Germany, and somewhat lower participation in Italy and Mexico. On the other hand, the data on remembered participation in the schools show a sharp contrast between the United States and the other four countries. This is true for informal participation within the school, but especially true for the opportunities for formal participation in school political discussions.

Consider the remembered ability of our respondents to participate informally within the school. To what extent did they have the opportunity to express their opinions? Tables 4 and 5 report the proportions of respondents who say they felt free to complain if they believed they were treated unfairly, as well as the proportions who remember actually complaining. As Table 4 indicates, American respondents report most often that they felt free to complain of unfair treatment and report least often that it was better not to talk to the teacher. In the other nations the pattern is rather mixed. Italian respondents report least often that they felt free to complain, and the British respondents report most frequently that it was better not to speak up. And Table 5 brings out the same pattern. While equal proportions of American respondents remember having actually complained as remember having never complained, in each of the other four nations the proportion reporting that they never

TABLE 5

Actual Discussion of Unfair Treatment or Disagreement with Teacher, by Nation
(in per cent)

Per Cent who Remember this occurred	U.S.	U.K.	Germany	Italy	Mexico
Occasionally or often	46	36	30	32	38
Never	46	57	58	56	58
Don't know, don't remember, and other	8	7	12	12	4
Total per cent	100	100	100	100	100
Total number	969	963	953	907	783

TABLE 6

Freedom to Participate in School Discussions and Debates, by Nation
(in per cent)

Per Cent who Remember they	U.S.	U.K.	Germany	Italy	Mexico
Could and did participate	40	16	12	11	15
Could but did not participate	15	8	5	4	21
Could not participate	34	68	68	56	54
Don't know and other	11	8	15	29	10
Total per cent	100	100	100	100	100
Total number	969	963	953	907	783

complained is substantially larger than the proportion reporting that they did complain.

But the sharpest difference in school participation is observed if one considers more formal opportunities to participate. Here the distinction between education in the United States and education elsewhere is immediately apparent. Respondents were asked whether children in their school were given the opportunity to discuss and debate political and social issues. If they reported that there were such discussions, then they were asked if they themselves took part. The results to these two questions are reported in Table 6. In the United States 40 per cent of the respondents report that there were such discussions and that they took part. In the other nations the percentage so reporting is much smaller, ranging from 16 per cent in Britain to 11 per cent in Italy. Clearly, the amount of explicit training for political participation in the schools is much higher in the United States than elsewhere.[9]

The data reported above suggest that there are differences among the nations in the frequency with which young people have an opportunity to participate in decisions. Before considering the relationship between authority patterns in nonpolitical and political situations, it is important to look more closely at the distribution of patterns of authority within the nations. Modes of participation in the family, for instance, may not be uniform throughout society; certain social strata may allow more participation than others. In fact, these differences among social strata may account for a good deal of the differences among the nations. And just as important as the class differences in patterns of authority are the changes that these patterns undergo over time. If participation within nonpolitical decision making fosters a sense of political competence, then it is relevant for an assessment of the future of democracy to see how these authority relationships change. We shall therefore consider the way in which social class groups and age groups within each nation differ in the extent to which members have experiences with participation.

Class and Early Participation. Our data suggest that authority patterns in the family and the school vary substantially among different social groups. Our survey unfortunately contained no index of the social status of the respondent's parents, and we must use certain information about the respondent to infer this. Perhaps the most useful though far from exact index is the respondent's educational level, for one may assume that the amount of education an individual receives is related to the social status of his parents.

In all five nations the frequency with which respondents report that they were able to participate in decisions within the family or at school—both their freedom to complain about decisions and the actual complaining they remember doing—rises with level of education. On the question of whether the respondent remembers ever protesting a family decision he did not like, the data in Table 7 indicate how closely such remembered protest is related to educa-

[9] For some important qualifications of these points, see the data reported below in this chapter on differences among educational and age groups.

tional level. The distinction is particularly sharp between those with primary education or less and those with secondary education; the difference between those with secondary education and those who attained some higher education is somewhat less; and in Britain and Italy the percentages of remembered protest decline as one moves from the secondary to the university level.

Due to their retrospective nature and to the fact that the measure of family social status is crude, the data must be interpreted with great caution; yet they do suggest strongly that experience with fam-

TABLE 7

Per Cent Reporting Actual Protests about Family Decisions, by Nation and Education

Nation	Total (%)	(No.)*	Prim. or Less (%)	(No.)	Some Sec. (%)	(No.)	Some Univ. (%)	(No.)
United States	66	(970)	50	(339)	72	(447)	75	(188)
Great Britain	62	(957)	56	(593)	72	(322)	54	(24)
Germany	45	(955)	42	(790)	64	(124)	77	(26)
Italy	53	(995)	46	(692)	69	(245)	67	(54)
Mexico	41	(923)	38	(800)	53	(99)	74	(23)

* Numbers in parentheses refer to the bases upon which percentages are calculated.

ily authority patterns differs among the social classes. Those of higher social status are more likely to participate in family decisions. If such experience facilitates the growth of democratic political competence in later life, one of the many reasons for the generally lower political competence of those with low educational attainment may be that these people are usually raised in families that do not nourish the expectation that one can make one's voice heard in decisions.

A similar class difference is observable in school participation (see Tables 8 and 9). Respondents with higher education remember informal participation (complaining about unfair treatment) and formal participation (classroom discussion) much more frequently than do those of lower educational attainment. For example, 25 per cent of the Italian respondents who did not get beyond primary school report that they remember complaining about unfair treatment, in contrast with 44 per cent of those who reached secondary school. And the differences are as sharp within each of the nations. Even more striking are the differences among social groups in the frequency of remembered formal participation in classroom discussions (as reported in Table 8). In each nation the frequency of re-membered participation is about three or four times as great among respondents with some secondary education as it is among those with only primary education.[10]

At first glance one may wonder at this class difference in school

TABLE 8

Per Cent Reporting Actual Discussion of Unfair Treatment or Disagreement with Teacher, by Nation and Education

Nation	Total (%)	(No.)*	Prim. or Less (%)	(No.)	Some Sec. (%)	(No.)	Some Univ. (%)	(No.)
United States	46	(959)	32	(339)	52	(447)	55	(188)
Great Britain	36	(963)	31	(593)	44	(322)	58	(24)
Germany	31	(953)	26	(790)	52	(124)	81	(26)
Italy	32	(907)	25	(604)	44	(245)	57	(54)
Mexico	38	(783)	32	(656)	63	(103)	81	(24)

* Numbers in parentheses refer to the bases upon which percentages are calculated.

TABLE 9

Per Cent Reporting Actual Participation in School Discussions and Debates, by Nation and Education

Nation	Total (%)	(No.)*	Prim. or Less (%)	(No.)	Some Sec. (%)	(No.)	Some Univ. (%)	(No.)
United States	40	(970)	17	(339)	50	(442)	57	(188)
Great Britain	16	(963)	7	(593)	26	(322)	46	(24)
Germany	12	(953)	7	(790)	34	(124)	42	(26)
Italy	11	(907)	6	(604)	22	(245)	22	(54)
Mexico	15	(783)	9	(656)	37	(103)	54	(24)

* Numbers in parentheses refer to the bases upon which percentages are calculated.

participation. Don't individuals of varying social classes often attend the same schools, and isn't school policy often made for a geographic area and not for specific social groups? If this is the case, one would not expect children of various social classes to differ in their school

[10] The same qualifications apply to these data as apply to the data on family partici-pation. Further, although the questions reported in Tables 8 and 9 dealt with the primary school, those respondents with higher education may have been unable to separate the two levels of educational experience and may be reporting later ex-perience.

The limited size of our sample makes it impossible to deal more intensively with varying types of schools. Sharp differences probably exist among types of British secondary schools, for instance. The socializing effects on British public school students of their relations *among themselves* would be a fascinating and significant topic to explore.

experiences. But though this may be partially true (unlike the situation with the family), there are a number of ways in which class differentials might be introduced. In the first place, children of varying social classes do not attend the same schools; this may be due to neighborhood differences or to the fact that those in upper-status families will more often attend private schools. And the opportunities to participate may be uneven among the various types of schools.[11] Furthermore, even if children from a variety of social backgrounds attend the same schools and are in the same classroom, the school may favor the participation of those of higher status. In life-history interviews, for instance, when respondents were asked to expound more fully on their school experiences, a large number of respondents from lower-status families in all five nations commented on the differential treatment that teachers gave to children of different social backgrounds.[12] And lastly, children from higher-status homes may be better equipped and more highly motivated to participate within the school, if given the opportunity, than are children from lower status homes. For if we can expect individuals to generalize from their family experiences to the political system— if their earliest attitudes toward authority determine some of their later attitudes toward political authority—the same pattern should hold between the family and the school. And higher-status children do have greater opportunity to participate within the family.

The implications of these data are significant. If experience with nongovernmental patterns of authority is indeed a source of political attitudes, then the sharp differences in political attitudes that one observes among respondents from various social backgrounds may originate in their early experiences with authority. We shall return to this question below.

One further point must be made about the distribution of school and family participatory experiences among those with varying educational backgrounds. In our earlier discussion of the national differences in the frequency with which respondents report remembered opportunities to participate within the family, we found a

[11] As Eckstein points out (*op. cit.*), as one moves from the secondary modern schools in Britain to the grammar and public schools, especially the latter, one finds social situations that allow boys greater degrees of freedom and responsibility.

[12] A British skilled worker, for instance, commented that teachers ". . . favored someone from a better home, because they had all the books and so forth that they needed to learn"; while a German laborer said that teachers ". . . spent much more time with the rich farmers' children. After school the teacher would help these children. . . . He did not do that with the poor children."

rough parallel between the frequencies of reported ability to participate in politics and remembered participatory family experiences. Both were most frequent in the United States and Britain and least frequent in Italy and Mexico. And within the schools we found the contrast between the United States and the other four nations to be the clearest pattern. But if one considers the data in Tables 7, 8, and 9, it becomes clear that much of the difference in school and family experiences seems to be due to the differing distributions of educational attainment among the nations. As Table 7 indicates, the national differences in remembered family participation are only faintly mirrored in the data for respondents with no more than primary school education, and not mirrored at all at higher educational levels. The remembered informal participation in schools (reported in Table 8) shows little systematic national difference within each educational group. It is, in fact, only with formal participation in school debates (Table 9) that any sharp national difference persists—and this is the clear contrast between the frequency of participation in the United States and in other nations.

Thus those with higher education in all five nations seem to receive somewhat greater opportunities to participate in nonpolitical situations than do those with lower educational attainment. And when one considers respondents of similar educational backgrounds, cross-national differences in opportunities to participate become insignificant.

Age and Early Participation. Perhaps even more significant than the differences among social classes in the degree to which individuals have opportunities to participate in family and school decisions are the differences among generations. Our data strongly suggest that patterns of family and school participation have been changing over time, and, what is most important, that they have been changing in the same direction in all five nations. These data are presented in Tables 10, 11, and 12, which show the frequencies with which respondents at various ages remember complaining about a family decision they did not like, remember protesting a decision made by the teacher, and remember taking part in formal class discussions.

The most striking characteristic of the data in these tables is that there is change in a similar direction in all five nations. The older the respondent, the less likely he is to report opportunities to participate. In almost every instance the two groups over fifty years of age report school and family participation least frequently. Despite the

TABLE 10

Per Cent Reporting Actual Protests about Family Decisions, by Nation and Age

Nation	Total % No.*	18-25 % No.	26-30 % No.	31-35 % No.	36-40 % No.	41-50 % No.	51-60 % No.	61- % No.
United States	66 (970)	85 (122)	82 (89)	74 (90)	72 (97)	69 (175)	53 (155)	48 (241)
Great Britain	62 (957)	74 (81)	75 (95)	72 (112)	69 (138)	66 (194)	52 (170)	40 (167)
Germany	45 (955)	65 (115)	54 (81)	53 (99)	48 (115)	42 (177)	41 (182)	29 (186)
Italy	53 (995)	57 (162)	58 (120)	60 (112)	55 (113)	56 (188)	42 (166)	39 (134)
Mexico	41 (923)	35 (183)	41 (173)	43 (119)	43 (130)	48 (146)	39 (114)	35 (58)
Year of birth		1934-41	1929-34	1924-29	1919-24	1909-19	1900-09	before 1900
Years at age 16		1950-57	1945-50	1940-45	1935-40	1925-35	1916-25	before 1916

* Numbers in parentheses refer to the bases upon which percentages are calculated.

TABLE 11

Per Cent Reporting Actual Discussion of Unfair Treatment or Disagreement with Teacher, by Nation and Age

Nation	Total % No.*	18-25 % No.	26-30 % No.	31-35 % No.	36-40 % No.	41-50 % No.	51-60 % No.	61- % No.
United States	46 (959)	66 (122)	63 (89)	52 (90)	48 (97)	45 (175)	41 (155)	29 (241)
Great Britain	36 (963)	52 (81)	43 (95)	35 (112)	35 (139)	40 (194)	35 (172)	25 (170)
Germany	31 (953)	45 (115)	37 (81)	31 (99)	33 (115)	33 (177)	21 (182)	24 (186)
Italy	32 (907)	54 (158)	38 (114)	32 (108)	28 (111)	24 (178)	22 (148)	24 (90)
Mexico	38 (783)	46 (155)	43 (147)	41 (101)	45 (110)	34 (124)	29 (97)	13 (49)

* Numbers in parentheses refer to the bases upon which percentages are calculated.

TABLE 12

Per Cent Reporting Actual Participation in School Discussions and Debates, by Nation and Age

Nation	Total % No.*	18-25 % No.	26-30 % No.	31-35 % No.	36-40 % No.	41-50 % No.	51-60 % No.	61- % No.
United States	40 (970)	68 (122)	60 (89)	49 (90)	47 (97)	44 (175)	30 (155)	15 (24)
Great Britain	16 (963)	42 (81)	26 (95)	17 (112)	15 (138)	15 (194)	9 (170)	5 (167)
Germany	12 (955)	38 (115)	6 (81)	16 (99)	16 (115)	9 (177)	4 (182)	2 (186)
Italy	10 (995)	22 (162)	11 (120)	11 (112)	9 (113)	7 (188)	7 (166)	3 (134)
Mexico	12 (783)	16 (155)	15 (147)	14 (133)	13 (144)	12 (160)	5 (124)	1 (61)

* Numbers in parentheses refer to the bases upon which percentages are calculated.

wide disparities in the recent histories of these nations, the differences in their social structures and in overall levels of participation and competence, all five appear to be experiencing a similar secular trend toward a less authoritarian school and family system.[13]

Despite the general similarity of pattern in the five nations, there are some interesting differences in the regularity of change in family and school participation over time. In the United States one observes a relatively gradual increase in the frequency of remembered participation; the data seem to indicate that this change has been going on steadily over the last generations. A similar pattern of gradual change over time is apparent in the data about family participation (Table 10) for Great Britain and Germany and, to a lesser extent, Italy. Despite political and social vicissitudes, which at times may have slowed changes in family structure, there appears to be a relatively steady movement toward a participatory family in these three nations. Increases in school participation, on the other hand (Tables 11 and 12), seem to have occurred in two stages in Britain, Germany, and Italy: during the post-World War I period and again in the post-World War II period, with relatively little change for those respondents who attended school roughly from the mid-1920's to the end of the Second World War. This pattern is what one might expect in Germany and Italy, where institutional change was arrested by the Nazi and Fascist regimes. And indeed, the sharp changes in the postwar generation suggest the degree to which old, imposed forms of school training have been replaced by new forms. The similarity in the British pattern may be explained by the modifications in secondary education following both world wars.

In Mexico changes in family and school authority patterns appear to have been the slowest. There is a steady increase in the frequency of reported participation in school decisions as one moves from older to younger respondents, but the changes are much more gradual than in the other nations. And in relation to family participation, there appears to be little regular pattern in the responses reported in Table 10. Nevertheless, the cross-national uniformity is impressive. All

[13] The fact that older respondents are more likely to have forgotten whether they could participate does not seem to be the reason for age differences in reported participation. For this pattern of age differences holds even if we consider the proportion who remember being able to participate of those respondents who were able to remember if they participated or not. Thus the age differential obtains even when we control for the factor of worse memory among older respondents. Furthermore, older respondents report more frequently than the younger that they remember *not* being able to participate.

the patterns of authority outside the realm of politics appear to be changing in the same direction: toward greater participation. Furthermore, they appear to change somewhat independently of the political system. This is at least the inference one can draw from the relatively steady change in patterns of family authority—especially in Germany—since the early part of the century. On the other hand, the arrested change in school authority pattern in Italy and Germany suggests that these patterns are more likely to be affected by the political system.

What we may be observing in this general trend toward greater participation in the school and family are certain aspects of the industrialization, urbanization, and modernization processes in Europe and the United States. The last century has seen a dramatic shift from agricultural to industrial employment, from rural to urban residence, and a sharp rise in educational levels. This has meant by and large a shift from the extended, patriarchal family to the nuclear family, the emancipation of women, and the development of greater individual autonomy. The striking point about these general changes in patterns of social authority and individual participation is that they do not immediately, or even necessarily, spill over into the political sphere. They do, however, have political consequences. We shall return to these below.

Job Participation. Thus far we have looked at nonpolitical participation in the early lives of our respondents. But though much of the politically relevant experience with authority patterns occurs in the preadult years, it is also likely that these experiences continue beyond childhood. Opportunities to participate in adult life, as well as preadult opportunities in family and school, can affect one's expectations of chances to participate politically. In particular, participation at work ought to have a significant effect on the individual's belief in his ability to participate politically. Though job participation comes later in life than participation in family and school, and therefore at an age when the individual's attitudes are probably less malleable, the very fact that it is contemporary with political participation suggests that disparities between the patterns of authority would lead to greater strains to bring them into harmony with each other.

How much opportunity do individuals have to participate in decisions at their place of work? While this question could be asked

341

only of those respondents who were employed in some enterprise where there was someone in authority over them, the question had this advantage over those about the family and the school: it was not retrospective. Respondents were asked, not about experiences in the

TABLE 13
Consulted about Job Decisions, by Nation
(in per cent)

Per Cent Saying they are Consulted	U.S.	U.K.	Germany	Italy	Mexico
Sometimes or often	78	80	68	59	61
Rarely or never	21	19	29	36	38
Don't know and other	1	–	3	5	–
Total per cent	100	100	100	100	100
Total number*	428	470	369	314	277

* Smaller bases because not all respondents had people in authority over them in their jobs.

TABLE 14
Freedom to Protest Job Decisions, by Nation
(in per cent)

If They Disagreed with Job Decision, They Would	U.S.	U.K.	Germany	Italy	Mexico
Feel free to protest	82	89	75	55	70
Feel uneasy about protest	4	4	8	13	4
Better not to protest	13	6	10	22	26
Don't know and other	1	–	7	12	–
Total per cent	100	100	100	100	100
Total number	428	470	369	314	277

past, but about their current job situation. One can therefore attribute greater reliability to these responses.

Table 13 reports the responses to this question. British and American respondents report most frequently (80 per cent and 78 per cent, respectively) that they are consulted when decisions are made on the job. At the other extreme, Mexican and Italian respondents least often report that they are consulted (though in both countries the percentages are more than half). In Germany the proportion of respondents who report consultation lies in-between. A similar pattern is found in Table 14, which reports the extent to which respondents say they feel free to protest on the job if a decision is made of which they do not approve. Again the freedom to participate is most frequently reported in the United States and Britain, followed by Germany. In this case, however, there is a sharp difference between Mexico and Italy, with the Italian respondents much less frequently saying that they feel free to participate.

The pattern of perceived ability to participate on the job is rounded out by data in Table 15, which show the extent to which respondents report they actually have complained about decisions.

TABLE 15

Actual Protests about Job Decisions, by Nation
(in per cent)

Per Cent who say	U.S.	U.K.	Germany	Italy	Mexico
They have protested	62	67	57	54	37
They haven't protested	38	32	37	41	63
Don't know and other	–		6	5	–
Total per cent	100		100	100	100
Total number	428	470	369	314	277

Such complaints are reported most frequently in the United States and Britain, and are somewhat less common in Italy and Germany. Mexican workers report the smallest frequency of complaining.[14]

The opportunity to participate at work is also unevenly distributed throughout the various occupations. Some occupations, apparently, allow a wider scope than others for worker participation. This fact is clearly reflected in Tables 16 and 17, which report the frequency of ability to participate in decisions at one's place of work, for four occupational categories. As Table 16 indicates, in general, the higher the status of the occupation, the more likely the individual is to be consulted on decisions. In all five nations skilled workers report more frequent consultation than do unskilled workers, and white-collar workers report either more frequent consultation than skilled workers (in Germany, Mexico, and Italy) or about as much consultation (the United States and Britain). And those in professional or managerial positions (who nevertheless have someone in a

[14] Mexicans frequently say that they would feel free to protest—yet they rarely do so. This may be another manifestation of the aspirational character of the Mexican pattern of participation: a high belief in one's efficacy, not matched by actual experience in participation.

position of authority over them) report even more frequent consultation.

This finding is not, of course, unexpected. One would assume that those with higher skills would, on the basis of technical competence

TABLE 16

Per Cent Saying They Are Usually or Sometimes Consulted about Job Decisions, by Nation and Occupation

Nation	Total %	No.[a]	Unskilled %	No.	Skilled %	No.	White Collar %	No.	Professional & Managerial %	No.
United States	78	(428)	69	(102)	82	(87)	78	(120)	87	(54)
Great Britain	79	(470)	68	(129)	82	(172)	81	(80)	95	(42)
Germany	68	(370)	50	(84)	66	(93)	83	(75)	95	(20)
Italy	58	(311)	40	(112)	67	(46)	78	(95)		b
Mexico	61	(277)	48	(35)	61	(120)	69	(78)	70	(17)

[a] Numbers in parentheses refer to the bases upon which percentages are calculated.
[b] Too few cases.

TABLE 17

Per Cent Saying They Feel Free to Protest Job Decisions, by Nation and Occupation

Nation	Total %	No.[a]	Unskilled %	No.	Skilled %	No.	White Collar %	No.	Professional & Managerial %	No.
United States	82	(428)	71	(92)	85	(71)	81	(139)	87	(55)
Great Britain	93	(470)	81	(129)	91	(172)	96	(80)	95	(42)
Germany	75	(370)	70	(84)	72	(93)	83	(75)	100	(20)
Italy	55	(311)	38	(112)	61	(46)	74	(96)		b
Mexico	70	(277)	59	(35)	66	(120)	83	(78)	85	(17)

[a] Numbers in parentheses refer to the bases upon which percentages are calculated.
[b] Too few cases.

alone, be more frequently consulted by those in authority over them. Furthermore, this may reflect, not merely technical requirements, but a different set of social relations between unskilled workers and their supervisors and those with higher-status occupations and their supervisors. In any case, it is clear that the nature of the occupation has a similar effect in each nation on the participatory opportunities that are afforded. This holds true, not only for consultation by supervisors, but for individuals' feelings of freedom to protest decisions they do not like.

Whatever the reason for the increase in participatory opportunities as one ascends the occupational scale, the implications for political participation are clear. In the first place, those in higher-status jobs are more likely to receive the sort of training in participation that we have suggested may be related to political participation. And second, economic advance and a shift in the distribution of the labor force toward a higher proportion of skilled, white-collar, technical and managerial personnel may be accompanied by the development of a more competent citizenry. What this implies for the development of democratic political participation is not self-evident, however. Increased work-place participation creates a strain and a potential competence to which political systems tend to respond; but the response may take forms other than increased opportunities for real political participation.

The data in Tables 16 and 17 suggest an important qualification about the national differences in the frequencies of work-place participation. As with family and school participation, it appears that work-place participation is in part a function of the distribution of occupational types in each nation, as well as a function of national "style." The national differences within each matched occupational group often appear to be quite a bit smaller than for the entire samples. But this is particularly so on the level of the white-collar occupations. Among white-collar workers and those in professional or management positions, opportunities to participate are fairly uniform in all nations. On the blue-collar levels of skilled and unskilled workers, sharp national differences persist. This suggests that on the higher-status occupational levels—whether because of the demands of the job or because democratic ideologies are more widespread here—a uniform cross-national pattern of participation exists. The effects of national affiliation are more apparent on lower occupational levels.[15]

The materials thus far presented suggest that participation in family, school, and job is related to patterns of political participation in each nation. In general, respondents in the two nations where frequency of political participation seems to be highest (the United States and Britain) also report most frequently that they were able

[15] For a similar point in relation to educational level, see chapter 13 below.

to participate in nonpolitical decisions. And respondents in Italy and Mexico, where the overall levels of political participation tend to be low, generally report the least frequent participatory experience in nonpolitical situations. However, the data also suggest that the relationship between political and nonpolitical participation may be more complicated. For instance, British respondents report levels of school participation that are somewhat similar to those in Germany, Italy, and Mexico, and quite different from that in the United States. On the other hand, the clearest parallel to the data on political participation exists in the data on job participation. Those nations with the most political participation also appear to afford the greatest opportunities for work-place participation, the distinction being especially sharp on the blue collar level. This latter point is important, for the data on job participation represent the only evidence on nonpolitical participation contemporaneous with adult political participation. The data on family and school participation are often information about the distant past. This suggests that the patterns of authority perceived by an individual as most similar are those adult patterns of authority, political and nonpolitical, to which he is contemporaneously exposed—thus democracy in both may develop simultaneously. Let us consider these questions more directly.

Social Participation and Civic Competence

Family Participation and Civic Competence. Our main interest in nongovernmental patterns of authority—those of the family, school, and place of work—is in the effect that these patterns have on the political attitudes and behavior of those who have been exposed to them. Specifically, we want to know if a sense of ability is in some way transferred from the more limited sphere of participation in nonpolitical decisions to the larger one of participation in politics; or, put another way, is the member of a democratic family more likely to be a democratically competent citizen?

In order to assess the impact that participation within the family has on later political competence, we divided our respondents into three groups: those who consistently reported that they had had participatory opportunities in the family; those who consistently reported that they had had no such opportunity, and those who remember more mixed patterns of participation.[16] These were then com-

---

[16] Grouped together as family participants are respondents who report that they had some influence on family decisions, that they would have felt free to protest a decision

pared in terms of their position on the scale of subjective political competence. There are a number of reasons why this scale was chosen as the dependent variable. In the first place, one would expect participation within the family to have an effect on the individual's subjective perception of his ability to participate in politics. Therefore, if opportunities to participate within the primary group affect political competence, this effect ought to be most apparent in the individual's feeling of mastery in the political sphere. Other aspects of political competence, such as political activity or knowledge of politics, cannot be as directly affected by a process of generalization from the family level. Activity or knowledge may be more easily inhibited by a lack of objective opportunities to take an active part or to acquire knowledge. But the subjective feeling that one can participate, while not completely independent of the external political situation, is certain to be relatively more independent than those other attributes. Furthermore, the individual's perception of his ability to participate is a significant political attitude. As was shown in Chapter 9, this subjective perception is intimately related to political behavior, to positive identification with the political system, and to the acceptance of democratic attitudes. If, then, participation within the family can foster a sense of political competence, we can safely say that such nonpolitical participation will have some effect on the extent of democratic political orientations within a nation.

As the data in Table 18 indicate, there is a connection between remembered ability to participate in family decisions and current political competence. In all five nations those who remember consistently being able to express themselves in family decisions tend to score highest in subjective political competence. In the United States, where the scores on the subjective competence scale tend to be highest, 70 per cent of the respondents who report that they were able to participate in the family are in the highest three groups on the subjective competence scale, whereas 47 per cent of those who report that they were not able to participate are in these highest three groups. Similarly in Mexico, where the scores on subjective

---

they did not like, and that they remember actually protesting. Nonparticipants report that they had no influence, that they did not feel free to protest, and that they do not remember protesting. Those with a mixed pattern of participation answered some of the items positively and some negatively—for instance, that they had some influence on family decisions but did not feel free to complain.

TABLE 18

Per Cent who scored Highest in Subjective Competence[a] among Respondents who Report Varying Degrees of Participation in Family Decisions, by Nation and Education

Nation	Total						Primary or Less						Secondary or More					
	Partic.		Mixed		Nonpartic.		Partic.		Mixed		Nonpartic.		Partic.		Mixed		Nonpartic.	
	%	No.[b]	%	No.	%	No.	%	No.	%	No.	%	No.	%	No.	%	No.	%	No.
United States	70	(377)	67	(462)	47	(89)	58	(144)	56	(264)	42	(73)	77	(233)	80	(198)	69	(16)
Great Britain	70	(359)	63	(479)	51	(93)	67	(186)	59	(313)	45	(71)	73	(165)	70	(154)	76	(17)
Germany	52	(233)	50	(449)	42	(164)	46	(163)	45	(381)	42	(153)	66	(67)	75	(65)	[45	(11)]
Italy	46	(242)	41	(462)	34	(169)	35	(132)	37	(311)	31	(143)	59	(109)	50	(149)	52	(25)
Mexico	50	(126)	41	(598)	26	(199)	51	(85)	39	(524)	24	(191)	48	(41)	57	(73)		c

a I.e., those who received three highest scores on the subjective competence scale
b Numbers in parentheses refer to the bases upon which percentages are calculated.
c Too few cases

competence are generally lowest, 50 per cent of those who participated in the family are in the three highest groups of the subjective competence scale, in contrast with 26 per cent of those who could not participate in the family. And the same pattern may be observed in the other three nations.

Since experiences with family authority patterns as well as sense of political competence vary with education, it is important to consider this relationship within matched educational groups. When we separate those with secondary education or better from those with no more than primary school instruction, an interesting qualification to our earlier generalization becomes apparent. The relationship between remembered ability to participate within the family and subjective political competence persists among those with lower educational attainment (though in Italy and Germany only to a slight extent), but not among those in the higher educational group. In all five countries family participation is generalized to political participation among those with primary school education. But among those with higher education there is little apparent connection between the two variables.

This finding suggests an important qualification to any hypothesis about the extent of generalization between family experience and political participation. Apparently, the degree to which such generalization takes place depends on other factors. The fact that generalization from family to polity does not apply to those on higher education levels suggests that family participation may be of least significance among those who ordinarily would be expected to have most subjective political competence. Among those with higher education, political competence develops for a number of reasons. For one thing, these people will have greater skill than others in political participation; they will be more likely to have been taught norms that foster political participation. Furthermore, the general social expectation is that those with higher educational attainment will be politically competent. And, of course, they are more likely to mingle with others who consider themselves politically competent. If, then, their family training is not such as to foster participation, there are other factors that can substitute for it.

On the other hand, those with lower educational attainment are both less likely to have learned participatory skills or the norm that one ought to participate and less likely to find themselves in situations where they are expected to be politically competent. And

349

where there is no presumption in favor of political competence, generalization from the family level can have, as it were, greater marginal effect. If political participation receives support outside the family sphere, family participation becomes less crucial as a determinant of political involvement.

To some extent this proposition is supported by the relationship between family participation and political competence within various age groups. One might expect that the longer ago the family participation occurred, the less its impact on political attitudes: thus the relationship between the two variables would be weakest among older respondents and strongest among the younger. However, our discussion of the relationship between the two forms of participation on the two educational levels suggest the opposite result: that the relationship is strongest among older respondents, who were brought up when norms of political and family participation were weakest. Insofar as levels of participation have been changing over time, political participation was a less salient norm and family participation in decisions was relatively infrequent when the older respondents were growing up. Those who were able to participate in family decisions received a deviant form of political socialization and therefore differed from their age peers in terms of their political attitudes. In more recent times, however, when both the family patterns and the more general political norms support political participation, family participation has less of a differential effect on political behavior.

The data in Table 19 support this conclusion. In the United States, Britain, and Germany, the relationship between family participation and political competence is strongest among those in the oldest age group; in the United States and Germany, in fact, there appears to be little if any relationship between family experience and political competence among respondents under fifty years of age.[17]

In any case, the fact that family participation appears to have little effect on political competence among those with higher education in the United States, Britain, and Germany, as well as among those Americans and Germans under fifty years of age, suggests that whatever effect family participation has on political competence, it is not a universal one and it may be offset by other factors.[18]

[17] In Mexico and Italy, on the other hand, no discernable age difference appears.

[18] Another interpretation of the results must be mentioned here. It is possible that some of the relationship between family participation and sense of political competence is an artifact of the interview situation. The questions about political

TABLE 19

Per Cent who scored Highest in Subjective Competence[a] among Respondents who Report Varying Degrees of Participation in Family Decisions, by Nation and Age

	18-30						31-50						51 and older					
	Partic.		Mixed		Nonpartic.		Partic.		Mixed		Nonpartic.		Partic.		Mixed		Nonpartic.	
Nation	%	No.[b]	%	No.	%	No.	%	No.	%	No.	%	No.	%	No.	%	No.	%	No.
United States	72	(129)	69	(71)	c	(8)	73	(151)	68	(170)	72	(25)	62	(97)	65	(221)	41	(56)
Great Britain	71	(86)	66	(83)	c	(5)	71	(188)	66	(221)	63	(27)	67	(87)	57	(174)	44	(59)
Germany	53	(80)	45	(91)	56	(16)	49	(94)	55	(199)	49	(57)	55	(60)	45	(158)	35	(91)
Italy	46	(84)	42	(139)	38	(37)	51	(99)	42	(203)	35	(71)	37	(59)	41	(120)	30	(61)
Mexico	63	(33)	43	(212)	29	(60)	46	(68)	46	(261)	28	(86)	47	(25)	29	(124)	19	(53)

a I.e., those who received three highest scores on subjective competence scale
b Numbers in parentheses refer to the bases upon which percentages are calculated.
c Too few cases

To sum up the relationship between family participation and sense of political competence: there is some connection between democracy in the family and democratic behavior in politics. Those who had the opportunity to participate in the family are somewhat more likely than others to feel politically competent. But the relationship is a complex one, in which a number of intervening variables can blunt the impact of this democratic training on political attitudes. Family participation is not generalized to political participation among those with higher education, and in several countries this generalization is not made by our younger respondents. The reason may be that the respondents whose political behavior is not affected by their family training do not need that training as a means of induction into a feeling of political competence. Younger respondents and those with higher education are subjected to numerous pressures leading to a sense of political competence, and the marginal effect of family participation is, under these circumstances, not very great.

School Participation and Civic Competence. Much of what has been said about the impact that family participation has on the sense of political competence may be said about the impact of school participation. The opportunity to participate within the school appears to have a definite effect upon one's position on the subjective competence scale. But the variety of types of participation within the school—particularly the difference between informal participation (protesting a decision) and formal participation (taking part in classroom discussions)—allows us to look somewhat more closely at the way in which participation in the school affects political competence.

Consider first the effect of remembered ability to participate informally in decisions in the school. In order to group our respondents according to the extent to which they report they were able to

competence were asked near the beginning of the interview, those on family participation near the end. Yet respondents may have upgraded or downgraded their memories of family experiences to match their reports of their current competence in politics. One would expect this to have happened especially among those whose memories of family experiences are dimmest; and this might explain the closer relationship between political and family competence among those in the older age groups and perhaps among those with lower educational attainment.

If this were the case, it would cast doubt on the validity of our connection between experience with nonpolitical authority and political attitudes. Some data reported in note 20 below, however, suggest that this relationship cannot be explained away as an artifact of the interview.

protest decisions, we divided them (on the basis of their responses to three questions) into three groups: those who consistently answered that they could participate in this way; those who consistently answered that they could not so participate, and those who gave mixed responses.[19] In many ways this parallels our grouping of respondents according to the extent of their family participation. And in many ways the data on informal school participation resemble those on informal family participation. As Table 20 indicates, those who remember that they were able to protest effectively within the school are most likely to be high on the scale of subjective competence. And to take again the nations with the highest and lowest overall rates of subjective political competence: in the United States 75 per cent of those who report that they were able to participate within the school are in the top three categories of the subjective competence scale, in contrast with 54 per cent of those who report that they could not participate; while in Mexico 52 per cent of the school participants are in the top three subjective competence categories, in contrast with 24 per cent of the nonparticipants.

But as with the data on participation in the family, it is important to consider the educational groups separately. If one looks at the relationship between school participation and political competence within higher and lower educational groups, a result strikingly similar to that found in regard to family participation appears. Informal participation within the school appears to be more closely associated with political competence among those with limited education than among those who achieved somewhat higher education. The distinction between those with primary school education and those with secondary education or more is not as sharp as it was in connection with family participation, but the distinction is clear nevertheless. In all five countries the extent of school informal participation is associated with a high score on the subjective

[19] The three questions were:

"*1*. If you felt you had been treated unfairly in some way or disagreed with something the teacher had said, did you feel free to talk to the teacher about it, a bit uneasy about it, or was it better not to talk to the teacher?

"*2*. Would it have made any difference?

"*3*. Do you remember ever doing this?"

Those who said they felt free to protest, that it might have made a difference, and that they remember protesting are listed as participants. Those who replied negatively to the three items are the nonparticipants. The remainder of the respondents are in the mixed category. Those who could not remember have been omitted from the table.

TABLE 20

Per Cent who scored Highest in Subjective Competence[a] among Respondents who Report Varying Degrees of Informal School Participation, by Nation and Education

Nation	Total						Primary or Less						Secondary or More					
	Partic. %	No.[b]	Mixed %	No.	Nonpartic. %	No.	Partic. %	No.	Mixed %	No.	Nonpartic. %	No.	Partic. %	No.	Mixed %	No.	Nonpartic. %	No.
United States	75	(252)	67	(496)	54	(158)	66	(100)	58	(257)	42	(109)	80	(152)	77	(239)	78	(49)
Great Britain	70	(187)	66	(462)	56	(265)	68	(102)	62	(274)	53	(187)	74	(79)	73	(177)	63	(73)
Germany	53	(186)	49	(436)	44	(229)	48	(133)	45	(361)	44	(229)	67	(52)	73	(70)	57	(23)
Italy	51	(128)	46	(385)	32	(478)	43	(60)	42	(236)	28	(393)	59	(68)	53	(146)	54	(84)
Mexico	52	(177)	45	(376)	24	(205)	49	(118)	43	(319)	24	(197)	56	(59)	55	(57)		[c]

[a] I.e., those who received three highest scores on subjective competence scale
[b] Numbers in parentheses refer to the bases upon which percentages are calculated.
[c] Too few cases

competence scale among those in the lower educational group. Among those with higher education, on the other hand, the relationship between school participation and political competence is either not a direct one (as in Mexico, Italy, and the United States), or is weaker than the one among primary-school respondents (as in the other two nations).

Again as with family participation, this phenomenon may reflect the relative absence of other factors that might foster political competence among those with lower education. School training in participation has a greater marginal effect than it would have if there were—as there are among those with higher education—other factors that could substitute for this training.

Whereas this general hypothesis received some confirmation from the data on the relationship between family participation and political competence, by age groups, the data on the relationship between school participation and political competence, by age groups, are more ambiguous. According to our hypothesis, school participation would have the greatest effect on the subjective political competence of older respondents. Among these, as compared to younger respondents, training for participation would be rarer and they would not be exposed to as many other pressures leading to political competence. As the data in Table 21 indicate, participation within the school has a positive relationship with sense of political competence, usually on all age levels. In the United States and Mexico this relationship is the clearest, and in the other nations there is a tendency for the relationship to exist within specific age groups. In Germany and Britain the hypothesis that school participation has the greatest impact upon older respondents is partially confirmed, for the relationship between school participation and political competence drops somewhat in the lowest age group. In Italy, however, the pattern is reversed: school participation and sense of political competence appear to be more closely associated among those in the younger two age groups.

In general, as with family participation and political competence, there does appear to be some relationship between school experiences and political attitudes, but the relationship is not a strong one. School participation seems to affect the sense of political competence among some groups more than among others. Our earlier hypothesis—that the impact of nonpolitical participation upon political competence is greatest among those who, for other

355

TABLE 21

Per Cent who Scored Highest in Subjective Competence[a] among Respondents who Report Varying Degrees of Informal School Participation, by Nation and Age

Nation	18-30						31-50						51 and older					
	Partic.		Mixed		Nonpartic.		Partic.		Mixed		Nonpartic.		Partic.		Mixed		Nonpartic.	
	%	No.[b]	%	No.	%	No.	%	No.	%	No.	%	No.	%	No.	%	No.	%	No.
United States	72	(90)	69	(102)	47	(15)	81	(88)	68	(205)	64	(53)	72	(74)	64	(189)	48	(90)
Great Britain	66	(41)	66	(105)	58	(31)	75	(87)	68	(222)	62	(113)	68	(60)	63	(137)	49	(120)
Germany	46	(54)	51	(95)	50	(34)	61	(85)	52	(184)	46	(80)	47	(47)	45	(158)	40	(115)
Italy	46	(54)	42	(184)	37	(94)	65	(48)	46	(167)	35	(195)	39	(26)	52	(84)	27	(189)
Mexico	50	(82)	43	(139)	26	(74)	50	(78)	51	(164)	29	(83)	67	(17)	38	(73)	14	(48)

[a] I.e., those who received three highest scores on subjective competence scale
[b] Numbers in parentheses refer to the bases upon which percentages are calculated.

reasons, would be expected to be less politically competent—receives some support from a comparison of educational groups, but somewhat less support from a comparison of age groups.[20]

Thus far we have considered the effect of rather informal participation within family and school on the sense of political competence. We have been concerned in both social situations with the respondent's remembered ability to protest an unfair decision. But in connection with school participation we are also interested in the effect of more formal opportunities to participate. Does experience in classroom discussion and debate increase the probability that an individual will feel subjectively competent to influence the government? The data in Table 22 indicate that one can answer

[20] The same caveat raised above—that reports of childhood participation may have been upgraded or downgraded by individuals to match their current level of political competence—applies to the data on school participation. As we mentioned above, we cannot completely eliminate this possibility, but we can control somewhat for this (conscious or unconscious) tendency of some individuals.

We do this by considering the relationship between family participation and political competence only among those respondents who *report mixed experiences within the school*. Selecting this group allows us to isolate respondents who probably are not adjusting their answers to achieve consistency. For one thing, their answers about school authority patterns indicate that they do not necessarily report consistency in authority patterns. Second, those within this group who are participants or nonparticipants in the family can hardly be accused of remembering only that which maintains consistency, for their answers on family authority patterns are necessarily inconsistent with those on school authority patterns.

Table A reports the relationship between family participation and sense of political competence among those respondents who report mixed patterns of school participation. (The categories are defined as on Tables 18 and 20 above.)

TABLE A

Per Cent who scored Highest in Subjective Competence[a] among Respondents who Report Varying Degrees of Participation in Family Decisions, by Nation[b]

Nation	Partic. (%)	(No.)[c]	Mixed (%)	(No.)	Nonpartic. (%)	(No.)
United States	69	(188)	68	(251)	49	(39)
Great Britain	76	(184)	61	(238)	52	(29)
Germany	59	(115)	48	(223)	42	(66)
Italy	52	(81)	48	(214)	41	(54)
Mexico	46	(54)	51	(227)	34	(70)

[a] I.e., those who received three highest scores on subjective competence scale
[b] Only those who reported *mixed* experiences with school participation are included in this table.
[c] Numbers in parentheses refer to the bases upon which percentages are calculated.

In all cases, the relationship between family participation and political competence remains among those who remember mixed school experiences. Those who did not

357

with a qualified "yes." In the United States, Britain, Germany, and Mexico, on both levels of educational attainment, and in Italy among those with primary education, remembered participation in school discussions and debates is related to an increased sense of political efficacy. Those respondents who remember that they could and did participate in these discussions tend to score higher on the scale of subjective competence than do those respondents who remember that they could not participate. In the United States, for instance, 76 per cent of those who say that they could and did participate in school discussions score in the upper half of the subjective competence scale, in contrast with 63 per cent of those who report that they had no such opportunity. And in Mexico the respective percentages are 59 and 39.

---

participate in the family are much less likely to score high on the subjective competence scale than are those who did participate in the family.

The reverse test can be made with the data on school participation. Using the same logic, we can consider the relationship between school participation and political competence among those respondents who report a *mixed participation situation in the family*. The results are in Table B.

TABLE B

Per Cent who scored Highest in Subjective Competence[a] among Respondents who Report Varying Degrees of Informal School Participation, by Nation[b]

Nation	Partic. (%) (No.)[c]		Mixed (%) (No.)		Nonpartic. (%) (No.)	
United States	76	(94)	68	(251)	61	(84)
Great Britain	80	(85)	61	(238)	56	(136)
Germany	56	(85)	49	(224)	54	(99)
Italy	52	(50)	48	(216)	32	(196)
Mexico	53	(111)	50	(223)	23	(136)

[a] I.e., those who received three highest scores on subjective competence scale

[b] Only those who reported *mixed* experiences with school participation are included in this table.

[c] Numbers in parentheses refer to the bases upon which percentages are calculated.

As with the data on family participation, the relationship between school participation and political competence remains even when we consider only those who report mixed experiences within the family. The one exception is the data for Germany, which show relatively little difference in the frequency of high political competence between those who remember being able to participate in the schools and those who do not so remember. But in the other four nations the relationship is as strong within the subgroup that remembers mixed family patterns of authority as within the total sample.

These two tables suggest that a tendency to seek consistent answers is not the explanation for the relationship we find between experience with nonpolitical authority and the sense of political competence. The relationship is more than an artifact of the interview situation.

TABLE 22

Per Cent who scored Highest in Subjective Competence[a] among Respondents who Report Varying Degrees of Formal School Participation, by Nation and Education

Nation	Total						Primary or Less						Secondary or More					
	Could and Did Participate in Discussions		Could and Did Not		Could Not		Could and Did		Could and Did Not		Could Not		Could and Did		Could and Did Not		Could Not	
	%	No.[b]	%	No.	%	No.	%	No.	%	No.	%	No.	%	No.	%	No.	%	No.
United States	76	(387)	53	(144)	63	(329)	63	(125)	45	(91)	57	(218)	83	(262)	66	(53)	75	(111)
Great Britain	78	(139)	46	(75)	61	(651)	76	(45)	63	(40)	59	(462)	80	(94)	66	(35)	66	(189)
Germany	70	(109)	43	(49)	47	(650)	60	(57)	42	(39)	45	(568)	80	(52)	50	(10)	62	(82)
Italy	63	(81)	46	(26)	45	(415)	59	(34)	44	(16)	40	(335)	65	(47)	50	(10)	66	(80)
Mexico	59	(111)	39	(176)	39	(491)	62	(61)	34	(146)	38	(445)	55	(50)	59	(30)	48	(46)

[a] I.e., those who received three highest scores on subjective competence scale
[b] Numbers in parentheses refer to the bases upon which percentages are calculated.

One interesting point is apparent in Table 22. In general, the respondents who score the lowest on the subjective competence scale are not those who report that they had no opportunity to participate in discussions and debates. Rather, those who report that there were such opportunities but that *they did not take advantage of them* tend to score as low as or lower than those who had no such opportunities. In the United States and Germany on both educational levels, in Mexico on the lower educational level, and in Italy on the higher educational level, those who report that they could have but did not participate receive generally lower scores on the subjective competence scale than those who were not afforded such opportunities.

This fact suggests a qualification to our earlier findings. We are dealing here with more than the impact of the objective situation within the school upon a later sense of political competence. The reason why those who did not take advantage of the opportunities to participate are even lower in their level of subjective political competence than are those who were not even given the opportunity may well lie in certain individual characteristics that affect both the respondent's participation in the school and his sense of political competence. Given the opportunity to participate, those who did not do so are likely to be nonparticipants for personal reasons. Perhaps it is lack of self-confidence or skill; perhaps there are social reasons, such as membership in a relatively less privileged group. These reasons may be independent of the participation opportunities in the school.

The data on formal opportunities to participate suggest, therefore, that some of the generalization phenomena we observe—that is, the apparent transfer of participatory experience in family and school to the political sphere—may not result from the impact of a participatory family or school system on political attitudes. Rather, the degree of participation in the school and the family, as well as the level of subjective competence in political matters, may *both* derive from the same psychological or social factors. This qualification about the meaning of our findings is apparent in the data on formal school participation. But it may apply even more strongly to the previously reported data on the impact of remembered informal participation on political competence. Whether or not a child feels free to protest or actually does protest in family or school is not determined solely by the adult-created authority

structure of the family or school. Rather, family or school participation and political self-confidence may both be affected by the
extent to which the child has a strong ego.

Thus our data on the impact of family and school participation
on later political attitudes suggest, at best, that there is some connection. But how strong the connection is, under what circumstances it is more or less close, and the process by which the connection is made are questions that cannot yet be answered.

So far, we have been concentrating mostly on the latent effects of
family and school experiences upon political competence. We have
been discussing the effects on political attitudes, not of direct formal
teaching, but of the generalization from experiences in family or
school to politics. Even in the case of the opportunity for formal
discussion in the classroom, the significant aspect was the discussion
itself, not the subject matter of the discussion. One may ask, however, whether direct teaching, too, might not have significant effects on political attitudes. The data in Table 23 suggest an answer.

In this table the level of subjective political competence of one
group (those respondents who report that time was spent in their
school in teaching about politics and government) is compared with
that of another (those who report that they were not so taught).
The data suggest that manifest teaching about politics can increase
an individual's sense of political competence, but that this depends
upon the content of the teaching. In the United States, Britain, and
Mexico, those who were taught about politics are more likely than
the others to score high on the subjective competence scale. The
pattern in Germany and Italy is quite different. In Germany those
with primary education are somewhat more likely to feel politically
competent if they were taught about politics in the school, while
those with secondary education or better are somewhat less likely to
feel highly politically competent if they remember such teaching.
In Italy those with primary school education are somewhat less
likely to feel politically competent if they remember political
teaching, while this teaching apparently makes no difference
among those with higher education. While there is a relatively
clear connection between manifest political teaching and political
competence in the United States, Britain, and Mexico, there is no
clear connection in the two nations whose educational systems were
dominated for much of the life span of our respondents by antidemocratic philosophies. This contrast suggests strongly that mani-

TABLE 23

Per Cent who scored Highest in Subjective Competence[a] by whether they were Taught in School about Government, by Nation and Education

	Total				Primary or Less				Secondary or More			
	Remember being Taught about Government		Were Not Taught		Taught about Government		Not Taught		Taught about Government		Not Taught	
Nation	%	No.[b]	%	No.	%	No.	%	No.	%	No.	%	No.
United States	72	(710)	47	(260)	62	(320)	41	(198)	80	(390)	66	(62)
Great Britain	73	(370)	58	(523)	70	(168)	55	(370)	76	(185)	67	(146)
Germany	52	(580)	43	(214)	48	(458)	39	(190)	66	(119)	75	(24)
Italy	45	(365)	49	(303)	36	(202)	45	(192)	56	(162)	56	(109)
Mexico	44	(578)	27	(103)	41	(462)	30	(93)	56	(116)		c

[a] I.e., those who received three highest scores on subjective competence scale
[b] Numbers in parentheses refer to the bases upon which percentages are calculated.
c Too few cases

fest teaching about politics can have an impact, and this impact will depend a good deal on the content of what is taught.

Job Participation and Political Competence. The data so far presented suggest that there is some relationship between family and school experiences and an individual's later political attitudes. But as we have suggested, the formation of political attitudes continues after the individual becomes an adult and enters his political role. Attitudes change, new experiences can have political effects. If early authority experiences can affect political attitudes, so can authority experiences in later life. Individuals are exposed to a wide range of these experiences, be it in the family, in church, voluntary association, or at work. Can these later relationships and experiences affect an individual's sense of political competence? If, for instance, an adult has the opportunity to participate in decisions in his contemporary nonpolitical relationships, will he generalize from these experiences and believe that he can participate in his public life? Conversely, will those who are given little opportunity of mastery over decisions in their day-to-day lives generalize this to a belief in their lack of political ability?

These questions are similar to those we raised about participatory opportunities in the family and the school. Essentially we are interested in the extent to which a democratic political system depends upon democratic substructures in the society. Do democratic political orientations (which include the attitude that one can be a participant in political decisions) depend upon opportunities to participate in nonpolitical social relationships? Of crucial significance here are the opportunities to participate in decisions at one's place of work. The structure of authority at the work place is probably the most significant—and salient—structure of that kind with which the average man finds himself in daily contact. Furthermore, this form of participation may have a heightened effect on political participation because authority patterns in the work place, while probably a mixture of formal and informal authority, have a larger formal component than, say, authority patterns within the family.

As reported earlier, there is some parallel between the frequency with which respondents report that they can participate in decisions made at work and the frequency with which respondents are politically competent. And the data in Table 24 indicate that this parallel does indeed reflect a relationship between the extent of opportunities to participate in job decisions and the extent of subjective

TABLE 24

Per Cent who scored Highest in Subjective Competence[a] among Respondents who Report Varying Degrees of Formal Participation in Job Decisions, by Nation and Occupation

Nation	Total[b]				Unskilled				Skilled				White Collar			
	Consulted on the Job[c]		Not Consulted		Consulted		Not Consulted		Consulted		Not Consulted		Consulted		Not Consulted	
	%	No.	%	No.	%	No.	%	No.	%	No.	%	No.	%	No.	%	No.
United States	75	(334)	62	(94)	70	(70)	53	(32)	73	(71)	69	(16)	82	(93)	63	(27)
Great Britain	71	(372)	52	(98)	74	(88)	54	(41)	71	(140)	50	(30)	75	(65)	[60]	(15)
Germany	58	(253)	38	(116)	55	(42)	26	(42)	52	(61)	44	(32)	61	(62)	[46]	(13)
Italy	57	(181)	35	(130)	49	(45)	31	(67)	74	(31)	[40]	(15)	55	(76)	52	(21)
Mexico	51	(170)	45	(107)	26	(17)	43	(18)	48	(74)	53	(46)	47	(55)	45	(23)

a I.e., those who received three highest scores on subjective competence scale

b The total columns refer to job holders of all kinds. The occupational breakdown into unskilled, skilled, and white collar has been selective and does not include all job holders in the total columns.

c Numbers in parentheses refer to the bases upon which percentages are calculated.

political competence. In each nation those who report that they are consulted about decisions on their job are more likely than the others to score high on the scale of subjective political competence. And as Table 25 indicates, the same relationship exists between informal job participation (freedom to protest) and sense of political competence. Those respondents who report that they feel free to protest decisions are more likely to feel subjectively competent to influence the government.

Unlike many of the relationships between family and school

TABLE 25

Per Cent who scored Highest in Subjective Competence[a] among Respondents who Report Varying Degrees of Informal Participation in Job Decisions, by Nation

Nation	Can and Have Protested (%) (No.)[b]		Can But Have Not Protested (%) (No.)		Cannot Protest (%) (No.)	
United States	76	(240)	77	(107)	55	(76)
Great Britain	74	(295)	60	(121)	50	(48)
Germany	64	(183)	46	(83)	34	(65)
Italy	58	(125)	53	(45)	35	(108)
Mexico	54	(86)	46	(122)	41	(86)

[a] I.e., those who received three highest scores on subjective competence scale
[b] Numbers in parentheses refer to the bases upon which percentages are calculated.

participation and political competence, the relationships between competence on the job and subjective political competence remain strong even within matched educational groups. Whereas the impact of family or school participation on political competence appeared to decrease among those with higher educational attainment, the impact of job participation remains strong on both educational levels. And as Table 24 indicates, though there are differences in the degree to which individuals in various types of occupation can participate in decisions on the job, this participation has a positive effect on political competence among occupations at all levels. Among unskilled workers, skilled workers, and white-collar workers (the only occupational strata with enough cases to make this analysis feasible), those who report that they are consulted in decisions at their place of work, compared with those who are not consulted, report higher levels of subjective political competence. This is the case in all nations but Mexico, where the relationship between the two forms of participation is less clear.

It is, of course, impossible to conclude that there is a unidirectional flow of influence from patterns of participation on the job to patterns of participation in politics. It is quite likely that opportunities for job and political participation have a reciprocal effect on each other: that is, the relationship between perceived ability to participate on the job and perceived ability to participate in politics may represent, not merely a generalization from the work place to the political sphere, but a generalization in the other direction as well. Demands to participate in job decisions are often justified by the political norms of democratic participation. And the individual whose political experience includes chances to participate in decisions will be less likely to accept unquestioningly the authority relationships at his place of work. In any case, our data suggest a tendency toward homogeneity between job and political authority patterns: those who are oriented to participate in one area will be oriented to participate in the other. Whether job participation leads to democratic political orientations, or vice versa, is difficult to tell; but the evidence is strong that these two develop closely together and mutually support each other.

The Cumulative Effect of Participatory Experiences. There is evidence that the impact of participation in nonpolitical decision making—at home, school, and job—is cumulative. The individual who has consistent opportunities for nonpolitical participation—compared with someone whose ability to participate in one nonpolitical area is not matched by an ability to participate in another nonpolitical area—is more likely to generalize this to political participation.

Consider the respondents who report that they had the opportunity to participate in family or school decisions. One would assume that this opportunity to participate will probably be generalized into subjective political competence, if it is not thwarted by experience with authority situations in which one cannot participate. This hypothesis is supported by the data in Tables 26 and 27. In Table 26, individuals who could and could not participate in family decisions are then divided into those who can and cannot participate in decisions on the job. The results are clear. Among those who report that they were able to take part in family decisions, those who can also take part in job decisions are more likely to score high in subjective political competence than are those whose ability to participate in family is not matched by a present

366

ability to participate in job decisions. In Britain, for instance, 75 per cent of those whose family participation is matched by participatory opportunities at work score in the highest three cells of the

TABLE 26

Per Cent who scored Highest in Subjective Competence[a] among Respondents who Report Varying Degrees of Participation in Family and Job Decisions, by Nation

| Nation | Family Participants | | | | Family Nonparticipants | | | |
| | Job Partic. | | Job Nonpartic. | | Job Partic. | | Job Nonpartic. | |
	(%)	(No.)[b]	(%)	(No.)	(%)	(No.)	(%)	(No.)
United States	77	(242)	70	(61)	70	(80)	45	(31)
Great Britain	75	(270)	58	(64)	64	(92)	37	(30)
Germany	61	(144)	38	(52)	59	(81)	37	(49)
Italy	60	(120)	44	(70)	50	(48)	24	(41)
Mexico	56	(72)	52	(44)	43	(97)	45	(62)

[a] I.e., those who received three highest scores on subjective competence scale
[b] Numbers in parentheses refer to the bases upon which percentages are calculated.

TABLE 27

Per Cent who scored Highest in Subjective Competence[a] among Respondents who Report Varying Degrees of Participation in School Discussions and Job Decisions, by Nation

| Nation | School Participants | | | | School Nonparticipants | | | |
| | Job Partic. | | Job Nonpartic. | | Job Partic. | | Job Nonpartic. | |
	(%)	(No.)[b]	(%)	(No.)	(%)	(No.)	(%)	(No.)
United States	83	(195)	67	(55)	63	(126)	56	(34)
Great Britain	77	(163)	34	(32)	67	(192)	57	(61)
Germany	67	(110)	38	(39)	53	(125)	36	(69)
Italy	57	(67)	42	(33)	55	(116)	38	(78)
Mexico	57	(60)	52	(40)	38	(82)	51	(90)

[a] I.e., those who received three highest scores on subjective competence scale
[b] Numbers in parentheses refer to the bases upon which percentages are calculated.

subjective competence scale, in contrast with 58 per cent of those respondents whose family participation is not backed up by job participation. And as Table 27 indicates, the same cumulative effect exists in connection with school and job participation. Those who could participate in school decisions and can now participate in job decisions are more likely to be politically competent than are those whose school participation is not supported by later job participation. Taking Britain as our example again, we find the relationship even more striking. Seventy-seven per cent of the respondents who report being able to participate both in school and job decisions are in the top three groups of our subjective competence scale, in contrast with 34 per cent of those who were able to participate in the school but cannot participate on the job. This relationship however, holds for only four out of five of the nations. The Mexican data show little of this cumulative effect.

Conclusion

A major element of a democratic political orientation is the belief that one has some control over political elites and political decisions. This belief has many roots. An individual might base his estimate of his capacity to influence the government upon direct experience with that government. Opportunities to participate in decisions might convince him of his competence, while thwarted influence attempts might lead to the opposite conclusion. Or he might base his subjective competence on more indirect evidence about the operations of the political system. He might observe others attempting to influence politics and learn from their experience; or he might learn from the estimates that he hears others make of the extent to which the "ordinary man" can influence politics. In these ways he will form his political beliefs from his observation of politics or from his exposure to others' views of politics.

Without denying the importance of the political system itself as a source of individuals' attitudes toward that system, this chapter has attempted to seek some of the nonpolitical sources of the belief that one has a voice in governmental affairs. One such source is experience with authority figures outside the governmental sphere. From these experiences the individual generalizes to politics. If in all his social relationships he is afforded no opportunity to participate meaningfully in decisions, he may derive from this a general belief in his incapacity to control any decisions, including political decisions. On the other hand, if he finds authority figures in social situations amenable to influence, he may come to believe that authority figures in politics will also be amenable to his influence.

The data presented in this chapter suggest that there is indeed a generalization from the nonpolitical sphere to the polity. If an individual has had the opportunity to participate in the family, in school, or at work, he is more likely than someone who did not have the same opportunities to consider himself competent to influence the government. But this conclusion must be presented with some caution. As we pointed out in this chapter, the relationship between nonpolitical participatory experience and political attitudes is by no means unambiguous. It appears stronger among some groups than among others. And many respondents manifest a sense of political competence though they had little participatory experience outside of politics, while others are not politically competent despite social experiences that should have furthered such competence. This lack of a strong, unambiguous relationship is not surprising. There is, after all, quite a gap in time between the ability to participate within the family and one's ability to participate in politics. The authority structures differ in nature, and this might impede generalizations from the primary group to the political system. Furthermore, each type of political system interacts differently with the expectations that an individual brings with him from nonpolitical experiences. No matter what opportunities he has to participate outside of politics, his generalization from these experiences to politics will be inhibited in a political system that is recognized as authoritarian. The difference between nonpolitical and political authority patterns may cause some strain or discontent, but the differences may not lead to a sense of competence. Experience with nonpolitical authority patterns may affect an individual's political attitudes by creating a set of predisposed responses to stimuli. The individual who has had opportunities for nonpolitical participation, compared with someone who has not had these opportunities, will be more likely to choose a participatory response *if* a political situation arises in which there is some chance to participate. An individual who has had a voice in family, school, or job decisions is more likely to accept the belief that he is a competent citizen *if* there is any other basis for the belief. Nonpolitical experiences with participation increase the individual's availability for an active political role and increase the likelihood that he will believe in his political influence.

The data in this chapter, however, allow us to go a bit further in specifying the way in which nonpolitical experiences create predispositions. Three points may be made about the effects of nonpolitical authority patterns on political attitudes: these effects are *cumulative,* other *social factors may substitute* for them, and they appear to be in a *rank order of importance.*

369

The cumulative effect that nonpolitical participation has upon political participation was suggested in Tables 26 and 27. And certainly this kind of effect is to be expected. If one finds one's self consistently in social situations where one has a voice over decisions, this is more likely to result in a general sense of competence than if the experience with participation in one area is not matched by similar experiences in other areas.

Second, other social factors may substitute for experience within the school or family. In particular, our data suggest that education on the secondary level or above can replace family participation, and to some extent school participation, as a factor leading toward political competence. This implication may be drawn from the fact that among those with education beyond the primary school, experiences with school participation have little impact on political competence, and experiences with family participation have no impact. Those with higher education, this suggests, do not need the push toward a sense of political competence that participatory family and school experiences might provide, for there are so many other factors that operate to make them politically competent.

But though a higher level of education may be able to substitute for family or school participation, it is interesting to note that job participation, though it can reinforce that which is learned in the family and the school, cannot replace it. This is seen in Table 26 and 27. Even among those who have the opportunity to participate on the job (the respondents in the first and third columns of these two tables), it makes a difference whether or not they were previously able to participate in the family and the school. Though they have current opportunities to participate, if they could not participate in the family or in the school, they are less subjectively competent in politics than are those who could participate previously. And this is true in all the nations.

Why is it that a higher level of education can substitute for family or school participation, while work-place participation cannot do so? If we may speculate, the reason may lie in the fact that education above the primary level represents a many-sided experience which can, in a large number of ways, increase an individual's potentiality to participate. The processes whereby higher educational attainment affects political competence are varied: they may be intellectual processes, as when one learns a set of skills useful for participation; they may be the inculcation of participatory norms through direct teaching of those norms; they may involve

370

social pressures, as when educational attainment places one in a social situation in which one is expected to participate. These processes are different from those by which one generalizes from family and school authority patterns to politics; and they may, therefore, be little affected by what experiences the individual has had with family and school participation. Even if his nonpolitical participation is such that it would tend to counteract the factors that foster participation derived from his educational level, the fact that these are different types of influences on his level of participation would minimize the conflict between them.

Somewhat different is the relationship between school and family participation, on the one hand, and work-place participation, on the other. Work-place participation does not have as broad an effect upon one's sense of political competence as educational attainment does; it is a much narrower factor, which does not produce as basic a set of changes in one's intellectual capabilities, values, or social situation. Furthermore, it acts upon political competence much the same way that experience in participation in the family or school does: through a process of generalizing one's capabilities from one field to the other. Because of this, it is likely that work-place participation, insofar as its effects tend to be in the opposite direction from the effects of school or family participation, will conflict with the other experiences. It will therefore be more likely to dampen the effect of family or school participation rather than replace them.

The last point that must be made is that the impact of nonpolitical participation on political attitudes differs from one nonpolitical area to another. There appears to be a rank order in the strength of connection between nonpolitical types of participation and political competence: the connection becomes stronger as one moves from family to school to job participation. When we considered the relationship between family participation and sense of political competence within high and low educational groups, we found that it weakened somewhat among those with primary education or less and disappeared among those with more than primary education. Between school participation and sense of political competence, on the other hand, the relationship is not weaker on the lower educational level; and though it is weaker in all nations on the higher level, a positive relationship still persists within three of the five nations. In contrast to the situation with family and school participation, the relationship between job participation and political competence remains strong on both educational levels—even among those with secondary education or better. And we might add here, since it is relevant to the general argument that will be made, that the generalization of participatory experiences from voluntary association to the polity shows a similar relationship. As was pointed out in Chapter 11, those who are active participants in voluntary associations are more likely than passive members to be politically competent; and this relationship is apparent on both educational levels.

This rank order in the strength of the relationship between the various modes of nonpolitical participation and political attitudes suggests an important specification of the way in which nonpolitical participation affects political attitudes. The individual's experiences at work and in voluntary associations differ basically from those in the family and the school in that they are closer—in time as well as structure—to the polity. Job and group memberships are contemporaneous with political participation. More important, perhaps, is the fact that the mode of participation within the work place or voluntary association comes closer in form to political modes of participation than does participation within the family or the school. Authority patterns in the work place and voluntary association are mixtures of formal and informal patterns. The bases of the authority hierarchy include incumbency of formal positions within the organization as well as technical and "human relations" skills. This is in many ways similar to patterns of political authority; in any case, more similar than are the patterns in the family or the school. In the latter two institutions authority patterns are "naturally" hierarchical, depending to a large extent on age differentials. Furthermore, especially in the family, the patterns of authority tend to be informal and implicit. In terms of formality of authority patterns, the school, rather than the home, more closely approximates the political system. And, there exists in the school, in comparison to the family, a closer connection between participation and sense of political competence.

There are several reasons for this rank order. In the first place, as Eckstein has suggested, the closer a social structure is to the political system, the more likely there is to be a strain toward congruence between the two authority patterns.[21] If the social structure and

[21] Eckstein, *op. cit.*, means by the "closeness" of a structure to the political system both its closeness in terms of time and its closeness in terms of the extent to which the

the political system are close, it is difficult for the individual to segregate his roles in the two systems. But if, as with the family and, to a lesser extent, the school, they are relatively remote from the political system, he may with less strain be able to isolate his non-political experiences with authority from his political experiences with authority.

The hierarchical connection between nonpolitical authority patterns and attitudes toward political authority suggests another conclusion: that in a relatively modern and diversified social system socialization in the family and, to a lesser extent, in the school represents inadequate training for political participation. As Eisenstadt has suggested, in societies where the main adult roles are non-familial—that is, where they are universalistic, functionally specific, and achievement oriented—roles learned within the particularistic, diffuse, and ascriptive family will not be harmonious with later adult roles. The performance of these roles within the family will not ensure the attainment of full social maturity, nor will they prepare the child adequately for participation within the larger social system.

In situations of this sort, other socializing agencies will come to play significant roles,[22] especially, it seems, in relation to the political system. In a society with a specialized political system, the transfer from family to polity will be more difficult, and there is likely to be less congruence between the two.[23] Our data tend to support these generalizations. Family experiences do play a role in the formation of political attitudes, but the role may not be central; the gap between the family and the polity may be so wide that other social experiences, especially in social situations closer in time and in structure to the political system, may play a larger role. Further-

---

structure is involved in political and governmental affairs. But the extent to which systems are similar in the degree of formality of authority patterns and in the criteria for authority positions is also relevant.

[22] S. N. Eisenstadt, *From Generation to Generation*, Glencoe, Ill., 1956, chap. i. A similar argument is made by Helmut Schelsky, *Die Skeptische Generation: Eine Soziologie der Deutschen Jugend*, Dusseldorf-Köln, 1957, chaps. ii and iii.

[23] See Robert A. Levine, "The Role of the Family in Authority Systems: A Cross-cultural Application of the Stimulus-generalization Hypothesis," *Behavioral Science*, v (1960), pp. 291-96. Levine finds that among the Gussi of Kenya—a stateless political system with segmentary patrilineages—there is a high degree of generalization of attitudes from the family to the political system. In contrast with modern systems, says Levine, the transfer in Kenya occurs because the scope and norms of the political system resemble those in the family. Thus the shift from family to political participation involves fewer discontinuities than in modern political systems.

more, these other experiences may also interact with family or school experiences. Sometimes they may dampen or heighten the effects of that early socialization training. At other times—the experience with higher levels of education was our example here—they may substitute for it.

This discussion suggests that it may be difficult to draw the implications of one of the major findings in this chapter: that patterns of participation have been changing relatively uniformly over time in the direction of greater opportunities for participation in family and school. This change will increase the individual's "availability" for political participation. But whether or not this will lead to an increase in effective political participation is problematic.

PART IV

PROFILES OF POLITICAL CULTURE

CHAPTER 13

GROUP DIFFERENCES IN
POLITICAL ORIENTATION

THE populations of nations are composed of many subgroups—social classes, religious and ethnic groups, age groups, and the like. In our survey we sought to isolate a number of group characteristics that we believed might be correlated with differences in political orientation. In this chapter we shall comment in detail on two of these: education and sex. In all five of our countries, educational level is the variable that has the strongest relationship with political attitudes. Differences in the political attitudes and behavior of women are important in understanding the role of the family and political socialization patterns in different kinds of political systems. We shall comment more briefly on the effects of social class and religion.

The theme we are pursuing here is of great importance for understanding the functioning of political systems. For the stability and performance of democratic political systems it matters a great deal how men and women, occupational and income groups, educational and religious groups are oriented toward the political structure. If, for example, women are predominantly parochials, or subjects, this will have important implications for the role of the family in the political system. If relatively uneducated strata of the population, or the low income groups, or the Catholic elements of the population are predominantly parochials, or subjects, this will affect the interest groups and party system, and the communications and electoral processes.

We have already introduced the theme of political subculture both in our theory and in reporting our findings. In our theory we stressed that most political cultures are heterogeneous; that they are "mixes." A predominantly democratic culture will contain subjects and parochials as well as citizens, and a predominantly subject culture will contain parochials and may contain some citizens as well as subjects. We differentiated two kinds of subculture: those based on differences in structural orientation and those based on differences in policy orientation. Our study has stressed the structural aspects of political culture, and in what follows we shall be primarily concerned with the extent to which subnational groupings differ in their orientations to the structure of the political system.

As we reported above, the subcultural patterns of the five countries came out most sharply in the realm of partisanship. In Italy, for example, the members of the left and right parties had predominantly antagonistic images of each other, and the social distance between political parties, as reflected in attitudes toward interparty marriage, was greater than in the other countries. We observed similar tendencies, though not so extreme, in Mexico, Germany, and Britain. Partisanship was least sharp and fragmented in the United States. Where political parties are pitted against one another with a strong and exclusive antagonism, we may say the political culture is fragmented. The clerical right and the Communist left in Italy are oriented differently toward politics in both a structural and policy sense, and these differences are associated with sharp differences in life style and social values. Where antagonism is characteristic only of the extreme wings of political parties, or only of a minority of militants; where the bulk of left and right party supporters share common structural orientations and many policy orientations; and where primary groups can bear the impact of partisan differences, the political culture is predominantly consensual. Or, more precisely, we may say that the shared orientations moderate the impact of the unshared ones; that a common political culture contains subcultural tendencies. That subcultural tendencies in the United States and Britain are contained in a widely shared culture of social trust, civic cooperativeness, and open partisanship is reported a number of times above (see Chapters 5, 7, and 10).

In our examination of the political orientations of demographic groups, we are in two respects limited by our data. First, reliable comparisons of demographic subgroupings would have required a larger sample. With our sample of approximately 1,000 in each country, we rapidly run out of cases as we introduce controls to determine whether a particular attitude difference results from a demographic characteristic other than the one under examination. The second limitation is more serious: the substance of our interview stressed attitudes toward the structure of political systems, rather than policy orientations or social attitudes and styles of life. Subcultural differences are ideological as well as structural, and they are associated with social ideologies and life patterns; thus we shall be able to develop the relationship between demographic groups and political subcultural tendencies in only a limited way. Briefly, we shall be able to show only how educational and social class groups, men and women, and religious groups constitute political subcultures within the framework of our parochial-subject-citizen classification.

Education and Political Orientation

Throughout this study we have reported differences among several educational groups. As in most other studies of political attitudes, our data show that educational attainment appears to have the most important demographic effect on political attitudes. Among the demographic variables usually investigated—sex, place of residence, occupation, income, age, and so on—none compares with the educational variable in the extent to which it seems to determine political attitudes. The uneducated man or the man with limited education is a different political actor from the man who has achieved a higher level of education.

There are a number of reasons for this. One reason, of course, is that educational differences are associated with differences in other social characteristics. Individuals who have achieved higher education, compared with those who have not, are likely to have higher incomes, to be in higher-status occupations, to be males, and so on— and all these characteristics tend in the same attitudinal direction. But even when these additional factors are controlled, respondents of lower and higher education still differ substantially in political attitudes. The main reason for this is probably that education has so many different kinds of effects. For one thing, people do *learn* in schools: they learn specific subjects as well as skills useful for political participation. And they learn the norms of political participation as well. Much of this learning may be through direct teaching; some of it may be more indirect. Not only does education influence political perspectives, it also places the individual in social situations where he meets others of like educational attainment, and this tends to reinforce the effect of his own education.

The way in which education affects an individual's political attitudes was discussed in Chapter 12. Here we concentrate, not on the

379

process by which education acts upon political orientation, but on the specific ways in which those who have achieved education differ in their political orientations from those who have not. For this purpose, it is useful to have data from more than one nation. We can ask whether there are uniform differences among educational groups observable in all nations, or whether the nations differ in this respect. Does education create differing political subcultures in each nation, and, if so, does the educated subculture differ in the same way from the uneducated subculture in all the nations?

Since most of the data pertaining to education have been presented in other parts of the text, we need only summarize those findings here. Three types of differences between the political orientations of the more and the less educated respondents can be discerned. First, there are those political orientations that are strongly affected by higher education—and affected the same way in all five nations. Second, there are some political attitudes that change relatively little from one educational group to another. Here, too, there is cross-national uniformity, but the uniformity lies in the absence of differences in attitude among educational groups. Third, there are some political orientations upon which educational level has a different effect from nation to nation. In some nations those with higher education have a higher frequency of a particular orientation; in other nations it is those with lower education who have the higher frequency of the same orientation; or in one nation educational groups differ in their frequency of the particular orientation, while in other nations they will not so differ.

It is of great interest, and among the most important facts we discovered, that most of the relationships between education and political orientation are of the first type: educational groups differ from one another substantially, and in a similar way, in each nation. The manifestations of this cross-national uniformity are the following:

(1) The more educated person is more aware of the impact of government on the individual than is the person of less education (Chapter 3);

(2) The more educated individual is more likely to report that he follows politics and pays attention to election campaigns than is the individual of less education (Chapter 3);

(3) The more educated individual has more political information (Chapter 3);

(4) The more educated individual has opinions on a wider range of political subjects; the focus of his attention to politics is wider (Chapter 3);

(5) The more educated individual is more likely to engage in political discussion (Chapter 4);

(6) The more educated individual feels free to discuss politics with a wider range of people (Chapter 4). Those with less education are more likely to report that there are many people with whom they avoid such discussions;

(7) The more educated individual is more likely to consider himself capable of influencing the government; this is reflected both in responses to questions on what one could do about an unjust law (Chapter 7) and in respondents' scores on the subjective competence scale (Chapter 9).

The above list refers to specifically political orientations, which vary the same way in all five nations. In addition, our evidence shows that:

(8) The more educated individual is more likely to be a member —and an active member—of some organization (Chapter 11); and

(9) The more educated individual is more likely to express confidence in his social environment: to believe that other people are trustworthy and helpful (Chapter 10).

In all nine relationships the differences between those with relatively little education and those who are more highly educated are substantial. In all the nations, in almost all the cases, those with no more than primary education and those with some university training differ by at least twenty percentage points, and often by substantially more, in the frequency with which a particular attitude is held. The attitude dimensions affected this way are ones that common sense and previous research would lead us to expect: information about politics and awareness of the activities of the government, for example. Yet the findings deserve some emphasis, for they illustrate that, despite national differences in political history and the current context of politics, and despite wide differences in the educational and social systems, strikingly uniform cross-national patterns can be found.

In each of these nations, it would seem, the educated classes possess the keys to political participation and involvement, while those with less education are less well equipped. In each nation the educated classes are more likely to be cognitively aware of politics (to be aware of the impact of government, to have information about government, to follow politics in the various media); to have political opinions on a wide range of subjects; and to engage in political discussions. The more highly educated are also more likely to consider themselves competent to influence the government and free to engage in political discussions. This set of orientations, widely distributed among those with high education and much less widely distributed among those with low education, constitutes what one might consider the minimum requirements for political participation. More complex attitudes and behavior depend upon such basic orientations as awareness of the political system, information about it, and some exposure to its operations. It is just this basic set of orientations that those of limited education tend not to have.

It is interesting, furthermore, that the orientations that distinguish the educated from the relatively uneducated tend, with one exception, to be affectively neutral. So far we have not shown either that educated individuals necessarily support the political system more, or that they are more hostile to it. We have merely shown that they are more aware of it. Nor do we know the content of the political discussions that go on on the higher educated level: we know only that there are more such discussions on that level than on any other. The educated individual is, in a sense, available for political participation. Education, however, does not determine the content of that participation.

Though educational differences in political orientation show a striking cross-national uniformity, this does not imply that differences among nations disappear when one considers matched educational groups. As we have pointed out, respondents on various educational levels within each nation differ from one another in the same way as the total samples of the populations differ from one another. The primary-educated Mexican is still different from the primary-educated German or Briton. But perhaps the most striking point is that within each nation the same relationship between those with more and less education obtains. Within each nation the more educated segment is more fully involved in the political system, is more fully a participant in politics. The less educated segment is less likely to take a full participating role.

But there is evidence that educational level does affect the *degree* of difference among the nations. On all the measures of political cognition or participation listed above—awareness of governmental impact, exposure to politics, political information, range of political opinions, subjective political competence, political participation— respondents on the higher educational levels tend to be more similar to one another than are the respondents on the lower educational levels. In general, the range between the nation where political participation is most frequent (United States) and the one where it is less frequent (Italy) is greatest among respondents with little education and least among those with higher education. This national difference among the former group is not always great, but it can be observed fairly consistently on all the measures listed above. Thus the university-educated respondents in Italy may differ from the university-educated respondents in the United States, but they are more like each other than are the Italians and Americans who did not get beyond primary education.

That higher education tends to reduce national differences suggests that the nature of political culture is greatly determined by the distribution of education. We have seen in Chapter 12 that education can substitute for family participation and, to some extent, for school participation as well: that is, the subjective competence of the more educated individual is less dependent on family or school participation than is the competence of the less educated individual. And the more highly educated segments of all five nations show a cross-national uniformity in political orientation. Educational systems vary, yet there is a certain uniformity in the educational experience; thus these people share a common experience. Those with less education share less of a common cross-cultural experience with one another and are more affected by the particular history and culture of their own national systems. To say that education replaces national differences is of course an exaggeration; national differences persist, as we have said, even among the highly educated; moreover, the generalization being made here applies only to specific political orientations. Nevertheless, the highly educated participate in politics, no matter what their nation; participation by the less educated depends more heavily upon nation.

The highly educated show another cross-national uniformity: compared with the less educated, they participate more frequently in voluntary associations. We would expect this from educated respondents as they pursue professional activities or certain kinds of leisure activity. But beyond that, the finding demonstrates the way in which the potentialities for political participation can accumulate within this segment of society. Not only does education itself increase political participation; it also places the individual in an organizational situation which further heightens his participation.

We referred above (p. 381) to one exception in this first class of orientations that are uniformly affected by education. This is trust and confidence in the social environment. We have to qualify our comment that only cognitive awareness and political competence are increased by education in all five countries, for educated people appear to have trust in the social environment. And insofar as this trust is an important precondition of the capacity to join with others to effect political goals, we may stress even further the importance of education as a factor affecting democratic capabilities. It may not be too much to say that it produces a protocivic tendency. (We shall show below, however, that certain crucial components of the civic culture are not affected by education.)

We turn now to the second class of political orientations: those that the relatively uneducated share with the more educated in all five nations. One example of such an attitude was reported in Chapter 6. There we saw that the norm that one ought to be a participant in the local community is found somewhat more frequently within the highly educated segments of society than among those with lower education, but this difference is relatively small compared with the other differences listed above. Similarly, we reported in Chapter 5 that the frequency with which individuals say favorable things about opposition party supporters does increase with education, but again the increase is neither consistent nor great. Both the more and less educated parts of each nation have relatively similar evaluations of opposition party supporters. And in the example of the strategy of influence, in particular the belief that one can cooperate with others in attempting to influence the government (discussed extensively in Chapters 7 and 10), there is almost no difference among the educational levels. Within each nation, local competents on all educational levels showed roughly the same frequency of cooperative competence. These three dimensions that are relatively unaffected by education—the norm that one ought to participate, the strategy to be employed in participating, and the degree of antagonism between the supporters of political parties—are not neutral political orientations. As political orientation becomes loaded with affective and evaluative content, we begin to find relatively great uniformity within each nation, and less difference among the educational sub-groups. Of particular interest is the fact that interparty antagonism and cooperative competence do not differ as much among the educational levels as does the more neutral, interpersonal activity of engaging in political discussion.

We have been saying that the educational groups in each nation differ less in their evaluations of the political potentialities of their fellow citizens than they do in their evaluatively neutral participation and cognition of politics. This can be shown if we can reconsider one of the orientations of the first type: the frequency with which respondents indicate that they avoid political discussion. Those on the lower levels of education more frequently say that there are many individuals with whom they avoid political discussions. This might be taken to mean that their evaluations of the political environment differ from those of the more educated; that in each nation the less educated, compared with the more educated, are more likely to find that environment hostile or dangerous or unpleasant. The major reason for this educational difference in evaluation of the political system is the cognitive capability of each group. In giving their reasons for avoiding political discussion, those with lower education are more likely than those with higher education to say that they consider themselves too ignorant or ill-informed. The more educated are somewhat more likely to cite their belief that such discussions are useless: that other people are not interested or have already made up their minds. On the other hand, reasons that would imply a negative evaluation of the political environment—such reasons as the "unpleasantness" of political controversy, the danger that one might get into trouble with the authorities by expressing one's point of view, or that one might suffer some economic loss—are given with about equal frequency by respondents in all levels of education.

In subjective and cognitive competence, then, the more educated respondents in each nation exist more fully within the political system. But when it comes to norms of political behavior or feelings about politics or partisanship, the various educational groups within each nation are more like one another. To illustrate this point, we shall consider those attitudes in our survey where education seems to have a different impact from one nation to another. We found this inconsistent pattern in three dimensions:

(1) In the United States and Britain those who are relatively more educated are more likely to express pride in the political aspects of their nation than are those with somewhat less education; a similar but smaller difference exists in Mexico; in Germany and Italy, however, there is no such difference between the education groups (Chapter 4);

(2) The sense of administrative competence—the extent to which individuals think they will be treated fairly and have their point of view considered—varies hardly at all between the educational groups in the United States and Britain; it varies slightly more in Germany, and substantially in Mexico and Italy (Chapter 4). Despite a uniform pattern in each nation (in each case those with higher education are more likely to have a sense of administrative competence), the variation and the degree of difference between the upper and lower educational levels suggests that the relationship belongs in this third group of political orientations: where the national differences between the educational groups are not uniform; and

(3) The relationship between the affective tone of election campaigns and educational attainment presents a mixed cross-national pattern (Chapter 5). In the United States, Britain, and Mexico, the more highly educated express more general satisfaction with their electoral participation, and also more frequently express the other three feelings we asked about: anger at election campaigns, enjoyment of election campaigns, and the feeling that these campaigns are silly or ridiculous. In Germany those with higher education more frequently express anger at election campaigns; but in their expression of satisfaction, as well as in the other two affective orientations to elections, they do not differ in any systematic way from those with lower education. In Italy, on the other hand, though anger, enjoyment, and the feeling that elections are silly increase in frequency as one moves up the educational ladder, the sense of satisfaction at electoral participation does not increase in this way.

In summary, we can say that in all five countries the less educated strata of the population tend to constitute subject and parochial subcultures. Pure parochials, in the sense defined in our classification are rarely encountered among the respondents in our five countries. The overwhelming majority have had some exposure to governmental authority. The closest approximation of parochialism occurs among uneducated women particularly in Italy and Mexico. And here it is more normative and affective than cognitive. That is, in these countries, and to some extent in the others, political awareness and involvement are not considered appropriate to the female role. Hence we encounter uneducated women who know vaguely of the existence of government and politics, but who are uninvolved with them and take their indifference for granted.

The uneducated in our five countries who are oriented to government and politics are frequently oriented as subjects rather than as citizens. They tend more frequently to recognize the impact of government and to expect equal treatment by bureaucratic authority than to engage in political discussion or follow politics and election campaigns. But here there are national differences of some importance. In the United States, Britain, and Germany, large proportions of the uneducated (though much smaller than the educated) are oriented toward political input as well as governmental output. In other words, there are substantial numbers of citizens among them. In Italy and Mexico, on the other hand, the uneducated are far less frequently oriented toward politics and political participation. They tend to be subjects in their orientation, and at the level of illiteracy they approach parochialism.

But we have been speaking thus far only of the cognitive and competence dimensions, where education has fairly uniform effects from country to country. If we look at these dimensions where education has little or no effect, or where its effects differ from country to country, we must qualify the propositions we have made regarding the parochial and subject tendencies among the uneducated. Thus in the United States and Britain the uneducated tend to share with the educated a common affective and normative allegiance to the political system, even though they differ sharply in the incidence of awareness and subjective competence. In Germany and Italy the uneducated tend to share with the educated a normative and affective alienation from the political system. The Mexican pattern is more complex, resembling the American and British in some respects, and the German and Italian in others.

Women and Political Orientation

Some of the advocates of feminine suffrage a few decades ago made exaggerated claims about the consequences of granting equal political rights to women. A polity that included women as active participants would, they said, abolish poverty, protect family life, and raise educational and cultural standards; an international society made up of nations in which women had the suffrage would not tolerate war. Certainly these expectations have not been realized. Wherever the consequences of women's suffrage have been studied, it would appear that women differ from men in their political behavior only in being somewhat more frequently apathetic, parochial, conservative, and sensitive to the personality, emotional, and esthetic aspects of political life and electoral campaigns.[1]

Lane, in explaining this feminine political pattern, argues: "The culture emphasizes moral, dependent, and politically less competent images of women, which reduce their partisanship and sense of political effectiveness and define a less active political role for them."[2] It would appear from the context that Lane is referring to American culture, where this characterization of the feminine image, though applicable, is less applicable than in most—if not all—other nations. Perhaps it is this failure in the literature to appreciate the cultural and national differences in the political orientations and behavior of women that leaves our understanding of the problem in an unsatisfactory condition.

Our data, on the whole, confirm the findings reported in the literature. In each of the countries we studied, men showed higher frequencies and higher intensities than women in practically all the indices of political orientation and activity that we employed. However, when we compare one country with another, it is quite clear that the feminine political patterns differ. We suggest that these differences have important implications for the functioning of political systems, and that these implications are not simply of the parochial, apathetic, conservative, and "emotional" sort referred to in the literature. Even if these patterns persist, and in all likelihood they will, they are probably not the most important consequences of the enfranchisement of women.

The Open and the Closed Family. In Chapter 10 we showed that leisure activities differ among the five countries. Americans and Britons report much more frequently than Germans, Italians, and

[1] See Robert E. Lane, *Political Life*, pp. 209 ff.; Maurice Duverger, *The Political Role of Women;* Fred W. Greenstein, "Sex-Related Political Differences in Childhood," *The Journal of Politics*, XXIII (1961), pp. 353 ff.; M. Dogan and J. Narbonne, *Les Françaises Facent à la Politique*, Paris, 1955; Gabriele Bremme, *Die Politische Rolle der Frau in Deutschland.*

[2] *Op. cit.*, p. 215.

Mexicans that they spend their free time in organized or social activities. What is most interesting is the fact that these relatively higher frequencies seem to derive from the rate of social interaction among American and British women (see Table 1). Thus the percentages of men who choose political, community, religious, and social forms of free-time activity are similar in the United States, Britain, and Germany—while it is the American and British women who most frequently report these types of leisure activities. In Italy and Mexico neither men nor women seem to want to interact or actually to interact with others in their community.

TABLE 1

Per Cent who Choose Outgoing Leisure Activities,[a] by Nation and Sex

Nation	Total (%)	(No.)[b]	Male (%)	(No.)	Female (%)	(No.)
United States	40	(970)	24	(455)	54	(515)
Great Britain	30	(963)	22	(460)	37	(503)
Germany	16	(955)	18	(449)	13	(506)
Italy	7	(995)	6	(471)	9	(524)
Mexico	11	(1,007)	8	(355)	13	(652)

[a] For text of question, see Ch. 10, pp. 262-63.
[b] Numbers in parentheses refer to the bases upon which percentages are calculated.

Needless to say, these figures do not cover the whole gamut of social interaction. The respondents were asked to exclude their occupational and family interests. Nevertheless, the findings are striking. They suggest a type of family in the United States and Britain that is open to the community, and open via both men and women. When we recall that the proportion of respondents in the United States and Britain who trust other people and have confidence in the safety of social relations is much higher than it is in Germany, Italy, and Mexico, we may add a significant item to the social interaction pattern. The higher rate of social interaction in the United States and Britain seems to be associated with a sense of safety and responsiveness in the community—a sense that is shared equally by American and British men and women.

Women and Political Participation. It remains to show that the relative "openness" of the American and British family is associated with the political orientations and roles of American and British women. We may begin with some of our indices of political activity.

389

Table 2 records the proportions of male and female respondents in the five countries who report that they discuss politics. If we look at the total columns, it is clear that, though in all five countries men more frequently than women say they discuss politics, in the United States and Britain the differences in frequency are rather small. Around two-thirds of the women in each country say they discuss politics; Germany, Mexico, and Italy follow in order of frequency. At the level of primary education or less, the differences between the sexes are more pronounced in all five countries. Nevertheless, well

TABLE 2
Per Cent who Discuss Politics, by Sex and Education

Nation	Total				Primary or Less				Secondary or More			
	Male		Female		Male		Female		Male		Female	
	%	No.*	%	No.	%	No.	%	No.	%	No.	%	No.
United States	83	(455)	70	(515)	73	(248)	57	(269)	95	(207)	83	(246)
Great Britain	77	(459)	63	(503)	74	(277)	56	(340)	83	(182)	75	(163)
Germany	77	(442)	46	(499)	74	(352)	42	(440)	88	(90)	74	(59)
Italy	47	(471)	18	(524)	36	(293)	13	(403)	64	(178)	37	(121)
Mexico	55	(355)	29	(652)	49	(285)	26	(592)	77	(67)	56	(60)

* Numbers in parentheses refer to the bases upon which percentages are calculated.

over half of the less well-educated American and British women report that they discuss politics, as compared with 42 per cent of the German, 26 per cent of the Mexican, and 13 per cent of the Italian women.

At the level of secondary education or higher, the proportions of women who discuss politics in the United States, Britain, and Germany reach or exceed three-quarters. The increase in Mexico is substantial; while in Italy, though the increase from primary to secondary is large, only a little more than one-third of the educated feminine population report that they talk politics. The German figures are of particular interest. At the level of secondary education, German women discuss politics as frequently as British women and only a little less frequently than the American. However, German women in general feel more restricted in their political communications, as is shown in Table 3. While American and British men and women resemble each other in their sense of freedom to discuss politics, almost two-thirds of the German women report feeling severely restricted, as compared with 48 per cent of the

German men. The Italian pattern is similar to the German, while the Mexican falls in the middle of the five nations.

What this would seem to suggest is that in the United States and Britain, where women report high rates of social interaction in their communities, and where they report almost as frequently as men that they feel free to discuss politics, the family becomes part of the system of political communications. In Italy, on the other hand, the general rate of political discussion is low, and particularly low among

TABLE 3

Feelings of Freedom or Restriction in Discussing Politics, by Sex and Nation
(in per cent)

Per Cent who Feel	U.S. M.	U.S. F.	U.K. M.	U.K. F.	Germany M.	Germany F.	Italy M.	Italy F.	Mexico M.	Mexico F.
They must avoid talking to many or almost all people	34	40	31	31	48	61	43	59	45	41
They can talk to anyone or most people	66	60	66	62	46	30	50	25	47	38
Don't know and other	0	0	3	7	6	9	7	16	8	21
Total per cent	100	100	100	100	100	100	100	100	100	100
Total number of cases	455	515	460	503	449	506	471	524	355	652

women; here, too, it would appear that when men engage in political discussion, they tend to do so outside the home: in the café, on the street, or in their places of work. In Germany and Mexico, which seem to present an intermediate pattern, educated women in particular engage in political discussion at a relatively high rate. In Germany the rate of political discussion among educated women is as high as it is among American and British women; the rate among uneducated German women is substantially below that of their American and British counterparts.

Our hypothesis, that American and British families tend to be involved in the political communications system, is supported by our data on voluntary association membership. Thus Table 4 shows us that more than two-thirds of the American men and almost half of the American women in our sample are members of voluntary associations (civic organizations, interest groups, church groups, social groups, and the like). One-quarter or more of the American men and of the women have at some time been officers of voluntary associa-

391

tions. In Britain proportionately fewer women are members of organizations, and only a small percentage have ever been officers of such groups. In Germany the differences between men and women

TABLE 4
Membership in Voluntary Associations, by Sex and Education
(in per cent)

Nation and Sex		Officer	Member	Either	Neither	Total %	Total No.
U.S.	M.	28	40	68	32	100	455
	F.	25	22	47	53	100	515
U.K.	M.	21	45	66	34	100	459
	F.	7	23	30	70	100	503
German	M.	12	55	67	33	100	442
	F.	2	22	24	76	100	499
Italian	M.	10	31	41	59	100	471
	F.	4	15	19	81	100	524
Mexican	M.	14	29	43	57	100	355
	F.	3	12	15	85	100	652
PRIMARY OR LESS							
U.S.	M.	18	42	60	41	101	248
	F.	17	23	40	60	100	269
U.K.	M.	16	47	63	37	100	277
	F.	5	19	24	76	100	340
German	M.	9	57	66	34	100	352
	F.	2	19	21	80	101	440
Italian	M.	5	32	37	62	99	299
	F.	2	14	16	84	100	403
Mexican	M.	15	23	38	62	100	285
	F.	2	11	13	87	100	592
SECONDARY OR MORE							
U.S.	M.	40	39	79	22	101	207
	F.	34	21	55	45	100	246
U.K.	M.	29	42	71	29	100	182
	F.	10	32	42	58	100	163
German	M.	24	48	72	28	100	90
	F.	5	46	51	49	100	59
Italian	M.	18	29	47	53	100	178
	F.	9	18	27	73	100	121
Mexican	M.	31	29	60	40	100	67
	F.	6	21	27	73	100	60

in their organizational activity are greater than in Britain, while in Italy and Mexico the proportion of female organizational members is lowest of all.

In all five countries the percentages of organizational members increase with education. The German frequencies for both men and women exceed the British and are almost as high as the American. Perhaps the most interesting findings in the table are the figures for educated American women. Thirty-four per cent have held office in voluntary associations at one time or another. In Italy and Mexico, organizational membership is quite low even among the better educated women, (27 per cent).

TABLE 5

Per Cent High Scorers[a] in Political Information Test, by Sex and Nation

	Total				Primary or Less				Secondary or More			
	Male		Female		Male		Female		Male		Female	
Nation	%	No.[b]	%	No.	%	No.	%	No.	%	No.	%	No.
United States	59	(455)	40	(515)	45	(248)	25	(269)	77	(207)	61	(246)
Great Britain	60	(459)	36	(503)	54	(277)	30	(340)	70	(182)	52	(163)
Germany	71	(442)	51	(499)	66	(352)	38	(440)	90	(90)	88	(59)
Italy	32	(471)	14	(524)	27	(293)	4	(403)	66	(178)	46	(121)
Mexico	43	(355)	15	(652)	32	(285)	9	(592)	77	(67)	52	(60)

[a] High scorers on information can name at least two party leaders and two ministries or cabinet positions.
[b] Numbers in parentheses refer to the bases upon which percentages are calculated.

TABLE 6

Per Cent Low Scorers[a] in Following Politics and Political Campaigns, by Sex and Education

	Total				Primary or Less				Secondary or More			
	Male		Female		Male		Female		Male		Female	
Nation	%	No.[b]	%	No.	%	No.	%	No.	%	No.	%	No.
United States	16	(455)	23	(515)	25	(248)	36	(269)	6	(207)	9	(246)
Great Britain	31	(459)	48	(503)	34	(277)	54	(340)	27	(182)	35	(163)
Germany	20	(442)	45	(499)	24	(352)	49	(440)	8	(90)	22	(59)
Italy	52	(471)	81	(524)	60	(293)	88	(403)	39	(178)	60	(121)
Mexico	37	(355)	66	(652)	40	(285)	70	(592)	28	(67)	35	(60)

[a] Low scorers neither follow politics nor pay attention to political campaigns.
[b] Numbers in parentheses refer to the bases upon which percentages are calculated.

Political Awareness and Information. In the purely cognitive dimensions of political awareness and information, a somewhat different pattern emerges. German women are as frequently well informed about politics as British women (see Table 5). At the level of secondary education German women seem much more frequently well informed than American and British women. It is of interest that Italian women with secondary education almost reach the British frequency, and Mexican women equal it.

In Table 6 we report the frequencies of low scores among men and women on our political awareness questions. The "low scorers" are those who report that they neither follow politics nor pay attention to campaigns. German women are more frequently politically aware than the British, while Italian women appear to be the least frequently aware of all: eighty-one per cent score low on following politics and political campaigns. At the level of secondary education the percentage of low scorers drops in all countries. But again German educated women have a higher frequency of political awareness than do British women of similar education. Italian women, even on and above the level of secondary education, continue to have an exceptionally high "unaware" frequency (60 per cent).

TABLE 7

Per Cent who Acknowledge Duty to Participate in Local Community, by Sex and Nation

Nation	Total				Primary or Less				Secondary or More			
	Male		Female		Male		Female		Male		Female	
	%	No.*	%	No.	%	No.	%	No.	%	No.	%	No.
United States	52	(455)	50	(515)	37	(248)	42	(269)	70	(207)	59	(246)
Great Britain	43	(459)	36	(503)	43	(277)	33	(340)	42	(182)	43	(163)
Germany	31	(442)	16	(499)	29	(359)	16	(440)	40	(90)	22	(59)
Italy	14	(471)	6	(524)	9	(293)	5	(403)	22	(178)	12	(121)
Mexico	31	(355)	24	(652)	29	(285)	22	(592)	39	(67)	36	(60)

* Numbers in parentheses refer to the bases upon which percentages are calculated.

In the dimension of pure cognition, compared with that of participation, we have a reversal in the ranking of national female performance, as well as in the ranking of nations. Just as Germans in general rank higher in political cognition than do the British, so do German women exceed British women in frequency of cognition. On the other hand, the Italian pattern persists in the cognitive dimension, even among educated Italian women. Six out of ten educated Italian women report that they never or infrequently follow politics and political campaigns—a proportion almost twice that of their Mexican counterparts.

Political Responsibility and Competence. Sex differences in political obligation and competence fall into a pattern that tends to support our earlier hypothesis about the role of women in Britain and the United States. Thus Table 7 shows that almost equal proportions of American men and women say that ordinary people have an obligation to participate actively in the public affairs of their local communities. In Britain the overall percentage is somewhat lower and the difference between men and women somewhat greater. But in Germany the female frequency drops to half that of the male. German women acknowledge political obligations in the local community less frequently than do Mexican women. The sense of local obligation among Italian men and women has an extremely low frequency; indeed, it appears to be almost nonexistent among Italian women.

Education clearly increases the frequency of political obligation in all five countries. But in this dimension, too, we have found

TABLE 8
Per Cent who Report Subjective Political Competence (Local and National),
by Nation and Sex

	Local				National			
	Male		Female		Male		Female	
Nation	%	No.*	%	No.	%	No.	%	No.
United States	81	(455)	83	(515)	77	(455)	72	(515)
Great Britain	83	(459)	72	(503)	70	(459)	56	(503)
Germany	72	(442)	53	(499)	49	(442)	27	(499)
Italy	62	(471)	41	(524)	38	(471)	19	(524)
Mexico	62	(355)	46	(652)	46	(355)	33	(652)

* Numbers in parentheses refer to the bases upon which percentages are calculated.

evidence to support our hypothesis that relatively educated American and British men and women have similar frequencies, while in Germany and Italy substantial differences persist among secondary-educated men and women. In Germay 22 per cent of the secondary-educated women, as compared to 40 per cent of the secondary-educated men, acknowledge political obligation in the local community. In Italy the figure for males is 22 per cent; for females, 12 per cent. The Mexican pattern is very similar to the British, with 39 per cent of the educated males and 36 per cent of the educated females acknowledging local obligations.

If we examine the responses to our questions on the sense of competence to influence local and national governments, several points may be made (Table 8). In all five countries women as well as men more frequently feel locally competent than nationally competent; and this difference is especially noticeable among women. But despite this universal trend, almost three-fourths of the American female respondents express a sense of national competence. In Germany, while 53 per cent of the women express local competence, only 27 per cent express national competence; and the Italian figures are, respectively, 41 per cent and 19 per cent. Mexican women express national competence somewhat more frequently than do German women. As these data suggest, the view that female political competence tends to be limited to the local community seems to be true of the continental European countries, but much less true of the United States and Britain.

Education raises the frequency of subjective political competence at both the local and national levels in all five countries. And it raises it for both males and females. The majority of the better-educated women in all five countries express a sense of competence to influence their local governments. But the Italian percentage of locally competent, educated women is lowest of all: 52 per cent (n: 121), as compared with 87 per cent (n: 246) for educated American women, 83 per cent (n: 163) for the British, 82 per cent (n: 159) for the German, and 68 per cent (n: 60) for Mexican educated women. Women's sense of competence to influence the national government also increases universally with education. However, the better-educated Italian women express national political competence infrequently (25 per cent, n: 121). In the dimension of local and national competence, educated German women show frequencies almost as high as those of American and British women.

Feelings Toward Nation and Politics. Here we have measures of emotional involvement in politics for men and women. One of these measures, discussed in detail in Chapter 4, is pride in nation. There we pointed out that the incidence of pride in the political aspects of the nation was high in the United States and Britain, fairly high in Mexico, and very low in Germany and Italy. The female patterns resemble the overall national patterns. Thus 91 per cent (n: 515) of the American women express political pride, as compared with 61 per cent (n: 563) of the British women, 26 per cent (n: 652) of Mexican women, 15 per cent (n: 499) of German women, and 3 per cent (n: 523) of Italian women.

We are able to ascertain an apathy rate from our series of questions on feelings during election campaigns. If we define as politically apathetic those who report none of the three feelings of enjoyment, anger, and contempt during election campaigns, the following pattern emerges (Table 9): in all five countries the female apathy rate is higher than the male. In Germany it is almost double the male rate; in Mexico both proportions are high and more nearly equal; in Italy the rates are very high for both men and women, with almost two-thirds of the women manifesting apathy. In the United States 14 per cent of the women and 9 per cent of the men are apathetic; in Britain the percentages are 32 for women and 20 for men.

Education reduces the rate of apathy among women in all countries. Nevertheless, apathy is characteristic of almost one-half of the secondary-educated Italian women (n: 121), as compared with 29 per cent (n: 163) of the better-educated women in Britain, 24 per

TABLE 9
Per Cent who Report No Feelings about Election Campaigns, by Sex and Nation

Nation	Male (%)	(No.)*	Female (%)	(No.)
United States	9	(455)	14	(515)
Great Britain	20	(459)	32	(503)
Germany	24	(442)	44	(499)
Italy	46	(471)	62	(524)
Mexico	30	(355)	48	(652)

* Numbers in parentheses refer to the bases upon which percentages are calculated.

cent (n: 59) of those in Germany, 22 per cent (n: 60) of those in Mexico, and 10 per cent (n: 246) of those in America.

Women and the Political System. In summary, we may say that American women and, to a somewhat lesser extent, British women tend to be active and involved in their communities, both in an informal and in an organizational sense. They are trustful of their social surroundings, politically informed, observant, and emotionally involved in the political scene. They acknowledge the obligation to participate actively in local political affairs, they feel competent to exercise influence over their government, and they take pride in the political characteristics of their nations. Except in the dimension of political awareness and knowledge, German women manifest lower frequencies than do American and British women. But except in the dimensions of social interaction, pride in nation, and local community obligation, educated German women manifest frequencies similar to those of American and British women. Mexican women show an uneven pattern: relatively low in the dimensions of participation and knowledge, they equal or surpass the German female rates in the obligation and national competence dimensions, and they are relatively high in national pride. The Italian feminine pattern is almost consistently low in all the political dimensions discussed here.

If we consider these data from the point of view of the political systems in the five countries, it is evident that we have to revise older theories of the role of women in democracy. These theories have tended to treat the sex differential in the same way that they treat other demographic categories, such as income, occupation, education, and the like. What they have overlooked is the fact that the great majority of adults are married; that they create families, raise children, and help to "socialize" these children into their adult roles and attitudes. Thus the political characteristics of women affect the family as a unit in the political system and affect the way in which the family performs the political socialization function. In all five countries, of course, the overwhelming majority of politicians, civil servants, and political activists are men. But it makes a great deal of difference whether women tend to live outside the political system in an intra-mural family existence, which is generally the case in Italy and among the relatively uneducated German and Mexican women, or within the political system, which tends to be the case in the United States and Britain. Duverger's comment that women ". . . have the mentality of minors in many fields and, particularly in politics, they usually accept paternalism on the part of men. The man—husband, fiancé, lover, or myth—is the mediator between them and the political world"[3] is an essentially continental European comment, and even here Duverger may be commenting more on the past and present than on the future.

While our data do not permit us to demonstrate it directly and explicitly, we are suggesting that in the United States and Britain the family tends to be a part of the political system, that events and issues in the polity tend to be transmitted into the family via both marriage partners, and that political discussion tends to be frequent and reciprocal, rather than male-dominated. Furthermore, we suggest that the problems of family life, the needs of women and children are more directly and effectively transmitted into the polity through this kind of politically open family. The esthetic quality and emotional tone of political life are probably also affected by the

---

[3] Duverger, *op. cit.*, p. 129. For comments on Duverger, and an analysis of differences in the socialization of American boys and girls, which affect male and female adult political patterns, see Greenstein, *op. cit.*, p. 370.

political competence and activity of women in the United States and Britain. We would suggest, too, that a family that is open to reciprocal discussion of political issues provides a type of political socialization that enables children to develop *within the family itself* a sense of political competence and obligation, and to learn to tolerate the ambiguities of politics and political controversy.

From this point of view, politically competent, aware, and active women seem to be an essential component of the civic culture. The significance of the political emancipation of women is not in the suffragette's dream of women in cabinets, parliaments, at the upper levels of the civil service, and the like; nor is it in Duverger's conception of the dependent minor. March has shown that there tends to be a division of labor between husbands and wives in the kinds of issues on which they take the initiative.[4] Greenstein has shown that American boys are more politically aware and informed than girls,[5] and he suggests how differential political socialization in the family produces these sexual differences. He also points out, correctly, that there are inherent limitations in the adult female role, which set an outer boundary to political participation for the great majority of women. What a purely American study would not bring to light is the fact that, by comparison with continental European women, American and British women tend to "live in" the community and the polity; and this has considerable significance for the functioning of the polity. We have only suggested what these consequences may be.

That the role of the passive and parochial woman may be on the way out, even in Italy, is suggested by two pieces of evidence. We have already seen that awareness and participation are greater among educated than among uneducated women. Thus we may assume that the increasingly wide distribution of educational opportunities in all five countries will eventually weaken the traditional female status. Relevant to this problem is a recent question that was asked in another survey conducted in a number of different countries, including Britain, Germany, and Italy. The question was: "Are you of the opinion that women should have the same political and legal rights as men or not?" The responses reveal the popular *norms* regarding the status of women, the rights and powers they

[4] James G. March, "Husband-Wife Interaction Over Political Issues," *The Public Opinion Quarterly*, XVIII (1953-54), pp. 461-70.
[5] *Op. cit.*, pp. 365 ff.

should have, rather than their current attitudes and performance. If acknowledgement of the norm of female equality is any indication of future changes in attitude and behavior, then our hypothesis about the general trend toward the open and participatory family receives support. Seventy-nine per cent of the British respondents of both sexes, 65 per cent of the Italians, and 62 per cent of the Germans answered the question affirmatively.[6]

Other Demographic Patterns

The many studies of voting behavior, party preference, and attitudes on political issues have shown that these patterns depend heavily on social position: occupation, income, and social status. The sorts of attitudes we have been concerned with—political awareness, competence, activity, and affect—are also influenced by socio-economic status. Individuals with lower income or with lower-status jobs are less likely to be involved in politics, to be well informed, to be active. However, though economic position does have a general cross-national effect on attitudes, this effect is neither as clear nor as strong as that of education. When education is held constant, differences among economic groups decline. Still, a fairly uniform relationship does remain: the man higher in the economic heirarchy, just like the more educated man, is more likely to be politically competent and active.

The relation between religion and political attitudes is more complex. Lenski, in his detailed analysis of differences in attitudes and behavior among religious groups in the Detroit area, makes the point that Catholics tend to be more traditional in their social orientations than Protestants and Jews. They are less frequently achievement oriented, and morally and intellectually less autonomous. They are more conservative on matters of social and religious morality. In the field of public policy, he reports, Catholics tend to be more "welfare" oriented than Protestants, and they give less support to civil rights.[7]

In the dimensions covered in our survey, there is some slight support for Lenski's thesis that Catholics are more traditional than Protestants, yet the differences are so small as to be negligible. Far more important is the finding that in the three of our countries

[6] *DIVO Presse Dienst,* Cologne, April 2, 1958.
[7] Gerhard Lenski, *The Religious Factor,* Garden City, New York, 1961, chaps. 4 and 8.

where both denominations are present in substantial numbers—the United States, Britain, and Germany—Protestants and Catholics have similar structural political orientations. In other words, the two denominations do not constitute political subcultures in the structural sense of the term. Certainly in all three countries there is a strong relation between denominational and party preference. And had our study included public policy issues, especially those on which the denominations tend to be divided, or had it included moral and social issues, then greater differences would probably have come to light.

Other demographic characteristics, such as age, region, and city size have been treated only in specific contexts in our study. We are unable to treat them more systematically because of the priorities of our research design. We were concerned primarily with national rather than subcultural patterns, and with attitudes toward the political system rather than public policy. Investigation of the phenomena of political subcultures and of their relation to demographic characteristics requires a research design of its own.

CHAPTER 14

FIVE POLITICAL CULTURES

IN previous chapters we have presented our data dimension by dimension. We began with knowledge and awareness of the various aspects of government and politics in our five countries; then we turned to political emotion and involvement, the sense of political obligation and competence, and social attitudes and experiences in other authority contexts that might have effects on political attitudes. Our concern was, not only to describe differences among our countries, but to discern what relations existed among these attitude dimensions.

An analytical procedure such as this tends to obscure the wholeness of individual countries and the reality of the human beings who constitute them. We turn now to a configurative and clinical method of exposition, presenting summary country profiles and illustrative case histories. For each nation we shall briefly summarize the pattern of attitudes found. In the next chapter we shall attempt to relate these patterns of attitudes to a theory of the functioning of democratic government. The cases of individual respondents are, like all individual cases, unique; and they do not lend themselves easily to generalization. They are presented here as illustrations of the patterns of attitudes analyzed in previous chapters.

Italy: An Alienated Political Culture

The picture of Italian political culture that has emerged from our data is one of relatively unrelieved political alienation and of social isolation and distrust. The Italians are particularly low in national pride, in moderate and open partisanship, in the acknowledgement of the obligation to take an active part in local community affairs, in the sense of competence to join with others in situations of political stress, in their choice of social forms of lei-

402

sure-time activity, and in their confidence in the social environment.

If we consider Italian political history, these tendencies are not surprising. Before unification Italy had experienced centuries of fragmentation and external tyranny in which allegiant subject and citizen could not develop. In the brief century of her national history Italians have learned to associate nationalism with humiliation, and constitutionalism and democracy with ineffectiveness. Her liberating experiences—the *Risorgimento* and the resistance to Fascism in World War II—were incomplete and deeply divisive in their effects. Thus Italians tend to look upon government and politics as unpredictable and threatening forces, and not as social institutions amenable to their influence. The political culture of Italy does not support a stable and effective democratic system; but these characteristics are quite understandable in the light of her political history.[1]

We may add two more features to this description of the Italian political culture. Italian national and political alienation rests on social alienation. If our data are correct, most Italians view the social environment as full of threat and danger. Thus the social fabric sustains neither an allegiant political culture nor an allegiant pattern of political participation. And perhaps as sobering is the fact that the Italians are the most traditional of our five peoples in their attitudes toward family participation. The norms of the patriarchal family still persist among a large proportion of Italians. Though the younger age groups have experienced participatory family socialization patterns more frequently than have the older groups, these differences between generations are of a smaller order than in the United States, Britain, and Germany.

The striking economic improvements in recent years in Italy hold out some prospect of changes in social structure and political culture. Rapid industrial development will certainly weaken traditionalism, and rising standards of living, assuming equitable distribution, may increase social trust and confidence in the political system. But the present pattern is of a predominantly alienated political culture.

This alienation may or may not be accompanied by belief in some revolutionary alternative to the present Italian political system. Italian Communists may, by our definition, be viewed as participants: they are aware of and involved in politics and they have an active sense of their own political competence—this despite the fact

---

[1] For a detailed discussion of Italian political culture, see the study of Joseph La Palombara, *Interest Groups in Italian Politics*, chap. iv, Princeton, 1964.

that they would cease being participants in the same sense if their political party came into power. This is also true of the supporters of the Fascist right, insofar as they take an active part in public affairs. It is paradoxical that the majority of politically involved and informed Italians are opposed to the contemporary constitutional and democratic regime, and that the bulk of the support for this regime comes from Italians who are oriented as subjects or as parochials. We saw in Chapter 5 that Italy's largest political party, from which her governments have been drawn since World War II, rests in considerable part on the votes of politically uninvolved Catholic women.

Our case histories illustrate these significant currents in Italian political culture. We include two "alienated participants" of the left, a parochial woman, and an allegiant subject.

A Communist Housewife: An Alienated Participant. *This first Italian case illustrates a common form of participant orientation in Italy: the alienated participant. Political involvement is high and political memories are strong, but the memories are bitter and the attitude to the present system is hostile. And, as with most of the Italian alienated participants, this respondent is found on the extreme left.*

Signora M., a fifty-one-year-old carpenter's wife, lives in a small mountain village in central Italy. The carpentry shop is a family business and employs the husband, his two sons, and an apprentice. The family is having a hard time. Signora M. complained, "Artisans are in great trouble. . . . This part of the country should be treated as a distressed area. There is little work and we are badly off." Some of the men try to work in factories in a nearby city, but the high train fares cut into their earnings. Many of the small farmers have had to sell their farms. She is pessimistic about the future. "If things don't change, everything will get worse. There must be political changes so that we can at least hope for some improvement. Economic conditions are worse than they used to be. In the past, at least, the farmers were able to cultivate their fields and sell their produce. Even the artisans had more work." The village pharmacist, the doctor, the teacher, and perhaps four or five other families are comfortably off, she reports. Everyone else has reached a dead end. About fifty fields in the neighborhood have already been abandoned, due largely to government regulations limiting the amount of sugar beets that may be cultivated.

The M. family is on good terms with its neighbors and feels that their common experiences unite them. However, there is less mutual help than there used to be. Signora M. goes on to explain: "We don't help each other much because the town administration has forbidden any kind of assistance for the last five or six years. In 1947 we used to have public parties for those who were disabled or hospitalized for war injuries. We had public parties and collected money. Once, I remember, the poor farmers were each giving some little thing and we collected quite a lot of stuff that we brought to the hospital in Bologna in a wagon. We had all kinds of entertainment. Then the police came and said we had to have permission to do this, and we were prevented from doing anything. Today, with the present crisis, money circulates less, and one is more attached to the little one has."

Signora M.'s current political views appear to rest heavily on a number of vivid political memories. Her past was highly politically charged. Her father was a farmer. There were sixteen people in the family, and their poverty was extreme. Her father, her uncle, and the oldest son formed a kind of family council, and their word was law. The men were socialists, as was almost everyone in the area. Politics was a constant topic of discussion. She described a number of events that affected her political attitudes. One such event involved the fate of a cousin who was beaten and wounded by the Blackshirts. His mother attempted to protest, and she was mistreated and imprisoned. Shortly after that, the M.'s house was ransacked. She tells of similar episodes in the lives of her relatives and neighbors and adds, "When Fascism came, this was a socialist village. We have always been against Fascism and had a certain determination and resistance. That is why this village was particularly persecuted." The persecution, she reports, united the village, and there was much mutual help during the Fascist era.

During the Second World War, her husband volunteered to go to Poland as a laborer for two years in order to evade army service. Signora M. recalls the atrocities of the Germans, the skirmishes of local partisans, and the fear of Fascist reprisals. "All these facts stay with you, and you can never forget them. A few days ago, I had a nightmare that I was encircled by Germans, and I could see the faces of the SS men who were questioning me. They were trying to torture me. Twice I woke up and twice I had this dream. Sixteen years have passed since that time, but it shows that we haven't forgotten." At the time of the 1948 elections the whole village supported the Popular Front. "I have arrived at the conclusion that only the working class can bring the country, our country, forward."

She is intensely interested in politics "as are all the poor people. They have to be interested in politics." The others are "those that are deceived by the clergy, the priests." The family discusses politics vigorously, and Signora M. gives this as an example: "We have already started discussing the next local elections. We will see if, like the other times, there will be an invasion of priests and monks." There are no disagreements when the family discusses politics. "I am not ashamed to say, we are all Communists. We are all members of the party, except my youngest son. He shares our ideas, too, but he does not want to take part directly. . . . As for religion, we are Catholics, but we are not active. Our religion, our faith is in the ideas of the party. Religion is a fraud for those that believe in it. Unfortunately, it has too much importance in the country."

Signora M. explains her support of the Communist party by saying: "This party gives us a reason to live, a reason to hope for a better future, and the possibility of seeing slowly, slowly, that this future is coming nearer. . . . The Africans, those that were in colonies, are now getting their freedom. Many countries are going ahead with Socialism, and we too are beginning to advance along this road. The Communist party gives us this hope. What could we do if we didn't have this guide?"

She is dissatisfied with her government and finds that "it never intervenes when it should"; but she thinks that the local administration, at least, has tried harder. She adds, "The authorities should take a greater interest. They should consider that this is an underprivileged area and take measures accordingly." The central government, in her opinion, ". . . should do two things: it should industrialize the village and build some factories. We have a river that has plenty of water that could be used to make electrical power for industry. The government should also take agriculture into consideration. It should try to reactivate production instead of suppressing it. . . . But we know this government well enough. We can hope for no good."

The M.'s have occasional routine contacts with local officials and find that they "are all friends at the Town Hall. They are good people." They have talked to some of their provincial deputies, but Signora M. adds, "With the deputies it is for the honor of talking to them more than anything, but with the [local] officials we talk about everything . . . they are always interested." Signora M. believes that a good citizen should take part in his local political party organization. On the national level he "should be a respectful citizen and pay his taxes." If she had any complaint, she would feel free to protest to her local government as an individual, but she would approach any part of the central government only as a member of a group.

A Tailor in Southern Italy: An Alienated Participant. *This case also illustrates a pattern of left-wing participant alienation. But unlike Signora M., Signor S. is not as closely committed to a particular political party of the left.*

Signor S. is a thirty-one-year-old tailor who lives with his wife and child in a small village in Calabria. Few of his neighbors can afford the services of a tailor, and the S.'s find it difficult to make ends meet. If he had to choose again, Signor S. would want to become a bricklayer. The work may be seasonal, but it is in demand, and bricklayers are fortunate in being covered by social security.

Signor S. is a Catholic, but seldom attends church. He sees religion as a moral force. In describing his neighbors, he mentions their extreme poverty and hopelessness. The land does not produce enough, and much of it lies uncultivated. The young people try to learn a trade and go north. There are a few rich absentee landlords who may visit their property for two or three weeks out of the year. Signor S. gets along well with all his neighbors. He does not consider them completely trustworthy, but he knows that he can always count on their help.

Signor S.'s memories of the Fascist era are less personal and intense than were Signora M.'s, but his experiences left him with the opinion that "dictatorships are always evil. Even in a small place like this, the mayor was like a dictator. He had a little house outside the village and could call a woman and would tell her, 'Tomorrow morning, you have to bring some wood to my house!' I'd like to see the mayor come to my house now and tell my wife what to do! I'd tell him, 'Get a servant or tell your wife to do it. I am the boss in my house!' Today, at least, one can defend one's self. . . . I tried not to take an active part in the *Balilla,* but I noticed that, as I was poor, the sons of the big shots in the party would always order me to do the lowest jobs, such as picking up rags in the village to send to the soldiers. I couldn't have protested. If I had tried to, I should probably have been beaten. Today, such things don't happen any more. They made me hate dictatorships."

Signor S. supports the parties of the left in general, though he refuses to say specifically for which party he has voted in the past. His views of the Communist party are ambiguous. "After Fascism, we had great hopes that the Communist party would achieve a better life for the workers after so many years of injustice. But after 1947, when the Communists had won the local election, the situation did not improve. There was no work. Many people had to leave the country. I was young then, but I remember well the great commotion in the country. There was even a battle. Elections seem to be less animated nowadays." He says he has always been interested in politics: "Poor people have to be interested, as no one takes an interest in them. Therefore, they have to be able to protest."

He adds, "I believe that a democratic government is good. Everybody likes liberty, especially after the bad period of dictatorship that we have been through, but I would like to see more social reforms. That's why I lean towards those parties that know what the Italian people need. I would like more social justice and less fraud. . . ."

Signor S.'s political commitment appears to be to a general policy rather than to a particular party. As he puts it: "I don't know what parties are best, but I am against those that defend the interests of the rich against a better life for the working class." He hopes that his son, too, will have an active interest in politics and will support a pro-working-class party. He would approve if his son became a Communist or a Socialist, but would also permit him to support the Christian Democrats if that party defended working-class interests. He would "try to get his son away" from the MSI, should he be attached to it.

The S. family discusses politics often, but one can discuss them freely only within a narrow group. Signor S. says, "We talk about all the unjust things that happen, but only among ourselves in the family. It is not wise to discuss the subject in the workshop, where someone may overhear it. Then people would become suspicious and we might lose the order."

Signor S. thinks that the central government could improve many things and adds, "First of all, there should be a reform of the bureaucracy and less corruption among the officials. . . . So many laws, even good ones, are not put into practice. Then there is the problem of the [public] health service. We have a nurse here and also a doctor who comes once a week . . . but he is always in a hurry and doesn't pay much attention to us. My wife brought our boy to see him and he just told her to give him some medicine; she didn't have a chance to explain anything. Every time that he is sick, I have to take him to a private practitioner. . . . When my child was born, we had to have a specialist come as my wife was very sick. The doctor told me, 'Let us do things in a friendly way, just give me thirty-thousand lire.' I finished paying the bills only last year. It's not right—people without money should get help. The government should provide less expensive houses, too."

As far as the area as a whole is concerned, he says, "I would like to see better conditions. I don't mean that everyone should be the same. If people have cars or luxuries, they should keep them, of course. But I mean the working class—the small artisans, the farmers, the laborers—they should have better living conditions, as they have in the North. Among the poor, many children have to leave school, even if they are bright. We lose many youngsters that way."

His sense of alienation and isolation from the government is reflected in the fact that he has little hope of immediate improvement. "The government in Rome is not interested in the South. . . . Even the political parties are usually more interested in the North. So we have no one to defend us, to give us courage. We are isolated and in the hands of corrupt local officials and capitalists. There are people with money here, but they are different from the ones that you have in the North. Here, the rich people don't invest their money but put it in the bank and get the interest that the bank gives them, so that the poor people remain poor, and there is never any work. . . . Chances would be better if there was a party interested in social reform, a party of the left." He still hopes that there will be changes on the national level, but has no faith in his local administration and in "bureaucracy."

His alienation is reflected as well in a sense of futility about his ability to influence the government, coupled with a belief that such influence is available only to a small group with money and connection. If a nation-wide unjust law were passed, he thinks that he might "ask why"; but a local law ". . . we have to accept. There is not much we can do." He finds that the only way of influencing his government is through personal and family connections, and "the officials pay more attention to those who have money." Approaching one's parliamentary deputy would be useless.

A Parochial Housewife. *This is an example of an Italian parochial woman, deeply religious and almost completely apolitical.*

Signora O. is a fifty-five-year-old widow living in an old apartment house in a large industrial city; she supports herself by renting rooms to students and other young people. Her husband, who died some years ago, was an interpreter in a business office. She has no children.

Signora O. says that life is quite different for young people today. They have more opportunities, but they are spoiled and immature and try to dominate their families. Her own life has always centered in her home and her husband. "I've always stayed at home. I never had to think of anything. My husband did not want me to work. He would say, 'You don't need to work; leave that to others.'" In her free time she likes to watch television. "It's the only pleasant thing that interests me."

Signora O. is a Catholic and attends church regularly. She believes that one cannot live without faith and that religion is important as a guide to proper conduct. She knows little about her neighbors, although most of them have lived in the same apartment house for the last thirty years and are close to her in age and economic circumstances. Her views of her neighbors are ambiguous. She supposes she is the "friend of everybody and nobody." She wants to trust people but says there are "vicious types" whom one cannot trust. She believes that her neighbors would probably be willing to help her, but she is glad that she has never needed their help.

Her childhood was spent in a slum district in the same city where she attended public primary and trade schools. The most important event in Signora O.'s life was her husband's death. Political events have touched her life only distantly. She was not interested in the era of Fascism, but "heard about" the war in Ethiopia and was glad that she was in no way affected by it, as her husband was not drafted. Her feelings are stronger about the Second World War. Her husband was in the army, and her worry and fear were such that they made her physically ill. She remembers the disorganization and horror of the immediate postwar era, but becomes vague again when discussing the 1948 elections. She says, "I might have voted. I think so, but I don't know. You know, we women! . . ."

She reports no interest in politics at all. "I have never taken any interest in it. What was important to me was my family." Her parents and her husband did not care for politics either. At school "there were patriotic songs; I sang them because I liked to sing." She says, "Women like me and peaceful people like my husband" are not interested in politics. "I just ask that they leave me in peace." If she had any children, she is sure that "they would be nonpolitical like me and like their father," but she does feel that a government is necessary because "a country needs a guide, just as a family needs a father or a mother." She finds it hard to discuss the local or national government, other than to indicate that it is remote and complicated and probably important. She says with certainty, "It doesn't affect my life at all." She has no idea how tax funds are used but thinks that they are being spent "in the right way." She does not know what the government could do to improve her life, other than to "do something" to help her economically, since her income is small. She has never had any contact with a government bureau or official and does not know anyone who might have. Signora O.'s sense of civic competence and responsibility matches her other parochial attitudes. If she were desperate, she supposes that she might turn to someone in the government, but she does not know to whom. She is not sure what she might be able to do about an unjust law, as she "knows very few people." Such things are best handled through personal or family connections. If she had dealings with any local government office or a police station, she thinks that she might be listened to, but is not sure whether she would be treated fairly. Signora O. believes that a good citizen is the person "who minds his own business and does his own job without bothering anyone."

A Town Messenger: An Allegiant Subject. This is the case of an Italian who has a sense of identification with the present political system. He considers it a step forward for Italy and considers himself well treated under it.

Signor B. is a fifty-one-year-old town government employee; the town is in Southern Italy. He is married and has had ten children, only four of whom are still living. His twenty year old daughter helps with the work at home, and the boys, ages 13, 9, and 8, go to school. He used to work as a shoemaker but could not manage on his earnings. He now works for the town government as a messenger and handyman. Occasionally he plays the organ in one of the neighboring churches, and in his free time he likes to listen to the radio, watch television, and read newspapers. His heroes are Verdi, Rossini, and Pope Pius XII.

411

These are Signor B.'s ideas on family life: "I make the decisions as head of the family. . . . The children listen and keep quiet. They don't have enough education yet to understand the importance of the family; they have to think about going to school and that is enough." He and his wife often talk about politics and discuss the news they have heard on the radio. There are no disagreements and Signor B.'s opinion dominates. "My wife is sure that whatever I say is correct."

He goes to church regularly, and in the evenings he listens to the Rosary program on the radio. Religion is of great importance to him, and he feels that "it should be and will be of great importance for all the people on earth, for God has so established in his Gospel."

The family lives in a working-class neighborhood. There are many laborers, who try to emigrate, and artisans, who are more comfortably off. There are few well-to-do people. He does not count himself among the poor and is content with his situation. He has many friends in the neighborhood when he visits from time to time, but he tries not to get too close to them and he does not trust them too freely. He has seen people deceive their friends and knows of treachery and murder. He finds that some families in their street will help each other and exchange greetings and presents on special occasions, but others are selfish and hostile.

Unlike many of his countrymen, Signor B. views the present political system in Italy favorably. He considers the main event of his life to have been the coming to power of the present government in 1948: ". . . families didn't go hungry any more. It was a good event, a triumphant event. Dictatorship was a real cross for us. We were at the point of locking up our mouths—not on account of Mussolini, but on account of the Fascists. The anti-Fascists were purged and beaten. I had to go to war to keep my family from starving. People were lining up at the military district office to be able to go to war sooner. . . . There were two armies at the time: the Blackshirts and the regular army. The militia men earned six lire a day and the soldiers, five lire. This is how hatred and vengeance began. . . .

"Yes, I went to Africa. I had to fight for food. . . . There was no work. To buy cigarettes we used to get two or three boys together and try to get a few cents to buy one cigarette between us. . . . I never knew the taste of milk or coffee when I was a child, but now we are never without them. Every now and then we see a thousand-lire bill, but in those days several weeks would go by when we would never even cook. Nowadays, a father can earn something, even if it is not

412

every week. Today conditions are better because the government has given people over sixty a pension. They don't die of hunger any more, like our fathers. This pension is a great thing for both men and women—that is the kind of progress our present government is making."

B.'s sense of allegiance appears to derive from his family background, his religious views, and his sense of the effectiveness of governmental output. When he was a child, his parents would discuss the various parties and tell him "to be obedient and follow a right-wing party, never a left-wing one, as a party of the right could not do foolish things and believed in the Divinity." The Christian Democratic government has been good to him. He has a local government job and his children have been sent to a vacation camp near Rome through the good offices of a friend in the government.

Signor B. supports the Christian Democrats, as they are "a right-wing party that has given satisfaction to everyone by eliminating slavery and instituting the Mass for Holy Peace. . . . It has given more importance to religion, it has given a better living to the priests by augmenting their salaries . . . it has built new offices, has widened the field of education and has instituted works of charity." Signor B. used to belong to the Fascist party, in order to have some degree of freedom and a chance at a job. He believes that most Italians support the parties of the right because they respect God and are grateful to Him. Some people believe blindly in Communist promises, but a "good Christian would never belong to that party."

He thinks that the central government is quite effective, citing public housing projects as an example. As far as his family is concerned, the government has been good to him. "My wife was almost blind. I told the mayor and he asked a minister, and immediately I got satisfaction. My request was granted. And I wasn't the only one, many other people have to thank the government for taking care of people who have been abandoned."

He thinks that the local administration is active, too. They put pressure on the provincial government for building programs and public works. The mayor goes to the provincial capital once a week in order to get results. Signor B. thinks that taxes are being used for public works projects and various improvements, but he wishes that far more could be done for Calabria. New industries and more jobs are needed, and the region still feels underprivileged and abandoned.

Signor B. has a sense of competence, but it is a form of administrative or "subject" competence. He has had good relations with the members of his town government, but as an employee and friend. And he is confident of the future, too: "If I needed something, I am sure that they would give me satisfaction, as a friend, as they have done in the past." Yet he believes that he could do nothing if he felt threatened by some harmful law, as "reason against force is not worth anything."

Mexico: Alienation and Aspiration

What have been most striking in the Mexican pattern of political culture are the imbalances and inconsistencies. Mexico is lowest of all five countries in the frequency with which impact and significance are attributed to government and in its citizens' expectations of equal and considerate treatment at the hands of the bureaucracy and police. At the same time, the frequency with which Mexicans express pride in their political system is considerably higher than that of the Germans or Italians. And the objects of this pride tend predominantly to be the Mexican Revolution and the presidency. Furthermore, what sense of participation there is appears to be relatively independent of a sense of satisfaction with governmental output. As was pointed out in Chapter 9, those Mexicans with a high sense of subjective competence are no more likely than those with low competence to evaluate specific governmental performance favorably, though they are more likely to express general system affect. In Mexico, then, participant orientation appears to have outrun subject orientation, and the role of participant tends to be isolated from a sense of allegiance in the subject sense.

Much of this isolation and imbalance may be explained by Mexican political history. Before 1910 the Mexican political system was primarily an exploitative, extractive one. Prerevolutionary parochialism was based on tradition; more, it represented a protective reaction against an exploitative central regime, and against predatory local chieftains and guerrilla bands. Thus historical experience and personal memory sustain an alienation from governmental authority, and these specific memories are consistent with contemporary authority trends in the various institutions of Mexican society.

The Mexican Revolution of 1910 represented a break with the past, for the government began to affect the population materially and favorably. But corruption and authoritarianism persist. The result, according to Scott, is an ambivalence in authority reactions. Mexicans have had direct experience with bureaucratic authority, and they reject that authority as corrupt and arbitrary. At the same time, there exists the myth of the benign Revolution and *presidencialismo,* the institutional charisma that the Mexican presidency has acquired in recent decades.[2]

There is another striking inconsistency in the Mexican data: high frequencies in subjective political competence are coupled with the lowest frequencies of all five countries in political performance (as measured by political information scores, voluntary association membership, and political activity). On the one hand, Mexicans have been exposed to a revolutionary ideology that places a high value on political participation. Exposure to these norms may create a tendency toward overestimating the competence of the self; a tendency to confuse aspiration with performance. On the other hand, the high rate of social mobility in Mexico, the discontinuous patterns of socialization associated with it, and the value conflicts that result from it create a high incidence of personal-identity crises comparable to the situation described by Pye in his Burmese study.[3] The personality aspects of this mobility are value conflict and a fragile self-esteem that typically produces over- and underestimation of the self. This may account for the inconsistency in Mexican responses: high self-appraisal of competence, coupled with cognitive inadequacy and political inexperience.

Nevertheless, these civic aspirational tendencies in Mexican political culture are important evidence that the democratic aspiration of the Mexican Revolution and the political elite is meaningful to the population. The norms have begun to take root among large numbers of Mexicans. And increasingly the Mexican political system offers opportunities for political experience that may begin to consolidate these aspirations.

[2] Robert E. Scott, *The Modernization of Political Culture in Mexico,* a paper prepared for the Summer Institute on Political Systems and Political Development, Committee on Comparative Politics, Social Science Research Council, 1962. On the basis of social psychological and anthropological studies, Scott argues that the majority of Mexicans are oriented to the political system as subjects. But the Mexican subject orientation is ambivalent: it is characterized by both strong dependency needs and rejective and rebellious tendencies. Scott describes this ambivalence as one that pervades all authority relations in Mexican society—family, school, work group, and governmental-political system. The authority syndrome involves an exploitative and dominative exercise of power by those in authority positions, and a rebellious-dependency reactions by those in subordinate roles.
[3] Pye, *Politics, Personality, and Nation Building.*

415

A Mexican Stonemason: An Alienated Subject/Aspiring Citizen. *This case illustrates the several levels of Mexican political attitudes: a sense of national identity and pride, coupled with rejection of the actual operation of politics and government.*

Sr. M., a forty-seven-year-old stonemason, lives in one of the poorer neighborhoods of a large Mexican provincial city on the central plateau. Childless, he and his wife share one large room in a rundown adobe *vecindad,* which houses three other families. Although electricity has recently been installed, there is no running water. The cement floor of the building is somewhat of a luxury in that part of the city, but it is marred by mud and puddles that have been washed in by the rain from a refuse pile behind the house.

Sr. M. has had no schooling. He is a master mason and has five men working under him. He is content with his work, saying, "I do not complain of our Lord's will," even though his income is modest and his work irregular. He takes pride in his craftsmanship and in his thrift. If he had had the chance, he would have preferred a technical or professional career, but he is proud to have worked his way up from the level of a poor farmer's son.

In many ways Sr. M. prefers the past, when ". . . there was more respect for older people. Nowadays, young people do not show respect to anyone, not even to their parents. They get together to cause trouble in the streets." He believes that the man of the house should have the final word in family decisions and that children should not be consulted, because "they still cannot reason and cannot give opinions."

Sr. M. attends church every Sunday. "To me religion means that, for example, when I go home from work, I pray to our Lord to protect me and let nothing harmful happen to me, either at work or out in the streets, and that I may always have a job and earn my daily bread. . . . Religion has to have the first place, in that one must believe that one is a Catholic and must love God above everything. God gives us life, and it is He who allows us to go on living."

His neighbors are small farmers and craftsmen. Most of them are quite poor. Sr. M. does not feel that he can trust them. They gossip, he says, and are interested only in themselves; they are not apt to help each other. "Those who have money do not care to help people outside their own family. It has happened to me that when I needed money, I tried to borrow it from others—but I can get it only if I can put up some security."

Sr. M. combines a strong sense of national pride as a Mexican with more negative views about the actual operation of the government. He has strong nationalistic feelings. About the recent Guatemalan crisis, he says, "When they killed a Mexican in Guatemala because he was Mexican, as I am, it affected me very much in my love for my race. Guatemala should never have done this to a Mexican." Yet he is not interested in current politics and public affairs. "I gain absolutely nothing from such activities." Sr. M. feels that those who are interested in politics are the "ambitious people who want a job where they can make more money and work less than factory workers." "Humble people, peasants" do not care about politics.

This combination of rejection of the more immediate manifestations of politics and satisfaction on the symbolic level is seen in M.'s attitudes toward parties and government. He supports the PRI because, as he says, "In general, it is the party that wins, and because if I want to vote for any other party I am not allowed to. To me it does not represent anything. I vote because I am a citizen. The idea is to put in the presidents of the Republic, so that they may help their people in matters, such as not letting prices go up and providing many jobs." Sr. M. does not know anything about any other political parties. He thinks that government is necessary because "even with a government, people kill each other. Without a government, people would kill and kill without fear."

He thinks that the federal government has done a fairly good job in providing schools and jobs and in keeping prices down. He is proud of his country and of "President Lopez Mateos, who is doing what is needed for the welfare of the country, such as seeing to it that there are no food shortages for the people and that we live in a free country and . . . have no war."

His views of local government are more negative. "We have asked them for a sewage system and schools here, and the government has not helped us at all and has improved the place only by giving us public electricity. We have no water in this part of town. My wife has to go and bring it from the other side of town." Sr. M. feels that tax funds are being used to "build pavements, to pay government employees, and build houses for mayors and governors," and he wishes that it were spent for water and sewage systems instead. "They should expropriate the power plant and the telephone company so that the money that these companies make may go into the funds of the President, where they can benefit the people of Mexico—such as raising workmen's wages in order to avoid the many strikes that are about to break out. . . ."

Sr. M. is not politically active, nor is he much interested in such activity. He would contact a government official only ". . . if I had some kind of recommendation to work, that is, if I had a card to see him and do some mason's job at his house." He does not discuss politics with anyone, "because sometimes people poke fun at what you say." If necessary, he might "send someone" to petition on his behalf to a justice of the peace or a local representative. If the matter were serious, he might join a protest committee. On the national level, however, he feels that one "can do nothing because one cannot oppose the federal government. They are the ones who govern and they will say, 'There, there, nothing can be done about it and that's final.'" The best a man can do, Sr. M. feels, is to "look after his family, seeing to it that they do not lack anything at home."

A Mexican Farm Worker: An Alienated Subject/Aspiring Citizen. *Sr. P. is also alienated from the operation of the political system. But as with many such Mexicans, his alienation is tempered by pride in the system and some civic aspiration.*

Sr. P. is a thirty-seven-year-old Mexican farm worker with three years of education. He lives with his wife and three children in a small, deteriorating one-room adobe house, simply furnished and lacking in modern sanitary facilities. During the interview he was dressed in plain workclothes and wore no shoes.

Sr. P. works as a day laborer on a small farm. At first he said that he is content with his work and gets along well with his fellow workers, but as he continued to speak, a more critical attitude came to the fore: there is really no future in this work, it is a "dead-end" job, the work is hard, and the pay very low; he would have preferred to be an automobile mechanic or, perhaps, a sculptor. The farm owner is short-tempered. Sometimes his orders make little sense, but the workers are not able to voice their opinions.

Sr. and Sra. P. discuss their family problems together, but Sr. P. has the final decision. He does not expect his children to participate until they have reached adulthood, but he will consult them on school matters since that is an area in which a child should not be forced.

He is a practising Catholic and attends church weekly. Religion to him means "a brake against humanity's committing any stupid-

418

ities, not to do evil against any neighbors, not to kill, not to wound, not to offend others." He is more religious now than he was in his younger years.

His neighbors are unskilled laborers, most of them quite poor. He is apt to mistrust people and tells of an experience in a tax collector's office. "An employee of the Government Collector's Office kept my money and made me pay again, because when I went to pay, he didn't give me the receipt and stole the money." He also claims that people are not helpful, either; they care only for their own families.

Sr. P.'s political memories are of the potentialities for change through politics as well as of the danger of politics. He vividly recalls ". . . the administration of Governor Rafael Avila Camacho, because it improved conditions for the people. They paid very few taxes and prices went down so that what one earned went further than it does now." But he also remembers the time when his father "was thrown into jail because of a political conflict growing out of the land reform program. He was an agrarian commissioner and got involved in a change of governors. He was on the losing side."

He has no interest in public affairs and does not consider himself "capable of taking part in politics. I spend my time earning a living for my family." He says that farm workers and unskilled workers are not interested in politics, and he names some local government employees, seed and food merchants, and industrialists as examples of people who are interested. While he discusses politics with his neighbors from time to time, he reports he could not do this freely with anyone holding a government position, because such a person is of a different class. "I could speak [only] with the humbler class, like ourselves, because I am not equal to those in the other group."

Like many Mexican respondents, Sr. P. has negative views about government and politics. It is an alien and hostile world. Government officials as a group, he thinks, have a harmful influence on the country. ". . . all those in the government, like deputies, governors, mayors and aldermen of this city—they don't worry about the lower classes." He states that he supports no party, but he became vocal in his denunciation of the PRI: "It imposes its candidates . . . the government officials favor the industrialists and the commercial interests, lowering their taxes by half. And we poor, who have a minimal share in the land or business, are those who have to pay any taxes they assign to us. The PRI through its officials is leading the people to unhappiness because everything is expensive and taxes are very high. They impose government officials just as they please. . . . I might possibly support a party of the people that really would nominate government candidates popularly. It would be a party that would remove all the taxes and assessments and would lower the prices of such items as seeds, vegetables, articles of prime necessity. It would be different in that it would make everything cheaper and not impose government officers. . . . The PRI is carrying the people to misery. It represents a monopoly of government officials, throughout the Republic. . . . People who support it include industrialists, big businessmen, the rich, the unions, and directors of workers' organizations who force their members to work for the PRI." He would feel "disgusted" if his children supported the PRI.

What contact Sr. P. has had with the government—his experience at the local tax office—has confirmed his negative view of it. He was cheated and treated unfairly. The people who were better dressed were given priority and the humbler ones kept waiting. Nevertheless, his view of his potential competence is not all negative. He has never approached any elected representative, but he thinks that if he had any personal request, he might ask for an interview with the governor or mayor during the proper office hours and receive a satisfactory response. On the other hand, if he were faced with some harmful local or national law, he would feel quite powerless. He adds that on the national level any attempt at recourse would be totally "impossible, as this law would have been established by the President of the Republic and I would have to support it."

But, Sr. P. does have some sense of civic obligation and quite a bit of pride in the political system. He believes that a good citizen should "give his vote to some candidate for mayor or governor" and should make voluntary donations of money to the schools. He is proud of Mexico's progress, of its laws abolishing slavery, of the people's freedom, although he feels that the country is still far from reaching the goals of the Revolution. And he has great admiration for "President of the Republic, Don Adolfo Lopez Mateos, for his activities in favor of the nation. He has built large schools and irrigation works and has provided many roads."

A Mexican Radio Technician: An Aspiring Citizen/Alienated Subject. *Sr. C. is on a somewhat higher economic and educational*

420

level than the first two Mexicans. Like them, he is alienated from much of what the government does. But his alienation is not as thoroughgoing. He sees benefits as well, and he has, as the others do, a strong sense of pride in his nation.

Sr. C. is a forty-year-old Mexican radio operator and technician who lives in a medium-sized city. He is married and has five children. He is satisfied with his salary and working conditions. His coworkers are friendly, and although his superior is quite strict, he finds that his personal needs are always taken into account. In his spare time Sr. C. likes to do home repairs and take care of his car. He likes to read a daily newspaper, listen to the radio, and read a magazine about once a week.

Sr. C. hopes and believes that his children will be even more successful in life than he has been, since there are more educational opportunities open to children these days. "It is due to two things. One is the progress of science in the world and the other, the progress of our country." He believes in a democratic family life. When decisions are to be made, he chooses "the logical and reasonable one. This is the one that carries the most weight. It does not matter whether it comes from my wife, my son, or anyone else." Children should participate in family discussions "as soon as they can use their reason, at five or six years of age, without being overtaxed or confused with superfluous or inappropriate matters." As for his children's future, Sr. C. adds, "I have tried to let them know of the variety of paths that they could take, and if I notice any inclination by one of them towards some line, I encourage as far as I am able." The older children take part in family discussions, although Sr. C.'s opinions tend to dominate. This does not particularly please him. "Perhaps my children allow themselves to be guided too much by me."

He is a practicing Catholic: "My parents' religious teachings are good enough to guide my life"; but he feels far less religious than he did as a child. While religion should have an important place in the life of his country, he does not want it to interfere in political affairs. He thinks that there are many religious fanatics who try to influence the government, and he adds, "Their fanaticism does not allow them to see the reality of the progressive aims of the majority of Mexicans."

Sr. C.'s neighbors are mostly businessmen, professional people, and office workers. He knows almost all of his neighbors and tends to trust them. "In general, people like to cooperate as much as they can to help towards better living conditions for the community. I believe that, without going out of our way, we all wish to live happily together—except, naturally, some. In general, people are honest. For example, if you were to lose something, people would bring it to you . . . When there is a family problem, such as sickness, the neighbors quickly come to our help. . . . In general, I think these [good] relations depend on one's self, but, naturally, one must encourage them."

Sr. C. went to primary school and trade school and continued to take advanced technical training in the evenings. His most outstanding memories are of personal events, an illness that kept him out of the army, a particularly good job offer. His main political memory consists of a general feeling of disappointment over corruption and the slowness of economic progress. "There is, for instance, the devaluation of our currency . . . our income was greatly reduced . . . also the handling of public affairs, such as petroleum, the fraudulent way in which the popular vote is counted, and so on. These are reasons for discouragement for those of us who have hopes for our country."

Of the church-state conflict of 1925, Sr. C. says, "At that time, we saw it as a vile insult to our religious beliefs. But the events that took place at that time had an influence on my present way of thinking— the Church should not interfere in government affairs." The Second World War he remembers mainly in personal terms. "I had planned to open up a radio store . . . and I had to postpone it, hoping that business conditions would become more favorable, but it has not been feasible so far. . . . [I saw] that many great interests were at play, and that it is not true, as is usually said, that politics aspires to a goal of justice and equity—but, rather, that it involves ambitions for power."

Sr. C. reports that he has some interest in government and politics, particularly in ". . . whatever concerns me as an ordinary citizen. I consider that I lack the skill to participate actively in political affairs. My interest has always been one of complying as an ordinary citizen." However, he is well informed in political matters and believes that he understands them fairly well. He thinks that idealistic, patriotic citizens, as well as some who seek only their personal benefit, have some interest in politics. The apathetic and the ignorant do not care at all. He supports the PRI, saying, "Of all the bad [parties], I think that the least bad one is the PRI. It stands for the revolutionary movement, the ideals of the Revolution, and the betterment of the underprivileged."

Sr. C. has had no government contacts, but he has a sense of competence. If he ever needed to, he would approach a local official through a friend or would present his "protest to him personally and also to the person above him; for example, making him realize that this is a heavy tax for the people who make so many sacrifices . . . basing [my protest], naturally, on the laws of our constitution." If he had dealings with a government office or the police, he would expect to be treated as well as anyone else, but that would not mean that he would be given much consideration. Sr. C. thinks that he could have no influence over national officials. He says, "My personal opinion would not count in a case like that. It so happens that if a harmful law is issued, they have already taken everything into account."

Sr. C. has a strong attachment to the political system, despite his negative views. He believes that a good Mexican citizen should love his country, behave respectfully toward other people, and work hard for his country's welfare. In his local community the good citizen "makes friends with persons of high status, is an active member of a political party, but, above all, cultivates friendships with persons of high position in the locality. . . ." He is proud of his country: its natural beauties, its industrialization, the hard work of its peasants, its intellectuals and scientists. He feels that the ideals of the Mexican Revolution have not yet been attained, but he believes that they will lead to "social justice. All those men who were victims of the land-owners and the rich rose up and rid themselves of that heavy burden, freeing themselves of the abuses and slavery to which they were subjected."

And the men he admires most are all in public life. "General Cardenas—because of his many moral qualities, integrity, love for his country and countrymen. He has helped young people to study . . . and he wanted to liberate all peasants. He is a very hard worker— very dynamic. He gets to work early. . . . The most daring feat he ever performed was to expropriate the Mexican oil fields. Don Jose Vasconcelos . . . and former President Ruiz Cortinez: for his patriotism, his humanitarianism, his hard work . . . he carried out all his promises. . . ."

423

A Mexican Factory Worker: An Aspiring Citizen. *Compared with the first three Mexicans, Sr. S. has a more positive view of the political system. In his eyes, it operates to benefit himself and the nation.*

Sr. S. is a forty-three-year-old factory worker living on the outskirts of a state capital in central Mexico. The area is still partly rural. Sr. S.'s house is a fair-sized, one-story farmhouse situated on an unpaved street. Sr. S. does "piece-work" on an assembly line in a shoe factory, where he is one of seven hundred workers. On the whole, he is satisfied with his job. "When there is a party in the house, the men from my department come. When we go out on an excursion, we talk about what we are doing in the factory, what we need there, and the like. For example, we are organizing a band." He has worked his way up to his present position from that of a brick carrier. As for the future, he says, "I've got some chance for advancement. Any time one wants to rise or move ahead, one can do so. All you need is money to give to the brother of someone like the chief of the department. One arranges these matters with money."

Sr. S. has ten children. Some are married and have moved away to the capital. They are working at skilled jobs. The middle ones are learning trades, and the younger ones are in primary school. Sr. S. believes that his children will have greater security than he has had, because they have had more education and live in a time of technical progress and increasing opportunity. When decisions have to be made in the S. family, both parents discuss the matter, but Sr. S. has the final word. He is somewhat inconsistent in his views on his children's participation. He thinks that some participation is good for a child when he has reached his middle teens, but he also thinks that children ought to obey. Regarding educational planning, however, Sr. S. adds: "My wife and I discuss it with the child involved, whether he wants to go on studying or whether he wants to work. We write to order a correspondence course, for example, to learn radio, television, or general mechanics, and he takes part in the discussion. For example, I say, 'Look son, you're going to study such and such, like studying mechanics,' and he decides on what I have told him."

The S. family is Catholic, but Sr. S. is not actively religious. The people in Sr. S.'s neighborhood are mostly skilled and white-collar workers. He considers himself to be "middle class, because we dress well, have our own house, and three of us have jobs. We have all the conveniences: water, light, drainage. We have radio and television." Sr. S. has a few friends among his neighbors, but he is fairly reserved.

He trusts people with some reservations and finds that some are helpful but others are not.

Sr. S. completed four years of primary school. In looking back over his life, his main memory is of "the misery, the lack of clothing, of food, and of money. This was because I came from a poor family." He still feels that this was a great handicap to him. His main political memory is of discussions about Benito Juarez, who was considered the father of his country in the government schools, but was deprecated or ignored in the Catholic ones. "This affected me because of the difference of opinions. While the Government wanted to do one thing, the Church wanted to do another."

Sr. S. reports that he discusses politics from time to time, and he adds, "I like politics, I am interested in it." He thinks union leaders have failed to safeguard the interests of the workers, and he remembers being interested from an early age in the economic benefits promised by politicians. He thinks everyone should be interested in politics because it helps to improve his economic situation. "With politics, one gets good leaders, presidents, governors. Politics is for the improvement of the people because from it comes the management of industry, of commerce, of imports and export. I see even that the street sweepers are interested, since they are organizing into unions." Sr. S. believes that only illiterates and those physically incapable of seeing the world around them are not interested in politics. He follows the news daily in the newspapers and over the radio and feels confident that he can understand it thoroughly. Yet he is reserved in discussing politics with outsiders, for not everyone might agree with his views. His factual knowledge is actually rather meager, but he feels that if he wanted to learn more about some issue, he would turn to someone better informed.

He supports the PRI, which, he says, has offered good candidates who have shown concern for the people and an ability to rule. He sees it as representing all classes and as supporting "the ideals and values of social improvement." He opposes the PAN, saying that it is supported by Catholics, illiterates, and misguided people in general. As far as his children's party choices are concerned, he would be proud if they joined the PRI, but would respect their decision without too much unhappiness if they turned to the PAN instead.

Sr. S. recalls the last election. He was pleased to vote for the PRI, and he adds, "One vote more in favor of my candidate! I felt proud. The federal soldiers were around the voting place. I marked my ballot, deposited it in the urn, and walked out. Everything very peaceful."

Sr. S. has had some of the routine government contacts of the average citizen and householder and has found them quite satisfactory. In general, though, he believes that while he could always expect fairness, he would rarely be listened to with any real consideration. He has never contacted any of his elected representatives but thinks that if he ever had any problem, he would work through his party. "I would do it through the PRI. For example, if I were involved in a traffic accident or a criminal case or if any member of my family were brought into court, I think they would arrange something for me because I am a citizen and have never been arrested nor had any kind of problem." Sr. S. feels that the duties of a good citizen are to join a local political center and to defend his country's flag and territory.

A Parochial/Alienated Mexican Housewife. *Sra. S. is little involved or interested in politics. What image she has of politics is of a hostile and alien realm—part of a larger, generally hostile environment.*

Sra. S. is a sixty-one-year-old Mexican housewife who lives in a medium-sized city: a market center for the surrounding farming area. The S.'s live in an old, rundown, working-class neighborhood. Their house is of unpainted adobe and has an uncovered earth floor. There is no electricity and no indoor sanitation of any kind. During the interview Sra. S. was suspicious, brusque, and unfriendly.

Sra. S. keeps house for her husband and herself, but whenever she has time she likes to "sleep, sew, embroider, and take care of her chickens." She does not read a newspaper or listen to the radio. Her husband works in a small brickyard, and while he finds the work quite hard, he is satisfied with his wages.

She thinks that her own life has changed for the worse. "Today I suffer more than before. One suffers a great deal in marriage. And then, life is very expensive—everything one needs to eat keeps going up in price. The shopkeepers want to swallow us alive." In the past there were chances for getting ahead, too, because "people weren't such bandits and not as unscrupulous as they are now. They used to have a conscience, but they don't any more. God gives more to some than to others."

Sra. S. discusses family problems with her husband, but he has the

426

final voice when a decision has to be reached. Sra. S. does not believe that children should participate in such matters until they are twenty years of age. In the meantime, "they should do as they are told."

She attends church regularly and belongs to two religious confraternities. She has become more religious as she has grown older.

The S.'s neighbors are mostly factory workers. Almost all of them are quite poor. "I am one of the poor ones—because God wanted to give me a poor life. I lack everything. The Lord in Heaven doesn't do much for the poor people." Sra. S. distrusts her neighbors: ". . . some of them try to rob you or break into your house and carry away away everything that they can find. . . . Besides, people are selfish. They don't speak to you and won't do any favors for you. People around here treat me badly. I asked them to lend me money and they wouldn't do it."

Sra. S.'s father was a miner who lived with his wife and twenty-three children in a one-room adobe house. The family accepted its poverty stoically and both parents were kind and friendly, if quite strict. Sra. S. did not attend school and did not want to. She was glad when she was old enough to leave home and begin her own life, and although she found it difficult to support herself, she still remembers those days as the high point in her life. She has no political memories —"I don't like to get mixed up in politics"—but she does recall the church-government conflict of the '20's. "I was sorry for the poor priests. It hurt me to see that they were persecuted."

She is not interested in politics. It does not affect her in any way. She says, ". . . rich people are interested—the ones who live in the center of town here, but those of us who live in this neighborhood, humble people, are not." She adds, "I have never gone around getting mixed up in politics because I don't know how to talk about politics and don't understand those things . . . I don't know anything about political parties." Sra. S. would not want her children to support a political party, either, for "it's better to keep out of trouble." She herself has voted only once, and then because "they took me along and convinced me that I should go and vote for a particular man for mayor." She is not interested in election campaigns and does not believe that they are needed.

Sra. S. is not sure exactly what the central government does, but she feels vaguely that it probably shows some concern for the poor by providing jobs for them. Personally, though, it does not affect her at all. She is not sure whether her local government affects her, either. As far as tax funds are concerned, she says that "they are used for those in the government, for the mayor—since he is the one who keeps the money." She would like to see the money used for local improvements instead. On the whole, she wishes that both the central and the local governments would improve the economic conditions of the people by providing more jobs, but she does not think there is much chance of that under this or any other administration.

Sra. S. has had no contact with any government official and cannot imagine the occasion ever arising. If she felt the need for further information, she believes that she could "ask the mayor because he is the one who controls such things." But in general she believes that such matters are too complicated for her to understand. If she were faced with some unjust law or regulation, she says that she would do ". . . nothing—because what can you do when you know nothing about such matters? And perhaps they would pay no attention." She would expect little fairness or attention at the local tax office or police station. She has no pride in her country, and says that the Mexican Revolution meant ". . . nothing more than going around stealing and violating girls. They were nothing but bandits."

Germany: Political Detachment and Subject Competence

Germany is a technologically advanced nation with a highly developed and widespread educational and communications system. It had a bitter and traumatic political history before the founding of the present republic: a humiliating defeat in World War I, an abortive experiment in democracy, the Nazi dictatorship, the devastation and national division at the end of World War II. Both her technological advance and her traumatic history are reflected in Germany's political culture.

The high level of development in the communications and educational fields is reflected in the fact that most Germans are aware of and well informed about politics and government. In a number of ways they take part in the political system. The frequency of voting is high, as is the belief that voting is an important responsibility of the ordinary man. And their level of exposure to political material in the mass media of communications is high. Furthermore, German political culture is characterized by a high level of confidence in the administrative branches of government and a strong sense of competence in dealing with them.

428

Yet the contemporary political culture also reflects Germany's traumatic political history. Awareness of politics and political activity, though substantial, tend to be passive and formal. Voting is frequent, but more informal means of political involvement, particularly political discussion and the forming of political groups, are more limited. Germans are often members of voluntary associations, but rarely active within them. And norms favoring active political participation are not well developed. Many Germans assume that the act of voting is all that is required of a citizen. And Germany is the only nation of the five studied in which a sense of administrative competence occurs more frequently than a sense of political competence. Thus, though there is a high level of cognitive competence, the orientation to the political system is still relatively passive—the orientation of the subject rather than of the participant.

Germany's traumatic political history affects other important characteristics of the political culture. Though there is relatively widespread satisfaction with political output, this is not matched by more general system affect. Germans tend to be satisfied with the performance of their government, but to lack a more general attachment to the system on the symbolic level. Theirs is a highly pragmatic—probably overpragmatic—orientation to the political system; as if the intense commitment to political movements that characterized Germany under Weimar and the Nazi era is now being balanced by a detached, practical, and almost cynical attitude toward politics. And the attitudes of the German citizen to his fellow political actors are probably also colored by the country's political history. Hostility between the supporters of the two large parties is still relatively high and is not tempered by any general social norms of trust and confidence. And the ability of Germans to cooperate politically also appears to have serious limitations.

A German Businessman: A "Detached" Subject. *Herr R. is politically informed, but remains deliberately aloof from politics.*

Herr R. is a forty-eight-year-old businessman. He works for his father, who supplies welding equipment to the shipping industry. The interview took place in an office in an old house near the waterfront, still surrounded by the debris of the last war. It is an old Hanseatic structure: dignified, and old-fashioned. The interviewer described the respondent as suave, well-dressed, intelligent, but quite reserved, especially at the beginning; as the interview progressed, he became freer in his replies.

429

His business is quite secure, but he is rather looking forward to the time when his father will retire and he can take over the firm and modernize it. Until then, he is more or less marking time. He is interested in music and in economics. The person he admires most is the physicist Weiszäcker. Herr R. is married and has two sons who are in their teens. Both boys will go to the university. One is interested in biology and the other one will follow in his father's footsteps and take an engineering degree.

He and his wife share their family decisions almost equally, with Herr R. having a slight edge, being the more experienced one. Herr R.'s sons are permitted to take part in family decisions. He thinks that it is a good idea to let children start doing so at about the age of fourteen.

Herr R. lives in a middle-class neighborhood and refers to himself as belonging either to the middle or the upper middle class. He has no close friends and no "social life," but feels that he can trust all the "old Hanseatic businessmen" in town and that people are generally helpful in small ways. When they are not, it is apt to be a matter of thoughtlessness rather than selfishness; everyone is so rushed today that he has little time to think of his neighbor. He grew up in the same neighborhood that he now lives in, and life was comfortable and secure. His father was very strict. He says it was the usual thing in those days for the father to have complete authority. His mother was more lenient and quite submissive to the head of the household. Decisions were made by his father, and the children were not expected to voice their opinions.

He recalls the various political events of his time with little feeling. His father had been a strong nationalist. The family saw the first world war as a holy crusade, but kept aloof from the tensions of the postwar era. In the '30's there were mixed feelings; they respected the NSDAP, he reports, although they did not approve of it entirely and remained largely noncommittal.

Herr R. feels detached from contemporary politics. "I have watched too many wrong decisions being made. I have become neutral and think that a united Europe would be the best solution. It means that we would have to become European nationals. . . ." He thinks that the only people really interested in politics are those who have special dealings with various government agencies; unfortunately, most people do not care, "because they cannot encompass everything and are not actually confronted with any questions that they ought to help decide." He does not discuss politics with anyone outside his own family. ". . . there is no point to it, and people are not competent, after all."

The most recent family political conversation he remembers was about the Eichmann trial, when he figured out mathematically that Eichmann could not possibly have killed all the people he is supposed to have—the number per day is an impossibility. This shows "how much nonsense people are supposed to swallow."

Herr R. supports no party. He prefers to keep aloof from partisan politics and to concentrate on the idea of a united Europe. He would like to see it as a third force in the world struggle for power. He prefers not to state which party he voted for at the last election. He describes his years of imprisonment in Russia and forced labor in the Crimea: "I had to work there as an engineer and saw what Russia is planning. I saw that everything is aimed solely toward technical progress in order to dominate the world. I served in the field of atomic science together with Russians and Germans. I saw how everyone is given his special task, how people are used in a rigid and one-sided manner, shut off from life, just in order to attain the required goal." Herr R. requested the interviewer not to ask him for any further details of his experiences, as he had signed an agreement with the Russians not to reveal any of the information he had gained.

Herr R. would let his sons choose any party they desired, but he would explain to them carefully the background and purposes of the DRP. He himself votes out of a sense of duty, but without any feeling of personal involvement. He follows election campaigns carefully, although he thinks that the country would be better off without them. He is often annoyed by election campaigns, sometimes contemptuous, never amused.

He attributes great importance to the government and orients to it very much as a subject. "After all, every regulation has the force of law and must be obeyed. Even though the citizen is touched only indirectly, we must do exactly as ordered. Think of the draft: the younger man must serve. Think of taxes; and so on." As far as the local government is concerned, Herr R. believes that it, too, affects him indirectly with its various laws and regulations. He says: "We don't realize how all of family life follows a life-scheme that has been determined by the state: from marriage, registration of children, the children's schooling, to death certificates."

Herr R. has had no contacts with his local or national representatives. He does not believe that he would ever approach them. If he had any problems, he would go to the appropriate government bureau in his city or write to the editor of *Der Spiegel*. He believes that a good citizen should vote and be ready to defend his country. Locally, he might join some citizen group in order to keep informed.

A German Headwaiter: An Allegiant Participant. *Herr Q. is an aware participant, satisfied with the politics of the Bonn Republic as well as with his role in it.*

Herr Q. is a German headwaiter working in a hotel in a large Bavarian city. He is thirty-five years old, married, and has two children in their early teens. The Q.'s live in a small, modern development house in the suburbs. The interview took place in the kitchen, which contains various modern electrical appliances and looks inviting with its dining corner and green plants.

He is proud of his work, having worked his way up from hotel trainee (three years) to steward with the North German Lloyd, merchant marine steward, hotel manager under the Occupation, bartender, and, finally, headwaiter in charge of table service for the entire hotel. He supervises twelve people and gets along well with all of them. He has considerable scope in planning, both for regular service and special functions, although his supervisor is in charge of work schedules.

If Herr Q. took some further training he could advance to the position of business manager, but even though his present salary is relatively modest, he has no further ambitions. "I should choose the same occupation again. You become quite a psychologist and connoisseur of people. You have many contacts, especially with people of foreign nationality, and your horizons expand—something that is not possible in other occupations." In his free time he enjoys reading and talking about politics and economics. The men he admires most are Adenauer and Erhard.

Herr Q.'s children are both attending public school. He is making careful plans for their future. His daughter has a bent for art and decoration and hopes to learn store window display. His son will become a television technician. He is interested in the field, and it should give him a good start in the army and in later life. He thinks that children have many more chances today. "My children shall choose whatever occupation appeals to them and for which they have the necessary interest and aptitude. Chances are better today, there is more scope socially, class barriers have disappeared, and views on child-rearing have changed. Children are being brought up to be independent human beings, and they are being permitted far more freedom in their choice of an occupation."

He and his wife share in making family decisions. "I discuss things with my wife. Both of us have sensible views and only want what is best for our family. Neither of us insists on always being right. Both our opinions have equal weight." Where exclusively adult matters are concerned, the children are not considered to be experienced enough to participate, but in things that concern them ". . . the children should have the feeling that they are taken seriously, and, besides, they should be brought up to be independent." Where the children's own future is concerned, Herr Q. puts it this way: "We ask the children and expect them to express their opinions and their wishes. If they are good ones we try to realize them, and if they are not we try to explain to the children what is not good about them. . . . In that way, they should develop their personalities and their independence as early as possible." In general, Herr Q. finds, family life is better than it was in the past. He is glad that women play a more important role than they have traditionally, and he feels that equality of the sexes makes for a more companionable family.

The Q.'s discuss politics frequently. Most recently, they talked about the American presidential election and relations between East and West.

He is a Catholic. He thinks that from the Church's point of view he would not be considered a good Catholic, but he feels that his belief in a higher being makes him a religious person. He sees religion as giving moral strength and support, and he has definite views on the role of the Church: "It should teach young people to be ethical and moral, but it should keep away from politics, and it should revise many of its views. Many of the teachings of the Church are obsolete. The whole organization of the Church should adapt itself to the times. It should try to win over its young people in a modern and timely manner without compulsion and without dogma. . . . Because of the developments of our times, we have stopped believing many of the things the Church has taught us. For instance, today we explore the universe and we send rockets to the moon. The kind of heaven that the Bible talks about has not been discovered. All that contributes to making us more critical of everything that is said by the Church and, finally, we free ourselves completely from all dogma. Nevertheless, in a certain sense, we are still religious and believe in a higher being."

Occupationally, Herr Q.'s neighborhood is quite mixed. There are farmers, businessmen, civil servants, and technical and commercial employees. He has not lived in the area for very long and does not know many people, but he has pleasant neighborly relations with many. He finds that everyone in the area is decent enough to be trusted, but does not think one can generalize nowadays: there has been so much mobility and mixing since the war. As far as neighborly help is concerned, people have become more careful, but they are still glad to lend tools to a neighbor or do similar small services.

Herr Q. attended elementary and secondary schools for eight years. The teachers were strict and not always fair. They were mostly National Socialists. The children were taught that Hitler was their savior, that the Fatherland was above all, and that they must be ready to give their life for it. The main events in his life so far have been political ones: specifically, the rise of National Socialism, the war, and the experiences of the postwar era. He finds that his entire thinking was changed and influenced by these events, particularly the postwar ones. He says: "The collapse of the Reich, my dealings with American officers, the growing awareness of German atrocities in the concentration camps—all that took away my illusions. I became more sober, more thoughtful, more careful, more suspicious. One lost one's idealistic attitude and one's confidence in politics." The Hitler period ". . . had a great effect on us when we heard and saw that Germany was playing an important role again and that the people were better off and everyone had enough work. We had the feeling that politics were something idealistic. When things kept getting worse, we became more and more thoughtful and wondered about the whole basis of the thing—especially the bombings, where women and children had to suffer as much as the soldiers at the front. Sometimes we simply could not decide any more between good and evil. We could not understand that the Americans could bomb our cities and attack defenseless women and children." He says of the Occupation: "Through my work I had many opportunities to meet Americans, and when I realized more and more what atrocities had been committed by the Germans in the concentration camps, the whole idealistic house of cards collapsed."

He likes to discuss political questions, and if there is no discussion going he will try to get one started. Today, he finds, everybody who

434

has an open mind is interested in politics. The number of those who do not care is constantly decreasing, and the few remaining ones will be just those who "don't want to hear or see anything, who want to shut themselves off from the outside world and only want to live within their own small, tightly limited, work-a-day existence." He follows the news in the daily press and the radio. He can discuss politics freely with everyone except extreme nationalists, whom he considers too rigid and too one-sided to talk to.

Herr Q. supports the CDU but wants it understood that he opposes a one-party system. There should be as much diversity of political thought as possible. He finds that the CDU has "a clear and worthwhile aim: the creation of a democratic Germany in which freedom and law and the desires of the individual stand in first place." He thinks that the CDU has kept all its promises, so far, and has remained true to its principles. The party he opposes particularly is the DRP. He considers it a neo-Nazi party and does not ever want such a group to come into power again.

He thinks that government is very important. ". . . just as a train cannot be without an engineer, a business without a boss, or a man without a head, so a state cannot be without a government." He feels that government is responsible for maintaining the security and stability of the country and for seeing that he and his family can live and prosper in peace. The local government, too, is effective. Herr Q. cites some specific examples of local services, and adds, "The local government sees to it that we can lead a life of human dignity."

In his work he meets many government officials, including high governmental officials. Whenever he can, he tries to engage them in conversation and learn about their work and their problems. If he had any personal difficulties, however, he would not contact his Bundestag deputy, for he feels the man's influence would be too limited. As an individual he puts his faith in administrative officials rather than elected ones. But if he were concerned with some large-scale national problem, he would seek like-minded people and work through his political party. He thinks a good citizen should take a part in his local government, attend meetings, and voice his opinions. As a good German he should do his work well, pay his taxes, vote, and be ready to defend his country.

A German Farmer's Widow: A Subject/Parochial. *Frau P. is interested mostly in her family and farm. Politics is for men. Though*

435

she votes, her political affiliation is largely a reflection of her religious views.

Frau P. is a fifty-nine-year-old German farmer's widow. She has eight grown children of whom three, one son and two daughters, have stayed at home and are helping her to run the farm. Her village consists of scattered, medium-sized farms. The houses are mostly old and simple, but well kept. There are few modern conveniences. One can see orchards and vegetable gardens but no flowers or trimmed hedges. The interview took place in Frau P.'s kitchen, which is small and dark and contains no furniture other than a coal stove, a table, and three chairs.

Frau P.'s life is centered in her family, her farm, her church. She cannot imagine what she might like to do if she had any free time, since she has never had any. Things have not changed very much for farmers. Those children who cannot stay on the farm do have an easier time in finding work, but for girls and women especially, farm work will continue as it always has. Her views on family life are conservative. Children should not participate in making decisions until they are about eighteen years of age, and even then they cannot be expected to have the necessary experience. Actually, there are few things to be decided: the family stays on the farm, there are very few major purchases, and children are not expected to discuss their future plans as long as they are "too young."

She is a Catholic and goes to church every Sunday. It is natural for her to be a Catholic, to believe, and to fulfill her obligations. She knows that everyone around her believes in God and is a Catholic, although in the cities, she thinks, it may be different.

Some of the men of the village—those whose farms are small— work in the peat bogs in the summer, and some others have begun to work in town, largely in the building trades. There are a few refugees who have found quarters in various farmhouses, but none of these developments have yet made much impact on the village. She knows all the "old" residents. They get along well, but there is no actual visiting. She rarely leaves her home, but in times of need and at harvest time people will get together and help each other.

Politics does not bulk large in her memory. She remembers that during the First World War people would come from the city in search of food, and that during the Weimar Republic farm prices were low and the farmers suffered. Hitler's rise to power did not change things in the village, except that farm prices rose again. The

436

Second World War brought worries: "war is always terrible." One of Mrs. P.'s sons was wounded. During the Occupation people again came from town, hoping to buy food. As a child she was taught to love her country and the Kaiser, but she has hardly ever discussed politics or government. Those things are for men only. Actually, in her village even the men do not often discuss politics. As farmers they are kept busy enough with their work.

Her political affiliation largely reflects her religious views. She supports the CDU because "we are all Catholic here, after all." She does not know whether there are any parties that she would disapprove of. She is sure that her children will choose the CDU. She voted last year because ". . . we have to around here. They always come and call for us."

She thinks that government affects her little. Occasionally, there may be an increase in old-age pensions or some farm subsidy, but that is all. Locally, new roads are being built and everyone has to pay taxes. Frau P. does not know for what other purposes tax money may be used. She does not wish for any improvements by any branch of the government and believes that they are doing as well as they can with the funds available. She is satisfied with the administration of her village. She knows the village constable and also the mayor, who is one of the neighboring farmers. She thinks that they are doing their job well, but regards them as neighbors rather than as government officials.

Frau P. reads a daily newspaper and occasionally listens to the news over the radio. If she wanted further clarification she would turn to her son or to the mayor. She discusses politics rarely and then only with her son. She feels competent as a local citizen and believes that one should speak up at local council meetings, but she does not think that she could do anything about a national problem.

A Refugee Housewife: A Subject. *Frau A. is not politically involved and would prefer to leave such problems to others; they are not for women. As with many German respondents, political memories are ambiguous and painful.*

Frau A. is a refugee housewife from Saxony, now settled with her family in a Bavarian tourist town. Her husband is a railroad conductor. They have three children ranging in age from six to twenty years.

She is very dissatisfied with modern family life. She thinks women ought to be more feminine, more passive, and should be the "soul"

437

of the family. The modern "career woman" is offensive to her, and she thinks that children nowadays have no standards. The flashiness and luxury of the tourists who visit their town also offend her sense of values. Frau A. would like to trust people, but she feels that one has to be careful. Except for a small spiritual elite who are willing to help, people are generally selfish.

Her father was a poorly paid civil servant, who supplemented his income by acting as a building superintendent in a boarding school in return for free accommodations. She attended a Catholic school, where the discipline was severe. "The Catholic teachers were terribly strict. There were many beatings—even in the eighth grade; I still remember that I always thought that my soul was in danger, since the chaplain and the teacher were one and the same person for many of the subjects, and I was quite an individual and was often beaten when I did something against his will." At home, when she complained about school there was little comfort. "Father just wouldn't believe me, and when I said something, he would beat me again, in the bargain."

During the Nazi period her family supported the Hitler regime. ". . . the world would not leave us a German honor. We all resented that, and even my brothers began to favor Hitler." When the Nazis came to power, "I thought that Germany's resurrection had come at last. . . . Away with dreadful party quarrels! At last, I thought, our people is achieving national consciousness, knows what has to be done in order to live . . . as a united people." As the Nazi era progressed, Frau A. felt thrilled that "decency, morals, and discipline were going to return to our confused times, but then, when everyone was supposed to march in formation, everything to be regimented, I realized what we were faced with." Of the Second World War she says, "The bombings, fire everywhere, the collapse, the neglect and confusion, the moral and ethical degeneration, all that depressed and horrified me. Could we still believe in anything —and in what?"

She says of the Occupation, "That, too, shocked me. To seduce young girls with chocolate, to try to make an American colony of us . . . where can you still find life's values? That, only that, occupied my thoughts."

After leaving Saxony, Frau A. withdrew from the Catholic Church and joined a small Protestant sect. Her group meets once or twice a week to study the Bible, break bread, and pray together.

She gave up Catholicism when she found out ". . . what miserable Christianity is behind it all . . . when as refugees we had no bed, nothing, and asked for help, they refused. They would not even let us sleep on the floor. What sham Christianity—the things I could tell you!"

Of contemporary German society she says, "We have done much, politically, but now we must approach the inner person. I find these times so upsetting. They remind me of a kind of inflation. . . . Where is the people's capital? Everything is thrown away with abandon. People travel to Italy—they have nothing, they are nothing, but they throw their money out of the window. The government does nothing. Surely, Adenauer must realize what is going on. Pensioners get eighty DM. a month, and young things doing some mechanical work earn four hundred to eight hundred DM. . . ."

She reports no interest in politics. The people who are interested are mainly businessmen, church people, and those who have direct dealings with the government. Most people do not care, especially those who have lost everything. She supports no political party. "The CDU is too Catholic, the SPD is too godless. And not the FDP—I just don't know what to say." She might favor a party that combined the best qualities of all three. Her children will have freedom of choice, although she will draw their attention to the shortcomings of the various parties, especially those that are one-sided and radical. Frau A. herself has never voted, "out of inner conviction." She avoids discussing politics with others, as she considers most people too one-sided in their views and unable to see things from a national point of view.

Frau A. does not find that the national government has much effect on her life, except perhaps through its laws. Nor does the local government touch her much. "It's just that the children have to go to school and we have to obey the traffic regulations. . . . Otherwise, we really have nothing to do with it."

Frau A. thinks that a good citizen should be active in philanthropic work, such as the Red Cross; he should be honorable, unselfish, hardworking, and pay his taxes fairly. If she had any complaint against her local government, she would go or write to the proper bureau and present her point of view. She feels sure of a courteous reception. If the threat of injustice came from Bonn, however, she would feel powerless to act. She is sure that it is only special interest groups, industry, capital, the Church, who have influence.

439

The United States: A Participant Civic Culture

The pattern of political culture found in the United States approximates what we have labeled the civic culture. There are several significant components of this cultural pattern. In the first place, the role of the participant is highly developed and widespread. As our data show, respondents in the United States, compared with those in the other four nations, are very frequently exposed to politics. They report political discussion and involvement in political affairs, a sense of obligation to take an active part in the community, and a sense of competence to influence the government. They are frequently active members of voluntary associations. Furthermore, they tend to be affectively involved in the political system: they report emotional involvement during political campaigns, and they have a high degree of pride in the political system. And their attachment to the political system includes both generalized system affect as well as satisfaction with specific governmental performance.

The civic culture, though, is a mixed and incorporative culture. The participant role is highly developed, but the more passive roles of subject and parochial persist, and are fused with the political system. That these other orientations temper the performance of the participant role can be shown by the fact that primary affiliations are important in setting the political style of participation in the United States. They are both an influence resource, providing individuals with what we have called a reserve of influence, and an important link in the political communications process. Moreover, the ability to cooperate with one's fellow citizens, which the use of informal groups as a political resource reflects, appears to depend upon a more general social trust and confidence that permeate the political system. This social trust is also seen in the "open" pattern of partisanship in the United States. Though there is emotional involvement in the outcome of elections, this does not mean complete rejection of one's political opponent.

The civic culture, then, is characterized by balance among the parochial, subject, and participant roles. But though the American political culture comes close to this balance, the data suggest that there is some imbalance in the direction of the participant role. As was suggested in Chapter 8, participant orientation in the United States appears better developed than subject orientation and to some extent dominates it. Subject competence seems to depend upon po-

440

litical competence; those Americans who feel competent in bureaucratic authority contexts are likely to be those who feel competent in political contexts. In the specific measures of subject competence —expectations of consideration by bureaucratic and police authority —the Americans drop to third place among our five countries, below Britain and Germany. This cultural imbalance, we have suggested, is the result of American historical experience with governmental and bureaucratic authority—an experience that began with distrust and revolution against the British Crown, and that has been consolidated by the American tendency to subject all governmental institutions, including the judiciary and bureaucracy, to direct popular control.

An American Stenographer: An Allegiant Participant. *Miss E. illustrates that civic norms may be fairly well developed by the time an individual first enters an adult political role.*

Miss E. is an eighteen-year-old American girl, living in a small country town in the South. She lives at home and is engaged to be married. She had a short working experience as a stenographer in a lawyer's office, but found the legal terminology difficult. She adds: "I just don't like working in an office. I'd rather be a plain housewife, and that's what I'm planning to be." She does remember her employer quite fondly: "He was just as nice as he could be, not hard-boiled. I guess I was pretty dumb, but he always joked with me and put up with whatever I did."

Miss E. is one of four children. She is used to having her father have the final word in family decisions, but feels free to state her views. She thinks that perhaps young people do not have quite enough voice in family decisions, but then adds: "Oh, I guess they do, really! It's just that sometimes we think we don't."

Miss E.'s main outside interest is her Baptist church. She attends services and meetings about three times a week and is a member of two church organizations as well as the YWCA. Of religion she says: "I think it should be very important. I believe our leaders should be good men and look to God for help, but I think it's wrong to say that they should belong to one church or can't belong to another. I think it's all right for a Catholic to be President, because one of the things that we were always taught was that this country was founded for the religious freedom, and even if our preacher says we shouldn't have a Catholic I don't see why not."

Miss E.'s neighbors are mostly rural working class. The majority, including her father, are employed at a large local paper mill, but there are still some full-time farmers and farm laborers in the area. The neighborhood is stable and friendly. Miss E. says: "When there's sickness in the family or a death, all the neighbors come in and help. The family below us had a fire, and the people for miles around brought clothes and furniture, money too, to help them get started over." Miss E.'s childhood is still too recent for her to have much perspective on it. She knows that they have become a little more prosperous of late and were able to build a new five-room house a few years ago. She describes her father as the stricter parent: "He was the one we all minded. We kind of jumped when he told us to do something. He was good to us though, and he was a lot of fun. He was pretty strict, but not any stricter than we needed. Mama was the one who always took our part, and she'd listen to us more." The children were permitted some participation in the family decisions that concerned their future, but they had little to say in matters such as family purchases. Miss E. was fairly content, though. She says: "I never thought much about it. I just knew we always got along fine. We never though they were too hard on us, or almost never. Maybe, they wouldn't let us do everything we thought we ought to, but they were probably right."

Miss E. has happy memories of her elementary and high school days. She says of her teachers: "They were very sweet. They helped you all they could. They seemed to be able to make the children mind without being too hard on them." Miss E. remembers that there was "a student council. There was a student from every home-room on it, and they took any problems the students had to the council, where the council voted on the problems." The school was quite active in the areas of government and civics. Miss E. says: "They taught us a lot! Especially in my last year, we studied current events and we had an awfully good course in American history, and at the end of the year we took up the study of the government—what the different branches are, what each one does, and what the different duties are. We were taught to understand our government and re-spect it. In elementary school, especially, we had patriotic programs —about Washington, Lincoln, and great men in the South."

The subject of politics is very much on the family's mind at the moment. Miss E. says: "It's the main subject around here this year. Our most recent discussion was yesterday. It was whether a Catholic should be elected President. There was a crowd around here, including two preachers, and we discussed it pretty strong. . . . We all speak our minds. Mama is interested and reads a lot, and of course Daddy has always liked it." The family disagrees at times, and Miss E. recalls: "In the Democratic primary for governor, Daddy was for one man, and Mama and I were for another. Mama and Daddy both voted the way they pleased for different candidates."

Miss E. finds that she is beginning to be very interested in politics at this time, as it is an election year. She says: "I guess it's because Mama and Daddy talk about it a lot. Then there's a lot on TV and in the papers about it now. I think it's sort of exciting." She finds that the people who care about politics are the ones "who are well informed, people who read, and people who have been brought up in families where their parents talk about it." Of the kind of people who are not interested in politics Miss E. says: "They are mainly people who aren't educated, but sometimes education isn't the main thing, for lots of people with education are just careless or indifferent or something. They just don't take any interest in politics, but I think everybody should. Well, if you're really interested in your country, you ought to be interested in electing good people."

Miss E. considers herself a Democrat, although she is still too young to vote. She says: "I guess it's because my family are Democrats. I've always thought it stands for the little people. . . . But I feel that when I have children they can make up their own minds. If they felt like being Republicans, I'd feel they had good reasons." Miss E. feels particularly strongly about religion as an issue in the coming election. She says: "It don't seem fair to me to hold anyone's religion against them. If they believe in God, I don't see why Jesus wouldn't save a Catholic too, and our country is supposed to have religious freedom, and it just makes me mad what they are telling about Catholics. Of course, I don't know much about Catholics, but I just don't believe what they are saying is all so, that they worship idols and that they are worse than Communists."

Miss E. is well informed on the uses of tax funds and is on the whole satisfied with the ways in which tax money is being used. She has had some routine official contacts, at the local Social Security Office for instance, and she found the officials "in every way as nice as could be." She remembers her father's writing to the governor about some state problem and receiving a pleasant and courteous reply. She feels that she would always be treated with friendliness and consideration by any government official.

Miss E. thinks that a good citizen should vote and should take part in community, church, and school affairs. He "should be loyal and obey the laws. He should be patriotic, be proud of his country, and do whatever he can to keep it free." If she disapproved of some ordinance of her local government, Miss E. would "talk to them, go to see them, and tell them I didn't approve of it. I could get up a petition if they would let me—if I was old enough." On the national level she would write to her congressman. Miss E. takes pride in her country, and says: "We have freedom. It's a democracy. We can worship as we feel we want to. We have a good government, and we are one of the great powers in the world. We can elect the people we want to to run the government."

A Retired Civil Engineer: An Allegiant Participant. *Mr. C. is politically aware and has a relatively well developed sense of competence. He is generally allegiant to the system, but his strong views lead to some serious reservation and to a fairly high level of hostility to political opponents.*

Mr. C. is a retired civil engineer living in a small town. He is married and has three grown sons. Mr. C. finds that life has changed considerably since he was young: "It's been the general changes in the economy and system of government, and other things: they're all different. When we were young we didn't buy unless we had enough money to pay for it. Nowadays, you buy and then pay if and when you can. This country is up to its neck in credit. . . ."

In talking about family problems in general, Mr. C. feels that today "kids have too much rope" and should be brought up more strictly. They should be permitted to voice their opinions at home in matters concerning their eduction or their future, but nowadays they "just do as they please and the parents let them."

Mr. C. is a Protestant and considers himself to be a religious person. He has strong and varied feelings about the general role of religion. He says: "It should occupy a prominent place in the life of the country. I don't believe in prohibiting the reading of the Bible in schools. . . . I believe in the separation of church and state, yet I believe that some part of religion should be recognized by the government, and those who don't like it should get the hell out. I believe that Jews and other non-Christians should be tolerated, but

444

they should not dictate to the government what religious policies should be. The principle is: this country is Christian. I don't believe in public support of Catholic schools."

Mr. C. grew up in the same town in which he lives now. He knows most of the people in it, considers many of them his friends, but does little actual visiting. He trusts people but finds most of them quite selfish. His father was a small storekeeper who, though his income was limited, managed to support his wife and son. Mr. C. remembers that "father was a good person. He got along very well with other people. He was a good businessman. I admire him for being a good worker. He was well trusted by those in town. My mother was strict as far as the family was concerned. She and father were religious and were both active in religious work." Mr. C. found that he could talk freely to both parents and was allowed a voice in personal matters, such as clothing or school decisions. Mr. C. remembers that people were more helpful in those days. "Now they want to know what they can get out of it, maybe because of changes in employer-employee relationships. Before unions there was cooperation."

Mr. C. admired his teachers at school: "They were well prepared and well trained scholastically, and they had discipline. They didn't spare the rod. Of course, it's not the teachers' fault today. The parents will have them in jail if they dare touch their child. . . . There was one teacher who was able to teach me more than the others. He was a very strict disciplinarian." At college Mr. C. was a member of a politics club. He remembers: "We talked politics, and one thing that I noticed is that action is too slow in a democratic form of government. I don't know what can be done about it."

Mr. C. has a wide range of political memories: "I was a Republican because my father was. I don't know today—the parties are different from when I was a boy. Parties should have different names, maybe Conservative and Liberal, something like that. I have always been concerned with the outcome of all the socialist principles that you hear nowadays—Social Security and things like that. I am wondering what the end result will be." Mr. C. remembers all specific political events clearly and with firm convictions. He finds that the First World War was a Democratic device to get the country out of economic trouble, and that the Depression was a natural consequence and unconnected with politics. He opposed the New Deal: "I felt the New Deal came from underneath the deck. . . . Because of it, I made up my mind never to work for a Democrat." The Second

445

World War ". . . was probably unavoidable, but again it was a Democratic administration" and ". . . we should have let Hitler and Stalin knock each other off." Of the Korean War Mr. C. says: "I thought it was a mistake of President Truman to get rid of Mac-Arthur"; and of the desegregation decision: "I'm in favor of the Negro having just as good schools as the white, but I'm not in favor of mixing them up. The good Lord didn't make white and black with the idea of mixing them up so you can't tell the difference."

Mr. C. is vitally interested in politics, and the family has lively political discussions. Mr. C. recalls the last Fourth of July, when the whole family was together and everyone discussed Cuba, Communism, and the presidential campaign, with special reference to the religion of the candidates. Everyone talked; parents, sons, and daughters-in-law. Opinions varied, but the discussion was amiable. He gives as his reason for political interest: "It's everybody's duty. Whatever is done has an effect on everybody, individually and collectively." He finds that all alert and public-spirited people care, but he has contempt for what he calls "professional politicians." He supports the Republican party, as he considers himself "by nature a conservative"; and he criticizes the Democratic party for "all those socialistic principles: social security, fixing of minimum wages, the support of unions. . . . I can't understand why a working man should tell an employer what he's going to do, what he's going to pay." He would not like to see his children join the Democratic party.

Mr. C. never misses an election. He has had some routine contacts with tax officials and with a state senator and in both cases found the officials cordial and quite helpful. Mr. C. finds that a good citizen "should take office if called upon and should be active in social and charitable affairs in his community. He should support the country morally and financially and should support those elected officials who are trying to enforce the laws." If you disapprove of some local ordinance, Mr. C. says that you should "fight against it in your conversations and get your ideas across to other people." In a national matter he would write to his congressman or try to have a political candidate commit himself before election. The things he admires most in his country are "its freedom of speech and religion, its freedom in general."

A Widow: An Aspiring/Active Participant. *Mrs. P. shares with many other Americans civic participatory norms and pride in the*

446

political system. She also has a sense of political competence and involvement, though much of this is new to her. Her view of the performance of the system is more mixed, however, for what she desires is a full sense of participation.

Mrs. P. is a sixty-year-old Southern Negress who is widowed and shares a small house with her brother. She is quite poor, and her house is old and badly in need of repair. As she looks back on her life, she finds that everything is much easier than it used to be. She says: "When I was a child you did good to get three years of schooling because they had hardly any schools in the country, and when they did, it did not last but about four or five months out of a year. There was no kind of entertainment at all. The only work you could find was in somebody else's field, and that did not pay anything much. Today there are better schools; a person can get as much education as he wants now. The houses are more modern and convenient, and there are more jobs to be had, too. The government helps with the schools. There used not to be anything but church schools. There are more industries, and that makes more jobs. People have more money to spend and are buying more."

Mrs. P. feels close to her church. She attends services "every time the church doors are opened," is the superintendent of the "Sabbath School," and belongs to various church groups. She believes that religion should have the highest place in the country, and says: "People were more religious when I was a child. They had good old-fashioned revivals, and people really tried to live by the Bible and keep the Sabbath holy. People wash, iron, and do everything else on the Sabbath now. There are so many works of the devil to get peoples' minds off religion now—the picture shows, television, and all kinds of gimmicks."

In Mrs. P.'s neighborhood there are working- and middle-class people, but she counts herself among the poorer ones. She finds everyone around her to be pleasant and friendly, and she mentions: "I do missionary work and have never been refused help for someone less fortunate when I have asked these people for help."

Mrs. P.'s father was a cotton farmer. She recalls: "We had plenty of food because we grew everything, but there was never any money for anything." There were five children in the family, who all felt very close to each other, but Mrs. P. remembers her father as being very strict. "It was better to obey him than to put up a fuss. I don't think he had a soft spot anywhere. He was the supreme law in our

447

house. There were no decisions to make; he stated the facts, and that was that. My mother was very sweet and timid. I have never remembered her losing her temper. She was not a very strict person, but we obeyed her because we loved her so." The neighbors in the area were mostly farmers, and "they were very, very poor. Some were even almost starving." People helped one another at harvest time and in times of illness, but the houses were too far apart for any social visiting.

As a child Mrs. P. completed only a few years of primary school, but after her husband died she felt that she wanted to graduate from elementary school, at least. She attended evening classes for adults until she completed the equivalent of eight years of education. She has pleasant memories of one teacher, who "had so much patience with us because it was harder for adults to catch on to the book learning. She was so understanding." Mrs. P. adds: "I got enough education to hold a decent conversation and to give me confidence in myself."

Mrs. P. lists three people whom she admires especially: "Mr. E., a Jewish businessman of our city, who is very generous and thoughtful to all people, and especially to our race. Mr. Abraham Lincoln, who came up in poverty but did not let that be an obstacle to himself— he succeeded in spite of all, and Booker T. Washington, because he established that wonderful institution, Tuskegee College, for the colored people."

The greatest event in Mrs. P.'s life was her coming to the industrial city of B. and meeting her future husband there. Mrs. P.'s most outstanding political memory is of the election of Franklin D. Roosevelt. She says: "I never paid politics any attention until Roosevelt got elected. We had had such a hard time while Hoover was in office, and things began to get better so fast after Roosevelt got in that I began to notice the different parties. Then, too, I got a radio, and they would have the news on the radio, and a lot of things I would read in the newspaper but I didn't understand what I read, but when they would talk about it over the radio it would be clearer in my mind, and I would kind of keep up an interest in politics."

Mrs. P. remembers the Depression vividly: "Everybody nearly starved to death, and some folks did starve. That was during Hoover's time, and they even had soup lines to feed the folks, and the bakeries were giving away bread to keep people from starving. I ate it many a day, and that was all. I almost starved too, because there was no work for anyone. The Republicans were starving us poor folks to death, and I ain't had nothing to do with a Republican since. But when my husband finally got something to do with the WPA, it wasn't much money, but it gave us our self-respect back. . . . I said: 'May God bless Mr. Roosevelt and the Democrats, too.' "

Mrs. P. was first pleased and then disillusioned by the school desegregation decision: "I said, now some children won't have to ride half-way around the country before day in the morning to get to school. They can go to school right in their community, be it white or colored. But that was the biggest lie I ever told, because then the bombings started all over the country. I said the Republicans have really done it this time—just plain messed up. They passed a law, but did nothing to see that the law was carried out. They could *make* all these Southern places let the children go to school nearest their home and not go by the color of their skin."

Mrs. P. takes a great deal of interest in politics. She has recently registered as a voter. Referring to the first cross-section interview, she told the interviewer: "When you came before and asked all those questions I was really ashamed because I wasn't a voter. After that I started going to the civic meeting out here so I could learn how to vote, and then I went down and passed, and now I am a voter." She finds that "all thinking people" are interested in politics. When asked what political party she opposes, she mentions the Communist party. "They stand for the overthrow of the United States, and, according to the papers, it is backed by Russia. I don't want no part of the Russian way, and I think we have a good country as a whole." While Mrs. P. will vote Democratic in her first national election, she would let her children choose their own party. "It would be their privilege to vote as they saw fit." For additional information on some political problem, Mrs. P. would turn to her "minister, who is good about explaining things I don't understand," as well as to newspapers and the radio. She does not think that the national government has much effect, but reports in detail how local services and regulations touch her life. She approves of the way tax funds are spent, but wishes for better street maintenance in her neighborhood. She has had contacts with tax officials and staff members of a city hospital and clinic and found that she was treated very fairly. As a member of an organization called "The Christian Movement," she has tried to combat "local laws which take away a colored citizen's human and civil rights"; but the group's protests have been ignored.

449

Mrs. P. says that a good citizen should be "informed and should know who the officials are who run the affairs of the town." He should serve his country in every way possible, especially in times of war, and should "live a spiritually clean life." If she disapproved of some federal law, she would write to her senator. On the local level she would ". . . discuss it and let other people whom you come in contact with know about it being unjust or harmful." She adds, "Well, if enough see it my way, I can get up a petition." As far as her country as a whole is concerned, Mrs. P. is proud of "our beautiful churches, schools, and buildings, and our democratic form of government."

A Parochial American Housewife. *Typical of many American female parochials, Mrs. W. is interested mostly in religion and in her family and private life. Politics is explicitly a "man's business." Yet one finds at least the norms of civic participation and some sense that the political system is amenable to influence—at least by her husband if not by her.*

Mrs. W. is a middle-aged American housewife who lives in a small southern town. Now that her daughter is grown, her main outside interests are church work, gardening, and her grandchildren. Her husband is a manual laborer in a large paper mill, where he is well paid and contented. They find that their lives are serene and unchanging, although the last few years have brought some additional comforts for everyone. The people she admires most are Billy Graham and the actress Loretta Young.

The W.'s like to make their family decisions jointly, with Mr. W. having the final word whenever that is necessary. They feel that children should be permitted to participate when they become about fifteen years old. They discuss politics on occasion. Mrs. W. adds: "My son-in-law and my husband do it mostly. Sometimes me and my daughter talk some, but we let the men do most of the talking." Mrs. W. is a religious woman. She attends her Baptist church twice on Sundays and goes to prayer meetings three times during the week. She is a member of the Church's Women's Society and feels that religion should have first place in the country. She says: "If a people don't put God first, that country is bound to fall."

Mrs. W. finds all the people in her area to be good neighbors. They help each other in times of need and can all be trusted. She herself was born in a small isolated mountain village, where her father was a tenant farmer. There were five children, and although the family was poor, it "managed" and was content. Mrs. W. remembers that her "father wasn't a hard man, but, of course, he made us mind." She describes her mother as sweet, gentle, and patient. The children were occasionally consulted on their plans for the future, but little other participation was expected of them.

The neighbors in those days were as friendly as they are today, but were perhaps a little more dependent on each other for help. Mrs. W. attended a small, three-teacher country school. The teachers were strict but fair, and Mrs. W. felt free to approach them.

Mrs. W.'s main memories are all personal ones: her mother's death, her marriage, the birth of her daughter. Political matters have left little trace. Of the Second World War she remembers "nothing but that there was one." However, she does recall the Supreme Court's desegregation decision. She does not approve of it, and says: "I don't believe God meant us to be mixed up, and if them people up North would mind their business we would mind ours." On the whole, she is not interested in politics, and adds: "Men are, mostly. People that is out in public life more, like teachers. I just never did follow it much. Women that have their work to do don't have too much time for things like that." If Mrs. W. did want some further information on a political issues she would ask her husband, or "I might try to understand what was in the papers or ask the preacher to explain it."

Mrs. W. was "raised" a Democrat, but she reports that "my husband is a Republican—so I guess I am." She does not vote. "I guess there is a lot of women like me that just never got in the habit of voting. I let my husband do that." She believes that the government has probably quite a lot of influence on people's lives and mentions social security, tobacco growers' quotas, roads, and schools. As far as tax funds are concerned, she believes that "the politicians get a lot." She adds: "I think there is a lot of waste. We have to pay taxes to Washington and to North Carolina and the county, but I reckon I ought not to complain. We're better off than people in other places. A missionary told us that we had more real rich people than in other countries." She is satisfied with her government and finds that only the schools might be in need of improvement. She has had no government contacts, but recalls the time her husband was involved in a minor automobile collision and found that "the patrolman was real nice."

451

Mrs. W. feels that as a good citizen you "should do your part. . . . You should take an interest in things—school things—and I think you can do a lot of good if you do your part of church work." You owe your country "honesty, not to impose on other people, and your vote." If Mrs. W. disagreed with some local ordinance, she thinks that she could go to the court house. She says: "I could stand up for my beliefs. I could go to the county officers, but I'd probably get my husband to go." In a national matter Mrs. W. finds: "I could vote against it if it was put to a vote. I could write a letter to my congressman."

Mrs. W. is proud of her country: "Of our freedom; well, we are free. We can do what we please if we don't break the law. Of our churches; nearly everybody is a Christian and we can go to whatever church we please. Of our homes; we can make them as nice as we can afford to or are willing to work for, we can raise our children according to what we think is the right thing and not have to be told how to raise them or what to teach them. That's what I'm proud of."

A Miner: An Allegiant Subject. Mr. F. is an example of an allegiant subject. He is relatively satisfied with governmental output, and has no desire for a greater participant role. The political norms he subscribes to involve obedience and passivity.

Mr. F. is a Southern Negro miner of near-retirement age, living in a small, shabby, but well-kept cottage in a mining area. He is content with his work and finds that the mine has "taken care of him all these years." He has little leeway on the job and believes: "It's better not to make suggestions, and I know I ain't, it's too close to pension time. . . . When they give orders they don't care how the orders affect you, just so you get the company's work done. . . . I get along fine because I know my place, as the old saying goes." Nevertheless, Mr. F. finds that life is better than it was. "The children get much better education than when I was a child—they can do a thousand different jobs."

Mr. F. is a religious man. He attends his Baptist church twice a month and thinks that "all our leaders should be religious people." At home he and his wife reach all their family decisions jointly and discuss politics on occasion. They never disagree because, as Mr. F. says, "Neither of us know what we are talking about. I know just what little I can read and understand and what I can see and hear on television and radio and what the men say at work." Mr. F. is reluctant to discuss politics with outsiders. "I would not talk with anybody who did not understand at all and was just looking for an argument. Sometimes white people will ask you what you think about things, and if you differ they will try to force their idea on you and get angry if you stick to your idea." In his free time, however, Mr. F. enjoys learning about the outside world. His main reaction is newspaper reading, listening to the radio, and watching television. He has great admiration for the Reverend Martin Luther King and President Eisenhower.

Mr. F.'s neighbors are all connected with the mine in some way, and they are all quite poor. They help and trust each other, though, and Mr. F. feels that "people have a sort of kinship feeling in small areas." (As an example, he says: "We have been helping that man and his family up there in that third house almost a year now and will keep on helping till he is back on his feet again. Everybody here has been good to them—money, food, and medicines, our time and energy.")

Mr. F. grew up in considerable poverty in a mining camp shack. He was one of six children and does not remember his father, but he recalls that his mother "was very strict, and if you did not pay what she said any mind, she could really whip you good. She did not like to visit other people's homes and thought that they should keep their children at home, too." Mr. F.'s uncle, however, was devoted to the family, and Mr. F. remembers him as a man "who really understood children." Mr. F.'s mother did not permit her children to take part in any family decisions, and Mr. F. recalls, "We never had any say in anything, and every child has a mind of its own, and after you get to a certain age you just want to use your mind sometimes. . . ."

The F.'s neighbors were poor and quite friendly, but they were looked down upon by the townspeople. Even the teachers "always seemed to look down on us children because we were mining camp children. They associated us with loudness and roughness. . . . You know, all the week end when the mines are closed the people have a good time drinking, dancing, playing cards, eating, and the camp is just a loud place then. The teachers were from town, and they just could not understand this mining camp life. They thought we and our parents were worthless. But there has been some good folk raised in the camp—school teachers and everything."

Mr. F. remembers his uncle's kindness as the most important event in his life. As the most important political event, he recalls "the election of Roosevelt. He made things better for the miners—in fact, all working people. We got social security protection, safer mines, more health benefits, and unemployment compensation. It made me take a little interest in politics and specially the Democratic party." Mr. F. still remembers the Depression more clearly than any other event. "I nearly starved to death and you never caught up with yourself with what little money you made. . . . I did like everybody else; I blamed the conditions on the Republicans and still do. The Republicans is for the rich man and big business and not for the working man or the poor man." Mr. F. recalls the Second World War and the Korean War in terms of prosperity, because of the increased need for steel at the time. As far as the Supreme Court's desegration decision is concerned, Mr. F. thinks: "I said it was just going to bring on a lot of troubles, and it did."

Mr. F. has "just a little" interest in politics. He says, "I feel what will be will be, anyway." He finds that it is the uneducated people, the people like himself, who have little interest. It is the educated, politicians, and business people who know and care about politics. However, Mr. F. strongly favors the Democratic party. When asked if there is a political party he opposes, he mentions the Communists and says, "According to what I hear and read about the Communist party I would not have any interest. It stands for doing away with the American way of life. Everybody will be working for the state and take what the state gives you." If Mr. F. had children, he would permit them to support any party they chose.

Mr. F. has never voted. He believes that the federal government affects his life in no way, and thinks that only the President has an effect on the country as a whole. The local government, however, "makes all of the town rules and laws we have to go by . . . it serves you and furnishes you police protection." Mr. F. knows how taxes are used for local services and finds those services to be adequate on the whole. He does wish for some improvements in housing and general living conditions and thinks that the national government under the Democrats might bring about some change; but to hope for that kind of help from the local government "would be like daydreaming. I mean, they are not much concerned about the people."

Mr. F. has had no direct government contacts. If he were dissatisfied with any local situation, he would feel powerless to correct it. He says, "I could not do anything but talk against it, but I don't see where that would do much good." In a national matter Mr. F. believes that he could not do anything either, but on second thought he finds that "I could get some of my friends and we could write a letter to Senator H. and let him know we did not think the law was a good one." Mr. F. considers the obligations of the good citizen to be passive. A good citizen is one who "obeys the laws of his town, votes, if he is a registered voter, and pays whatever taxes he is supposed to pay," who defends his country in times of war and who "obeys the rules." Mr. F. is proud of his country. He says, "It's a free country. You can worship in any church you want to. You can work anywhere and buy what you want with your money. It is a beautiful country."

Great Britain: A Deferential Civic Culture

The political culture in Great Britain also approximates the civic culture. The participant role is highly developed. Exposure to politics, interest, involvement, and a sense of competence are relatively high. There are norms supporting political activity, as well as emotional involvement in elections and system affect. And the attachment to the system is a balanced one: there is general system pride as well as satisfaction with specific governmental performance.

Furthermore, the British political culture, like the American, fuses parochial and subject roles with the role of participant. Primary groups are relatively open to the political process and available as influence resources, and the political culture is permeated by more general attitudes of social trust and confidence. Open patterns of partisanship predominate. To some extent, the British political culture represents a more effective combination of the subject and participant roles. As was suggested in Chapter 8, the development of the participant orientation in Britain did not challenge and replace the more deferential subject orientations, as was the tendency in the United States. Despite the spread of political competence and participant orientations, the British have maintained a strong deference to the independent authority of government. Thus the British political culture, like the American, approximates the balanced civic culture; but the balance is weighted somewhat differently from that in the United States. If in the latter country there tends to be too much weight placed on the participant role, in Britain the deferrential subject role is more strongly developed and widespread.

A British White-Collar Worker: An Allegiant Participant. *Mr. E. is a well-informed and participant citizen. He is attached to the Labour Party, but this involves disagreement with rather than hostility toward the Conservatives.*

Mr. E. is a fifty-two-year-old white-collar worker in the editorial office of a newspaper in a Northern industrial city. He is married and has two school-aged children. His outside interests are wide and include arts and crafts, music, reading, and politics. He is a member of a trade union, and the people he most admires are Bertrand Russell, Henry James, and Fred Hoyle.

Mr. E. believes in a democratic family life and feels that children should often be brought into family discussions. "Otherwise they feel resentful that decisions affecting them were taken over their heads. . . . You have to make them feel they are playing a part, when, in reality, they are being guided." Mr. E. considers himself an agnostic, although he is willing to grant religion an important place in the country. He lives in a working-class neighborhood where he has several friends whom he visits and entertains on occasion. He finds that everyone around him is pleasant and more than willing to help in time of need. He cites as an example, "When my wife was in the hospital my youngest boy can be said almost to have lived in the house of my neighbors."

Mr. E.'s father was a railway employee who had a difficult time supporting his three children. Mr. E. recalls that both his parents were friendly and easygoing. He does not remember his schooldays as having been remarkable, except that he had one teacher who "recognized me as an individual, something that had never happened to me before. It had a most profound effect." There was no discussion of politics at school, but Mr. E. remembers that patriotism was inculcated by "the slanting of history and by emphasis on the celebration of national events, such as the Coronation and Empire Day."

Mr. E. recalls all the political events of his life clearly, and he remembers first becoming interested in politics when he came to London as a young man and met a number of politically conscious people. He feels sure that "every reasonably well-educated person is interested in politics, including such people as shop stewards, trade union officials, and people of that kind." He reads two newspapers daily, news magazines regularly, and listens to radio news programs. He supports the Labour party because, "Ideally, socialism means what the word implies, that is, the requirement for people to live together, help each other, and to be just to each other. That's what Socialism stands for, ideally. Unfortunately, Socialists have to make short-term decisions which are not truly socialistic." Mr. E. explains his opposition to the Conservative party in these terms: "Going back to the nineteenth century they were always opposed to social progress, but the Conservative party today—one must be just—is a good deal more liberal than it was. Indeed, the left wing of the Conservative party is very similar to the right wing of the Socialist party. But in the last analysis, they stand in the way of progress." On the whole, Mr. E. finds that the influence of the "Establishment" is excessive, but thinks that the monarchy should be retained to provide a desirable element of "romance."

Mr. E. feels that government affects everyone, and he cites several examples on the national and local levels. He is well informed on tax matters, but wishes that less money might be spent on defense. "If we could reduce it by fifty per cent, the standard of living in this country would take a great upward leap immediately. . . . It is a political matter. It depends on whom we are afraid of." However, Mr. E. thinks that there is little chance of a change of policy in this area, "because this country is living under the illusion that it is a great power. This is no longer true. We should accept our situation, as do, for example, the Swedes and Norwegians."

Mr. E. has had some routine contacts with public officials and says about them, "I was very well satisfied. I thought I was treated fairly and with courtesy and honesty." He wrote to his Member of Parliament to voice his objections at the time of the Suez crisis and was reasonably satisfied with the reply, considering that the local member was a Conservative. The M.P. "supported the Suez venture, but he gave what I thought was a reasoned defense of it."

Mr. E. feels that every citizen has an obligation, first of all, to vote; but it should be an informed vote. He should obey the law, pay his taxes, and be prepared to defend his country. If his local government passed some undesirable law, Mr. E. thinks that he might attend a Council meeting and protest, or write a letter to his local councilor, for "after all, you helped to put him in." In a national matter he would always act through his Member of Parliament. Mr. E. is proud that his country is what he calls a "sophisticated democracy."

A Housewife: An Allegiant Participant. *Mrs. D., while in no sense deeply committed politically, does have a strong interest in politics, a set of political views, and a feeling of competence.*

Mrs. D. is a middle-class Englishwoman in her late thirties. She is married and has a fourteen-year-old daughter and a twelve-year-old son. She is not eager to be interviewed, as she is rather reserved. She says that she does not like to "generalize" or theorize, but she is cooperative and thoughtful in her answers. She is attractive and well dressed, friendy and articulate. Her house is a large semidetached one in a somewhat drab and definitely "unfashionable" neighborhood. The garden is large and well cared for, and the living room is plain and comfortable.

Mrs. D.'s outside interests are cultural ones. She likes to read and is vitally interested in music and the theater; she is a member of a music club. The person she admires most is Dr. Schweitzer, both as a musician and as a medical missionary.

Mrs. D.'s husband, whom she met while studying at the Royal Academy of Music, is a pianist and composer. He plays the piano for a dance band, does arrangements, and works for the BBC and for film companies. He plays in the band with some reluctance, but on the whole he is content and financially successful.

The D.'s two children both go to private schools. Mrs. D. feels that her daughter's life will not be too different from her own, but her son is likely to do very well. He is enterprising and determined and has the strength of character to "get ahead." Mrs. D. thinks that he is lucky to be a boy, and that men have more opportunities than women. They don't get bogged down with domestic life. The girl will just marry and have a family and be a housewife. She adds ". . . I'm rather a strong feminist. I think women should have a more important place in family life, not to be relegated to the kitchen so much. I'm rather in favor of women being allowed to have a job if they want one, once the children are older, and if it can be done without too much work on the woman's part." Meanwhile, both children will have more "advantages" than their parents had, and more than many of the neighborhood children. Mrs. D. feels that private education is valuable and that money still makes a difference.

Most important, though, is the parents' ambition for their children.

In the matter of family decisions, Mr. and Mrs. D. discuss things freely, but the final decision rests with Mr. D. The children's wishes are taken into consideration. They may comment, and they should understand what is at stake. They are expected to become full members of the family unit. Mrs. D. stresses that they will never be "pushed" where their educations and futures are concerned.

Mrs. D. is a member of the Church of England. She does not consider herself a religious person and attends church only a few times a year. She has had a rather strict religious upbringing, but in her adult life she has not found the fulfillment in religion that she had hoped for. She does feel that religion is needed as a foundation for life and a guide to standards.

The D.'s have lived in their neighborhood for less than five years. They are somewhat out of their element, living near the railroad station in a drab working- and lower-middle-class area. Mrs. D. has few contacts with her neighbors. Though she has a few close friends in other parts of town. Some of the neighborhood people who have worked for her have proved unreliable, and there has been one instance of theft. It hurts Mrs. D. to think that there are people whom one can't trust. She finds that people in general tend to be selfish, but again excludes her own small circle of friends.

Mrs. D.'s childhood was not entirely happy. Her father, a career army officer, died when she was six years old. She only remembers that he was "wonderful"—but almost a stranger. Her mother was left with four small children to raise. Years of "genteel poverty" and relative social isolation followed. The family moved to a small bungalow in a neighborhood of pensioners and other middle-class people in straitened circumstances. Mrs. D. remembers her mother as rather cold and reserved, strict and quick-tempered. This was partly compensated for by her generosity and sense of humor. Mrs. D., however, became shy and withdrawn and learned to keep her problems to herself. She was not consulted on family matters and did not think that anything she would say could have any influence anyway. There was no political bias at school, but the children were encouraged to be patriotic. History was taught from a patriotic point of view. At home politics was never discussed. The family was Conservative. An interest in current affairs was not encouraged, and Mrs. D. does not recall hearing her mother ever discuss politics.

She herself first became aware of politics during the Spanish Civil War. Many of the boys she knew were going to Spain to fight. Mrs. D. feels that she was at a particularly impressionable age at that time. She began to ponder about world affairs, about Communism and Fascism. Domestic affairs interested her less. Her next political experience was membership in a women's branch of the armed services during the Second World War. She feels that it made her "more broad-minded and more thoughtful."

Mrs. D.'s Conservative convictions were strengthened during the postwar Labour government. "I remember the terrible feeling of depression around us and how I hated the Labour government, blaming it for all my troubles . . . no coal, no fuel." During the Suez crisis Mrs. D. strongly supported the Conservative government and felt that the Prime Minister should have been given more backing.

About her current political interests Mrs. D. says: "I'm not an avid follower of government. I do read newspapers. I do take quite a big interest. As my own party is in, I'm quite happy to let them get on with it. But if Labour were in, I would take much more interest, I suppose. . . . Surely, just about every mature person must be interested in politics, although many young people are not." She finds that the Conservative party is best, as it favors no class, but is fair to everyone. She feels that it is competent in foreign affairs. She opposes most strongly the Communist party for its ideas of state ownership, its regimentation, compulsion, and tendency to violence. She would be very pleased if her children chose the Conservative party, would not mind if they turned out to be Liberals, but would be very upset if they chose Labour. She would hope that they would "come to their senses" as time went on. Most of Mrs. D.'s friends are Conservatives, but she feels that she can discuss politics with anyone, regardless of party.

Mrs. D. feels strongly that both the local and the national government have an effect on people's lives. She is well informed about government functions and is satisfied that the government is doing its best for everyone. The country's standard of living is better than ever before. She wishes (with a rueful laugh) that the income tax might be lowered, but thinks that the government will eventually see to that, if it possibly can. "They realize that the best incentive to hard work is a good income."

Mrs. D. feels that she is effective as a citizen. She knows that if she had some request or some criticism to make, she could write to her local representative or a Member of Parliament. She thinks that she would be quite likely to do so. She adds: "I think they'd be interested in what I had to say and would listen to my point of view." As far as the obligations of a citizen are concerned, Mrs. D. thinks that it is good to be active in party politics, and that one should be willing to give up an occasional evening to go to meetings, and so on. A good citizen should also back up his country in the event of war, and he owes it financial support. Mrs. D. is proud of the standard of living and especially of the level of education that her country has achieved.

A Factory Worker: An Allegiant Participant. *This British worker manifests a high sense of competence coupled with some dissatisfaction with governmental output and a strong class attachment.*

Mr. V. is a factory worker who, after twenty-five years on the assembly line, has recently been promoted to the job of parts inspector. He is a union shop steward, and it is up to him to pass on grievances to his superiors in the union. He is not entirely content with his union's effectiveness. "We lose more battles than we win. They consider themselves before us. They can dictate conditions. If they can, they consider us, but their own interests are always number one."

Mr. V. is married and has one son of school age for whom he has great hopes. Times are better now, and "There is nothing to stop a working-class child getting right to the top if he has the ability." He believes that children should be treated with consideration and respect and should take part in family decisions "as soon as they can talk. It gives them a background and confidence." Besides, "if you try to force them into anything it burns something up inside them and they don't put all they have into it."

The V.'s attend church on occasion, and Mr. V. sees his religion as "ruling his conscience"; but he also finds that "religion has too much power in this country. The church should not play such a domineering part. They interfere too much in government affairs. The Sunday Observance laws are all wrong. . . ."

The neighborhood in which the V.'s live is slated for slum clearance and is considered rather a "rough" quarter. Mr. V. is quite reserved, socially, but wishes that the people in his neighborhood were as pleasant and friendly as those in his native Yorkshire. In re-

461

calling his youth, he describes his early poverty. "It was pretty grim. I used to go to school with one clog and one boot on. We got enough food but no extras and very little clothing. My father was too domineering. He was the big stick at home but he humbled himself to his superiors too much for what he got out of life. He seemed to crawl to people." Mr. V.'s mother also was "very domineering and strict. She never kissed us or gave us affection. She was hard." Mr. V. was not consulted in family matters, and he remembers, "I should have liked to have been brought into the picture more, but it was unheard of, and I was too scared to do anything about it." The situation was relieved by the helpfulness of the neighbors. Mr. V. could go to them for advice, and, besides, everyone was so poor that their very survival depended on mutual help. At school, Mr. V. remembers, his teachers were "very strict but they were fair. But students that were cleverer got better treatment. They favored someone from a better home because they had all the books that they needed to learn."

As the major events in his life, Mr. V. recalls a childhood operation and his marriage. He adds wistfully, "Had my wife been more interested in politics, I could have gone ahead, as I got on the local union committee where we used to live and would love to have really gone further. But your wife must come up to the top with you, and my own isn't interested—although I wouldn't change her!" As far as his specific political memories are concerned, Mr. V. recalls being out of work for many months during the Depression. He says, "It just endorsed my view that the workers must have a fairer deal. I felt that the Conservative method was oppressive." In 1945 ". . . we were in for a great time. I think it could have gone on, but we shall never go back to the '30's, because Labour has too much power for that, even now. The Conservatives will never have the upper hand again." All political events have served to strengthen Mr. V.'s basic opinions. He has been interested in politics for as long as he can remember, "because of the unfairness I saw as a child—the very rich and the very poor. This made me burn up and I felt I must help to remedy it. . . . My father was a Conservative and he had nothing, and I felt it was unjust. It riled me to see him look up to his superiors when he had nothing, so I automatically turned to Labour. . . ." Mr. V. regrets that the "lower classes" have little interest in politics: "If everyone would use their vote we should have level government, but some of the workers don't care and don't vote." At the last parliamentary election he was sorry to see everyone so apathetic. "I thought there wasn't enough excitement going on." (The seat, a former Labour stronghold, was subsequently won by a Conservative.) Mr. V. finds that Labour stands for "equality, freedom from injustice, and a fair deal for all," and that the Conservatives "conserve": they keep what they have and do not share it with anyone else. He hopes that his son will follow in his footsteps. As far as the monarchy is concerned, Mr. V. is not opposed to it. "They are harmless in a way, although expensive. They are a figurehead and do a good job on these tours. Better for trade, when other countries have seen our Queen."

Mr. V. has had various minor government contacts and has found the officials courteous and efficient. One request was denied, but Mr. V. admits that he "didn't seem to have a good cause." To inform himself on some complex government issue, Mr. V. would go to the district organizer of his union, write to his M.P., or read newspapers and government publications. He finds that "all people should take an active part in their own local government by going to local meetings and getting to know how the affairs of the town are run." If things were not going well, he would attend his "trades union branch meeting and get them to send a protest. I'd write to the local paper myself." If he had any complaints on the national level, he would get his union to petition Parliament, or "form a discussion group and try to get public opinion on my side." He finds that a good Englishman owes his country respect and pride. He himself is "proud of our own way of life, tradition, and free speech. We're not like the Iron Curtain countries. I am proud to belong to the working class, taking the history over the last twenty years."

A Baker: An Allegiant Subject/Participant. *Mr. H. is a good illustration of the deferential British participant. This is reflected in his support for the Conservative party despite his working-class position, and in his attitudes toward government and politics.*

Mr. H. is a fifty-three-year-old Englishman living in a large industrial city in the North of England. He works in a bakery, is married and the father of eight grown children. His home, which he and his wife share with their married daughter and her family, is on a small, rough street of old terrace houses. The interview took place in the front parlor, a small, amply furnished room, containing dining and living room pieces, the family's good china in a glass-fronted cabinet and other showpieces that they value. Mr. H. is a small, alert looking man, neatly dressed, thoughtful in his answers, and quite interested in the interview as a whole.

Mr. H. used to be in charge of seventy workers at his factory, but has recently changed to a job with less responsibility. He has enjoyed both ways of working, but now that his children are grown, he seems to prefer to "take it easy." He has pleasant relations with the foremen and with the bakery manager, who are ". . . all decent enough blokes of our own kind. They were once our workmates. . . ." The main decisions, however, are made by the directors, and working conditions are negotiated for by the union. The younger men in the bakery have a good chance of getting ahead, but Mr. H. is content to remain on his present level. He went to work in the depths of the Depression, has been able to improve his financial status steadily ever since, and considers himself quite fortunate.

Mr. H.'s great pride is his family. His sons are able and ambitious and are all doing skilled work. One, a fireman, is studying mathematics at night school, another, a baker, is learning to become a production manager. The others are equally hard working and versatile. The two unmarried girls are working in stores. Mr. H. remembers, "We had to work hard just to exist, but if they work hard they can't go wrong. Chances for young men today are great. We were too old at thirty-five or forty. Now they don't care a damn as long as you can do the job." The family has remained very close. Mr. H. is proud of having done a good job as a father, and says, "They have set off to a wonderful start. They've been helped a lot and I'm proud of that. If they were doing something, they would come and ask my advice and they'd take it, and that is something very, very few people can say. . . . I think I do more for my children than other parents do." When family problems come up, the whole family discusses them, but Mr. H. has the final word. He adds, with evident satisfaction, "Everything gets discussed, but all have their share of discussion—I allow everybody to speak for themselves, that is why I am such a popular dad. I never believe in bringing anybody down." He feels that children should start participating as soon as they are capable of carrying on a conversation, even if they are only twelve years old. Mr. H. has strong feelings about family life in general. "There should be a lot more unity with families, and there would not be half the unrest. If a family can't agree among themselves, how can they go out into the world and agree with everyone else?"

Mr. H. is a member of the Church of England, but as he works on Sundays he cannot attend services. He does not consider himself actually religious, but tries to be a good Christian. He finds that religion is important and should pervade family life, but indicates that there is religious friction in his part of town and that it is best not to discuss the subject publicly.

The H.'s live in a stable working- and lower-middle-class neighborhood. There are workers in the building trades, electricians, firemen, policemen, and school teachers. Mr. H. mentions that people are sociable but mind their own business. He has lived in the area for nineteen years. He has no friends or acquaintances, but apparently this is due to the fact that his working hours run almost entirely counter to everyone else's. He trusts people freely, and finds that he has never known anyone to do anything dishonest. His wife seems to be in closer touch with the neighbors and attests to the fact that everyone is helpful in times of need. When she was sick there were many offers of practical help.

Mr. H.'s father was an iron molder who had a very difficult time supporting his twelve children. Mr. H. remembers that he was "very, very pleasant" and "liked to make you believe that he was strict, but in the wrong places." His mother was the stronger parent; she was small but strict and determined. Her husband was glad to leave all decisions to her. The children had no voice in family decisions and were expected "to put up with it, right or wrong." The neighbors were mostly skilled workers. Mr. H.'s parents got along well with everyone, and his mother, especially, was very sociable and a friend to everyone. However, one did have to be careful in trusting people. There was much poverty and "conditions made people desperate. In some places people went in and took a neighbor's food. One would have to be very desperate to do that." People were not in a position to help each other, either. They could barely keep their own heads above water, and Mr. H. cannot recall a single neighbor who would have been in a position to help anyone outside his own family.

Mr. H.'s schooling was affected by an accident he had when he was five years old. He was in and out of hospitals for the next five years, and could not walk properly until he was nine. He has been slightly handicapped ever since, although this is hardly noticeable now. He liked his teachers but has few other memories of his school days.

Mr. H. cannot take an active interest in politics because of his

465

working hours, but has always "kept up" with what was going on in the world. He reads a daily newspaper and listens to the radio. He discusses politics frequently, but thinks it is better not to talk in a crowd where you might get mixed reactions. He does not report vivid political memories. He remembers occasional political conversations at home. He was aware of the Depression, but was fortunate to be in a trade that was not too severly affected. He disapproved of the King's abdication in 1936, feeling that he had shirked his responsibility and taken the easy way out.

The Second World War meant long hours of work for Mr. H. He recalls leaving for work at dawn and walking home after midnight. When the Labour government came into power, Mr. H. did not feel directly affected, but nevertheless, he disapproved strongly. "I just don't think the Labour party is smart enough for the job." He found that Sir Anthony Eden "got a rotten deal" over the Suez and should have been supported instead of criticized. He still admires Sir Anthony more than anyone. Mr. H. is a firm patriot. At school ". . . we always had the National Anthem on every occasion, and Scripture and prayers. You were told to love your own country. We were always told our own country was the best, and I still believe it."

Mr. H. supports the Conservative party, as ". . . they are the right people in the right place." He finds that Labour stands for peace at any price, and that seems to him an unworthy goal. He has no interest in their domestic policies. However, his children are quite free to choose their own parties, and even if they chose Labour he would assume that they knew what they were doing. He votes with a feeling of satisfaction, and while he does not become deeply involved in campaigns, he rather enjoys them at times.

Mr. H. feels that the central government affects his life in many ways. "That is where your life is worked out. They can make it pleasant or unpleasant." He refers especially to the Exchequer, "the one man everybody must remember." Locally, the government is equally effective. Mr. H. knows that there is much "red tape" involved in housing matters and that there is some injustice, but as a homeowner he does not have any definite facts and does not want to accuse anyone unfairly.

Mr. H. is a believer in the monarchy, equating it to some extent with democracy. "I'm against handing power to one man. In other countries they'd be better off if they had a king or a queen instead of one-man powers, which is all dictatorship is." Mr. H.'s information about taxes is vague, but he supposes that the matter is in capable hands. He finds that the government as a whole is doing well, too. "They are doing their best [to improve conditions]. It's as much to their interest as it is to ours." He knows that any improvements take a long time, but is content that his children will reap the benefits of much that is being done today. He has had only social contacts with government officials, but recalls that other men in his family have. His eldest brother was a local council member in another town and was the head of the local Conservative party.

If he felt strongly enough about some issue, Mr. H. would send a letter of complaint to his Member of Parliament, but with some reservations as to its success. If there were some local problems, he could form a committee of protest. As a citizen he feels that he owes loyalty to his country and a watchful eye over public finances to his local community. He is "proud of the way his country is run and of the policy to help those who cannot help themselves."

A Garment Worker: An Allegiant Subject/Parochial. Mrs. K. sees all political problems in personal terms. She has little political interest and no sense of competence.

Mr. K. is a fifty-two-year-old English garment worker who is married and has four children. She and her family live in a narrow, five-room terrace house that is badly in need of repair on the outside. Their neighborhood consists of similar and rather drab terrace houses, a large school, and various pubs and liquor stores. There is some small industry. Inside, the K.'s house is clean and freshly decorated. The living room is tiny and crowded, but newly papered with wallpaper in a modern design. It is freely used as a family room and not considered a "parlor." The interviewer describes Mrs. K. as a small, rather tense woman, who did not find it easy to answer questions of the kind contained in the interview, although she seemed to be quite articulate at other times.

Now that three of her children are grown and two of them have left home, Mrs. K. has returned to part-time work in a small dressing-gown factory employing six workers. She finds her coworkers friendly and companionable, but describes herself as rather shy and quite unambitious. She finds it hard to generalize about today's life, but thinks that perhaps her children will have an easier time and will be able to own their own homes. Education has improved

467

too, and people have more material things, but Mrs. K. is not sure what has caused these changes. She considers her own situation rather unsatisfactory and does not feel that it is apt to change in the future.

Mr. and Mrs. K. discuss their family problems together, but Mrs. K. confides that she usually has the final word. She does not feel that children should have a share in such conversations since their parents usually know better what is good for them, but she is not willing to see them "pushed around," either. She does not consider herself a religious person, but tries to lead a Christian life and goes to church on special occasions.

The K.'s find that their neighbors are of the "poorer classes," largely workers in the building trades and some white-collar workers. Mrs. K. knows many of the people in the area, but "just to say 'good morning' to, not to visit one another's houses." She will chat occasionally with her two closest neighbors. In general, Mrs. K. feels, people cannot be trusted. They will twist your words around and gossip. Some of them may be all right, but it is best to keep to one's self and not take any chances. People are not very helpful either. "You hear of people helping neighbors; they just don't seem to around here. . . . When I came to live here, my husband went into the army, I was going to have Paul, but no one offered to help."

Mrs. K.'s father was a janitor in an apartment building. The family was poor and the parents did not get along well together. There were three children, but Mrs. K. has lost touch with her brother and sister. Mrs. K. does not go into much detail about her childhood. Her parents separated, she was raised by an aunt and knew much poverty, deprivation, and neglect. She does remember vaguely that people were more sociable in those days and were inclined to help each other.

Mrs. K. left school at the age of fourteen. She liked her teachers, although they were not especially interested in her, and she remembers going on a week's school journey. It stands out in her mind as her only childhood holiday. The children were taught to be patriotic and Empire Day was an important holiday. There was a pageant with children dressed in the various national costumes of the Empire, but Mrs. K. was never chosen to participate.

Mrs. K. has only the vaguest memories of the various political events of her lifetime. Her husband was overseas during the war and she was on her own with her children, but she does not feel that politics was in any way connected with that situation. As for the advent of the Labour government, "Didn't they bring in the allowance for children? Well, I thought . . . I think they tried to do a lot of good, anyway." The Suez crisis brought personal worries, Mrs. K.'s eldest son was in the paratroopers, and there was a chance that he might have to go overseas. Again, Mrs. K. feels that these were personal troubles and in no way due to the political situation. Mrs. K. is not greatly interested in politics and says, "I haven't got the time to go to listen to the meetings to understand things, I just go and vote how I think and leave it at that." She does not follow the news in the papers or on the radio and feels that the various issues are usually too complicated for her to understand. She cannot think who might be interested in politics, unless it is people who have more education.

Mrs. K. supports the Labour party. "I think it stands more for the poorer classes than for the upper classes." However, she is not sure just what its program is or how it differs from the Conservative party on specific issues. She finds campaigns to be rather a waste of time but votes out of a sense of duty, "I just felt I had a vote and I must use it." She will let her children support any party of their choice.

Mrs. K. thinks that a government is needed ". . . to make the decisions. . . . There are them that are in the know of things, and they run the country." She is not sure how effective her government is and in what ways it might touch her own life. She is not sure just what sorts of things tax funds are used for, and can think of nothing that the government could do to improve life for her and her family or the country at large. In the past, she has had some contact with public health personnel and was glad to be given advice and help at the local children's clinic. She thinks that she might write to her Member of Parliament if anything should happen to "particularly upset" her and does not think that she would be ignored. They would try to do something to help her. However, she does not feel equally confident about the police and various other government bureaus, where she thinks that she would get little attention. Mrs. K. does not feel that she could affect the course of government in any way or that her views could be important. She feels that she owes her country loyalty and her vote, and, in return, she is proud of the fact that it is a welfare state.

469

PART V

CONCLUSION

CHAPTER 15

THE CIVIC CULTURE AND
DEMOCRATIC STABILITY

THUS FAR we have concentrated upon one aspect of political systems: that which we call political culture. The bulk of this book has dealt with the similarities and differences in the patterns of political attitudes found in the five nations. We have attempted to describe these similarities and differences as well as to explain them; to relate political attitudes to the structure of politics and to general attitudes toward people and society. In all this the political culture has been the focus of our attention. When other aspects of the political system have been brought into the discussion, it has usually been because of their impact on the political culture. But an important question remains to be dealt with: what is the impact of a political culture on the political system of which it is a part?

The five nations we have studied are democracies, though quite different from one another in their characteristics and their political histories. We shall therefore consider the way in which political culture affects democratic government; more specifically, we shall ask how far it goes toward creating and maintaining stable and effective democracy. Is there a democratic political culture—a pattern of political attitudes that fosters democratic stability, that in some way "fits" the democratic political system? To answer this question we must look at the political culture in the two relatively stable and successful democracies, Great Britain and the United States. As we have said, the political cultures of these two nations approximate the civic culture. This pattern of political attitudes differs in some respects from the "rationality-activist" model, or the model of political culture which, according to the norms of democratic ideology, would be found in a successful democracy. Civics texts would have us believe that the problem facing the citizen in a democracy is, to quote

473

the title of a recent book in the field, *How to Be an Active Citizen.*[1] According to this rationality-activist view, a successful democracy requires that citizens be involved and active in politics, informed about politics, and influential. Furthermore, when they make decisions, particularly the important decision of how to cast their vote, they must make them on the basis of careful evaluation of evidence and careful weighing of alternatives. The passive citizen, the non-voter, the poorly informed or apathetic citizen—all indicate a weak democracy. This view of democratic citizenship stresses activity, involvement, rationality. To use the terminology we have developed, it stresses the role of the participant and says little about the role of the subject or parochial.

Recent studies of political behavior call the rationality-activist model into question, for it is becoming clear that citizens in democracies rarely live up to this model. They are not well informed, not deeply involved, not particularly active; and the process by which they come to their voting decision is anything but a process of rational calculation.[2] Nor does this model accurately represent the civic culture we have found in Britain and the United States. It is true—and this point is both substantively important as well as indicative of the usefulness of comparative data—that the informed, involved, rational, and active citizen is more frequently found in the successful than in the unsuccessful democracies. The characteristics of the rationality-activist model of democratic citizenship are indeed components of the civic culture; but the point to be stressed here is that they are only *part* of that culture.

The civic culture is a mixed political culture. In it many individuals are active in politics, but there are also many who take the more passive role of subject. More important, even among those performing the active political role of the citizen, the roles of subject and parochial have not been displaced. The participant role has been added to the subject and parochial roles. This means that the active citizen maintains his traditional, nonpolitical ties, as well as his more passive political role as a subject. It is true that the rationality-activist model of the citizen does not imply that participant orientations replace subject and parochial ones; but by not mention-

---

[1] Paul Douglass and Alice McMahon, *How to be an Active Citizen*, Gainesville, Fla., 1960.

[2] See, for instance, Berelson *et al.*, *Voting*, chap. xiv; Campbell *et al.*, *The American Voter*, chap. x, and Julian L. Woodward and Elmo Roper, "Political Activity of American Citizens," *American Political Science Review*, XLIV (1950), pp. 872-85.

ing the latter two roles explicitly, it does imply that they are ir-relevant to the democratic political culture.

Actually, these two orientations do more than persist: they play an important part in the civic culture. In the first place, the parochial and subject orientations modify the intensity of the in-dividual's political involvement and activity. Political activity is but one part of the citizen's concerns, and usually not a very important part at that. The maintainance of other orientations limits the extent of his commitment to political activity and keeps politics, as it were, in its place. Furthermore, not only do the parochial and subject orientations persist side by side with the participant orienta-tions, but they penetrate and modify the participant orientations. Primary affiliations, for instance, are important in the patterns of citizen influence. In addition, a diffuse set of social attitudes and interpersonal attitudes tends to affect the content of the political attitudes—to make them less intense and divisive. Penetrated by primary group orientations and by general social and interpersonal attitudes, political attitudes are not solely the results of articulated principle and rational calculation.

How can we explain the discrepancy between the ideals of the rationality-activist model and the patterns of political attitudes we actually find, even in the more stable and successful democracies? One possible explanation, and the one most often found in the literature on civic education, is that this discrepancy is evidence for the malfunctioning of democracy. Insofar as people do not live up to the ideal of the active citizen, democracy is a failure. If one be-lieves that the realities of political life should be molded to fit one's theories of politics, such an explanation is satisfactory. But if one holds to the view that theories of politics should be drawn from the realities of political life—a somewhat easier and probably more useful task—then this explanation of the gap between the rationality-activist model and democratic realities is less acceptable. From the latter point of view, one would probably argue that the gap exists because the standards have been set unreasonably high. Given the complexity of political affairs, given the other demands made upon an individual's time, and given the difficulty of obtaining informa-tion necessary for making rational political decisions, it is no wonder that the ordinary citizen is not the ideal citizen. In the light of an individual's nonpolitical interests, it might be quite irrational to invest in political activity the time and effort needed to live up to the rationality-activist model. It may just not be worth it to be that good a citizen.

But though a completely activist political culture may be a utopian ideal, there may be other, more significant reasons why an intricately mixed civic culture is found in the more successful democracies. The civic culture, which sometimes contains apparently contradictory political attitudes, seems to be particularly appropriate for democratic political systems, for they, too, are mixtures of contradictions. Harry Eckstein has suggested that a democratic political system requires a blending of apparent contradictions—he calls them "balanced disparities"—if it is to function effectively. On the one hand, a democratic government must govern; it must have power and leadership and make decisions. On the other hand, it must be responsible to its citizens. For if democracy means anything, it means that in some way governmental elites must respond to the desires and demands of citizens. The need to maintain this sort of balance between governmental power and governmental responsiveness, as well as the need to maintain other balances that derive from the power/responsiveness balance—balances between consensus and cleavage, between affectivity and affective neutrality —helps explain the way in which the more mixed patterns of political attitudes associated with the civic culture are appropriate for a democratic political system.[3]

Power and Responsiveness

The maintenance of a proper balance between governmental power and governmental responsiveness represents one of the most important and difficult tasks of a democracy. Unless there is some control of governmental elites by nonelites, it is hard to consider a political system democratic. On the other hand, nonelites cannot themselves rule. If a political system is to be effective—if it is to be able to initiate and carry out policies, adjust to new situations, meet internal and external challenges—there must be mechanisms whereby governmental officials are endowed with the power to make

[3] The contradictory demands placed upon democratic political systems have been stressed in some as yet unpublished lectures by Professor Harry Eckstein, upon which this chapter draws. The authors are grateful for the opportunity to see his notes on this subject. That democratic systems are called upon to pursue apparently opposing goals is also stressed in Berelson *et al., op. cit.,* chapter xiv, and in Parsons, "Voting and the Equilibrium of the American Political System," in Burdick and Brodbeck (eds.), *American Voting Behavior,* Glencoe, Ill., 1959.

authoritative decisions. The tensions produced by the need to pursue the opposing goals of governmental power and governmental responsiveness become most apparent in times of crisis. Wars, for instance (hot or cold), have often shifted the balance so far in the direction of governmental power and authority as to cause concern about the preservation of democratic responsiveness. Yet if the balance is not so shifted, it is argued that democratic governments may succumb to external challenges.

Crises bring to the fore the problem of maintaining an adequate balance, but the problem exists in the day-to-day running of a democracy. How can a governmental system be constructed so that a balance is maintained between power and responsiveness? As E. E. Schattschneider has put it, "The problem is not how 180 million Aristotles can run a democracy, but how we can organize a community of 180 million ordinary people so that it remains sensitive to their needs. This is a problem of *leadership, organization, alternatives, and systems of responsibility and confidence.*"[4] In trying to resolve this problem, political scientists have usually spoken in terms of the structure of electoral conflict. An electoral system, designed to turn power over to a particular elite for a limited period of time, can achieve a balance between power and responsiveness: the elites obtain power, yet this power is limited by the periodic elections themselves, by the concern for future elections during the interelection period, and by a variety of other formal and informal checks. For a system of this sort to work, there must obviously be more than one party (or at least some competing elite group with the potentiality of gaining power) to make the choice among elites meaningful; and at the same time there must be some mechanism whereby an elite group can exercise effective power—perhaps by the giving of all power to the victorious party in a two-party system, or by the formation of workable coalitions among a group of parties. Most of the debate on the most appropriate electoral system for a democracy (proportional representation, single member districts, or some mixed form) has revolved around two questions: how to maximize the competing goals of power and responsiveness, and how to decide which goal deserves greater stress.[5] There has also been

[4] E. E. Schattschneider, *The Semi-Sovereign People,* New York, 1960, p. 138. Italics in original.

[5] On this continuing debate, see, among others, Enid Lakeman and James D. Lambert, *Voting in Democracies,* London, 1955; F. A. Hermens, *Democracy or Anarchy,* South Bend, Ind., 1941, and M. Duverger, *Political Parties,* London, 1954.

much concern over the proper organization of political parties to maximize both of these goals. This concern clearly motivated the members of the American Political Science Association's Committee on Political Parties, when, in their report, they called for a political party system that is ". . . democratic, responsible, and effective—a system that is accountable to the public, respects and expresses differences of opinion, and is able to cope with the great problems of modern government."[6]

The tension between power and responsiveness can be managed to some extent by the structure of partisan conflict. But our main interest is in the relationship between this tension and political culture, particularly the civic culture. Can the set of attitudes held by citizens help to maintain the delicate balance between the contradictory demands placed on a democratic system? This concentration upon the political attitudes of ordinary citizens does not imply a rejection of the important role of political structures or of elite attitudes and behavior. These are important as well, and we shall return to them below when we consider the way in which the attitudes of ordinary citizens and of elites interact.

The tension between governmental power and responsiveness has a parallel in the conflicting demands made upon the citizens of a democratic system. Certain things are demanded of the ordinary citizen if elites are to be responsive to him: the ordinary citizen must express his point of view so that elites can know what he wants; he must be involved in politics so that he will know and care whether or not elites are being responsive, and he must be influential so as to enforce responsive behavior by the elites. In other words, elite responsiveness requires that the ordinary citizen act according to the rationality-activist model of citizenship. But if the alternate pole of elite power is to be achieved, quite contradictory attitudes and behavior are to be expected of the ordinary man. If elites are to be powerful and make authoritative decisions, then the involvement, activity, and influence of the ordinary man must be limited. The ordinary citizen must turn power over to elites and let them rule. The need for elite power requires that the ordinary citizen be relatively passive, uninvolved, and deferential to elites. Thus the demo-

6 "Toward a More Responsible Two Party System," a report of the Committee on Political Parties, of the American Political Science Association, *American Political Science Review*, XLIV (1950), Special Supplement, p. 17.

cratic citizen is called on to pursue contradictory goals: he must be active, yet passive; involved, yet not too involved; influential, yet deferential.[7]

Norms, Perceptions, and Activity

The data presented in this book suggest some ways in which these conflicting demands might be managed. The crucial cases for our analysis are clearly Britain and the United States, for if there is some pattern of attitudes that can allow this tension to be managed, one might expect it to act most effectively within the relatively more stable democracies. It is in these two nations that we found the closest approximation to the civic culture. Our data suggest that in two broad ways the civic culture maintains the citizen's active-influential role as well as his more passive role: on the one hand, there is in the society a *distribution* of individuals who pursue one or the other of the conflicting citizen goals; on the other hand, certain *inconsistencies in the attitudes of an individual* make it possible for him to pursue these seemingly conflicting goals at the same time. Let us first consider the inconsistencies within the individual.

As our survey showed, there exists a gap between the *actual political behavior* of our respondents, on the one hand, and their *perceptions of their capacities to act* and their *obligations to act,* on the other. Respondents in Britain and the United States manifest high frequencies of what we have called subjective political competence. As was reported in Chapter 7, a large proportion considers itself able to influence the decisions of the local government, and a substantial, though not quite as large, proportion feels the same way about the activities of the national government. Yet this high

[7] It should be clear that the tension described here is not the same as that between the obligations of the citizen and the obligations of the subject, as discussed in chap. i. There we dealt with the fact that the democratic citizen has a set of role expectations within the input structure of the political system. He is expected to participate in some ways in decisions. At the same time he has "subject" obligations toward the output aspects of the political system. He is expected to abide by decisions once they are made. This mixture, too, is part of the civic culture. But the tension described in this section is not between an individual's role in relation to the input structure (i.e., as citizen) and his role in relation to the output structure (i.e., as subject)—a tension that at least in theory appears fairly easy to resolve. Rather, the tension described here is between two modes of relating to the input structures. The citizen has both to be influential and to affect the course of policy; at the same time he must be noninfluential and allow political elites to make decisions independently. Thus the tension we are describing lies within the role of citizen.

479

estimation of one's competence as an influential citizen is certainly not matched by actual political behavior. In the first place, only a small proportion of those respondents who say the could influence the government report that they have ever attempted such influence. And even if those who think they could influence governmental decisions were to attempt to do so—which is unlikely—they would almost certainly not have the success that they believe they would have. It is clearly an exaggeration when forty per cent of American respondents or twenty-four per cent of the British say that there is some likelihood that an attempt of theirs to influence the national legislature would be successful.

A similar gap exists between the sense of obligation to participate in political life and actual participation. As reported in Chapter 6, a much higher proportion of respondents says that the ordinary man has some obligation to participate in the affairs of his local community than in fact does participate; and again the pattern is clearest in the United States and Britain. As one respondent, quoted in Chapter 6, put it, "I'm saying what [one] ought to do, not what I do." And there is evidence that this position is far from rare. Certainly, the sense of obligation to take some part in one's community affairs is not matched by the importance attributed to such activity by respondents. The proportion saying that one has such obligations is in each nation much larger than the proportion that, when asked to report on its free-time activities, reports participation in community affairs. Fifty-one per cent of the American respondents report that the ordinary man ought to take some active part in the affairs of his community. But when asked what they do in their free time, only about ten per cent of the American respondents mention such activities (See Table 10-1). And when Gillespie and Allport asked a somewhat differently phrased question of youth in the United States, only about one in five said that he expected community participation to be a source of satisfaction.[8] This suggests that though there is a widespread norm that one ought to participate within the community, active participation is far from the most significant activity to most people. It is not what most people do in their spare time, nor is it the major source of satisfaction, joy, and excitement.

These two gaps—between a high perception of potential influence

[8] James M. Gillespie and Gordon W. Allport, *Youth's Outlook on the Future,* New York, 1955, p. 57.

and a lower level of actual influence, and between a high frequency of expressed obligation to participate and the actual importance and amount of participation—help explain how a democratic political culture can act to maintain a balance between governmental elite power and governmental elite responsiveness (or its complement, a balance between nonelite activity and influence and nonelite passivity and noninfluence). The comparative infrequency of political participation, its relative lack of importance for the individual, and the objective weakness of the ordinary man allow governmental elites to act. The inactivity of the ordinary man and his inability to influence decisions help provide the power that governmental elites need if they are to make decisions. But this maximizes only one of the contradictory goals of a democratic system. The power of the elites must be kept in check. The citizen's opposite role, as an active and influential enforcer of the responsiveness of elites, is maintained by his strong commitment to the norm of active citizenship, as well as by his perception that he can be an influential citizen. This may be in part a myth, for it involves a set of norms of participation and perceptions of ability to influence that are not quite matched by actual political behavior. Yet the very fact that citizens hold to this myth—that they see themselves as influential and as obligated to take an active role— creates a potentiality of citizen influence and activity. The subjectively competent citizen, as was pointed out in Chapter 7, has not necessarily attempted to influence the government, but he is *more likely* to have made such attempts than is the citizen who does not consider himself competent.[9]

A citizen within the civic culture has, then, a reserve of influence. He is not constantly involved in politics, he does not actively oversee the behavior of political decision makers. But he does have the potential to act if there is need. This reserve of influence—influence potential that is inactive and uncommitted to the political system —was best illustrated by the data, presented in Chapter 7, on the ability of citizens to create political structures in time of need. The citizen is not a constant political actor. He is rarely active in political groups. But he thinks that he can mobilize his ordinary social environment, if necessary, for political use. He is not the active citizen: he is the potentially active citizen.

[9] On the importance of the democratic myth, see, V. O. Key, Jr., *Public Opinion and American Democracy*, New York, 1961, p. 547.

481

Yet the intermittent and potential character of the citizen's political activity and involvement depends upon steadier, more persistent types of political behavior. By living in a civic culture, the ordinary man is more likely than he would be otherwise to maintain a steady and high rate of exposure to political communications, to be a member of an organization, and to engage in informal political discussion. These activities do not in themselves indicate an active participation in the decision-making process of a society; but they do make such participation more possible. They prepare the individual for intervention in the political system; and more important perhaps, they create a political environment in which citizen involvement and participation are more feasible.

We have been saying that inconsistencies within attitudes and inconsistencies between attitudes and behavior, rather than the one-sided attitudes of the rationality-activist model, can maintain the tension between citizen activity and citizen passivity. But now we must ask whether these inconsistencies cause instability in the civic culture. Much of the recent theorizing about attitude formation emphasizes the strain toward consistency or consonance among the beliefs, attitudes, and behavior of an individual; there now exists a large body of data to support the theory that cognitive inconsistencies will produce a stress toward the reduction of those inconsistencies.[10] But as we have seen, the balance between citizen influence and citizen passivity *depends upon the inconsistencies* between political norms and perceptions, on the one hand, and political behavior, on the other. This inconsistency, however, creates no undue strain within the citizen; for politics, as much of our data suggest and as the data from many other studies confirm, is not the uppermost problem in his mind. Compared with other concerns, politics is usually invested with relatively little affect or involvement. Thus inconsistencies among attitudes or between attitudes and behavior can be more easily tolerated, for they can be overlooked or ignored. As Rosenberg and Abelson have put it, ". . . potential imbalance will remain undiscovered by an individual unless he is motivated to

[10] Some of the important literature developing this theory includes: Leon Festinger, *A Theory of Cognitive Dissonance*, Evanston, Ill., 1957; F. Heider, *The Psychology of Interpersonal Relations*, New York, 1958; C. E. Osgood, C. J. Suci, and P. H. Tannenbaum, *The Measurement of Meaning*, Urbana, Ill., 1957, and M. J. Rosenberg *et al.*, *Attitude Organization and Change*, New Haven, Conn., 1960. See also the special issue of the *Public Opinion Quarterly* on attitude change, xxiv (Summer 1960), especially the articles by Zajonc, Cohen, Rosenberg, and Osgood.

think about the topic and in fact does so."[11] Because politics has little importance for them, few citizens are motivated to think about their influence or their political activities.

That politics has relatively little importance for citizens is an important part of the mechanism by which the set of inconsistent political orientations keeps political elites in check, without checking them so tightly as to make them ineffective. For the balance of inconsistent orientations would be more diffcult to maintain if the issues of politics were always considered important by the citizens. If issues arise that individuals consider important, or if some relatively severe dissatisfaction with government occurs, the individual will be motivated to think about the topic and thus will be under greater pressure to resolve the inconsistency—to make attitudes and behavior consonant with each other. One way he may do this is to bring his behavior into line with norms and perceptions by becoming politically active. Thus the inconsistency between attitudes and behavior acts as a latent or potential source of political influence and activity.

To say that the civic culture maintains the balance between power and responsibility suggests a further point about democratic politics. It suggests why unresolved political issues of great importance eventually create instability in a democratic political system. The balance between activity and passivity can be maintained only if the issues of politics are relatively mild. If politics becomes intense, and if it remains intense because of some salient issue, the inconsistency between attitude and behavior will become unstable. But any relatively permanent resolution of the inconsistency is likely to have unfortunate consequences. If behavior is brought into line with attitudes, the amount of attempted control of elites by nonelites will create governmental ineffectiveness and instability. On the other hand, if attitudes change to match behavior, the resulting sense of impotence and noninvolvement will have damaging consequences for the democratic quality of the political system.

However, this does not suggest that all important issues damage a democratic political system. It is only when issues become intense and remain intense that the system may be made unstable.[12] If

[11] Milton J. Rosenberg and Robert F. Abelson, "Analysis of Cognitive Balancing," in Rosenberg *et al., op. cit.*, chap. iv, p. 121.

[12] It is important to stress the term *issues* used in this connection. Not all salient political events are issues, i.e., points of dispute. This model applies best to those political disputes in which individuals are involved and have relatively specific demands

significant issues arise only sporadically *and* if the government is able to respond to the demands stimulated by these issues, an equilibrium can be maintained between citizen influence and government influence. In ordinary times, citizens are relatively uninterested in what governmental decisions makers do, and the latter have the freedom to act as they see fit. However, if an issue becomes prominent, citizen demands on officials will increase. If officials can respond to these demands, the importance of politics will fall again and politics will return to normal. Furthermore, these cycles of citizen involvement, elite response, and citizen withdrawal may tend to reinforce the balance of opposites needed for democracy. Within each cycle, the citizen's perception of his own influence is reinforced; at the same time the system adjusts to new demands and thereby manifests its effectiveness. And the system may become generally more stable through the loyalty engendered by participation and effective performance.[13]

These cycles of involvement are an important way of maintaining the balanced inconsistencies between activity and passivity. If the constant involvement and activity associated with salient issues would eventually make the maintenance of the balance difficult, so, too, would the complete absence of involvement and activity. The balance can be maintained over time only if the gap between activity and passivity is not too wide. If the belief in one's political

---

that they would like satisfied by the government. The content of some political events may be so distant from the individual that, though he may consider the events important, he is in no position to formulate demands relevant to them; thus even if the issue is significant, he will exert less pressure on political elites than he would on other issues. (Warren Miller has found that there is a closer relationship between the views of constituents and their Congressmen on such subjects as civil rights and welfare than on foreign policy. The relatively greater distance of foreign policy issues from the ordinary man might explain this. See Miller, "Policy Preferences of Congressional Candidates and Constituents", paper delivered at the meetings of the American Political Science Association, September 1961.)

Some political crises that are not issues—i.e., not subjects of disputes among the citizens of a nation or between the citizens and the elites—may lead to an increased involvement in political affairs that is not coupled with increased demands for influence over decisions. Wars, for instance, may unite a population behind the elites and, by triggering off feelings of loyalty, lead to demands for strong leadership rather than for chances to participate in decisions. This type of situation may have unstabilizing consequences for democracy, although the consequences will be different from those spelled out above. In this case, the stress on loyalty and the demand for strong leadership may lead to a reduction of citizen control over governmental elites.

[13] For an example of such a cyclical pattern of disinterest-involvement-influence-withdrawal, see William K. Muir, Jr., *Defending the "Hill" Against Metal Houses*, 1955, cited in Dahl, *Who Governs?*, chap. xvi. See Dahl, chap. xxviii, for a general discussion relevant to our argument.

competence is not reinforced occasionally, it is likely to fade. Or, if the belief is maintained in a purely ritual manner, it will not represent potential influence or be a check on decision makers. This, perhaps, is what characterizes the "aspirational" political competence observable in Mexico. Mexican respondents manifest relatively high levels of subjective political competence, especially in comparison to their very low levels of "administrative" competence, exposure to communications, and the like. Furthermore, they quite frequently mention group-forming strategies. But as we have seen, their sense of competence is not matched by experience in political action. There is a gap between the subjective perception of competence and actual political behavior, as there is in the United States and Britain. But the gap is much wider. In the United States, for instance, thirty-three per cent of those respondents who say they believe they can influence the local government have actually tried to do so, as have eighteen per cent of the British local competents. But among the Mexican local competents, only nine per cent report such experience. Thus the perception-behavior gap may be so wide as to make difficult the performance of the dual functions of furthering citizen control and maintaining citizen passivity. For the democratic "myth" to be an effective political force, it cannot be pure myth. It must be an idealization of real behavioral patterns. Where, as perhaps in Mexico, it has very little relation to reality, it cannot function as part of a balanced civic culture.[14]

We have so far dealt with the way in which activity and passivity may be balanced within the individual citizen. But this balance is maintained, not merely by the set of attitudes individuals have, but by the distribution of attitudes among different types of political actors in a system: some individuals believe that they are competent and some do not; some individuals are active and some are not. This variation in beliefs and activity among individuals also helps enforce the power-responsiveness balance. This can be seen if we consider the equilibrium mechanism described above: an issue becomes salient, activity rises, and balance is restored by a governmental response that reduces the salience of the issue. One reason that an increasingly prominent issue and the consequent rise in

[14] If the ordinary man's belief in his competence is to be reinforced, it may not be necessary for him to be personally involved in successful influence activity vis-a-vis the government. It may be enough simply that he be aware of others engaged in such activity. But the likelihood that an individual will see others attempting to influence the government will naturally depend upon how frequently people make such attempts.

political activity are kept from straining the political system is that the prominence of the issue rarely increases for all citizens at once. Rather, it is particular groups that show a rise in political activity, while the rest of the citizens remain inactive. In this way the amount of citizen activity at any one point in time is not so great as to strain the system.

The above discussion is based upon our data on the attitudes of ordinary citizens. But if a mechanism such as the one we postulate is to work, the attitudes of elites must complement those of non-elites. The decision maker must believe in the democratic myth— that ordinary citizens ought to participate in politics and that they are in fact influential. If the decision maker accepts this view of the role of the ordinary citizen, his own decisions serve to maintain the balance between governmental power and responsiveness. On the one hand, he is free to act as he thinks best because the ordinary citizen is not pounding on his door with demands for action. He is insulated by the inactivity of the ordinary man. But if he shares the belief in the influence potential of the ordinary man, his freedom to act is limited by the fact that he believes there *will* be pounding on his door if he does not act in ways that are responsive. Furthermore, if he shares the view that the ordinary man ought to participate in decisions, he is under pressure to act responsively because he believes that such citizen influence is legitimate and justified. Though our data cannot demonstrate this, there is reason to believe that political elites share the political culture of the nonelite; that in a society with a civic culture they, as well as non-elites, hold the attitudes associated with it.[15] Elites are, after all, part of the same political system and exposed to many of the same political socialization processes as are nonelite. And studies have shown that political and community leaders, as well as those of higher social status, are more likely than those of lower status to accept the norms of democracy.[16]

[15] Yet there are important ways in which elites differ from the general population in their political attitudes; see chap. i, p. 27. Further, there are probably differences in autonomy between British and American political elites; see below, for some comments on these differences.

[16] Relevant here are our data on the effect of educational differences on the differences in attitudes among respondents. Also relevant is the finding in Samuel Stouffer's, *Communism, Conformity, and Civil Liberties*, New York, 1955, to the effect that community leaders are more tolerant and more accepting of democratic norms than are nonleaders. Several studies of German public opinion support this general finding. See, for instance, Erich Reigrotski, *Soziale Verflechtungen in der Bundesrepublik*, Part

The consideration of elite attitudes suggests another mechanism whereby elite responsiveness can be enforced while the activity and involvement of the ordinary citizen remain low. The pattern of citizen influence is not always, or even predominantly, one of stimulus (the citizen or group of citizens make a demand) followed by response (the governmental elite acts to satisfy the demand). Rather, the well-known "law of anticipated reactions" may operate here. A good deal of citizen influence over governmental elites may entail no activity or even conscious intent of citizens. On the contrary, elites may anticipate possible demands and activities and act in response to what they anticipate. They act responsively, not because citizens are actively making demands, but in order to keep them from becoming active.[17]

Within the civic culture, then, the individual is not necessarily the rational, active citizen. His pattern of activity is more mixed and tempered. In this way he can combine some measure of competence, involvement, and activity with passivity and noninvolvement. Furthermore, his relationship with the government is not a purely rational one, for it includes adherence—his and the decision maker's—to what we have called the democratic myth of citizen competence. And this myth has significant consequences. For one thing, it is not pure myth: the belief in the influence potential of the average man has some truth to it and does indicate real behavioral potential. And whether true or not, the myth is believed.

The Management of Affect

We have discussed the way in which the civic culture balances involvement and activity with indifference and passivity. But the balance achieved by the civic culture goes further. Not only must involvement and activity be balanced by a measure of their opposites, but the *type* of political involvement and activity must itself

---

2, and *Basic Orientation and Political Thinking of West German Youth and Their Leaders,* DIVO Institute Frankfurt am Main-Bad Godesberg, 1956.

Political leaders in democracies must express agreement with the democratic myth in public. Of course, much of this may be lip service. But the requirement that they give public support to this set of beliefs also puts pressure on them to accept the beliefs—unless hypocrisy is a conscious value among political elites. As the studies in cognitive dissonance have shown, the requirement that an individual make a certain kind of public declaration creates pressures to change his private beliefs in that direction. See Rosenberg *et al., op. cit.,* and Festinger, *op. cit.*

[17] See chap. 7 for a discussion of "anticipatory" and other forms of influence.

be balanced. In particular, there appears to be a need for a balanced affective orientation to politics; or rather, there must be a balance between instrumental and affective orientations to politics. Politics must not be so instrumental and pragmatic that participants lose all emotional involvement in it. On the other hand, the level of affective orientation to politics ought not to become too intense.

There are several reasons why this balance, rather than a maximization of either pragmatism or passion, is needed in an effective democracy. In the first place, political commitment, if it is to be dependable, cannot be completely unemotional. Loyalty to a political system, if it is based on purely pragmatic considerations of the effectiveness of that system, represents, as Lipset has suggested, a rather unstable basis of loyalty, for it is too closely dependent upon system performance.[18] If it is to remain stable in the long run, the system requires a form of political commitment based upon more general attachment to the political system—a commitment we have called "system affect." Furthermore, as Eckstein suggests, a purely pragmatic and unemotional political involvement implies a politics of opportunism; a politics that will probably lead to cynicism.[19] On the other hand, if an affective commitment to politics or to a particular political group is too intense, this can have unfortunate consequences for a democracy. In the first place, an intense emotional involvement in politics endangers the balance between activity and passivity, for that balance depends on the low salience of politics. Second, such intense involvement tends to "raise the stakes" of politics: to foster the sort of mass, messianic movements that lead to democratic instability.[20] Furthermore, the consequences can be harmful whether the commitment is to the system as a whole and the incumbent elites or only to particular subgroups in society. It is clear that intense commitment to particular political parties or groups can produce an unstabilizing level of fragmentation in the system. But even an intense commitment to the political system and to the incumbent elites is likely to have harmful effects. If citizens are to maintain some control over political elites, their loyalty to the system and to the elites must not be complete and unquestioning. Furthermore, the civic culture implies the maintenance of the more traditional parochial roles along with the role of citizen. The

[18] Lipset, *Political Man*, pp. 77-83.
[19] Eckstein uses as an example of this the politics of *Trasformismo* of pre-World War I Italy. See his *Theory of Stable Democracy*, p. 33.
[20] See Kornhauser, *op. cit.*

preservation of a sphere of activity that is outside of politics is important if one is to have the balanced participation of the civic culture.[21]

Participation in politics, this suggests, ought to be neither purely instrumental nor purely affective. The political participant ought to receive both instrumental and emotional gratifications from his participation. And this balanced involvement in politics again appears to characterize the civic culture in the two more successful democracies. As was discussed in Chapter 8, in the United States and Britain the more the respondent considers himself capable of participating in politics, the more likely he is to receive affective satisfaction from the political system and to evaluate positively the instrumental performance of that system. In contrast, the other three nations show patterns of unbalanced participation. In Germany and Italy the sense of ability to participate is accompanied by a higher evaluation of the instrumental effectiveness of the system but not by a deeper general commitment. In Mexico the opposite is true: sense of participation is accompanied by greater pride in the system but not a higher evaluation of its performance. In Italy and Germany, commitment to the political system is largely pragmatic, and is based on little emotional commitment. In Mexico there may be an unrealistic attachment to symbols, coupled with the absence of a belief in instrumental rewards of politics.

Consensus and Cleavage

Our data suggest another way in which the political cultures of the more successful democracies are characterized by a balanced type of commitment. As was reported at various places throughout this volume, respondents in the United States and Britain more frequently than respondents in the other three nations express pride in their political system and feel satisfaction when voting. They are

[21] This helps explain the way in which nonissue crises—that is, political events which, though considered important and salient by the population, do not involve citizen demands for influence over governmental decisions—may destroy the balance of the civic culture. It was suggested in note 11 that they destroy the balance by increasing demands for leadership and therefore shifting the balance away from elite responsiveness. Crises of this sort may upset the balance of the civic culture in another way: by increasing the amount of loyalty to the system to such a high level that it is considered "unpatriotic" to question the actions of elites. When this stage is reached, democracy is obviously in danger. Furthermore, a crisis such as a war may destroy the balance within the civic culture between the parochial and the citizen roles. Too much of life —including the nonpolitical sphere of relations—may become political.

489

more likely to report interest in politics and actually to discuss politics. And they are more likely to report some emotional involvement in political campaigns. All these indicate a comparatively high level of political involvement. Yet the political involvement in these two countries is tempered in intensity by its subordination to a more general, overarching set of social values. As the data in Chapter 10 suggest, attitudes of interpersonal trust and cooperation are more frequent in the United States and Britain than in the other nations. More important, these general social attitudes penetrate into the realm of politics. The role of social trust and cooperativeness as a component of the civic culture cannot be overemphasized. It is, in a sense, a generalized resource that keeps a democratic polity operating. Constitution makers have designed formal structures of politics that attempt to enforce trustworthy behavior, but without these attitudes of trust, such institutions may mean little. Social trust facilitates political cooperation among the citizens in these nations, and without it democratic politics is impossible. It probably also enters into a citizen's relation with political elites. We argued earlier that the maintenance of elite power was essential in a democracy. We would now add that the sense of trust in the political elite—the belief that they are not alien and extractive forces, but part of the same political community—makes citizens willing to turn power over to them.

Furthermore, these general social attitudes temper the extent to which emotional commitment to a particular political subgroup leads to political fragmentation. This general set of social attitudes, this sense of community over and above political differences, keeps the affective attachments to political groups from challenging the stability of the system. Furthermore, it acts as a buffer between the individual and the political system, and thereby reduces the "availability" (in Kornhauser's use of the word) of the ordinary citizen for involvement in unstabilizing mass movements.[22] These norms—particularly those that say that political criteria are not to be applied to all situations—place a limit on politics. They indicate that certain social relationships are not to be dominated by political considerations. And in this way they allow the individual to maintain a certain degree of independence from the political system.

This brings us to a further balance that must be maintained within a democratic political system: that between consensus and cleavage.[23]

[22] *The Politics of Mass Society*, Chap. 2.
[23] The significance of this balance is also stressed by Eckstein, Berelson, and Parsons. See the references in note 3 above.

Without some meaningfully structured cleavage in society, it is hard to see how democratic politics can operate. If democracy involves at some point a choice among alternatives, the choice must be about something. If there were no cleavage, if people did not combine into meaningfully opposed political groupings, this would suggest ". . . a community in which politics was of no real importance to the community,"[24] and one in which the alternation of political elites meant little. Too much agreement would mitigate against the enforcement of elite responsiveness. Yet if cleavage went too far, ". . . a democratic society . . . would probably be in danger of its existence. The issues of politics would cut so deeply, be so keenly felt, and, especially, be so fully reinforced by other social identifications of the electorate . . ." as to threaten democracy.[25] There must be what Parsons has called a "limited polarization" of society.[26] If there is no consensus within society, there can be little potentiality for the peaceful resolution of political differences that is associated with the democratic process. If, for instance, the incumbent elite considered the opposition elite too threatening, it is unlikely that the incumbents would allow a peaceful competition for elite position.

This balance between consensus and cleavage is managed within the civic culture by a mechanism similar to the one that managed the balance between activity and passivity: that is, an inconsistency between norms and behavior. This is illustrated by the data presented on attitudes toward primary group membership and partisan affiliation (reported in Chapters 5 and 10). On the one hand, as all studies of voting behavior indicate, primary groups tend to be homogeneous in the partisan sense; families, friendship groups, workplace groups tend to be composed of people of like political views. And, what may be more important evidence for their partisan homogeneity, if there is some heterogeneity of political views within the group, there will be pressure toward attitude change to produce homogeneity.[27] This existent homogeneity attests to the existence of cleavage in the political system. If partisan affiliation was not closely

---

[24] Berelson *et al., op. cit.*, p. 319.

[25] *Ibid.*

[26] Parsons, in Burdick and Brodbeck, eds., *American Voting Behavior*, p. 92.

[27] This homogeneity is partly due to the fact that members of a primary group tend to share similar social characteristics that affect their vote. They tend to be members of the same class, residential area, and so forth. But even when these characteristics are held constant, the political composition of the primary group has a strong residual effect on the individual's political attitudes; see Berelson *et al., op. cit.*, pp. 88-93 and 137-38; and Herbert McCloskey and Harold E. Dahlgren, "Primary Group Influence on Party Loyalty," *American Political Science Review*, LIII (1960), pp. 757-76.

correlated with primary group affiliation, it is hard to see how there could be any basis for meaningful political competition, for partisan affiliation would then be unimportant as well as unrelated to basic social groupings in society. On the other hand, the cleavage produced by this existent correlation between primary group affiliation and partisan affiliation is tempered in the United States and Britain by the consensual norm (discussed in Chapters 5 and 10) that one's primary group *ought not* to be politicized. Though one's most intimate associates tend to be of like political affiliation (and if they are not, there will be pressure for attitudes to change until they are), this cleavage is balanced by a general social norm that places some relationships (in theory, if not in practice) above politics. Again, the civic culture allows a balance between apparently contradictory demands through the mixture of a set of norms (that primary groups be nonpartisan) and actual behavior (that primary groups are indeed homogeneous in the partisan sense) that are themselves in contradiction one with the other.

This is but one example of the way in which the civic culture manages cleavage in society. In general, this management of cleavage is accomplished by subordinating conflicts on the political level to some higher, overarching attitudes of solidarity, whether these attitudes be the norms associated with the "rules of the democratic game" or the belief that there exists within the society a supraparty solidarity based on nonpartisan criteria.[28]

This balance, furthermore, must be maintained on the elite as well as the citizen level. Though our data are not relevant here, it is quite likely that similar mechanisms operate on the elite level as well. The elaborate formal and informal rules of etiquette in the legislatures of Britain and the United States, for example, foster and indeed require friendly relations (or at least friendly words) between the supporters of the opposing parties. And this tempers the intensity of partisanship. It is not that partisanship is destroyed as a significant force; rather, it is kept in its place by more general norms of social relationships.

In sum, the most striking characteristic of the civic culture as it has been described in this volume is its mixed quality. It is a mixture in the first place of parochial, subject, and citizen orientations. The orientation of the parochial to primary relationships, the passive political orientation of the subject, the activity of the citizen, all

[28] See Parsons, *op. cit.*, p. 100.

merge within the civic culture. The result is a set of political orientations that are managed or balanced. There is political activity, but not so much as to destroy governmental authority; there is involvement and commitment, but they are moderated; there is political cleavage, but it is held in check. Above all, the political orientations that make up the civic culture are closely related to general social and interpersonal orientations. Within the civic culture the norms of interpersonal relationships, of general trust and confidence in one's social environment, penetrate political attitudes and temper them. The mixture of attitudes found in the civic culture, we have argued in this chapter, "fits" the democratic political system. It is, in a number of ways, particularly appropriate for the mixed political system that is democracy.

Political Culture and Stable Democracy

That the civic culture is appropriate for maintaining a stable and effective democratic political process can best be appreciated if we consider the impact of deviations from this model. We can begin by considering again the United States and Britain. We have argued that these two nations most closely approximate the model of the civic culture, but that in important respects they differ from each other in the way in which they approximate the model. Both nations achieve a balance of the active and passive roles of the citizen, but whereas in the United States the balance appears to be weighted somewhat in the direction of the active, participant pole, in Britain it tends somewhat in the direction of the subject, deferential pole. While in the United States the development of participant orientations has tended to overshadow the subject role, in Britain strong subject orientations have persisted despite the development of more active participant orientations. Though the British citizen became an active participant, he did not lose his respect for the independent authority of government to the extent that this occurred in the United States.

The kind of balance between active and passive orientations is in turn reflected in the way in which the political system balances governmental power and governmental responsiveness. In Britain the persisting deferential and subject orientations foster the development of strong and effective governments and the maintenance of an efficient and independent administrative structure. Americans, on

493

the other hand, tend to be uneasy with a powerful government—and their uneasiness is reflected in the institutional structures of government as well as in the strain of immobility that often pervades the American political process. On the other hand, one can argue that the balance in Britain is tilted too far in the opposite direction. It is possible that deference to political elites can go too far, and that the strongly hierarchical patterns in British politics—patterns that have often been criticized as limiting the extent of democracy in that nation—result from a balance weighted too heavily in the direction of the subject and deferential roles.

In comparison with Great Britain and the United States, Germany, Italy, and Mexico have relatively lower levels of social and interpersonal trust. More important, what social trust there is does not penetrate into political relationships, which tend to represent a separate and autonomous realm of attitudes. The absence of general social attitudes that penetrate the political realm inhibits the ability of citizens to cooperate with each other in their relations with the government. Thus their ability to influence the government in time of need—in particular, their ability to create *ad hoc* political structures for this purpose—is limited. Furthermore, their lack of ability to cooperate politically reflects a more general inability to enter political bargains, to collaborate, and to aggregate interests. The society divides up into closed and relatively hostile camps; or, to use our terminology, the balance between consensus and cleavage appears to be heavily weighted toward the latter. In these three nations, and especially in the first two, where the pattern of fragmentation coincides with partisan affiliation, the political culture seems to be unbalanced in the direction of political cleavage. This is not to argue that Germany and Italy may not be moving toward a reduction of political fragmentation. Certainly in Gemany the current political party system represents a much lower level of fragmentation and interparty hostility than existed under the Weimar Republic. But at present the balance appears to lie in the direction of cleavage rather than consensus, and this in turn affects the operation of the political system.

Perhaps the most significant deviations from the civic culture occur in the political participation and commitment in these three nations. In the ideal civic culture the activity and involvement of the citizen are balanced by a measure of passivity and noninvolvement. Similarly, the commitment itself is balanced, combining a

494

commitment to the actual operation and performance of the government as well as to the political system per se. But in Germany, Italy, and Mexico, there are important deviations from these ideal patterns, and the deviations differ from one country to another.

In Germany a passive subject orientation persists and has not yet been balanced by a participant orientation. Our German respondents appear more at ease in dealing with the output side of governmental activity, where government becomes administration rather than politics. Political activity tends to be more formal than informal—exposure to mass media, voting, formal but inactive membership in voluntary associations. Within these dimensions the activity levels are high, but they are not matched in frequency by more informal political discussions or group-forming influence strategies. Furthermore, the commitment to the system is heavily oriented to the output of the system. Those who consider themselves competent to participate in political decisions are more likely to be satisfied with governmental output, but their more general attachment to the system, or what we call system affect, is not likely to be any higher. And in general, though the satisfaction with governmental operations is relatively high, the attachment to the system is much lower. In Germany, then, the balance of the political culture is weighted in the direction of the subject role and of passive forms of participation. The government is viewed largely as an agency of administration. And the attachment to the political system is closely related to the ability of the government to satisfy pragmatic needs.

The response patterns in Italy are similar to those in Germany in certain important respects. As in Germany, the type of commitment to the political system is closely related to governmental output without being balanced by system affect. But Italian response patterns differ from the German, for the sense of subject allegiance is not present. If the German does not fully participate as an influential citizen in the input side of government, he does consider himself capable of acting effectively as a subject within an administrative context. The Italian, on the other hand, is more likely to be thoroughly alienated both as participant and as subject.

In some respects the Mexican political culture represents the most interesting imbalanced pattern of commitment and involvement. In this country the role of allegiant subject is least well developed. The Mexicans are more alienated from governmental output than are respondents in any of the other four nations—and this is so especially in terms of administrative output. Yet this alienation does not involve the more consistent pattern of alienation found in Italy. There is a relatively high level of system affect, especially connected with the symbols of the Mexican Revolution. Furthermore, there is a participant orientation toward the input side of the political system. But the type of participant orientation is what we have called an aspirational one. The level of subjective political competence is relatively high, but is unmatched by performance. This gap between perceived ability to influence the government and actual experience with such influence is also a feature of the civic culture, but the gap in Mexico is much wider than in the United States and Britain. And the relatively high level of political information, exposure to mass media and political communications upon which the American and British sense of political competence rests is also missing in Mexico. In Mexico, therefore, the balance between subject and participant orientations is heavily weighted in the direction of the participant. And the orientation to participation is not a balance of aspiration and performance where the former supports the latter, as in the civic culture; instead, it is a concentration on aspiration in which the performance remains unfulfilled.

Germany, Italy, and Mexico deviate from the civic culture in three different ways, but in each country the deviations create a political culture incongruent with an effective and stable democratic political system. In Germany the lack of commitment to the political system that is relatively independent of system output suggests that the stability of the system may be in doubt if the level of output becomes less satisfactory. There is little capital of "system affect" to draw upon if governmental performance should weaken. Furthermore, weakness of the participant role in Germany, especially the lack of an informal participatory culture, suggests that too much reliance is placed upon hierarchical leadership. Though the formal political institutions of democracy exist in Germany and though there is a well-developed political infrastructure—a system of political parties and pressure groups—the underlying set of political attitudes that would regulate the operation of these institutions in a democratic direction is missing.

In Mexico relatively high levels of system affect are coupled with a lack of experience with political input and an almost total rejection of political output. But the aspirational aspect of the Mexican political culture suggests a potentiality for a civic culture, for the orientation to participation is present. But if the German political system lacks the capital of system affect that might allow it to weather crises, the Mexican system may be described as living off its capital of system affect. Unless the output performance of the system can match the aspirations of the citizens (and what is relevant is not the objective level of output, but the evaluation of its adequacy by the citizens), then the Mexican pattern, too, may have within it the seeds of instability.

Italy suggests an even higher level of instability. While Germany and Mexico have some of the components of the civic culture, Italy lacks both the passive output satisfaction of the Germans and the aspirational input satisfaction of the Mexicans. The potential for the development of a civic culture would appear lowest here.

These considerations ought not to be taken as predictions of the future of the three political systems. We are spelling out differing potentialities, but we have concentrated on too narrow an aspect of the political system to allow prediction. To a considerable extent the future of these nations will be affected by the nature of their political cultures, but other factors will also have important consequences. International events, which have been outside our purview, will certainly have significant effects both on the political cultures of these nations and on their performance and stability. The future of German democracy rests in part on tendencies within the political culture, but it rests as well on the resolution of the East-West conflict; and Italy's political future is not unaffected by these tensions. And certainly since the advent of Castroism in Cuba, the impact of the external environment upon Mexico's political culture and structure has become especially important. The political cultures of these nations will play important roles in mediating these external impacts, but the weight of these impacts make it difficult for us, as students of political culture, to predict the future.

The Sources of the Civic Culture

This study began with a concern for understanding the development of political democracy. Our concern was occasioned by the large number of nations in which the realization of such a political system is an overt yet difficult goal. We refer, not only to the new nations of the world, but to many older nations that have for a long time been attempting to create a stable pattern of democratic insti-

497

tutions. The statesmen who attempt to create political democracy often concentrate upon the creation of a formal set of democratic governmental institutions and the writing of a constitution. Or they may concentrate upon the formation of a political party to stimulate the participation of the masses. But the development of a stable and effective democratic government depends upon more than the structures of government and politics: it depends upon the orientations that people have to the political process—upon the political culture. Unless the political culture is able to support a democratic system, the chances for the success of that system are slim.

The civic culture appears to be particularly appropriate for a democratic political system. It is not the only form of democratic political culture, but it seems to be the one most congruent with a stable, democratic system. It may therefore be useful to consider how it is transmitted from generation to generation. The first point that may be made is that it is not taught, in any complete sense of the term, in the schools. Civics training in the United States stresses a kind of citizen behavior that is closer to the rationality-activist model than to the civic culture. This is an important component of the civic culture, but it is only one component. In Great Britain, where there is also a close approximation of the civic culture, there is relatively little explicit attempt to inculcate either the pattern of norms and behavior associated with the civic culture or the pattern associated with the rationality-activist model. There is little explicit philosophy concerning what makes a "good British subject" and how children ought to be trained for their role as citizens. The point is not that the explicit training in the schools plays no role in the creation of a civic culture; it is, rather, that it may play only a minor role.

That the civic culture is not transmitted solely by explicit indoctrination is not surprising. Its attitudes and behavior combine in a complicated, subtle way; it is a culture that is characterized to some extent by inconsistencies and the balancing of opposites. One important component of the civic culture is the set of attitudes concerning confidence in other people—a diffuse, partially inconsistent pattern that does not lend itself readily to explicit teaching. How, then, can it be transmitted from generation to generation?

Our consideration of political socialization in Chapter 12 suggests an answer. The civic culture is transmitted by a complex process that includes training in many social institutions—family, peer group, school, work place, as well as in the political system itself. Furthermore, the types of experience within these institutions vary. Individuals learn political orientations through intentional teaching, as in a school civics class; but they also learn through overtly political experiences that are not intended to be lessons in politics, as when the child overhears parents discussing politics or when he observes the action of the political system. Or the training in political orientations may be neither explicit nor political in content, as when the individual learns about authority from participating in authority structures in the family or the school or when he learns about the trustworthiness of others from his early contact with adults.

So broad a pattern of political socialization provides an excellent way to inculcate the subtleties that comprise the civic culture. Insofar as some of the teaching is implicit, inconsistencies among orientations can be passed on without recognition. And insofar as many types of political training occur simultaneously, one may learn different aspects of the political culture from different sources. This kind of learning can minimize the strain that might result if orientations toward activity and passivity (to take one example of the opposing political attitudes of the civic culture) were introduced from a single source. Thus through his own participation in family and school and through the manifest teaching of the norms of political participation, the child may learn to expect opportunities to participate in decisions. Yet at the same time, his exposure to the necessarily hierarchical patterns of authority in family and school will temper this expectation of mastery over his political environment. Similarly, what he learns in civics textbooks about the need for political activity and for a politics of idealism will be tempered by what he observes of the actual political behavior and attitudes of adults. And this mixed set of orientations developed in childhood will be further modified by later, direct experiences with politics. His expectations and norms about participation will interact with the opportunities that the political system offers for participation, with the importance he himself places on particular issues, and with the demands that other roles place upon him.

A major part of political socialization, then, involves direct exposure to the civic culture and the democratic polity themselves. In this way each new generation absorbs the civic culture through exposure to the political attitudes and behavior of the preceding generation.

499

The preceding discussion, on the problem of transferring the civic culture from generation to generation, applies mostly to those nations where the civic culture already exists. But this is not the problem of the new nations. If a civic culture is to be created in these nations, it must be newly created. How can this be done? Such a question takes us well beyond the scope of our data, yet the characteristics of the civic culture and the political histories of the nations in which it has developed suggest two points. First, the civic culture emerged in the West as a result of a gradual political development—relatively crisis-free, untroubled, and unforced. Second, it developed by fusion: new patterns of attitudes did not replace old ones, but merged with them.

The reasons why this pattern of historical development facilitated the emergence of a civic culture are clear. It is a political culture of moderation. In it there is awareness of political issues, yet such issues are not the most salient for the ordinary man; there is involvement in politics, but the involvement is not intense. These political attitudes can only appear, one can argue, where political development has been relatively untroubled; where the stakes of politics are high enough to involve more and more people in the political process, but not so high as to force them to enter into politics as if into a battle to protect their interests from dangerous adversaries.

Less obvious, but also implied by the nature of the civic culture, are the reasons why it developed by fusion. For it is a mixed culture, combining parochial, subject, and participant orientations. Its development must be one in which the newer orientations to political participation merge with the older two orientations but do not replace them.

There are, as we have seen, two aspects to this fusion. On the one hand, the orientations associated with the diffuse patterns of traditional authority are not completely replaced by the newer, more differentiated patterns of political orientation. And second, the more active role of participant does not replace the more passive roles of parochial and the subject. The result is the type of civic culture found in the United States and Britain, where the political system is permeated by diffuse and general social values. For this permeation to continue, the development of a modern polity, with its functional, specific political units and its structured form of political competition, must not take place in a way that will shake the original community. These older orientations must be carried on into the modern system.

Similarly, the development of political democracy, with the spread of opportunities for the ordinary man to participate in the political decision-making process, cannot completely destroy the subject orientation to politics if there is to be a civic culture. The new way of making political decisions through participation of citizens does not so much replace the old mode of governmental operations as supplement it. In this way the blend of activity and passivity that characterizes the civic culture can be created.

The Future of the Civic Culture

This gradual, fusional growth of the civic culture has generally occurred in a political system whose problems have been spread over time. A variety of new groups have wanted entry into full participation, but not all groups at once. Major social issues have had to be resolved, but at different times. This gradualness of political change characterizes British and, to a lesser extent, American political history. The problem in the new nations of the world is that such gradualness is not possible. There is great demand for participation in politics from many who were only recently parochials. Tremendous problems of social change must be faced all at once. And what may be most crucial: the very acts of creating national boundaries and national identity must go on at the same time. A slow political development may foster a civic culture, but what the new nations of the world lack is the time for this gradual development.

These new nations are seeking to accomplish in a brief period of time what took centuries to consummate in the West. Is it possible to find substitutes for this gradual and fusional process of political change? There is no clear answer to this question, and one can only speculate. If our study has taught us anything, it is that there is no simple formula for the development of a political culture conducive to the maintenance of democracy. However, several conclusions do emerge that have a bearing on this problem.

The most obvious substitute for time would be education. Our data have shown education to be the most important determinant of political attitudes; and it is also the most manipulable. The great advantage of education is that skills that may take years to develop for the first time can be passed on much more easily once there are some who possess them. Education, as our data have shown, can develop a number of the major components of the civic culture. It can train individuals in the skills of political participation. They can be taught how to gather information; they can be brought into contact with the mass media; they can learn the formal structure of politics, as well as the importance of governmental and political institutions. And it is possible to communicate through education the explicit norms of democratic participation and responsibility.

But our data also show that education can create only some of the components of the civic culture. The schools can teach the cognitive skills connected with participation, but can they teach the underlying social attitudes that are an important component of the civic culture? Can education teach social trust and confidence? Can it foster the permeation of the political process by these social attitudes? And can the curious mixture of activity and passivity, involvement and indifference, of parochial, subject, and participant orientations be communicated through formal education? Our analysis of the relationship between the socialization processes and the creation of a civic culture suggests that formal education may not adequately substitute for time in the creation of these other components of the civic culture.

One way to supplement formal education might be to develop other channels of political socialization. As was suggested above, the very existence of a large number of channels of political socialization fosters the inculcation of the mixed pattern of attitudes of the civic culture. It increases the variety of political orientations that can be transmitted. More important, experience with a multitude of socializing agencies can train the individual to deal with varied roles at the same time—to schedule and balance his political orientations. And this ability to handle numerous roles is a major component of the civic culture. Some important socializing agencies are the family, the work place, and voluntary associations. Perhaps as these institutions change and develop in the new nations, the channels of socialization for the civic culture will broaden. As the family becomes more participant and open to the political process —and our data suggest that this is a function of modernization— new opportunities to foster civic attitudes may develop. Similarly, occupational changes that accompany industrialization, as well as the development of a structure of voluntary associations, may increase the channels of socialization.

But even the opening of these new channels may not be enough for the development of a civic culture. Such channels may foster attitudes toward participation, but their importance in the creation of social trust and affective commitment to the system is more questionable. If these socializing agencies are in a fragmented political system, for example, the affect developed might be one of alienation, and the interpersonal trust might not be translatable into politically relevant trust. What is required is a process by which individuals can come to develop a sense of common political identity; an identity that implies common affective commitment to the political system, as well as a sense of identity with one's fellow citizens. Participation and cognitive skills are not enough to create a political community in which one trusts and can cooperate politically with one's fellow citizens, and in which one's attachment to the political system is deep and affective.

The problem, then, is to develop, along with the participation skills that schools and other socializing agencies can foster, affective commitment to the political system and a sense of political community. How this might come about is suggested if we consider for a moment the patterns of political culture in Germany and Mexico, two nations that are particularly relevant here. In Germany we find a high level of political cognition. What is missing is system affect and a sense of ability to cooperate with one's fellow citizens. In Mexico we find the educational and cognitive components weaker, but there is system affect and a highly developed sense of identity as Mexicans. And this sense of identity is accompanied by a sense of ability to cooperate politically—or at least the aspiration for such cooperation. Mexico lacks the developed educational system that produces the high levels of cognitive political skills in Germany, but it has what Germany lacks to produce a high level of system affect. Mexico has had a symbolic, unifying event: the Mexican Revolution. This revolution, as we have argued, is the crucial event in the development of the Mexican political culture, for it created a sense of national identity and a commitment to the political system that permeates almost all strata of the society.

If a new nation is to create a civic culture, it needs both the unifying symbols and system affect that the Mexican Revolution has provided, as well as the cognitive skills that exist in Germany. There must be a symbolic event, or a symbolic, charismatic leader, or some other means of creating commitment and unity at the symbolic

503

level. But also important are expanding educational opportunity, experiences in industrial contexts, and exposure to the media of communication, to political parties, and voluntary associations. Governmental performance, too, has a crucial effect on the growth of a civic culture. As the German and Mexican cases illustrate, the development of stable political commitment may hinge upon the ability of the political system, especially in its formative stages, to produce output that satisfies the expectations of the members of the system. Only in this way can a stable and balanced commitment to the system be created and maintained.

Stated in these terms, the difficulties confronting efforts to create effective democratic processes and the orientations necessary to sustain them in the developing areas may appear to be insurmountable. What seems to be called for is the simultaneous development of a sense of national identity, subject and participant competence, social trust, and civic cooperativeness. The resources available to the elites of the new nations are scarce, and there are limits on the capacity of these societies to assimilate these resources rapidly and effectively. Other goals compete for the same resources. We cannot properly sit in judgment of those leaders who concentrate their resources on the development of social overhead capital, industrialization, and agricultural improvement, and who suppress disruptive movements or fail to cultivate democratic tendencies. Nor can we properly condemn those who, when confronted with the enormous range and pressure of the problems of modernization, are unable to make the necessary painful choices and thus permit their societies and political processes to drift into chaos. Few Western statesmen have ever been called upon to cope with such a range of issues and choices all at once.

What our study enables us to argue is that *any* approach to modernization has within it some of the seeds of the civic culture. Any set of modernizing priorities will place heavy stress on education; and rising levels of education will create some of the components of a civic culture. Thus an imaginative approach to education may serve to increase its civic dividends. The probability is also high that any approach to modernization will tend to enlarge the urban-industrial sector of the society. And we know that the urban-industrial family and occupations have within them civic potentialities. Broadly speaking, we can say that these core processes of modernization—education and industrialization—create a democratic opportunity; the problem then becomes, what *other* investments of energy, resources, and imagination can consolidate these tendencies and potentialities, and what are their relative costs?

The answers to these questions are not readily available. It is only in recent decades that political science has turned its attention to a realistic and serious analysis of the nature of democratic and other types of political process. We are only beginning to develop a theory of political systems and political change that might be of use to democratic statesmen in the new nations. What we have done in this book is to spell out methodically the mixture of attitudes that support a democratic system. If it can create a more sober and informed appreciation of the nature and complexity of the problems of democratization, it will have served its purpose.

APPENDICES

APPENDIX A

SAMPLING AND SAMPLE ERROR

THE DATA in this book are based on five independent samples, each carried on in one of the nations. The samples are similar in design, for all are stratified, multistage, probability samples. The most important characteristic of this kind of sample is that for each family in each nation there was the same chance that one of its members aged eighteen or over would fall within the sample. In Mexico, due to technical considerations as well as problems of cost, the sample was limited to cities over ten thousand in population. Within these cities, however, random techniques were used. (A comparison of the Mexican results with those for cities of the same size in the other four nations suggests that this difference in the sample does not distort the results. In most cases the national differences reported would probably be even greater had the Mexican sample included smaller communities.) The choice of families and the choice of respondent within each family were strictly random and therefore outside the interviewer's control.

Within the framework of this broad similarity there were differences in the sampling techniques used in each country and in the experiences with each sample. In order to specify the nature of the samples, it would be best to quote directly from the reports on the sampling prepared by the research agencies in each of the nations.

GERMANY (DIVO Institute, Frankfort):
                    The Sample
1. Description of the Sampling Method
   This study is based on a stratified, multistage, random sample of the West German population between the ages of eighteen and eighty.
   The first step in the selection procedure was to select the communities from a complete list of all communities in the country. To accomplish this, two strata were formed: the first included all communities with less than two thousand inhabitants, the second contained all communities of two thousand or more inhabitants. Beginning from the north of Germany and gradually descending to the southern parts, we broke each stratum down into smaller units—so-called cells—according to the percentage of total population living in each stratum: in the first, thirty-eight cells, and in the second, sixty-two cells—all cells of one stratum enclosing about the same number of inhabitants. Using random numbers, we selected a sample point from each cell, following the cumulated sequence of inhabitants. When the communities of the sample had been

thus determined, the households to be contacted were systematically selected from a central register of inhabitants (*Einwohnermeldekartei*) in each community; a random number was used as a starting point. In the selected households all members aged eighteen years and older were listed in unique order of succession. From this list the person to be questioned was determined, again by the use of random numbers. Substitutions were not allowed.

The sample is based on 1,296 addresses. Number of completed interviews: 955.

2. Results

	Number of Cases	Percentage
Completed interviews	955	74
Households without members between 18 and 79 years of age	13	1
Unoccupied dwelling units	44	3
Nonexistent addresses	14	1
Not at home	123	9
Refusals	134	10
Respondent physically or mentally unable to give interview	9	1
Other	4	—
Total addresses assigned:	1,296	99%

3. Representativeness of the Sample

Census figures are used for comparison with the results of the survey. All figures shown are percentages.

Church Membership	Census 13.9.1959	Sample
Roman Catholic	45.2	42
Protestant	51.2	52
Jew	0.1	0
Other/None	3.5	6
	100	100

Age	1.1.1959	
18-25	16.1	12
26-30	8.9	8
31-35	9.3	10
36-40	9.2	12
41-50	16.6	19
51-60	18.9	19
60 and over	21.0	20
	100	100

Size of Town	1.7.1958	
Less than 5,000	36.7	37
5,000-19,999	16.1	19
20,000-49,999	9.8	6
50,000-99,999	6.4	10
100,000 and over	31.0	28
	100	100

Region of Country	1.7.1958	
Schleswig-Holstein, Niedersachsen	17.1	17
Nordrhein-Westfalen, Rheinland-Pfalz	36.5	37
Hessen, Baden-Württemberg	23.5	22
Bayern	18.1	19
Hamburg-Bremen	4.8	5
	100	100

Sex	1.1.1959	
Male	45.6	47
Female	54.4	53
	100	100

ITALY (Istituto Italiano Dell'Opinione Pubblica, Milan):
The Sample

A random sample of persons to be interviewed was obtained by a system of multistage, stratified sampling:

Stage 1. Stratification and selection of provinces;

Stage 2. Stratification and selection of communes within the provinces selected in stage 1;

Stage 3. Selection of persons resident in the communes selected in stage 2.

In the following paragraphs we give a full illustration of the sampling method pursued in its three successive stages.

1. First stage of Sampling: Stratification and Selection of the Provinces

(A) *Stratification.* The whole Italian territory was subdivided into ninety-two provinces. These provinces were stratified as follows: first, the ninety-two provinces were classified into four main geographical strata, corresponding in turn to the four main geographical divisions of Italy. The provinces belonging to each of these four main strata were then further stratified on the basis of eight nongeographical variables, which express some of the social, economic, and political characteristics of the Italian provinces.

(B) *Selection.* From each of the total of thirteen strata, one province was randomly selected. Since the population varies a great deal from province to province, the selection was carried out with probability proportionate to size: that is, by allotting to every province a probability proportionate to the number of residents over the age of eighteen.

2. Second Sampling Stage: Stratification and Selection of Communes

The commune was chosen as the sampling unit for the second stage; it represents the smallest territorial unit in the Italian administrative system.

Within every province selected in the first stage, communes were stratified according to the size of their populations, as follows:

1. Up to 10,000 inhabitants
2. From 10,000 to 30,000
3. From 30,000 to 50,000
4. From 50,000 to 100,000
5. Over 100,000 inhabitants

From the total of thirteen provinces forty-nine strata were obtained, and from each of these a commune was selected at random; this selection was also made by assigning to the communes a probability proportionate to their size: that is, to the number of inhabitants over eighteen years of age.

3. *Third Sampling State: Selection of Persons*

The total size of the sample was fixed at 1,500 units. In view of the particular difficulties involved in the survey, it was thought best to provide for a reserve oversample equal to fifty per cent of the number of successful interviews.

The sample was divided among the thirteen provinces and then among the communes selected from each province in proportion to the size of the corresponding strata.

The sample assigned to each commune was divided into two parts, in proportion to the population of those twenty-one years and over, and to the population between the ages of eighteen and twenty-one.

As regards the population of twenty-one and over, the random selection was made by means of systematic sampling from the general electoral registers. It was considered preferable to use these registers and to avoid an intermediate selection from a few electoral areas, in order to obtain the widest distribution of the sample within the territory of the commune and, consequently, maximum variability of the persons interviewed.

Because the sample is "self-weighting"—the sampling at the first and second stages was carried out with probability proportionate to the size of each unit (provinces and communes)—the overall probability of selection has turned out to be the same for all the Italian electors.

As regards the sample of persons between the ages of eighteen and twenty-one, it was not possible to make a selection by means of official records of population. An empirical system of selection was therefore adopted, by which the interviewers selected persons exclusively from the families or the houses of the electors selected at random. This system, though not a strictly random one, made it possible almost completely to eliminate the risk of bias due to selection by the interviewer; furthermore, it must be remembered that persons between the ages of eighteen and twenty-one represent barely seven and one-half per cent of the whole sample.

Results of the Calls

	Number	%	
Completed Interviews	995	74	
Failed Interviews	350	26	
Not at home 3rd visit	172		13
Refusal	178		13
Available persons	1,345	100	

Unavailable persons	227	
Away on holiday		36
Unknown, moved, incorrect address		165
Deceased or invalids		26
Total sample	1,572	

It is pointed out that of the total number of persons available (i.e., excluding deceased, invalids, unknown, moved, incorrect addresses and those away on holidays) interviews were conducted with 74 per cent, two-thirds at the first visit. The 26 per cent of failures (not a high percentage when the particular features of the questionnaire are considered) are distributed equally between absences at the third visit and refusals. Almost the same results were obtained in all the provinces.

Geographical Distribution	Cases	Sample %	Universe %
Northern Italy	469	47.1	47.0
Central Italy	192	19.3	18.8
Southern Italy	223	22.4	22.9
Italian Islands	111	11.2	11.3
	995	100.0	100.0

City Size	Cases	%	%
Up to 10,000 inhabitants	326	48.9	44.0
From 10,000 to 50,000	430	27.1	26.7
Over 50,000	239	24.0	29.3
	995	100.0	100.0

Sex	Cases	%	%
Males	471	47.3	48.0
Females	524	52.7	52.0
	995	100.0	100.0

Age	Cases	%	%
18-25	162	16.3	17.5
26-35	232	23.3	20.9
36-60	466	46.8	43.9
Over 60	135	13.6	17.7
	995	100.0	100.0

Education	Cases	%	%
No schooling	88	8.8	9.6
Primary school	605	60.8	56.0
Secondary school			
Lower middle school	147	14.8	17.3
Higher middle school	97	9.8	12.0
University	54	5.4	5.1
Other	4	0.4	–
	995	100.0	100.0

MEXICO (International Research Associates of Mexico, Mexico City):
The Sample

The universe for this study consisted of the adult population (twenty-one years of age or over) residing in all Mexican cities of ten thousand population or more, as of government estimates for June 1958. Mexico City, being by far the most populous metropolitan center, and two other key population centers, Guadalajara and Monterrey, were arbitrarily included in the sample. (Metropolitan Mexico City is defined as Mexico City proper plus the adjoining areas of Coyoacán, Atzcapotzalco, and Mixcoac.)

For the selection of the interior cities, the nation was divided into five urbanization strata, in accordance with Mexican census data. The strata were:

1. Mexico City
2. Cities of 300,000 or more (Guadalajara and Monterrey)
3. Cities of 100,000 to 299,999
4. Cities of 30,000 to 99,999
5. Cities of 10,000 to 29,999

A total of twenty-seven specific localities (cities) was selected and distributed randomly within these strata, in such a manner as to insure proper geographical distribution throughout the five regions of Mexico as defined by the Mexican census. Localities randomly selected within strata were chosen with probability proportionate to size.

A calculation of the proportion of interviews that should derive from each stratum was made in accordance with census data. Groups of interviews in proportion to these data were assigned, within the gross sample, to each stratum accordingly. The size of these groups varies among strata but remains constant within each stratum.

Shown below are interview group size and the relationship of completed interview totals to population distribution in cities of ten thousand or more population. It will be noticed that Mexico City was undersampled. A proportionate distribution of one thousand interviews within the universe studied would have given 372 interviews to Mexico City. In order to allow for greater interior city coverage, however, Mexico City's normal portion of interviews was cut by one half: that is, only 186 interviews were anticipated for Mexico City, while the remaining 186 were distributed proportionately throughout the interior cities.

Upon tabulation, these Mexico City interviews were upweighted by a factor of 2.5 in order to bring them once again to their true proportion within the sample as a whole.

Each group of interviews was assigned to 10 blocks in stratum 2; 9 blocks in stratum 3; 5 blocks in stratum 4, and 3 blocks in stratum 5, thus providing an average cluster size of six completed interviews in all interior cities.

The assignment of interviews in each city (both for Mexico City and the interior cities) was made through the use of the latest block maps available. The following procedure was used:

1. The blocks were numbered in serpentine fashion;

2. A random number was chosen (the block corresponding to the number was the first sample block);

3. All subsequent blocks were chosen by adding a skipping ratio (the ratio of total blocks in each city to the number of sample blocks desired) to the previous number used. Thus the second block included in the

Stratum	Expected Size of Interview Group, After Mortality	Number of Interview Groups (cities)	Total Anticipated Completions	Total Interviews Completed
1	186	1	186	191
2	60	2	120	117
3	54	5	270	270
4	30	8	240	230
5	18	11	198	200
Total		27	1,014	1,008

Stratum	Sample Distribution, before Weighting (in %)	Approximate Population Each Stratum	Population Distribution (in %)	Sample Distribution, after Weighting (in %)
1	18.9	4,500,000	37.2	36.9
2	11.6	1,093,000	9.0	9.0
3	26.8	2,382,000	19.7	20.8
4	22.8	2,407,000	19.9	17.8
5	19.8	1,727,000	14.3	15.4
Total	100.0	12,109,000	100.0	100.0

sample was that which corresponded to the sum of the second block number and the skipping ratio, and so on;

4. The above procedure was continued in a circular manner (first block succeeding the last) until the desired number of sample blocks was chosen.

In Mexico City, where population data by district are available, the city was stratified by district and blocks, assigned in accordance with known district population. Selection of households to be interviewed was made within districts, as described above, for assignment within cities where no district population data exist.

A complete list of all households on each of the blocks chosen for the city was compiled.

The number of interviews assigned to each block was calculated by multiplying the total number of interviews for the city by the ratio that households on a given block bore to the total number of households on all sample blocks for the city (or, in the case of Mexico City, for each district).

In each group of blocks in the sample the specific households to be

515

interviewed were chosen in the same manner as blocks were chosen, as described above.

The choice of respondent within a household was made by having the interviewer first list all members of the household twenty-one years of age and over, and then choose the appropriate respondent by means of a table of random number, printed on the questionnaire itself. A member of the household was defined as a person who usually sleeps at that address. Thus a servant who had her own room and lived with the family would be a member of the household, but a servant who only worked in the house during the day and went elsewhere to sleep at night was not considered a resident.

One respondent was selected in each household, regardless of family size.

The universe of study was purposely oversampled in order to allow for an estimated mortality of approximately forty per cent. At the outset, a minimum of one initial visit and two call-backs were made in an effort to locate and interview the respondent originally selected. No substitutes were taken. During the course of the field work, however, it was found that two call-backs would not be sufficient to achieve the minimum number of completed interviews desired in certain cities. In Mexico City, for example, it was necessary to make a maximum of five call-backs because of the extremely high mortality experienced after only two. In interior cities, however, an average maximum of three call-backs was sufficient to achieve the minimum number of interviews desired. An analysis of respondent mortality follows:

	%
Completed interviews	60
Refusals	14
Absentees	26
Total	100

UNITED KINGDOM (Research Services Ltd., London):
The Sample

The sample design was a multistage probability sample, with the Electoral Register used as a sampling frame. The Register is the most comprehensive list of names and addresses of persons available in Great Britain for sampling purposes, and it was used in the way described below to select a sample of electors (i.e., those whose names appear on the Register).

The Electoral Register can also be considered a list of households; from this a sample of households can be chosen and nonelectors in the households interviewed. Nonelectors include all those ineligible to vote: e.g., persons under the age of twenty-one (and for our purposes not younger than eighteen years), peers, aliens, lunatics and criminals, and those who for any reason have been omitted from the Register.

The sampling design was of four stages. First, a sample of parliamentary constituencies was chosen; then from each constituency two wards were selected. These wards were broken down into several polling districts and we selected one polling district from each ward. From these polling districts individual names were taken from the Register. At each stage the method of selection of units was random in the technical statistical sense, i.e., by systematic sampling with a random start.

First Stage

Constituencies were chosen as the first stage unit since they vary less in population size than do administrative districts. It was decided to use forty constituencies (seven per cent of all constituencies). All the constituencies in each of the Registrar General's twelve regions were listed in the following way:

1. Constituencies situated in towns of two hundred thousand population and over were placed in a separate group and were listed in the order of the ratio of Labour/non-Labour vote in the 1955 general election. This ratio is closely connected with social class: the higher the proportion of the Labour vote, the lower the social class of the constituency.

2. The remaining constituencies were listed by the use of the same ratio to establish a ranking order. This ensured that a correct proportion of large towns was included in the sample, and also ensured that there should be a fair reflection of constituencies of differing social class structure.

Second Stage

This stage was to select two wards (into which each constituency is divided for purposes of electoral administration) for each selected constituency. This followed similar lines to the process of selecting constituencies.

Third Stage

Each ward is divided into polling districts. The polling districts in each ward are listed in alphabetical order. The number of electors in each polling district were listed cumulatively and one polling district was randomly selected.

Fourth Stage

For each polling district a systematic selection of individuals was made: that is, names were taken at fixed intervals. This procedure gives a well-spread sample of electors, but special provision had to be made to obtain a sample of nonelectors.

For one of the two polling districts in the selected constituency twenty names were selected (by dividing the total number of electors by nineteen and taking half the remainder as a starting point).

For the other polling district thirty-two names were selected in a similar manner, but of these, twelve were treated as samples of households, and all electors living in those twelve households were listed. At these households attempts were made to interview only a nonelector. Whenever more than one nonelector was found to be living in a single household, the birthday rule was used to select the one to be interview: that is, the nonelector whose birthday was nearest to the day of the interview. In this way a proportion of nonelectors in each constituency was to be obtained.

For electors the required quota was twelve interviews per polling district. To achieve this, the interviewers were instructed to first attempt to contact fourteen of the twenty names selected for each polling district. The remaining six names were to be used as reserves in case of refusals and noncontacts.

Results

In all, 1,600 names of electors were drawn and 480 households for nonelectors. Nine hundred and thirty-seven (59 per cent) elector interviews were obtained and 30 (6 per cent) nonelector interviews. There were 663 (41 per cent) unproductive elector calls and 450 (94 per cent) unproductive nonelector calls. The bulk of the unproductive calls among nonelectors were due to the fact that there were no nonelectors residing in the household. Of the 450 unproductive nonelector calls (94 per cent of the 480 nonelector calls), 427 (89 per cent of the total nonelector calls) were households without members in the 18 to 20 age group. For electors the bulk of the unproductive calls (265 out of 663) were refusals. Given the type of survey, the refusal rate is of an order to be expected. The following table presents the sample results for electors.

	Cases	%
Completed interviews	937	59
Refusals	265	16
Out or no reply	189	12
Other reasons (away, sick, dead, premises empty, or demolished, not known at address, miscellaneous)	209	13
Total elector calls	1600	100

Representatives of the Sample:
Comparison of Sample with the 1951 Census

Age	Total Sample (963)		1951 Census (35,990,200)	
	No.	%	'00	%
18-25	81	8.4	51,692	14.4
26-30	95	9.9	37,601	10.4
31-35	112	11.6	32,748	9.1
36-40	139	14.3	37,688	10.5
41-50	194	20.4	72,215	20.1
51-60	172	17.8	56,347	15.7
60 and over	170	17.6	71,611	19.8

The figures available for direct comparison are those of the 1951 census. Later figures are not directly comparable, since our age breakdown intervals do not conform to those used in official statistical tables. The 1951 census gave population figures for each year of age and therefore a direct comparison could be made.

The survey figures are low for the young age groups (eighteen to

518

twenty-five). This is partly accounted for by the low contact rate for this group. The reasons for this are several. Possibly they live away from home but do not register their new address; they also tend to be out a great deal more than those in older age groups. Further, armed forces voters registered at their home address were not drawn in the sample.

Regional and social grade breakdowns are compared below with the figures obtained from a large random sample (n: 17,706), which has been weighted to bring it into line with the census figures.

Region	Citizenship Survey 963	%	Weighted Figures 17,706	%
South of England	395	41.0	7,252	40.9
Wales	58	6.0	984	5.7
Midlands	126	13.1	2,818	15.8
North of England	290	30.1	4,867	27.0
Scotland	94	9.8	1,785	10.6
Social Grade	963	%	17,706	%
AB	151	15.6	2,626	15.3
C1	146	15.2	3,092	16.7
C2	323	33.5	5,502	33.6
DE	343	35.7	6,486	34.4

UNITED STATES (National Opinion Research Center, Chicago):
Sample Design

The individuals designated for interview were selected through a process of stratified, multistage, probability sampling. Through this procedure each family in the United States had an equal chance of having one of its members aged eighteen or older fall within the sample.

The first stage sampling units were standard metropolitan areas and individual nonmetropolitan counties. The approximately three thousand such units in the United States were grouped into sixty-six strata as nearly equal in population as feasible. The goal was to make the composition of each stratum homogeneous with respect to the demographic characteristics of the areas classified therein. Among the variables entering into the stratification were: geographic location, size of the largest municipality within the unit, median family income, proportion of the working population employed in the mining or manufacturing industries, and the racial composition of the population. From each of the sixty-six strata one primary sampling unit was selected, with probability proportionate to an estimate of its mid-1953 population. Among approximately half the strata, the selections of primary sampling units were independent. For the remaining half of the strata, variance reducing procedures, such as the Goodman-Kish controlled selection technique, were employed.

Within each primary sampling unit, a sample of localities was systematically selected with probabilities proportionate to 1950 population. For this stage, incorporated places were ordered on the basis of their population, and the unincorporated portions of each minor civil division were appended at the end of the listing. Generally, two or three localities were selected from each primary sampling unit that represented one of the less populous strata, and a larger number of localities from each primary sampling unit representing one of the more populous strata.

Within the larger cities, census tracts were ordered on the basis of median family income, and two or more were selected systematically, with probability proportionate to the number of occupied dwelling units they contained. In smaller municipalities and in unincorporated areas, census enumeration districts served as third-stage units. These units were sampled with probability proportionate to population.

Within each of the third-stage units, one or two segments were selected with probability proportionate to the number of occupied dwelling units. By this process, 461 segments were selected. Thus each segment produced, on the average, approximately two interviews.

In the larger cities, square blocks generally served as segments and the census *Block Statistics* volumes provided measures of size. In smaller places, field counts were employed to obtain approximate measures of size. In areas with urban street patterns, small groupings of contiguous blocks were designated as segments. In open-country areas, segments were small areas bounded by roads or streams so that their limits could be readily identified in the field.

The dwelling units in each segment were then prelisted in a specified geographic order. A sampling ratio was computed for each segment such that the product of the segment's probability and the within-segment sampling ratio was equal over all segments. The reciprocal of this sampling ratio was applied in the systematic sampling of the dwelling units within a segment.

Upon visiting a dwelling unit thus selected, the interviewer enumerated all persons eighteen years of age or older residing there. In cases of dwelling units occupied by more than one family, the members of each of the families were enumerated on a separate questionnaire. For each dwelling unit the interviewer was assigned a specific selection table to be employed in determining which member of each family was thereby strictly random and outside the interviewer's control. No substitutions were allowed at any stage of the process.

The sample was designed in such a fashion as to correct automatically for shifts in the population that had occurred since the 1950 census and for errors in prelisting discovered during the course of interviewing. In that sense, the sample is self-weighting and unbiased.

Since only one person was interviewed from each family, individuals from one-adult families are somewhat overrepresented in the sample and individuals from families containing three or more adults are correspondingly underrepresented. Considerable past experience with surveys dealing with similar subjects-matter has shown that this distortion has only a negligible effect on estimates derived from this type of sample.

Field Performance

It was of course not possible to conduct an interview with every individual selected for the sample. The following table indicates the out-come of the field operations with respect to the sample.

	Cases	%
Completed interviews	970	83.3
Refusals	120	10.3
Break-offs	9	0.8
Not at home	26	2.2
Misc. (too ill to be interviewed, language barriers, senility, moved between initial call and call-back for interview)	39	3.4
	1,164	100.0

Estimates are available from the Bureau of the Census pertaining to several of the variables measured in the citizenship survey. All figures shown are percentages.

Sex	Census 18 + years of age July 1, 1959	Citizenship Survey
Male	47.5	46.9
Female	52.5	53.1
	100.0	100.0

Region of Resident	Census 14 + years of age March 1959	Citizenship Survey
Northeast	26.9	25.8
Midwest	28.4	27.7
South	29.8	32.4
West	14.9	14.1
	100.0	100.0

Race	Census 18 + years of age July 1, 1959	Citizenship Survey
White	90.0	89.4
Non-White	10.0	10.6
	100.0	100.0

Age	Census July 1, 1959	Citizenship Survey
18-25	14.9	12.6
26-30	9.7	9.2
31-35	10.7	9.3
36-40	10.8	10.0
41-50	19.6	18.1
51-60	15.5	16.0
61 and over	18.8	24.8
	100.0	100.0

	Census	
	20+ years of age	*Citizenship*
Type of Residence	*April 1959*	*Survey*
Standard metropolitan area	59.2	60.6
Other territory	40.8	39.4
	100.0	100.0

	Census	
	18+ years of age	*Citizenship*
Marital Status	*March 1959*	*Survey*
Single	14.3	11.6
Married	72.2	72.6
Divorced, separated	4.4	4.8
Widowed	9.1	11.0
	100.0	100.0

	Census	
	18+ years of age	*Citizenship*
Educational Attainment	*March 1959*	*Survey*
No schooling	2.0	1.1
Completed 1-4 years	5.4	5.7
Completed 5-7 years	11.6	10.8
Completed 8 years	15.8	17.2
Completed 9-11 years	19.2	18.4
Completed 12 years	29.3	27.4
Completed 1-3 years college	9.1	11.1
Completed 4 or more years college	7.6	8.3
	100.0	100.0

	Distribution of	
	Families	*Citizenship*
Family Income	*1959*	*Survey*
Under $1,000	5.1	8.4
$1,000-$1,999	8.3	9.5
$2,000-$2,999	9.3	10.4
$3,000-$4,999	21.8	22.8
$5,000-$7,499	29.1	27.8
$7,500-$9,999	14.2	10.3
$10,000-$14,999	9.1	7.9
$15,000 and over	3.1	2.9
	100.0	100.0

Life-History Sample

Respondents for the follow-up life-history interviews were selected from those interviewed in the cross-section survey. No attempt was made to select these reinterviews on a random basis. Rather, the respondents from the cross-section survey were divided into several "political types" based upon their answers to the first interview. The political types differed largely in the extent to which they were active and involved in politics. An attempt was then made to reinterview some of each political type in each nation. The respondents were selected in such a way as to provide some distribution of demographic characteristics within each political type. (The demographic characteristics used were sex, age, education, city size, party vote, occupation, and region.) In several cases this involved an overrepresentation of certain deviant types—highly educated males who were relatively inactive in politics or poorly educated women who were active. The original plan was to obtain 125 such reinterviews in each nation. In some cases this was not possible, and the following number of reinterviews were obtained: Germany 135; Italy 121; Mexico 120; United Kingdom 114, and United States 49.

Sampling Error

All sample surveys are subject to sampling error. Sampling error is the difference between the attributes of the sample and the attributes of the population from which the sample is drawn. Such errors cannot be eliminated, but with random sampling it is possible to make some estimate of the probable magnitude of these errors. Such estimates are usually made through the use of tests of statistical significance. With these tests we can tell how close the true proportion of an attribute in a population is likely to be to the sample proportion (say, 95 per cent of the time), or what the chances are that a particular difference between two groups could be due to sampling error. As a convention, differences so large that they could have been due to sampling error only one out of twenty times (95 per cent level) are generally accepted as statistically significant.

The application of such tests of significance to the sort of material discussed in this book must be approached with caution. There are two reasons. On the one hand, the tests may not be rigorous enough. They may lead to the acceptance of findings as statistically significant that have little significance statistically or otherwise. On the other hand, the tests may be too rigorous. They may lead in some cases to the rejection of statistically insignificant findings that ought not to be dismissed from consideration.[1]

Tests of statistical significance may overstate the importance of the findings in a number of ways. In the first place, of course, statistical significance is not a measure of the substantive significance of the finding. It merely indicates that a particular difference is unlikely to be due to chance errors in the sample. A difference of one per cent in the proportions of two groups having a particular attribute may be statistically significant if the sample is large enough, but it may be of no substantive significance. Similarly, tests of statistical significance are not tests of association. One cannot infer a high level of association from a high level of significance.

[1] The usefulness of statistical significance for surveys such as ours is being currently debated among statisticians. See the opposing views of H. Selvin, "A Critique of Tests of Significance in Survey Research," *American Sociological Review*, XXII (1957), pp. 519-27, and L. Kish, "Some Statistical Problems in Research Design," *ibid.*, XXIV (1959), pp. 328-38.

Most important, perhaps: such tests of significance are more appropriate for the sort of research in which rigorously defined hypotheses are being tested, and less appropriate for more exploratory research in which many of the relationships commented upon "emerge" from an *a posteriori* inspection of the data. With a large enough number of differences to inspect, the researcher is sure to find some that are statistically significant by chance alone. If, for instance, one has twenty paired comparisons, the chances are that in two out of three cases of these sets of comparisons, at least one difference will be statistically significant by chance, even if there are actually no differences in the population sampled. This problem would be most serious in our data when, say, the national differences in the proportion having a particular attribute were being compared. Since there are five nations, there are ten possible pairs that can be compared, and a statistically significant difference between one of the pairs is quite likely to arise by chance alone. It is only when the particular difference is predicted that it can be considered statistically significant. Since this study was exploratory, we have not hesitated to report interesting results that emerge from the data, though in most cases the differences that are reported and stressed are those that were expected at the beginning of the study. However, this limitation on the use of statistical tests ought to be kept in mind.

Lastly, statistical tests, because they deal only with random sampling errors, may overstate the validity of a finding. They do not deal with other sources of error—in interviewing, coding, translation, and so forth—that may not vary in random way. In general, then, one ought to use tests of statistical significance with great caution lest they give one a false sense of scientific security.

On the other hand, the tests of statistical significance may understate the scientific validity of our findings. This is particularly true because few conclusions are drawn in this volume on the basis of a single difference. Rather, we have concentrated much more on the pattern of differences among a variety of groups as well as a variety of measures. For instance, we have five independent national samples. The chances of a difference coming out the same way in all five nations due to sampling error—say, the chances of more highly educated respondents being more politically active in all five nations—would be about $(\frac{1}{2})^5$, no matter what the level of significance of any pair. If each of the five differences was significant at the ninety per cent level (to take a less rigorous figure than ordinarily used), the chance of all five pairs coming out in the same direction would be $1/10^5$ or one in one hundred thousand. Many of our tables are of the form in which a series of comparisons are reported. Many tables, for instance, show that within each nation and on the two educational levels (in ten groups, that is) a consistent pattern of differences is found: e.g., members of organizations are more likely than those who are not members to engage in political conversations. The chance that all ten comparisons will come out in the same direction is about two in one thousand, and the chance that nine of the paired comparisons will come out in the same direction is about two in one hundred. (And the chances of the differences coming out in the *predicted* direction are one-half as great as those cited above—one out of one thousand and one out of one hundred, respectively.) In fact, the chance of eight paired comparisons coming out the same way is less than one in ten, and the chance of eight comparisons coming out in the predicted way is less than one in twenty.

The general conclusion of this discussion seems to be that the value of tests of statistical significance for a study of this sort is dubious. The criticisms of such tests that have been made in the literature would seem to apply even more strongly to our five-nation study. However, for those readers who desire to apply tests of significance to our data, we include the following two formulas. When they are used, it ought to be kept in mind that too much weight ought not to be placed on the discovery that a particular difference is or is not statistically significant. If found to be significant, it must still be subject to the qualifications listed above. If not statistically significant, it may still be part of a pattern of responses that is significant. The patterning of responses in a variety of groups is probably the most useful test for the significance of the findings.[2]

---

[2] If the reader wishes to apply tests of statistical significance to the data in this study, the following formulas can be used. These assume that, due to the clustering in the national samples, the sampling error is greater than it would be in a simple random sample of this size. For all five samples used, it appeared safe to consider the standard errors of the estimates to be twice those derived from a simple random sample.

For estimating the sampling error of a particular proportion:

$$\text{S.E. (.05 level)} = 4\sqrt{\frac{pq}{n}}$$

For estimating the sampling error of the difference between two proportions:

$$\text{S.E. (difference at .05 level)} = 4\sqrt{\left(\frac{n_1 p_1 + n_2 p_2}{n_1 + n_2}\right)\left(\frac{n_1 q_1 + n_2 q_2}{n_1 + n_2}\right)\left(\frac{1}{n_1} + \frac{1}{n_2}\right)}$$

Where p = proportion of sample having attribute
$q = 1\text{-}p$
n = number of cases on which proportion is based and the subscripts $_1$ and $_2$ refer to the subgroups being compared (when using the second formula).

APPENDIX B

INTERVIEW SCHEDULES

THE following are composite versions of the cross-section and life-history interviews. Separate forms were prepared for each nation. These differed in some details, but were essentially the same as those below.

CROSS-SECTION SURVEY
INTRODUCTION IN ARRANGING INTERVIEW

My name is———————. I work for the———————. We are doing a survey for a large-university in order to find out how people in different countries feel about their government and about political affairs. We want to know what people feel about government in such countries as Italy, Germany, England, the United States—and also here in (COUNTRY OF INTERVIEW). We would like to know how they differ in their attitudes and in what ways they are similar.

I was hoping that you might help us in this. The interview will take about an hour. I was wondering if we could make an appointment for some time when it was convenient for you. It would help us out a lot.

INTRODUCTION AT TIME OF ACTUAL INTERVIEW

It was very kind of you to let me ask you these questions. Let me tell you something more about what we are doing. I mentioned that this interview is part of a large international study concerned with how people of all different walks of life think and feel about their country and political affairs. The purpose of the study is scientific: it is being done for a university. We want to know both what people's attitudes are and how they are formed.

Before we get into the details of the interview, I'd like to ask you some questions about your background and interests.

1a. Where were you born?

1b. What was the size of the town where you were born?

2. How long have you lived in this town (city)?

3. Do you intend to stay in this town (city)?

4a. Are you married?

4b. (IF EVER MARRIED) How many children do you have?

5. We'd like to start out by talking about some of your more general interests. Now aside from your work and your family, what are the activities that interest you most, that you spend your free time on? (FOR PEOPLE WHO MENTION ONLY ONE THING) Is there anything else? (FOR THOSE WHO SAY THEY HAVE NO FREE TIME) If you had more free time and opportunity, which activities would you like to engage in?

6a. All of us have ideas about what people should be like. Here is a list of characteristics you might find in people (HAND LIST 1). Could you select the quality you admire most?

List 1

Does his job well
Active in public and social affairs
Ambitious, wants to get ahead
Generous, considerate of others
Thrifty, saving
Lets no one take advantage of him
Keeps himself to himself
Respectful, doesn't overstep his place

6b. Which would be next?

7. Some people say that most people can be trusted. Others say you can't be too careful in your dealings with people. How do you feel about it?

8. Aside from people you know personally, of all the people you hear or read about, could you name one or more individuals you admire very much? (PROBE, IF NEEDED) Is there someone in particular?

9a. Here are some important problems facing the people in this country (HAND LIST 2). Would you please read through this list and tell me which one you feel is most important to you, personally?

List 2

Spiritual and moral betterment
Making ends meet
Government control and regulation of business
Eliminating inequality and injustice
Foreign affairs, national defense
Improving conditions for your family

9b. Which one is next?

10. Public issues often arise that are complex and hard to understand. Suppose such an issue arose that might affect your own way of life—such as a law concerning taxes or an international crisis that might lead to war—but you didn't understand this issue fully. What would you do to find out more about it? (IF ONLY ONE ANSWER GIVEN) Is there anything else?

11a. Do you follow the accounts of political and governmental affairs? Would you say you follow them regularly, from time to time, or never? (IF NEVER OR DON'T KNOW, SKIP TO Q. 12)
ASK 11b, 11c, and 11d ONLY IF RESPONDENT FOLLOWS THE ACCOUNTS OF POLITICAL AND GOVERNMENTAL AFFAIRS:

11b. What about newspapers—do you follow accounts of political and governmental affairs in the newspapers nearly every day, about once a week, from time to time, or never?

11c. What about on the radio or television? Do you listen to accounts of public affairs nearly every day, about once a week, from time to time or never?

11d. What about magazines? Do you read about public affairs in magazines about once a week, from time to time, or never?

12. What about talking about public affairs to other people? Do you do that nearly every day, once a week, from time to time, or never?

13a. If you wanted to discuss political and governmental affairs, are there some people you definitely *wouldn't* turn to, that is, people with whom you feel it is better *not* to discuss such topics? About how many people would you say there are with whom you would *avoid* discussing politics?

13b. (IF RESPONDENT AVOIDS POLITICAL DISCUSSIONS) Why do you avoid these discussions?

14. Some people say that politics and government are so complicated that the average man cannot really understand what is going on. In general, do you agree or disagree with that?

15. How do you feel about this? Thinking of the important national and international issues facing the country, how well do you think you can understand these issues?

16. How about local issues in this town or part of the country? How well do you understand them?

17. Many people we've interviewed have said that they have trouble understanding political and governmental affairs. Which of the reasons on this list (HAND LIST 3) best explains why this happens? (IF NEEDED) Which is the *major* reason?

List 3

The problems are too complex

People don't care and don't try

Those in power don't help people to understand

18a. One sometimes hears that some people or groups have so much influence over the way the government is run that the interests of the majority are ignored. Do you agree or disagree that there are such groups?

18b. (IF AGREEMENT OR PARTIAL AGREEMENT) Who or what groups?

19. We know that the ordinary person has many problems that take his time. In view of this, what part do you think the ordinary person ought to play in the local affairs of his town or district? (IF NEEDED) What *specifically* ought he to do?

20. People speak of the obligations that they owe to their country. In your opinion, what are the obligations that every man owes his country?

21. Speaking generally, would you say that most people are more inclined to help others, or more inclined to look out for themselves?

22. Suppose a regulation were being considered by (SPECIFY MOST LOCAL GOVERNMENTAL UNIT: TOWN, VILLAGE, ETC.) that you considered very unjust or harmful. What do you think you could do? (IF NEEDED) Anything else?

23. If you made an effort to change this regulation, how likely is it that you would succeed?

528

24. If such a case arose, how likely is it that you *would actually* try to do something about it?

25. Have you ever done anything to try to influence a local decision?

26. Suppose a law were being considered by (SPECIFY APPROPRIATE NATIONAL LEGISLATURE FOR EACH NATION) that you considered to be very unjust or harmful. What do you think you could do? (IF NEEDED) Anything else?

27. If you made an effort to change this law, how likely is it that you would succeed?

28. If such a case arose, how likely is it you *would actually* try to do something about it?

29. Have you ever done anything to try to influence an act of (SPECIFY NATIONAL LEGISLATURE)?

30a. Suppose several men were trying to influence a government decision. Here is a list of things they might do (HAND LIST 4). The first man works through personal and family connections with government officials. The second one writes to government officials explaining his point of view. The third tries to get people interested in the problem and to form a group. The fourth man works through his party. A fifth man organizes a protest demonstration. Which one of these methods do you think would be the most effective?

30b. Which method would be least effective?

List 4

    Working through personal and family connections
    Writing to government officials
    Getting people interested, forming a group
    Working through a political party
    Organizing a protest demonstration

31a. Thinking now about the national government in (LONDON, BONN, ETC.), about how much effect do you think its activities, the laws passed and so on, have on your day-to-day life? Do they have a great effect, some effect or none?

31b. On the whole, do the activities of the national government tend to improve conditions in this country, or would we be better off without them?

32a. Now take the local government: about how much effect do you think its activities have on your day-to-day life? Do they have a great effect, some effect, or none?

32b. On the whole, do the activities of the local government tend to improve conditions in this area, or would we be better off without them?

33. Here is a different type of question. Speaking generally, what are the things about this country that you are most proud of as an American (MEXICAN, GERMAN, ETC.)?

34. Suppose there were some question that you had to take to a government office—for example, a tax question or housing regulation. Do you think you would be given equal treatment? I mean, would you be treated as well as anyone else?

529

35. If you explained your point of view to the officials, what effect do you think it would have? Would they give your point of view serious consideration, would they pay only a little attention, or would they ignore what you had to say?

36a. (ITALY AND GERMANY) Under our present system of government, as you know, the President has little to do with the actual running of the country. Government affairs are conducted by the Prime Minister, his Cabinet, and Parliament. Some people say that there is really no need for the presidency. What do you think? Is the presidency needed or not?

36b. (IF RESPONDENT SAYS THE PRESIDENCY IS NEEDED) Here is a list of reasons that people have given as to why the presidency is needed (HAND LIST 5). Which of these do you think is the most important?

36c. Which is next in importance?

List 5

A nation needs someone to symbolize it to foreign countries;

People get real pleasure out of following the activities of the President;

A nation, like a family, needs a respected figure at its head;

The President is needed to appoint the Prime Minister and to open Parliament;

A nation needs someone at its head who stands above political conflict.

36a. (UNITED KINGDOM) Under our present system of government, as you know, the Queen has little to do with the actual running of the country. Government affairs are conducted by the Prime Minister, his Cabinet, and Parliament. Some people say that there is really no need for the monarchy. What do you think? Is the monarchy needed or not?

36b. (IF RESPONDENT SAYS THE MONARCHY IS NEEDED) Here is a list of reasons which people have given as to why the monarchy is needed (HAND LIST 5). Which of these do you think is the most important?

36c. Which is next in importance?

List 5

A nation needs someone to symbolize it to foreign countries;

People get real pleasure out of following the activities of the Queen;

A nation, like a family, needs a respected figure at its head;

The Queen is needed to appoint the Prime Minister and to open Parliament;

A nation needs someone at its head who stands above political conflict.

36a. (UNITED STATES) Now I would like to ask you a question about the presidency. Some people say that the President should be above political party conflicts. Others say that he should be an active leader of his own party. Which view do you think is correct?

36b. Why do you say that?

37a. If you had some trouble with the police—a traffic violation maybe, or being accused of a minor offense—do you think you would be given equal treatment? That is, would you be treated as well as anyone else?

37b. If you explained your point of view to the police, what effect do you think it would have? Would they give your point of view serious consideration, would they pay only a little attention, or would they ignore what you had to say?

38a. (GERMANY, ITALY, MEXICO, AND UNITED KINGDOM) Now we would like to find out something about your party preference and how you vote. Are you currently a member of any political party or organization? (IF MEMBER, SKIP TO Q. 39a.)

38b. Were you ever a member?

38c. Do you consider yourself a supporter of any particular political party? (IF SUPPORTER, SKIP TO Q. 39a.)

38d. Towards which political party do you lean?

38a. (UNITED STATES) Now we would like to know something about your party preferences and how you vote. Do you consider yourself a supporter of a particular political party? (Which party?) (IF NECESSARY TO EXPLAIN "SUPPORTER," SAY: Do you think of yourself generally as a Democrat, a Republican, an independent, or what?)

38b. (IF INDEPENDENT OR NO PARTY) Toward which party do you lean?

38c. (IF SUPPORTS OR LEANS TOWARD ANY PARTY) Are you a member of any political club or organization? (Which club or organization is that?)

38d. (ASK EVERYONE) Have you ever been active in a political campaign? That is, have you ever worked for a candidate or party, contributed money, or done any other active work?

39a. (IF RESPONDENT IS A MEMBER OF, SUPPORTS, OR LEANS TOWARD, A POLITICAL PARTY) You say you are a (member of, support, lean toward—SELECT APPROPRIATE ONE) of the —————— party. What about your friends and acquaintances? Would you say that all of your friends support the same party, that most of them do, that some of them do, or that almost none support the same party?

39b. (IF RESPONDENT IS NEITHER A PARTY MEMBER NOR A SUPPORTER, AND LEANS TOWARD NO PARTY) You say you don't support any political party. What about your friends and acquaintances? Do most of them support a political party, do some support a political party, do only a few support some party, or do none support a party?

40. If you can remember, will you tell me how you voted in the last three national (U.K.: GENERAL) elections? (SPECIFY YEARS)

41. What party do you usually vote for in local elections?

42. (IF RESPONDENT HAS NOT VOTED IN ANY OF THE LAST THREE GENERAL ELECTIONS OR ANY RECENT LOCAL ELECTIONS, SKIP TO Q. 44) In general elections do you usually know *definitely* how you will vote *before the electoral campaign* starts, do you *sometimes* have doubts as to how to vote, or do you *usually* have doubts about what party or candidate to support?

43. Which one of these statements comes *closest* to describing your feelings when you go to the polls to cast your ballot? (HAND LIST 6)

List 6

I get a feeling of satisfaction out of it
I do it only because it is my duty
I feel annoyed, it's a waste of time
I don't feel anything in particular

44. What about the campaigning that goes on at the time of a national election: do you pay much attention to what goes on, just a little, or none at all?

45. Some people feel that campaigning is needed so the public can judge candidates and issues. Others say that it causes so much bitterness and is so unreliable that we'd be better off without it. What do you think: is it needed or would we be better off without it?

46. Do you ever get angry at some of the things that go on in election campaigns? Do you *often* get angry, do you *sometimes* get angry or do you *never* get angry?

47. Do you ever find election campaigns to be pleasant and enjoyable? Do you *often*, do you *sometimes*, or do you *never* find them pleasant and enjoyable?

48. Do you ever find election campaigns silly or ridiculous? Do you *often, sometimes,* or *never* find them silly or ridiculous?

49. Suppose a son or daughter of yours was getting married. How would you feel if he or she married a supporter of the _____ (ASK OF ALL LISTED PARTIES) party? Would you be pleased, would you be displeased, or would it make no difference?

50. We're interested in what sorts of people support and vote for the different parties. If you had to generalize, which expressions in this list (HAND LIST 7) come closest to describing the kinds of people who vote for the _____ (ASK OF ALL LISTED PARTIES) party?

List 7

People interested in national strength and independence
Selfish people, interested in their own welfare at the expense of others'
Intelligent people
Religious people
Betrayers of freedom and the country's welfare
Ignorant and misguided people
Fascists, militarists (U.K.: imperialists)
People interested in the welfare of humanity
Atheists, godless people

51. The _____ party now controls the national government. Do you think that its policies and activities would ever seriously endanger the country's welfare? Do you think that this *probably* would happen, that it *might* happen, or that it *probably wouldn't* happen?

52. Let me ask you about some other parties that might some day take control of the government. If the _____ (ASK OF ALL LISTED PARTIES) party were to take control of the government, how likely is it that it would seriously endanger the country's welfare? Do you think that this would *probably* happen, that it *might* happen, or that it probably *wouldn't* happen?

53. We are also interested in how well known the national leaders of the various political parties are in this country. Could you name three leaders of the _____ party? Could you name three leaders of the _____ party? Could you tell me the name of a leader from the _____ party? (NUMBER OF PARTIES AND LEADERS VARIED FROM NATION TO NATION)

54a. Now we would like to ask you a few questions about your family life. We're interested in how decisions were made in your family when you were a child, let's say when you were sixteen. Here's a list of ways of making family decisions (HAND LIST 8). By and large, how were decisions made in your family?

List 8

By and large, *father* made the decision
By and large, *mother* made the decision
Both parents acted *together*
Each parent acted *individually*

54b. What about decisions on the punishment of children for misbehavior? How were these made? (SAME LIST)

55a. (IF NOT MARRIED, SKIP TO Q. 56) How does this compare with your present family? In general, how are decisions made in your family now? (HAND LIST 9)

List 9

By and large, *husband* makes the decision
By and large, *wife* makes the decision
Both act *together*
Each acts *individually*

55b. What about the punishment of children for misbehavior? (SAME LIST)

55c. And on deciding how to vote? (SAME LIST)

56. When your parents made decisions affecting you, how well did you think they understood your needs? Did they understand them very well, fairly well, not so well, or not at all? (IF RESPONDENT ASKS: QUESTION REFERS TO RESPONDENT'S VIEW *AT THE TIME*, NOT LOOKING BACK NOW)

57. As you were growing up, let's say when you were around sixteen, how much influence do you remember having in family decisions affecting yourself? Did you have much influence, some, or none at all?

58a. At around the same time, if a decision were made that you didn't like, did you feel *free* to complain, did you feel a little *uneasy* about complaining, or was it *better not* to complain?

58b. If you complained, did it make any difference in your parents' decision? Did it make a lot of difference, some, or none?

58c. At that time do you remember ever actually complaining—do you remember doing this often, once in a while, or never?

59. Were you satisfied or dissatisfied with the amount of influence you had in family decisions when you were about sixteen?

60. In general, how much voice do you think children of sixteen should have in family decisions?

61. We would like to find out something about your education. How far did you get with your education?

62. What sort of primary school did you go to—was it public (U.K.: STATE), private (U.K.: PUBLIC), or a church school?

63. What about your husband (or wife)—how far did he (she) get with his (her) education?

64. Do you remember how much time was spent in your school in studying current events and the government of the country? Was there a lot of time spent on this, a little, or none at all?

65. Here is a list of things that children may be taught at school (HAND LIST 10). Which was stressed the most in your school?

List 10

Have faith in leaders
Obey the law
How the government is run
Love your country

66a. In some schools the children are encouraged to discuss and debate political and social issues and to make up their own minds. How was it in your school—how much chance did the children have to express their opinion? A lot, some, or none at all?

66b. (IF A LOT OR SOME) Did you take part in these discussions and debates?

67. What about your teachers—how interested were they in you as an individual? Did they take a lot of interest, some, or none at all?

68. Did your teachers in school treat everyone fairly, or were some treated better than others?

69a. If you felt you had been treated unfairly in some way or disagreed with something the teacher had said, did you feel *free* to talk to the teacher about it? Did you feel a bit *uneasy* about talking to the teacher? Or was it better *not* to talk to the teacher?

69b. Would your talking to the teacher have made any difference? A lot, some, or none?

69c. Do you remember ever doing this? Often, occasionally, or never?

70a. (IF RESPONDENT DID NOT GO BEYOND PRIMARY SCHOOL, SKIP TO Q. 71) In some secondary schools the students participate in running school affairs; in others, the teachers decide everything. How was it in your school—did the students participate a great deal, some, very little, or not at all?

70b. (IF GREAT DEAL OR SOME PARTICIPATION) How about *you*—did you participate a great deal, some, or not at all?

71. Do you think it is a good idea to let students take some part in running the school?

72. Now I'd like to ask you another kind of question. Here are things that people say, and we want to find out how other people feel on these things. I'll read them one at a time, and you just tell me offhand whether you *agree* or *disagree*.

A. The way people vote is the main thing that decides how things are run in this country.

B. If you don't watch yourself, people will take advantage of you.

C. A few strong leaders would do more for this country than all the laws and talk.

D. All candidates sound good in their speeches, but you can never tell what they will do after they are elected.

E. Human nature is fundamentally cooperative.

F. People like me don't have any say about what the government does.

G. The individual owes his first duty to the state and only secondarily to his personal welfare.

H. No one is going to care much what happens to you, when you get right down to it.

73. When a new Prime Minister (MEXICO AND UNITED STATES: PRESIDENT) comes into office, one of the first things he must do is appoint people to cabinet positions and ministries. Could you tell me what some of these cabinet positions are? (IF NEEDED) Can you name any others? (PROBE UNTIL RESPONDENT NAMES FIVE CABINET POSITIONS OR UNTIL HE KNOWS NO MORE)

74a. Now could you tell me something about your present job? What do you do for a living?

74b. (IF HOUSEWIFE) What does your husband do for a living?

74c. (IF UNEMPLOYED OR RETIRED) What do (did) you usually do for a living?

75. (IF NOT CURRENTLY EMPLOYED, SKIP TO Q. 81) Is there anyone in a position of authority over you in your day-to-day work?

76. We'd like to find out how decisions are made on your job. When decisions are made affecting your own work, do those in authority over you ever consult you about them? Do they *usually* consult you, do they *sometimes* consult you, does this happen *rarely,* or are you *never* consulted?

77. If a decision were made affecting your own work that you disagreed with strongly, what would you do—would you feel *free* to complain, would you feel *uneasy* about complaining, or is it better to accept the decision and *not* complain?

78. If you did complain, would it do any good?

79. Have you ever actually complained about such a decision?

80. The way things are, do you think that those who run the place where you work take your interests and needs into account when they make decisions, or do they ignore your interests?

81. Thinking about the economic situation of your family in general —the money you earn, the chances for advancement, etc.—do you think it is satisfactory or not?

82. How do you think it will change in the next ten years?

83a, b. Are you a member of any organizations now (trade or labor unions, business organizations, social groups, professional or farm organizations, cooperatives, fraternal or veterans' groups, athletic clubs, political, charitable, civic, or religious organizations) or any other organized group? (IF NEEDED) Which ones?

535

83c. (IF A MEMBER OF SOME ORGANIZATION NOW) Have you ever been an officer in this (one of these) organization(s)?

83d. (IF A MEMBER OF SOME ORGANIZATION) Are any of the organizations you belong to in any way concerned with governmental, political, or public affairs? For instance, do they take stands on or discuss public issues or try to influence government actions?

84a. We'd like to ask about your religious affiliation. Do you belong to any church? (IF NEEDED) Which one?

84b. (IF YES) About how often do you attend services?

85. How old are you?

86. Could you please place your family income in one of the following income groups? (HAND LIST 11; EQUIVALENTS IN EACH NATION)

List 11

Under $1,000
$ 1,000–$ 1,999
$ 2,000–$ 2,999
$ 3,000–$ 4,999
$ 5,000–$ 7,499
$ 7,500–$ 9,999
$10,000–$14,999
$15,000 and over

TO BE FILLED OUT BY INTERVIEWER AT CLOSE OF INTERVIEW

87. Place of interview
88. Size of town where interview takes place
89. Region of country
90. Sex
91. Race
92. Interviewer rating of respondent's socio-economic class
93. Articulateness of respondent
94. Attitude of respondent toward interview

APPENDIX C

POLITICAL LIFE-HISTORY INTERVIEW

1. Could you tell me something about your present job—what do you do for a living? PROBE FOR FULL DESCRIPTION OF JOB: Could you describe the work you do?)

    1a. IF *RETIRED OR UNEMPLOYED,* ASK QUESTIONS 2–13 ABOUT JOB LAST HELD OR USUALLY HELD

    1b. IF *HOUSEWIFE,* SKIP 2–14 AND ASK 14–18

    1c. IF *SELF-EMPLOYED,* ARTISAN, PROFESSIONAL, FARMER, OR IN *MANAGERIAL POSITION,* SKIP 2–13 AND ASK 19–22

    2–14 *NOT FOR HOUSEWIVES OR SELF-EMPLOYED*

2. How big is the firm you work for? How many employees does it have? How many are in the branch where you work?

3. In general, how satisfied are you with your work? (IF SATISFIED) In what way? (IF NOT SATISFIED) In what way?

4. How well do you get along with your fellow workers? Do you have pleasant relations with them?

5. We'd like to find out how decisions are made on your job. When decisions are made affecting your own work, do you have any voice in those decisions?

    5a. (IF YES) How much voice do you have? In what way? Can you give me any examples?

    5b. (IF NO) Who makes the decisions? Can you give me any examples?

6. How satisfied are you with the way decisions are made on your job?

7. When such decisions are made, do you think that your interests are taken into account? (IF YES) In what way? (IF NO) In what way?

8. How well do you get along with the people who supervise your work?

9. What is your supervisor like as a person?

10. What is his authority like? (IF NEEDED) Is he strict?

11. How good are your chances for advancement in your present job?

12. If you were starting your working life over, would you take up the same work again?

    12a. (IF NO) Why not? What sort of work would you do?

13. Could you tell me what other jobs you have had?

SKIP TO 23

14–18 FOR HOUSEWIVES ONLY

14. Could you tell me something about your husband's job—what does he do for a living? (PROBE FOR FULL DESCRIPTION: Can you describe the work he does?)

IF HUSBAND UNEMPLOYED OR RETIRED, ASK 15–19 ABOUT JOB LAST OR USUALLY HELD

15. Do you know how big the firm is where he works? (IF YES) About how many employees does it have?

16. In general, how satisfied is your husband with his job? (IF YES) In what way? (IF NO) In what way?

17. If your husband could start his working life over again, would you like to see him take up the same work again?

17a. (IF NO) Why not? What sort of work would you like to have seen him take up?

18. Could you tell me what other jobs your husband has held?

SKIP TO 23

19–22 *FOR SELF-EMPLOYED, PROFESSIONALS, FARMERS, AND MANAGERS ONLY*

19. How satisfied are you with the work you do? (IF YES) In what way? (IF NO) In what way?

20. How good are your chances for advancing and improving your life through your work?

21. If you were starting your life's work over again, would you take up the same work?

21a. (IF NO) Why not? What sort of work would you take up?

22. Can you tell me what other jobs you have had?

23. How many children do you have?

IF *NO CHILDREN*, SKIP 24–29 AND ASK 29–32.

24–29 *FOR THOSE WITH CHILDREN ONLY*

24. How old are they? Are they boys or girls?

25. INTERVIEWER NOTE: GET FULL DESCRIPTION OF CHILDREN'S PRESENT ACTIVITIES—THE JOBS THEY HAVE, THE SCHOOLS THEY GO TO, AND SO FORTH. FOR INSTANCE: Do they still live at home? Are they still in school? Are they working?

26. Think now of the life you have led and of the lives your children will lead. Do you think there will be a difference between the life you led and the lives your children will lead?

IF *A DIFFERENCE*, ASK 26a, b, c

26a. In what way will there be a difference? (Will their occupations be different?)

26b. Will their lives be better or worse than yours?

26c. What would you say is the cause of this difference?

IF *NO DIFFERENCE*, ASK 26d, e

26d. In what ways will they be the same?

26e. Why do you think there will be no difference?

27. Think now of the chances your children have to *improve* their lives. How do these chances compare with your chances to improve your life when you were a child?

27a. In what way are they (better, worse, the same)? (CHOOSE APPROPRIATE WORD BASED ON ANSWER TO 27.)

27b. What would you say is the reason for this?

28. Consider the chances that are open to your children to improve their lives. How do these chances compare with those of *other young people* in this town (neighborhood, IF IN A LARGE CITY)?

28a. Are there some young people whose chances to improve their lives are better than those of your children? (IF YES) Who are they?

28b. Are there some whose chances are not as good as those of your children? (IF YES) Who are they?

28c. (IF DIFFERENCES MENTIONED IN 28, 28a, or 28b) What are the reasons for these differences?

SKIP TO 32

29 *FOR THOSE WITH NO CHILDREN ONLY*

29. Think now of life today and life when you were a child. Do you think there is a great difference between life today and life when you were a child?

IF A DIFFERENCE, ASK 29a, b, c

29a. In what way is there a difference?

29b. Do you think life is better or worse?

29c. What would you say is the cause of this difference?

IF NO DIFFERENCE, ASK 29d, e

29d. In what ways is life the same?

29e. Why do you think there is no difference?

30. Think now of the chances people had to *improve* their lives when you were a child and the chances that one has today. How do the chances to *improve* one's life today compare with those when you were a child?

30a. In what way are they (better, worse, the same)? (CHOOSE APPROPRIATE WORD BASED ON ANSWER TO 30.)

30b. What would you say is the reason for this?

31. Consider the chances that are open to you today to improve your own life. How do these chances compare with those of other people in this town (neighborhood, IF IN A LARGE CITY)?

31a. Are there some people whose chances to improve their lives are better than your own? (IF YES) Who are they?

31b. Are there some whose chances are not as good as your own? (IF YES) Who are they?

31c. (IF DIFFERENCES MENTIONED IN 31, 31a, or 31b) What are the reasons for these differences?

32. When an important problem comes up in your family, like buying a new piece of furniture or deciding whether to move to a new place, how do you go about solving the problem?

32a. Which members of the family discuss it?

32b. Whose opinion has the most weight?

33, 33a *FOR THOSE WITH CHILDREN OF SCHOOL AGE OR OLDER ONLY*

33. Do your children have a voice in these decisions?

33a. How much part do they take in the discussions? (IF NONE) Why not? (IF SOME PART) Do you think this is a good thing?

539

34. In general, do you think it is a good thing that children take part in family discussions?

34a. (IF YES) At what age should they start taking part?

34b. (IF NO) Why not?

35–36 *FOR THOSE WITH CHILDREN ONLY*

35. How are decisions made in matters affecting the children—matters such as deciding on their education and their futures?

35a. Which members of the family discuss it?

35b. Whose opinion has the most weight?

35c. Should children be consulted on matters of this sort? (IF YES) Why? (IF NO) Why not?

36. Do you ever discuss political or governmental affairs in your family? I mean, do you talk about politics? (IF NO, SKIP TO 38.)

36a, b, c *FOR THOSE WHO SAY THEY DISCUSS POLITICS*

36a. Can you remember the last time you discussed such topics? (IF YES) When was it? What was the topic?

36b. When you discuss politics, who takes part? Whose opinion in the family has the greatest weight?

36c. Are there differences of opinion? (IF YES) Can you recall any examples? How are the differences worked out?

37. Consider now family life in general in this country. Are there any changes that you would like to see in family life?

38. Do you think that, in general, children have too much voice in family decisions or not enough?

39. What is your religion?

39a. (IF SOME RELIGION NAMED) How often do you attend services?

40. Do you consider yourself a religious person?

41. What does religion mean to you?

42. What place do you think religion should occupy in the life of the country?

43. Think back to when you were a child. How does your religious life today differ from what it was then? (IF NEEDED) Are you more or less religious now?

INTERVIEWER NOTE: QUESTIONS 44–50 ARE TO BE ASKED ABOUT THE LOCAL AREA IN WHICH THE RESPONDENT LIVES. THE INTERVIEWER SHOULD SELECT AN APPROPRIATE TERM TO USE FOR THAT AREA—"IN THIS TOWN," "IN THIS NEIGHBORHOOD," "IN THIS SECTION OF THE CITY." WE WANT THESE QUESTIONS TO BE ABOUT THE RESPONDENT'S CLOSE AND IMMEDIATE SOCIAL ENVIRONMENT. WE ARE INTERESTED IN AN AREA SMALL ENOUGH SO THAT THE RESPONDENT WOULD HAVE AT LEAST SOME KNOWLEDGE OF THE PEOPLE IN IT—FOR INSTANCE, BE ABLE TO RECOGNIZE THEM (NOT NECESSARILY GREET THEM) IF HE PASSED THEM ON THE STREET. IN A SMALL VILLAGE THIS MAY BE THE ENTIRE VILLAGE. IN A CITY IT MAY BE THE

LOCAL NEIGHBORHOOD OR QUARTER, OR PERHAPS JUST A FEW ADJACENT APARTMENT HOUSES. THE INTERVIEWER WILL HAVE TO USE HIS JUDGMENT IN SELECTING THE APPROPRIATE TERM TO BE USED IN 44–50.

44. I would like to ask a few questions about the people who live around here, in this (area, SELECT TERM AS DIRECTED ABOVE). What kinds of work do the people in this (area) do?

45. What sorts of classes and economic groups are there in this (area)? (IF NEEDED) Are there many rich or many poor?

45a. (IF DIFFERENT GROUPS MENTIONED) What group do you and your family fit into? Why this particular group?

46. Do you know many of the people around here?

47. Do you have many friends in this (area)?

48. Do you visit many of the people around here?

49. Some people say that most people can be trusted. Others say that you can't be too careful in your dealings with people. Thinking now of the people in this (area), which statement do you think applies? (IF NEEDED) Do you think that most people can be trusted or do you think that you can't be too careful in your dealings with others?

IF RESPONDENT SELECTS EITHER ALTERNATIVE—EITHER PEOPLE CAN BE TRUSTED OR ONE MUST BE CAREFUL—ASK 49a, b

49a. Why do you say that?

49b. Can you think of any incidents that would illustrate this?

IF BOTH STATEMENTS TRUE—SOME CAN BE TRUSTED AND SOME NOT—ASK 49c, d, e

49c. Which people can be trusted?

49d. With whom can't you be too careful?

49e. Can you remember any incidents that illustrate this?

ASKED OF EVERYONE

49f. Do you think that what you say applies only to people in this (area), or does it apply to people in general?

49g. (IF STATEMENTS ABOUT THE AREA DO NOT APPLY TO PEOPLE IN GENERAL) In what way is there a difference between people around here and others?

50. Some people are inclined to help others. Other people look out for themselves. Thinking again of the people in this (area), which statement do you think applies? (IF NEEDED) Are most people helpful or do most look out for themselves?

IF RESPONDENT SELECTS EITHER ALTERNATIVE—EITHER PEOPLE ARE HELPFUL OR THEY LOOK OUT FOR THEMSELVES—ASK 50a, b

50a. Why do you say that?

50b. Can you remember any incidents that illustrate this?

IF BOTH STATEMENTS ARE TRUE—SOME ARE HELPFUL AND OTHERS ARE NOT—ASK 50c, d

50c. Which people are helpful?

50d. Which people are not helpful?

ASKED OF EVERYONE

50e. Do you think that what you say applies only to people in this (area) or does it apply to people in general?

50f. (IF STATEMENTS ABOUT THE AREA DO NOT APPLY TO PEOPLE IN GENERAL) In what way is there a difference between people around here and others?

51. Think back now to your childhood. What did your father do for a living when you were a child?

52. Where did you live?

53. What was the house like? Can you describe it?

54. Can you remember what it was like economically when you were a child? (IF NEEDED) Did you always have the things that were necessary?

55. Do you remember if your parents ever discussed their economic situation? (IF YES) What did they say?

55a. Were they satisfied or dissatisfied with their economic situation?

56. How many brothers and sisters did you have? Were they older or younger?

57. How did you get along with them?

58. Did anyone else live in the household besides your parents and your brothers and sisters?

59. What was your father like as a person?

60. What was his authority like? (IF NEEDED) Was he strict?

61. What was your mother like as a person?

62. What was her authority like? (IF NEEDED) Was she strict?

63. If you had some problem, when you were younger and living with your parents, to whom did you go to talk it over? (IF SOMEONE MENTIONED) Could you do this freely?

64. When some problem came up in the family when you were a child, such as moving to another house or deciding on the future of one of the children, how was the problem solved?

64a. Who discussed the problem?

64b. Who had the main voice in the decision? Whose opinion had the most weight?

65. What about the children—did they have any voice in family discussions?

65a. (IF THEY HAD SOME VOICE) Which problems could they discuss?

66. As a child, were you satisfied with the way in which decisions were made in your family? In what way?

67. I would like to ask you a few questions about the (town or neighborhood) you lived in when you were a child. (INTERVIEWER: SELECT APPROPRIATE TERM USING DIRECTIONS FOR QUESTIONS 44–50) When you were a child, what sort of work did most of the people who lived near you do for a living?

68. What sort of classes or economic groups were there in your (local area) when you were a child? (IF NEEDED) Were there many rich or many poor?

IF DIFFERENT GROUPS MENTIONED, ASK 68a, b, c

68a. Did your parents ever discuss this? (IF YES) What did they say?

68b. Were you aware of this at the time?

68c. Which group did your parents fit into? Why that particular group?

69. Did your parents know many of the people who lived near them?

70. How did the people get along? (PROBE) Can you give any examples?

71. Some people say that most people can be trusted. Others say that you can't be too careful in your dealings with people. Thinking now of the people in the (local area) where you lived as a child, which statement do you think applies? (IF NEEDED) Could most of the people be trusted, or was it better to be very careful in your dealings with others?

IF RESPONDENT SELECTS EITHER ALTERNATIVE—EITHER PEOPLE COULD BE TRUSTED OR ONE HAD TO BE CAREFUL —ASK 71a, b

71a. Why do you say that?

71b. Can you remember any incidents that would illustrate this?

IF BOTH STATEMENTS ARE TRUE—SOME COULD BE TRUSTED AND OTHERS NOT—ASK 71c, d, e

71c. Which people could be trusted?

71d. With which ones was it better to be careful?

71e. Can you remember any incidents that illustrate this?

72. Some people are inclined to help others. Other people look out for themselves. Thinking again of the people in the (local area) where you lived as a child, which statement do you think applies? (IF NEEDED) Were most of the people inclined to help others or did most look out for themselves?

IF RESPONDENT SELECTS EITHER ALTERNATIVE—EITHER PEOPLE ARE HELPFUL OR THEY LOOK OUT FOR THEM- SELVES—ASK 72a, b

72a. Why do you say that?

72b. Can you remember any incidents that would illustrate that?

IF BOTH STATEMENTS ARE TRUE—SOME WERE HELPFUL AND OTHERS NOT—ASK 72e, f, g

72e. Which people were helpful?

72f. Which people were not helpful?

72g. Can you remember any incidents that illustrate this?

73. We'd like to know about your education. How far did you get with your education?

73a. IF *NO SCHOOLING,* SKIP 74–90

73b. IF *ELEMENTARY SCHOOL ONLY,* ASK 74–81 AND SKIP 82–90

73c. IF *ELEMENTARY AND SECONDARY SCHOOLS,* ASK 74–90. 74–82 *FOR THOSE WHO ATTENDED ELEMENTARY SCHOOL (INCLUDING THOSE WHO WENT ON TO SECONDARY SCHOOL)*

74. What sort of elementary school did you go to—was it public (U.K.: STATE), private (U.K.: PUBLIC), or a church school? (IF RESPOND-

ENT ATTENDED MORE THAN ONE, ASK QUESTIONS 75–82 ABOUT THE ONE HE REMEMBERS BEST.)

75. What were the teachers like?

76. Is there any particular teacher that stands out in your memory? (IF YES) In what way?

77. Did you feel that the teachers were interested in you as a person?

78. Did you feel free to talk to them?

79. What was the authority of the teachers like? How strict were they? Were they fair?

80. How well did you get along with your fellow students?

81. Was there any sort of school government run by the students?

81a. (IF YES) Could you describe it? Were you active in it?

IF NO SECONDARY SCHOOL, SKIP TO 90

82–90 *FOR THOSE WHO ATTENDED SECONDARY SCHOOL*

82. What sort of secondary school did you attend—was it public (U.K.: STATE), private (U.K.: PUBLIC), or a church school? (IF RESPOND-ENT ATTENDED MORE THAN ONE, ASK QUESTIONS 83–90 ABOUT THE ONE HE REMEMBERS BEST.)

83. What were the teachers like?

84. Is there any particular teacher that stands out in your memory? (IF YES) In what way?

85. Did you feel that the teachers were interested in you as a person?

86. Did you feel free to talk to them?

87. What was the authority of the teachers like? How strict were they? Were they fair?

88. How well did you get along with your fellow students?

89. Was there any sort of school government run by the students?

89a. (IF YES) Could you describe it? Were you active in it?

90. Looking back over your life as a whole, what would you say are some of the most important events that affected your life? (IF NEEDED: events you remember very well; events that changed your life?)

90a. (IF SOME EVENT MENTIONED) In what way did this event affect you?

91. We are interested in the way in which the events of a person's life influence the way he acts and feels about politics and government. Can you remember any event that had an effect on how you feel about politics and government? (IF NEEDED) Are there any experiences in your life that changed your views on politics?

91a. (IF SOMETHING MENTIONED) What was this event? How did it affect you?

The section of the life-history interview dealing with political memories was of course different for each one of the five countries. We include the British version (QUESTIONS 92–99) for illustrative purposes.

INTERVIEWER NOTE: QUESTIONS 92–98 ARE ABOUT SPE-CIFIC EVENTS THE RESPONDENT MAY HAVE EXPERIENCED. IF RESPONDENT IS CLEARLY TOO YOUNG TO HAVE EXPERI-ENCED SOME OF THESE EVENTS, SUCH AS WORLD WAR I, DO

NOT ASK ABOUT THAT EVENT BUT NOTE ON THE INTER-
VIEW FORM THAT RESPONDENT WAS TOO YOUNG.

92. Do you remember anything about World War I?

92a. (IF YES) How did it affect you at the time?

92b. (IF YES TO 92) Did it affect how you felt about politics? (IF
YES) In what way?

93. Do you remember anything about the General Strike of 1926?

93a. (IF YES) How did it affect you at the time?

93b. (IF YES TO 93) Did it affect how you felt about politics? (IF
YES) In what way?

94. Do you remember anything about the depression of the 1930's?

94a. (IF YES) How did it affect you at the time?

94b. (IF YES TO 94) Did it affect how you felt about politics? (IF
YES) In what way?

95. Do you remember anything about the abdication of the King in
1936?

95a. (IF YES) How did it affect you at the time?

95b. (IF YES TO 95) Did it affect how you felt about politics? (IF
YES) In what way?

96. Do you remember anything about World War II?

96a. (IF YES) How did it affect you at the time?

96b. (IF YES TO 96) Did it affect the way you felt about politics? (IF
YES) In what way?

97. Do you remember anything about the Labour party policies after
1945?

97a. (IF YES) Did they affect you at the time?

97b. (IF YES TO 97) Did it affect the way you felt about politics? (IF
YES) In what way?

98. Do you remember anything about the Suez campaign of 1956?

98a. (IF YES) How did it affect you at the time?

98b. (IF YES TO 98) Did it affect the way you felt about politics? (IF
YES) In what way?

99. What about your family—did anything happen in your family
when you were growing up that affected your views about politics?

99a. (IF YES) What was the event? How did it affect your views?

100. Do you remember any discussions of politics in your family when
you were growing up—I mean, did anyone talk about politics or government?

100a. (IF YES) What were the discussions about?

100b. (IF YES TO 100) Who took part in the discussions?

101. Can you remember what you were taught in school about politics
or government? (IF YES) What were you taught?

102. Were you taught in school to be patriotic? (IF YES) How was this
done? What exactly were you taught?

102a. Was there any organization of a patriotic nature for the students? (IF YES) Would you describe it? Were you active in this organization?

103. Is there anything else that we have not yet discussed that you feel affected your views on government? (PROBE) Perhaps something that happened in your town or neighborhood, or something that happened at your work?

103a. (IF YES) What was it? How did it affect you?

104. About how much interest do you take in political and governmental affairs?

IF LITTLE OR NO INTEREST, ASK 104a, b

104a. Why aren't you interested in political and governmental affairs?

104b. Was there ever a time when you were more interested in these things than you are today? (IF YES) Why did you lose interest?

IF SOME OR MUCH INTEREST, ASK 104c, d

104c. Why are you interested in political and governmental affairs?

104d. Can you remember when you first became interested? (IF YES) What made you become interested at that time?

105. Speaking generally, what sort of a person do you think is interested in politics?

106. What sort of a person do you think is not interested in politics?

107. By and large, with what political party are you sympathetic?

IF SYMPATHETIC TO A PARTY, ASK 107a, b

107a. Why do you favor this party? What does it stand for?

107b. Have you ever supported another party? (IF YES) What made you change?

IF NOT SYMPATHETIC TO A PARTY, ASK 107c, d, e

107c. Why are you not now sympathetic with any party?

107d. Have you ever been sympathetic to a particular political party? (IF YES) Which party? Why did you lose sympathy with it?

107e. What kind of party would you support if it existed in this country? (IF NEEDED) What would the party stand for that you would support? How would it differ from the present parties?

108. Are there any political parties in this country that stand for things that you oppose? (PROBE IF NEEDED) Are there any parties that have ideas or activities that you oppose?

IF PARTY NAMED, ASK 108a, b, c, d

108a. Which party (or parties) is this?

108b. What does it (they) stand for?

108c. Why do you oppose it (them)?

108d. What sorts of people support this party (parties)?

BRITISH VERSION [Questions 109–112]

109. Suppose a son or daughter of yours (IF NEEDED: if you had one) joined one of the political parties. How would you feel about it? For instance, suppose your child joined the Conservative party. How would you feel about it?

110. Suppose your child joined the Labour party? How would you feel about it?

111. What about the Liberal party?

112. (QUESTION 112 OMITTED IN BRITAIN) [In other nations referred to minor parties.]

113. Can you remember the last time you voted? (IF YES) When was it?

113a. (IF REMEMBERS LAST TIME VOTED) How did you feel when you went to the polls to cast your ballot? (IF NEEDED) Can you remember what went through your mind?

114. Some people say that governments are really unnecessary and that people would get along better without them. What do you think?

115. Think now about the central government—the ministries and Parliament in (LONDON, BONN, etc.). How much effect do its activities have on the lives of the (BRITISH, GERMANS, etc.)?

115a. (IF THEY HAVE SOME EFFECT) Can you give me any examples?

116. In what ways do the activities of the government in (LONDON, BONN, etc.) affect your own life and the life of your family?

117. Think now about the local government (SPECIFY MOST LOCAL GOVERNMENTAL UNIT: TOWN, VILLAGE, *GEMEINDE*, COUNTY, etc.). How much effect do its activities have on the lives of the people around here?

117a. (IF THEY HAVE SOME EFFECT) Can you give me any examples?

118. In what ways do the activities of the local government affect your life and the life of your family?

119. What sorts of things are the taxes you pay used for?

120. Is there any way you think they could be put to better use? (IF YES) In what way?

121. Is there anything that you think the national government in (LONDON, BONN, etc.) could do to improve conditions for the people of this country? (IF YES) What, for instance?

122. You have spoken to us about your way of life and that of your family. Is there anything that the national government could do to improve conditions for you and your family? (IF YES) What, for instance? *IF SOME IMPROVEMENTS MENTIONED IN ANSWER TO 121 OR 122, ASK 123, 124, 124a, b*

123. How good are the chances that these improvements would be made under the present government? Why?

124. Would the chances be better under some other government—perhaps under a different political party?

124a. (IF CHANCES BETTER UNDER ANOTHER GOVERNMENT OR PARTY) Under which party? (Under what kind of government?)

124b. How likely is it that such a government (party) will get into power?

125. How about the local government—is there anything that it could do to improve conditions for the people around here? (IF YES) What, for instance?

126. Is there anything the local government could do to improve conditions for you and your family? (IF YES) What, for instance?

127. Have you ever had any personal contact with people in government—I mean, people in government offices, ministries, local officials, health officials, tax officials, police officials, or any others? (IF YES) With which ones?

IF RESPONDENT HAS HAD SUCH CONTACTS, ASK 127a, b, c, d

127a. What were the contacts about?

127b. How satisfied were you with the treatment you received? In what way?

127c. Did the officials seem efficient?

127d. Did you think you were treated fairly, that is, as well as anyone else? (IF NOT TREATED FAIRLY) In what way weren't you treated fairly?

IF RESPONDENT HAS HAD NO CONTACTS WITH GOVERN-MENT OFFICIALS, ASK 127e, f, g

127e. Do you know anyone who has had such contacts? (IF YES) Who was it?

127f. What were the contacts about?

127g. Do you know whether the person was satisfied or unsatisfied with the contacts? In what way?

128. Have you ever spoken to or written a letter to your representative in Parliament or your representative on the local council?

IF RESPONDENT HAS CONTACTED REPRESENTATIVE, ASK 128a, b, c

128a. What was the contact about?

128b. What sort of response did you receive?

128c. Were you satisfied with the response?

IF RESPONDENT HAS NEVER CONTACTED REPRESENTATIVE, ASK 129

129. Do you know anyone who has spoken to or written to his representative in Parliament or on the local council? (IF YES) Who was it?

IF RESPONDENT KNOWS SOMEONE, ASK 129a, b, c

129a. What was the contact about?

129b. Do you know what sort of response was received?

129c. Do you know how satisfied the person was with the response?

130. Under what circumstances might you contact your representative in Parliament or on the local council?

131. If you did contact your representative, what sort of response do you think you would get?

AFTER THE INTERVIEW, INTERVIEWER SHOULD FILL OUT THE FOLLOWING FORM DESCRIBING THE SETTING OF THE INTERVIEW. THE DESCRIPTION SHOULD BE AS DETAILED AND PRECISE AS POSSIBLE.

1. What was the neighborhood like in which the interview took place? What were the buildings like near the building in which the interview took place? How old were they? Were they in good repair?

2. What was the building like in which the interview took place? How old was it? Was it in good repair? Did many other people live in it? (DESCRIBE THE BUILDING FULLY.)

3. What was the room or apartment like in which the interview took place? How was it furnished? Was it neat and in order? What objects were there in it—a television set? a radio? (DESCRIBE THE ROOM AS FULLY AS POSSIBLE.)

4. What was the respondent like? What was he wearing? Was he doing anything during the interview? What was his attitude toward the interview? How self-confident and articulate was he? (DESCRIBE RESPONDENT AS FULLY AS POSSIBLE.)

5. Was anyone else present during the interview? Who were they?

6. At what time of day did the interview take place, and how long did it last?

7. Are there any other details you think might be useful in understanding the respondent?

LIST OF TABLES AND FIGURES

Tables

554

555

556

Figures

INDEX